STANDARD GUIDE TO

GOLDEN AGE COMICS

ALEX G. MALLOY AND STUART W. WELLS III

Published by

kp books
An Imprint of F+W Publications

700 East State Street • Iola, WI 54990-0001
715-445-2214 • 888-457-2873

Our toll-free number to place an order or obtain
a free catalog is (800) 258-0929.

Library of Congress Catalog Number: 2005922947
ISBN: 0-89689-181-X
Designed by Stuart W. Wells III
Edited by Kristine Manty
Printed in China

A-1 Comics N#

Batman 3-D #1

Canteen Kate #1

CONTENTS

Xmas Comics, 2nd Series #7

Yellowjacket Comics #8

Zorro #15

Preface 2005

By Alex G. Malloy & Stuart W. Wells III

The Golden Age of comic books started in the late 1930s, just at the onset of World War II. Much of the rest of the current popular culture, including color movies, television, and paperback books, also started at virtually the same moment. Graphical story-telling worked beautifully for most of the genres then popular in pulp magazines, movies, and cartoons, including westerns, mysteries, sci-fi and war stories, but the real innovation was the super-hero story. Vision seekers, comic publishers, artists, writers and creators conceived this new American genre.

The popularity of comics in the market place exploded in World War II and continued through the post war era. Collecting of Golden Age Comics started early, and has not stopped over the subsequent 60+ years. The best early comics have been recognized as fine art, and collectors now seeking Golden Age comics are paying astonishing prices.

We can thank the creators for establishing, fine tuning and producing the Super-hero, Science Fiction, the War Hero, Funny Animal (such as Disney and Looney Tunes), Horror, Drama and Romantic Adventure, and for bringing classic literature to the populace in Classic Comics. Current hot publishers include Timely, especially titles like *Jumbo* and *Planet Comics*, DC, early Fiction House, Centaur, Lev Gleason, and MLJ Magazines. EC is ever popular, with its titles benefiting from a strong crossover collector base of fans interested in top artists, horror and science fiction stories, and, of course, *MAD* magazine. The early Baby Boomers are now the primary group that buy Golden Age comics.

The paper shortages in 1944-45, due to World War II, resulted in smaller print runs for most comics. The issues from this period should see new price increases when the collectors realize this. Romance comics also have the potential of further increases in value. They are far scarcer than their super-hero counterparts, especially in high grade. Atlas-Marvel love romances and teenage romances are good examples. Millie the Model and related titles are currently in strong demand.

Work by the best artists continues to be highly sought. The covers of Alex Schomburg from World War II are very hot. Other popular early artists include Lou Fine, Simon & Kirby, Bill Everett, Leonard B. Cole, Bernie Krigstein, Bob Powell, Will Eisner and George Tuska. Post war era artists such as Wally Wood, Carl Barks, Walt Kelly, Bill Ward, Alex Toth, Matt Baker, Frank Frazetta, Joe Orlando, Johnny Craig, Jack Davis, Graham Ingles, Al Williamson, and Bill Elder are also in demand.

As with any collectible, the three key words are condition, condition, and condition. With the advent of CGC, the third party grading guide, sales of Golden Age comics have risen to impressive heights, mirroring the exceptional price increases in the U. S. coin market when coins were encapsulated and graded by independent experts some years ago. The new collector can venture into buying and selling with confidence. Investors have entered the market, bringing new big money into the collecting realm. High grade comics are harder and harder to locate. Collectors also seek so called "pedigree comics," especially those from the Mile High collection, as well as ones from the Allentown, San Francisco, Larson, Bethlehem, Boston, White Mountain and Gaines collections.

This book follows the listing system and format we devised in the early days of "Comic Values Monthly" (started in 1986) and *Comics Values Annual* (now in its 13th edition). Comics are covered in numerical order, with keys to artists, happenings, character appearances, etc. Prices in this guide are for strict standards like CGC grading, not like the grading standards of comics in the '80s and '90s.

Special thanks is extended to Paul Kennedy and Don Gulbrandsen at KP Books for saying 'Go' to this project. Great appreciation to Ed Jaster, director of acquisitions at Heritage Comics, and Ben Samuels for writing the introduction. Lastly, special thanks to Heritage Comics for its market report, and letting us use many of its fine comic cover illustrations.

Alex G. Malloy and Stuart W. Wells III

GOLDEN AGE MARKET REPORT

by Ed Jaster and Ben Samuels

Heritage Comics Auctions

The Golden Age comic market looks as strong as ever. At the top of the heap are the usual suspects: key issues from mainstream superhero titles featuring characters like Batman, Superman, Captain America, the Human Torch, Wonder Woman, Flash, and the Spectre — and the higher the grade, the better! The sale of *Marvel Comics* #1 (Denver pedigree) CGC VF+ 8.5 off-white pages for $172,500 in August 2005, and the sale of *Detective Comics* #38 (Allentown pedigree) CGC NM 9.4 off-white pages for $126,500 in May 2005, shows that there is plenty of competition for these high-end comics.

Key Archie-related comics are still in much demand, and can be very challenging to locate. Early Archie appearances in *Pep*, *Archie* #1, and *Jughead* #1 are as good as money in the bank. The early Disney Four Color key issues are also showing very healthy demand. File copies and bound volumes are proving to be especially popular.

Classic EC horror and science fiction titles are still holding strong, and demand is as strong as ever for *MAD* comics and the first

Marvel Comics #1, © Marvel Comics Group, and Detective Comics #38, © DC Comics, Inc.

few magazine issues. The market for some Quality titles like *Police*, *Plastic Man*, *Military*, and *Modern Comics* still show that current Overstreet values are somewhat inflated, but we see this as an opportunity for buyers to get good deals on books with fantastic work by artists like Jack Cole, Will Eisner, and Lou Fine.

The Mile High pedigree of Edgar Church still commands a healthy premium among collectors, but for many collectors a comic's CGC grade will trump the provenance of many "lesser" pedigrees. Another market segment that deserves note are comics with restoration, which seem to making a comeback as collectors re-adjust their attitudes and realize that a nice-looking book with restoration, at a reasonable price, can be a great addition to most collections!

Overall, the market for Golden Age comics looks very stable, and for the "best of the best," prices continue to rise with no limit in sight. High-grade, key Golden Age books are harder and harder to come by, as they find homes in permanent collections. Collectors of high-grade books know what they want, and they're willing to pay for it. The competition for the really nice books is very fierce, especially for key issues. There's no arguing with the fundamental economics of the hobby; as long as demand outweighs supply, prices will continue to rise.

Wonderworld Comics #15, © Fox Features Syndicate, cover by Lou Fine & Police Comics #57, © Quality Comics Group, cover by Jack Cole.

Marvel Mystery Comics #46, $2,700
Marvel Timely 1943.

Captain America #3, $17,000
Marvel Timely 1941.

Covers by Alex Schomburg

Sub-Mariner #11, $4,500
Marvel Timely 1943.

The Fighting Yank #11, $1,500
Nedor 1945.

Exciting Comics #62, $1,000,
Nedor 1948.

Startling Comics #50, $1,100,
Better Publications 1948.

Covers by "Xela" (Alex Schomburg)

Thrilling Comics #70, $900,
Better Publications 1948.

Wonder Comics #15, $1,700,
Better Publications 1947.

Seven Seas Comics #4, $1,200
Universal Phoenix 1947.

The Saint #4, $800
Avon 1948.

Covers by Matt Baker

Phantom Lady #16, $3,200
Fox Features Syndicate 1948.

Flyin' Jenny #2, $350
Pentagon Publishing 1947.

Blue Beetle #52, $1,700,
Fox Features Syndicate 1948.

Dagar Desert Hawk #15, $1,000,
Fox Features Syndicate 1948.

Covers by Jack Kamen

Brenda Starr #14 (#2), $5,000,
Four Star Publications 1948.

All Top Comics #10, $1,500,
Fox Features Syndicate 1948.

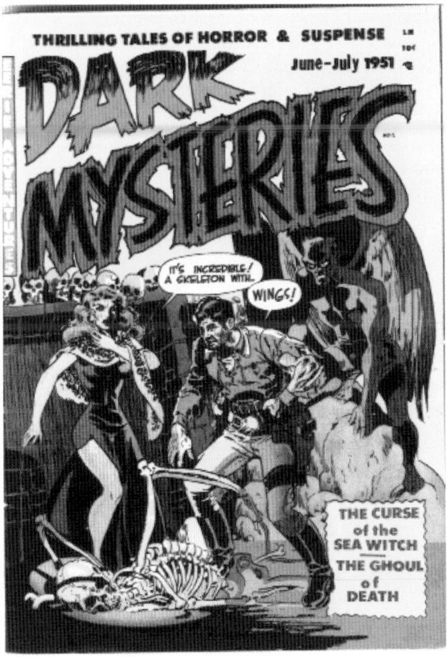

Dark Mysteries #1, $1,500
Master Publications 1951.

Judy Canova #23 (#1), $350
Fox Features Syndicate 1950.

Covers by Wally Wood

My Experience #19, $400
Fox Features Syndicate 1949.

Famous Gangsters #2, $450
Avon 1951.

Jumbo Comics #73, $350,
Fiction House 1945.

Rangers Comics #31, $400,
Fiction House 1946.

Covers by Joe Doolin

Planet Comics #51, $1,200,
Fiction House 1948.

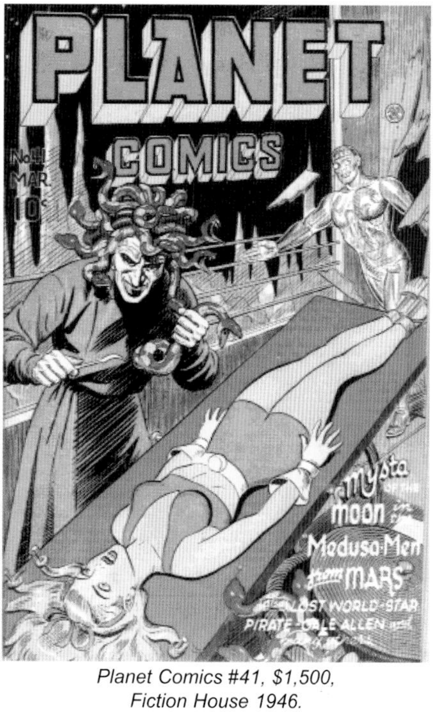

Planet Comics #41, $1,500,
Fiction House 1946.

Zoot #11, $900, Fox Features
Syndicate 1947, cover by Jack Kamen.

Wings Comics #91, $900,
Fiction House 1948, cover by Bob Lubbers.

Untie Me You Fiends!

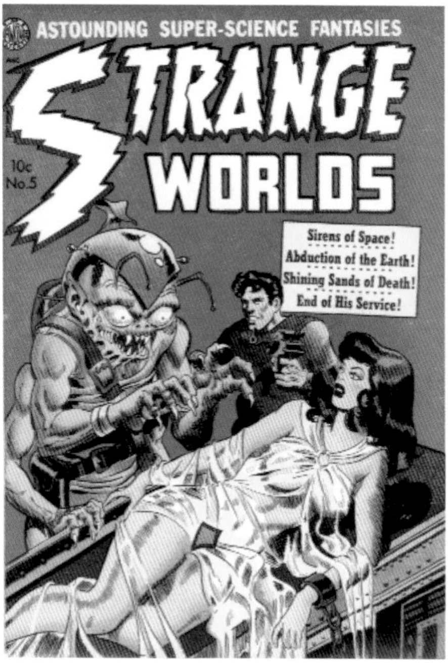

Strange Worlds #5, $2,400,
Avon 1951, cover by Wally Wood.

Adventure Comics #39, $3,000,
DC Comics 1939.

Planet Comics #46, $1,500,
Fiction House 1947, cover by Joe Doolin.

Seven Seas #6, $1,000, Universal Phoenix
Feature 1947, cover by Matt Baker.

Girls to the Rescue!

Black Cat #15, $375,
Harvey Publications 1949, cover by Lee Elias.

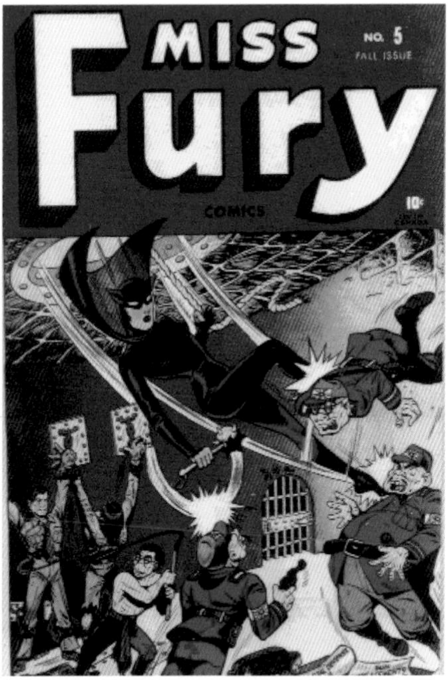

Miss Fury #5, $1,300,
Marvel Timely 1945, cover by Alex Schomburg.

Blonde Phantom #14, $1,500,
Marvel Timely 1947, cover by Syd Shores.

Fight Comics #41, $1,000,
Fiction House 1945, cover by Joe Doolin.

Wheel of Doom!

Mister Mystery #6, $800,
Aragon Magazines 1952, cover by Mortellaro.

Rangers Comics #25, $450,
Fiction House 1945, cover by Lee Elias.

Heroic Comics #3, $750,
Eastern Color 1940, cover by Bill Everett.

Captain Marvel Adventures #21, $1,700, Fawcett
1942, cover by C. C. Beck.

Heroes to the Rescue!

Strange Adventures #12 , $1,000,
DC Comics 1951, cover by Gil Kane.

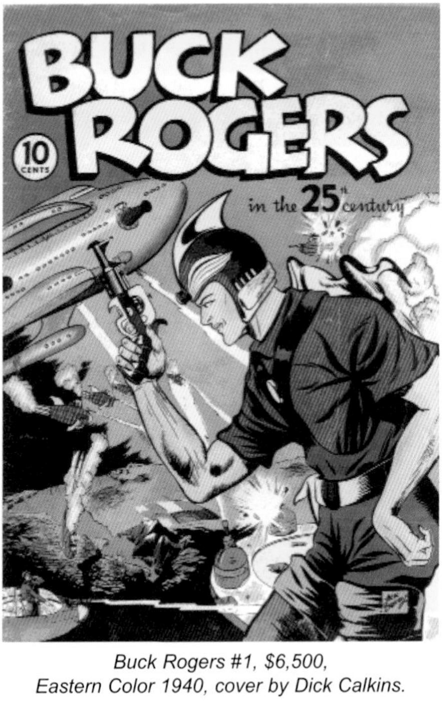

Buck Rogers #1, $6,500,
Eastern Color 1940, cover by Dick Calkins.

Junior #15, $1,000, Fox Features Syndicate 1948, cover by Al Feldstein.

Al Capp's Wolf Gal #1, $500, Toby Press 1951, cover by Al Capp.

Here's Looking at You, Kid!

Sunny America's Sweetheart #11, $2,000, Fox Features 1947, cover by Al Feldstein.

Torchy #4, #1,400, Quality Publications 1950, cover by Gill Fox.

Son of Sinbad #1, $500, St. John Publications 1950, cover by Joe Kubert.

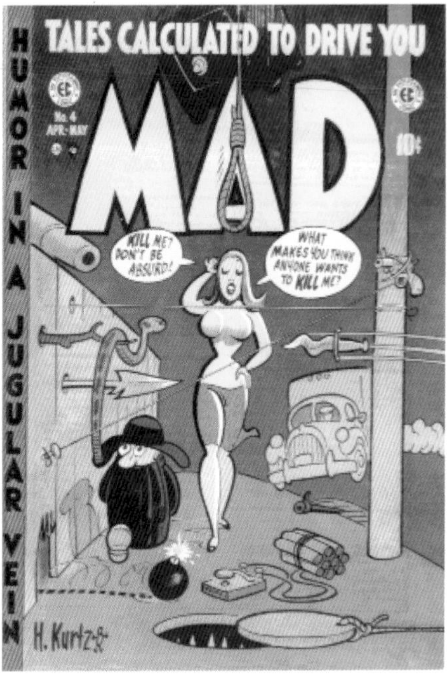

MAD Magazine #4, $2,500, EC Comics 1953, cover by Harvey Kurtzman.

Famous Artists

Two-Fisted Annual 1953 (#2), $1,400, EC Comics 1953, cover by Jack Davis.

Tales From the Crypt #32, $1,500, EC Comics 1952, cover by Jack Davis.

Blue Beetle #54, $1,800,
Fox Features Syndicate 1948.

Moon Girl and the Prince #1, $1,400,
EC Comics 1947, cover by Johnny Craig.

Famous Artists

Love Diary #1, $400,
Quality Comics 1949, cover by Bill Ward.

Zoot Comics #16, $650, Fox Features
Syndicate 1948, cover by Victor Fox.

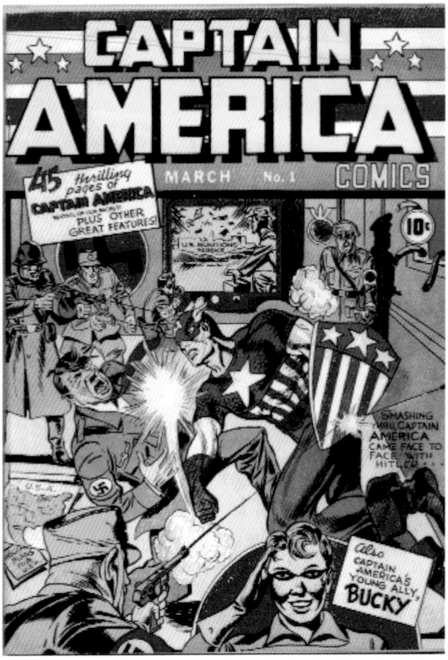

Captain America #1, $135,000,
Marvel Timely 1941, cover by Jack Kirby.

Whiz Comics #30, $1,400,
Fawcett Publications 1942, cover by C. C. Beck.

Famous Artists

National Comics #7, $3,500,
Quality Publications 1941, cover by Lou Fine.

Walt Disney Comics and Stories #167, $150,
Dell Publications 1954, cover by Carl Barks.

A-1 Comics #69 (The Ghost Rider #9), $600, Magazine Ent. 1952, cover by Dick Ayers.

A-1 Comics #47 (Thunda #1), $2,200, Magazine Ent. 1952, cover by Frank Frazetta.

Famous Artists

Captain America Comics #66, $3,300, Marvel Timely 1948, cover by Syd Shores.

Sub-Mariner Comics #23, $2,200, Marvel Timely 1947, cover by Syd Shores.

Walt Disney's Comics and Stories #109, $275., Dell Publ. 1950, cover by Carl Barks.

The Marvel Family #37, $350, Fawcett Publications 1949, cover by C. C. Beck.

Famous Artists

Target Comics #5, $9,000, Novelty Press 1940, cover by Bill Everett.

Donald Duck #26, $800, Dell Publishing 1952, cover by Carl Barks.

Pogo Possum #10, $450,
Dell Publishing Co. 1952, cover by Walt Kelly.

Animal Fables #7, $1,200,
EC Comics 1947, cover by Al Fago.

Famous Artists

Holiday #7, $275,
Star 1952, cover by L. B. Cole.

Walt Disney's Comics and Stories #22, $750,
Dell 1942, cover by Carl Buettner.

GRADING GUIDE

In David Brin's science fiction–fantasy novel, *The Practice Effect*, things improve with use. You start with a crudely made tool and keep using it until it becomes a fine instrument. If our world worked that way, you could read your Golden Age comics as often as you liked and they would just get better looking each time. Unfortunately, our world does not work that way, and reading your comics (along with just about everything else) causes comics to deteriorate.

Even if you could protect your comics from external light, heat, cold, moisture, pressure and everything else, you couldn't protect them from their own paper. Most comic books were printed on pulp paper, which has a high acid content. This means that the paper slowly turns brittle with age, no matter what you do to it, short of special museum-style preservation.

Very old, well-preserved comics are coveted collector's items. In most cases, people did not save their comic books for future generations. They read them and discarded them. Comic books were considered harmless ephemera for children. When these children outgrew their comics, their parents often threw them away. If everybody kept all of their comics, comics would not be valuable because everybody would have them scattered about the house!

The value of any comic depends on scarcity, popularity and condition. Scarcity increases with age and popularity depends on the whim of the public — only condition automatically decreases with age. Newer comics are generally available in near-mint condition, so newer comics in lesser condition have little collector potential. However, older comics are scarce, so they are still collectible in less than near-mint condition, but the value is obviously less. This is a basic tenet of all collectibles. A car is more valuable with its original paint. A baseball card is more valuable if it has not been marred by bicycle spokes. Coke bottles, stamps, coins, and toys in good condition are all more valuable than their abused counterparts. Comic books are no exception.

New comic book collectors should learn how to assess the prospective value of a comic in order to protect themselves from being fleeced by unscrupulous dealers or hucksters. Yet, a majority of dealers, especially store owners, can be considered reliable judges of comic grade. Because comic retail may be their primary source of income, certain dealers are particularly adept at noticing comic book imperfections, especially in issues they intend to purchase. As such, hobbyists and collectors must understand that dealers need to make a minimum profit on their investments. Buying collectible comics entails certain risks. Therefore, dealers must scrutinize a comic to determine if the particular book will stand a chance of resale. Well-preserved comics are invariably more desirable to dealers because they are more desirable to collectors.

There are eight standard comic grades: mint, near mint, very fine, fine, very good, good, fair, and poor. Clearly, these eight grades could be split into even finer categories when haggling over an exceptionally rare or coveted Golden Age comic. In most cases, however, comic books can be evaluated using these eight standard grades. The values listed in this book are all for comics in "Near Mint" condition. The grading/price chart given at the back of this book should be used to adjust this price for comics in different grades.

For many Golden Age comic issues, there are no known mint condition examples, but most issues have a few near mint copies in the hands of collectors. Many of these come from a few "pedigree" sources like the famous mile-high collection. There are, however, some issues where no known example is in near mint condition. To be consistent, the value listed in this price guide is still for a "near mint" copy, even if no such copy exists. The grading/price chart in the back will still yield a price for the lesser grades that actually exist. And, who knows, maybe there is another treasure trove of old comics somewhere — maybe you'll even be the one who finds it!

Mint (CGC 9.5 or above)

Finding old comics in mint condition is almost impossible because of inferior storage techniques and materials. In the early days of collecting, few people anticipated that the very boxes and bags in which they stored their comics were contributing to decay. Acid from bags, backing boards, and boxes eat away at many comics.. Mint condition comics usually fetch prices higher than price guide listings. Mint comics can sell for 120% or more of the listed price.

Mint comics are perfect comics and allow no room for imperfections. Pages and covers must be free of discoloration, wear, and wrinkles. A mint comic is one that looks like it just rolled off the press. Staples and spine must meet perfectly without cover "rollover." The cover must be crisp, bright, and trimmed perfectly. The staples must not be rusted and the cover should not have any visible creases. The interior pages of a mint comic are equally crisp and new. A mint comic must not show any signs of age or decay. Because of the paper stock used on many older comics, acid and oxygen cause interior pages to yellow and flake.

Near Mint (CGC 9.4)

A near mint comic and a mint comic are close siblings, with their differences slight, even to an experienced eye. Most of the new comics on the shelf of the local comic shop are in near mint condition. These are comics that have been handled gingerly to preserve the original luster of the book. Near mint comics are bright, clean copies with no major or minor defects. Slight stress lines near the staples and perhaps a very minor printing defect are permissible. Corners must still be sharp and devoid of creases. Interior pages of newsprint stock should show almost no discernible yellowing. Near mint comics usually trade for 100% of the listed price, with just a small discount for slightly lower grades.

Very Fine (CGC 8.0)

A very fine comic is one that is routinely found on the shelves and back issue bins of most good direct market comic shops. This grade comic has few defects, none of them major. Stress around the staples of a very fine comic are visible but not yet radical enough to create wrinkles. Both the cover and interior pages should still be crisp and sharp, devoid of flaking and creases. Interior pages may be slightly yellowed from age.

Most high-quality older comics graded as very fine can obtain 80-90% of listed prices. More, if the comic is the highest-graded comic known to exist.

Fine (CGC 6.0)

Fine comics are often issues that may have been stored carefully under a bed or on a shelf by a meticulous collector. This grade of comic is also very desirable because it shows little wear and retains much of its original sharpness. The cover may be slightly off center from rollover. The cover retains less of its original gloss and may even possess a chip or wrinkle. The comers should be sharp but may also have a slight crease. Yellowing begins to creep into the interior pages of a comic graded as fine.

Fine comics are respectable additions to collections and sell for about 40-60% of the listed price.

Very Good (CGC 4.0)

A very good comic may have been an issue passed around or read frequently. This grade is the common condition of older books. Its cover will probably have lost some luster and may have two or three creases around the staples or edges. The corners of the book may begin to show the beginnings of minor rounding and chipping, but it is by no means a damaged or defaced comic. Comics in very good condition sell for about 30-40% of listed price.

Good (CGC 2.0)

A good comic is one that has been well read and is beginning to show its age. Although both front and back covers are still attached, a good grade comic may have a number of serious wrinkles and chips. The corners and edges of this grade comic may show clear signs of rounding and flaking. There should be no major tears in a good comic nor should any pages be clipped out or missing. Interior pages may be fairly yellowed and brittle. Good comics sell for about 15-25% of the listed price.

Fair (CGC 1.0)

A fair comic is one that has definitely seen better days and has considerably limited resale value for most collectors. This comic may be soiled and damaged on the cover and interior. Fair comics should be completely intact and may only be useful as a reading copy, or a comic to lend to friends. Fair comics sell for about 10-20% of the listed price.

Poor

Comics in poor condition are generally unsuitable for collecting or reading because they range from damaged to unrecognizable. Poor comics may have been water damaged, attacked by a small child, or worse, perhaps, gnawed on by the family pet! Interior and exterior pages may be cut apart or missing entirely. A poor comic sells for about 5-15% of the listed price.

Sniffing Out Grades

Despite everything that is mentioned about comic grading, the process remains relative to the situation. A comic that seems to be in very good condition may actually be a restored copy. A restored copy is generally considered to be in between the grade it was previous to restoration and the grade it has become. Many collectors avoid restored comics entirely.

Each collector builds his collection around what he believes is important. Some want every issue of a particular series or company. Others want every issue of a favorite artist or writer. Because of this, many collectors will purchase lower-grade comics to fill out a series or to try out a new series. Mint and near mint comics are usually much more desirable to hardcore collectors. Hobbyists and readers may find the effort and cost of collecting only high-grade comics financially prohibitive.

Getting artists or writers to autograph comics has also become a source of major dispute. Some collectors enjoy signed comics and others consider those very comics defaced! The current trends indicate that most collectors do enjoy signed comics. A signature does not usually change the grade of the comic.

As mentioned, comic grading is a subjective process that must be agreed upon by the buyer and seller. Buyers will often be quick to note minor defects in order to negotiate a better price. Sellers are sometimes selectively blind to their comic's defects.

Abel, Jack	JA
Addeo, Stephen	StA
Alcala, Alfredo	AA
Anderson, Murphy	MA
Andriola, Alfred	AlA
Andru, Ross	RA
Ashe, Edd	EA
Avison, Al	AAv
Ayers, Dick	DAy
Bailey, Bernard	BBa
Bailey, M	MBi
Baker, Kyle	KB
Baker, Matt	MB
Barks, Carl	CB
Barry, Dan	DBa
Battlefield, Dennis	DB
Battlefield, Ken	KBa
Beck, C. C.	CCB
Berg, Dave	DBe
Berger, Charles	ChB
Biggs, Geoffrey	GB
Binder, Jack	JaB
Bingham, Jerry	JBi
Biro, Charles	CBi
Blum, Alex	AB
Bolle, Frank	FBe
Boring, Wayne	WB
Bossart, William	WmB
Braithwaite, Doug	DBw
Brewster, Ann	ABr
Briefer, Dick	DBr
Brodsky, Allyn	AyB
Burgos, Carl	CBu
Burnley, Jack	JBu
Burns, Robert	RBu
Buscema, John	JB
Cady, Harrison	HCa
Cameron, Don	DCn
Cameron, Lou	LC
Campbell, Stan	StC
Cardy, Nick	NC
Carlson, George	GCn
Castrillo, Anthony	ACa
Chestney, Lillian	LCh
Citron, Sam	SmC
Colan, Gene	GC
Cole, Jack	JCo
Cole, Leonard B.	LbC
Colletta, Vince	ViC
Collins, Mike	MC
Colon, Ernie	EC
Cooper, Sam	SCp
Costanza, Peter	PrC
Craig, Johnny	JCr
Crandall, Reed	RC
Cuidera, Chuck	CCu
Davis, Bob	BD
Davis, Jack	JDa
Del Bourgo, Maurice	MDb
Dillin, Dick	DD
Disbrow, Jay	JyD
Ditko, Steve	SD
Dougherty, H.	HD
Dresser, Larry	LDr
Drucker, Mort	MD
Duursema, Jan	JD
Eisner, Will	WE
Elder, Bill	BE
Elias, Lee	LEl
Evans, George	GE
Evans, Ray	REv
Everett, Bill	BEv
Fabry, Glenn	GF
Fago, Al	AFa
Feldstein, Al	AF
Fine, Lou	LF
Finnocchiaro, Sal	SF
Fiske, J.	JFe
Flemming, Homer	HFl
Flessel, Creig	CF
Forte, John	JF
Foster, Hal	HF
Fox, Gill	GFx
Fox, Matt	MF
Frazetta, Frank	FF
Frese, George	GFs
Froehlich, August	AgF
Fujitani(Fuje), Bob	BF
Giacoia, Frank	FrG
Giordano, Dick	DG
Glanzman, Sam	SG
Goldberg, Rube	RuG
Gottfredson, Floyd	FG
Gould, Chester	ChG
Grandmetti, Jerry	JGr
Griffiths, Harley	HyG
Guardineer, Fred	FGu
Guinan, Paul	PGn
Gulacy, Paul	PG
Gustavson, Paul	PGv
Harmon, Jim	JHa
Harrison, Simon	SHn
Hart, Ernest	EhH
Hearnes, David	DvH
Hearne, Jack	JH
Heath, Russ	RH
Hebbard, Robert	RtH
Heck, Don	DH
Hibbard, E.E.	EHi
Hicks, Arnold	AdH
Hing, T. F.	TFH
Hogarth, Burne	BHg
Hughes, Adam	AH
Hultgren, Ken	KHu
Infantino, Carmine	CI
Ingles, Graham	GrI
Iorio, Medio	MI
Isherwood, Geoff	GI
Jaffee, Al	AJ
Jenney, Robert	RJ
Johnson, Walter	WJo
Kaluta, Mike	MK
Kamen, Jack	JKa
Kane, Bob	BKa
Kane, Gil	GK
Katz, Jack	JKz
Kelly, Walt	WK
Kiefer, Henry C.	HcK
Kildale, Malcolm	MKd
Kinsler, Everett R.	EK
Kirby, Jack	JK
Krenkel, Roy	RKu
Krigstein, Bernie	BK
Kubert, Joe	JKu
Kurtzman, Harvey	HK
Lamme, Bob	BbL
LaRocque, Greg	GrL
Larsen, Erik	EL
Lavery, Jim	JLv
Lawrence, Terral	TLw
Leonard, Lank	LLe
Livingstone, Rolland	RLv
Lubbers, Bob	BLb
Maneely, Joe	JMn
Manning, Russ	RsM
Maxwell, Stanley	StM
Mayer, Sheldon	ShM
McCann, Gerald	GMc
McWilliams, Al	AMc
Meagher, Fred	FMe
Meskin, Mort	MMe
Messmer, Otto	OM
Miller, Steve	SM
Moe, C. S.	CSM
Moldoff, Sheldon	SMo
Mooney, Jim	JM
Morales, Lou	LM
Moreira, Ruben	RMo
Morisi, Pete	PMo
Morrow, Gray	GM
Mortimer, Win	WMo
Moskowitz, Seymour	SMz
Nodel, Norman	NN
Noonan, Dan	DNo
Nostrand, Howard	HN
Novick, Irv	IN
Orlando, Joe	JO
Oskner, Bob	BO
Oughton, Thomas	TO
Palais, Rudy	RP
Paul, Frank R.	FP
Payne, Pop	PP
Perlin, Don	DP
Plastino, Al	APl
Polseno, Jo	JP
Powell, Bob	BP
Premaini, Bruno	BPr
Prezio, Victor	VP
Quinlan, Charles	CQ
Raboy, Mac	MRa
Ramsey, Ray	RR
Rasmussen, H	HR
Raymond, Alex	AR
Rico, Don	DRi
Robinson, James	JeR
Roea, Doug	DgR
Rogers, Boody	BRo
Romita, John	JR
Ross, David	DR
Rubano, Aldo	ARu
Sahle, Harry	HSa
Sale, Tim	TSe
Saltares, Javier	JS
Saunders, Norm	NS
Schaffenberger, Kurt	KS
Schomburg, Alex	ASh
Schrotter, Gustav	GS
Sekowsky, Mike	MSy
Severin, John	JSe
Sherman, Jim	JSh
Shores, Syd	SSh
Shuster, Joe	JoS
Siegel & Shuster	S&S
Silvestri, Mark	MS
Sim, Dave	DS
Simon & Kirby	S&K
Simon, Allen	ASm
Simon, Joe	JSm
Sinnott, Joe	JSt
Smith, Fran	FSm
Sparling, Jack	JkS
Spector, Irving	IS
Starr, Leonard	LSt
Stein, Marvin	MvS
Streeter, Lin	LnS
Swan, Curt	CS
Tallarico, Tony	TyT
Tartaglione, John	JTg
Thompson, Bud	BTh
Thorne, Frank	FT
Torres, Angelo	AT
Toth, Alex	ATh
Trapain, Sal	ST
Tuska, George	GT
Ulmer, Al	AU
Van Buren, Raeburn	RvB
Vincent, A	AVi
Waldinger, Morris	MsW
Waldman, Ed	EW
Ward, Bill	BWa
Warren, Jack A.	JW
Webb, Robert	RWb
Whiteman, Ezra	EzW
Whitman, Bill	BWh
Whitney, Ogden	OW
Wiacek, Bob	BWi
Wildey, Doug	DW
Williams, J.H.	JWi
Williamson, Al	AW
Willingham, Bill	BWg
Wilson, Gahan	GW
Woggin, Bill	BWo
Wolverton, Basil	BW
Wood, Bob	BoW
Wood, Wally	WW
Woodbridge, George	GWb
Woodring, Jim	JWo
Zansky, Louis	LZ

GENERAL ABBREVIATIONS FOR COMICS LISTINGS

Adaptation	Adapt.
Appearance of	A:
Anniversary	Anniv.
Annual	Ann.#
Art & Cover	(a&c)
Artist	(a)
Back-Up Story	BU:
Beginning of	B:
Birth of	b:
Cameo Appearance	C:
Cover	(c)
Crossover with	x-over
Death/Destruction of	D:
Edition	Ed.
Ending of	E:
Features	F:
Giant Size	G-Size
Identity Revealed	IR:
Introduction of	I:
Joins of	J:
King Size	K-Size
Leaving of	L:
New Costume	N:
No Issue Number	N#
Origin of	O:
Painted Cover	P(c)
Part	pt. or Pt.
Photo cover	Ph(c)
Preview	Prev.
Reprinted issue	rep.
Retold	rtd.
Return/Revival of	R:
Story, or, Written by	(s)
Special	Spec.
Team-up	T.U.
Versus	V: or vs.
Wedding of	W:
With	w/
Without	w/o

AA	Alfredo Alcala
AAv	Al Avison
AB	Alex Blum
ABr	Ann Brewster
ACa	Anthony Castrillo
AdH	Arnold Hicks
AF	Al Feldstein
AFa	Al Fago
AgF	August Froehlich
AH	Adam Hughes
AlA	Alfred Andriola
AJ	Al Jaffee
AMc	Al McWilliams
APl	Al Plastino
AR	Alex Raymond
ARu	Aldo Rubano
ASh	Alex Schomburg
ASm	Allen Simon
AT	Angelo Torres
ATh	Alex Toth
AU	Al Ulmer
AVi	A. Vincent
AW	Al Williamson
AyB	Allyn Brodsky
BBa	Bernard Bailey
BbL	Bob Lamme
BD	Bob Davis
BE	Bill Elder
BEv	Bill Everett
BF	Bob Fujitani(Fuje)
BHg	Burne Hogarth
BK	Bernie Krigstein
BKa	Bob Kane
BLb	Bob Lubbers
BO	Bob Oskner
BoW	Bob Wood
BP	Bob Powell
BPr	Bruno Premaini
BRo	Boody Rogers
BTh	Bud Thompson
BW	Basil Wolverton
BWa	Bill Ward
BWg	Bill Willingham
BWh	Bill Whitman
BWi	Bob Wiacek
BWo	Bill Woggin
CB	Carl Barks
CBi	Charles Biro
CBu	Carl Burgos
CCB	C. C. Beck
CCu	Chuck Cuidera
CF	Creig Flessel
ChB	Charles Berger
ChG	Chester Gould
CI	Carmine Infantino
CQ	Charles Quinlan
CS	Curt Swan
CSM	C. S. Moe
DAy	Dick Ayers
DB	Dennis Battlefield
DBa	Dan Barry
DBe	Dave Berg
DBr	Dick Briefer
DBw	Doug Braithwaite
DCn	Don Cameron
DD	Dick Dillin
DG	Dick Giordano
DgR	Doug Roea
DH	Don Heck
DNo	Dan Noonan
DP	Don Perlin
DR	Ross, David
DRi	Don Rico
DS	Dave Sim
DvH	David Hearnes
DW	Doug Wildey
EA	Edd Ashe
EC	Ernie Colon
EhH	Ernest Hart
EHi	E.E. Hibbard
EK	Everett R. Kinsler
EL	Erik Larsen
EW	Ed Waldman
EzW	Ezra Whiteman
FBe	Frank Bolle
FF	Frank Frazetta
FG	Floyd Gottfredson
FGu	Fred Guardineer
FMe	Fred Meagher
FP	Frank R. Paul
FrG	Frank Giacoia
FSm	Fran Smith
FT	Frank Thorne
GB	Geoffrey Biggs
GC	Gene Colan
GCn	George Carlson
GE	George Evans
GF	Glenn Fabry
GFs	George Frese
GFx	Gill Fox
GI	Geoff Isherwood
GK	Gil Kane
GM	Gray Morrow
GMc	Gerald McCann
GrI	Graham Ingles
GrL	Greg LaRocque
GS	Gustav Schrotter
GT	George Tuska
GW	Gahan Wilson
GWb	George Woodbridge
HCa	Harrison Cady
HcK	Henry C. Kiefer
HD	H. Dougherty
HF	Hal Foster
HFl	Homer Flemming
HK	Harvey Kurtzman
HN	Howard Nostrand
HR	H. Rasmussen
HSa	Harry Sahle
HyG	Harley Griffiths
IN	Irv Novick
IS	Irving Spector
JA	Jack Abel
JaB	Jack Binder
JB	John Buscema
JBi	Jerry Bingham
JBu	Jack Burnley
JCo	Jack Cole
JCr	Johnny Craig
JD	Jan Duursema
JDa	Jack Davis
JeR	James Robinson
JF	John Forte
JFe	J. Fiske
JGr	Jerry Grandmetti
JH	Jack Hearne
JHa	Jim Harmon
JK	Jack Kirby
JKa	Jack Kamen
JkS	Jack Sparling
JKu	Joe Kubert
JKz	Jack Katz
JLv	Jim Lavery
JM	Jim Mooney
JMn	Joe Maneely
JO	Joe Orlando
JoS	Joe Shuster
JP	Jo Polseno
JR	John Romita
JRo	Jerry Robinson
JS	Javier Saltares
JSe	John Severin
JSh	Jim Sherman
JSm	Joe Simon
JSt	Joe Sinnott
JTg	John Tartaglione
JW	Jack A Warren
JWi	J.H. Williams
JWo	Jim Woodring
JyD	Jay Disbrow
KB	Kyle Baker
KBa	Ken Battlefield
KHu	Ken Hultgren
KS	Kurt Schaffenberger
LbC	Leonard B. Cole
LC	Lou Cameron
LCh	Lillian Chestney
LDr	Larry Dresser
LEl	Lee Elias
LF	Lou Fine
LLe	Lank Leonard
LM	Lou Morales
LnS	Lin Streeter
LSt	Leonard Starr
LZ	Louis Zansky
MA	Murphy Anderson
MB	Matt Baker
MBi	M. Bailey
MC	Mike Collins
MD	Mort Drucker
MDb	Maurice Del Bourgo
MF	Matt Fox
MI	Medio Iorio
MK	Mike Kaluta
MKd	Malcolm Kildale
MMe	Mort Meskin
MRa	Mac Raboy
MS	Mark Silvestri
MsW	Morris Waldinger
MSy	Mike Sekowsky
MvS	Marvin Stein
NC	Nick Cardy
NN	Norman Nodel
NS	Norm Saunders
OM	Otto Messmer
OW	Ogden Whitney
PG	Paul Gulacy
PGn	Paul Guinan
PGv	Paul Gustavson
PMo	Pete Morisi
PP	Pop Payne
PrC	Peter Costanza
RA	Ross Andru
RBu	Robert Burns
RC	Reed Crandall
REv	Ray Evans
RH	Russ Heath
RJ	Robert Jenney
RKu	Roy Krenkel
RLv	Rolland Livingstone
RMo	Ruben Moreira
RP	Rudy Palais
RR	Ray Ramsey
RsM	Russ Manning
RtH	Robert Hebbard
RuG	Rube Goldberg
RvB	Raeburn Van Buren
RWb	Robert Webb
S&K	Simon & Kirby
S&S	Siegel & Shuster
SCp	Sam Cooper
SD	Steve Ditko
SF	Sal Finnocchiaro
SG	Sam Glanzman
ShM	Sheldon Mayer
SHn	Simon Harrison
SmC	Sam Citron
SM	Steve Miller
SMo	Sheldon Moldoff
SMz	Seymour Moskowitz
SSh	Syd Shores
ST	Sal Trapain
StA	Stephen Addeo
StC	Stan Campbell
StM	Stanley Maxwell
TFH	T. F. Hing
TLw	Terral Lawrence
TO	Thomas Oughton
TSe	Tim Sale
TyT	Tony Tallarico
ViC	Vince Colleta
VP	Victor Prezio
WB	Wayne Boring
WE	Will Eisner
WJo	Walter Johnson
WK	Walt Kelly
WmB	William Bossart
WMo	Win Mortimer
WW	Wally Wood

GENERAL ABBREVIATIONS FOR COMICS LISTINGS

A:	**Appearance of**
(a)	**Artist**
Adapt.	**Adaptation**
Anniv.	**Anniversary**
Ann.#	**Annual**
(a&c)	**Art & Cover**
B:	**Beginning of**
b:	**Birth of**
BU:	**Back-Up Story**
C:	**Cameo Appearance**
(c)	**Cover**
D:	**Death/Destruction of**
Ed.	**Edition**
E:	**Ending of**
F:	**Features**
G-Size	**Giant Size**
I:	**Introduction of**
IR:	**Identity Revealed**
J:	**Joins of**
K-Size	**King Size**
L:	**Leaving of**
N:	**New Costume**
N#	**No Issue Number**
O:	**Origin of**
P(c)	**Painted Cover**
Ph(c)	**Photo cover**
Prev.	**Preview**
pt. or Pt.	**Part**
rep.	**Reprinted issue**
R:	**Return/Revival of**
rtd.	**Retold**
(s)	**Story, or Written by**
Spec.	**Special**
T.U.	**Team-up**
V: or vs.	**Versus**
W:	**Wedding of**
w/	**With**
w/o	**Without**
x-over	**Crossover with**

GOLDEN AGE VALUES

A-1 COMICS

Magazine Enterprises, 1944

N# F:Kerry Drake,BU:Johnny Devildog & Streamer Kelly . . 300.00
1 A:Dotty Driple,Mr. EX,Bush Berry and Lew Loyal 150.00
2 A:Texas Slim & Dirty Dalton, The Corsair,Teddy Rich, Dotty Dripple,Inca Dinca,Tommy Tinker Little Mexico and Tugboat . . . 100.00
3 same 100.00
4 same 100.00
5 same 100.00
6 same 100.00
7 same 100.00
8 same 100.00
9 Texas Slim Issue 125.00
10 Same characters as issues #2–#8 . . . . 100.00
11 Teena 150.00
12 Teena 100.00
13 JCr,Guns of Fact and Fiction, narcotics & junkies featured . 400.00
14 Tim Holt #1. . . . . 1,100.00
15 Teena 100.00
16 Vacation Comics 75.00
17 Tim Holt #2, E:"A-1" on cover . 500.00
18 Jimmy Durante, Ph(c). 650.00
19 Tim Holt #3 . . . . 400.00
20 Jimmy Durante Ph(c) 600.00
21 OW,Joan of Arc movie adapt. . 400.00
22 Dick Powell (1949) 350.00
23 Cowboys N' Indians #6. . . . . . 175.00
24 FF(c),LbC,Trail Colt #1 . . . . . . 600.00
25 Fibber McGee & Molly (1949). 125.00
26 LbC, Trail Colt #2 . . . . 500.00
27 GhostRider#1,O:GhostRider 1,500.00
28 Christmas (Koko & Kola #6) . . . 75.00
29 FF(c), Ghost Rider #2 . . . . . 1,100.00
30 BP, Jet Powers #1 . . . . 600.00
31 FF,Ghost Rider #3,O:Ghost Rider 1, 100.00
32 AW,GE,Jet Powers #2 . . . . . . 550.00
33 Muggsy Mouse #1 . . . . 100.00
34 FF(c),Ghost Rider #4 . . . . . . 1,100.00
35 AW,Jet Powers#3 . . . . 550.00
36 Muggsy Mouse #2 . . . . 125.00
37 FF(c),Ghost Rider #5. . . . . . 1,100.00
38 AW,WW,Jet Powers#4, Drugs 900.00
39 Muggsy Mouse #3 . . . . 100.00
40 Dogface Dooley #1. . . . . 100.00
41 Cowboys 'N' Indians #7 . . . . . 100.00
42 BP,Best of the West #1. . . . . . 700.00
43 Dogface Dooley#2 . . . . 75.00
44 Ghost Rider #6 . . . . 500.00
45 American Air Forces #5 . . . . . 200.00
46 Best of the West #4 . . . . 650.00
47 FF,Thunda #1. . . . . 2,200.00
48 Cowboys N' Indians #8. . . . . . 150.00
49 Dogface Dooley #3 . . . . 75.00
50 BP,Danger is Their Business #11 . . . . 200.00
51 Ghost Rider #7 . . . . 500.00
52 Best of the West #3 . . . . 400.00
53 Dogface Dooley #4 . . . . 75.00
54 BP,American Air Forces #6. . . 100.00
55 BP,U.S. Marines #5. . . . . 100.00
56 BP,Thunda #2 . . . . 350.00
57 Ghost Rider #8, Drugs 600.00
58 American Air Forces #7 . . . . . 100.00
59 Best of the West #4 . . . . 350.00
60 The U.S. Marines #6. . . . . 100.00
61 Space Ace #5 . . . . 900.00
62 Starr Flagg #5. . . . . 600.00
63 FF,Manhunt #13 . . . . 550.00
64 Dogface Dooley #5 . . . . 75.00
65 BP,American Air Forces #8 . . . 100.00
66 Best of the West #5 . . . . 350.00
67 American Air Forces #9 . . . . . 100.00
68 U.S. Marines #7 . . . . 100.00
69 Ghost Rider #9, Drugs 600.00
70 Best of the West #6 . . . . 350.00
71 Ghost Rider #10 . . . . 500.00
72 U.S. Marines #8 . . . . 100.00
73 BP,Thunda #3 . . . . 300.00
74 BP,American Air Forces #10. . 100.00
75 Ghost Rider #11 . . . . 400.00
76 Best of the West #7 . . . . 250.00
77 LbC,Grl,Manhunt #14 . . . . 450.00
78 BP,Thunda #4 . . . . 300.00
79 American Air Forces #11. . . . . 100.00
80 Ghost Rider #12, Bondage(c). 500.00
81 Best of the West #8 . . . . 200.00
82 BP,Cave Girl #11. . . . . 700.00
83 BP,Thunda #5 . . . . 250.00
84 Ghost Rider #13 . . . . 400.00
85 Best of the West #9 . . . . 200.00
86 BP,Thunda #6 . . . . 250.00
87 Best of the West #10 . . . . 200.00
88 Bobby Benson's B-Bar-B #29. 150.00
89 BP,Home Run #3,Stan Musial. 275.00
90 Red Hawk #11 . . . . 200.00
91 BP,American Air Forces #12. . 100.00
92 Dream Book of Romance #5 . 175.00
93 BP,Great Western #8 . . . . 300.00
94 FF,White Indian #11 . . . . 350.00
95 BP,Muggsy Mouse #4. . . . . 75.00
96 BP,Cave Girl #12 . . . . 500.00
97 Best of the West #11 . . . . 200.00
98 Undercover Girl #6 . . . . 600.00
99 Muggsy Mouse #5 . . . . 75.00
100 Badmen of the West #1 . . . . 325.00
101 FF,White Indian #12 . . . . 325.00
101(a) BP(c),FGu, Dream Book of Romance #6, Marlon Brando 300.00
103 BP,Best of the West #12. . . . 200.00
104 FF,White Indian #13 . . . . 325.00
105 Great Western #9 . . . . 200.00
106 BP,Dream Book of Love #1 . 200.00
107 Hot Dog #1 . . . . 125.00
108 BP,LbC,Red Fox #15 . . . . . . 350.00
109 BP,Dream Book of Romance 150.00
110 Dream Book of Romance #8 150.00
111 BP,I'm a Cop #1 . . . . 200.00
112 Ghost Rider #14 . . . . 400.00
113 BP,Great Western #10 . . . . . 175.00
114 Dream Book of Love #2 . . . . 150.00
115 Hot Dog #2 . . . . 100.00
116 BP,Cave Girl #13. . . . . 500.00
117 White Indian #14. . . . . 175.00
118 BP(c),Starr Flagg– Undercover Girl #7 . . . . 550.00
119 Straight Arrow's Fury #1 . . . . 225.00
120 Badmen of the West #2 . . . . 250.00
121 Mysteries of the Scotland Yard #1. . . . . 250.00
122 Black Phantom #1. . . . . 550.00
123 Dream Book of Love #3 . . . . 125.00
124 Hot Dog #3 . . . . 100.00
125 BP,Cave Girl #14 . . . . 500.00
126 BP,I'm a Cop #2. . . . . 150.00
127 BP,Great Western 200.00
128 BP,I'm a Cop #3 . . . . 150.00
129 The Avenger #1 . . . . 600.00
130 BP,Strongman #1 . . . . 325.00
131 BP,The Avenger #2. . . . . 450.00
132 Strongman #2 . . . . 300.00

A-1 Comics #27
© Magazine Enterprises

A-1 Comics #56
© Magazine Enterprises

A-1 Comics #61
© Magazine Enterprises

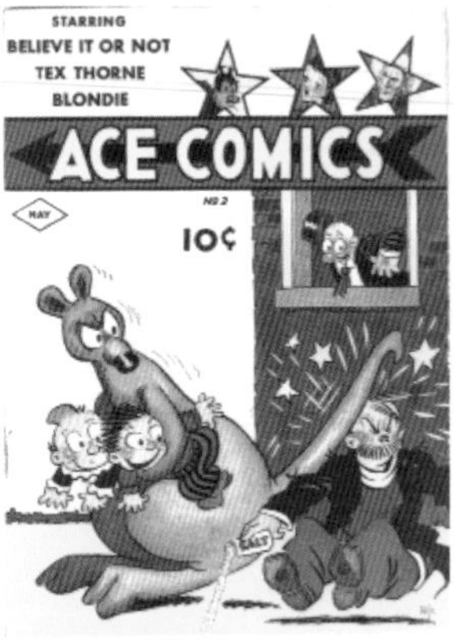

Ace #2
© David McKay Publications

Aces High #4
© EC Publications

Action Comics #17
© DC Comics

133 BP,The Avenger #3 . . . . 450.00
134 Strongman #3 . . . . 300.00
135 White Indian #15 . . . . 175.00
136 Hot Dog #4 . . . . 100.00
137 BP,Africa #1 . . . . 350.00
138 BP,Avenger #4 . . . . 450.00
139 BP,Strongman #4, 1955 . . . . 300.00

ABBIE AN' SLATS

United Features Syndicate, March–Aug., 1948

1 RvB(c) 250.00
2 RvB(c) 175.00
3 RvB(c) 150.00
4 Aug., 1948 . . . . 150.00
N# 1940,Earlier Issue 600.00
N# 500.00

ABBOTT AND COSTELLO

St. John Publishing Co., Feb., 1948

1 PP(c), Waltz Time 800.00
2 Jungle Girl and Snake(c) 450.00
3 Outer Space (c) 300.00
4 MD, Circus (c) 250.00
5 MD,Bull Fighting (c) 250.00
6 MD,Harem (c) 250.00
7 MD,Opera (c) 250.00
8 MD,Pirates (c) 250.00
9 MD,Polar Bear (c) 250.00
10 MD,PP(c),Son of Sinbad tale . 300.00
11 MD 200.00
12 PP(c), Movie issue 250.00
13 Fire fighters (c) 200.00
14 Bomb (c) 200.00
15 Bubble Bath (c) 200.00
16 thru 29 MD . . . . @175.00
30 thru 39 MD . . . . @150.00
40 MD,Sept., 1956 . . . . 150.00
3-D #1, Nov., 1953 . . . . 500.00

ACE COMICS

David McKay Publications, April, 1937

1 JM, F:Katzenjammer Kids . . 5,000.00
2 JM, A:Blondie 1,500.00
3 JM, A:Believe It Or Not 1,000.00
4 JM, F:Katzenjammer Kids . . 1,000.00
5 JM, A:Believe It Or Not 1,000.00
6 JM, A:Blondie 750.00
7 JM, A:Believe It Or Not 750.00
8 JM, A:Jungle Jim 750.00
9 JM, A:Blondie 750.00
10 JM, F:Katzenjammer Kids 700.00
11 I:The Phantom series 1,200.00
12 A:Blondie, Jungle Jim 600.00
13 A:Ripley's Believe It Or Not . . 500.00
14 A:Blondie, Jungle Jim 500.00
15 A:Blondie 475.00
16 F:Katzenjammer Kids 475.00
17 A:Blondie 475.00
18 A:Ripley's Believe It Or Not . . 475.00
19 F:Katzenjammer Kids 475.00
20 A:Jungle Jim 475.00
21 A:Blondie 450.00
22 A:Jungle Jim 450.00
23 F:Katzenjammer Kids 450.00
24 A:Blondie 450.00
25 . . . . 450.00
26 O:Prince Valiant 1,500.00
27 thru 36 . . . . @450.00
37 Krazy Kat Ends 350.00
38 thru 40 . . . . @350.00
41 thru 59 . . . . @300.00
60 thru 69 . . . . @250.00
70 thru 89 . . . . @150.00
90 thru 99 . . . . @125.00
100 . . . . 150.00
101 thru 109 . . . . @125.00
110 thru 119 . . . . @100.00
120 thru 143 . . . . @100.00
144 Phantom covers begin 125.00
145 thru 150 . . . . @100.00
151 Oct.–Nov., 1949 . . . . 125.00

ACES HIGH

E.C. Comics, March–April, 1955

1 GE(a&c),JDa,WW,BK 500.00
2 GE(a&c),JDa,WW,BK 300.00
3 GE(a&c),JDa,WW,BK 250.00
4 GE(a&c),JDa,WW,BK 250.00
5 GE(c),JDa,WW,BK 250.00

ACTION

DC Comics, June, 1938

1 JoS,I&O:Superman;Rescues Evelyn Curry from electric chair . 500,000.00
2 JoS,V:Emil Norvell 60,000.00
3 JoS,V:Thorton Blakely 40,000.00
4 JoS,V:Coach Randall 25,000.00
5 JoS,Emergency of Vallegho Dam 25,000.00
6 JoS,I:Jimmy Olsen, V:Nick Williams 25,000.00
7 JoS,V:Derek Niles 50,000.00
8 JoS,V:Gimpy 15,000.00
9 JoS,A:Det.Captain Reilly . . 15,000.00
10 JoS,Superman fights for prison reform 30,000.00
11 JoS,Disguised as Homer Ramsey 7,500.00
12 JoS,Crusade against reckless drivers 8,000.00
13 JoS,I:Ultra Humanite 15,000.00
14 JoS,BKa,V:Ultra Humanite, B:Clip Carson 8,000.00
15 JoS,BKa,Superman in Kidtown 15,000.00
16 JoS,BKa,Crusade against Gambling 8,000.00
17 JoS,BKa,V:Ultra Humanite. 12,000.00
18 JoS,BKa,V:Mr.Hamilton O:Three Aces 8,000.00
19 JoS,BKa,V:Ultra Humanite B:Superman (c) 12,000.00
20 JoS,BKa,V:Ultra Humanite. 10,000.00
21 JoS,BKa,V:Ultra Humanite. 10,000.00
22 JoS,BKa,War between Toran and Galonia 10,000.00
23 JoS,BKa,SMo,I:Lex Luthor 16,000.00
24 JoS,BKa,BBa,SMo,FGu,Meets Peter Carnahan 10,000.00
25 JoS,BKa,BBa,SMo, V:Medini 10,000.00
26 JoS,BKa,V:ClarenceCobalt 10,000.00
27 JoS,BKa,V:Mr & Mrs.Tweed 6,000.00
28 JoS,BKa,JBu,V:Strongarm Bandit 6,000.00
29 JoS,BKa,V:Martin 7,000.00
30 JoS,BKa,V:Zolar 6,000.00
31 JoS,BKa,JBu,V:Baron Munsdorf 4,000.00
32 JoS,BKa,JBu,I:Krypto Ray Gun V:Mr.Preston 4,000.00
33 JoS,BKa,JBu,V:Brett Hall, O:Mr. America 4,000.00
34 JoS,BKa,V:Jim Laurg 4,000.00
35 JoS,BKa,V:Brock Walter . . . 4,000.00
36 JoS,BKa,V:StuartPemberton 4,000.00
37 JoS,BKa,V:Commissioner Kennedy, O:Congo Bill 3,900.00
38 JoS,BKa,V:Harold Morton . . 3,900.00
39 JoS,BKa,Meets Britt Bryson 3,900.00
40 JoS,BKa,Meets Nancy Thorgenson 3,900.00
41 JoS,BKa,V:Ralph Cowan, E:Clip Carson 3,500.00
42 V:Lex Luthor,I&O:Vigilante . . 5,000.00
43 V:Dutch O'Leary,Nazi(c) . . . 3,500.00
44 V:Prof. Steffens,Nazi(c) 3,500.00
45 V:Count Von Henzel, I:Stuff,Nazi(c) 3,500.00
46 V:The Domino 3,500.00

 All comics prices listed are for *Near Mint* condition.

Action Comics #56
© DC Comics

Action Comics #112
© DC Comics

Action Comics #160
© DC Comics

47 V:Lex Luthor—1st app. w/super powers,I:Powerstone 5,000.00
48 V:The Top 3,200.00
49 I:Puzzler 3,200.00
50 Meets Stan Doborak 3,200.00
51 I:Prankster 4,000.00
52 V:Emperor of America 4,500.00
53 JBu,V:Night-Owl 3,500.00
54 JBu,Meets Stanley Finchcomb 3,500.00
55 JBu,V:Cartoonist Al Hatt 3,500.00
56 V:Emil Loring 3,500.00
57 V:Prankster 3,500.00
58 JBu,V:Adonis 3,500.00
59 I:Susie Thompkins,Lois Lane's niece 3,500.00
60 JBu,Lois Lane-Superwoman 3,500.00
61 JBu,Meets Craig Shaw 3,500.00
62 JBu,V:Admiral Von Storff 3,500.00
63 JBu,V:Professor Praline 3,500.00
64 I:Toyman 3,500.00
65 JBu,V:Truman Treadwell 3,500.00
66 JBu,V:Mr.Annister 3,500.00
67 JBu,Superman School for Officer's Training 3,500.00
68 A:Susie Thompkins 3,500.00
69 V:Prankster 3,500.00
70 JBu,V:Thinker 3,500.00
71 Superman Valentine's Day Special 3,000.00
72 V:Mr. Sniggle 3,000.00
73 V:Lucius Spruce 3,000.00
74 Meets Adelbert Dribble 3,000.00
75 V:Johnny Aesop 3,000.00
76 A Voyage with Destiny 3,000.00
77 V:Prankster 3,000.00
78 The Chef of Bohemia 3,000.00
79 JBu,A:J. Wilbur Wolfingham 3,000.00
80 A:Mr. Mxyzptlk (2nd App) 3,500.00
81 Meets John Nicholas 3,000.00
82 JBu,V:Water Sprite 3,000.00
83 I:Hocus and Pocus 3,000.00
84 JBu,V:Dapper Gang 3,000.00
85 JBu,V:Toyman 3,000.00
86 JBu,V:Wizard of Wokit 3,000.00
87 V:Truck Hijackers 3,000.00
88 A:Hocus and Pocus 3,000.00
89 V:Slippery Andy 3,000.00
90 JBu,V:Horace Rikker and the Amphi-Bandits 3,000.00
91 JBu,V:Davey Jones 900.00
92 JBu,V:Nowmie Norman 900.00
93 Superman Christmas story 900.00
94 JBu,V:Bullwer 'Bull' Rylie 900.00
95 V:Prankster 900.00
96 V:Mr. Twister 900.00
97 A:Hocus and Pocus 900.00
98 V:Mr. Mxyzptlk, A:Susie Thompkins 3,500.00
99 V:Keith Langwell 900.00
100 I:InspectorErskineHawkins. 1,300.00
101 V:Specs Dour,A-Bomb(c) 1,900.00
102 V:Mr. Mxyzptlk 1,400.00
103 V:Emperor Quexo 1,400.00
104 V:Prankster 1,400.00
105 Superman Christmas story 1,400.00
106 Clark Kent becomes Baron Edgestream 1,400.00
107 JBu,A:J.Wilbur Wolfingham 1,400.00
108 JBu,V:Vince Vincent 1,400.00
109 V:Prankster 1,400.00
110 A:Susie Thompkins 800.00
111 Cameras in the Clouds 800.00
112 V:Mr. Mxyzptlk 1,400.00
113 Just an Ordinary Guy 1,400.00
114 V:Mike Chesney 1,400.00
115 Meets Arthur Parrish 1,400.00
116 A:J. Wilbur Wolfingham 1,400.00
117 Superman Christmas story 1,400.00
118 Execution of Clark Kent 1,400.00
119 Meets Jim Banning 1,400.00
120 V:Mike Foss 1,400.00
121 V:William Sharp 1,400.00
122 V:Charley Carson 1,400.00
123 V:Skid Russell 1,400.00
124 Superman becomes radioactive 1,200.00
125 V:Lex Luthor 750.00
126 V:Chameleon 1,200.00
127 JKu,Superman on Truth or Consequences 2,100.00
128 V:'Aces' Deucey 2,000.00
129 Meets Gob-Gob 2,000.00
130 V:Captain Kidder 2,000.00
131 V:Lex Luthor 2,000.00
132 Superman meets George Washington 2,000.00
133 V:Emma Blotz 2,000.00
134 V:Paul Strong 2,000.00
135 V:John Morton 2,000.00
136 Superman Show-Off! 2,000.00
137 Meets Percival Winter 2,000.00
138 Meets Herbert Hinkle 2,000.00
139 Clark Kent...Daredevil! 2,000.00
140 Superman becomes Hermit 2,000.00
141 V:Lex Luthor 2,000.00
142 V:Dan the Dip 2,000.00
143 Dates Nikki Larve 2,000.00
144 O:Clark Kent reporting for Daily Planet 2,000.00
145 Meets Merton Gloop 2,000.00
146 V:Luthor 2,000.00
147 V:'Cheeks' Ross 2,000.00
148 Superman, Indian Chief 2,000.00
149 The Courtship on Krypton!. 2,000.00
150 V:Morko 2,000.00
151 V:Mr.Mxyzptlk,Lex Luthor and Prankster 2,000.00
152 I:Metropolis Shutterbug Society 2,100.00
153 V:Kingpin 2,000.00
154 V:Harry Reed 2,000.00
155 V:Andrew Arvin 2,000.00
156 Lois Lane becomes Superwoman,V:Lex Luthor 1,800.00
157 V:Joe Striker 1,800.00
158 V:Kane Korrell O:Superman (retold) 2,500.00
159 Meets Oswald Whimple 1,800.00
160 I:Minerva Kent 1,800.00
161 Meets Antara 1,800.00
162 V:'IT!' 1,800.00
163 Meets Susan Semple 1,800.00
164 Meets Stefan Andriessen 1,800.00
165 V:Crime Czar 1,800.00
166 V:Lex Luthor 1,800.00
167 V:Prof. Nero 1,800.00
168 O:Olaf 1,800.00
169 Caveman Clark Kent! 1,800.00
170 V:Mad Artist of Metropolis . 1,800.00
171 The Secrets of Superman . 1,800.00
172 Lois Lane..Witch! 1,800.00
173 V:Dragon Lang 1,800.00
174 V:Miracle Twine Gang 1,800.00
175 V:John Vinden 1,800.00
176 V:Billion Dollar Gang 1,800.00
177 V:General 1,800.00
178 V:Prof. Sands 1,800.00
179 Superman in Mapleville 1,800.00
180 V:Syndicate of Five 1,800.00
181 V:Diamond Dave Delaney . 1,200.00
182 Return from Planet Krypton 1,200.00
183 V:Lex Luthor 1,200.00
184 Meets Donald Whitmore 1,200.00
185 V:Issah Pendleton 1,200.00
186 The Haunted Superman 1,200.00
187 V:Silver 1,200.00
188 V:Cushions Raymond gang 1,200.00
189 Meets Mr.& Mrs. Vandeveir 1,200.00
190 V:Mr. Mxyzptlk 1,200.00
191 V:Vic Vordan 1,200.00
192 Meets Vic Vordan 1,200.00
193 V:Beetles Brogan 1,200.00
194 V:Maln 1,200.00
195 V:Tiger Woman 1,200.00
196 Superman becomes Mental Man 1,200.00
197 V:Stanley Stark 1,200.00

Action Comics #209
© DC Comics

Action Comics #271
© DC Comics

Adventure Comics #33
© DC Comics

198 The Six Lives of Lois Lane 1,200.00
199 V:Lex Luthor 1,200.00
200 V:Morwatha 1,200.00
201 'V:Benny the Brute 1,200.00
202 Lois Lane's X-Ray Vision 1,000.00
203 Meets Pietro Paresca 1,000.00
204 Meets Sam Spulby 1,000.00
205 Sergeant Superman 1,000.00
206 Imaginary story F:L.Lane 1,000.00
207 Four Superman Medals! 1,000.00
208 V:Mr. Mxyzptlk 1,000.00
209 V:'Doc' Winters 1,000.00
210 V:Lex,I:Superman Land 1,000.00
211 Superman Spectaculars 1,000.00
212 V:Thorne Varden 1,000.00
213 V:Paul Paxton 1,000.00
214 Superman,Sup.Destroyer! 1,000.00
215 I:Superman of 2956 1,000.00
216 A:Jor-El 1,000.00
217 Meets Mr&Mrs.Roger Bliss 1,000.00
218 I:Super-Ape from Krypton 1,000.00
219 V:Art Shaler 1,000.00
220 Interplanetary Olympics 1,000.00
221 V:Jay Vorrell 800.00
222 The Duplicate Superman 800.00
223 A:Jor-El 800.00
224 I:Superman Island 800.00
225 The Death of Superman 800.00
226 V:Lex Luthor 800.00
227 Man with Triple X-Ray Eyes 800.00
228 A:Superman Museum 800.00
229 V:Dr. John Haley 800.00
230 V:Bart Wellins 800.00
231 Sir Jimmy Olsen, Knight of Metropolis 800.00
232 Meets Johnny Kirk 800.00
233 V:Torm 800.00
234 Meets Golto 800.00
235 B:Congo Bill, B:Tommy Tomorrow 800.00
236 A:Lex Luthor 800.00
237 V:Nebula Gang 800.00
238 I:King Krypton,the Gorilla 800.00
239 Superman's New Face 800.00
240 V:Superman Sphinx 800.00
241 WB,A:Batman,Fortress of Solitude (Fort Superman) 700.00
242 I&O:Brainiac 5,000.00
243 Lady and the Lion 700.00
244 CS,A:Vul-Kor,Lya-La 700.00
245 WB,V:Kak-Kul 700.00
246 WB,A:Krypton Island 700.00
247 WB,Superman Lost Parents 700.00
248 B&I:Congorilla 700.00
249 A:Lex Luthor 700.00
250 WB,The Eye of Metropolis 700.00
251 E:Tommy Tomorrow 700.00
252 I&O:Supergirl 5,000.00
253 B:Supergirl 1,300.00
254 I:Adult Bizarro 1,000.00
255 I:Bizarro Lois 800.00
256 Superman of the Future 500.00
257 WB,JM,V:Lex Luthor 500.00
258 A:Cosmic Man 500.00
259 A:Lex Luthor,Superboy 500.00
260 A:Mighty Maid 500.00
261 I:Streaky,E:Congorilla 500.00
262 A:Bizarro 500.00
263 O:Bizarro World 600.00
264 V:Bizarro 500.00
265 A:Hyper-Man 500.00
266 A:Streaky,Krypto 500.00
267 JM,3rd A:Legion,I:Invisible Kid 1,200.00
268 WB,A:Hercules 400.00
269 A:Jerro 400.00
270 CS,JM,A:Batman 500.00
271 A:Lex Luthor 400.00
272 A:Aquaman 400.00
273 A:Mr.Mxyzptlk 400.00
274 A:Superwoman 400.00
275 WB,JM,V:Braimiac 400.00
276 JM,6th A:Legion,I:Brainiac 5, Triplicate Girl,Bouncing Boy 700.00
277 CS,JM,V:Lex Luthor 300.00
278 CS,Perry White Becomes Master Man 300.00
279 JM,V:Hercules,Samson 300.00
280 CS,JM,V:Braniac, A:Congorilla 300.00
281 JM,A:Krypto 300.00
282 JM,V:Mxyzptlk 300.00
283 CS,JM,A:Legion of Super Outlaws 400.00
284 A:Krypto,Jerro 300.00
285 JM,Supergirl Existence Revealed, C:Legion (12th app.) 400.00
286 CS,JM,V:Lex Luthor 250.00
287 JM,A:Legion 250.00
288 JM,A:Mon-El 250.00
289 JM,A:Adult Legion 250.00
290 JM,C:Phantom Girl 250.00
291 JM,V:Mxyzptlk 250.00
292 JM,I:Superhorse 250.00
293 JM,O:Comet-Superhorse 300.00
294 JM,V:Lex Luthor 250.00
295 CS,JM,O:Lex Luthor 250.00
296 V:Super Ants 250.00
297 CS,JM,A:Mon-El 250.00
298 CS,JM,V:Lex Luthor 250.00
299 O:Superman Robots 250.00
300 JM,A:Mxyzptlk 300.00

REAL ADVENTURE COMICS

Gillmor Magazines, Apr. 1955

1 100.00

Becomes:

ACTION ADVENTURE

Gillmor Magazines, June–Oct., 1955

2 100.00
3 100.00
4 100.00

ACTUAL CONFESSIONS

See: LOVE ADVENTURES

ACTUAL ROMANCES

Marvel, Oct., 1949

1 150.00
2 Photo Cover 100.00

ADVENTURE COMICS

DC Comics, Nov., 1938–83

[Prev: New Adventure Comics]

32 CF(c) 7,000.00
33 CF(c),BKa 4,000.00
34 FGu(c) 4,000.00
35 FGu(c) 4,000.00
36 Giant Snake(c) 4,000.00
37 CF,Rampaging Elephant(c) 4,000.00
38 Tiger(c) 4,000.00
39 Male Bondage(c) 3,000.00
40 CF(c),1st app. Sandman 90,000.00
41 Killer Shark(c) 15,000.00
42 CF,Sandman(c) 30,000.00
43 CF(c) 9,000.00
44 CF,FGu,Sandman(c) 15,000.00
45 FGu(c) 9,000.00
46 CF,Sandman(c) 14,000.00
47 Sandman (c) 14,000.00
48 1st app.& B:Hourman 60,000.00
49 SMo(c),BKa,CF 6,000.00
50 Hourman(c) 6,000.00
51 BBa(c),Sandman(c) 9,000.00
52 BBa(c),Hourman(c) 5,500.00
53 BBa(c),1st app. Minuteman 5,500.00
54 BBa(c),Hourman(c) 5,500.00
55 BBa(c),same 5,500.00
56 BBa(c),same 5,500.00
57 BBa(c),same 5,500.00
58 BBa(c),same 5,500.00
59 BBa(c),same 5,500.00

Adventure Comics #57
© DC Comics

Adventure Comics #138
© DC Comics

Adventure Comics #161
© DC Comics

60 Sandman(c) 4,800.00
61 CF(c),JBu,Starman(c) 25,000.00
62 JBu(c),JBu,Starman(c). 7,000.00
63 JBu(c),JBu,same 5,000.00
64 JBu(c),JBu,same 5,000.00
65 JBu(c),JBu,same 5,000.00
66 JBu(c),JBu,O:Shining Knight, Starman(c) 5,500.00
67 JBu(c),JBu,O:Mist 5,000.00
68 JBu(c),JBu,same 5,000.00
69 JBu(c),JBu,1st app. Sandy, Starman(c) 5,000.00
70 JBu(c),JBu,Starman(c). 5,000.00
71 JBu(c),JBu,same 5,000.00
72 JBu(c),S&K,JBu,Sandman. 30,000.00
73 S&K(c),S&K,I:Manhunter . . 31,000.00
74 S&K(c),S&K,You Can't Escape Your Fate-The Sandman . . 5,000.00
75 S&K(c),S&K,Sandman and Sandy Battle Thor. 5,000.00
76 S&K(c),Sandman(c),S&K. . . 5,000.00
77 S&K,(c),S&K,same. 5,000.00
78 S&K(c),S&K,same 5,000.00
79 S&K(c),S&K,Manhunter . . . 12,000.00
80 S&K(c),Sandman(c),S&K. . . 5,000.00
81 S&K(c),MMe,S&K,same. . . . 3,000.00
82 S&K(c),S&K,Sandman X-Mas story 3,000.00
83 S&K(c),S&K,Sandman Boxing(c),E:Hourman 3,000.00
84 S&K(c),S&K 3,000.00
85 S&K(c),S&K,Sandman in The Amazing Dreams of Gentleman Jack 3,000.00
86 S&K(c),Sandman(c). 3,000.00
87 S&K(c),same 3,000.00
88 S&K(c),same 3,000.00
89 S&K(c),same 3,000.00
90 S&K(c),same 3,000.00
91 S&K(c),JK 3,000.00
92 S&K(c) 2,000.00
93 S&K(c),Sandman in Sleep for Sale. 2,000.00
94 S&K(c),Sandman(c). 2,000.00
95 S&K(c),same 2,000.00
96 S&K(c),same 2,000.00
97 S&K(c),same 2,000.00
98 JK(c),Sandman in Hero of Dreams. 2,000.00
99 JK(c). 2,000.00
100JK(c&a) 2,000.00
101 S&K(c) 2,000.00
102 S&K(c) 2,000.00
103 B:Superboy stories,(c),BU: Johnny Quick,Aquaman,Shining Knight,Green Arrow 5,000.00
104 S&S,ToyTown USA 1,900.00
105 S&S,Palace of Fantasy . . . 1,500.00
106 S&S,Weather Hurricane . . 1,500.00
107 S&S,The Sky is the Limit. . 1,500.00
108 S&S,Proof of the Proverbs 1,500.00
109 S&S,You Can't Lose 1,500.00
110 S&S,The Farmer Takes it Easy. 1,500.00
111 S&S,The Whiz Quiz Club. . 1,500.00
112 S&S,Super Safety First . . . 1,500.00
113 S&S,The 33rd Christmas . . 1,400.00
114 S&S,Superboy Spells Danger 1,400.00
115 S&S,The Adventure of Jaguar Boy 1,400.00
116 S&S,JBu,Superboy Toy Tester 1,400.00
117 S&S,JBu,Miracle Plane . . . 1,400.00
118 S&S,JBu,The Quiz Biz Broadcast 1,400.00
119 WMo,JBu,Superboy Meets Girls 1,400.00
120 S&S,JBu,A:Perry White; I:Ringmaster 1,500.00
121 S&S,Great Hobby Contest. 1,600.00
122 S&S,Superboy-Super-Magician 1,800.00
123 S&S,Lesson For a Bully. . . 1,600.00
124 S&S,Barbed Wire Boys Town 1,200.00
125 S&S,The Weight Before Christmas 1,200.00
126 S&S,Superboy:Crime Fighting Poet 1,200.00
127 MMe,O:Shining Knight; Super Bellboy 1,200.00
128 WMo,How Clark Kent Met Lois Lane 1,200.00
129 WMo,Pupils of the Past . . . 1,200.00
130 WMo,Superboy Super Salesman 1,200.00
131 WMo,The Million Dollar Athlete 1,200.00
132 WMo,Superboy Super Cowboy. 1,200.00
133 WMo,Superboy's Report Card 1,200.00
134 WMo,Silver Gloves Sellout 1,200.00
135 WMo,The Most Amazing of All Boys 1,200.00
136 WMo,My Pal Superboy . . . 1,200.00
137 WMo,Treasure of Tondimo. 1,200.00
138 WMo,Around the World in Eighty Minutes 1,200.00
139 WMo,Telegraph Boy 1,200.00
140 Journey to the Moon 1,200.00
141 WMo,When Superboy Lost His Powers 1,200.00
142 WMo,The Man Who Walked With Trouble 1,200.00
143 WMo,Superboy Savings Bank, A:Wooden Head Jones . . . 1,200.00
144 WMo,The Way to Stop Superboy 1,200.00
145 WMo,Holiday Hijackers . . . 1,200.00
146 The Substitute Superboy . . 1,200.00
147 Clark Kent,Orphan 1,200.00
148 Superboy Meets Mummies 1,200.00
149 Fake Superboys. 1,200.00
150 FF,Superboy's Initiation . . . 1,100.00
151 FF,No Hunting(c). 850.00
152 Superboy Hunts For a Job. 1,000.00
153 FF,Clark Kent,Boy Hobo . . 1,100.00
154 The Carnival Boat Crimes . 1,000.00
155 FF,Superboy-Hollywood Actor. 1,100.00
156 The Flying Peril 1,000.00
157 FF,The Worst Boy in Smallville 1,100.00
158 The Impossible Task 1,000.00
159 FF,Superboy Millionaire?. . 1,100.00
160 Superboy's Phoney Father . . 950.00
161 FF. 1,100.00
162 Super-Coach of Smallville High!. 1,000.00
163 FF,Superboy's Phoney Father. 1,100.00
164 Discovers the Secret of a Lost Indian Tribe!. 1,000.00
165 Superboy's School for Stunt Men! 1,000.00
166 Town That Stole Superboy. 1,000.00
167 Lana Lang, Super-Girl! . . . 1,100.00
168 The Boy Who Out Smarted Superboy. 1,000.00
169 Clark Kent's Private Butler. 1,000.00
170 Lana Lang's Big Crush 900.00
171 Superboy's Toughest Tasks . 900.00
172 Laws that Backfired 900.00
173 Superboy's School of Hard Knocks 900.00
174 The New Lana Lang! 900.00
175 Duel of the Superboys 900.00
176 Superboy's New Parents! . . . 900.00
177 Hot-Rod Chariot Race! 900.00
178 Boy in the Lead Mask. 900.00
179 World's Whackiest Inventors 900.00
180 Grand Prize o/t Underworld . 900.00
181 Mask for a Hero 900.00
182 Super Hick from Smallville . . 800.00
183 Superboy and Cleopatra. . . . 800.00

Adventure Comics #195
© DC Comics

Adventure Comics #250
© DC Comics

Adventure Into Mystery #1
© Marvel Comics Group

184 Shutterbugs of Smallville . . . 800.00
185 The Mythical Monster 800.00
186. . . . . 800.00
187 25th Century Superboy. 800.00
188 Bull Fighter from Smallville 800.00
189 Girl of Steel(Lana Lang) 800.00
190 The Two Clark Kents 800.00
191 . . . . 800.00
192 Coronation of Queen Lana Lang 800.00
193 Superboy's Lost Costume. . . 800.00
194 Super-Charged Superboy. . . 800.00
195 Lana Lang's Romance on Mars! 800.00
196 Superboy vs. King Gorilla . . . 800.00
197 V:Juvenile Gangs 800.00
198 Super-Carnival from Space. . 800.00
199 Superboy meets Superlad . . 800.00
200 Superboy and the Apes! . . 1,000.00
201 Safari in Smallville! 750.00
202 Superboy City, U.S.A. 750.00
203 Uncle Superboy! 750.00
204 Super-Brat of Smallville 750.00
205 Journey of the Second Superboy! 750.00
206 The Impossible Creatures. . . 750.00
207 Smallville's Worst Athlete . . . 750.00
208 Rip Van Winkle of Smallville? 750.00
209 Superboy Week! 750.00
210 I:Krypto,The Superdog from Krypton. 8,000.00
211 Superboy's Amazing Dream! 600.00
212 Superboy's Robot Twin. 600.00
213 Junior Jury of Smallville!. . . . 600.00
214 A:Krypto 1,100.00
215 Super-Hobby of Superboy . . 500.00
216 The Wizard City 500.00
217 Farewell to Smallville 500.00
218 Two World's of Superboy . . . 500.00
219 Rip Van Wrinkle of Smallville 500.00
220 Greatest Show on Earth A:Krypto. 600.00
221 The Babe of Steel. 500.00
222 Superboy's Repeat Performance 500.00
223 Hercules Junior. 500.00
224 Pa Kent Superman 500.00
225 Bird with Super-Powers 500.00
226 Superboy's Super Rival! 500.00
227 Good Samaritan of Smallville 500.00
228 Clark Kent's Body Guard . . . 500.00
229 . . . . 500.00
230 Secret o/t Flying Horse. 450.00
231 Super-Feats of Super-Baby . 450.00
232 House where Superboy was Born 450.00
233 Joe Smith, Man of Steel 450.00
234 1,001 Rides of Superboy . . . 450.00
235 Confessions of Superboy . . . 450.00
236 Clark Kent's Super-Dad 450.00
237 Robot War of Smallville 450.00
238 Secret Past of Superboy's Father. 450.00
239 Super-Tricks of the Dog of Steel. 450.00
240 Super Teacher from Krypton. 450.00
241 Super-Outlaw of Smallville . . 450.00
242 The Kid From Krypton 450.00
243 Super Toys from Krypton . . . 450.00
244 Poorest Family in Smallville . 450.00
245 The Mystery of Monster X . . 450.00
246 Girl Who Trapped Superboy. 450.00
247 I&O:Legion. 10,000.00
248 Green Arrow 400.00
249 CS,Green Arrow 400.00
250 JK,Green Arrow 400.00
251 JK,Green Arrow 400.00
252 JK,Green Arrow 400.00
253 JK,1st Superboy & Robin T.U. 600.00
254 JK,Green Arrow 400.00
255 JK,Green Arrow 400.00
256 JK,O:Green Arrow 1,200.00
257 CS,LEI,A:Hercules,Samson . 350.00
258 LEI,Aquaman,Superboy 350.00
259 I:Crimson Archer. 350.00
260 1st S.A. O:Aquaman 1,400.00
261 GA,A:Lois Lane. 300.00
262 O:Speedy 300.00
263 GA,Aquaman,Superboy 300.00
264 GA,A:Robin Hood 300.00
265 GA,Aquaman,Superboy 300.00
266 GA,I:Aquagirl. 300.00
267 N:Legion(2nd app.) 1,800.00
268 I:Aquaboy 300.00
269 I:Aqualad,E:Green Arrow . . . 450.00
270 2nd A:Aqualad,B:Congorilla . 300.00
271 O:Lex Luthor rtd 450.00
272 I:Human Flying Fish 300.00
273 Aquaman,Superboy 300.00
274 Aquaman,Superboy 300.00
275 O:Superman/Batman T.U. rtd. 400.00
276 Superboy,3rd A:Metallo. 300.00
277 Aquaman,Superboy 300.00
278 Aquaman,Superboy 300.00
279 CS,Aquaman,Superboy 300.00
280 CS,A:Lori Lemaris. 300.00
281 Aquaman,Superboy E:Congorilla. 300.00
282 5th A:Legion,I:Starboy. 400.00
283 I:Phantom Zone 400.00
284 CS,JM,Aquaman,Superboy . 250.00
285 WB,B:Bizarro World 350.00
286 I:Bizarro Mxyzptlk 350.00
287 I:Dev-Em,Bizarro Perry White, Jimmy Olsen 250.00
288 A:Dev-Em 250.00
289 Superboy. 250.00
290 8th A:Legion,O&J:Sunboy, I:Brainiac 5 . . . . 400.00
291 A:Lex Luthor 250.00
292 Superboy,I:Bizarro Lucy Lane, Lana Lang 250.00
293 CS,O&I:Marv-El,I:Bizarro Luthor 350.00
294 I:Bizarro M.Monroe,JFK 300.00
295 I:Bizarro Titano 250.00
296 A:Ben Franklin,George Washington 250.00
297 Lana Lang Superboy Sister . 250.00
298 The Fat Superboy. 250.00
299 I:Gold Kryptonite. 250.00
300 B:Legion,J:Mon-El, E:Bizarro World 1,000.00

ADVENTURE INTO MYSTERY

Marvel Atlas, 1956–57

1 BP,BEv(c),Future Tense 500.00
2 Man on the 13th Floor 300.00
3 Next Stop Eternity 300.00
4 BP,AW, The Hex 300.00
5 JO,BEv,The People Who Weren't 300.00
6 The Wax Man 300.00
7 AT,BEv(c). 300.00
8 AT,JWo,TSe 300.00

ADVENTURE IS MY CAREER

Street & Smith Publ., 1944

n# U.S.Coast Guard Academy. . . 300.00

ADVENTURES

St. John Publishing Co., Nov. 1949–Feb. 1950

1 Adventures in Romance 350.00
2 Spectacular Adventures 500.00

Adventures in 3-D #1
© Harvey Publ.

Adventures into the Unknown #39
© American Comics Group

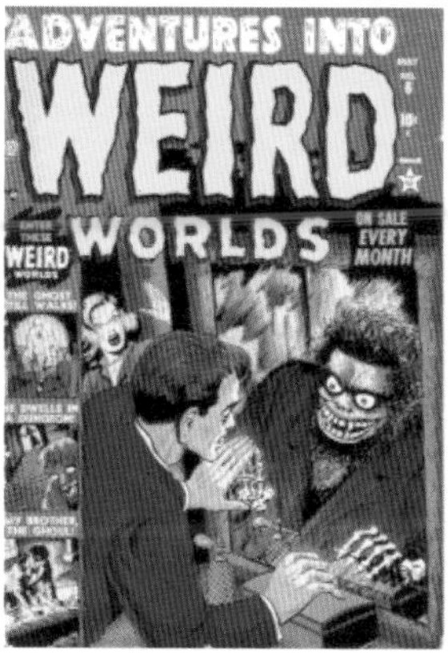

Adventures Into Weird Worlds #6
© Marvel Comics Group

ADVENTURES FOR BOYS

Bailey Enterprises, Dec. 1954

n# 100.00

ADVENTURES IN 3-D

Harvey Publications, Nov. 1953–Jan 1954

1 with glasses. 350.00
1a rep. O'Dells Adventures in 3-D. 300.00
2 with glasses. 300.00

ADVENTURES INTO DARKNESS

Standard Publications, Aug., 1952

5 JK(c), ATh 700.00
6 GT, JK 500.00
7 JK(c) 500.00
8 ATh. 500.00
9 JK,ATh 500.00
10 JK,ATh,MSy 450.00
11 JK,ATh,MSy 450.00
12 JK,ATh,MSy 450.00
13 Cannibalism feature 600.00
14 . . . . 350.00

ADVENTURES INTO TERROR

See: JOKER COMICS

ADVENTURES INTO THE UNKNOWN!

American Comics Group, Fall 1948

1 FGu, Haunted House (c) . . . 5,000.00
2 Haunted Island (c) 2,000.00
3 AF, Sarcophagus (c). 2,000.00
4 Monsters (c). 950.00
5 Monsters (c). 950.00
6 Giant Hands (c) 900.00
7 Skeleton Pirate (c). 900.00
8 Horror. 900.00
9 Snow Monster 900.00
10 Red Bats. 900.00
11 Death Shadow 900.00
12 OW(c) 900.00
13 OW(c),Dinosaur 500.00
14 OW(c),Cave 500.00
15 Red Demons. 500.00
16 OW(c). 400.00
17 OW(c),The Thing Type 600.00
18 OW(c),Wolves. 500.00
19 OW(c),Graveyard 500.00
20 OW(c),Graveyard 500.00
21 OW(c),Bats and Dracula. 400.00
22 Death 400.00
23 OW(c),Bats 400.00
24 Swamp Monster 400.00
25 . . . . 400.00
26 DW(s) 400.00
27 AW,RKu,OW(c). 500.00
28 thru 37. . . . . @400.00
38 A-Bomb. 600.00
39 thru 49. . . . . @500.00
50 Giant fly (c) 500.00
51 H. Lazarus 500.00
52 H. Lazarus, 3-D-ish. 500.00
53 thru 55. . . . . @500.00
56 H. Lazarus 500.00
57 SMo,OW(c). 500.00
58 H. Lazurus 500.00
59 3-D-ish 400.00
60 . . . . 300.00
61 OW,Rocket ship (c). 300.00
62 thru 69. . . . . @250.00
70 thru 79. . . . . @250.00
80 thru 90. . . . . @200.00
91 AW 250.00
92 thru 95. . . . . @150.00
96 AW 225.00
97 thru 99 . . . . @150.00
100 JB 200.00
101 thru 106. . . . . @150.00
107 AW 225.00
108 thru 115 . . . . @150.00
116 AW,AT 225.00
117 thru 127. . . . . @150.00
128 AW,Forbidden Worlds. 150.00
129 thru 151. . . . . @150.00
152 JCr 150.00
153 A:Magic Agent. 150.00
154 O:Nemesis 200.00
155 Nemesis 125.00
156 A:Magic Agent. 125.00
157 thru 167. . . . . @125.00
168 JB,SD, Nemesis 125.00
169 Nemesis vs. Hitler. 150.00
170 thru 174, Aug., 1967 . . . . . @125.00

ADVENTURES INTO WEIRD WORLDS

Marvel, Jan., 1952–June, 1954

1 RH,GT,The Walking Death . . 1,400.00
2 GT,JMn,Thing in the Bottle . . . 600.00
3 JMn,The Thing That Waited . . 500.00
4 BEv,RH,TheVillageGraveyard . 500.00
5 BEv,I Crawl Thru Graves. 500.00
6 The Ghost Still Walks 500.00
7 OW,Monsters In Disguise 500.00
8 DAy,Nightmares. 500.00
9 Do Not Feed 500.00
10 BEv,Down In The Cellar 500.00
11 JMn,Phantom 450.00
12 GT,Lost In the Graveyard 450.00
13 JeR,DRi,Where Dead Men Walk. 450.00
14 A Shriek In the Night. 450.00
15 GT,Terror In Our Town 450.00
16 The Kiss of Death. 450.00
17 RH,He Walks With A Ghost . . 450.00
18 Ivan & Petroff 450.00
19 It Happened One Night. 450.00
20 JMn,The Doubting Thomas . . 450.00
21 JF,What Happened In the Cave,Hitler. 500.00
22 JMn,RH,Vampire's Partner . . . 450.00
23 JMn,The Kiss of Death. 300.00
24 JF,Halfway Home 300.00
25 BEv,JSt,The Mad Mamba 300.00
26 DAy,Good-Bye Earth. 300.00
27 The Dwarf of Horror Moor. . . . 600.00
28 DW,Monsters From the Grave 500.00
29 Bone Dry. 250.00
30 JSt,The Impatient Ghost 250.00

ADVENTURES IN WONDERLAND

Lev Gleason Publications, April, 1955

1 . . . . 200.00
2 . . . . 150.00
3 and 4 . . . . @125.00
5 Christmas. 150.00

THE ADVENTURES OF ALAN LADD

DC Comics, 1949–51

1 Ph(c). 1,500.00
2 Ph(c) 900.00
3 Ph(c) 550.00
4 Ph(c) 550.00
5 Ph(c),inc.Destination Danger. . 500.00
6 Ph(c) 500.00
7 RMo(c&a). 500.00
8 Grand Duchess takes over . . . 500.00
9 Deadlien in Rapula 500.00

Adventures of Bob Hope #11
© DC Comics

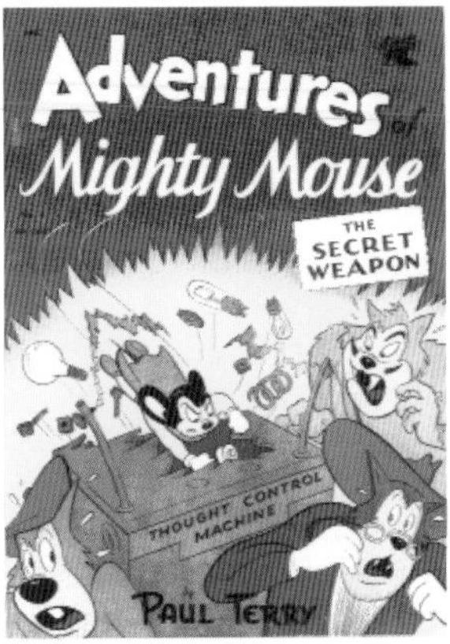

Adventures of Mighty Mouse #4
© St. John Publishing Co.

Adventures of Rex, The Wonderdog
#18 © DC Comics

ADVENTURES OF ALICE
Civil Service Publ., 1945–46

1 In Wonderland 300.00
2 Through the Looking Glass . . . 200.00
3 Monkey Island 200.00

THE ADVENTURES OF BOB HOPE
DC Comics, 1951

1 Ph(c) 3,000.00
2 Ph(c) 1,500.00
3 Ph(c) 1,000.00
4 Ph(c) 1,000.00
5 thru 10 . . . . @750.00
11 thru 20 . . . . @600.00
21 thru 40 . . . . @400.00
41 thru 60 . . . . @300.00
61 thru 90 . . . . @150.00
91 thru 93 . . . . @125.00
94 C:Aquaman 150.00
95 1st Superhip 150.00
96 thru 105 . . . . @125.00
106 thru 109 NA . . . . @200.00

ADVENTURES OF DEAN MARTIN AND JERRY LEWIS
DC Comics, 1952–57

1 . . . . 2,700.00
2 . . . . 1,000.00
3 . . . . 750.00
4 . . . . 750.00
5 . . . . 750.00
6 thru 10 . . . . @750.00
11 thru 20 . . . . @500.00
21 thru 40 . . . . @300.00

Becomes:

ADVENTURES OF JERRY LEWIS
DC Comics, 1957

41 thru 55 . . . . @250.00
56 thru 69 . . . . @200.00
70 thru 87 . . . . @150.00
88 A:Bob Hope 150.00

THE ADVENTURES OF HOMER COBB
Say/Bart Prod., Sept. 1947

1 . . . . 500.00

ADVENTURES OF HOMER GHOST
Marvel Atlas, June–Aug., 1957

1 . . . . 250.00
2 . . . . 250.00

ADVENTURES OF LITTLE ORPHAN ANNIE COMICS
Giveaway 1940–42

N#(1) 600.00
N#(2) 500.00
N#(3) 500.00

MIGHTY MOUSE ADVENTURES
St. John Publishing Co., Nov., 1951

1 Mighty Mouse Adventures 400.00

Becomes:

ADVENTURES OF MIGHTY MOUSE
St. John Publishing Co., Nov., 1951

2 Menace of the Deep 400.00
3 Storm Clouds of Mystery 300.00
4 Thought Control Machine 300.00
5 Jungle Peril 300.00
6 'The Vine of Destruction' 250.00
7 Space Ship(c) 250.00
8 Charging Alien(c) 250.00
9 Meteor(c) 200.00
10 'Revolt at the Zoo' 200.00
11 Jungle(c) 200.00
12 A:Freezing Terror 200.00
13 A:Visitor from Outer Space . . . 200.00
14 V:Cat 200.00
15 . . . . 200.00
16 . . . . 200.00
17 . . . . 200.00
18 May, 1955 . . . . 200.00

ADVENTURES OF MIGHTY MOUSE
See: TERRY-TUNES COMICS

ADVENTURES OF OZZIE AND HARRIET
DC Comics, 1949–50

1 Ph(c) 1,500.00
2 . . . . 900.00
3 thru 5 . . . . @750.00

ADVENTURES OF PATORUZU
Green Publishing Co., 1946

N# 125.00

ADVENTURES OF PINKY LEE
Marvel Atlas, July, 1955

1 . . . . 400.00
2 . . . . 300.00
3 thru 5 . . . . @275.00

THE ADVENTURES OF PIPSQUEAK
Archie Publications Sept. 1959–July 1960

34 . . . . 125.00
35 thru 39 . . . . @100.00

ADVENTURES OF REX, THE WONDER DOG
DC Comics, 1952–59

1 ATh 2,000.00
2 ATh 1,000.00
3 ATh 900.00
4 . . . . 800.00
5 . . . . 800.00
6 thru 10 . . . . @600.00
11 Atom Bomb 700.00
12 thru 20 . . . . @400.00
21 thru 46 . . . . @300.00

ADVENTURES OF ROBIN HOOD
See: ROBIN HOOD

THE ADVENTURES OF BIG BOY
Marvel Timely Comics, 1956

1 . . . . 1,500.00

 All comics prices listed are for *Near Mint* condition.

Adventures of the Big Boy #15
© Marvel Comics Group

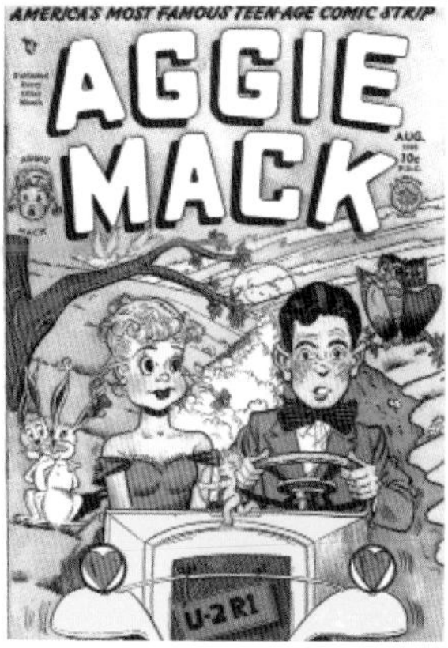

Aggie Mack #2
© Four Star Comics

Air Ace Vol2, #1
© Street & Smith

2 .... 900.00
3 .... 500.00
Becomes:

ADVENTURES OF THE BIG BOY

Marvel Timely Comics, 1956

4 .... 450.00
5 .... 400.00
6 .... 300.00
7 .... 300.00
8 .... 300.00
9 .... 300.00
10 .... 300.00
11 thru 20 .... @200.00
21 thru 30 .... @125.00
31 thru 40 .... @75.00
41 thru 50 .... @60.00
51 thru 60 .... @50.00
61 thru 70 .... @50.00

ADVENTURES OF THE DOVER BOYS

Close-up/Archie 1950

1 .... 150.00
2 .... 150.00

ADVENTURES OF THE FLY

Archie Publications/ Radio Comics, 1959–65

1 JSm/JK,O:Fly,I:SpiderSpry A:Lancelot Strong/Shield .. 1,000.00
2 JSm/JK,DAy,AW 600.00
3 JDa, O:Fly 500.00
4 V:Dazzler NA panel 300.00
5 A:Spider Spry 200.00
6 V:Moon Men 200.00
7 A:Black Hood 225.00
8 A:Lancelot Strong/Shield 225.00
9 A:Lancelot Strong/Shield I:Cat Girl 200.00
10 A:Spider Spry 200.00
11 V:Rock Men 125.00
12 V:Brute Invaders 125.00
13 I:Kim Brand 125.00
14 I:Fly-Girl(Kim Brand) 150.00
15 A:Spider 125.00
16 A:Fly-Girl 125.00
17 A:Fly-Girl 125.00
18 A:Fly-Girl 125.00
19 A:Fly-Girl 125.00
20 O:Fly-Girl 150.00
21 A:Fly-Girl 100.00
22 A:Fly-Girl 100.00
23 A:Fly-Girl,Jaguar 100.00
24 A:Fly-Girl 100.00
25 A:Fly-Girl 100.00
26 A:Fly-Girl,Black Hood 100.00
27 A:Fly-Girl,Black Hood 100.00
28 A:Black Hood 100.00
29 A:Fly-Girl,Black Hood 100.00
30 A:Fly-Girl,R:Comet 150.00
31 A:Black Hood, Shield, Comet . 150.00

AFTER DARK

Sterling Comics, May–Sept. 1955

6 .... 125.00
7 .... 100.00
8 .... 100.00

AGGIE MACK

Four Star Comics/ Superior Comics, Jan., 1948

1 AF,HR(c),Johnny Prep 600.00
2 JK(c) 300.00
3 AF,JK(c) 300.00
4 AF, Johnny Prep 400.00
5 AF,JK(c) 300.00
6 AF,JK(c) 275.00
7 AF,Burt Lancaster on cover ... 325.00
8 AF,JK(c), Aug., 1949 .... 275.00

BILL BARNES

Street & Smith Publ.,July, 1940

1 (Bill Barnes Comics) 1,500.00
Becomes:

BILL BARNES, AMERICA'S AIR ACE

Street & Smith Publ., 1940

2 Second Battle Valley Forge ... 750.00
3 A:Aviation Cadets 500.00
4 Shotdown(c) 500.00
5 A:Air Warden, Danny Hawk ... 500.00
6 A:Danny Hawk,RocketRodney. 400.00
7 How to defeat the Japanese .. 400.00
8 Ghost Ship 400.00
9 Flying Tigers, John Wayne ... 425.00
10 I:Roane Waring 400.00
11 Flying Tigers 400.00
12 War Workers 400.00
Becomes:

AIR ACE

Street & Smith Publ., Jan., 1944

2-1 Invades Germany 600.00
2-2 Jungle Warfare 450.00
2-3 A:The Four Musketeers 200.00
2-4 A:Russell Swann 200.00
2-5 A:The Four Musketeers 200.00
2-6 Raft(c) 200.00
2-7 BP, What's New In Science . 200.00
2-8 XP-59 .... 200.00
2-9 The Northrop P-61 .... 200.00
2-10 NCG-14 .... 200.00
2-11 Whip Launch 200.00
2-12 PP(c) 200.00
3-1 .... 150.00
3-2 Atom and Its Future 150.00
3-3 Flying in the Future 150.00
3-4 How Fast Can We Fly 150.00
3-5 REv(c) 150.00
3-6 V:Wolves 150.00
3-7 BP(c), Vortex of Atom Bomb 400.00
3-8 BP,Feb.–March, 1947 ...... 175.00

AIRBOY

See: AIR FIGHTERS COMICS

AIR FIGHTERS COMICS

Hillman Periodicals, Nov., 1941

1 I:Black Commander (only App) 5,000.00
2 O:Airboy A:Sky Wolf 7,000.00
3 O:Sky Wolf and Heap 4,000.00
4 A:Black Angel, Iron Ace 3,500.00
5 A:Sky Wolf and Iron Ace 2,500.00
6 Airboy's Bird Plane 2,700.00
7 Airboy Battles Kultur 2,500.00
8 A:Skinny McGinty 2,200.00
9 A:Black Prince, Hatchet Man 2,200.00
10 I:The Stinger 2,200.00
11 Kida(c) 2,200.00
12 A:Misery 2,200.00
2-1 A:Flying Dutchman 2,400.00
2-2 I:Valkyrie 2,700.00
2-3 Story Panels (c) 1,000.00
2-4 V:Japanese 1,000.00
2-5 Air Boy in Tokyo 1,000.00
2-6 'Dance of Death' 1,000.00
2-7 A:Valkyrie 1,000.00
2-8 Airboy Battles Japanese ... 1,000.00
2-9 Airboy Battles Japanese ... 1,000.00
2-10 O:Skywolf 1,200.00
Becomes:

Airboy Comics Vol. 4 #5
© Hillman Periodicals

Airboy Comics Vol. 10 #4
© Hillman Periodicals

Al Capp's Wolf Gal #2
© Toby Press

AIRBOY COMICS

Hillman Periodicals, Dec., 1945

2-11 . . . . 1,200.00
2-12 A:Valykrie 800.00
3-1 . . . . 600.00
3-2 . . . . 600.00
3-3 Never published
3-4 I:The Heap 500.00
3-5 Airboy 500.00
3-6 A:Valykrie 500.00
3-7 AMc,Witch Hunt 500.00
3-8 A:Condor. 550.00
3-9 O:The Heap 550.00
3-10 . . . . 500.00
3-11 . . . . 500.00
3-12 Airboy missing 650.00
4-1 Elephant in chains (c). 600.00
4-2 I:Rackman 450.00
4-3 Airboy profits on name 450.00
4-4 S&K 500.00
4-5 S&K,The American Miracle . 450.00
4-6 S&K,A:Heap and Flying Fool. 450.00
4-7 S&K 450.00
4-8 S&K,Girlfriend captured 450.00
4-9 S&K,Airboy in Quick Sand . . 450.00
4-10 S&K,A:Valkyrie 450.00
4-11 S&K,A:Frenchy 450.00
4-12 FBe. 500.00
5-1 LSt 400.00
5-2 I:Wild Horse of Calabra 400.00
5-3 . . . . 400.00
5-4 Cl 400.00
5-5 Skull on cover. 400.00
5-6. . . . . 400.00
5-7. . . . . 400.00
5-8 Bondage (c) 400.00
5-9 Zoi,Row 400.00
5-10 A:Valykrie,O:The Heap 450.00
5-11 Airboy vs. The Rats. 400.00
5-12 BK,Rat Army captures Airboy 400.00
6-1. . . . . 400.00
6-2. . . . . 400.00
6-3. . . . . 400.00
6-4 Airboy boxes. 500.00
6-5 A:The Ice People 400.00
6-6 . . . . 400.00
6-7 Airboy vs. Chemical Giant . . 400.00
6-8 O:The Heap 400.00
6-9 . . . . 400.00
6-10 . . . . 400.00
6-11 . . . . 400.00
6-12 . . . . 400.00
7-1 . . . . 400.00
7-2 BP. 400.00
7-3 BP. 500.00
7-4 I:Monsters of the Ice. 400.00
7-5 V:Monsters of the Ice 400.00
7-6 . . . . 400.00
7-7 Mystery of the Sargasso Sea 400.00
7-8 A:Centaur 400.00
7-9 I:Men of the StarlightRobot. . 400.00
7-10 O:The Heap 400.00
7-11 . . . . 400.00
7-12 Airboy visits India 400.00
8-1 BP,A:Outcast and Polo Bandits. 400.00
8-2 BP,Suicide Dive (c). 400.00
8-3 BK, I:The Living Fuse. 400.00
8-4 A:Death Merchants of the Air 400.00
8-5 A:Great Plane from Nowhere 400.00
8-6 . . . . 400.00
8-7 . . . . 400.00
8-8 . . . . 400.00
8-9 . . . . 400.00
8-10 A:Mystery Walkers 400.00
8-11 . . . . 400.00
8-12 . . . . 450.00
9-1 . . . . 350.00
9-2 A:Valykrie 300.00
9-3 A:Heap (c). 300.00
9-4 A:Water Beast, Frog Headed Riders 350.00
9-5 A:Heap vs.Man of Moonlight 300.00
9-6 Heap (c) 300.00
9-7 Heap (c) 300.00
9-8 Heap (c) 350.00
9-9 . . . . 350.00
9-10 Space (c) 350.00
9-11 . . . . 350.00
9-12 Heap (c) 350.00
10-1 Heap (c) 350.00
10-2 Ships on Space 300.00
10-3 . . . . 350.00
10-4 May, 1953 . . . . 350.00

ALARMING TALES

Harvey Publications, 1957–58

1 JK,JK(c) 400.00
2 JK,JK(c) 300.00
3 JK. 275.00
4 JK,BP. 275.00
5 JK,AW 275.00
6 JK 275.00

AL CAPP'S DOGPATCH COMICS

Toby Press, June, 1949

1 . . . . 350.00
2 A:Daisy. 250.00
3 . . . . 225.00
4 Dec., 1949 . . . . 225.00

AL CAPP'S SHMOO

Toby Press, July, 1949

1 100 Trillion Schmoos 550.00
2 Super Shmoo(c). 400.00
3 . . . . 400.00
4 . . . . 400.00
5 April, 1950 . . . . 400.00

AL CAPP'S WOLF GAL

Toby Press, 1951

1 Pin-Up 500.00
2 1952. . . . . 450.00

ALGIE

Timor Publ. Co., Dec. 1953

1 Teen-age 125.00
1a reprint. 125.00
2 . . . . 100.00
3 . . . . 100.00

ALICE

Ziff-Davis Publ. Co., 1952

10 New Adventures in Wonderland 400.00
11 (#2) 350.00

ALL-AMERICAN COMICS

DC Comics, 1939–48

1 B:Hop Harrigan,Scribbly,Mutt&Jeff, Red,White&Blue,Bobby Thatcher, Skippy,Daiseybelle,Mystery Men of Mars,Toonerville 10,000.00
2 B:Ripley's Believe It or Not. . 5,000.00
3 Hop Harrigan (c). 3,500.00
4 Flag(c). 3,500.00
5 B:The American Way 3,500.00
6 ShM(c),Fredric Marchin in The American Way 3,000.00
7 E:Bobby Thatcher,C.H. Claudy's A Thousand Years in a Minute 3,000.00
8 B:Ultra Man. 5,500.00

All-American Comics #24
© DC Comics

All-American Comics #65
© DC Comics

All-American Western #117
© DC Comics

9 A:Ultra Man 3,000.00
10 ShM(c),E:The American Way, Santa-X-Mas(c) 3,000.00
11 Ultra Man(c) 3,000.00
12 E:Toonerville Folks 2,500.00
13 The Infra Red Des'Royers . . 2,500.00
14 Ultra Man 2,500.00
15 E:Tippie and Reg'lar Fellars 3,000.00
16 O&1st App:Green Lantern, B:Lantern(c) 220,000.00
17 SMo(c) 30,000.00
18 SMo(c) 25,000.00
19 SMo(c),O&I: Atom, E:Ultra Man 30,000.00
20 I:Atom's Costume,Hunkle becomes Red Tornado . . . 10,000.00
21 E:Wiley of West Point & Skippy 6,000.00
22 SMo(c),F:Green Lantern . . . 5,800.00
23 E:Daieybelle 6,000.00
24 E:Ripley's Believe It or Not . 8,000.00
25 O&I:Dr. Mid-Nite 20,000.00
26 O&I:Sargon the Sorcerer . . . 7,000.00
27 I:Doiby Dickles 7,000.00
28 F:Green Lantern 3,000.00
29 ShM(c) 3,000.00
30 ShM(c) 3,000.00
31 Adventures of the Underfed Orphans 3,000.00
32 . . . . 2,500.00
33 . . . . 2,500.00
34 . . . . 2,500.00
35 Doiby discovers Lantern's ID 2,500.00
36 Auto Racing (c) 2,500.00
37 . . . . 2,500.00
38 ShM,V:A Modern Napoleon . 2,500.00
39 . . . . 2,500.00
40 Doiby Dickles idol(c) 2,500.00
41 . . . . 2,000.00
42 ShM 2,000.00
43 . . . . 2,000.00
44 I Accuse the Green Lantern! 2,000.00
45 . . . . 2,000.00
46 Riddle of Dickles Manor 2,000.00
47 Hop Harrigan meets the Enemy,(c) 2,000.00
48 . . . . 2,000.00
49 Doiby Dickles Cab 2,000.00
50 E:Sargon 2,000.00
51 Murder Under the Stars 1,500.00
52 . . . . 1,500.00
53 Green Lantern delivers the Mail 1,500.00
54 . . . . 1,500.00
55 The Riddle of the Runaway Trolley 1,500.00
56 V:Elegant Esmond 1,500.00
57 V:The Melancholy Men 1,500.00
58 . . . . 1,500.00
59 The Story of the Man Who Couldn't Tell The Truth 1,500.00
60 . . . . 1,500.00
61 O:Soloman Grundy,Fighters Never Quit 9,000.00
62 Da Distrik Attorney 1,300.00
63 . . . . 1,300.00
64 A Bag of Assorted Nuts! 1,300.00
65 The Man Who Lost Wednesday 1,300.00
66 The Soles of Manhattan! . . . 1,300.00
67 V:King Shark 1,300.00
68 F:Napoleon & Joe Safeen . . 1,300.00
69 Backwards Man! 1,300.00
70 JKu,I:Maximillian O'Leary, V:Colley, the Leprechaun . . 1,300.00
71 E:Red,White&Blue,The Human Bomb 1,200.00
72 B:Black Pirate 1,200.00
73 B:Winkey,Blinky&Noddy, Mountain Music Mayhem . . 1,200.00
74 . . . . 1,200.00
75 . . . . 1,200.00
76 Spring Time for Doiby 1,200.00
77 Hop Harrigan(c) 1,200.00
78 . . . . 1,200.00
79 Mutt & Jeff 1,200.00
80 . . . . 1,200.00
81 . . . . 1,200.00
82 . . . . 1,200.00
83 Mutt & Jeff 1,200.00
84 The Adventure of the Man with Two Faces 1,200.00
85 . . . . 1,200.00
86 V:Crime of the Month Club . 1,200.00
87 The Strange Case of Professor Nobody 1,200.00
88 Canvas of Crime 1,200.00
89 O:Harlequin 1,700.00
90 O:Icicle 1,700.00
91 Wedding of the Harlequin . . 1,700.00
92 The Icicle goes South 1,700.00
93 Double Crossing Decoy 1,700.00
94 A:Harlequin 1,700.00
95 The Unmasking of the Harlequin 1,700.00
96 ATh(c),Solve the Mystery of the Emerald Necklaces! . 1,700.00
97 ATh(c),The Country Fair Crimes 1,700.00
98 ATh,ATh(c),End of Sports! . . 1,700.00
99 ATh,ATh(c),E:Hop Harrigan . 1,700.00
100 ATh,I:Johnny Thunder 3,000.00
101 ATh,ATh(c),E:Mutt & Jeff . . 2,500.00
102 ATh,ATh(c),E:GrnLantern . . 7,000.00

Becomes:

ALL-AMERICAN WESTERN

DC Comics, 1948–52

103 A:Johnny Thunder,The City Without Guns, All Johnny Thunder stories 1,400.00
104 ATh(c),Unseen Allies 800.00
105 ATh(c),Hidden Guns 700.00
106 ATh(c),Snow Mountain Ambush 700.00
107 ATh(c),Cheyenne Justice . . . 700.00
108 ATh(c),Vengeance of the Silver Bullet 400.00
109 ATh(c),Secret of Crazy River 400.00
110 ATh(c),Ambush at Scarecrow Hills 400.00
111 ATh(c),Gun-Shy Sheriff 400.00
112 ATh(c),Double Danger 400.00
113 ATh(c),Johnny Thunder Indian Chief 400.00
114 ATh(c),The End of Johnny Thunder 400.00
115 ATh(c),Cheyenne Mystery . . . 400.00
116 ATh(c),Buffalo Raiders of the Mesa 400.00
117 ATh(c),V:Black Lightnin 300.00
118 ATh(c),Challenge of the Aztecs 300.00
119 GK(c),The Vanishing Gold Mine 300.00
120 GK(c),Ambush at Painted Mountain 300.00
121 ATh(c),The Unmasking of Johnny Thunder 300.00
122 ATh(c),The Real Johnny Thunder 300.00
123 GK(c),Johnny Thunder's Strange Rival 300.00
124 ATh(c),The Iron Horse's Last Run 300.00
125 ATh(c),Johnny Thunder's Last Roundup 300.00
126 ATh(c),Phantoms of the Desert 300.00

Becomes:

ALL-AMERICAN MEN OF WAR

DC Comics, 1952–66

127 (0) 2,000.00

All-American Men of War #8
© DC Comics

All-American Men of War #57
© DC Comics

All-American Men of War #88
© DC Comics

128 (1) IN, ... 1,200.00
2 JGr(c),Killer Bait. 900.00
3 Pied Piper of Pyong-Yang 800.00
4 JGr(c),The Hills of Hate. 800.00
5 One Second to Zero 800.00
6 IN(c),Jungle Killers. 700.00
7 IN(c),Beach to Hold 700.00
8 IN(c),Sgt. Storm Cloud. 700.00
9 . . . . 700.00
10 . . . . 700.00
11 JGr(c),Dragon's Teeth. 700.00
12 . . . . 600.00
13 JGr(c),Lost Patrol 600.00
14 IN(c),Pigeon Boss. 600.00
15 JGr(c),Flying Roadblock 600.00
16 JGr(c),The Flying Jeep 600.00
17 JGr(c),Booby Trap Ridge 600.00
18 JKu(c),The Ballad of Battling Bells 600.00
19 JGr(c),IN,Torpedo Track 500.00
20 JGr(c),JKu,Lifenet to Beach Road. 500.00
21 JGr(c),IN,RH,The Coldest War. 500.00
22 JGr(c),IN,JKu,Snipers Nest . . 500.00
23 JGr(c),The Silent War. 500.00
24 JGr(c),The Thin Line. 500.00
25 JGr(c),IN,For Rent-One Foxhole 500.00
26 Dial W-A-R 500.00
27 JGr(c),RH,Fighting Pigeon . . . 500.00
28 JGr(c),RA,JKu,Medal for A Dog 500.00
29 IN(c),JKu,Battle Bridges 500.00
30 JGr(c),RH,Frogman Hunt 500.00
31 JGr(c),Battle Seat. 400.00
32 JGr(c),RH,Battle Station 400.00
33 JGr(c),IN,Sky Ambush 400.00
34 JGr(c),JKu,No Man's Alley . . . 400.00
35 JGr(c),IN, Battle Call. 400.00
36 JGr(c),JKu,Battle Window. . . . 400.00
37 JGr(c),JKu,The Big Stretch. . . 400.00
38 JGr(c),RH,JKu,The Floating Sentinel 400.00
39 JGr(c),JKu,The Four Faces of Sgt. Fay. 400.00
40 JGr(c),IN,Walking Helmet. . . . 400.00
41 JKu(c),RH,JKu,The 50-50 War 300.00
42 JGr(c),JKu,Battle Arm. 300.00
43 JGr(c),JKu,Command Post. . . 300.00
44 JKu(c),The Flying Frogman . . 300.00
45 JGr(c),RH,Combat Waterboy . 300.00
46 JGr(c),IN,RH,Tank Busters . . . 300.00
47 JGr(c),JKu,MD,Battle Freight . 300.00
48 JGr(c),JKu,MD,Roadblock . . . 300.00
49 JGr(c),Walking Target. 300.00
50 IN,RH,Bodyguard For A Sub. . 300.00
51 JGr(c),RH,Bomber's Moon . . . 250.00
52 JKu(c),RH,MD,Back Seat Driver 250.00
53 JKu(c),JKu,Night Attack 250.00
54 JKu(c),IN,Diary of a Fighter Pilot. 250.00
55 JKu(c),RH,Split-Second Target 250.00
56 JKu,IN,RH,Frogman Jinx 250.00
57 Pick-Up for Easy Co. 250.00
58 JKu(c),RH,MD,A Piece of Sky 250.00
59 JGr(c),JKu,The Hand of War . 250.00
60 JGr(c),The Time Table 250.00
61 JGr(c),IN,MD,Blind Target. . . . 250.00
62 JGr(c),RH,RA,No(c) 250.00
63 JGr(c),JKu,Frogman Carrier . . 250.00
64 JKu(c),JKu,RH,The Other Man's War 250.00
65 JGr(c),JKu,MD,Same Old Sarge 250.00
66 JGr(c),The Walking Fort 250.00
67 JGr(c),RH,A:Gunner&Sarge, The Cover Man 700.00
68 JKu(c),Gunner&Sarge, The Man & The Gun 300.00
69 JKu(c),A:Tank Killer, Bazooka Hill 300.00
70 JKu(c),IN,Pigeon Without Wings 250.00
71 JGr(c),A:Tank Killer,Target For An Ammo Boy 200.00
72 JGr(c),A:Tank Killer,T.N.T. Broom 200.00
73 JGr(c),JKu,No Detour 200.00
74 The Minute Commandos 200.00
75 JKu(c),Sink That Flattop 200.00
76 JKu(c),A:Tank Killer, Just One More Tank 200.00
77 JKu(c),IN,MD,Big Fish-little Fish 200.00
78 JGr(c),Tin Hat for an Iron Man 200.00
79 JKu(c),RA,Showdown Soldier. 200.00
80 JGr(c),RA,The Medal Men . . . 200.00
81 JGr(c),IN,Ghost Ship of Two Wars. 150.00
82 IN(c),B:Johnny Cloud, The Flying Chief 300.00
83 IN(c),Fighting Blind 250.00
84 IN(c),Death Dive 150.00
85 RH(c),Battle Eagle 150.00
86 JGr(c),Top-Gun Ace 150.00
87 JGr(c),Broken Ace 150.00
88 JGr(c),The Ace of Vengeance 150.00
89 JGr(c),The Star Jockey. 150.00
90 JGr(c),Wingmate of Doom . . . 125.00
91 RH(c),Two Missions To Doom 125.00
92 JGr(c),The Battle Hawk 125.00
93 RH(c),The Silent Rider 125.00
94 RH(c),Be Brave-Be Silent. . . . 125.00
95 RH(c),Second Sight For a Pilot 125.00
96 RH(c),The Last Flight of Lt. Moon 125.00
97 IN(c),A Target Called Johnny . 125.00
98 The Time-Bomb Ace 125.00
99 IN(c),The Empty Cockpit. 125.00
100 RH(c),Battle o/t Sky Chiefs. . 125.00
101 RH(c),Death Ship of Three Wars 100.00
102 JKu(c),Blind Eagle-Hungry Hawk 100.00
103 IN(c),Battle Ship-Battle Heart 100.00
104 JKu(c),The Last Target 100.00
105 IN(c),Killer Horse-Ship 100.00
106 IN(c),Death Song For A Battle Hawk 100.00
107 IN(c),Flame in the Sky 100.00
108 IN(c),Death-Dive of the Aces 100.00
109 IN(c),The Killer Slot. 100.00
110 RH(c),The Co-Pilot was Death. 100.00
111 RH(c),E:Johnny Cloud, Tag–You're Dead. 100.00
112 RH(c),B:Balloon Buster,Lt. Steve Savage-Balloon Buster 100.00
113 JKu(c),The Ace of Sudden Death 100.00
114 JKu(c),The Ace Who Died Twice. 100.00
115 IN(c),A:Johnny Cloud, Deliver One Enemy Ace-Handle With Care 100.00
116 JKu(c),A:Baloon Buster, Circle of Death. 100.00
117 Sept.–Oct., 1966. . . . . 100.00

ALLEY OOP

Standard Comics, Sept. 1947–Oct. 1949

10 . . . . 350.00
11 . . . . 300.00
12 . . . . 300.00
13 . . . . 300.00
14 . . . . 300.00
15 . . . . 300.00
16 . . . . 300.00
17 . . . . 300.00
18 . . . . 300.00

All-Famous Crime #9 (#2)
© Star Publications

All-Flash #32
© DC Comics

All Good Comics #1
© Fox Publications

(The Adventures of) ALLEY OOP

Argo Publications, 1955–56

1 ... 200.00
2 ... 150.00
3 ... 150.00

ALL-FAMOUS CRIME

Star Publications, May, 1951

1 LbC(c) (8) ... 350.00
2 LbC(c) (9) ... 500.00
3 LbC(c) (10) ... 325.00
4 LbC(c) (4) Law Crime ... 300.00
5 LbC(c) (5) ... 300.00

Becomes:

ALL-FAMOUS POLICE CASES

Feb., 1952

6 LbC(c) ... 325.00
7 LbC(c) ... 300.00
8 LbC(c) Marijuana ... 300.00
9 LbC(c) ... 250.00
10 thru 15 LbC(c) ... @250.00
16 Sept., 1954 ... 250.00

ALL-FLASH

DC Comics, 1941–47

1 EHi,O:Flash,I:The Monocle. 30,000.00
2 EHi,The Adventure of Roy Revenge ... 10,000.00
3 EHi,The Adventure of Misplaced Faces ... 4,000.00
4 EHi,Tale of the Time Capsule 4,000.00
5 EHi,The Case of the Patsy Colt! Last Quarterly ... 3,000.00
6 EHi,The Ray that Changed Men's Souls ... 2,700.00
7 EHi,Adventures of a Writers Fantasy, House of Horrors . 2,700.00
8 EHi,Formula to Fairyland! ... 2,700.00
9 EHi,Adventure of the Stolen Telescope ... 2,700.00
10 EHi,Case of the Curious Cat 2,700.00
11 EHi,Troubles Come in Doubles ... 2,500.00
12 EHi,Tumble INN to Trouble, Becomes Quarterly on orders from War Production Board O:The Thinker ... 2,500.00
13 EHi,I:The King ... 2,500.00
14 EHi,I:Winky,Blinky & Noddy Green Lantern (c) ... 2,600.00
15 EHi,Secrets of a Stranger .. 2,500.00
16 EHi,A:The Sinister ... 2,500.00
17 Tales of the Three Wishes .. 2,500.00
18 A:Winky,Blinky&Noddy B:Mutt & Jeff reprints ... 2,500.00
19 No Rest at the Rest Home . 2,500.00
20 A:Winky, Blinky & Noddy ... 2,500.00
21 I:Turtle ... 2,000.00
22 The Money Doubler, E:Mutt & Jeff reprints ... 2,000.00
23 The Bad Men of Bar Nothing 2,000.00
24 I:Worry Wart,3 Court Clowns Get Caught ... 2,000.00
25 I:Slapsy Simmons, Flash Jitterbugs ... 2,000.00
26 I:The Chef,The Boss,Shrimp Coogan,A:Winky, Blinky & Noddy ... 2,000.00
27 A:The Thinker, Gangplank Gus Story ... 2,000.00
28 A:Shrimp Coogan, Winky, Blinky & Noddy ... 2,000.00
29 The Thousand-Year Old Terror, A:Winky, Blinky & Noddy .. 2,500.00
30 The Vanishing Snowman ... 2,000.00
31 A:Black Hat,Planet of Sport . 2,000.00
32 I:Fiddler,A:Thinker ... 2,500.00

ALL FOR LOVE

Prize-Feature Publications, 1957–59

Vol. 1
1 ... 150.00
2 thru 6 ... @100.00
Vol. 2
1 thru 6 ... @100.00
Vol. 3
1 thru 4 ... @100.00

ALL FUNNY COMICS

DC Comics, 1943–48

1 Genius Jones ... 750.00
2 same ... 350.00
3 same ... 250.00
4 same ... 250.00
5 thru 10 ... @250.00
11 Genius Jones ... 250.00
12 same ... 250.00
13 same ... 200.00
14 ... 200.00
15 ... 200.00
16 A:DC Superheroes ... 500.00
17 thru 23 ... @200.00

ALL GOOD COMICS

Fox Publications, 1946

1 ... 400.00

ALL GOOD COMICS

R. W. Voight/ St. John Publishing, 1949

N# Giant ... 1,500.00

ALL GREAT

Fox Features, 1946

1 Crazy Horse, etc. ... 500.00

ALL GREAT COMICS See: DAGAR, DESERT HAWK

ALL HERO COMICS

Fawcett Publications, March, 1943

1 A:Capt. Marvel Jr.,Capt. Midnight,Ibis, Golden Arrow and Spy Smasher ... 3,000.00

ALL HUMOR COMICS

Comic Favorites, Inc. (Quality Comics) Spring 1946

1 ... 350.00
2 PG Atomic Tot ... 200.00
3 I:Kelly Poole ... 150.00
4 thru 7 ... @ 150.00
8 PG ... 150.00
9 ... 150.00
10 ... 150.00
11 thru 17 ... @125.00

ALL LOVE

Ace Periodicals, May 1949

26 ... 125.00
27 LbC ... 250.00
28 thru 32 ... @100.00

ALL LOVE ROMANCES See: SCREAM COMICS

ALL-NEGRO COMICS

June,1947

1 ... 9,000.00

All-New Comics #13
© Harvey Publications

All Select Comics #11
© Marvel Comics Group

All-Star Comics #1
© DC Comics

ALL-NEW COMICS

Family Comics (Harvey Publ.) Jan., 1943

1 A:Steve Case, Johnny Rebel I:Detective Shane 5,000.00
2 JKu,O:Scarlet Phantom 2,000.00
3 Nazi War. 1,800.00
4 AdH 1,500.00
5 Flash Gordon 1,800.00
6 ASh(c),I:Boy Heroes and Red Blazer 1,800.00
7 JKu,ASh(c),A:Black Cat & Zebra 1,800.00
8 JKu,A:Shock Gibson. 1,800.00
9 JKu,A:Black Cat 1,800.00
10 ASh(c),JKu,A:Zebra 1,800.00
11 BP,A:Man in Black, Girl Commandos 1,800.00
12 JKu. 1,500.00
13 Stuntman by S&K, A:Green Hornet&(c) 1,600.00
14 BP,A:Green Hornet 1,200.00
15 Smaller size, Distributed by Mail, March–April, 1947. 2,000.00

ALL PICTURE ALL TRUE LOVE STORY

St. John Publ. Co. 1952

1 MB,Romance on Route 202 . . 600.00
2 MB 375.00

ALL ROMANCES

Ace Periodicals, 1949–50

1 . . . . 150.00
2 . . . . 135.00
3 . . . . 100.00
4 . . . . 100.00
5 . . . . 100.00
6 . . . . 100.00

ALL SELECT COMICS

Marvel Timely, (Daring Comics) Fall, 1943

1 ASh(c),B:Capt.America,Sub-Mariner, Human Torch;WWII 25,000.00
2 ASh(c),A:Red Skull,V:Axis Powers 10,000.00
3 ASh(c),B:Whizzer,V:Axis. . . . 7.000.00
4 ASh(c),V: Axis 4,500.00
5 ASh(c),E:Sub-Mariner,V:Axis 4,500.00
6 ASh,A:The Destroyer,V:Axis . 3,200.00
7 ASh,MSu,E:Whizzer,V:Axis. . 3,200.00
8 ASh(c),MSu,V:Axis Powers . 3,200.00
9 ASh(c),V:Axis Powers. 3,200.00
10 ASh(c),E:Capt.America,Human Torch;A:The Destroyer 3,200.00
11 SSh, I:Blonde Phantom, A:Miss America. 4,200.00
Becomes:

BLONDE PHANTOM

Marvel, 1946

12 SSh, B:Miss America; The Devil's Playground . . . 2,500.00
13 SSh,B:Sub-Mariner;Horror In Hollywood. 1,600.00
14 SSh,E:Miss America;Horror At Haunted Castle 1,500.00
15 SSh,The Man Who Deserved To Die 1,500.00
16 SSh,A:Capt.America,Bucky; Modeled For Murder. 2,000.00
17 Torture & Rescue. 1,600.00
18 SSh,Jealously,Hate&Cruelty 1,600.00
19 SSh(c),Killer In the Hospital. 1,600.00
20 Blonde Phantom's Big Fall . 1,600.00
21 SSh,Murder At the Carnival. 1,600.00
22 V: Crime Bosses 1,600.00
Becomes:

LOVERS

Marvel, 1949

23 Love Stories 350.00
24 My Dearly Beloved 200.00
25 The Man I Love. 200.00
26 thru 29. . . . . @150.00
30 MK. 200.00
31 thru 36 . . . . @150.00
37 . . . . 300.00
38 BK 300.00
39 . . . . 150.00
40 . . . . 150.00
41 BEv 200.00
42 thru 65 . . . . @150.00
66 . . . . 125.00
67 ATh 150.00
68 thru 86 Aug., 1957. . . . . @125.00

REAL SPORTS COMICS

Hillman Periodicals, 1948

1 BP,Boxing (c) 600.00
Becomes:

ALL SPORTS COMICS

Hillman Periodicals, 1949

2 BP,BK,Football (c) 550.00
3 Basketball (c). 450.00
Becomes:

ALL-TIME SPORTS COMICS

Hillman Periodicals, 1949

4 Auto Racing (c) 350.00
5 BP,Baseball (c), Ty Cobb. 325.00
6 Horse Racing (c) 300.00
7 BK, Baseball (c), W. Johnson . 300.00

ALL-STAR COMICS

DC Comics, 1940–51

1 B:Flash,Hawkman,Hourman, Sandman,Spectre,Red White & Blue. 26,000.00
2 B:Green Lantern and Johnny Thunder 10,000.00
3 First meeting of Justice Society with Flash as Chairman . . 65,000.00
4 First mission of JSA 10,000.00
5 V:Mr. X,I:Hawkgirl 8,000.00
6 Flash Leaves 5,500.00
7 Green Lantern Becomes Chairman, L:Hourman, C:Superman, Batman & Flash 6,000.00
8 I:Wonder Women;Starman and Dr. Mid-Nite Join,Hawkman Becomes Chairman 60,000.00
9 JSA in Latin America. 6,000.00
10 C:Flash & Green Lantern, JSA Time Travel story 6,000.00
11 Wonder Women joins; I:Justice Battalion 8,000.00
12 V:Black Dragon society 5,000.00
13 V:Hitler 5,000.00
14 JSA in Occupied Europe . . . 5,000.00
15 I:Brain Wave,A:JSA's Girl Friends. 5,000.00
16 Propaganda/relevance issue 2,400.00
17 V:Brain Wave 2,400.00
18 I:King Bee 2,500.00
19 Hunt for Hawkman. 2,400.00
20 I:Monster 2,400.00
21 Time Travel Story. 2,500.00
22 Sandman and Dr. Fate Leave, I:Conscience, Good Fairy. . 2,500.00
23 I:Psycho-Pirate. 2,500.00
24 Propaganda/relevance issue, A:Conscience&Wildcat,Mr.Terrific; L:Starman & Spectre; Flash & Green Lantern Return. . . 2,500.00
25 JSA whodunit issue 3,000.00
26 V:Metal Men from Jupiter. . . 4,000.00
27 Handicap issue,A:Wildcat . . 4,000.00
28 Ancient curse comes to life . 4,000.00
29 I:Landor from 25th Century . 4,000.00

All comics prices listed are for *Near Mint* condition.

All Star Western #62
© DC Comics

All Surprise #2
© Marvel Comics Group

All Top Comics #12
© Fox Features Syndicate

30 V:Brain Wave 4,000.00
31 V:Zor 4,000.00
32 V:Psycho-Pirate 2,300.00
33 V:Soloman Grundy,A:Doiby Dickles, Last appearance Thunderbolt 5,600.00
34 I:Wizard 2,000.00
35 I:Per Degaton. 2,000.00
36 A:Superman and Batman. . . 6,000.00
37 I:Injustice Society of the World 3,000.00
38 V:Villians of History, A:Black Canary. 4,000.00
39 JSA in Magic World, Johnny Thunder leaves . . . 2,500.00
40 A:Black Canary,Junior Justice Society of America 2,500.00
41 Black Canary joins,A:Harlequin, V:Injustice Society of the World 2,500.00
42 I:Alchemist 2,400.00
43 V:Interdimensional gold men 2,400.00
44 I:Evil Star 2,400.00
45 Crooks develop stellar JSA powers 2,400.00
46 Comedy issue 2,400.00
47 V:Billy the Kid. 2,400.00
48 Time Travel story 2,400.00
49 V:Comet-Being Invaders . . . 2,400.00
50 V:Flash's Classmate 3,800.00
51 V:Diamond Men from Center of the Earth. 2,400.00
52 JSA Disappears from Earth for Years 2,400.00
53 Time Travel issue. 2,400.00
54 Circus issue 2,400.00
55 JSA Fly to Jupiter. 2,400.00
56 V:Chameleons from 31st Century. 2,400.00
57 I:Key. 3,100.00

Becomes:

ALL STAR WESTERN

DC Comics, April-May, 1951

58 Trigger Twins 800.00
59 . . . . 500.00
60 . . . . 500.00
61 thru 64 ATh . . . . @400.00
65 . . . . 400.00
66 . . . . 450.00
67 GK,B:Johnny Thunder 500.00
68 thru 81. . . . . @250.00
82 thru 98. . . . . @250.00
99 FF 250.00
100 . . . . 250.00
101 thru 104. . . . . @200.00
105 O:JSA, March, 1987 . . . . 200.00
106 and 107. . . . . @200.00
108 O:Johnny Thunder 400.00
109 thru 116. . . . . @200.00
117 CI,O:Super-Chief. 250.00
118 . . . . 200.00
119 . . . . 200.00

ALL STAR WESTERN
See: WEIRD WESTERN TALES

ALL SURPRISE

Marvel Timely, Fall, 1943

1 (fa),F:Super Rabbit,Gandy, Sourpuss 400.00
2 . . . . 200.00
3 . . . . 150.00
4 thru 10 . . . . @150.00
11 HK. 150.00
12 Winter, 1946 . . . . 150.00

ALL TEEN COMICS
See: ALL WINNERS COMICS

ALL-TIME SPORTS COMICS
See: ALL SPORTS COMICS

ALL TOP COMICS

William H. Wise Co., 1944

N# 132pgs.,A:Capt. V,Red Robbins 500.00

ALL TOP COMICS

Fox Features Syndicate, Spring 1946

1 A:Cosmo Cat, Flash Rabbit . . . 300.00
2 . . . . 150.00
3 . . . . 125.00
4 . . . . 125.00
5 . . . . 125.00
6 . . . . 125.00
7 . . . . 125.00
7a 125.00
8 JKa(c),I:Blue Beetle 3,600.00
9 JKa(c),A:Rulah 1,800.00
10 JKa(c),A:Rulah. 1,500.00
11 A:Rulah,Blue Beetle. 1,600.00
12 A:Rulah,Jo Jo,Blue Beetle . . 1,600.00
13 A:Rulah 1,600.00
14 A:Rulah,Blue Beetle. 2,000.00
15 A:Rulah 1,600.00
16 A:Rulah,Blue Beetle. 1,600.00
17 A:Rulah,Blue Beetle. 1,600.00
18 A:Dagar,Jo Jo 1,000.00

Becomes:

MY EXPERIENCE

Fox Features Syndicate 1949–50

19 WW. 400.00
20 . . . . 125.00
21 WW. 400.00
22 WW. 350.00

Becomes:

JUDY CANOVA

Fox Features Syndicate, May, 1950–Sept., 1950

23 (1)WW(a&c) 350.00
24 (2)WW(a&c) 350.00
3 JO,WW(a&c) 350.00

ALL TOP COMICS

Green Publ., 1957–59

6 1957 Patoruzu the Indian 100.00
6 1958 Cosmo Cat. 100.00
6 1959 Atomic Mouse 100.00
6 1959 Little Eva 100.00
6 Supermouse (c) 100.00

ALL-TRUE CRIME
See: OFFICIAL TRUE CRIME CASES

ALL-TRUE DETECTIVE CASES

Avon Periodicals, 1954

1 WW 350.00
2 EK(c),JKa. 250.00
3 JKa. 250.00
4 JKa. 300.00
N# (5) JK,JKu 700.00

ALL TRUE ROMANCE

Artful/Comic Media, 1951

1 . . . . 300.00

All Winners Comics #8
© Marvel Comics Group

Journey Into Unknown Worlds #14
© Marvel Comics Group

All Western Winners #2
© Marvel Comics Group

2 . . . . 150.00
3 . . . . 150.00
4 . . . . 150.00
5 . . . . 150.00
6 WW 300.00
7 . . . . 125.00
8 . . . . 125.00
9 . . . . 125.00
10 . . . . 125.00
11 thru 13 . . . . @100.00
14 Marijuana 125.00
15 thru 27 . . . . @100.00
28 LbC 200.00
29 thru 34 . . . . @100.00

ALL WINNERS COMICS

Marvel Timely, Summer, 1941

1 S&K,BEv,B:Capt.America & Bucky, Human Torch & Toro,Sub-Mariner A:The Angel,Black Marvel 42,000.00
2 S&K,SSh, B:Destroyer, Whizzer. 10,000.00
3 BEv,Bucky & Toro Captured . 7,000.00
4 BEv,AAv,Battle For Victory For America 7,500.00
5 AAv,V:Nazi Invasion Fleet. . . 5,000.00
6 SSh,AAv,V:Axis Powers,A: Black Avenger. 6,000.00
7 V:Axis Powers. 4,500.00
8 V:Axis Powers. 4,200.00
9 V:Nazi Submarine Fleet 4,200.00
10 V:Nazi Submarine Fleet. . . . 4,500.00
11 V: Nazis 2,700.00
12 ASh(c),A:Red Skull,E:Destroyer; Jap P.O.W. Camp. 3,500.00
13 ASh(c),V:Japanese Fleet . . . 3,000.00
14 ASh(c),V:Japanese Fleet . . . 3,000.00
15 ASh(c),Jap Supply Train . . . 3,000.00
16 ASh(c),In Alaska V:Gangsters 3,000.00
17 V:Gansters;Atomic Research Department 3,000.00
18 ASh(c),V:Robbers;Internal Revenue Department 3,200.00
19 ASh(c),SSh,I:All Winners Squad, Fall, 1946 . . . . 10,000.00
21 SSh,AAv,A:All-Winners Squad; Riddle of Demented Dwarf. 7,500.00

Becomes:

ALL TEEN COMICS

Marvel, 1947

20 F:Georgie,Willie, Mitzi,Patsy Walker. 200.00

Becomes:

TEEN COMICS

Marvel, 1947

21 HK,A:George,Willie,Mitzi, Patsy Walker, Hey Look 200.00
22 A:George,Willie,Margie, Patsy Walker 125.00
23 SSh,A:P.Walker,Cindy,George 125.00
24 . . . . 150.00
25 thru 27. . . . . @125.00
28 . . . . 150.00
29 . . . . 125.00
30 HK,Hey Look. 150.00
31 thru 34. . . . . @125.00
35 May, 1950 . . . . 125.00

Becomes:

JOURNEY INTO UNKNOWN WORLDS

Marvel Atlas, Sept., 1950

36(1) RH,End of the Earth. . . . 4,000.00
37(2) BEv,GC,When Worlds Collide. 1,800.00
38(3) GT,Land of Missing Men 1,500.00
4 MSy,RH,Train to Nowhere . . 1,000.00
5 MSy,Trapped in Space 1,000.00
6 GC,RH,World Below the Atlantic 1,000.00
7 BW,RH,JMn,House That Wasn't. 1,500.00
8 RH,JMn,The Stone Thing . . . 1,000.00
9 MSy,JSt,The People Who Couldn't Exist 1,000.00
10 The Undertaker 1,000.00
11 BEv,Frankie Was Afraid 700.00
12 BK,Last Voice You Hear 700.00
13 The Witch Woman 600.00
14 BW,BEv,CondemnedBuilding1,200.00
15 JMn,They Crawl By Night . . 1,200.00
16 JMn,Scared to Death 600.00
17 BEv,GC,RH,The Ice Monster Cometh 700.00
18 The Broth Needs Somebody . 700.00
19 MF,GC,The Long Wait 700.00
20 GC,RH,The Race That Vanished 600.00
21 MF,JMn,JSt,Decapitation 450.00
22 thru 32. . . . . @450.00
33 SD,The Man in the Box 450.00
34 MK,AT,DAy 350.00
35 AT,MD 350.00
36 thru 44 . . . . @400.00
45 AW,SD. 400.00
46 & 47. . . . . @400.00
48 GW,GM 400.00
49 JF,JMn. 400.00
50 JDa,RC 400.00
51 WW,SD,JSe 400.00
52 . . . . 400.00
53 RC,BP. 400.00
54 AT,BP 400.00
55 AW,RC,BEv. 400.00
56 BEv 400.00
57 JO 250.00
58 MD,JMn. 250.00
59 AW,Aug., 1957 . . . . 350.00

ALL WINNERS COMICS

Marvel, [2nd Series], Aug., 1948

1 SSh,F:Blonde Phantom,A:Capt.Am. Sub-Mariner,Human Torch 5,000.00

Becomes:

ALL WESTERN WINNERS

Marvel, 1948–49

2 SSh,B,I&O:Black Rider, B:Two-Gun Kid, Kid-Colt . . 1,200.00
3 Black Rider V: Satan 600.00
4 Black Rider Unmasked 600.00

Becomes:

WESTERN WINNERS

Marvel, 1949

5 I Challenge the Army 600.00
6 The Mountain Mystery 500.00
7 Ph(c) Randolph Scott 500.00

Becomes:

BLACK RIDER

Marvel, 1950–55

8 Ph(c) of Stan Lee,B:Black Rider; Valley of Giants 800.00
9 SSh,JMn,Wrath of the Redskin 500.00
10 O:Black Rider 550.00
11 Redmen on the Warpath. 300.00
12 GT,The Town That Vanished. . 300.00
13 SSh,The Terrified Tribe. 300.00
14 The Tyrant of Texas 300.00
15 Revolt of the Redskins 250.00
16 . . . . 250.00
17 . . . . 250.00
18. . . . . 250.00
19 SSh,GT,A:Two-Gun Kid 250.00
20 GT. 300.00
21 SSh,GT,A:Two-Gun Kid 250.00
22 SSh,DAy(c),A:Two-Gun Kid . . 250.00
23 SSh,A:Two-Gun Kid 250.00
24 SSh,JSt. 250.00
25 SSh,JSt,A:Arrowhead 250.00
26 SSh,A:Kid-Colt 250.00

All Your Comics #1
© Fox Features Syndicate

Amazing Adventures #1
© Ziff-Davis Publications

Amazing-Man Comics #8
© Centaur Publications

27 SSh,JMn(c),A:Kid-Colt 300.00
Becomes:

WESTERN TALES OF BLACK RIDER

Marvel, 1955

28 JSe,D:Spider. 300.00
29 . . . . 200.00
30 . . . . 200.00
31 . . . . 200.00
Becomes:

GUNSMOKE WESTERN

Marvel, 1955–63

32 MD,MB,F:Kid Colt,Billy Buckskin 300.00
33 MD 200.00
34 MB. 175.00
35 GC. 200.00
36 AW,GC 200.00
37 JDa 175.00
38 . . . . 150.00
39 GC. 150.00
40 AW 175.00
41 thru 43. . . . . @125.00
44 AT 125.00
45 & 46. . . . . @125.00
47 JK 150.00
48 & 49. . . . . @125.00
50 JK,RC 200.00
51 JK 150.00
52 thru 54. . . . . @125.00
55 & 56 MB . . . . @125.00
57 Two Gun Kid. 100.00
58 & 59. . . . . @100.00
60 Sam Hawk (Kid Colt) 125.00
61 RC. 150.00
62 thru 67 JK . . . . @100.00
68 . . . . 100.00
69 JK 100.00
70 . . . . 100.00
71 JK 125.00
72 O:Kid Colt 125.00
73 JK 135.00
74 thru 76. . . . . @100.00
77 JK,July, 1963 . . . . 150.00

ALL YOUR COMICS

R.W. Voight, 1944

1 Red Robbins 350.00

ALL YOUR COMICS

Fox Features, 1946

1 . . . . 300.00

AMAZING ADVENTURE FUNNIES

Centaur Publ,. 1940

1 BEv,The Fantom of the Fair . 4,000.00
2 rep.After Fantoman. 2,500.00
Becomes:

FANTOMAN

Aug., 1940

2 The Fantom of the Fair. 3,000.00
3 . . . . 2,500.00
4 Red Blaze. 2,500.00

AMAZING ADVENTURES

Ziff-Davis Publ., Co., 1950

1 MA,WW, Asteroid Witch 1,500.00
2 MA,ASh(c),Masters of Living Flame. 700.00
3 MA,The Evil Men Do 700.00
4 Invasion of the Love Robots . . 700.00
5 MA,Secret of the Crater-Men. . 700.00
6 BK,Man Who Killed a World . . 750.00

AMAZING COMICS

Marvel Timely, 1944

1 ASh(c),F:Young Allies,Destroyer, Whizzer, Sergeant Dix 4,000.00
Becomes:

COMPLETE COMICS

2 ASh(c),F:Young Allies,Destroyer, Whizzer Sergeant Dix; 3,200.00

AMAZING DETECTIVE CASES

Marvel Atlas, Nov., 1950

3 Detective/Horror Stories 350.00
4 Death of a Big Shot 200.00
5 . . . . 200.00
6 Danger in the City 200.00
7 . . . . 175.00
8 . . . . 175.00
9 GC, The Man Who Wasn't . . . 175.00
10 GT. 175.00
11 The Black Shadow 350.00
12 MSy,BK, Harrigan's Wake. . . . 350.00
13 BEv,JSt,. 400.00
14 Hands Off; Sept., 1952. . . . . . 350.00

AMAZING GHOST STORIES

See: WEIRD HORRORS

AMAZING-MAN COMICS

Centaur Publications, Sept., 1939–Feb., 1942

5 BEv,O:Amazing Man. 40,000.00
6 BEv,FT,B:The Shark 8,000.00
7 BEv,I:Magician From Mars . . 6,000.00
8 BEv, Cat-Man as Woman . . . 5,000.00
9 BEv,FT,A:Eternal Monster. . . 5,000.00
10 BEv,FT. 3,500.00
11 BEv,I:Zardi 3,500.00
12 SG(c) 3,200.00
13 SG(c) 3,200.00
14 FT,B:Reef Kinkaid, Dr. Hypo 2,500.00
15 FT,A:Zardi 2,400.00
16 AAv,Mighty Man's Powers Revealed 2,500.00
17 FT,A:Dr. Hypo 2,400.00
18 FT,BLb(a),SG(c). 2,400.00
19 FT,BLb(a),SG(c). 2,400.00
20 FT,BLb(a),SG(c). 2,400.00
21 FT,O:Dash Dartwell 2,500.00
22 A:Silver Streak, The Voice . . 3,000.00
23 I&O:Tommy the AmazingKid 2,200.00
24 B:King of Darkness, Blue Lady 2,200.00
25 A:Meteor Marvin. 3,200.00
26 A:Meteor Marvin,ElectricRay 3,200.00

AMAZING MYSTERIES

Marvel-Comics, 1949–50

32 The Isle of No Return 1,500.00
33 The Thing in the Vault. 750.00
34 Photo(c) 400.00
35 Photo(c) 400.00

AMAZING MYSTERY FUNNIES

Centaur Publications, 1938

1 Skyrocket Steele in Year X . . 8,000.00
2 WE,Skyrocket Steele 4,500.00
3 . . . . 2,700.00
(#4) WE,bondage (c) 2,600.00
2-1(#5) 2,400.00
2-2(#6) Drug use. 2,000.00
2-3(#7) Air Sub DX 2,000.00
2-4(#8) Sand Hog 2,000.00
2-5(#9) 3,000.00
2-6(#10) 2,000.00
2-7(#11) Fantom of Fair, scarce 7,500.00
2-8(#12) Speed Centaur 3,200.00
2-9(#13) 2,000.00
2-10(#14) 2,000.00
2-11(#15)Robot(c). 2,000.00

Amazing Mystery Funnies #19
© Centaur Publications

2-12(#16) BW,I:Space Patrol . . 4,000.00
3-1(#17) I:Bullet 2,000.00
18 Fantom of Fair 2,000.00
19 BW,Space Patrol 2,200.00
20 . . . . 1,800.00
21 thru 24 BW,Space Patrol . @2,200.00

AMAZING WILLIE MAYS
Famous Funnies, 1954
1 Willie Mays(c) 1,400.00

AMERICA IN ACTION
Dell Publishing Co., 1942
1 . . . . 400.00

THE AMERICAN AIR FORCES
Flying Cadet Publ., 1944–45
1 War (c) 300.00
2 War (c) 400.00
3 War (c) 400.00
4 War (c) 250.00
Continues in *A-1 Comics*. See #45, #54, #58, #65, #67, #74, #79, #91

AMERICAN GRAPHICS
Henry Stewart, 1954
1 Indian Legends 200.00
2 . . . . 150.00

AMERICAN LIBRARY
David McKay Publ., 1943
(#1) Thirty Seconds Over Tokyo, movie adapt. 600.00
(#2) Guadalcanal Diary 500.00
3 Look to the Mountain 250.00
4 The Case of the Crooked Candle (Perry Mason) 250.00
5 Duel in the Sun 250.00
6 Wingate's Raiders 250.00

AMERICA'S BEST COMICS
Nedor/Better/Standard Publications, Feb., 1942
1 ASh(c),B:Black Terror, Captain Future, The Liberator,Doc Strange . 4,500.00
2 O:American Eagle 2,000.00
3 B:Pyroman 1,500.00
4 A:Doc Strange, Jimmy Cole . 1,100.00

America's Best Comics #9
© Nedor/Standard Publications

5 ASh(c),A:LoneEagle, Cap.Future 1,100.00
6 A:American Crusader 1,100.00
7 ASh(c),A:Hitler,Hirohito 1,800.00
8 The Liberator ends 1,100.00
9 ASh(c),Fighting Yank 1,500.00
10 ASh(c),American Eagle 1,100.00
11 ASh(c) Hirihito & Tojo(c). . . . 1,500.00
12 Red Cross (c). 1,100.00
13 Fighting Yank 1,100.00
14 Last American Eagle app. . . 1,100.00
15 ASh(c),Fighting Yank 1,100.00
16 ASh(c),Fighting Yank 1,100.00
17 ASh(c),Doc Strange carries football 1,100.00
18 Fighting Yank,Bondage(c) . . 1,100.00
19 ASh(c),Fighting Yank 1,100.00
20 ASh(c),vs. the Black Market 1,100.00
21 ASh(c),Infinity (c) 1,100.00
22 A:Captain Future 1,000.00
23 B:Miss Masque 1,150.00
24 Miss Masque,Bondage (c). . 1,150.00
25 A:Sea Eagle 750.00
26 A:The Phantom Detective. . . . 750.00
27 Pyroman,ASh(c) 750.00
28 A:Commando Cubs, Black Terror 750.00
29 ASh(c),A:Doc Strange. 750.00
30 ASh(c).Xela. 750.00
31 ASh(c),Xela,July, 1949 . . . . . . 750.00

AMERICA'S BIGGEST COMICS BOOK
William H. Wise, 1944
1 196 pgs. A:Grim Reaper, Zudo, Silver Knight, Thunderhoof, Jocko and Socko,Barnaby Beep,Commando Cubs 700.00

Becomes:

AMERICA'S FUNNIEST COMICS
William H. Wise, 1944
2 Funny Animal. 500.00
N# (3). 500.00

AMERICA'S GREATEST COMICS
Fawcett Publications, Fall 1941
1 MRa(c),A:Capt. Marvel, Bulletman,Spy Smasher and Minute Man. 6,500.00
2 F:Capt. Marvel 3,000.00

America's Greatest Comics #4
© Fawcett Publications

3 F:Capt. Marvel 2,500.00
4 B:Commando Yank. 2,000.00
5 Capt.Marvel in 'Lost Lighting' 2,000.00
6 Capt.Marvel fires Machine Gun 2,000.00
7 A:Balbo the Boy Magician. . . 2,000.00
8 A:Capt.Marvel Jr.,Golden Arrow, Summer 1943 . . . . . 2,000.00

ANCHORS ANDREWS
St. John Publ. Co. 1953
1 MB,Navy Humor 225.00
2 thru 4 . . . . @75.00

ANDY COMICS
See: SCREAM COMICS

ANDY DEVINE WESTERN
Fawcett Publ. 1950
1 Photo (c) 800.00
2 . . . . 675.00

ANGEL
Dell Publishing Co., Aug., 1954
(1) *see Dell Four Color #576*
2 . . . . 100.00
3 thru 16 . . . . @75.00

ANIMAL ADVENTURES
Timor Publ./Accepted Publ. 1953–54
1 Funny Animal. 100.00
1a rep.. . . . . 90.00
2 . . . . 90.00

ANIMAL ANTICS
DC Comics, 1946–49
1 B:Racoon Kids. 600.00
2 . . . . 300.00
3 thru 10 . . . . @175.00
11 thru 23. . . . . @125.00

ANIMAL COMICS
Dell Publishing Co., 1942
1 WK,Pogo. 1,700.00
2 Uncle Wiggily(c),A:Pogo. . . . 1,000.00
3 Muggin's Mouse(c),A:Pogo . . . 750.00
4 Uncle Wiggily(c). 500.00
5 Uncle Wiggily(c). 750.00
6 Uncle Wiggily. 500.00

Animal Fables #6
© E.C. Comics

Annie Oakley & Tagg #4
© Dell Publishing Co.

Apache #1
© Fiction House Magazines

7 Uncle Wiggily 500.00
8 WK,Pogo 600.00
9 WK,War Bonds(c),A:Pogo 600.00
10 WK,Pogo 600.00
11 WK,Pogo 400.00
12 WK,Pogo 400.00
13 WK,Pogo 400.00
14 WK,Pogo 400.00
15 WK,Pogo 400.00
16 Uncle Wiggily 250.00
17 WK,Pogo(c) 300.00
18 WK,Pogo(c) 300.00
19 WK,Pogo(c) 300.00
20 WK,Pogo 250.00
21 WK,Pogo(c) 300.00
22 WK,Pogo 200.00
23 WK,Pogo 200.00
24 WK,Pogo(c) 200.00
25 WK,Pogo(c) 200.00
26 WK,Pogo(c) 200.00
27 thru 30 WK,Pogo(c) . . . . . . @200.00

ANIMAL FABLES

E.C. Comics, July–Aug., 1946

1 B:Korky Kangaroo,Freddy Firefly
Petey Pig & Danny Demon . 600.00
2 B:Aesop Fables 375.00
3 . . . . 300.00
4 . . . . 300.00
5 Firefly vs. Red Ants 300.00
6 . . . . 300.00
7 O:Moon Girls,Nov.–Dec.1947 1,200.00

ANIMAL FAIR

Fawcett Publications, March, 1946

1 B:Captain Marvel Bunny,
Sir Spot 500.00
2 A:Droopy, Colonel Walrus 350.00
3 . . . . 250.00
4 A:Kid Gloves, Cub Reporter . . 250.00
5 thru 7 . . . . @250.00
8 thru 10 . . . . @200.00
11 Feb., 1947 . . . . 200.00

ANIMATED COMICS

E.C. Comics, 1948

1 Funny Animal 1,200.00

ANIMATED MOVIE-TUNES

Marvel-Margood Publ., 1945

1 Super Rabbit 300.00
2 Super Rabbit 300.00

Becomes:

MOVIE TUNES

Marvel-Margood Publ., 1946

3 . . . . 135.00

Becomes:

FRANKIE

Marvel-Margood, 1946–48

4 . . . . 200.00
5 . . . . 125.00
6 . . . . 125.00
7 . . . . 125.00
8 . . . . 125.00
9 . . . . 125.00
10 . . . . 100.00
11 . . . . 100.00

Becomes:

FRANKIE & LANA

Marvel-Margood, 1949

12 . . . . 100.00
13 . . . . 100.00
14 . . . . 100.00
15 . . . . 100.00

Becomes:

FRANKIE FUDDLE

Marvel-Margood, 1949

16 . . . . 100.00
17 . . . . 100.00

ANNIE OAKLEY

Marvel Timely, Spring, 1948

1 A:Hedy Devine 750.00
2 CCB,I:Lana,A:Hedy Devine . . 500.00
3 . . . . 350.00
4 . . . . 350.00
5 . . . . 300.00
6 . . . . 300.00
7 . . . . 300.00
8 . . . . 300.00
9 AW, ... 300.00
10 . . . . 250.00
11 June, 1956 . . . . 250.00

ANNIE OAKLEY & TAGG

Dell Publishing Co., 1953

(1) *see Dell Four Color #438*
(2) *see Dell Four Color #481*
(3) *see Dell Four Color #575*
4 . . . . 250.00
5 . . . . 200.00
6 thru 10 . . . . @150.00
11 thru 18 . . . . @125.00

APACHE

Fiction House Magazines, 1951

1 . . . . 300.00

APACHE KID

Marvel-Comics, 1950–52

1 (53) 500.00
2 . . . . 300.00
3 . . . . 250.00
4 . . . . 250.00
5 . . . . 250.00
6 . . . . 150.00
7 RH 200.00
8 thru 10 . . . . @150.00
11 RH 125.00
12 . . . . 125.00
13 RH 125.00
14 thru 19 . . . . @100.00

Becomes:

WESTERN GUNFIGHTERS

Marvel Atlas, 1956–57

20 GC,JSe 150.00
21 RC 150.00
22 WW,BP 250.00
23 AW 200.00
24 ATh 200.00
25 GM 100.00
26 GC 100.00
27 GC,JSe 100.00

APACHE TRAIL

America's Best, 1957

1 . . . . 125.00
2 GT 85.00
3 . . . . 75.00
4 . . . . 75.00

APPROVED COMICS

St. John Publishing Co., 1954

1 The Hawk 125.00
2 Invisible Boy 200.00
3 Wild Boy of the Congo 100.00
4 Kid Cowboy 100.00
5 Flyboy 100.00
6 MB,BK,Daring Adventures 150.00
7 The Hawk 100.00
8 BP,Crime on the Run 125.00
9 MB,Western Bandit Trails 125.00
10 Dinky Duck 100.00
11 MB,Fighting Marines 150.00
12 Northwest Mounties 150.00

Archie #27
© Archie Publications

Archie's Girls Betty and Veronica #26
© Archie Publications

Archie's Pal Jughead #4
© Archie Publications

ARCHIE COMICS

MLJ Magazines, Winter, 1942-43

1 I:Jughead & Veronica	25,000.00
2	5,000.00
3	3,500.00
4	1,800.00
5	1,800.00
6 Christmas issue	1,300.00
7 thru 10	@1,400.00
11 thru 15	@900.00
16 thru 19	@800.00

Archie Publications, 1946

20	850.00
21	550.00
22 thru 31	@525.00
32 thru 42	@350.00
43 thru 50	@225.00
51 A:Katy Keene	175.00
52 thru 64	@150.00
65 thru 70 A:Katy Keene	@150.00
71	100.00
72 thru 74 A:Katy Keene	@125.00
75 thru 99	@100.00
100	100.00
101 thru 122	@100.00
123 UFO,Vampire	75.00
124 thru 130	@75.00
131 thru 145	@60.00
146 thru 182	@60.00
183 Caveman Archie	60.00
184	60.00
185 I:The Archies Band	75.00
186 thru 195	@50.00
196 I:Cricket O'Dell	75.00
197 thru 200	@50.00
201 thru 228	@50.00
229 Lost Child	50.00
230 thru 260	@30.00
261 thru 300	@30.00

ARCHIE'S GIANT SERIES MAGAZINE

Archie Publications, 1954

1	1,700.00
2	1,000.00
3	700.00
4	650.00
5	650.00
6 thru 10	@500.00
11 thru 20	@300.00
21 thru 29	@175.00
30 thru 35	@125.00

ARCHIE'S GIRLS BETTY AND VERONICA

Archie Publications, 1950

1	3,000.00
2	1,500.00
3	650.00
4	600.00
5	600.00
6 thru 10	@500.00
11 thru 15	@400.00
16 thru 20	@350.00
21	275.00
22 thru 29	@250.00
30 thru 40	@200.00
41 thru 50	@175.00
51 thru 60	@125.00
61 thru 70	@110.00
71 thru 74	@100.00
75 Devil	200.00
76 thru 90	@100.00
91 thru 99	@100.00
100	100.00

ARCHIE'S JOKE BOOK MAGAZINE

Archie Publications, 1953

1	1,500.00
2	650.00
3	500.00
15 thru 19	@300.00
20 thru 25	@175.00
26 thru 35	@150.00
36 thru 40	@125.00
41 1st NA art	300.00
42 & 43 TV Personalities	@125.00
44 thru 48 NA	@150.00
49 thru 60	@60.00

ARCHIE'S MADHOUSE

Archie Publications, 1959–69

1	350.00
2	175.00
3 thru 5	@125.00
6 thru 10	@100.00
11 thru 16	@75.00
17 thru 21	@50.00
22 I:Sabrina	350.00
23 thru 25 Sabrina	@125.00
26 thru 30	@50.00
31 thru 33 Sabrina	@60.00
34	50.00
35	50.00
36 Salem Cat & Sabrina	100.00
37 Sabrina	75.00
38 thru 66	@50.00

ARCHIE'S MECHANICS

Archie Publications, 1954

1	1,200.00
2	650.00
3	500.00

ARCHIE'S PAL, JUGHEAD

Archie Publications, 1949

1	2,000.00
2	1,000.00
3	600.00
4	550.00
5	550.00
6	400.00
7 thru 10	@325.00
11 thru 15	@250.00
16 thru 20	@175.00
21 thru 30	@125.00
31 thru 39	@100.00
40 thru 50	@100.00
51 thru 60	@65.00
61 thru 70	@65.00
71 thru 80	@45.00
81 thru 99	@40.00
100	40.00

ARCHIE'S PALS 'N' GALS

Archie Publications, 1952–53

1	1,100.00
2	550.00
3	350.00
4	225.00
5	225.00
6	200.00
7	200.00
8 thru 10	@175.00
11 thru 15	@150.00
16 thru 20	@125.00
21 thru 30	@100.00

ARCHIE'S RIVAL REGGIE

Archie Publications, 1950

1	1,100.00
2	500.00
3	375.00

Arrowhead #4
© Marvel Comics Group

Astonishing #57
© Marvel Comics Group

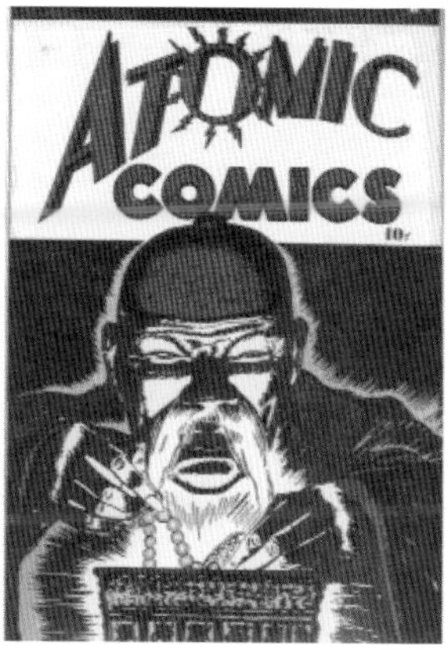

Atomic Comics #1
© Green Publishing Co.

4 . . . 350.00
5 . . . 350.00
6 . . . 275.00
7 . . . 250.00
8 thru 9 . . . @250.00
10 thru 14 A: Katy Keen . . . @200.00
15 . . . 160.00
16 Aug., 1954 . . . 175.00

ARIZONA KID

Marvel Atlas, March, 1951

1 RH,Coming of the Arizons Kid . 300.00
2 RH,Code of the Gunman . . . 150.00
3 RH(c) . . . 125.00
4 PMo . . . 125.00
5 PMo . . . 125.00
6 PMo,JSt,Jan., 1952 . . . 125.00

ARMY & NAVY COMICS
See: SUPERSNIPE COMICS

ARROW, THE

Centaur Publications, Oct., 1940–Oct., 1941

1 B:Arrow, BLb(c) . . . 6,000.00
2 BLb(c) . . . 2,500.00
3 O:Dash Dartwell,Human Meteor, Rainbow, Bondage(c) . . . 2,500.00

ARROWHEAD

Marvel, April, 1954

1 JSt,Indian Warrior Stories . . . 200.00
2 JSt . . . 125.00
3 JSt . . . 125.00
4 JSt,Nov., 1954 . . . 125.00

MARVEL BOY

Marvel, Dec., 1950

1 RH,O:Marvel Boy,Lost World 1,700.00
2 BEv,The Zero Hour . . . 1,200.00

Becomes:

ASTONISHING

Marvel, 1951

3 BEv,Marvel Boy,V:Mr Death . 1,500.00
4 BEv,Stan Lee,The Screaming Tomb . . . 1,100.00
5 BEv,Horror in the Caves of Doom . . . 1,100.00
6 BEv,My Coffin is Waiting E:Marvel Boy . . . 1,100.00
7 JR,JMn,Nightmare . . . 500.00
8 RH,Behind the Wall . . . 500.00
9 RH(c),The Little Black Box . . . 500.00
10 BEv,Walking Dead . . . 500.00
11 BF,JSt.Mr Mordeau . . . 350.00
12 GC,BEv,Horror Show . . . 350.00
13 BK,MSy,Ghouls Gold . . . 500.00
14 BK,The Long Jump Down . . . 500.00
15 BEv(c),Grounds for Death . . . 350.00
16 BEv(c),DAy,SSh,Don't Make a Ghoul of Yourself . . . 350.00
17 Who Was the Wilmach Werewolf? . . . 350.00
18 BEv(c),JR,Vampire at My Window . . . 350.00
19 BK,Back From the Grave . . . 350.00
20 GC,Mystery at Midnight . . . 350.00
21 Manhunter . . . 275.00
22 RH(c),Man Against Werewolf . 275.00
23 The Woman in Black . . . 300.00
24 JR,The Stone Face . . . 300.00
25 RC,I Married a Zombie . . . 300.00
26 RH(c),I Died Too Often . . . 275.00
27 . . . 275.00
28 TLw,No Evidence . . . 275.00
29 BEv(c),GC,Decapitation(c) . . . 275.00
30 Tentacled eyeball story . . . 350.00
31 JMn . . . 225.00
32 A Vampire Takes a Wife . . . 225.00
33 SMo,JMn . . . 225.00
34 JMn,Transformation . . . 225.00
35 . . . 225.00
36 Pithecanthrope Giant . . . 225.00
37 BEv,TLw,Poor Pierre . . . 225.00
38 The Man Who Didn't Belong . . 175.00
39 . . . 175.00
40 . . . 175.00
41 MD . . . 175.00
42 TLw . . . 175.00
43 BP,JR . . . 175.00
44 RC,BP . . . 190.00
45 BK . . . 190.00
46 . . . 190.00
47 BK,JO,BEv . . . 190.00
48 BP . . . 175.00
49 BEv . . . 175.00
50 DCn . . . 175.00
51 . . . 175.00
52 GM . . . 175.00
53 SD,JF,BEv . . . 190.00
54 BEv . . . 190.00
55 BEv . . . 200.00
56 JMn,JK . . . 175.00
57 JR . . . 200.00
58 JF,JO . . . 175.00
59 TSe,BEv . . . 175.00
60 JF,BEv . . . 175.00
61 GM,JO,JR,BEv . . . 175.00
62 MD,BEv . . . 175.00
63 BEv,August, 1957 . . . 175.00

ATOM-AGE COMBAT

St. John Publ. Co., 1952–53

1 Buck Vinson . . . 1,200.00
1a rep. (1958) . . . 350.00
2 Flying Saucer . . . 500.00
3 . . . 450.00
4 . . . 350.00
5 Flying Saucer . . . 350.00

ATOM-AGE COMBAT

Fago Magazines, 1959

2 Nuclear Sub,A-Bomb . . . 325.00
3 Space Missile . . . 225.00

ATOMAN

Spark Publications, Feb., 1946

1 JRo,MMe,O:Atoman,A:Kid Crusaders . . . 1,500.00
2 JRo,MMe . . . 800.00

ATOMIC BOMB

Jay Burtis Publ., 1945

1 . . . 1,500.00

ATOMIC COMICS

Green Publishing Co., Jan., 1946

1 S&S,A:Radio Squad, Barry O'Neal . . . 2,200.00
2 MB,A:Inspector Dayton, Kid Kane . . . 1,100.00
3 MB,A:Zero Ghost Detective . . 800.00
4 JKa(c), July–Aug., 1946 . . . 800.00

ATOMIC COMICS

Daniels Publications, 1946 (Reprints)

1 A:Rocketman,Yankee Boy, Bondage (c),rep. . . . 750.00

ATOMIC MOUSE

Capital Stories/ Charlton Comics, March, 1953

1 AFa,O:Atomic Mouse . . . 500.00
2 AFa,Ice Cream (c) . . . 150.00

Atomic War! #4
© Ace-Junior Books

Authentic Police Cases #4
© St. John Publ. Co.

Avon One-Shots, An Earthman on Venus © Avon Periodicals

3 AFa,Genie and Magic Carpet (c) 125.00
4 AFa 125.00
5 AFa,A:Timmy the Timid Ghost 125.00
6 thru 10 Funny Animal . . . . @100.00
11 thru 14 Funny Animal . . . . @100.00
15 A:Happy the Marvel Bunny . . . 100.00
16 Funny Animal,Giant 75.00
17 thru 30 Funny Animal . . . . @75.00
31 thru 36 Funny Animal . . . . @75.00
37 A:Atom the Cat 75.00
38 thru 40 Funny Animal . . . . @50.00
41 thru 53 Funny Animal . . . . @30.00
54 June, 1963 . . . . 30.00

ATOMIC RABBIT
Charlton Comics, 1955–58

1 . . . . 350.00
2 . . . . 150.00
3 . . . . 100.00
4 . . . . 100.00
5 . . . . 100.00
6 . . . . 100.00
7 . . . . 100.00
8 . . . . 100.00
9 . . . . 100.00
10 . . . . 100.00
11 . . . . 150.00

Becomes:

ATOMIC BUNNY

12 . . . . 150.00
13 thru 18 . . . . @100.00
19 Dec., 1959 . . . . 100.00

ATOMIC THUNDERBOLT, THE
Regor Company, Feb., 1946

1 I:Atomic Thunderbolt, Mr. Murdo 1,200.00

ATOMIC WAR!
Ace-Junior Books, 1952–53

1 Atomic explosion (c) 2,000.00
2 . . . . 1,600.00
3 A-Bomb 1,600.00
4 . . . . 1,600.00

ATOM THE CAT
See: BO

ATTACK
Youthful Mag./Trojan, 1952

1 Violence 500.00
2 . . . . 250.00
3 Bondage 300.00
4 RKu 250.00

Becomes:

ATOMIC ATTACK
Youthful Magazines, 1953

5 . . . . 250.00
6 . . . . 200.00
7 . . . . 200.00
8 . . . . 200.00
5 thru 8 . . . . @ 200.00

ATTACK
Charlton Comics, 1958–59

54 . . . . 150.00
55 thru 60 . . . . @100.00

AUTHENTIC POLICE CASES
St. John Publ. Co., 1948

1 Hale the Magician 600.00
2 Lady Satan, Johnny Rebel . . . 350.00
3 A:Avenger 600.00
4 Masked Black Jack 350.00
5 JCo 350.00
6 JCo,MB(c) 650.00
7 thru 10 . . . . @275.00
11 thru 15 . . . . @275.00
16 thru 23 . . . . @175.00
24 thru 28 Giants . . . . @375.00
29 thru 38 . . . . @150.00

AVIATION AND MODEL BUILDING
See: TRUE AVIATION PICTURE STORIES

AVIATION CADETS
Street & Smith Publ., 1943

1 . . . . 200.00

AVON ONE-SHOTS
Avon Periodicals, 1949-1953 {Listed in Alphabetical Order}

1 Atomic Spy Cases 500.00
N# WW,Attack on Planet Mars . 1,500.00
1 Bachelor's Diary 450.00
1 Badmen of the West 450.00
N# Badmen of Tombstone 200.00
1 EK,Behind Prison Bars 375.00
2 Betty and Her Steady 125.00
N# EK,Blackhawk Indian Tomahawk War 225.00
1 EK,Blazing Sixguns 200.00
1 EK,Butch Cassidy 225.00
N# Chief Crazy Horse 235.00
N# FF,AW,EK,Chief Victorio's Apache Massacre 550.00
N# City of the Living Dead 750.00
1 Complete Romance 475.00
N# Custer's Last Fight 225.00
1 EK(c),Dalton Boys 225.00
N# GT(c),Davy Crockett 225.00
N# The Dead Who Walk 800.00
1 Diary of Horror,Bondage(c) . . . 700.00
N# WW,Earth Man on Venus . . 2,000.00
1 Eerie, bondage (c) 1,200.00
1 EK,Escape from Devil's Island 500.00
N# EK,Fighting Daniel Boone . . . 250.00
N# EK(c),For a Night of Love . . . 375.00
1 WW,Flying Saucers 1,400.00
N# Flying Saucers. 700.00
1 Going Steady with Betty 150.00
N# Hooded Menace 800.00
N# EK,King of the Badmen of Deadwood 175.00
1 King Solomon's Mines 500.00
N# EK(c),Kit Carson & the Blackfeet Warriors 100.00
N# EK,Last of the Comanches . . 200.00
N# EK,Masked Bandit 200.00
1 WW,Mask of Dr. Fu Manchu. 1,500.00
N# EK,Night of Mystery 600.00
1 WW,JKu,Outlaws of the Wild West 400.00
1 JKu,Out of this World 1,000.00
N# EK,Pancho Villa 275.00
1 EK,Phantom Witch Doctor 700.00
1 Pixie Puzzle Rocket to Adventureland 150.00
1 EK,Prison Riot,drugs 500.00
N# EK,Red Mountain Featuring Quantrell's Raiders 350.00
N# Reform School Girl 2,000.00
1 Robotmen of the Lost Planet 1,700.00
N# JO,WW(c),Rocket to the Moon 1,700.00
N# JKu,Secret Diary of Eerie Adventures 2,700.00
1 EK,Sheriff Bob Dixon's Chuck Wagon 175.00
1 Sideshow 400.00

Babe #7
© Prize Publications

Baffling Mysteries #8
© Ace Magazines

Bang-Up Comics #2
© Progressive Publications

1 JKu,Sparkling Love 275.00
N# Speedy Rabbit 100.00
1 EK(c)Teddy Roosevelt & His Rough Riders 225.00
N# The Underworld Story 350.00
N# EK(c),The Unknown Man. . . . 350.00
1 EK,War Dogs of the U.S. Army 175.00
N# EK(c),White Chief of the Pawnee Indians. 200.00
N# Women to Love 700.00

AWFUL OSCAR
See: OSCAR

BABE
Prize/Headline Feature, June–July, 1948

1 BRo 300.00
2 BRo 175.00
3 BRo 150.00
4 thru 9 BRo . . . . @125.00

BABE RUTH SPORTS COMICS
Harvey Publications, April, 1949

1 BP 500.00
2 BP,Baseball 350.00
3 BP,Joe DiMaggio(c) 400.00
4 BP,Bob Feller(c). 325.00
5 BP,Football(c) 325.00
6 BP,Basketball(c). 325.00
7 BP 250.00
8 BP,Yogi Berra. 325.00
9 BP,Stan Musial(c). 300.00
10 . . . . 300.00
11 Feb., 1951. . . . . 250.00

BABY HUEY, THE BABY GIANT
Harvey Publications, 1956–80

1 . . . . 800.00
2 . . . . 350.00
3 Anti-Pep Pills 250.00
4 . . . . 150.00
5 . . . . 150.00
6 thru 10 . . . . @100.00
11 thru 20. . . . . @75.00
21 thru 40. . . . . @50.00
41 thru 60. . . . . @35.00
61 thru 79. . . . . @30.00

80 . . . . 30.00
81 thru 95 giant size. . . . . @35.00
96 Giant size 30.00
97 Giant size 30.00
98 . . . . 20.00
99 . . . . 15.00

BADMEN OF THE WEST
See: A-1 COMICS

BADGE OF JUSTICE
See: CRIME AND JUSTICE

INDIAN BRAVES
Ace Periodicals, 1951

1 Green Arrow. 150.00
2 . . . . 75.00
3 . . . . 65.00
4 . . . . 65.00

Becomes:

BAFFLING MYSTERIES
Periodical House/ Ace Mag., 1951–55

5 GC,MSy. 450.00
6 MSy 325.00
7 . . . . 300.00
8 LC 300.00
9 . . . . 300.00
10 . . . . 300.00
11 GC. 300.00
12 . . . . 275.00
13 . . . . 275.00
14 . . . . 275.00
15 . . . . 275.00
16 LC 275.00
17 LC 275.00
18 LC. 275.00
19 . . . . 275.00
20 LC,Bondage 350.00
21 LC. 275.00
22 LC,MSy. 300.00
23 Bondage 300.00
24 reprint 200.00
25 reprint 200.00

Becomes:

HEROES OF THE WILD FRONTIER
Ace Periodicals, 1956

27 (1) 100.00
2 . . . . 100.00

BANG-UP COMICS
Progressive Publ., 1941

1 CosmoMan, Lady Fairplay, O:Buzz Balmer 1,700.00
2 Buzz Balmer 1,000.00
3 Buzz Balmer 1,000.00

BANNER COMICS
Ace Magazines, Sept., 1941

3 B:Captain Courageous, Lone Warrior. 1,800.00
4 JM(c),Flag(c) 1,500.00
5 . . . . 1,500.00

Becomes:

CAPTAIN COURAGEOUS COMICS
March, 1942

6 I:The Sword 1,500.00

THE BARKER
Quality Comics Group, 1946–49

1 Circus. 150.00
2 . . . . 125.00
3 . . . . 125.00
4 . . . . 125.00
5 . . . . 125.00
6 . . . . 100.00
7 . . . . 100.00
8 . . . . 100.00
9 . . . . 100.00
10 . . . . 100.00
11 thru 15 . . . . @ 100.00

BARNEY BAXTER
Argo Publ., 1956

1 . . . . 125.00
2 . . . . 125.00

BARNEY GOOGLE & SNUFFY SMITH
Toby Press, 1951–52

1 . . . . 150.00
2 . . . . 100.00
3 . . . . 100.00
4 HK 100.00

BARNYARD COMICS
Animated Cartoons, June, 1944

1 (fa) 300.00
2 (fa) 250.00

Barnyard Comics #5
© Animated Cartoons

Batman #8
© DC Comics

Batman #61
© DC Comics

3 (fa) 150.00
4 (fa) 150.00
5 (fa) 150.00
6 thru 12 (fa) . . . . @125.00
13 FF(ti) 150.00
14 FF(ti) 150.00
15 FF(ti) 150.00
16 . . . . 125.00
17 FF(ti) 125.00
18 FF,FF(ti) 150.00
19 FF,FF(ti) 150.00
20 FF,FF(ti) 150.00
21 FF(ti) 125.00
22 FF,FF(ti) 150.00
23 FF(ti) 125.00
24 FF,FF(ti) 150.00
25 FF,FF(ti) 150.00
26 FF(ti) 125.00
27 FF(ti) 125.00
28 . . . . 100.00
29 FF(ti) 125.00
30 and 31 . . . . @100.00

Becomes:

DIZZY DUCK

32 Funny Animal 125.00
33 thru 39 . . . . @100.00

BASEBALL COMICS

Will Eisner Productions, Spring, 1949

1 WE,A:Rube Rocky 1,000.00

BASEBALL HEROS

Fawcett Publications, 1952

N# Babe Ruth (c) 1,500.00

BASEBALL THRILLS

Ziff-Davis Publ. Co., 1951

10 Bob Feller Predicts Pennant Winners 600.00
2 BP, Yogi Berra story 400.00
3 EK, Joe DiMaggio story, Summer 1952 . . . . 450.00

BASIL

St. John Publishing, 1953

1 F:Basil, The Royal Cat. 65.00
2 . . . . 40.00
3 . . . . 20.00
4 . . . . 20.00

BATMAN

DC Comics, Spring, 1940

1 I:Joker,Cat(Catwoman), V:Hugo Strange 175,000.00
2 V:Joker/Catwoman team . . 30,000.00
3 V:Catwoman 20,000.00
4 V:Joker 15,000.00
5 V:Joker 9,000.00
6 V:Clock Maker 6,500.00
7 V:Joker 6,200.00
8 V:Joker 6,000.00
9 V:Joker 6,000.00
10 V:Catwoman 6,000.00
11 V:Joker,Penguin 11,000.00
12 V:Joker. 5,000.00
13 V:Joker. 5,000.00
14 V:Penguin;Propaganda sty . 5,000.00
15 V:Catwoman 5,000.00
16 I:Alfred,V:Joker 8,500.00
17 V:Penguin 4,000.00
18 V:Tweedledum & Tweedledee 4,500.00
19 V:Joker. 5,000.00
20 V:Joker. 4,000.00
21 V:Penguin 4,000.00
22 V:Catwoman,Cavalier 4,000.00
23 V:Joker. 8,000.00
24 I:Carter Nichols, V:Tweedledum & Tweedledee. 3,000.00
25 V:Joker/Penguin team 4,000.00
26 V:Cavalier 2,700.00
27 V:Penguin 4,500.00
28 V:Joker. 2,500.00
29 V:Scuttler 2,500.00
30 V:Penguin,I:Ally Babble 2,500.00
31 I:Punch and Judy. 2,000.00
32 O:Robin,V:Joker. 2,000.00
33 V:Penguin,Jackall 2,300.00
34 A:Ally Babble 2,000.00
35 V:Catwoman 2,000.00
36 V:Penguin,A:King Arthur . . . 1,700.00
37 V:Joker. 2,400.00
38 V:Penguin 4,500.00
39 V:Catwoman,Xmas Story. . . 1,700.00
40 V:Joker. 2,500.00
41 V:Penguin 2,300.00
42 V:Catwoman 2,000.00
43 V:Penguin 2,000.00
44 V:Joker,A:Carter Nichols,Meets ancester Silas Wayne. 2,500.00
45 V:Catwoman 1,300.00
46 V:Joker,A:Carter Nichols, Leonardo Da Vinci 1,300.00
47 O:Batman,V:Catwoman 5,000.00
48 V:Penguin, Bat-Cave story . 1,700.00
49 I:Mad Hatter & Vicki Vale. . . 2,400.00
50 V:Two-Face,A:Vicki Vale . . . 1,400.00
51 V:Penguin 1,300.00
52 V:Joker. 1,300.00
53 V:Joker. 1,500.00
54 V:The Treasure Hunter 1,200.00
55 V:Joker. 1,800.00
56 V:Penguin 1,400.00
57 V:Joker. 1,200.00
58 V:Penguin 1,400.00
59 I:Deadshot 1,200.00
60 V:'Shark' Marlin 1,200.00
61 V:Penguin 1,300.00
62 O:Catwoman,I:Knight & Squire 2,000.00
63 V:Joker. 1,200.00
64 V:Killer Moth. 2,000.00
65 I:Wingman,V:Catwoman . . . 1,200.00
66 V:Joker. 1,000.00
67 V:Joker. 1,000.00
68 V:Two-Face,Alfred story 850.00
69 I:King of the Cats, A:Catwoman. 1,000.00
70 V:Penguin 850.00
71 V:Mr. Cipher 850.00
72 The Jungle Batman. 850.00
73 V:Joker,A:Vicki Vale 1,100.00
74 V:Joker 850.00
75 I:The Gorilla Boss 850.00
76 V:Penguin 850.00
77 The Crime Predictor 850.00
78 The Manhunter from Mars. . 1,100.00
79 A:Vicki Vale 850.00
80 V:Joker 850.00
81 V:Two-Face. 850.00
82 The Flying Batman 750.00
83 V:'Fish' Frye 750.00
84 V:Catwoman 1,000.00
85 V:Joker 750.00
86 V:Joker 750.00
87 V:Joker 750.00
88 V:Mr. Mystery 750.00
89 I:Aunt Agatha 750.00
90 I:Batboy. 750.00
91 V:Blinky Grosset 750.00
92 I:Ace, the Bat-Hound 750.00
93 The Caveman Batman 700.00
94 Alfred Has Amnesia 600.00
95 The Bat-Train 600.00
96 Batman's College Days 600.00
97 V:Joker 600.00
98 A:Carter Nichols,Jules Verne . 600.00
99 V:Penguin,A:Carter Nichols, Bat Masterson 600.00
100 Great Batman Contest. . . . 3,300.00
101 The Great Bat-Cape Hunt. . . 600.00

Batman #128
© DC Comics

Battle #11
© Marvel Comics Group

Battle Action #1
© Marvel Comics Group

102 V:Mayne Mallok	550.00
103 A:Ace, the Bat-Hound	550.00
104 V:Devoe	550.00
105 A:Batwoman	750.00
106 V:Keene Harper Gang	600.00
107 V:Daredevils	600.00
108 Bat-Cave Story	600.00
109 1,000 Inventions of Batman	600.00
110 V:Joker	550.00
111	450.00
112 I:Signalman	450.00
113 I:Fatman	450.00
114 I:Bat Ape	450.00
115	450.00
116	450.00
117	450.00
118	450.00
119	450.00
120	450.00
121 I:Mr.Zero (Mr.Freeze)	600.00
122	300.00
123 A:Joker	325.00
124 Mystery Seed from Space	300.00
125	300.00
126	300.00
127 A:Superman & Joker	325.00
128	300.00
129 O:Robin (Retold)	350.00
130	300.00
131 I:2nd Batman	250.00
132 Lair of the Sea-Fox	250.00
133	250.00
134	250.00
135	250.00
136 A:Joker, Bat-Mite	300.00
137 V:Mr. Marvel,The Brand	250.00
138 A:Bat-Mite	250.00
139 I:Old Batgirl	250.00
140 A:Joker	250.00
141 V:Clockmaster	250.00
142 Batman Robot Story	250.00
143 A:Bathound	250.00
144 A:Joker,Bat-Mite,Bat-Girl	250.00
145 V:Mr.50,Joker	300.00
146 A:Bat-Mite,Joker	300.00
147 Batman becomes Bat-Baby	200.00
148 A:Joker	250.00
149 V:Maestro	200.00
150 V:Biff Warner,Jack Pine	200.00
Ann.#1 CS,O:BatCave	1,100.00
Ann.#2	450.00
Ann.#3 A:Joker	450.00
Ann.#4	200.00
Ann.#5	200.00
Ann.#6	150.00
Ann.#7	150.00

BATTLE

Marvel Atlas, March, 1951

1 They called Him a Coward	350.00
2 The War Department Secrets	175.00
3 The Beast of the Bataan	125.00
4 JMn,I:Buck Private O'Toole	125.00
5 Death Trap Of Gen. Wu	125.00
6 RH, JMn	125.00
7 Enemy Sniper	125.00
8 A Time to Die	125.00
9 RH	100.00
10	100.00
11 SC	100.00
12 thru 21	@110.00
22	100.00
23 BK	100.00
24	100.00
25	100.00
26 JR	100.00
27	100.00
28 JSe	100.00
29	100.00
30	100.00
31 RH,JMn	100.00
32 JSe,GT	100.00
33 GC,JSe,JSt	100.00
34 JSe	100.00
35	100.00
36 BEv	100.00
37 RA,JSt	125.00
38 thru 46	@100.00
47 JO	100.00
48	100.00
49 JDa	100.00
50 BEv	100.00
51	100.00
52 GWb	100.00
53 BP	100.00
54	100.00
55 GC,AS,BP,AW,GWb	125.00
56	100.00
57	100.00
58	100.00
59 AT	100.00
60 A:Combat Kelly	100.00
61 JMn,A:Combat Kelly	100.00
62 A:Combat Kelly	100.00
63 SD	125.00
64 JK	125.00
65 JK	125.00
66 JSe,JK,JDa	125.00
67 JSe,JK,AS,JDa	125.00
68 JSe,JK,AW,SD	125.00
69 RH,JSe,JK,SW	135.00
70 BEv,SD; June, 1960	135.00

BATTLE ACTION

Marvel Atlas, Feb., 1952

1	300.00
2	150.00
3 JSt,RH	100.00
4	100.00
5	100.00
6 JeR	100.00
7 JeR	100.00
8 RH	125.00
9 thru 15	@100.00
16 thru 27	@100.00
28 GWb	100.00
29	100.00
30 GWb,Aug., 1957	100.00

BATTLE ATTACK

Stanmor Publications, 1952–55

1 War Combat	150.00
2	100.00
3	100.00
4	100.00
5	100.00
6	100.00
7	100.00
8	100.00

BATTLE BRADY

See: MEN IN ACTION

BATTLE CRY

Stanmor Publications, 1952–55

1	150.00
2	125.00
3	125.00
4 EC Copy	125.00
5	125.00
6	100.00
7	100.00
8	100.00
9	100.00
10	100.00
11 thru 20	@100.00

BATTLEFIELD

Marvel Atlas, April, 1952

1 RH, Slaughter on Suicide Ridge	250.00
2 RH	125.00
3 Ambush Patrol	125.00
4	125.00
5 Into the Jaws of Death	125.00

Battlefront #34
© Marvel Comics Group

Best Comics #4
© Better Publications

6 thru 10 . . . . @100.00
11 GC,May, 1953 . . . . 100.00

BATTLEFIELD ACTION
See: DYNAMITE

BATTLE FIRE
Stamfor Publications, 1955

1 War 150.00
2 . . . . 100.00
3 thru 7 . . . . @100.00

BATTLEFRONT
Standard Comics, 1952

5 ATh 175.00

BATTLEFRONT
Marvel Atlas, June, 1952

1 JeR,RH(c),Operation Killer . . . 325.00
2 JeR 200.00
3 JeR,Spearhead 125.00
4 JeR,Death Trap of General
Chun 125.00
5 JeR,Terror of the Tank Men . . . 125.00
6 A:Combat Kelly 125.00
7 A:Combat Kelly 125.00
8 A:Combat Kelly 125.00
9 A:Combat Kelly 125.00
10 A:Combat Kelly 125.00
11 thru 20 . . . . @100.00
21 thru 39 . . . . @100.00
40 AW 100.00
41 . . . . 100.00
42 AW 125.00
43 thru 48 Aug.,1957 . . . . @135.00

BATTLEGROUND
Marvel Atlas, Sept., 1954

1 . . . . 250.00
2 JKz 125.00
3 thru 8 . . . . @100.00
9 BK 100.00
10 . . . . 100.00
11 AW,GC,GT 125.00
12 MD,JSe 100.00
13 AW 100.00
14 JD 125.00
15 thru 17 . . . . @100.00
18 AS 125.00
19 JMn,JSe 100.00
20 Aug., 1957 . . . . 100.00

BATTLE REPORT
Excellent Publ./
Ajax-Farrell, 1952--53

1 . . . . 150.00
2 . . . . 100.00
3 . . . . 100.00
4 . . . . 100.00
5 . . . . 100.00
6 . . . . 100.00

BATTLE SQUADRON
Stanmor Publications, 1955

1 . . . . 125.00
2 . . . . 100.00
3 Iwo Jima flag 100.00
4 . . . . 100.00
5 . . . . 100.00

BATTLE STORIES
Fawcett Publications 1952–53

1 GE 175.00
2 . . . . 100.00
3 . . . . 100.00
4 . . . . 100.00
5 . . . . 100.00
6 thru 11 . . . . @100.00

BEANBAGS
Approved Comics
(Ziff-Davis), 1951–52

1 . . . . 125.00
2 . . . . 125.00

BEANIE THE MEANIE
Fago Publications, 1958

1 thru 3 . . . . @75.00

BEANY & CECIL
Dell Publishing Co., Jan., 1952

1 . . . . 250.00
2 . . . . 150.00
3 . . . . 150.00
4 . . . . 150.00
5 . . . . 150.00

BEE 29,
THE BOMBARDIER
Neal Publications, 1945

1 Funny Animal 350.00

BEN BOWIE & HIS
MOUNTAIN MEN
Dell Publishing Co., 1952

(1) *see Dell Four Color #443*
(2 thru 6) *see Dell Four Color*
7 . . . . 150.00
8 thru 10 . . . . @125.00
11 I:Yellow Hair 100.00
12 thru 17 . . . . @100.00

THE BERRYS
Argo Publications, 1956

1 . . . . 100.00

BEST COMICS
Better Publications, Nov., 1939

1 B:Red Mask 2,000.00
2 A:Red Mask, Silly Willie 1,200.00
3 A:Red Mask 1,200.00
4 Cannibalism story,
Feb., 1940 . . . . 1,500.00

BEST FROM BOY'S LIFE
Gilberton Company, 1957

1 . . . . 150.00
2 . . . . 100.00
3 . . . . 100.00
4 LbC 125.00
5 . . . . 100.00

BEST OF THE WEST
See: A-1 COMICS

BEST LOVE
Marvel-Manvis Publ., 1949
(Formerly: Sub-Mariner #32)

33 JKu 150.00
34 . . . . 100.00
35 BEv 125.00
36 BEv 125.00

BEST OF DENNIS
THE MENACE, THE
Hallden/Fawcett Publ.,
Summer, 1959–Spring, 1961

1 . . . . 150.00
2 . . . . 100.00
3 thru 5 . . . . @100.00

Best Western #58
© Marvel Comics Group

Beyond #4
© Ace Magazines

Big Shot Comics #13
© Columbia Comics Group

BEST ROMANCE

Visual Editions (Standard Comics), 1952

5 ATh,Photo(c) . . . 150.00
6 . . . 100.00
7 Photo(c) . . . 100.00

BEST WESTERN

Marvel, June, 1949

58 A:KidColt,BlackRider,Two-Gun Kid; Million Dollar Train Robbery . . . 325.00
59 A:BlackRider,KidColt,Two-Gun Kid;The Black Rider Strikes . . 300.00

Becomes:

WESTERN OUTLAWS & SHERIFFS

Marvel, 1949

60 PH(c),Hawk Gaither . . . 300.00
61 Ph(c),Pepper Lawson . . . 250.00
62 Murder at Roaring House Bridge . . . 250.00
63 thru 65 . . . @250.00
66 Hanging . . . 250.00
67 Cannibalism . . . 250.00
68 thru 72 . . . @225.00
73 June, 1952 . . . 225.00

BEWARE

See: CAPTAIN SCIENCE

BEWARE TERROR TALES

Fawcett Publications, 1952–53

1 . . . 900.00
2 . . . 700.00
3 . . . 600.00
4 . . . 600.00
5 . . . 600.00
6 . . . 600.00
7 . . . 550.00
8 . . . 750.00

THE BEYOND

Ace Magazines, 1950–55

1 Werewolf . . . 650.00
2 . . . 500.00
3 . . . 350.00
4 . . . 350.00
5 . . . 350.00
6 . . . 350.00
7 . . . 350.00
8 . . . 350.00
9 . . . 350.00
10 . . . 350.00
11 thru 20 . . . @300.00
21 thru 30 . . . @300.00

BIBLE TALES FOR YOUNG FOLK

Marvel/Atlas, 1953

1 . . . 300.00
2 BEv,BK . . . 250.00
3 . . . 175.00
4 JeR . . . 200.00
5 . . . 175.00

BIG ALL-AMERICAN COMIC BOOK

DC Comics, Dec., 1944

1 JKu . . . 20,000.00

BIG BOOK OF FUN COMICS

DC Comics, Spring, 1936

1 . . . 25,000.00

BIG CHIEF WAHOO

Eastern Color Printing, 1942–43

1 . . . 500.00
2 BWa(c),Three Ring Circus . . . 250.00
3 BWa(c) . . . 200.00
4 BWa(c) . . . 200.00
5 BWa(c),Wild West Rodeo . . . 200.00
6 A:Minnie-Ha-Cha . . . 150.00
7 . . . 125.00
8 . . . 100.00
9 . . . 100.00
10 . . . 125.00
11 thru 23 . . . @100.00

BIG JON AND SPARKIE

See: SPARKIE, RADIO PIXIE

BIG SHOT COMICS

Columbia Comics Group, May, 1940

1 MBI,OW,Skyman,B:The Face, Joe Palooka, Rocky Ryan . 4,000.00
2 MBi,OW,Marvelo (c) . . . 1,700.00
3 MBi,Skyman (c) . . . 1,500.00
4 MBi,OW,Joe Palooka (c) . . . 1,000.00
5 MBi,Joe Palooka (c) . . . 800.00
6 MBi,Joe Palooka (c) . . . 750.00
7 MBi,Elect Joe Palooka and Skyman . . . 700.00
8 MBi,Joe Palooka and Skyman dress as Santa . . . 700.00
9 MBi,Skyman . . . 700.00
10 MBi,Skyman . . . 700.00
11 MBi . . . 600.00
12 MBi,OW . . . 600.00
13 MBi,OW . . . 600.00
14 MBi,OW,O:Sparky Watts . . . 600.00
15 MBi,OW,O:The Cloak . . . 800.00
16 MBi,OW . . . 500.00
17 MBi(c),OW . . . 500.00
18 MBi,OW . . . 500.00
19 MBi,OW,The Face (c) . . . 450.00
20 MBi,OW,OW(c),Skyman cov. . 450.00
21 MBi,OW,A:Raja the Arabian Knight . . . 450.00
22 MBi,OW,Joe Palooka (c) . . . 450.00
23 MBi,OW,Sparky Watts (c) . . . 400.00
24 MBi,OW,Uncle Sam (c) . . . 600.00
25 MBi,OW,Hitler,Sparky Watts(c) 500.00
26 MBi,OW,Hitler,Devildog (c) . . . 450.00
27 MBi,OW,Skyman (c) . . . 450.00
28 MBi,OW,Hitler (c) . . . 800.00
29 MBi,OW,I:Captain Yank . . . 450.00
30 MBi,OW,Santa (c) . . . 450.00
31 MBi,OW,Sparky Watts (c) . . . 400.00
32 MBi,OW,B:Vic Jordan newspaper reps . . . 450.00
33 MBi,OW,Sparky Watts (c) . . . 400.00
34 MBi,OW . . . 400.00
35 MBi,OW . . . 400.00
36 MBi,OW,Sparky Watts (c) . . . 350.00
37 MBi,OW . . . 350.00
38 MBi,Uncle Slap Happy (c) . . . 350.00
39 MBi,Uncle Slap Happy (c) . . . 350.00
40 MBi,Joe Palooka Happy (c) . . 350.00
41 MBi,Joe Palooka . . . 300.00
42 MBi,Joe Palooka parachutes . 300.00
43 MBi,V:Hitler . . . 450.00
44 MBi,Slap Happy (c) . . . 300.00
45 MBi,Slap Happy (c) . . . 300.00
46 MBi,Uncle Sam (c),V:Hitler . . . 450.00
47 MBi,Uncle Slap Happy (c) . . . 300.00
48 MBi . . . 300.00
49 MBi . . . 250.00
50 MBi,O:The Face . . . 250.00
51 MBi . . . 250.00
52 MBi,E:Vic Jordan (Hitler cov) newspaper reps . . . 400.00

Big-3 #7
© Fox Features Syndicate

Big Town #11
© DC Comics

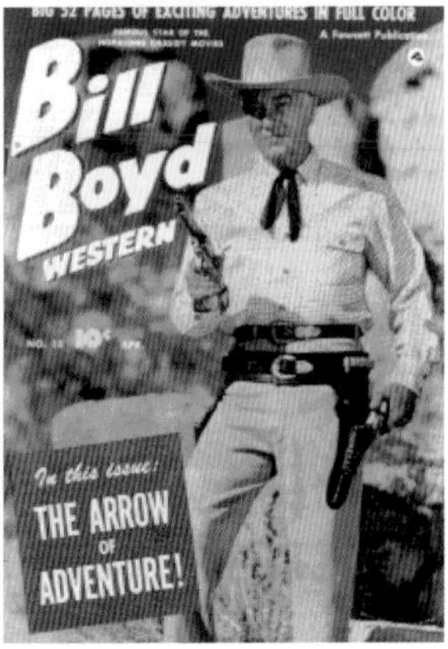

Bill Boyd Western #13
© Fawcett Publications

53 MBi,Uncle Slap Happy (c) . . . 225.00
54 MBi,Uncle Slap Happy (c) . . . 225.00
55 MBi,Happy Easter (c) 225.00
56 MBi 225.00
57 MBi 225.00
58 MBi 225.00
59 MBi,Slap Happy 225.00
60 MBi,Joe Palooka. 225.00
61 MBi 200.00
62 MBi 200.00
63 MBi 200.00
64 MBi,Slap Happy 200.00
65 MBi,Slap Happy 200.00
66 MBi,Slap Happy 200.00
67 MBi 200.00
68 MBi,Joe Palooka. 200.00
69 MBi 200.00
70 MBi,OW,Joe Palooka (c) 200.00
71 MBi,OW. 200.00
72 MBi,OW. 200.00
73 MBi,OW,The Face (c) 200.00
74 MBi,OW. 200.00
75 MBi,OW,Polar Bear Swim Club (c) 200.00
76 thru 80 MBi,OW . . . . @175.00
81 thru 84 MBi,OW . . . . @175.00
85 MBi,OW,Dixie Dugan (c). 175.00
86 thru 95 MBi,OW . . . . @150.00
96 MBi,OW,X-Mas (c) 150.00
97 thru 99 MBi,OW . . . . @150.00
100 MBi,OW,Special issue. 175.00
101 thru 103 MBi,OW . . . . @150.00
104 MBi, Aug., 1949 . . . . 175.00

BIG-3

Fox Features Syndicate, Fall 1940

1 B:BlueBeetle,Flame,Samson 4,500.00
2 A:BlueBeetle,Flame,Samson 2,000.00
3 same. 1,800.00
4 same. 1,600.00
5 same. 1,600.00
6 E:Samson, bondage (c) 1,500.00
7 A:V-Man, Jan., 1942 . . . . . . 1,500.00

THE BIG TOP COMICS

Toby Press, 1951

1 . . . . 135.00
2 . . . . 100.00

BIG TOWN

DC Comics, 1951–58

1 TV, radio tie-in. 1,100.00
2 . . . . 500.00
3 . . . . 350.00
4 . . . . 350.00
5 . . . . 350.00
6 . . . . 350.00
7 . . . . 350.00
8 . . . . 350.00
9 . . . . 350.00
10 . . . . 350.00
11 thru 20 . . . . @300.00
21 thru 30 . . . . @250.00
31 thru 40 . . . . @150.00
41 thru 50. . . . . @125.00

BILL BARNES, AMERICA'S AIR ACE

See: AIR ACE

BILL BATTLE, THE ONE-MAN ARMY

Fawcett Publications 1952–53

1 . . . . 200.00
2 . . . . 150.00
3 . . . . 150.00
4 . . . . 150.00

BILL BOYD WESTERN

Fawcett Publications, 1950

1 B:Bill Boyd, Midnite,Ph(c) 800.00
2 P(c) 500.00
3 B:Ph(c). 350.00
4 . . . . 300.00
5 . . . . 300.00
6 . . . . 300.00
7 . . . . 250.00
8 . . . . 250.00
9 . . . . 250.00
10 . . . . 250.00
11 . . . . 250.00
12 . . . . 235.00
13 . . . . 235.00
14 . . . . 235.00
15 thru 21. . . . . @235.00
22 E:Ph(c) 235.00
23 June, 1952 . . . . 250.00

BILL STERN'S SPORTS BOOK

Approved Comics, Spring-Summer, 1951

1 Ewell Blackwell 300.00
2 . . . . 250.00
2-2 EK Giant. 300.00

BILLY AND BUGGY BEAR

I.W. Enterprises, 1958

1 Funny animal. 100.00

BILLY BUCKSKIN WESTERN

Marvel Atlas, Nov., 1955

1 MD,Tales of the Wild Frontier . 250.00
2 MD,Ambush 150.00
3 MD,AW, Thieves in the Night . 200.00

Becomes:

2-GUN KID

Marvel, 1956

4 SD,A: Apache Kid 200.00

Becomes:

TWO-GUN WESTERN

Marvel, 1956

5 B:Apache Kid,Doc Holiday, Kid Colt Outlaw 250.00
6 . . . . 225.00
7 . . . . 225.00
8 RC 200.00
9 AW 200.00
10 . . . . 200.00
11 AW. 225.00
12 Sept., 1957,RC 200.00

BILLY BUNNY

Excellent Publications, 1954

1 . . . . 150.00
2 . . . . 100.00
3 . . . . 100.00
4 . . . . 100.00
Ann. #1 Christmas Frolics 225.00

BILLY THE KID

Charlton Publ. Co., 1957

9 . . . . 150.00
10 . . . . 125.00
11 O:Ghost Train 150.00
12 . . . . 125.00
13 AW,AT 150.00
14 . . . . 125.00
15 AW,O:Billy the Kid. 150.00
16 AW 150.00
17 . . . . 125.00
18 . . . . 125.00
19 . . . . 125.00

Billy the Kid Adventure Magazine #3
© Toby Press

Black Cat #8
© Harvey Publications

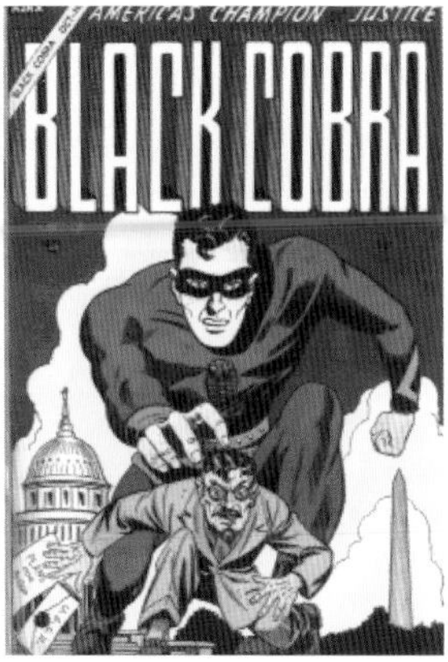

Black Cobra #1
© Ajax Farrell Publications

20 JSe 150.00
21 JSe 150.00
22 JSe 150.00
23 JSe 150.00
24 JSe 150.00
25 JSe 150.00
26 JSe 150.00
27 . . . . . 100.00
28 . . . . . 100.00
29 . . . . . 100.00
30 Masked Rider 125.00
31 thru 40 . . . . . @100.00

BILLY THE KID ADVENTURE MAGAZINE
Toby Press, Oct., 1950
1 AW(a&c),FF(a&c) 500.00
2 Photo (c) 200.00
3 AW,FF 500.00
4 . . . . . 125.00
5 . . . . . 125.00
6 FF,Photo (c) 250.00
7 Photo (c) 125.00
8 . . . . . 125.00
9 HK Pot-Shot Pete 150.00
10 . . . . . 125.00
11 . . . . . 100.00
12 . . . . . 100.00
13 HK 100.00
14 AW,FF 150.00
15 thru 21 . . . . . @100.00
22 AW,FF 125.00
23 thru 29 . . . . . @100.00
30 1955 . . . . . 100.00

BILLY THE KID AND OSCAR
Fawcett Publications, 1945–46
1 Funny animal 250.00
2 . . . . . 200.00
3 . . . . . 200.00

BILLY WEST
Visual Editions (Standard Comics), 1949–51
1 . . . . . 200.00
2 . . . . . 150.00
3 . . . . . 100.00
4 . . . . . 100.00
5 . . . . . 100.00
6 . . . . . 100.00
7 . . . . . 100.00
8 . . . . . 100.00
9 . . . . . 125.00

BINGO COMICS
Howard Publications, 1945
1 LbC,Drug 750.00

BINGO, THE MONKEY DOODLE BOY
St. John Publishing Co. 1951
1 . . . . . 125.00
1a rep. (1953) 100.00

BLACK CAT COMICS
Harvey Publications (Home Comics), June–July, 1946
1 JKu 1,200.00
2 JKu,JSm(c) 750.00
3 JSm(c) 450.00
4 B:Red Demon 450.00
5 S&K 550.00
6 S&K,A:Scarlet Arrow, O:Red Demon 550.00
7 S&K 550.00
8 S&K,B:Kerry Drake 500.00
9 S&K,O:Stuntman 550.00
10 JK,JSm 400.00
11 . . . . . 400.00
12 'Ghost Town Terror' 400.00
13 LEI 375.00
14 LEI 375.00
15 LEI 375.00
16 LEI 375.00
17 A:Mary Worth, Invisible Scarlet 375.00
18 LEI 375.00
19 LEI 375.00
20 A:Invisible Scarlet 375.00
21 LEI 375.00
22 LEI thru 26 . . . . . @375.00
27 X-Mas issue 350.00
28 I:Kit,A:Crimson Raider 350.00
29 Black Cat bondage (c) 350.00
Becomes:

BLACK CAT MYSTERY
Aug., 1951
30 RP,Black Cat(c) 500.00
31 RP 400.00
32 BP,RP,Bondage (c) 450.00
33 BP,RP,Electrocution (c) 450.00
34 BP,RP 300.00
35 BP,RP,OK, Atomic Storm 500.00
36 RP 400.00
37 RP 300.00
38 RP 300.00
39 RP 350.00
40 RP 300.00
41 . . . . . 300.00
42 . . . . . 300.00
43 BP 300.00
44 BP,HN,JkS,Oil Burning (c) 450.00
45 BP,HN,Classic (c) 600.00
46 BP,HN 300.00
47 BP,HN 300.00
48 BP,HN 300.00
49 BP,HN 300.00
50 BP,Rotting Face 1,200.00
51 BP,HN,MMe 300.00
52 BP 250.00
53 BP 250.00
Becomes:

BLACK CAT WESTERN
Feb., 1955
54 A:Black Cat & Story 350.00
55 A:Black Cat 250.00
56 same 250.00
Becomes:

BLACK CAT MYSTIC
Sept., 1956
58 JK,Starts Comic Code 325.00
59 KB 250.00
60 JK 275.00
61 Colorama, HN 250.00
62 . . . . . 175.00
63 JK 200.00
64 JK 225.00
65 April, 1963 . . . . . 225.00

BLACK COBRA
Farrell Publications (Ajax), 1954–55
1 . . . . . 500.00
2 (6) 350.00
3 . . . . . 300.00
Becomes:

BRIDES DIARY
Farrell Publications, 1955
4 . . . . . 150.00
5 . . . . . 100.00
6 . . . . . 100.00
7 . . . . . 100.00
8 . . . . . 100.00
9 . . . . . 125.00
10 . . . . . 125.00

Uncle Sam Quarterly #4
© Quality Comics Group

Blackhawk #27
© Comic Magazines

Blackhawk #72
© Comic Magazines

BLACK DIAMOND WESTERN
See: DESPERADO

BLACK FURY
Charlton Comics, 1955

1 . . . . 150.00
2 . . . . 100.00
3 thru 15 . . . . @100.00
16 thru 18 SD . . . . @150.00
19 and 20 . . . . @75.00
21 thru 56 . . . . @75.00
57 March-April, 1966 . . . . 60.00

UNCLE SAM QUARTERLY
Quality Comics Group, Fall, 1941

1 BE,LF(c),JCo,O:Uncle Sam . 6,000.00
2 LF&WE(c),DBe, Ray, Black Condor 3,500.00
3 GT(a&c) 2,700.00
4 GT,GF(c) 2,500.00
5 RC,GT 2,700.00
6 GT 2,500.00
7 Hitler, Tojo, Mussolini 2,700.00
8 GT 2,500.00

Becomes:

BLACKHAWK
Comic Magazines, Winter, 1944

9 Bait for a Death Trap 6,000.00
10 RC 1,850.00
11 RC 1,300.00
12 Flies to thrilling adventure . . 1,200.00
13 Blackhawk Stalks Danger . . 1,200.00
14 BWa 1,300.00
15 Patrols the Universe 1,200.00
16 RC,BWa,Huddles for Action 1,200.00
17 BWa,Prepares for Action . . . 1,500.00
18 RC(a&c),BWa,One for All and All for One 1,800.00
19 RC(a&c),BWa,Calls for Action 2,000.00
20 RC(a&c),BWa,Smashes Rugoth the Ruthless God . . 1,700.00
21 BWa,Battles Destiny Written in Blood 1,200.00
22 RC(a&c),BWa,Fear battles Death and Destruction 1,200.00
23 RC(a&c),BWa,Batters Down Oppression 1,200.00
24 RC(a&c),BWa 1,200.00
25 RC(a&c),BWa,V:The Evil of Mung 1,200.00
26 RC(a&c),V:Menace of a Sunken World 1,100.00
27 BWa,Destroys a War-Mad Munitions Magnate 1,100.00
28 BWa,Defies Destruction in the Battle of the Test Tube 1,100.00
29 BWa,Tale of the Basilisk Supreme Chief 1,100.00
30 BWa,RC(a&c),The Menace of the Meteors 1,100.00
31 BWa,RC(a&c),JCo,Treachery among the Blackhawks . . . 1,000.00
32 BWa,RC(a&c),A:Delya, Flying Fish 1,000.00
33 RC,BWa,A:The Mockers . . . 1,000.00
34 BWa,A:Tana,Mavis 1,000.00
35 BWa,I:Atlo,Strongest Man on Earth 1,000.00
36 RC(a&c),BWa,V:Tarya 750.00
37 RC(a&c),BWa,V:Sari,The Rajah of Ramastan 750.00
38 BWa 750.00
39 RC(a&c),BWa,V:Lilith 750.00
40 RC(a&c),BWa,Valley of Yesterday 750.00
41 RC(a&c),BWa 700.00
42 RC(a&c),BWa,V:Iron Emperor 700.00
43 RC(a&c),BWa,Terror from the Catacombs 700.00
44 RC(a&c),BWa, King of Winds . 700.00
45 BWa,The Island of Death 700.00
46 RC(a&c),BWa,V:DeathPatrol . 700.00
47 RC(a&c),BWa,War! 700.00
48 RC(a&c),BWa,A:Hawks of Horror,Port of Missing Ships . 700.00
49 RC(a&c),BWa,A:Valkyrie, Waters of Terrible Peace 700.00
50 RC(a&c),BWa,I:Killer Shark, Flying Octopus 750.00
51 BWa,V:The Whip, Whip of Nontelon 700.00
52 RC(a&c),BWa,Traitor in the Ranks 700.00
53 RC(a&c),BWa,V:Golden Mummy 700.00
54 RC(a&c),BWa,V:Dr. Deroski, Circles of Suicide 700.00
55 RC(a&c),BWa,V:Rocketmen . . 700.00
56 RC(a&c),BWa,V:The Instructor, School for Sabotage 700.00
57 RC(a&c),BWa,Paralyzed City of Armored Men 700.00
58 RC(a&c),BWa,V:King Cobra, The Spider of Delanza 700.00
59 BWa,V:Sea Devil 700.00
60 RC(a&c),BWa,V:Dr. Mole and His Devils Squadron 700.00
61 V:John Smith, Stalin's Ambassador of Murder 600.00
62 V:General X, Return of Genghis Kahn 600.00
63 RC(a&c),The Flying Buzz-Saws 600.00
64 RC(a&c),V:Zoltan Korvas, Legion of the Damned 600.00
65 Olaf as a Prisoner in Dungeon of Fear 600.00
66 RC(a&c),V:The Red Executioner, Crawler 600.00
67 RC(a&c),V:Future Fuehrer . . . 600.00
68 V:Killers of the Kremlin 500.00
69 V:King of the Iron Men, Conference of the Dictators . 500.00
70 V:Killer Shark 500.00
71 V:Von Tepp, The Man Who could Defeat Blackhawk O:Blackhawk 550.00
72 V:Death Legion 500.00
73 V:Hangman,The Tyrannical Freaks 400.00
74 Plan of Death 400.00
75 V:The Mad Doctor Baroc, The Z Bomb Menace 400.00
76 The King of Blackhawk Island 400.00
77 V:The Fiendish Electronic Brain 400.00
78 V:The Killer Vulture, Phantom Raider 400.00
79 V:Herman Goering, The Human Bomb 400.00
80 V:Fang, the Merciless, Dr. Death 400.00
81 A:Killer Shark, The Sea Monsters of Killer Shark 400.00
82 V:Sabo Teur, the Ruthless Commie Agent 400.00
83 I:Hammmer & Sickle, V:Madam Double Cross 400.00
84 V:Death Eye,Dr. Genius, The Dreaded Brain Beam . . . 400.00
85 V:The Fiendish Impersonator . 400.00
86 V:The Human Torpedoes 400.00
87 A:Red Agent Sovietta,V:Sea Wolf, Le Sabre,Comics Code 300.00
88 V:Thunder the Indestructible, The Phantom Sniper 300.00
89 V:The Super Communists 400.00
90 V:The Storm King, Villainess Who Smashed the Blackhawk Team 400.00

Blackhawk #109
© DC Comics

Blackhawk #148
© DC Comics

Black Knight #2
© Marvel Comics Group

91 Treason in the Underground . . 400.00
92 V:The World Traitor. 400.00
93 V:Garg the Destroyer, O:Blackhawk 350.00
94 V:Black Widow, Darkk the Destroyer 350.00
95 V:Madam Fury, Queen of the Pirates 350.00
96 Doom in the Deep. 350.00
97 Revolt of the Slave Workers . . 300.00
98 Temple of Doom 300.00
99 The War That Never Ended . . 300.00
100 The Delphian Machine 325.00
101 Satan's Paymaster 275.00
102 The Doom Cloud 275.00
103 The Super Race 275.00
104 The Jet Menace 275.00
105 The Red Kamikaze Terror . . 275.00
106 The Flying Tank Platoon . . . 275.00
107 The Winged Menace 275.00

DC Comics, 1957

108 DD,CCu,DD&CCu(c),The Threat from the Abyss A:Blaisie 650.00
109 DD,CCu,DD&CCu(c),The Avalance Kid 250.00
110 DD,CCu,DD&CCu(c),Mystery of Tigress Island 250.00
111 DD,CCu,DD&CCu(c),Menace of the Machines. 250.00
112 DD,CCu,DD(c),The Doomed Dog Fight. 250.00
113 DD,CCu,CCu(c),Volunteers of Doom. 250.00
114 DD,CCu,DD&CCu(c),Gladiators of Blackhawk Island. 250.00
115 DD,CCu,DD&CCu(c),The Tyrant's Return 250.00
116 DD,CCu,DD&CCu(c),Prisoners of the Black Island. 250.00
117 DD,CCu,DD&CCu(c),Menace of the Dragon Boat 250.00
118 DD,CCu,DD&SMo(c),FF,The Bandit With 1,000 Nets 260.00
119 DD,CCu,DD&SMo(c), V:Chief Blackhawk. 200.00
120 DD,CCu,DD&SMo(c),The Challenge of the Wizard 200.00
121 DD,CCu,DD&CCu(c),Secret Weapon of the Archer 200.00
122 DD,CCu,DD&CCu(c),The Movie That Backfired. 200.00
123 DD,CCu,DD&CCu(c),The Underseas Gold Fort. 200.00
124 DD,CCu,DD&CCu(c),Thieves With A Thousand Faces 200.00
125 DD,CCu,DD&CCu(c),Secrets o/t Blackhawk Time Capsule . 200.00
126 DD,CCu,DD&CCu(c),Secret of the Glass Fort 200.00
127 DD,CCu,DD&CCu(c),Blackie-The Winged Sky Fighter 200.00
128 DD,CCu,DD&CCu(c),The Vengeful Bowman 200.00
129 DD,CCu,DD&CCu(c),The Cavemen From 3,000 B.C. . . 200.00
130 DD,CCu,DD&SMo(c),The Mystery Missle From Space . 200.00
131 DD,CCu,DD&CCu(c),The Return of the Rocketeers . . . 150.00
132 DD,CCu,DD&CCu(c),Raid of the Rocketeers 150.00
133 DD,CCu,DD&CCu(c),Human Dynamo. 150.00
134 DD,CC,DD&CC(c),The Sinister Snowman 150.00
135 DD,CCu,DD&CCu(c),The Underworld Supermarket . . . 150.00
136 DD,CCu,DD&CCu(c),The Menace of the Smoke-Master 150.00
137 DD,CCu,DD&CCu(c),The Weapons That Backfired. . . . 150.00
138 DD,CCu,DD&SMo(c),The Menace of the Blob 150.00
139 DD,CCu,DD&CCu(c),The Secret Blackhawk 150.00
140 DD,CCu,DD&CCu(c),The Space Age Marauders. 150.00
141 DD,CCu,DD&CCu(c),Crimes of the Captive Masterminds . 100.00
142 DD,CCu,DD&CCu(c),Alien Blackhawk Chief 100.00
143 DD,SMo,DD&CCu(c),Lady Blackhawk's Rival 100.00
144 DD,CCu,DD&CCu(c),The Underworld Sportsmen 100.00
145 DD,CCu,DD&CCu(c),The Deadly Lensman 100.00
146 DD,CCu,DD&CCu(c),Black-hawk's Fantastic Fables 100.00
147 DD,SMo,DD&CCu(c),The Blackhawk Movie Queen. . . . 100.00
148 DD,CCu,DD&CCu(c),Four Dooms For The Blackhawks . 100.00
149 DD,CCu,DD&CCu(c),Masks of Doom. 100.00
150 DD,CCu,DD&SMo(c), Black-hawk Mascot from Space . . . 100.00
151 DD,CCu,Lost City 125.00
152 DD,CCu,DD&SMo(c),Noah's Ark From Space. 100.00
153 DD,CCu,DD&SMo(c), Boomerang Master 100.00
154 DD,CCu,DD&SMo(c),The Beast Time Forgot. 100.00
155 DD,CCu,DD&CCu(c),Killer Shark's Land Armada 100.00
156 DD,CCu,DD&SMo(c),Peril of the Plutonian Raider 100.00
157 DD,CCu,DD&SMo(c),Secret of the Blackhawk Sphinx 100.00
158 DD,CCu,DD&SMo(c),Bandit Birds From Space 100.00
159 DD,CCu,DD&SMo(c),Master of the Puppet Men. 100.00
160 DD,CCu,DD&CCu(c),The Phantom Spy. 100.00
161 DD,SMo,DD&SMo(c),Lady Blackhawk's Crime Chief. . . . 100.00
162 DD,CCu,DD&CCu(c),The Invisible Blackhawk 100.00
163 DD,CCu,DD&SMo(c), Fisherman of Crime. 100.00
164 DD,O:Blackhawk retold. 125.00
165 DD,V:League of Anti Blackhawks 100.00

BLACK HOOD
See: LAUGH COMICS

BLACK JACK
Charlton Comics, 1957–59

20 . . . . 125.00
21 . . . . 100.00
22 . . . . 125.00
23 AW,AT 125.00
24 SD. 135.00
25 SD. 135.00
26 SD. 135.00
27 . . . . 100.00
28 SD. 135.00
29 . . . . 100.00
30 . . . . 100.00

BLACK KNIGHT, THE
Toby Press, 1953

1 Bondage 400.00

BLACK KNIGHT, THE
Marvel Atlas, 1955–56

1 JMn,O: Crusader;The Black Knight Rides 1,500.00
2 JMn,Siege on Camelot 900.00

Black Magic #1
© Crestwood Prize Publications

Blackstone The Magician Detective #1
© E.C. Comics

Black Terror #18
© Better Publications

3 JMn,Black Knight Unmasked . 750.00
4 JMn,Betrayed 750.00
5 JMn,SSh,The Invincible Tartar. 750.00

BLACK MAGIC

Crestwood Publ., 1950–51

1 S&K,MMe 1,900.00
2 S&K,MMe 1,000.00
3 S&K,MMe. 900.00
4 S&K,MMe. 900.00
5 S&K,MMe. 900.00
6 S&K,MMe. 900.00
Volume 2, 1951
1 S&K,MMe. 500.00
2 MMe. 400.00
3 . . . . 400.00
4 S&K,MMe. 500.00
5 S&K,MMe. 500.00
6 . . . . 400.00
7 S&K,MMe. 500.00
8 MMe. 400.00
9 S&K,MMe. 500.00
10 . . . . 400.00
11 MMe 400.00
12 S&K,MMe 400.00
Volume 3, 1953
1 S&K,MMe. 400.00
2 S&K,MMe,AMc 400.00
3 S&K 400.00
4 S&K 400.00
5 S&K,MMe. 400.00
6 S&K,MMe. 400.00
Volume 4, 1954
1 S&K 400.00
2 S&K 400.00
3 S&K,SD(2nd work). 800.00
4 S&K,SD,eye damage. 600.00
5 S&K,SD 400.00
6 S&K,BP 350.00
Volume 5, 1956
1 S&K,MMe. 200.00
2 S&K,MMe. 200.00
3 S&K 200.00
4 S&K 200.00
5 S&K 200.00
6 S&K 200.00
Volume 6, 1957
1 JO 150.00
2 JO(c) 150.00
3 JO(c),GT 150.00
4 JO 150.00
5 JO(c) 150.00
6 JO(c) 150.00
Volume 7, 1958
1 LSt 150.00
2 JO 150.00
3 & 4 . . . . @150.00
5 AT,Hitler(c) 140.00
6 BP 125.00
Volume 8, 1961
1 BP 100.00
2 BP,SD 100.00
3 thru 5 BP . . . . @100.00

BLACK RIDER
See: ALL WINNERS COMICS

BLACK RIDER RIDES AGAIN

Marvel Atlas, Sept., 1957

1 JK,Treachery at Hangman's
Ridge 350.00

BLACKSTONE, MASTER MAGICIAN COMICS

Vital/Street & Smith Publ. 1946

1 . . . . 1,200.00
2 . . . . 1,000.00
3 . . . . 1,000.00

BLACKSTONE, THE MAGICIAN DETECTIVE

EC Comics, 1947

1 Happy Houlihans 750.00
Becomes:

BLACKSTONE, THE MAGICIAN

Marvel, May, 1948—Sept., 1948

2 B:Blonde Phantom 1,000.00
3 BO(c),bondage (c). 650.00
4 Bondage(c) 650.00

BLACK TERROR

Better Publications/
Standard, Winter, 1942-43

1 Bombing (c) 5,000.00
2 V:Arabs,Bondage(c) 2,000.00
3 V:Nazis,Bondage(c) 1,200.00
4 ASh(c),V:Sub Nazis 1,000.00
5 V:Japanese. 1,000.00
6 Air Battle 900.00
7 Air Battle,V:Japanese,
A:Ghost 900.00
8 V:Nazis 900.00
9 V:Japanese,Bondage(c) 1,000.00
10 ASh(c),V:Nazis 900.00
11 & 12 . . . . @800.00
13 ASh(c). 725.00
14 ASh(c). 800.00
15 ASh(c). 725.00
16 ASh(c). 725.00
17 ASh(c),Bondage(c) 800.00
18 ASh(c). 700.00
19 & 20 ASh. . . . . @700.00
21 ASh(c) 800.00
22 FF,ASh 700.00
23 ASh 700.00
24 Bondgae(c). 800.00
25 ASh. 700.00
26 GT,ASh(c) 700.00
27 MME,GT,ASh 700.00

BLAZE CARSON

Marvel, Sept., 1948

1 SSh(c),Fight,Lawman
or Crawl 300.00
2 Guns Roar on Boot Hill 225.00
3 A:Tex Morgan 225.00
4 SSh,A:Two-Gun Kid 225.00
5 A:Tex Taylor 250.00
Becomes:

REX HART

Marvel, 1949

6 CCB,Ph(c),B:Rex Hart,
A:Black Rider 300.00
7 Ph(c),Mystery at Bar-2 Ranch 200.00
8 Ph(c),The Hombre Who
Killed His Friends 200.00
Becomes:

WHIP WILSON

Marvel, 1950

9 Ph(c),B:Whip Wilson,O:Bullet;
Duel to the Death 800.00
10 Ph(c),Wanted for Murder 400.00
11 Ph(c) 400.00
Becomes:

GUNHAWK, THE

Marvel, 1950

12 The Redskin's Revenge 350.00
13 GT,The Man Who Murdered
Gunhawk 300.00
14 . . . . 250.00
15 . . . . 250.00
16 EC. 250.00
17 . . . . 250.00
18 JMn,Dec., 1951. . . . . 250.00

Blazing Comics #3
© Enwil Associates

Blondie Comics
© Harvey Publications

Blue Beetle #12
© Fox Features Syndicate

BLAZE, THE WONDER COLLIE

Marvel, Oct., 1949

2 Ph(c),Blaze-Son of Fury 300.00
3 Ph(c), Lonely Boy;Feb.,1950 . . 300.00

BLAZING COMICS

Enwil Associates/Rural Home, June, 1944

1 B:Green Turtle, Red Hawk, Black Buccaneer 1,000.00
2 Green Turtle (c) 700.00
3 Green Turtle (c) 650.00
4 Green Turtle (c) 650.00
5 March, 1945 . . . . 650.00
5a Black Buccaneer(c),1955. . . . 400.00
6 Indian-Japanese(c), 1955 . . . . 400.00

BLAZING WEST

B & I Publ./American Comics 1948

1 . . . . 250.00
2 . . . . 150.00
3 . . . . 150.00
4 O&I: Little Lobo 125.00
5 . . . . 100.00
6 . . . . 100.00
7 . . . . 100.00
8 . . . . 100.00
9 . . . . 100.00
10 . . . . 100.00
11 . . . . 100.00
12 . . . . 100.00
13 . . . . 100.00
14 O&I: The Hooded Horseman . 150.00
15 . . . . 125.00
16 . . . . 125.00
17 . . . . 125.00
18 . . . . 125.00
19 . . . . 125.00
20 . . . . 125.00

Becomes:

HOODED HORSEMAN

American Comics, 1952–54

21 . . . . 250.00
22 . . . . 200.00
23 . . . . 150.00
24 . . . . 150.00
25 . . . . 125.00
26 . . . . 150.00
27 . . . . 135.00

BLAZING WESTERN

Timor Publications, 1954

1 . . . . 200.00
2 thru 5 . . . . @100.00

BLONDE PHANTOM See: ALL-SELECT COMICS

BLONDIE COMICS

David McKay, Spring, 1947

1 . . . . 300.00
2 . . . . 150.00
3 . . . . 125.00
4 . . . . 125.00
5 . . . . 125.00
6 thru 10 . . . . @100.00
11 thru 15. . . . . @100.00

Harvey Publications, 1950

16 . . . . 150.00
17 thru 20. . . . . @125.00
21 thru 30. . . . . @100.00
31 thru 50. . . . . @100.00
51 thru 80. . . . . @100.00
81 thru 99. . . . . @100.00
100 . . . . 110.00
101 thru 124. . . . . @100.00
125 Giant, 80-pg. 125.00
126 thru 136 . . . . @100.00
137 Giant, 80-pg. 125.00
138 thru 139 . . . . @100.00
140 Giant, 80-pg. 125.00
141 thru 147 . . . . @100.00
148 Giant, 68-pg. 125.00
149 thru 154 . . . . @100.00
155 Giant, 68-pg. 125.00
156 . . . . 100.00
157 thru 159 Giant, 68-pg. . . . . @125.00
160 . . . . 100.00
161 thru 163 Giant, 68-pg. . . . . @125.00
See also: DAISY AND HER PUPS

BLOOD IS THE HARVEST

Catechetical Guild 1950

N# Comunist menace 2,000.00

BLUE BEETLE, THE

Fox Features Syndicate/ Holyoke Publ., Winter 1939

1 O:Blue Beetle,A:Master Magician 7,000.00
2 BP,Wonder World 2,500.00
3 JSm(c) 1,600.00
4 Mentions marijuana 1,500.00
5 GT,A:Zanzibar the Magician 1,300.00
6 B:Dynamite Thor, O:Blue Beetle 1,300.00
7 A:Dynamo 1,200.00
8 E:Thor,A:Dynamo 1,200.00
9 BP(c),A:Black Bird,Gorilla . . 1,200.00
10 BP(c),A:Black Bird, bondage(c) 1,200.00
11 BP(c),A:Gladiator 1,000.00
12 A:Black Fury. 1,000.00
13 B:V-Man 1,000.00
14 JKu,I:Sparky. 1,000.00
15 JKu. 1,000.00
16 . . . . 1,000.00
17 AyB,A:Mimic. 1,000.00
18 JKu,E:V-Man,A:Red Knight . 1,000.00
19 JKu,A:Dascomb Dinsmore. . 1,000.00
20 I&O:Flying Tiger Squadron . 1,000.00
21 . . . . 900.00
22 A:Ali-Baba 900.00
23 A:Jimmy DooLittle. 900.00
24 I:The Halo 900.00
25 . . . . 900.00
26 General Patton story 1,000.00
27 A:Tamoa 900.00
28 . . . . 800.00
29 . . . . 800.00
30 L:Holyoke 800.00
31 F:Fox. 775.00
32 Hitler (c) 900.00
33 Fight for Freedom 775.00
34 A:Black Terror,Menace of K-4 . 775.00
35 Threat From Saturn 775.00
36 The Runaway House 775.00
37 Inside the House. 775.00
38 Revolt of the Zombies. 775.00
39 . . . . 775.00
40 . . . . 775.00
41 A:O'Brine Twins 750.00
42 . . . . 750.00
43 . . . . 750.00
44 . . . . 750.00
45. . . . . 750.00
46 BP,A:Puppeteer. 750.00
47 JKa,V:Junior Crime Club . . . 1,700.00
48 JKa,A:Black Lace. 1,400.00
49 JKa. 1,400.00
50 JKa,The Ambitious Bride . . 1,400.00
51 JKa, Shady Lady 1,200.00
52 BP,JKa(c),Bondage (c) 1,700.00
53 JKa,A:Jack "Legs" Diamond,Bondage(c) 1,200.00
54 JKa,The Vanishing Nude . . . 1,800.00

Blue Bolt #11
© Funnies, Inc.

Blue Bolt #102
© Star Publications

Ghostly Weird Stories #120
© Star Publications

55 JKa. 1,100.00
56 JKa,Tri-State Terror 1,100.00
57 JKa,The Feagle Bros. 1,100.00
58 . . . . 200.00
59 . . . . 200.00
60 Aug., 1960 . . . . 225.00

BLUE BEETLE
See: THING!, THE

BLUE BOLT
Funnies, Inc./Novelty Press/ Premium Service Co, 1940

1 JSm,PGv,O:Blue Bolt 6,500.00
2 JSm,S&K 3,000.00
3 S&K,A:Space Hawk 2,500.00
4 S&K,BEv(c). 2,000.00
5 BEv,S&K,B:Sub Zero 2,000.00
6 JK,JSm 1,900.00
7 S&K,BEv 1,900.00
8 PGv,S&K(c) 1,900.00
9 . . . . 1,700.00
10 PGv,S&K(c) 1,700.00
11 BEv(c) 1,700.00
12 PGv 1,700.00
2-1 BEv(c),PG,O:Dick Cole & V:Simba 700.00
2-2 BEv(c),FGu,O:Twister 550.00
2-3 PGv,Cole vs Simba 400.00
2-4 BD 400.00
2-5 I:Freezum. 400.00
2-6 PGv,O:Sgt.Spook, Dick Cole . 350.00
2-7 BD,Lois Blake 350.00
2-8 BD 350.00
2-9 JW 350.00
2-10 JW 350.00
2-11 JW 350.00
2-12 E:Twister 350.00
3-1 A:115th Infantry 350.00
3-2 A:Phantom Sub 350.00
3-3 . . . . 350.00
3-4 JW(c) 250.00
3-5 Jor 250.00
3-6 Jor 250.00
3-7 X-Mas (c) 250.00
3-8 . . . . 250.00
3-9 A:Phantom Sub 250.00
3-10 DBa 250.00
3-11 April Fools (c). 250.00
3-12 . . . . 250.00
4-1 Hitler,Tojo,Mussolini (c) 600.00
4-2 Liberty Bell (c) 200.00
4-3 What are You Doing for Your Country 200.00
4-4 I Fly for Vengence 200.00
4-5 TFH(c) 200.00
4-6 HcK 200.00
4-7 JWi(c). 200.00
4-8 E:Sub Zero 200.00
4-9 . . . . 200.00
4-10 . . . . 200.00
4-11 . . . . 200.00
4-12 . . . . 200.00
5-1 thru 5-12. . . . . @175.00
6-1 . . . . 175.00
6-2 War Bonds (c) 175.00
6-3 . . . . 175.00
6-4 Racist(c). 300.00
6-5 Soccer (c) 175.00
6-6 thru 6-12. . . . . @175.00
7-1 thru 7-12. . . . . @175.00
8-1 Baseball (c) 175.00
8-2 JHa 175.00
8-3 JH 175.00
8-4 JHa 175.00
8-5 JH 175.00
8-6 JDo 175.00
8-7 LbC(c). 350.00
8-8 . . . . 175.00
8-9 AMc(c) 175.00
8-10 . . . . 175.00
8-11 Basketball (c). 200.00
8-12 . . . . 175.00
9-1 AMc,Baseball (c) 175.00
9-2 AMc 175.00
9-3 . . . . 175.00
9-4 JH 175.00
9-5 JH 175.00
9-6 LbC(c),Football (c). 300.00
9-7 JH 175.00
9-8 Hockey (c) 185.00
9-9 LbC(c),3-D effect 275.00
9-10 . . . . 175.00
9-11 . . . . 175.00
9-12 . . . . 175.00
10-1 Baseball (c),3-D effect. 200.00
10-2 3-D effect. 200.00

Star Publications, 1949

102 LbC(c),Chameleon 550.00
103 LbC(c),same 500.00
104 LbC(c),same 500.00
105 LbC(c),O:Blue Bolt Space, Drug Story 900.00
106 S&K,LbC(c),A;Space Hawk . 800.00
107 S&K,LbC(c),A;Space Hawk . 800.00
108 S&K,LbC(c),A:Blue Bolt 800.00
109 BW,LbC(c). 800.00
110 B:Horror (c)s,A:Target. 800.00
111 Weird Tales of Terror, A:Red Rocket 800.00
112 JyD 700.00
113 BW,JyD,A:Space Hawk. 700.00
114 LbC(c),JyD 700.00
115 LbC(c),JyD,A:Sgt.Spook 700.00
116 LbC(c),JyD,A:Jungle Joe . . . 700.00
117 LbC(c),A:Blue Bolt,Jo-Jo. . . . 700.00
118 WW,LbC(c),A:White Spirit . . . 700.00
119 LbC(c) 700.00

Becomes:

GHOSTLY WEIRD STORIES
Star Publications, Sept., 1953

120 LbC,A:Jo-Jo 750.00
121 LbC,A:Jo-Jo 700.00
122 LbC,A:The Mask,Sci-Fi. 750.00
123 LbC,A:Jo-Jo 600.00
124 LbC, Sept., 1954. . . . . 600.00

BLUE CIRCLE COMICS
Enwil Associates/ Rural Home, June, 1944

1 B:Blue Circle,O:Steel Fist 500.00
2 . . . . 350.00
3 Hitler parody (c) 400.00
4 . . . . 300.00
5 E:Steel Fist,A:DriftwoodDavey. 300.00
6 . . . . 300.00

BLUE RIBBON COMICS
MLJ Magazines, Nov., 1939

1 JCo,B:Dan Hastings, Richy-Amazing Boy 7,000.00
2 JCo,B:Bob Phantom, Silver Fox 3,000.00
3 JCo,A:Phantom,Silver Fox . . 2,500.00
4 O:Fox,Ty Gor,B:Doc Strong, Hercules 2,600.00
5 Gattling Gun (c) 1,500.00
6 Amazing Boy Richy (c) 1,400.00
7 A:Fox (c),Corporal Collins V:Nazis 1,400.00
8 E:Hercules 1,400.00
9 SCp,O&I:Mr. Justice 6,000.00
10 SCp,Mr. Justice (c) 2,500.00
11 CBi,MMe,SCp(c) 2,500.00
12 SCp,MMe,CBi,E:Doc Strong 2,500.00
13 CBi,IN,MMe,B:Inferno 2,500.00
14 MMe,CBi,SCp(c),A:Inferno . 2,200.00
15 A:Inferno,E:Green Falcon . . 2,200.00
16 SCp(c),O:Captain Flag 3,000.00
17 Captain Flag, V:Black Hand. 2,200.00
18 SCp(c),Captain Flag 2,000.00
19 Captain Flag (c). 2,000.00

Blue Ribbon Comics #12
© MLJ Magazines

Bob Colt #1
© Fawcett Publications

Bob Swift #5
© Fawcett Publications

20 Captain Flag V:Nazis (c) . . . 2,200.00
21 Captain Flag V:Death 2,000.00
22 Circus (c), March, 1942 . . . . 2,000.00

BLUE RIBBON COMICS
St. John Publications, Feb., 1949

1 Heckle & Jeckle 150.00
2 MB(c),Diary Secrets 250.00
3 MB,MB(c),Heckle & Jeckle . . . 150.00
4 Teen-age Diary Secrets 250.00
5 MB,Teen-age Diary Secrets. . . 350.00
6 Dinky Duck 100.00

BO
Charlton Comics, June, 1955

1 . . . . 100.00
2 . . . . 100.00
3 Oct., 1955 . . . . 100.00
Becomes:

TOM CAT
Charlton Comics, 1956

4 Funny animal-cat. 100.00
5 . . . . 75.00
6 . . . . 75.00
7 . . . . 75.00
8 . . . . 75.00
Becomes:

ATOM THE CAT
Charlton Comics, 1957–58

9 . . . . 100.00
10 . . . . 75.00
11 Atomic Mouse 125.00
12 Atomic Mouse 125.00
13 . . . . 75.00
14 . . . . 75.00
15 . . . . 75.00
16 . . . . 75.00
17 . . . . 75.00

BOB & BETTY & SANTA'S WISHING WELL
Sears-Roebuck Co., 1941

N# Giveaway 300.00

BOBBY BENSON'S B-BAR-B RIDERS
Parkway Publ. Co. (M.E. Entertainment), 1950

1 BP, Teen-age cowboy 750.00
2 BP 300.00
3 BP 250.00
4 BP 250.00
5 BP 250.00
6 BP 250.00
7 BP 250.00
8 BP 250.00
9 BP,FF(c). 500.00
10 BP. 200.00
11 BP,FF(c) 500.00
12 BP. 150.00
13 DAy,FF(c),A:Ghost Rider 500.00
14 DAy,A:Ghost Rider,bondage. . 400.00
15 DAy,A:Ghost Rider 350.00
16 photo(c). 200.00
17 . . . . 150.00
18 . . . . 150.00
19 . . . . 150.00

BOBBY COMICS
Universal Phoenix Features, 1946

1 . . . . 200.00

BOB COLT
Fawcett Publications, Nov., 1950

1 B:Bob Colt,Buck Skin 600.00
2 Death Round Train 400.00
3 Mysterious Black Knight of the Prairie 300.00
4 Death Goes Downstream 300.00
5 The Mesa of Mystery 300.00
6 The Mysterious Visitors 300.00
7 Dragon of Disaster 250.00
8 Redman's Revenge 250.00
9 Hidden Hacienda 250.00
10 Fiend from Vulture Mountain 250.00

BOB STEELE WESTERN
Fawcett Publications, 1950–52

1 Photo(c) 800.00
2 Ph(c); Dynamite Death 400.00
3 Ph(c); The Perilous Deadline. . 300.00
4 Ph(c); Six-Gun Menace 300.00
5 Ph(c); Murder on the Hoof. . . . 300.00
6 Ph(c); Range War 250.00
7 Ph(c); Tall Timber Terror 250.00
8 Ph(c); The Race of Death 250.00
9 Ph(c); Death Rides the Storm . 250.00
10 Ph(c); Draw...Or Die 250.00

BOB SWIFT
Fawcett Publications 1951–52

1 Boy sportsman. 150.00
2 . . . . 100.00
3 . . . . 100.00
4 . . . . 100.00
5 . . . . 100.00

BOLD STORIES
Kirby Publishing Co., 1950

1 WW,Near nudity (c) 2,200.00
2 GI,Cobra's Kiss 1,500.00
3 WW,Orge of Paris 1,500.00
4 Case of the Winking Buddha. . 800.00
5 It Rhymes with Lust. 800.00
6 Candid Tales, April, 1950. . . . . 800.00

BOMBER COMICS
Elliot Publishing Co., 1944

1 B:Wonder Boy,Kismet, Eagle Evans 1,500.00
2 Wonder Boy(c) Hitler 1,000.00
3 Wonder Boy-Kismet (c) 600.00
4 Hitler,Tojo, Mussolini (c) 1,200.00

BOOK OF ALL COMICS
William H. Wise, 1945

1 A:Green Mask,Puppeteer 600.00

BOOK OF COMICS, THE
William H. Wise, 1945

N# A:Captain V 600.00

BOOTS AND HER BUDDIES
Visual Editions (Standard Comics), 1948–49

5 Cowgirl. 250.00
6 . . . . 200.00
7 . . . . 225.00
8 . . . . 200.00
9 FF 450.00

BORDER PATROL
P.L. Publishing Co., 1951

1 Wild West. 200.00
2 . . . . 150.00
3 . . . . 150.00

Bo

The Bouncer #14
© Fox Features Syndicate

Boy Comics #59
© Lev Gleason Publications

Boy Commandos #29
© DC Comics

THE BOUNCER

Fox Features Syndicate, 1944

N# (10) 500.00
11 O:The Bouncer 400.00
12 . . . . 300.00
13 . . . . 300.00
14 rep. #(10) 300.00

BOY COMICS

Comic House, Inc.
(Lev Gleason Publ.) April, 1942

3 O:Crimebuster,Bombshell,Young Robin, B:Yankee Longago, Swoop Storm 7,000.00
4 Hitler,Tojo,Mussolini (c) 2,500.00
5 Crimebuster saves day (c) . 2,000.00
6 O:Iron Jaw & Death of Son, B:Little Dynamite 5,000.00
7 Hitler,Tojo,Mussolini (c) 2,000.00
8 D:Iron Jaw 2,100.00
9 I:He-She 2,000.00
10 Iron Jaw returns 2,300.00
11 Iron Jaw falls in love 1,800.00
12 Crimebuster V:Japanese . . . 1,000.00
13 V:New,more terrible Iron Jaw 1,000.00
14 V:Iron Jaw 1,000.00
15 I:Rodent,D:Iron Jaw 1,200.00
16 Crimebuster V:Knight 600.00
17 Flag (c),Crimebuster V:Moth 600.00
18 Smashed car (c) 550.00
19 Express train (c) 550.00
20 Coffin (c) 550.00
21 Boxing (c) 400.00
22 Under Sea (c) 400.00
23 Golf (c) 400.00
24 County insane asylum (c) 400.00
25 52 pgs 400.00
26 68 pgs 400.00
27 Express train (c) 450.00
28 E:Yankee Longago 450.00
29 Prison break (c) 450.00
30 O:Crimebuster,Murder (c) . . . 600.00
31 68 pgs 400.00
32 E:Young Robin Hood 400.00
33 . . . . 400.00
34 Suicide (c) & story 350.00
35 . . . . 300.00
36 . . . . 300.00
37 . . . . 300.00
38 . . . . 300.00
39 E:Little Dynamite 300.00
40 . . . . 300.00
41 thru 50 . . . . @275.00
51 thru 56 . . . . @250.00
57 B:Dilly Duncan 275.00
58 . . . . 250.00
59 . . . . 250.00
60 Iron Jaw returns 275.00
61 O:Iron Jaw,Crimebuster 300.00
62 A:Iron Jaw 275.00
63 thru 70 . . . . @200.00
71 E:Dilly Duncan 200.00
72 . . . . 200.00
73 . . . . 200.00
74 thru 79 . . . . @200.00
80 I:Rocky X 150.00
81 thru 88 . . . . @150.00
89 A:The Claw 200.00
90 same 200.00
91 same 200.00
92 same 200.00
93 The Claw(c),A:Rocky X 200.00
94 . . . . 150.00
95 . . . . 150.00
96 . . . . 150.00
97 . . . . 150.00
98 A:Rocky X 150.00
99 . . . . 150.00
100 . . . . 175.00
101 . . . . 175.00
102 . . . . 175.00
103 thru 118 . . . . @175.00
119 March, 1956 . . . . 175.00

BOY COMMANDOS

DC Comics, Winter, 1942–43

1 S&K,O:Liberty Belle;Sandman & Newsboy Legion 13,000.00
2 S&K,Hitler(c) 4,000.00
3 S&K,WWII(c) 1,700.00
4 WWII(c) 1,400.00
5 WWII(c) 1,400.00
6 S&K,WWII(c) 1,400.00
7 S&K,WWII(c) 900.00
8 S&K,WWII(c) 900.00
9 WWII(c) 1,000.00
10 S&K,WWII(c) 900.00
11 WWII(c) 900.00
12 WWII(c) 900.00
13 WWII(c) 900.00
14 . . . . 900.00
15 1st Crazy Quilt 800.00
16 . . . . 700.00
17 Science Fiction(c) 800.00
18 S&K 600.00
19 S&K 600.00
20 Science Fiction (c) 800.00
21 . . . . 500.00
22 Judy Canova 500.00
23 S&K,S&K,(c) 600.00
24 Superhero 600.00
25 superhero(c) 550.00
26 Science Fiction(c) 550.00
27 . . . . 600.00
28 . . . . 650.00
29 S&K story 600.00
30 Baseball Story 650.00
31 . . . . 600.00
32 A:Dale Evans(c) 650.00
33 . . . . 500.00
34 I:Wolf 500.00
35 . . . . 500.00
36 Sci-Fi(c),Nov.–Dec., 1949 . . . . 600.00

BOY DETECTIVE

Avon Periodicals, 1951–52

1 F:Dan Tayler 300.00
2 Vice Lords of Crime 200.00
3 Spy Menace 200.00
4 The Death Trap 200.00

BOY EXPLORERS
See: TERRY AND THE PIRATES

BOY MEETS GIRL

Lev Gleason Publ., 1950–52

1 Romance 200.00
2 . . . . 125.00
3 . . . . 100.00
4 . . . . 100.00
5 . . . . 100.00
6 . . . . 100.00
7 . . . . 100.00
8 . . . . 100.00
9 . . . . 100.00
10 . . . . 100.00
11 thru 24 . . . . @ 100.00

Becomes:

BOY LOVES GIRL

Lev Gleason Publ., 1952–56

25 Romance 100.00
26 . . . . 80.00
27 . . . . 80.00
28 . . . . 80.00
29 . . . . 80.00
30 . . . . 80.00
31 thru 57 . . . . @80.00

 All comics prices listed are for *Near Mint* condition.

Boys' Ranch #4
© Harvey Publications

Brave and the Bold #34
© DC Comics

Broadway Romances #1
© Quality Comics

BOYS' RANCH

Harvey Publications, 1950–51

1 S&K,F:Clay Duncan 1,000.00
2 S&K 750.00
3 S&K,MMe. 700.00
4 S&K 600.00
5 S&K,MMe. 400.00
6 S&K,MMe. 400.00

THE BRAIN

Sussex Publ. Co./Magazine Enterprises, 1956–58

1 . . . . 150.00
2 . . . . 100.00
3 . . . . 100.00
4 . . . . 100.00
5 . . . . 100.00
6 . . . . 100.00
7 . . . . 100.00

BRAVE AND THE BOLD

DC Comics, Aug.–Sept., 1955

1 JKu,RH,IN,I:VikingPrince,Golden Gladiator,Silent Knight 7,000.00
2 F:Viking Prince 2,500.00
3 F:Viking Prince 1,500.00
4 F:Viking Prince 1,500.00
5 B:Robin Hood 1,300.00
6 JKu,F:Robin Hood,E:Golden Gladiator 900.00
7 JKu,F:Robin Hood 900.00
8 JKu,F:Robin Hood 900.00
9 JKu,F:Robin Hood 900.00
10 JKu,F:Robin Hood 900.00
11 JKu,F:Viking Prince. 700.00
12 JKu,F:Viking Prince 700.00
13 JKu,F:Viking Prince 700.00
14 JKu,F:Viking Prince 650.00
15 JKu,F:Viking Prince 650.00
16 JKu,F:Viking Prince 650.00
17 JKu,F:Viking Prince 650.00
18 JKu,F:Viking Prince 650.00
19 JKu,F:Viking Prince 650.00
20 JKu,F:Viking Prince 650.00
21 JKu,F:Viking Prince 650.00
22 JKu,F:Viking Prince 650.00
23 JKu,O:Viking Prince 900.00
24 JKu,E:Viking Prince,Silent Knight 700.00
25 RA,I&B:Suicide Squad 850.00
26 F:Suicide Squad 600.00
27 Creature of Ghost Lake 600.00
28 I:Justice League of America,O:Snapper Carr . 10,000.00
29 F:Justice League 4,200.00
30 F:Justice League 3,000.00
31 F:Cave Carson 800.00
32 F:Cave Carson 500.00
33 F:Cave Carson 500.00
34 JKu,I&O:S.A. Hawkman. . . . 4,000.00
35 JKu:F:Hawkman. 1,000.00
36 JKu:F:Hawkman. 1,000.00
37 F:Suicide Squad 600.00
38 F:Suicide Squad 400.00
39 F:Suicide Squad 400.00
40 JKu,F:Cave Carson 300.00
41 F:Cave Carson 300.00
42 JKu,F:Hawkman 600.00
43 JKu,O:Hawkman. 700.00
44 JKu,F:Hawkman 600.00
45 CI,F:Strange Sports 200.00
46 CI,F:Strange Sports 200.00
47 CI,F:Strange Sports 200.00
48 CI,F:Strange Sports 200.00
49 CI,F:Strange Sports 200.00
50 F:GreenArrow & J'onnJ'onzz . 400.00

BRENDA STARR

Four Star Comics Corp./ Superior Comics Ltd., Sept., 1947

13(1) 3,500.00
14(2) JKa,Bondage (c) 5,000.00
2-3 . . . . 3,500.00
2-4 JKa,Operating table (c). . . . 3,500.00
2-5 Swimsuit (c) 2,000.00
2-6 . . . . 2,000.00
2-7 . . . . 2,000.00
2-8 Cosmetic (c) 2,000.00
2-9 Giant Starr (c) 2,000.00
2-10 Wedding (c) 2,000.00
2-11 . . . . 2,000.00
2-12 . . . . 2,000.00

BRICK BRADFORD

Best Books (Standard Comics) July, 1949

5 . . . . 350.00
6 Robot (c) 500.00
7 ASh(c) 200.00
8 . . . . 200.00

BRIDES DIARY

See: BLACK COBRA

BRIDES IN LOVE

Charlton Comics, 1956–65

1 . . . . 125.00
2 . . . . 100.00
3 thru 10 . . . . @75.00
11 thru 30 . . . . @75.00
31 thru 44 . . . . @60.00
45 . . . . 50.00

BRIDES ROMANCES

Quality Comics, 1953–56

1 . . . . 150.00
2 . . . . 125.00
3 . . . . 100.00
4 . . . . 100.00
5 . . . . 100.00
6 . . . . 100.00
7 . . . . 100.00
8 . . . . 100.00
9 . . . . 100.00
10 thru 23. . . . . @100.00

BROADWAY ROMANCES

Quality Comics Group, 1950

1 PG,BWa(a&c). 600.00
2 BWa,Glittering Desire 400.00
3 BL,Stole My Love. 200.00
4 Enslaved by My Past. 200.00
5 Flame of Passion,Sept.,1950 . 200.00

BRUCE GENTRY

Four Star Publ./ Visual Editions/ Superior, Jan., 1948

1 B:Ray Bailey reprints 900.00
2 Plane crash (c) 500.00
3 E:Ray Bailey reprints 500.00
4 Tiger attack (c) 400.00
5 . . . . 400.00
6 Help message (c) 400.00
7 . . . . 400.00
8 End of Marriage (c),July, 1949 400.00

BUCCANEERS

See: KID ETERNITY

BUCK DUCK

Marvel Atlas, June, 1953

1 (fa) stories 200.00
2 and 3 . . . . @100.00
4 Dec., 1953 . . . . 100.00

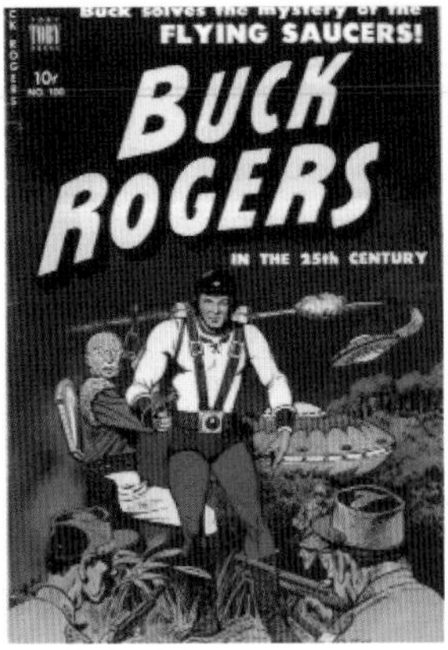

Buck Rogers #100
© Toby Press

Bugs Bunny Christmas Funnies #5
(1955) © Dell Publishing Co.

Bulletman #6
© Fawcett Publications

BUCK JONES

Dell Publishing Co., 1950

1 Buck Jones & Horse Silver . . . 250.00
2 . . . 150.00
3 . . . 100.00
4 . . . 100.00
5 . . . 100.00
6 . . . 100.00
7 . . . 100.00
8 . . . 100.00

BUCK ROGERS

Eastern Color Printing, Winter 1940

1 Partial Painted(c) . . . 6,500.00
2 . . . 2,400.00
3 Living Corpse from Crimson Coffin . . . 2,000.00
4 One man army of greased lightning . . . 1,900.00
5 Sky Roads . . . 1,700.00
6 Sept., 1943 . . . 1,700.00

Toby Press

100 Flying Saucers . . . 800.00
101 . . . 750.00
9 MA . . . 750.00

BUDDIES IN THE U.S. ARMY

Avon Periodicals, 1952–53

1 Fightin' Guys & Fabulous Gals 200.00
2 . . . 125.00

BUFFALO BILL

Youthful Magazines, 1950–51

2 Annie Oakley . . . 200.00
3 . . . 150.00
4 . . . 150.00
5 . . . 150.00
6 . . . 150.00
7 . . . 150.00
8 . . . 150.00
9 . . . 150.00

BUFFALO BILL PICTURE STORIES

Street & Smith Publ. 1949

1 . . . 250.00
2 . . . 250.00

BUFFALO BILL JR.

Dell Publishing Co., 1956

1 . . . 200.00
2 . . . 150.00
3 . . . 150.00
4 . . . 150.00
5 . . . 150.00
6 . . . 150.00
7 thru 13 . . . @125.00

BUGHOUSE

Ajax/Farrell, 1954

1 . . . 225.00
2 . . . 150.00
3 . . . 150.00
4 . . . 150.00

BUG MOVIES

Dell Publishing Co., 1931

1 . . . 600.00

BUGS BUNNY DELL GIANT EDITIONS

Dell Publishing Co. Christmas

1 Christmas Funnies (1950) . . . 350.00
2 Christmas Funnies (1951) . . . 300.00
3 Christmas Funnies (1952) . . . 250.00
4 Christmas Funnies (1953) . . . 200.00
5 Christmas Funnies (1954) . . . 200.00
6 Christmas Party (1955) . . . 175.00
7 Christmas Party (1956) . . . 185.00
8 Christmas Funnies (1957) . . . 185.00
9 Christmas Funnies (1958) . . . 185.00
1 County Fair (1957) . . . 200.00

Halloween

1 Halloween Parade (1953) . . . 200.00
2 Halloween Parade (1954) . . . 175.00
3 Trick 'N' Treat Halloween Fun (1955) . . . 185.00
4 Trick 'N' Treat Halloween Fun (1956) . . . 185.00

Vacation

1 Vacation Funnies (1951) . . . 325.00
2 Vacation Funnies (1952) . . . 275.00
3 Vacation Funnies (1953) . . . 250.00
4 Vacation Funnies (1954) . . . 200.00
5 Vacation Funnies (1955) . . . 200.00
6 Vacation Funnies (1956) . . . 175.00
7 Vacation Funnies (1957) . . . 175.00
8 Vacation Funnies (1958) . . . 175.00
9 Vacation Funnies (1959) . . . 175.00

BUGS BUNNY

Dell Publishing Co., 1942
see Four Color for early years

28 thru 30 . . . @130.00
31 thru 50 . . . @120.00
51 thru 70 . . . @100.00
71 thru 85 . . . @100.00
86 Giant-Show Time . . . 125.00
87 thru 100 . . . @100.00
101 thru 120 . . . @75.00
121 thru 140 . . . @50.00
141 thru 190 . . . @50.00
191 thru 245 . . . @50.00

BULLETMAN

Fawcett Publications, Summer, 1941

1 I:Bulletman & Bulletgirl . . . 7,000.00
2 MRa(c) . . . 3,000.00
3 MRa(c) . . . 2,500.00
4 V:Headless Horror, Guillotine (c) . . . 2,500.00
5 Riddle of Dr. Riddle . . . 2,500.00
6 V:Japanese . . . 1,500.00
7 V:Revenge Syndicate . . . 1,500.00
8 V:Mr. Ego . . . 1,500.00
9 V:Canine Criminals . . . 1,500.00
10 I:Bullet Dog . . . 1,700.00
11 V:Fiendish Fiddler . . . 1,100.00
12 . . . 1,000.00
13 . . . 1,000.00
14 V:Death the Comedian . . . 1,000.00
15 V:Professor D. . . . 1,000.00
16 VanishingElephant,Fall 1946 1,000.00

BULLS-EYE

Charlton Comics, 1954

1 S&K,Western Scout . . . 700.00
2 S&K . . . 600.00
3 S&K . . . 500.00
4 S&K . . . 500.00
5 S&K . . . 500.00
6 S&K . . . 450.00
7 S&K . . . 500.00

Becomes:

CODY OF THE PONY EXPRESS

Charlton Comics, 1955

8 F:Buffalo Bill Cody . . . 125.00
9 . . . 100.00
10 . . . 100.00

Becomes:

Buster Crabbe #3
© Famous Funnies

Buz Sawyer #3
© Standard Comics

Tex Granger #18
© Parents Magzine

OUTLAWS OF THE WEST

Charlton Comics, 1957

11	125.00
12	100.00
13	100.00
14 giant	150.00
15	100.00
16	100.00
17	100.00
18 SD	150.00
19 thru 40	@75.00

BULLS-EYE

See: SCOOP COMICS

BUSTER BEAR

Arnold Publications/ Quality Comics Group, 1953

1 Funny animal	150.00
2	125.00
3	100.00
4	100.00
5	100.00
6	100.00
7	100.00
8	100.00
9	100.00
10	100.00

BUSTER BROWN COMICS

Brown Shoe Co., 1945–59

1	1,000.00
2	350.00
3	250.00
4 scarce	400.00
5	250.00
6	250.00
7	250.00
8	250.00
9	250.00
10	250.00
11 thru 20	@100.00
21 thru 24	@100.00
25 RC	150.00
26 thru 36	@100.00
37 RC	150.00
38	100.00
39	100.00
40 RC	150.00
41 RC	150.00
42	100.00
43	100.00

BUSTER BUNNY

Animated Cartoons (Standard)/Pines, 1949

1 FF,Funny animal	150.00
2	100.00
3	100.00
4	100.00
5	100.00
6	100.00
7	100.00
8	100.00
9	100.00
10	100.00
11 thru 14	@100.00
15 racist(c)	125.00
16	100.00

BUSTER CRABBE

Famous Funnies, Nov., 1951

1 The Arrow of Death	650.00
2 AW&GE(c)	700.00
3 AW&GE(c)	800.00
4 FF(c)	900.00
5 AW,FF(a&c)	1,800.00
6 Sharks (c)	300.00
7 FF	350.00
8 Gorilla (c)	300.00
9 FF	350.00
10	300.00
11 Snakes (c)	250.00
12 Sept., 1953	250.00

BUSTER CRABBE

Lev Gleason Pub., 1953

1 Ph(c)	300.00
2 ATh	275.00
3 ATh	275.00
4 F. Gordon(c)	275.00

BUZ SAWYER

Standard Comics, June, 1948

1	300.00
2 I:Sweeney	250.00
3	250.00
4	250.00
5 June, 1949	250.00

BUZZY

DC Comics, 1944–58

1	500.00
2	300.00
3 thru 5	@250.00
6 thru 10	@150.00
11 thru 15	@150.00
16 thru 25	@150.00
26 thru 35	@125.00
36 thru 45	@100.00
46 thru 77	@100.00

CALLING ALL BOYS

Parents Magazine Institute Jan., 1946

1 Skiing	200.00
2 Roy Rogers Story	150.00
3 Peril Out Post	150.00
4 Model Airplane	150.00
5 Fishing	150.00
6 Swimming	150.00
7 Baseball	175.00
8 School	150.00
9 The Miracle Quarterback	150.00
10 Gary Cooper (c)	200.00
11 Rin-Tin-Tin (c)	150.00
12 Bob Hope (c)	250.00
13 Bing Cosby (c)	225.00
14 J. Edgar Hoover (c)	150.00
15 Tex Granger (c)	125.00
16	125.00
17 Tex Granger (c), May, 1948	125.00

Becomes:

TEX GRANGER

June, 1948

18 Bandits of the Badlands	125.00
19 The Seven Secret Cities	100.00
20 Davey Crockett's Last Fight	100.00
21 Canyon Ambush	100.00
22 V:Hooded Terror	100.00
23 V:Billy the Kid	100.00
24 A:Hector, Sept., 1949	100.00

CALLING ALL GIRLS

Parent Magazine Press, Inc., Sept., 1941

1	300.00
2 Virginia Weidler (c)	250.00
3 Shirley Temple (c)	300.00
4 Darla Hood (c)	150.00
5 Gloria Hood (c)	150.00
6	150.00
7	150.00
8	150.00
9 Flag (c)	150.00
10	150.00
11 Gary Cooper as Lou Gerrig	200.00
12 thru 20	@125.00

Ca

Camera Comics #2
© U.S. Camera Publishing Corp.

Candy #2
© William H. Wise

Captain Aero Comics #25
© Holyoke Publishing Co.

21 thru 39 . . . . @125.00
40 Liz Taylor 250.00
41 . . . . 100.00
42 . . . . 100.00
43 Oct., 1945 . . . . 100.00

CALLING ALL KIDS
Quality Comics, Inc., Dec./Jan., 1946

1 Funny Animal stories 150.00
2 . . . . 125.00
3 . . . . 100.00
4 . . . . 100.00
5 . . . . 100.00
6 thru 10 . . . . @100.00
11 thru 25 . . . . @100.00
26 Aug., 1949 . . . . 100.00

CAMERA COMICS
U.S. Camera Publishing Corp., July–Sept., 1944

1 Airfighter,Grey Comet 350.00
2 How to Set Up a Darkroom . . 300.00
3 Linda Lens V:Nazi (c) 300.00
4 Linda Lens (c) 250.00
5 Diving (c) 250.00
6 Jim Lane (c) 250.00
7 Linda Lens (c) 250.00
8 Linda Lens (c) 250.00
9 Summer, 1946 . . . . 250.00

CAMP COMICS
Dell Publishing Co., 1942

1 Ph(c),WK,A:Bugs Bunny 1,500.00
2 Ph(c),WK,A:Bugs Bunny 1,200.00
3 Ph(c),WK 1,000.00

CAMPUS LOVES
Comic Magazines (Quality Comics Group), 1949

1 BWa 500.00
2 BWa 400.00
3 Photo(c) 250.00
4 Photo(c) 250.00
5 Photo(c) 250.00

CAMPUS ROMANCES
Avon Periodicals/ Realistic Publ., 1949

1 . . . . 350.00
2 . . . . 300.00
3 . . . . 300.00

CANDY
William H. Wise, 1944–45

1 BW 600.00
1a rep.BW 100.00
2 BW 500.00
3 BW 500.00

CANDY
Quality Comics Group, 1947–56

1 JCo,Teen-age 375.00
2 JCo 300.00
3 JCo 150.00
4 JCo 150.00
5 JCo 150.00
6 thru 10 JCo . . . . @150.00
11 thru 20 JCo . . . . @125.00
21 thru 40 . . . . @100.00
41 thru 64 . . . . @100.00

CANNONBALL COMICS
Rural Home Publ. Co., 1945

1 Superhero, Crash Kid 1,400.00
2 Captive Prince 1,200.00

CANTEEN KATE
St. John Publishing Co., 1952

1 MB,Sexy babe 800.00
2 MB 600.00
3 MB 700.00

CAPTAIN AERO COMICS
Holyoke Publishing Co., 1941

1 B:Flag-Man&Solar,Master of Magic Captain Aero, Captain Stone 4,000.00
2 A:Pals of Freedom 1,600.00
3 JKu,B:Alias X,A:Pals of Freedom 1,600.00
4 JKu,O:Gargoyle, Parachute jump 1,600.00
5 JKu 1,500.00
6 JKu,Flagman,A:Miss Victory . 1,400.00
7 Alias X 900.00
8 O:Red Cross,A:Miss Victory . . 900.00
9 A:Miss Victory,Alias X 800.00
10 A:Miss Victory,Red Cross 750.00
11 A:Miss Victory 750.00
12 A:Miss Victory 750.00
13 A:Miss Victory 750.00
14 A:Miss Victory 750.00
15 AS(c),A:Miss Liberty 750.00
16 AS(c),Leather Face 500.00
17 LbC(c) 900.00
21 LbC(c) 900.00
22 LbC(c),I:Mighty Mite 900.00
23 LbC(c) 900.00
24 LbC(c) American Planes Dive Bomb Japan 1,200.00
25 LbC(c),Science Fiction(c) 700.00
26 LbC(c) 1,500.00

CAPTAIN AMERICA COMICS
Timely/Atlas, 1941–54

1 S&K,SSh,JK(c),Hitler(c),I&O:Capt. America & Bucky,A:Red Skull, B:Hurricane, Tuk 135,000.00
2 S&K,RC,AAv,Hitler(c), I:Circular Shield;Trapped in the Nazi Stronghold . . . 21,000.00
3 ASh(c),S&K,RC,AAv,Stan Lee's 1st Text,A:Red Skull, Bondage(c) 17,000.00
4 ASh(c),S&K,AAv,Horror Hospital 12,000.00
5 S&K,AAv,SSh,Ringmaster's Wheel of Death 10,000.00
6 S&K,AAv,SSh,O:Father Time, E:Tuk 8,200.00
7 S&K,SSh,A: Red Skull 10,000.00
8 S&K, The Tomb 7,000.00
9 S&K,RC,V:Black Talon 7,000.00
10 S&K,RC,Chamber of Horrors 7,000.00
11 AAv,SSh,E:Hurricane;Feuding Mountaneers 6,500.00
12 AAv,SSh,B:Imp,E:Father Time; Pygmie's Terror 6,000.00
13 AAv,O:Secret Stamp;All Out For America 6,500.00
14 AAv,V:Japs;Pearl Harbor Symbol cover 6,500.00
15 AAv,Den of Doom 6,500.00
16 AAv,A:R.Skull;CapA Unmasked 7,000.00
17 AAv,I:Fighting Fool; Graveyard 5,500.00
18 AAv,SSh,V:Japanese 5,500.00
19 AAv,V:Ghouls, B:Human Torch 5,000.00
20 AAv,A:Sub-Mariner,V:Nazis . 5,000.00
21 SSh(c),Bucky Captured 4,500.00
22 SSh(c),V:Japanese 4,500.00
23 SSh(c),V:Nazis 4,500.00
24 SSh(c),V:Black Dragon Society 4,500.00

 All comics prices listed are for *Near Mint* condition.

Captain America #35
© Marvel Comics Group

Captain Atom #3
© Nationwide Publishers

Captain Fearless Comics #2
© Helnit Publishing Co.

25 SSh(c),V:Japs;Drug Story . . 4,500.00
26 ASh(c),SSh,V:Nazi Fleet . . . 4,300.00
27 ASh(c),SSh,AAv,CapAm&Russians V:Nazis, E:Secret Stamp . . 4,300.00
28 ASh(c),SSh,Nazi Torture Chamber. 4,300.00
29 ASh(c),SSh,V:Nazis;French Underground. 4,300.00
30 SSh(c),Bucky Captured 4,300.00
31 ASh(c),Bondage(c). 4,000.00
32 SSh(c),V: Japanese Airforce 4,000.00
33 ASh(c),V:Nazis;BrennerPass 4,000.00
34 SSh(c),Bondage(c) 4,000.00
35 SSh(c),CapA in Japan 4,000.00
36 SSh(c),V:Nazis;Hitler(c). . . . 5,500.00
37 ASh(c),SSh,Captain America in Berlin, A:Red Skull 5,000.00
38 ASh(c),V:Japs;Bondage(c). . 4,200.00
39 ASh(c),SSh,V:Japs;Boulder Dam 4,200.00
40 SSh(c),V:Japs;Ammo Depot 4,200.00
41 ASh(c),FinalJapaneseWar(c) 4,000.00
42 ASh(c),SSh,V:BankRobbers 4,000.00
43 ASh(c),V:Gangsters 4,000.00
44 ASh(c),V:Gangsters 4,000.00
45 ASh(c),V:Bank Robbers 4,000.00
46 ASh(c),Holocaust(c). 4,500.00
47 ASh(c),Final Nazi War(c) . . . 4,500.00
48 ASh(c),V:Robbers 3,500.00
49 ASh(c),V:Saboteurs 3,500.00
50 ASh(c),V:Gorilla Gang 3,600.00
51 ASh(c),V:Gangsters 3,500.00
52 ASh(c),V:AtomBombThieves 3,500.00
53 ASh(c),V:Burglars 3,500.00
54 ASh(c),TV Studio, V:Gangsters 3,500.00
55 SSh,V:Counterfeiters 3,500.00
56 SSh(c),V:Art Theives 3,500.00
57 SSh,AAv,Symbolic CapA(c). 3,500.00
58 ASh(c),V:Bank Robbers 3,000.00
59 SSh(c)O:CapA Retold;Private Life of Captain America . . . 5,000.00
60 SSh,V:The Human Fly. 3,000.00
61 SSh(c),V:Red Skull; Bondage(c). 6,000.00
62 SSh(c),Kingdom of Terror . . 3,000.00
63 SSh(c),AAv,I&O:Asbestos Lady; The Parrot Strikes. 3,100.00
64 SSh,Diamonds Spell Doom . 3,200.00
65 SSh,AAv,Friends Turn Foes 3,200.00
66 SSh,O:Golden Girl;Bucky Shot 3,300.00
67 SSh,E:Toro(in Human Torch); Golden Girl Team-Up 3,200.00
68 A:Golden Girl;Riddle of the Living Dolls. 3,200.00
69 Weird Tales of the Wee Males, A:Sun Girl 3,200.00
70 A:Golden Girl,Sub-Mariner, Namora;Worlds at War. . . . 3,200.00
71 A:Golden Girl; Trapped 3,200.00
72 AAv,Murder in the Mind 3,200.00
73 The Outcast of Time 3,200.00
74 A:Red Skull;Capt.America's Weird Tales. 10,000.00
75 Thing in the Chest 3,200.00
76 JR(c),Capt.America,Commie Smasher 3,200.00
77 Capt.A,Commie Smasher . . 2,000.00
78 JR(c),V:Communists 2,000.00

CAPTAIN AND THE KIDS

United Features Syndicate, 1949

16 Kids humor 100.00
17 thru 32. . . . . @100.00
A1. . . . . 100.00
A2. . . . . 100.00
A3. . . . . 100.00

CAPTAIN ATOM

Nationwide Publishers, 1951 Mini-size

1 Scientific adventure 500.00
2 . . . . 250.00
3 . . . . 250.00
4 . . . . 250.00
5 . . . . 250.00
6 . . . . 250.00
7 . . . . 250.00

CAPTAIN BATTLE

New Friday Publ./ Magazine Press, Summer, 1941

1 B:Captain Battle,O:Blackout 3,000.00
2 Pirate Ship (c) 1,700.00
3 Dungeon (c) 1,500.00
4 *.may not exist*
5 V:Japanese, Summer, 1943 . . 900.00

CAPTAIN BATTLE, Jr.

Comic House, Fall, 1943

1 Claw V:Ghost, A:Sniffer 2,500.00
2 Man who didn't believe in Ghosts 2,000.00

CAPTAIN COURAGEOUS See: BANNER COMICS

CAPTAIN EASY

Standard Comics, 1939

N# Swash Buckler 2,100.00
10 . . . . 500.00
11 . . . . 300.00
12 . . . . 300.00
13 ASh(c). 300.00
14 . . . . 300.00
15 . . . . 300.00
16 ASh(c). 300.00
17 Sept., 1949 . . . . 300.00

CAPTAIN FEARLESS COMICS

Helnit Publishing Co., 1941

1 O:Mr. Miracle,Alias X,Captain Fearless Citizen Smith, A:Miss Victory 2,000.00
2 A:Border Patrol, Sept.,1941 . 1,500.00

CAPTAIN FLASH

Sterling Comics, Nov., 1954

1 O:Captain Flash 500.00
2 V:Black Knight 300.00
3 Beasts from 1,000,000 BC . . . 300.00
4 Flying Saucer Invasion 300.00

CAPTAIN FLEET

Approved Comics, Fall, 1952

1 Storm and Mutiny ...Typhoon . 250.00

CAPTAIN FLIGHT COMICS

Four Star Publications, March, 1944–Feb.-March, 1947

N# B:Captain Flight,Ace Reynolds, Dash the Avenger, ProfessorX 1,000.00
2 . . . . 500.00
3 . . . . 500.00
4 B:Rock Raymond Salutes America's Wartime Heroines. 500.00
5 Bondage (c),B:Red Rocket A:The Grenade 2,000.00
6 Girl tied at the stake 500.00
7 LbC(c),Dog Fight (c) 900.00
8 LbC(c),B:Yankee Girl, A:Torpedoman 900.00
9 LbC(c),Dog Fight (c) 900.00
10 LbC(c),Bondage (c) 900.00
11 LbC(c),Future(c). 2,000.00

Captain Gallant #3
© Charlton Comics

Captain Marvel Adventures #41
© Fawcett Publications

Captain Marvel Adventures #69
© Fawcett Publications

CAPTAIN GALLANT

Charlton Comics, 1955

1 Ph(c),Buster Crabbe 200.00
2 . . . . 150.00
3 . . . . 150.00
4 Sept., 1956 . . . . 150.00

CAPTAIN HOBBY COMICS

Export Publication Ent., 1948

1 Adventure. 125.00

CAPTAIN JET

Four Star Publ., May, 1952

1 Factory bombing (c). 300.00
2 Parachute jump (c) 200.00
3 Tank bombing (c) 175.00
4 Parachute (c) 175.00
5 . . . . 175.00

CAPTAIN KIDD

See: DAGAR, DESERT HAWK

CAPTAIN MARVEL ADVENTURES

Fawcett Publications, 1941

N# JK, B:Captain Marvel & Sivana 45,000.00
2 GT,JK(c),Billy Batson (c). . . . 7,000.00
3 JK(c),Thunderbolt (c) 4,000.00
4 Shazam(c) 3,000.00
5 V:Nazis 2,500.00
6 Solomon, Hercules, Atlas, Zeus, Achilles & Mercury (c) 2,000.00
7 Ghost of the White Room . . . 2,000.00
8 Forward America. 2,000.00
9 A:Ibac the Monster, Nippo the Nipponese, Relm of the Subconscious 2,000.00
10 V:Japanese 2,000.00
11 V:Japanese and Nazis 1,500.00
12 Joins the Army 1,400.00
13 V:Diamond-Eyed Idol of Doom 1,400.00
14 Nippo meets his Nemesis . . 1,400.00
15 Big "Paste the Axis" contest. 1,400.00
16 Uncle Sam (c), Paste the Axis. 1,400.00
17 P(c), Paste the Axis 1,200.00
18 P(c), O:Mary Marvel. 3,200.00
19 Mary Marvel & Santa (c) . . . 1,500.00
20 Mark of the Black Swastika 5,500.00
21 Hitler (c) 1,700.00
22 B:Mr. Mind serial, Shipyard Sabotage. 1,200.00
23 A:Steamboat 1,100.00
24 Minneapolis Mystery 1,100.00
25 Sinister Faces (c). 1,100.00
26 Flag (c). 1,100.00
27 Joins Navy 900.00
28 Uncle Sam (c). 900.00
29 Battle at the China Wall 900.00
30 Modern Robinson Crusoe . . . 900.00
31 Fights his own Conscience. . . 900.00
32 V:Mole Men, Dallas. 900.00
33 Mt. Rushmore parody (c), Omaha 800.00
34 Oklahoma City 800.00
35 O:Radar the International Policeman, Indianapolis 700.00
36 Missing face contest, St. Louis. 700.00
37 V:Block Busting Bubbles, Cincinnati. 700.00
38 V:Chattanooga Ghost, Rock Garden City 700.00
39 V:Mr. Mind's Death Ray, Pittsburgh 700.00
40 V:Ghost of the Tower,Boston . 700.00
41 Runs for President, Dayton . . 600.00
42 Christmas special, St. Paul. . . 600.00
43 V:Mr. Mind,I:Uncle Marvel, Chicago 600.00
44 OtherWorlds,Washington,D.C. 600.00
45 V:Blood Bank Robbers 600.00
46 E: Mr. Mind Serial, Tall Stories of Jonah Joggins. . . . 600.00
47 CCB,Shazam(c) 550.00
48 Signs Autographs (c) 550.00
49 V: An Unknown Killer 550.00
50 Twisted Powers 550.00
51 Last of the Batsons. 500.00
52 O&I:Sivana Jr.,V:Giant Earth Dreamer. 500.00
53 Gets promoted 500.00
54 Marooned in the Future, Kansas City 500.00
55 Endless String, Columbus . . . 500.00
56 Goes Crazy, Mobile 500.00
57 A:Haunted Girl, Rochester . . . 500.00
58 V:Sivana 500.00
59 CCB(c),PrC. 500.00
60 Man who made Earthquakes . 500.00
61 I&V: Oggar, the Worlds Mightiest Immortal 500.00
62 The Great Harness Race 500.00
63 Stuntman. 500.00
64 CCB(c&a),I:Lester the Imp . . . 500.00
65 V:Invaders from Outer Space . 500.00
66 Atomic War (c) 500.00
67 Hartford 400.00
68 Scenes from the Past, Baltimore 400.00
69 Gets Knighted 400.00
70 Horror in the Box 400.00
71 Wheel of Death. 400.00
72 CCB,Empire State Bldg.Ph(c). 400.00
73 Becomes a Petrophile. 400.00
74 Who is the 13th Guest 400.00
75 V:Astonishing Yeast Menace . 400.00
76 A:Atom Ambassador 400.00
77 The Secret Life 400.00
78 O:Mr. Tawny 450.00
79 O:Atom,A:World's Worst Actor 400.00
80 Twice told story 900.00
81 A:Mr. Atom 800.00
82 A:Mr. Tawny 400.00
83 Indian Chief. 400.00
84 V:Surrealist Imp 400.00
85 Freedom Train 400.00
86 A:Mr. Tawny 400.00
87 V:Electron Thief 400.00
88 Billy Batson's Boyhood 400.00
89 V:Sivana 400.00
90 A:Mr. Tawny 400.00
91 A:Chameleon Stone 400.00
92 The Land of Limbo 400.00
93 Book of all Knowledge 400.00
94 Battle of Electricity 400.00
95 The Great Ice Cap 400.00
96 V:Automatic Weapon 400.00
97 Wiped Out. 400.00
98 United Worlds 400.00
99 Rain of Terror 400.00
100 V:Sivana,Plot against the Universe 750.00
101 Invisibility Trap 350.00
102 Magic Mix-up 350.00
103 Ice Covered World of 1,000,000 AD. 350.00
104 Mr. Tawny's Masquerade . . . 350.00
105 The Dog Catcher 350.00
106 V:Menace of the Moon 350.00
107 V:Space Hunter. 350.00
108 V:Terrible Termites 350.00
109 The Invention Inventor 350.00
110 CCB(c),V:Sivana 350.00
111 The Eighth Sea,V:Vikings . . . 350.00
112 Worrybird. 350.00
113 Feud with Mr. Tawny. 350.00
114 V:The Ogre 350.00

 All comics prices listed are for *Near Mint* condition.

Captain Marvel Jr. #1
© Fawcett Publications

Captain Marvel Jr. #72
© Fawcett Publications

Captain Midnight #27
© Fawcett Publications

115 Mr. Tawny 350.00
116 Flying Saucer 400.00
117 Mr. Tawny bondage (c) 350.00
118 V:Weird Water Man. 350.00
119 Invisibility. 350.00
120 Voice heard round the world. 350.00
121 Origin retold 350.00
122 Atomic Fire 350.00
123 Dinosaur Dilemma 350.00
124 V:Discarded Instincts 350.00
125 V:Ancient Villain 350.00
126 The Creeping Horror. 350.00
127 Sivana's Voodoo Spell 350.00
128 . . . . 350.00
129 Robot Hunt 350.00
130 Double Doom 350.00
131 Station Whiz gets Atomic
Powers. 350.00
132 V:Flood 350.00
133 The Pressure Peril 350.00
134 Sivana's Capsule Kingdom. . 350.00
135 Perplexing Past Puzzle. 325.00
136 Witch of Haven Street. 325.00
137 Seven Deadly Sins 325.00
138 V:Haunted Horror 400.00
139 V:Red Crusher 325.00
140 Hand of Horror 325.00
141 Man Without a World 325.00
142 The Beauty in Black 325.00
143 Great Stone Face on Moon . 325.00
144 Stolen Shazam Powers 325.00
145 The Machines of Murder. . . . 325.00
146 The Unholy Spider 325.00
147 Thief From the Past 325.00
148 V:The World 325.00
149 Mr. Tawny Hermit 325.00
150 Captain Marvel's Wedding,
Nov., 1953 . . . . 650.00

CAPTAIN MARVEL JR.

Fawcett Publications, 1942

1 MRa(c),O:Captain Marvel, Jr.,
A:Capt. Nazi 8,000.00
2 MRa(c),O:Capt.Nippon,
V:Capt. Nazi 3,000.00
3 MRa(c),Parade to
Excitement 2,000.00
4 MRa(c),V:Invisible Nazi 1,600.00
5 MRa(c),V:Capt. Nazi 1,500.00
6 MRa(c),Adventure of Sabbac 1,300.00
7 MRa(c),City under the Sea . 1,300.00
8 MRa(c),Dangerous Double . 1,300.00
9 MRa(c),Independence (c) . . 1,400.00
10 Hitler (c). 1,500.00
11 MRa(c). 1,100.00
12 MRa(c),Scuttles the Axis
Isle in the Sky. 1,200.00
13 MRa(c),V:The Axis,Hitler,(c). 1,500.00
14 MRa(c),X-Mas (c), Santa wears
Capt. Marvel uniform 1,000.00
15 MRa(c),V:Capt. Nazi 1,100.00
16 MRa(c),A:Capt. Marvel,
Sivana, Pogo 1,000.00
17 MRa(c),Meets his future self 1,000.00
18 MRa(c),V:Birds of Doom . . . 1,000.00
19 MRa(c),A:Capt. Nazi &
Capt. Nippon 1,000.00
20 MRa(c),Goes on the Warpath 900.00
21 MRa(c),Buy War Stamps 700.00
22 MRa(c),Rides World's oldest
steamboat 700.00
23 MRa(c) 700.00
24 MRa(c),V:Weather Man 700.00
25 MRa(c),Flag (c). 700.00
26 MRa(c),Happy New Year 700.00
27 MRa(c),Jungle Thrills 700.00
28 MRa(c),V:Sivana's Crumbling
Crimes 700.00
29 MRa(c),Blazes a Wilderness
Trail 700.00
30 MRa(c) 700.00
31 MRa(c) 500.00
32 Keeper of the Lonely Rock . . . 500.00
33 . . . . 500.00
34/35 I&O:Sivana Jr. 500.00
36 Underworld Tournament 500.00
37 FreddyFreeman'sNews-stand. 500.00
38 A:Arabian Knight. 500.00
39 V:Sivana Jr., Headline Stealer 500.00
40 Faces Grave Situation 500.00
41 I:The Acrobat 400.00
42 V:Sivana Jr.. . . . . 400.00
43 BTh(c),V:Beasts on Broadway 400.00
44 Key to the Mystery 400.00
45 A:Icy Fingers. 400.00
46 BTh(c&a). 400.00
47 BTh(c),V:Giant o/t Beanstalk . 400.00
48 Whale of a Fish Story 400.00
49 BTh(c),V:Dream Recorder . . . 400.00
50 Wanted: Freddy Freeman . . . 400.00
51 The Island Riddle 350.00
52 A:Flying Postman 350.00
53 Atomic Bomb on the Loose. . . 400.00
54 V:Man with 100 Heads 350.00
55 Pyramid of Eternity 350.00
56 Blue Boy's Black Eye 350.00
57 MRa(c),Magic Ladder. 350.00
58 BTh(c),Amazing Mirror Maze . 350.00
59 MRa(c) 350.00
60 V:Space Menace 350.00
61 V:Himself. 300.00
62 V:Mr. Hydro. 300.00
63 V:Witch of Winter 300.00
64 thru 74. . . . . @300.00
75 V:Outlaw of Crooked Creek . . 300.00
76 thru 85. . . . . @300.00
86 Defenders of time 300.00
87 thru 89. . . . . @300.00
90 The Magic Trunk 300.00
91 thru 99. . . . . @300.00
100 V:Sivana Jr 300.00
101 thru 106. . . . . @300.00
107 The Horror Dimension 400.00
108 thru 118. . . . . @250.00
119 Condemned to Die, Electric
Chair, June, 1953 . . . . 250.00

CAPTAIN MIDNIGHT

Fawcett Publications, 1942

1 O:Captain Midnight,
Capt. Marvel (c) 6,000.00
2 Smashes Jap Juggernaut. . . 2,700.00
3 Battles Phantom Bomber . . . 2,400.00
4 Grapples the Gremlins 2,000.00
5 Double Trouble in Tokyo . . . 2,000.00
6 Blasts the Black Mikado . . . 1,500.00
7 Newspaper headline (c) 1,500.00
8 Flying Torpedoes
Berlin-Bound 1,500.00
9 MRa(c), Subs in Mississippi 1,500.00
10 MRa(c), Flag (c). 1,500.00
11 MRa(c), Murder in Mexico . . 1,500.00
12 V:Sinister Angels 1,500.00
13 Non-stop around the World . 1,500.00
14 V:King of the Villains 1,500.00
15 V:Kimberley Killer. 1,500.00
16 Hitler's Fortress Breached . . 1,500.00
17 MRa(c), Hello Adolf 1,500.00
18 Death from the Skies. 1,500.00
19 Hour of Doom for the Axis . . 1,500.00
20 Brain & Brawn against Axis 1,500.00
21 Trades with Japanese 1,000.00
22 Plea for War Stamps 1,000.00
23 Japanese Prison (c). 1,000.00
24 Rising Sun Flag (c) 1,000.00
25 Amusement Park Murder. . . 1,000.00
26 Hotel of Horror. 1,000.00
27 Death Knell for Tyranny. . . . 1,000.00
28 Gliderchuting to Glory 1,000.00
29 Bomb over Nippon. 1,000.00
30 . . . . 1,000.00
31 and 32. . . . . @600.00
33 V:Shark 600.00
34 thru 40. . . . . @600.00
41 thru 63. . . . . @500.00
64 V:XOG, Ruler of Saturn. 500.00

Ca

Captain Science #4
© Youthful Magazines

Captain Video #2
© Fawcett Publications

Casper The Friendly Ghost #5
© St. John Publishing

65 . . . . 500.00
66 V:XOG. 500.00
67 Fall, 1948 . . . . 500.00
Becomes:

SWEETHEARTS
Oct., 1948

68 Robert Mitchum 250.00
69 thru 110. . . . . @125.00
111 Ronald Reagan story 175.00
112 thru 118. . . . . @125.00
119 WW,Marilyn Monroe 600.00
120 Atomic Bomb story . . . . . @150.00
121 Liz Taylor. 200.00
122 Marjuana,1954 . . . . 150.00

CAPTAIN ROCKET
P.L. Publications, 1951

1 Sci-Fi 550.00

CAPTAIN SCIENCE
Youthful Magazines, 1950

1 WW,O:Captain Science, V:Monster God of Rogor . . 1,300.00
2 WW,V:Cat Men of Phoebus, Space Pirates 600.00
3 Ghosts from the Underworld . 600.00
4 WW,Vampires 1,200.00
5 WW,V:Shark Pirates of Pisces. 1,200.00
6 WW,V:Invisible Tyrants, bondage (c). 700.00
7 WW,Bondage(c) Dec., 1951 . . 700.00
Becomes:

FANTASTIC
Feb., 1952

8 Isle of Madness 500.00
9 Octopus (c) 400.00
Becomes:

BEWARE
June, 1952

10 SHn,Doll of Death. 700.00
11 SHn,Horror Head 500.00
12 SHn,Body Snatchers 500.00
Becomes:

CHILLING TALES
Dec., 1952

13 MF,Screaming Skull 900.00
14 SHn,Smell of Death 600.00
15 SHn,Curse of the Tomb 700.00
16 HcK,Mark of the Beast Bondage(c) 600.00
17 MFc(c),Wandering Willie, Oct.,1953. . . . . 700.00

CAPTAIN STEVE SAVAGE
Avon Periodicals
[1st Series] 1950

N# WW 500.00
2 EK(c),The Death Gamble . . . 300.00
3 EK(c),Crash Landing in Manchuria 250.00
4 EK(c),V:Red Raiders from Siang-Po 150.00
5 EK(c),Rockets of Death 150.00
6 Operation Destruction 150.00
7 EK(c),Flight to Kill 150.00
8 EK(c),V:Red Mystery Jet . . . 150.00
9 EK(c) 150.00
10 . . . . 150.00
11 EK(c). 150.00
12 WW. 225.00
13 . . . . 150.00

[2nd Series] Sept./Oct., 1954

5 . . . . 150.00
6 WW 200.00
7 thru 13 . . . . @150.00

CAPTAIN TOOTSIE & THE SECRET LEGION
Toby Press, 1950

1 Sci-Fi 400.00
2 . . . . 250.00

CAPTAIN VIDEO
Fawcett Publications, 1951

1 GE,Ph(c) From TV series . . . 1,600.00
2 Time When Men Could Not Walk 1,100.00
3 GE,Indestructible Antagonist 1,000.00
4 GE,School of Spies 1,000.00
5 GE,Missiles of Doom, photo (c). 1,000.00
6 GE,Island of Conquerors, Photo (c); Dec., 1951 . . . . 1,000.00

CAPTAIN WIZARD
Rural Home, 1946

1 Impossible Man 500.00

CARNIVAL
See: SCOOP COMICS

CARTOON KIDS
Marvel Atlas, 1957

1 JMn,A:Dexter the Demon, Little Zelda,Willie,Wise Guy 200.00

CASEY–CRIME PHOTOGRAPHER
Marvel, Aug., 1949

1 Ph(c),Girl on the Docks 300.00
2 Ph(c),Staats Cotsworth 250.00
3 Ph(c),He Walked With Danger 250.00
4 Ph(c),Lend Me Your Life 250.00
Becomes:

TWO GUN WESTERN
Marvel, [1st Series], 1950

5 JB,B,I&O:Apache Kid 300.00
6 JMn,The Outcast 225.00
7 Human Sacrifice 225.00
8 JR,DW,A:Kid Colt,Texas Kid, Doc Holiday 225.00
9 JMn,GM,A:Kid Colt,Marshall 'Frosty' Bennet Texas Kid . . . 225.00
10. . . . . 225.00
11 thru 14 JMn,June, 1952 . . . @150.00

CASPER CAT
I.W. Enterprises, 1958

1 Funny animal. 100.00

CASPER, THE FRIENDLY GHOST
St. John Publishing, 1949

1 O:Baby Huey 3,000.00
2 . . . . 1,500.00
3 . . . . 1,400.00
4 . . . . 1,000.00
5 . . . . 1,000.00

Harvey Publications

7 Baby Huey. 800.00
8 thru 9 Baby Huey. . . . . . . @500.00
10 I:Spooky 550.00
11 A:Spooky. 300.00
12 thru 18. . . . . @300.00
19 I:Nightmare 400.00
20 I:Wendy the Witch 2,000.00
21 thru 30. . . . . @250.00
31 thru 40. . . . . @200.00
41 thru 50. . . . . @150.00
51 thru 60. . . . . @150.00
61 thru 69. . . . . @150.00
70 July, 1958 . . . . 150.00

Catman Comics #24
© Holyoke Publishing Co.

Century of Comics N#
© Eastern Color Printing

Challengers of the Unknown #21
© DC Comics

CASPER'S GHOSTLAND

Harvey Publications, Winter, 1958-59

1 giant . . . 300.00
2 . . . 150.00
3 thru 10 . . . @125.00
11 thru 20 . . . @100.00

CATHOLIC COMICS

Catholic Publications, 1946–49

1 Sports . . . 550.00
2 Sports . . . 350.00
3 Sports . . . 300.00
4 thru 10 . . . @300.00
11 thru 20 . . . @250.00
21 thru 34 . . . @275.00

CATMAN COMICS

Helnit Publ. Co./ Holyoke Publ. Co./ Continental Magazine, 1941

1 O:Deacon&Sidekick Mickey, Dr. Diamond & Ragman,A:Black Widow, B:Blaze Baylor . . . 7,500.00
2 Ragman . . . 3,000.00
3 B:Pied Piper . . . 2,500.00
4 CQ . . . 2,400.00
5 I&O: The Kitten . . . 1,500.00
6 CQ . . . 1,500.00
7 CQ . . . 1,500.00
8 JKa, I:Volton . . . 1,800.00
9 JKa . . . 1,200.00
10 JKa,O:Blackout, B:Phantom Falcon . . . 1,200.00
11 JKa,DRi,BF,PzF . . . 1,200.00
12 Volton . . . 1,000.00
13 . . . 1,500.00
14 CQ . . . 1,000.00
15 Rajah of Destruction . . . 1,000.00
16 Bye-Bye Axis, Hitler . . . 1,500.00
17 Buy Bonds and Stamps . . . 1,000.00
18 Buy Bonds and Stamps . . . 1,000.00
19 CQ,Hitler,Tojo &Mussolini(c) 1,500.00
20 CQ,Hitler,Tojo &Mussolini(c) 1,500.00
21 CQ . . . 1,000.00
22 CQ . . . 1,000.00
23 CQ . . . 1,000.00
N# DRiV:Japanese,Bondage(c) 1,000.00
N# V:Demon . . . 1,000.00
N# LbC(c),A:Leather Face . . . 1,000.00
27 LbC(c),Flag (c),O:Kitten . . . 1,500.00
28 LbC(c),Horror (c) . . . 1,500.00
29 LbC(c),BF,RP . . . 1,500.00
30 LbC(c),BF,Bondage(c) . . . 1,500.00
31 LbC(c) . . . 1,500.00
32 LbC(c),RP,Aug., 1946 . . . 1,500.00

CAUGHT

Marvel-Vista Publications, 1956

1 JSe,Crime . . . 350.00
2 MD,JSe . . . 200.00
3 MMe,Al,JSe . . . 200.00
4 MMe,JSe . . . 200.00
5 RC,JSe,BK . . . 200.00

CAVALIER COMICS

Sture Ashberg Publ. 1945

1 Historic adventure . . . 250.00

CAVE GIRL

See: A-1 COMICS

CENTURY OF COMICS

Eastern Color Printing Co., 1933

N# . . . 60,000.00

CHALLENGER, THE

Interfaith Publications, 1945

N# O:The Challenger Club . . . 750.00
2 JKa . . . 600.00
3 JKa . . . 600.00
4 JKa,BF . . . 600.00

CHALLENGERS OF THE UNKNOWN

DC Comics, 1958

1 JK&JK(c),The Man Who Tampered With Infinity . . . 5,000.00
2 JK&JK(c),The Monster Maker . . . 1,600.00
3 JK&JK(c),The Secret of the Sorcerer's Mirror . . . 1,500.00
4 JK,WW,JK(c),The Wizard of Time . . . 1,000.00
5 JK,WW&JK(c),The Riddle of the Star-Stone . . . 1,000.00
6 JK,WW,JK(c),Captives of the Space Circus . . . 1,000.00
7 JK,WW,JK(c),The Isle of No Return . . . 1,000.00
8 JK,WW,JK&WW(c),The Prisoners o/t Robot Planet . 1,000.00
9 The Plot To Destroy Earth . . . 750.00
10 The Four Faces of Doom . . . 750.00
11 The Creatures From The Forbidden World . . . 600.00
12 The Three Clues To Sorcery . . 600.00
13 The Prisoner of the Tiny Space Ball . . . 600.00
14 O: Multi Man . . . 600.00
15 Lady Giant and the Beast . . . 600.00
16 Prisoners of the Mirage World 500.00
17 The Secret of the Space Capsules . . . 500.00
18 Menace of Mystery Island . . . 500.00
19 The Alien Who Stole a Planet. 500.00
20 Multi-Man Strikes Back . . . 500.00
21 Weird World That Didn't Exist. 500.00
22 The Thing In Challenger Mountain . . . 500.00
23 The Island In The Sky . . . 200.00
24 The Challengers Die At Dawn 200.00
25 Captives of the Alien Hunter . . 200.00
26 Death Crowns The Challenge King . . . 200.00
27 Master of the Volcano Men . . . 200.00
28 The Riddle of the Faceless Man . . . 200.00
29 Four Roads to Doomsday . . . 200.00
30 Multi-Man...Villain Turned Hero . . . 200.00
31 O:Challengers . . . 250.00

CHALLENGE TO THE WORLD

Catechetical Guild, 1950

N# The story of Fatima . . . 200.00

CHAMBER OF CHILLS

Harvey Publications/ Witches Tales, June, 1951

21 (1) AAv . . . 900.00
22 (2) AAv . . . 600.00
23 (3) Eyes Ripped Out . . . 600.00
24 (4) LEI,Bondage (c) . . . 700.00
5 LEI,Shrunken Skull, Operation Monster . . . 700.00
6 LEI,Seven Skulls of Magondi . 600.00
7 LEI,Pit of the Damned . . . 600.00
8 LEI,Formula for Death . . . 600.00
9 LEI,Bondage (c) . . . 500.00
10 LEI,AAv,Cave of Death . . . 500.00
11 AAv,Curse of Morgan Kilgane . 400.00
12 AAv,Swamp Monster . . . 400.00
13 AAv,The Lost Race . . . 550.00
14 LEI,Down to Death . . . 500.00
15 LEI,AAv,Nightmare of Doom . . 550.00

Chamber of Clues #28
© Harvey Publications

Charlie Chan #3
© Crestwood Prize

Cheyenne #8
© Dell Publishing Co.

16 LEI,Cycle of Horror . . . 550.00
17 LEI,Amnesia . . . 550.00
18 LEI,Hair Cut-Atom Bomb . . . 600.00
19 LEI,Happy Anniversary . . . 500.00
20 Shock is Struck . . . 500.00
21 LEI,BP,RP,Decapitation . . . 600.00
22 LEI,Is Death the End? . . . 550.00
23 LEI,BP,RP,Heartline . . . 550.00
24 LEI,BP,Bondage(c) . . . 600.00
25 LEI, . . . 400.00
26 LEI,HN,AAv,Captains Return . 400.00
Becomes:

CHAMBER OF CLUES

Feb., 1955

27 BP,A:Kerry Drake . . . 250.00
28 A:Kerry Drake . . . 150.00

CHAMPION COMICS

Worth Publishing Co., 1939

2 B:Champ, Blazing Scarab, Neptina, Liberty Lads, Jingleman . . . 3,500.00
3 . . . 2,000.00
4 Bailout(c) . . . 2,000.00
5 Jungleman(c) . . . 2,000.00
6 MNe . . . 2,000.00
7 MNe,Human Meteor . . . 2,000.00
8 JK . . . 3,000.00
9 JK,S&K . . . 3,000.00
10 JK,Bondage (c) . . . 3,000.00
Becomes:

CHAMP COMICS

Oct. 1940

11 Human Meteor . . . 2,500.00
12 Human Heteor . . . 2,200.00
13 Dragon's Teeth . . . 2,000.00
14 Liberty Lads . . . 2,000.00
15 RC,Liberty Lads . . . 2,000.00
16 Liberty Lads . . . 2,000.00
17 Liberty Lads . . . 2,000.00
18 Liberty Lads . . . 2,400.00
19 JSm,A:The Wasp . . . 2,500.00
20 S&K,A:The Green Ghost . . . 2,000.00
21 S&K . . . 1,500.00
22 A:White Mask . . . 1,500.00
23 Flag (c) . . . 1,800.00
24 Hitler,Tojo & Mussolini . . . 1,600.00
25 . . . 1,500.00
26 thru 29 . . . @1,500.00

CHARLIE CHAN

Crestwood, 1948–55

1 S&K(c),CI,Detective . . . 1,500.00
2 S&K . . . 1,000.00
3 S&K . . . 1,000.00
4 S&K . . . 1,000.00
5 S&K . . . 1,000.00

Charlton Comics, 1955

6 S&K . . . 750.00
7 . . . 500.00
8 . . . 500.00
9 . . . 500.00
Becomes:

ZAZA THE MYSTIC

Charlton Comics, 1956

10 Psychic revelations . . . 300.00
11 . . . 300.00
Becomes:

THIS MAGAZINE IS HAUNTED

Charlton Comics, 1957

12 . . . 450.00
13 . . . 650.00
14 The Green Man . . . 400.00
15 . . . 350.00
16 . . . 700.00
Becomes:

OUTER SPACE

Charlton Comics, 1958

17 AS,WW,Sci-Fi . . . 300.00
18 SD . . . 450.00
19 SD . . . 450.00
20 SD . . . 450.00
21 SD . . . 450.00
22 . . . 300.00
23 . . . 300.00
24 SD Machine Men of Mars . . . 300.00
25 . . . 300.00

CHARLIE McCARTHY

Dell Publishing Co., 1947

1 Ph(c) . . . 300.00
2 . . . 200.00
3 . . . 200.00
1 . . . 200.00
2 . . . 200.00
3 . . . 200.00
4 . . . 200.00
5 . . . 200.00
6 . . . 200.00
7 . . . 200.00
8 . . . 200.00
9 . . . 200.00

CHEYENNE

Dell Publishing Co., 1956

1 Ph(c) all . . . 350.00
2 . . . 250.00
3 . . . 200.00
4 thru 12 . . . @150.00
13 thru 25 . . . @100.00

CHEYENNE KID
See: WILD FRONTIER

CHIEF, THE

Dell Publishing Co., 1950

(1) *see Dell Four Color #290*
2 . . . 150.00

CHILDREN'S BIG BOOK

Dorene Publ. Co., 1945

N# Humor . . . 150.00

CHILLING TALES
See: CAPTAIN SCIENCE

CHIP 'N DALE

Dell Publishing, 1955–66

4 . . . 150.00
5 thru 10 . . . @100.00
11 thru 30 . . . @100.00

CHOICE COMICS

Great Comics, 1941

1 O:Secret Circle . . . 3,000.00
2 . . . 1,500.00
3 The Lost City . . . 2,000.00

CHRISTMAS CARNIVAL

Approved Comics (Ziff-Davis)/ St. John Publ., 1955

N# Santa . . . 500.00
2 . . . 300.00

CHUCKLE THE GIGGLY BOOK OF COMIC ANIMALS

R. B. Leffing Well Co., 1944

1 . . . 300.00

Cicero's Cat #2
© Dell Publishing Co.

Cisco Kid #17
© Dell Publishing Co.

Claire Voyant #4
© Pentagon Publishing

CICERO'S CAT

Dell Publishing Co., 1959

1 . . . . 150.00
2 . . . . 125.00

CINDERELLA LOVE

Approved Comics (Ziff-Davis)/ St. John Publ., 1951

1 (10) Romance 300.00
2 (11) RC 200.00
3 (12) 150.00
4 . . . . 150.00
5 . . . . 150.00
6 . . . . 150.00
7 Ph(c) 150.00
8 . . . . 150.00
9 EK 200.00
10 . . . . 150.00
11 . . . . 125.00
12 . . . . 125.00
13 Ph(c) 125.00
14 MB. 150.00
15 MB. 125.00
16 MB(c) 150.00
17 . . . . 125.00
18 . . . . 125.00
19 . . . . 125.00
20 . . . . 125.00
21 . . . . 125.00
22 . . . . 125.00
23 . . . . 125.00
24 . . . . 125.00
25 . . . . 125.00
26 MB(c) 150.00
27 MB(c) 150.00
28 . . . . 125.00
29 MB(c) 150.00

CINDY COMICS

See: KRAZY COMICS

CINEMA COMICS HERALD

Paramount/Universal/RKO/ 20th Century Fox Giveaways, 1941-43

N# Mr. Bug Goes to Town 300.00
N# Bedtime Story 200.00
N# Lady for a Night,J.Wayne . . . 350.00
N# Reap the Wild Wind 200.00
N# Thunderbirds 150.00
N# They All Kissed Me 150.00
N# Bombardier 200.00
N# Crash Dive 200.00
N# Arabian Nights. 150.00

CIRCUS COMICS

Farm Women's Publ., 1945

1 Clown, Funny Animal. 300.00
2 . . . . 200.00

CIRCUS COMICS

D.S. Publications, 1948

1 FF 500.00

CIRCUS OF FUN COMICS

A.W. Nugent Publ. Co., 1946

1 Funny animal. 250.00
2 . . . . 150.00
3 . . . . 150.00

CIRCUS THE COMIC RIOT

Globe Syndicate, June, 1938

1 BKa,WE,BW 10,000.00
2 BKa,WE,BW 6,000.00
3 BKa,WE,BW, Aug., 1938 . . . 5,000.00

CISCO KID COMICS

Bernard Bailey/ Swappers Quarterly, 1944

1 . . . . 700.00

CISCO KID, THE

Dell Publishing Co.

(1) *See Dell Four Color #292*
2 Jan., 1951 . . . . 550.00
3 thru 5 . . . . @350.00
6 thru 10 . . . . @300.00
11 thru 20. . . . . @250.00
21 thru 36 . . . . @200.00
37 thru 41 Ph(c)'s. . . . . . @375.00

CLAIRE VOYANT

Leader Publ./Visual Ed./ Pentagon Publ., 1946-47

N# 1,100.00
2 JKa(c) 800.00
3 Case of the Kidnapped
Bride 1,000.00
4 Bondage (c) 800.00

CLASSIC COMICS

(Becomes: CLASSIC ILLUSTRATED—1947)

Elliot Publishing, 1941–42 Gilberton Publications, 1942–60s

001-The Three Musketeers by Alexandre Dumas

10/41 **(—)** MKd(a&c),
Original,10¢ (c) Price 7,500.00
05/43 **(10)** MKd(a&c),
No(c)Price; rep 500.00
11/43 **(15)** MKd(a&c),Long
Island Independent Ed; 300.00
6/44 **(18/20)** MKd(a&c),
Sunrise Times Edition;rep . . . 200.00
7/44 **(21)** MKd(a&c),Richmond
Courier Edition;rep 175.00
6/46 **(28)** MKd(a&c);rep 150.00
4/47 **(36)** MKd(a&c),
New CILogo;rep 75.00
6/49 **(60)** MKd(a&c),CI Logo;rep . . 50.00
10/49 **(64)** MKd(a&c),CI Logo;rep . 50.00
12/50 **(78)** MKd(a&c),15¢(c)
Price; CI Logo;rep 30.00
03/52 **(93)** MKd(a&c),CI Logo;rep . 30.00
11/53 **(114)** CI Logo;rep. 25.00
09/56 **(134)** MKd(a&c),New
P(c),CI Logo,64 pgs;rep 30.00
03/58 **(143)** MKd(a&c),P(c),
CI Logo,64 pgs;rep 25.00
05/59 **(150)** GE&RC New Art,
P(c),CILogo;rep 30.00
03/61 **(149)** GE&RC,P(c),
CI Logo;rep 18.00

002-Ivanhoe by Sir Walter Scott

1941 **(—)** EA,MKd(c),Original . 3,500.00
05/43 **(1)** EA,MKd(c),word "Presents"
Removed From(c);rep 400.00
11/43 **(15)** EA,MKd(c),Long Island
Independent Edition;rep 250.00
06/44 **(18/20)** EA,MKd(c),Sunrise
Times Edition;rep. 200.00
07/44 **(21)** EA,MKd(c),Richmond
Courier Edition;rep 175.00
06/46 **(28)** EA,MKd(c),rep 150.00
07/47 **(36)** EA,MKd(c),New
CI Logo; rep. 100.00
06/49 **(60)** EA,MKd(c),CI Logo;rep 50.00
10/49 **(64)** EA,MKd(c),CI Logo;rep 40.00
12/50 **(78)** EA,MKd(c),15¢(c)
Price; CI Logo;rep 30.00
11/51 **(89)** EA,MKd(c),CI Logo;rep 25.00

Classic Comics #4
© Gilberton Publications

Classic Comics #5
© Gilberton Publications

Classic Comics #9
© Gilberton Publications

04/53 **(106)** EA,MKd(c),CI Logo;rep 20.00
07/54 **(121)** EA,MKd(c),CI Logo;rep 30.00
01/57 **(136)** NN New Art,New P(c),CI Logo;rep 30.00
01/58 **(142)** NN,P(c),CI Logo;rep. . 18.00
11/59 **(153)** NN,P(c),CI Logo;rep. . 18.00
03/61 **(149)** NN,P(c),CI Logo;rep. . 18.00

003-The Count of Monte Cristo by Alexandre Dumas

03/42 **(—)** ASm(a&c),Orig.. . . . 2,200.00
05/43 **(10)** ASm(a&c);rep. 400.00
11/43 **(15)** ASm(a&c),Long Island Independent Edition;rep 250.00
06/44 **(18/20)** ASm(a&c), Sunrise Times Edition;rep . . . 225.00
06/44 **(20)** ASm(a&c),Sunrise Times Edition;rep. 200.00
07/44 **(21)** ASm(a&c),Richmond Courier Edition;rep 175.00
06/46 **(28)** ASm(a&c);rep. 150.00
04/47 **(36)** ASm(a&c),New CI Logo; rep. 100.00
06/49 **(60)** ASm(a&c),CI Logo;rep . 60.00
08/49 **(62)** ASm(a&c),CI Logo;rep . 75.00
05/50 **(71)** ASm(a&c),CI Logo;rep . 50.00
09/51 **(87)** ASm(a&c),15¢(c) Price, CI Logo;rep 30.00
11/53 **(113)** ASm(a&c),CI Logo; rep25.00
11/56 **(—)** LC New Art,New P(c), CI Logo;rep. 25.00
03/58 **(135)** LC,P(c),CI Logo;rep . . 30.00
11/59 (153) LC,P(c),CI Logo;rep . . 18.00
03/61 (161) LC,P(c),CI Logo;rep . . 18.00

004-The Last of the Mohicans by James Fenimore Cooper

08/42 **(—)** RR(a&c),Original . . 1,800.00
06/43 **(12)** RR(a&c),Price Balloon Deleted;rep. 400.00
11/43 **(15)** RR(a&c),Long Island Independent Edition;rep 250.00
06/44 **(20)** RR(a&c),Long Island Independent Edition;rep 225.00
07/44 **(21)** RR(a&c),Queens Home News Edition;rep. 200.00
06/46 **(28)** RR(a&c);rep 150.00
04/47 **(36)** RR(a&c),New CI Logo; rep. 100.00
06/49 **(60)** RR(a&c),CI Logo;rep . . 50.00
10/49 **(64)** RR(a&c),CI Logo;rep . . 35.00
12/50 **(78)** RR(a&c),15¢(c) Price,CI Logo rep 35.00
11/51 **(89)** RR(a&c),CI Logo;rep . . 30.00
03/54 **(117)** RR(a&c),CI Logo;rep . 28.00
11/56 **(135)** RR,New P(c), CI Logo; rep. 28.00
11/57 **(141)** RR,P(c),CI Logo;rep. . 30.00
05/59 **(150)** JSe&StA New Art; P(c), CI Logo;rep. 35.00
03/61 **(161)** JSe&StA,P(c),CI Logo; rep 15.00

005-Moby Dick by Herman Melville

09/42 **(—)** LZ(a&c),Original . . . 2,400.00
05/43 **(10)** LZ(a&c),Conray Products Edition, No(c)Price;rep 500.00
11/43 **(15)** LZ(a&c),Long Island Independent Edition;rep 275.00
06/44 **(18/20)** LZ(a&c),Sunrise Times Edition;rep. 250.00
07/44 **(20)** LZ(a&c),Sunrise Times Edition;rep. 225.00
07/44 **(21)** LZ(a&c),Sunrise Times Edition;rep. 200.00
06/46 **(28)** LZ(a&c);rep 150.00
04/47 **(36)** LZ(a&c),New CI Logo;rep 100.00
06/49 **(60)** LZ(a&c),CI Logo;rep. . . 50.00
08/49 **(62)** LZ(a&c),CI Logo;rep. . . 55.00
05/50 **(71)** LZ(a&c),CI Logo;rep. . . 40.00
09/51 **(87)** LZ(a&c),15¢(c) Price, CI Logo;rep 30.00
04/54 **(118)** LZ(a&c),CI Logo;rep . . 25.00
03/56 **(131)** NN New Art,New P(c), CI Logo;rep. 35.00
05/57 **(138)** NN,P(c),CI Logo;rep. . 18.00
01/59 **(148)** NN,P(c),CI Logo;rep. . 18.00
09/60 **(158)** NN,P(c),CI Logo;rep. . 18.00

006-A Tale of Two Cities by Charles Dickens

11/42 **(—)** StM(a&c),Original . . 2,000.00
09/43 **(14)** StM(a&c),No(c) Price; rep. 400.00
03/44 **(18)** StM(a&c),Long Island Independent Edition;rep 275.00
06/44 **(20)** StM(a&c),Sunrise Times Edition;rep. 235.00
06/46 **(28)** StM(a&c);rep 150.00
09/48 **(51)** StM(a&c),New CI Logo; rep. 75.00
10/49 **(64)** StM(a&c),CI Logo;rep 40.00
12/50 **(78)** StM(a&c),15¢(c) Price, CI Logo; rep 30.00
11/51 **(89)** StM(a&c),CI Logo;rep. . 30.00
03/54 **(117)** StM(a&c),CI Logo;rep 25.00
05/56 **(132)** JO New Art,New P(c), CI Logo;rep. 35.00
09/57 **(140)** JO,P(c),CI Logo;rep . . 15.00
11/57 **(147)** JO,P(c),CI Logo;rep . . 15.00
09/59 **(152)** JO,P(c),CI Logo;rep . 250.00
11/59 **(153)** JO,P(c),CI Logo;rep . . 18.00
03/61 **(149)** JO,P(c),CI Logo;rep . . 18.00

007-Robin Hood by Howard Pyle

12/42 **(—)** LZ(a&c),Original . . . 1,400.00
06/43 **(12)** LZ(a&c),P.D.C. on(c) Deleted;rep. 350.00
03/44 **(18)** LZ(a&c),Long Island Independent Edition;rep 225.00
06/44 **(20)** LZ(a&c),Nassau Bulletin Edition;rep 250.00
10/44 **(22)** LZ(a&c),Queens City Times Edition;rep 225.00
06/46 **(28)** LZ(a&c),rep 150.00
09/48 **(51)** LZ(a&c),New CI Logo;rep 75.00
06/49 **(60)** LZ(a&c),CI Logo;rep. . . 35.00
10/49 **(64)** LZ(a&c),CI Logo;rep. . . 32.00
12/50 **(78)** LZ(a&c),CI Logo;rep. . . 32.00
07/52 **(97)** LZ(a&c),CI Logo;rep. . . 35.00
03/53 **(106)** LZ(a&c),CI Logo;rep. . 30.00
07/54 **(121)** LZ(a&c),CI Logo;rep. . 30.00
11/55 **(129)** LZ,New P(c), CI Logo;rep 35.00
01/57 **(136)** JkS New Art,P(c);rep . 30.00
03/58 **(143)** JkS,P(c),CI Logo;rep . . 18.00
11/59 **(153)** JkS,P(c),CI Logo;rep . 15.00
10/61 **(164)** JkS,P(c),CI Logo;rep . 15.00

008-Arabian Nights by Antoine Galland

03/43 **(—)** LCh(a&c),Original. . 2,200.00
09/43 **(14)** LCh(a&c);rep 750.00
01/44 **(17)** LCh(a&c),Long Island Independent Edition;rep 750.00
06/44 **(20)** LCh(a&c),Nassau Bulletin Edition,64 pgs;rep. . . 600.00
06/46 **(28)** LCh(a&c);rep 400.00
09/48 **(51)** LCh(a&c),New CI Logo; rep 400.00
10/49 **(64)** LCh(a&c),CI Logo;rep 300.00
12/50 **(78)** LCh(a&c),CI Logo;rep 250.00
10/61 **(164)** ChB New Art,P(c), CI Logo;rep 225.00

009-Les Miserables by Victor Hugo

03/43 **(—)** RLv(a&c),Original . . 1,300.00
09/43 **(14)** RLv(a&c);rep 400.00
03/44 **(18)** RLv(a&c),Nassau Bulletin Edition;rep 275.00

Classic Comics #11
© Gilberton Publications

Classic Comics #12
© Gilberton Publications

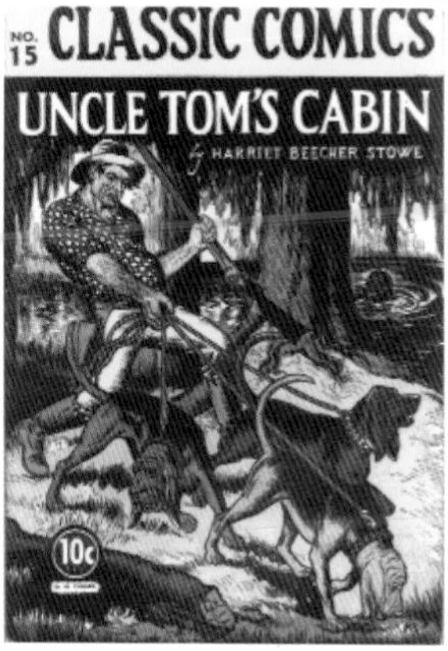

Classic Comics #15
© Gilberton Publications

06/44 **(20)** RLv(a&c),Richmond Courier Edition;rep 250.00
06/46 **(28)** RLv(a&c);rep 200.00
09/48 **(51)** RLv(a&c),New CI Logo; rep 100.00
05/50 **(71)** RLv(a&c),CI Logo;rep 75.00
09/51 **(87)** RLv(a&c),CI Logo, 15¢(c)Price;rep 60.00
03/61 **(161)** NN New Art,GMc New P(c), CI Logo;rep. 60.00

010-Robinson Crusoe
by Daniel Defoe

04/43 **(—)** StM(a&c),Original . . 1,100.00
09/43 **(14)** StM(a&c);rep 400.00
03/44 **(18)** StM(a&c),Nassau Bulletin Ed.,'Bill of Rights'Pge.64;rep. 300.00
06/44 **(20)** StM(a&c),Queens Home News Edition;rep. 250.00
??/45 **(23)** StM(a&c);rep 150.00
06/46 **(28)** StM(a&c);rep 150.00
09/48 **(51)** StM(a&c),New CI Logo; rep 75.00
10/49 **(64)** StM(a&c),CI Logo;rep. . 50.00
12/50 **(78)** StM(a&c),15¢(c) Price, CI Logo;rep 35.00
07/52 **(97)** StM(a&c),CI Logo;rep. . 32.00
12/53 **(114)** StM(a&c),CI Logo;rep 30.00
01/56 **(130)** StM,New P(c),CI Logo; rep 32.00
09/57 **(140)** SmC New Art,P(c), CI Logo; rep. 32.00
11/59 **(153)** SmC,P(c),CI Logo;rep 15.00
10/61 **(164)** SmC,P(c),CI Logo;rep 15.00

011-Don Quixote
by Miguel de Cervantes Saavedra

05/43 (—) LZ(a&c),Original . . . 1,300.00
03/44 **(18)** LZ(a&c),Nassau Bulletin Edition;rep 350.00
07/44 **(21)** LZ(a&c),Queens Home News Edition;rep. 250.00
06/46 **(28)** LZ(a&c);rep 150.00
08/53 **(110)** LZ,TO New P(c),New CI Logo;rep 50.00
05/60 **(156)** LZ,TO P(c),Pages Reduced to 48,CI Logo;rep . . . 30.00

012-Rip Van Winkle & The Headless Horseman
by Washington Irving

06/43 **(——)** RLv(a&c),Original. 1,200.00
11/43 **(15)** RLv(a&c),Long Island Independent Edition;rep 350.00
06/44 **(20)** RLv(a&c),Long Island Independent Edition;rep 250.00
10/44 **(22)** RLv(a&c),Queens City Times Edition;rep 225.00
06/46 **(28)** RLv(a&c);rep 150.00
06/49 **(60)** RLv(a&c),New CI Logo;rep 75.00
08/49 **(62)** RLv(a&c),CI Logo;rep 45.00
05/50 **(71)** RLv(a&c),CI Logo;rep. . 35.00
11/51 **(89)** RLv(a&c),15¢(c) Price, CI Logo;rep 30.00
04/54 **(118)** RLv(a&c),CI Logo;rep 32.00
05/56 **(132)** RLv,New P(c), CI Logo; rep. 35.00
05/59 **(150)** NN New Art;P(c), CI Logo; rep. 35.00
09/60 **(158)** NN,P(c),CI Logo;rep. . 20.00

013-Dr. Jekyll and Mr. Hyde
by Robert Louis Stevenson

08/43 **(—)** AdH(a&c),Original. . 2,000.00
11/43 **(15)** AdH(a&c),Long Island Independent Edition;rep 500.00
06/44 **(20)** AdH(a&c),Long Island Independent Edition;rep 275.00
06/46 **(28)** AdH(a&c),No(c) Price; rep. 225.00
06/49 **(60)** AdH,HcK New(c),New CI Logo,Pgs.reduced to 48;rep . . 75.00
08/49 **(62)** AdH,HcK(c),CI Logo;rep 45.00
05/50 **(71)** AdH,HcK(c),CI Logo;rep 40.00
09/51 **(87)** AdH,HcK(c),Erroneous Return of Original Date, CI Logo;rep 40.00
10/53 **(112)** LC New Art,New P(c), CI Logo;rep. 40.00
11/59 **(153)** LC,P(c),CI Logo;rep . . 20.00
03/61 **(161)** LC,P(c),CI Logo;rep . . 20.00

014-Westward Ho!
by Charles Kingsley

09/43 **(—)** ASm(a&c),Orig.. . . . 3,000.00
11/43 **(15)** ASm(a&c),Long Island Independent Edition;rep 750.00
07/44 **(21)** ASm(a&c);rep. 650.00
06/46 **(28)** ASm(a&c),No(c) Price; rep. 450.00
11/48 **(53)** ASm(a&c),Pages reduced to 48, New CI Logo;rep 400.00

015-Uncle Tom's Cabin
by Harriet Beecher Stowe

11/43 **(—)** RLv(a&c),Original . . 1,000.00
11/43 **(15)** RLv(a&c),Blank Price Circle, Long Island Independent Ed.;rep 350.00
07/44 **(21)** RLv(a&c),Nassau Bulletin Edition;rep 250.00
06/46 **(28)** RLv(a&c),No(c) Price; rep. 200.00
11/48 **(53)** RLv(a&c),Pages Reduced to 48, New CI Logo;rep 75.00
05/50 **(71)** RLv(a&c),CI Logo;rep. . 45.00
11/51 **(89)** RLv(a&c),15¢(c) Price, CI Logo;rep 45.00
03/54 **(117)** RLv,New P(c),CI Logo, Lettering Changes;rep. . 32.00
09/55 **(128)** RLv,P(c),"Picture Progress"Promotion,CI Logo;rep 22.00
03/57 **(137)** RLv,P(c),CI Logo;rep . 15.00
09/58 **(146)** RLv,P(c),CI Logo;rep . 15.00
01/60 **(154)** RLv,P(c),CI Logo;rep . 15.00
03/61 **(161)** RLv,P(c),CI Logo;rep . 17.00

016-Gulliver's Travels
by Johnathan Swift

12/43 **(——)** LCh(a&c),Original. 1,200.00
06/44 **(18/20)** LCh(a&c),Queen's Home News Edition,No(c)Price; rep 300.00
10/44 **(22)** LCh(a&c),Queen's Home News Editon;rep 225.00
06/46 **(28)** LCh(a&c);rep 150.00
06/49 **(60)** LCh(a&c),Pgs. Reduced To 48, New CI Logo;rep 75.00
08/49 **(62)** LCh(a&c),CI Logo;rep . 45.00
10/49 **(64)** LCh(a&c),CI Logo;rep . 45.00
12/50 **(78)** LCh(a&c),15¢(c) Price, CI Logo;rep 35.00
11/51 **(89)** LCh(a&c),CI Logo;rep. . 30.00
03/60 **(155)** LCh,New P(c),CI Logo; rep 35.00

017-The Deerslayer
by James Fenimore Cooper

01/44 **(——)** LZ(a&c),Original. . 1,000.00
03/44 **(18)** LZ(a&c),No(c)Price; rep 350.00
10/44 **(22)** LZ(a&c),Queen's City Times Edition;rep 200.00
06/46 **(28)** LZ(a&c);rep 150.00
06/49 **(60)** LZ(a&c),Pgs. Reduced to 48,New CI Logo;rep 75.00
10/49 **(64)** LZ(a&c),CI Logo;rep. . . 35.00
07/51 **(85)** LZ(a&c),15¢(c) Price, CI Logo;rep 30.00
04/54 **(118)** LZ(a&c),CI Logo;rep. . 28.00
05/56 **(132)** LZ(a&c),CI Logo;rep. . 25.00

Classic Comics #19
© Gilberton Publications

Classic Comics #21
© Gilberton Publications

Classic Comics #24
© Gilberton Publications

018-The Hunchback of Notre Dame
by Victor Hugo

03/44 **(—)** ASm(a&c),Original Gilberton Edition. 1,200.00
03/44 **(—)** ASm(a&c),Original Island Publications Edition . 1,000.00
06/44 **(18/20)** ASm(a&c),Queens Home News Edition;rep. 350.00
10/44 **(22)** ASm(a&c),Queens City Times Edition;rep 250.00
06/46 **(28)** ASm(a&c);rep. 225.00
06/49 **(60)** ASm,HcK New(c)8 Pgs. Deleted, New CI Logo;rep. . . . 75.00
08/49 **(62)** ASm,HcK(c),CI Logo;rep 40.00
12/50 **(78)** ASm,HcK(c),15¢(c) Price; CI Logo;rep 35.00
11/51 **(89)** ASm,HcK(c),CI Logo;rep 32.00
04/54 **(118)** ASm,HcK(c),CI Logo;rep 35.00
09/57 **(140)** ASm,New P(c),CI Logo; rep 32.00
09/58 **(146)** ASm,P(c),CI Logo;rep 32.00
09/60 **(158)** GE&RC New Art,GMc New P(c),CI Logo;rep 20.00

019-Huckleberry Finn
by Mark Twain

04/44 **(—)** LZ(a&c),Original Gilberton Edition 750.00
04/44 **(—)** LZ(a&c),Original Island Publications Company Ed. . . 800.00
03/44 **(18)** LZ(a&c),Nassau Bulletin Editon;rep 350.00
10/44 **(22)** LZ(a&c),Queens City Times Edition;rep. 250.00
06/46 **(28)** LZ(a&c);rep 200.00
06/49 **(60)** LZ(a&c),New CI Logo, Pgs.Reduced to 48;rep 75.00
08/49 **(62)** LZ(a&c),CI Logo;rep. . . 40.00
12/50 **(78)** LZ(a&c),CI Logo;rep. . . 35.00
11/51 **(89)** LZ(a&c),CI Logo;rep . . . 30.00
03/54 **(117)** LZ(a&c),CI Logo;rep. . 30.00
03/56 **(131)** FrG New Art,New P(c), CI Logo; rep 30.00
09/57 **(140)** FrG,P(c),CI Logo;rep . 20.00
05/59 **(150)** FrG,P(c),CI Logo;rep . 20.00
09/60 **(158)** FrG,P(c),CI Logo;rep . 20.00

020-The Corsican Brothers
by Alexandre Dumas

06/44 **(—)** ASm(a&c),Original Gilberton Edition 650.00
06/44 **(—)** ASm(a&c),Original Courier Edition. 550.00
06/44 **(—)** ASm(a&c),Original Long Island Independent Edition . . 550.00
10/44 **(22)** ASm(a&c),Queens City Times Edition;rep 275.00
06/46 **(28)** ASm(a&c);rep. 250.00
06/49 **(60)** ASm(a&c),No(c)Price, New CI Logo,Pgs. Reduced to 48;rep 225.00
08/49 **(62)** ASm(a&c),CI Logo;rep 165.00
12/50 **(78)** ASm(a&c),15¢(c) Price, CI Logo;rep 150.00
07/52 **(97)** ASm(a&c),CI Logo;rep 135.00

021-Famous Mysteries
by Sir Arthur Conan Doyle
Guy de Maupassant
& Edgar Allan Poe

07/44 **(—)** AdH,LZ,ASm(a&c), Original Gilberton Edition . . 1,300.00
07/44 **(—)** AdH,LZ,ASm(a&c), Original Island Publications Edition; No Date or Indicia 1,350.00
07/44 **(—)** AdH,LZ,ASm(a&c), Original Richmond Courier Edition. 1,100.00
10/44 **(22)** AdH,LZ,ASm(a&c), Nassau Bulletin Edition;rep . . 500.00
09/46 **(30)** AdH,LZ,ASm(a&c); rep 350.00
08/49 **(62)** AdH,LZ,ASm(a&c), New CI Logo;rep 300.00
04/50 **(70)** AdH,LZ,ASm(a&c), CI Logo;rep 275.00
07/51 **(85)** AdH,LZ,ASm(a&c), 15¢(c) Price,CI Logo;rep 250.00
12/53 **(114)** ASm,AdH,LZ,New P(c), CI Logo;rep. 250.00

022-The Pathfinder
by James Fenimore Cooper

10/44 **(—)** LZ(a&c),Original Gilberton Edition 600.00
10/44 **(—)** LZ(a&c),Original Island Publications Edition; . . 500.00
10/44 **(—)** LZ(a&c),Original Queens County Times Edition450.00
09/46 **(30)** LZ(a&c),No(c) Price;rep 200.00
06/49 **(60)** LZ(a&c),New CI Logo, Pgs.Reduced To 48;rep. 50.00
08/49 **(62)** LZ(a&c),CI Logo;rep. . . 45.00
04/50 **(70)** LZ(a&c),CI Logo;rep. . . 35.00
07/51 **(85)** LZ(a&c),15¢(c) Price, CI Logo;rep 32.00
04/54 **(118)** LZ(a&c),CI Logo;rep . . 30.00
05/56 **(132)** LZ(a&c),CI Logo;rep. . 30.00
09/58 **(146)** LZ(a&c),CI Logo;rep. . 35.00

023-Oliver Twist
by Charles Dickens
(First Classic by the Iger shop)

07/45 **(—)** AdH(a&c),Original . . . 700.00
09/46 **(30)** AdH(a&c),Price Circle is Blank;rep 450.00
06/49 **(60)** AdH(a&c),Pgs. Reduced To 48, New CI Logo;rep 50.00
08/49 **(62)** AdH(a&c),CI Logo;rep 45.00
05/50 **(71)** AdH(a&c),CI Logo;rep 35.00
07/51 **(85)** AdH(a&c),15¢(c) Price CI Logo;rep 32.00
04/52 **(94)** AdH(a&c),CI Logo;rep 32.00
04/54 **(118)** AdH(a&c),CI Logo;rep 30.00
01/57 **(136)** AdH,New P(c),CI Logo; rep. 30.00
05/59 **(150)** AdH,P(c),CI Logo;rep . 25.00
1961 **(164)** AdH,P(c),CI Logo;rep . 25.00
10/61 **(164)** GE&RC New Art,P(c), CI Logo;rep 35.00

024-A Connecticut Yankee in King Arthur's Court
by Mark Twain

09/45 **(—)** JH(a&c),Original 550.00
09/46 **(30)** JH(a&c),Price Circle Blank;rep 200.00
06/49 **(60)** JH(a&c),8 Pages Deleted,New CI Logo;rep 50.00
08/49 **(62)** JH(a&c),CI Logo;rep. . . 45.00
05/50 **(71)** JH(a&c),CI Logo;rep. . . 35.00
09/51 **(87)** JH(a&c),15¢(c) Price CI Logo;rep 30.00
07/54 **(121)** JH(a&c),CI Logo;rep. . 30.00
09/57 **(140)** JkS New Art,New P(c),CI Logo; rep. 35.00
11/59 **(153)** JkS,P(c),CI Logo;rep . 18.00
1961 **(164)** JkS,P(c),CI Logo;rep. . 15.00

025-Two Years Before the Mast
by Richard Henry Dana Jr.

10/45 **(—)** RWb,DvH,Original; . . 500.00
09/46 **(30)** RWb,DvH,Price Circle Blank;rep 200.00
06/49 **(60)** RWb,DvH,8 Pages Deleted,New CI Logo;rep 50.00
08/49 **(62)** RWb,DvH,CI Logo;rep . 45.00
05/50 **(71)** RWb,DvH,CI Logo;rep . 35.00
07/51 **(85)** RWb,DvH,15¢(c) Price CI Logo;rep 30.00

Classics Illustrated #26
© Gilberton Publications

Classics Illustrated #31
© Gilberton Publications

Classics Illustrated #33
© Gilberton Publications

12/53 **(114)** RWb,DvH,CI Logo;rep 28.00
05/60 **(156)** RWb,DvH,New P(c), CI Logo, 3 Pgs. Replaced By Fillers;rep 32.00

026-Frankenstein
by Mary Wollstonecraft Shelley
12/45 **(—)** RWb&ABr(a&c), Original 1,400.00
09/46 **(30)** RWb&ABr(a&c), Price Circle Blank;rep 400.00
06/49 **(60)** RWb&ABr(a&c), New CI Logo;rep 175.00
08/49 **(62)** RWb&ABr(a&c), CI Logo;rep 165.00
05/50 **(71)** RWb&ABr(a&c), CI Logo;rep 75.00
04/51 **(82)** RWb&ABr(a&c), 15¢(c) Price,CI Logo;rep 65.00
03/54 **(117)** RWb&ABr(a&c), CI Logo;rep 30.00
09/58 **(146)** RWb&ABr,NS New P(c), CI Logo; rep 35.00
11/59 **(153)** RWb&ABr,NS P(c),CI Logo; rep. 50.00
01/61 **(160)** RWb&ABr,NS P(c),CI Logo; rep. 16.00

027-The Adventures of Marco Polo
by Marco Polo & Donn Byrne
04/46 **(——)** HFl(a&c);Original. . . 550.00
09/46 **(30)** HFl(a&c);rep 200.00
04/50 **(70)** HFl(a&c),8 Pages Deleted, No(c) Price,New CI Logo;rep . 45.00
09/51 **(87)** HFl(a&c),15¢(c) Price,CI Logo;rep 30.00
03/54 **(117)** HFl(a&c),CILogo;rep. . 25.00
01/60 **(154)** HFl,New P(c),CI Logo;rep 25.00
1962 **(165)** HFl,P(c),CI Logo;rep . . 15.00

028-Michael Strogoff
by Jules Verne
06/46 **(—)** AdH(a&c),Original . . . 500.00
09/48 **(51)** AdH(a&c),8 Pages Deleted,New CI Logo;rep . . . 150.00
01/54 **(115)** AdH,New P(c),CI Logo; rep 45.00
03/60 **(155)** AdH,P(c),CI Logo;rep . 18.00

029-The Prince and the Pauper
by Mark Twain
07/46 **(—)** AdH(a&c),Original . . . 800.00
06/49 **(60)** AdH,New HcK(c),New CI Logo,8 Pages Deleted;rep. . . 100.00
08/49 **(62)** AdH,HcK(c),CILogo;rep 50.00
05/50 **(71)** AdH,HcK(c),CILogo;rep 35.00
03/52 **(93)** AdH,HcK(c),CILogo;rep 32.00
12/53 **(114)** AdH,HcK(c),CI Logo;rep 30.00
09/55 **(128)** AdH,New P(c),CI Logo; rep 30.00
05/57 **(138)** AdH,P(c),CI Logo;rep . 18.00
05/59 **(150)** AdH,P(c),CI Logo;rep . 18.00
1961 **(164)** AdH,P(c),CI Logo;rep . 18.00

030-The Moonstone
by William Wilkie Collins
09/46 **(—)** DRi(a&c),Original. . . . 550.00
06/49 **(60)** DRi(a&c),8 Pages Deleted,New CI Logo;rep . . . 100.00
04/50 **(70)** DRi(a&c),CI Logo;rep. . 65.00
03/60 **(155)** DRi,LbC New P(c), CI Logo;rep 90.00
1962 **(165)** DRi,LbC P(c),CI Logo; rep 35.00

031-The Black Arrow
by Robert Louis Stevenson
10/46 **(—)** AdH(a&c),Original . . . 450.00
09/48 **(51)** AdH(a&c),8 Pages Deleted,New CI Logo;rep 75.00
10/49 **(64)** AdH(a&c),CI Logo;rep 35.00
09/51 **(87)** AdH(a&c),15¢(c) Price;CI Logo;rep 30.00
06/53 **(108)** AdH(a&c),CI Logo;rep 28.00
03/55 **(125)** AdH(a&c),CI Logo;rep 27.00
03/56 **(131)** AdH,New P(c),CI Logo; rep 22.00
09/57 **(140)** AdH,P(c),CI Logo;rep . 20.00
01/59 **(148)** AdH,P(c),CI Logo;rep . 20.00
03/61 **(161)** AdH,P(c),CI Logo;rep . 20.00

032-Lorna Doone
by Richard Doddridge Blackmore
12/46 **(—)** MB(a&c),Original 550.00
10/49 **(53/64)** MB(a&c),8 Pages Deleted,New CI Logo;rep . . . 150.00
07/51 **(85)** MB(a&c),15¢(c) Price, CI Logo;rep 65.00
04/54 **(118)** MB(a&c),CI Logo;rep . 35.00
05/57 **(138)** MB,New P(c); Old(c) Becomes New Splash Pge.,CI Logo;rep 35.00
05/59 **(150)** MB,P(c),CI Logo;rep. . 20.00
1962 **(165)** MB,P(c),CI Logo;rep . . 20.00

033-The Adventures of Sherlock Holmes
by Sir Arthur Conan Doyle
01/47 **(—)** LZ,HcK(c),Original . 1,750.00
11/48 **(53)** LZ,HcK(c),"A Study in Scarlet" Deleted,New CI Logo;rep . . . 700.00
05/50 **(71)** LZ,HcK(c),CI Logo;rep 500.00
11/51 **(89)** LZ,HcK(c),15¢(c) Price,CI Logo;rep 400.00

034-Mysterious Island
by Jules Verne
02/47 (—) RWb&DvH,Original . . 600.00
06/49 **(60)** RWb&DvH,8 Pages Deleted,New CI Logo;rep 65.00
08/49 **(62)** RWb&DvH,CI Logo;rep 45.00
05/50 **(71)** RWb&DvH,CI Logo;rep 65.00
12/50 **(78)** RWb&DvH,15¢(c) Price, CI Logo;rep 35.00
02/52 **(92)** RWb&DvH,CI Logo;rep 35.00
03/54 **(117)** RWb&DvH,CI Logo; rep 35.00
09/57 **(140)** RWb&DvH,New P(c), CI Logo;rep 35.00
05/60 **(156)** RWb&DvH,P(c),CI Logo;rep 20.00
Becomes:

CLASSICS ILLUSTRATED
Gilberton Publications, 1947–60s

035-Last Days of Pompeii
by Lord Edward Bulwer Lytton
03/47 **(—)** HcK(a&c),Original 500.00
03/61 **(161)** JK,New P(c), 15¢(c)Price;rep 65.00

036-Typee
by Herman Melville
04/47 **(—)** EzW(a&c),Original. . . 275.00
10/49 **(64)** EzW(a&c),No(c)price, 8 pages deleted;rep. 90.00
03/60 **(155)** EzW,GMc New P(c);rep 35.00

037-The Pioneers
by James Fenimore Cooper
05/47 **(37)** RP(a&c),Original 300.00
08/49 **(62)** RP(a&c),8 Pages Deleted;rep 45.00
04/50 **(70)** RP(a&c);rep 35.00
02/52 **(92)** RP(a&c),15¢(c)price; rep 35.00
04/54 **(118)** RP(a&c);rep 30.00
03/56 **(131)** RP(a&c);rep 30.00
05/56 **(132)** RP(a&c);rep 30.00
11/59 **(153)** RP(a&c);rep 25.00

038-Adventures of Cellini
by Benvenuto Cellini
06/47 **(—)** AgF(a&c),Original . . . 400.00

Classics Illustrated #39
© Gilberton Publications

Classics Illustrated #44
© Gilberton Publications

Classics Illustrated #52
© Gilberton Publications

1961 **(164)** NN New Art,New P(c); rep 35.00

039-Jane Eyre by Charlotte Bronte
07/47 **(—-)** HyG(a&c),Original . . . 350.00
06/49 **(60)** HyG(a&c),No(c)Price, 8 pages deleted;rep. 50.00
08/49 **(62)** HyG(a&c);rep 45.00
05/50 **(71)** HyG(a&c);rep 35.00
02/52 **(92)** HyG(a&c),15¢(c) Price; rep. 32.00
04/54 **(118)** HyG(a&c);rep 32.00
01/58 **(142)** HyG,New P(c);rep. . . . 32.00
01/60 **(154)** HyG,P(c);rep. 32.00

040-Mysteries (The Pit & the Pendulum, The Adventures of Hans Pfall, Fall of the House of Usher) by Edgar Allan Poe
08/47 **(—-)** AgF,HyG,HcK(a&c), Original. 1,000.00
08/49 **(62)** AgF,HyG,HcK(a&c), 8 Pages deleted;rep 350.00
09/50 **(75)** AgF,HyG, HcK(a&c);rep. 300.00
02/52 **(92)** AgF,HyG,HcK(a&c) 15¢(c) Price;rep. 250.00

041-Twenty Years After by Alexandre Dumas
09/47 **(—-)** RBu(a&c),Original . . . 600.00
08/49 **(62)** RBu,HcK New(c),No(c) Price, 8 Pages Deleted;rep . . . 65.00
12/50 **(78)** RBu,HcK(c),15¢(c) Price; rep. 45.00
05/60 **(156)** RBu,DgR New P(c); rep 35.00

042-Swiss Family Robinson by Johann Wyss
10/47 **(42)** HcK(a&c),Original. . . . 300.00
08/49 **(62)** HcK(a&c),No(c)price, 8 Pages Deleted,Not Every Issue Has 'Gift Box' Ad;rep 75.00
09/50 **(75)** HcK(a&c);rep 35.00
03/52 **(93)** HcK(a&c);rep 32.00
03/54 **(117)** HcK(a&c);rep 30.00
03/56 **(131)** HcK,New P(c);rep. . . . 28.00
03/57 **(137)** HcK,P(c);rep. 28.00
11/57 **(141)** HcK,P(c);rep. 28.00
09/59 **(152)** NN New art,P(c);rep. . 28.00
09/60 **(158)** NN,P(c);rep 25.00

043-Great Expectations by Charles Dickens
11/47 **(—-)** HcK(a&c),Original . . 1,400.00
08/49 **(62)** HcK(a&c),No(c)price; 8 pages deleted;rep. 850.00

044-Mysteries of Paris by Eugene Sue
12/47 **(44)** HcK(a&c),Original . . 1,000.00
08/47 **(62)** HcK(a&c),No(c)Price, 8 Pages Deleted,Not Every Issue Has'Gift Box'Ad;rep 400.00
12/50 **(78)** HcK(a&c),15¢(c) Price; rep. 350.00

045-Tom Brown's School Days by Thomas Hughes
01/48 **(44)** HFl(a&c),Original, 1st 48 Pge. Issue 250.00
10/49 **(64)** HFl(a&c),No(c) Price;rep 60.00
03/61 **(161)** JTg New Art,GMc New P(c);rep 30.00

046-Kidnapped by Robert Louis Stevenson
04/48 **(47)** RWb(a&c),Original . . . 200.00
08/49 **(62)** RWb(a&c),Red Circle Either Blank or With 10¢;rep . 100.00
12/50 **(78)** RWb(a&c),15¢(c) Price; rep. 35.00
09/51 **(87)** RWb(a&c);rep. 32.00
04/54 **(118)** RWb(a&c);rep. 30.00
03/56 **(131)** RWb,New P(c);rep . . . 30.00
09/57 **(140)** RWb,P(c);rep 18.00
05/59 **(150)** RWb,P(c);rep 18.00
05/60 **(156)** RWb,P(c);rep 18.00
1961 **(164)** RWb,P(c),Reduced Pge. Wdth;rep 18.00

047-Twenty Thousand Leagues Under the Sea by Jules Verne
05/58 **(47)** HcK(a&c),Original. . . . 250.00
10/49 **(64)** HcK(a&c),No(c) Price; rep. 45.00
12/50 **(78)** HcK(a&c),15¢(c) Price; rep. 35.00
04/52 **(94)** HcK(a&c);rep 35.00
04/54 **(118)** HcK(a&c);rep 30.00
09/55 **(128)** HcK,New P(c);rep. . . . 30.00
07/56 **(133)** HcK,P(c);rep. 25.00
09/57 **(140)** HcK,P(c);rep. 18.00
01/59 **(148)** HcK,P(c);rep. 18.00
05/60 **(156)** HcK,P(c);rep. 18.00
62/63 **(165)** HcK,P(c);rep. 18.00
05/48 **(167)** HcK,P(c);rep. 18.00

048-David Copperfield by Charles Dickens
06/48 **(47)** HcK(a&c),Original. . . . 200.00
10/49 **(64)** HcK(a&c),Price Circle Replaced by Image of Boy Reading;rep. 45.00
09/51 **(87)** HcK(a&c),15¢(c) Price; rep. 35.00
07/54 **(121)** HcK,New P(c);rep. . . . 30.00
10/56 **(130)** HcK,P(c);rep. 18.00
09/57 **(140)** HcK,P(c);rep. 18.00
01/59 **(148)** HcK,P(c);rep. 18.00
05/60 **(156)** HcK,P(c);rep. 18.00

049-Alice in Wonderland by Lewis Carroll
07/48 **(47)** AB(a&c),Original. 250.00
10/49 **(64)** AB(a&c),No(c)Price; rep 75.00
07/51 **(85)** AB(a&c),15¢(c)Price; rep 50.00
03/60 **(155)** AB,New P(c);rep. 50.00

050-Adventures of Tom Sawyer by Mark Twain
08/48 **(51)** ARu(a&c),Original. . . . 225.00
09/48 **(51)** ARu(a&c),Original. . . . 250.00
10/49 **(64)** ARu(a&c),No(c) Price; rep. 35.00
12/50 **(78)** ARu(a&c),15¢(c) Price; rep. 30.00
04/52 **(94)** ARu(a&c);rep 30.00
12/53 **(114)** ARu(a&c);rep 30.00
03/54 **(117)** ARu(a&c);rep 25.00
05/56 **(132)** ARu(a&c);rep 25.00
09/57 **(140)** ARu,New P(c);rep. . . . 22.00
05/59 **(150)** ARu,P(c);rep. 25.00
10/61 **(164)** New Art,P(c);rep. 15.00

051-The Spy by James Fenimore Cooper
09/48 **(51)** AdH(a&c),Original, Maroon(c) 200.00
09/48 **(51)** AdH(a&c),Original, Violet(c). 175.00
11/51 **(89)** AdH(a&c),15¢(c) Price; rep. 35.00
07/54 **(121)** AdH(a&c);rep 30.00
07/57 **(139)** AdH,New P(c);rep. . . . 30.00
05/60 **(156)** AdH,P(c);rep. 18.00

052-The House of the Seven Gables by Nathaniel Hawthorne
10/48 **(53)** HyG(a&c),Original . . . 200.00
11/51 **(89)** HyG(a&c),15¢(c) Price; rep. 35.00
07/54 **(121)** HyG(a&c);rep 30.00
01/58 **(142)** GWb New Art,New P(c); rep. 35.00
05/60 **(156)** GWb,P(c);rep 18.00

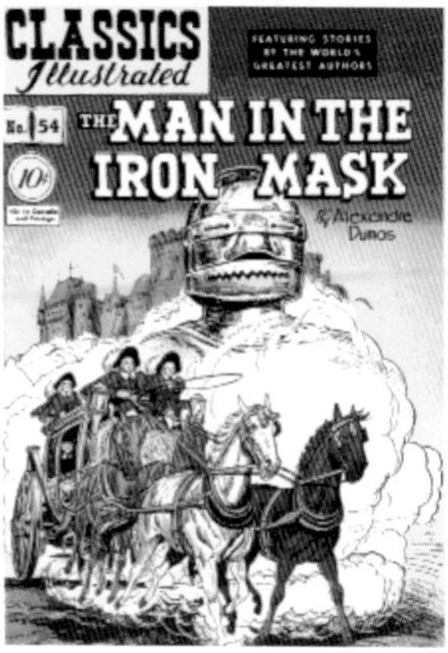

Classics Illustrated #54
© Gilberton Publications

Classics Illustrated #63
© Gilberton Publications

Classics Illustrated #68
© Gilberton Publications

053-A Christmas Carol by Charles Dickens
11/48 **(53)** HcK(a&c),Original. . . . 250.00

054-Man in the Iron Mask by Alexandre Dumas
12/48 **(55)** AgF,HcK(c),Original . . 200.00
03/52 **(93)** AgF,HcK(c),15¢(c) Price; rep. 45.00
09/53 **(111)** AgF,HcK(c);rep 60.00
01/58 **(142)** KBa New Art,New P(c); rep. 35.00
01/60 **(154)** KBa,P(c);rep. 18.00

055-Silas Mariner by George Eliot
01/49 **(55)** AdH,HcK(c),Original . . 200.00
09/50 **(75)** AdH,HcK(c),Price Circle Blank,'Coming next'Ad(not usually in reps.);rep. 45.00
07/52 **(97)** AdH,HcK(c);rep 32.00
07/54 **(121)** AdH,New P(c);rep. . . . 30.00
01/56 **(130)** AdH,P(c);rep. 18.00
09/57 **(140)** AdH,P(c);rep. 18.00
01/60 **(154)** AdH,P(c);rep. 18.00

056-The Toilers of the Sea by Victor Hugo
02/49 **(55)** AgF(a&c),Original. . . . 300.00
01/62 **(165)** AT New Art,New P(c); rep. 60.00

057-The Song of Hiawatha by Henry Wadsworth Longfellow
03/49 **(55)** AB(a&c),Original. 200.00
09/50 **(75)** AB(a&c),No(c)price,' Coming Next'Ad(not usually found in reps.);rep 50.00
04/52 **(94)** AB(a&c),15¢(c) Price;rep 35.00
04/54 **(118)** AB(a&c);rep 32.00
09/56 **(134)** AB,New P(c);rep 30.00
07/57 **(139)** AB,P(c);rep. 18.00
01/60 **(154)** AB,P(c);rep. 18.00

058-The Prairie by James Fenimore Cooper
04/49 **(60)** RP(a&c),Original 200.00
08/49 **(62)** RP(a&c);rep 75.00
12/50 **(78)** RP(a&c),15¢(c) Price In Double Circle;rep. 35.00
12/53 **(114)** RP(a&c);rep 30.00
03/56 **(131)** RP(a&c);rep 30.00
05/56 **(132)** RP(a&c);rep 30.00
09/58 **(146)** RP,New P(c);rep. 30.00
03/60 **(155)** RP,P(c);rep. 20.00

059-Wuthering Heights by Emily Bronte
05/49 **(60)** HcK(a&c),Original. . . . 225.00
07/51 **(85)** HcK(a&c),15¢(c) Price; rep. 50.00
05/60 **(156)** HcK,GB New P(c);rep 35.00

060-Black Beauty by Anna Sewell
06/49 **(62)** AgF(a&c),Original. . . . 200.00
08/49 **(62)** AgF(a&c);rep 225.00
07/51 **(85)** AgF(a&c),15¢(c) Price; rep 40.00
09/60 **(158)** LbC&NN&StA New Art, LbC New P(c);rep. 35.00

061-The Woman in White by William Wilke Collins
07/49 **(62)** AB(a&c),Original, Maroon & Violet(c)s. 200.00
05/60 **(156)** AB,DgR New P(c);rep 40.00

062-Western Stories (The Luck of Roaring Camp & The Outcasts of Poker Flat) by Bret Harte
08/49 **(62)** HcK(a&c),Original. . . . 200.00
11/51 **(89)** HcK(a&c),15¢(c) Price; rep. 40.00
07/54 **(121)** HcK(a&c);rep 32.00
03/57 **(137)** HcK,New P(c);rep. . . . 30.00
09/59 **(152)** HcK,P(c);rep. 20.00
10/63 **(167)** HcK,P(c);rep. 20.00

063-The Man Without a Country by Edward Everett Hale
09/49 **(62)** HcK(a&c),Original. . . . 200.00
12/50 **(78)** HcK(a&c),15¢(c)Price In Double Circles;rep. 40.00
05/60 **(156)** HcK,GMc New P(c); rep 35.00
01/62 **(165)** AT New Art,GMc P(c), Added Text Pages;rep. 32.00

064-Treasure Island by Robert Louis Stevenson
10/49 **(62)** AB(a&c),Original. 200.00
04/51 **(82)** AB(a&c),15¢(c) Price;rep 40.00
03/54 **(117)** AB(a&c);rep 32.00
03/56 **(131)** AB,New P(c);rep. 30.00
05/57 **(138)** AB,P(c);rep. 18.00
09/58 **(146)** AB,P(c);rep. 18.00
09/60 **(158)** AB,P(c);rep. 18.00

065-Benjamin Franklin by Benjamin Franklin
11/49 **(64)** AB,RtH,GS(Iger Shop), HcK(c),Original 200.00
03/56 **(131)** AB,RtH,GS(Iger Shop), New P(c) ;rep 35.00
01/60 **(154)** AB,RtH,GS(Iger Shop), P(c);rep 20.00

066-The Cloister and the Hearth by Charles Reade
12/49 **(67)** HcK(a&c),Original. . . . 400.00

067-The Scottish Chiefs by Jane Porter
01/50 **(67)** AB(a&c),Original. 200.00
07/51 **(85)** AB(a&c),15¢(c) Price;rep 40.00
04/54 **(118)** AB(a&c);rep 35.00
01/57 **(136)** AB,New P(c);rep. 32.00
01/60 **(154)** AB,P(c);rep. 20.00

068-Julius Caesar by William Shakespeare
02/50 **(70)** HcK(a&c),Original. . . . 200.00
07/51 **(85)** HcK(a&c),15¢(c) Price; rep. 40.00
06/53 **(108)** HcK(a&c);rep 32.00
05/60 **(156)** HcK,LbC New P(c);rep35.00
1962 **(165)** GE&RC New Art, LbC P(c);rep 35.00

069-Around the World in 80 Days by Jules Verne
03/50 **(70)** HcK(a&c),Original. . . . 200.00
09/51 **(87)** HcK(a&c),15¢(c) Price; rep. 45.00
03/55 **(125)** HcK(a&c);rep 32.00
01/57 **(136)** HcK,New P(c);rep. . . . 32.00
09/58 **(146)** HcK,P(c);rep. 20.00
09/59 **(152)** HcK,P(c);rep. 20.00
1961 **(164)** HcK,P(c);rep 20.00

070-The Pilot by James Fenimore Cooper
04/50 **(71)** AB(a&c),Original. 175.00
10/50 **(75)** AB(a&c),15¢(c) Price;rep 45.00
02/52 **(92)** AB(a&c);rep 32.00
03/55 **(125)** AB(a&c);rep 35.00
05/60 **(156)** AB,GMc New P(c);rep 30.00

071-The Man Who Laughs by Victor Hugo
05/50 **(71)** AB(a&c),Original. 250.00
01/62 **(165)** NN,NN New P(c);rep 125.00

072-The Oregon Trail by Francis Parkman
06/50 **(73)** HcK(a&c),Original. . . . 150.00
11/51 **(89)** HcK(a&c),15¢(c) Price; rep. 40.00

Classics Illustrated #75
© Gilberton Publications

Classics Illustrated #85
© Gilberton Publications

Classics Illustrated #91
© Gilberton Publications

07/54 **(121)** HcK(a&c);rep 32.00
03/56 **(131)** HcK,New P(c);rep. . . . 30.00
09/57 **(140)** HcK,P(c);rep. 20.00
05/59 **(150)** HcK,P(c);rep. 18.00
01/61 **(164)** HcK,P(c);rep. 18.00

073-The Black Tulip by Alexandre Dumas
07/50 **(75)** AB(a&c),Original. 550.00

074-Mr. Midshipman Easy by Captain Frederick Marryat
08/50 **(75)** BbL,Original 500.00

075-The Lady of the Lake by Sir Walter Scott
09/50 **(75)** HcK(a&c),Original. . . . 150.00
07/51 **(85)** HcK(a&c),15¢(c) Price; rep. 40.00
04/54 **(118)** HcK(a&c);rep 35.00
07/57 **(139)** HcK,New P(c);rep. . . . 35.00
01/60 **(154)** HcK,P(c);rep. 18.00

076-The Prisoner of Zenda by Anthony Hope Hawkins
10/50 **(75)** HcK(a&c),Original. . . . 150.00
07/51 **(85)** HcK(a&c),15¢(c) Price; rep 40.00
09/53 **(111)** HcK(a&c),rep 35.00
09/55 **(128)** HcK,New P(c);rep. . . . 35.00
09/59 **(152)** HcK,P(c);rep. 20.00
1962 **(165)** HcK,P(c);rep 18.00

077-The Illiad by Homer
11/50 **(78)** AB(a&c),Original. 175.00
09/51 **(87)** AB(a&c),15¢(c) Price;rep 40.00
07/54 **(121)** AB(a&c);rep 35.00
07/57 **(139)** AB,New P(c);rep. 35.00
05/59 **(150)** AB,P(c);rep. 20.00
1962 **(165)** AB,P(c);rep 18.00

078-Joan of Arc by Frederick Shiller
12/50 **(78)** HcK(a&c),Original. . . . 150.00
09/51 **(87)** HcK(a&c),15¢(c) Price; rep. 40.00
11/53 **(113)** HcK(a&c);rep 35.00
09/55 **(128)** HcK,New P(c);rep. . . . 35.00
09/57 **(140)** HcK,P(c);rep. 20.00
05/59 **(150)** HcK,P(c);rep. 20.00
11/60 **(159)** HcK,P(c);rep. 18.00

079-Cyrano de Bergerac by Edmond Rostand
01/51 **(78)** AB(a&c),Original,Movie Promo Inside Front(c) 175.00
07/51 **(85)** AB(a&c),15¢(c) Price;rep 40.00
04/54 **(118)** AB(a&c);rep 35.00
07/56 **(133)** AB,New P(c);rep. 35.00
05/60 **(156)** AB,P(c);rep. 30.00

080-White Fang by Jack London (Last Line Drawn (c)
02/51 **(79)** AB(a&c),Original. 175.00
09/51 **(87)** AB(a&c);rep 40.00
03/55 **(125)** AB(a&c);rep 35.00
05/56 **(132)** AB,New P(c);rep. 35.00
09/57 **(140)** AB,P(c);rep. 20.00
11/59 **(153)** AB,P(c);rep. 20.00

081-The Odyssey by Homer (P(c)s From Now on)
03/51 **(82)** HyG,AB P(c),Original . 175.00

082-The Master of Ballantrae by Robert Louis Stevenson
04/51 **(82)** LDr,AB P(c),Original. . 150.00

083-The Jungle Book by Rudyard Kipling
05/51 **(85)** WmB&AB,AB P(c), Original 150.00
08/53 **(110)** WmB&AB,AB P(c);rep 20.00
03/55 **(125)** WmB&AB,AB P(c);rep 20.00
05/56 **(134)** WmB&AB,AB P(c);rep 20.00
01/58 **(142)** WmB&AB,AB P(c);rep 20.00
05/59 **(150)** WmB&AB,AB P(c);rep 18.00
11/60 **(159)** WmB&AB,AB P(c);rep 18.00

084-The Gold Bug & Other Stories (Inc. The Telltale Heart & The Cask of Amontillado) by Edgar Allan Poe
06/51 **(85)** AB,RP,JLv,AB P(c), Original 200.00

085-The Sea Wolf by Jack London
08/51 **(85)** AB,AB P(c),Original . . 150.00
07/54 **(121)** AB,AB P(c);rep. 20.00
05/56 **(132)** AB,AB P(c);rep. 20.00
11/57 **(141)** AB,AB P(c);rep 20.00
03/61 **(161)** AB,AB P(c);rep. 18.00

086-Under Two Flags by Oiuda
08/51 **(87)** MDb,AB P(c),Original. 125.00
03/54 **(117)** MDb,AB P(c);rep 25.00
07/57 **(139)** MDb,AB P(c);rep 20.00
09/60 **(158)** MDb,AB P(c);rep 20.00

087-A Midsummer Nights Dream by William Shakespeare
09/51 **(87)** AB,AB P(c),Original . . 125.00
03/61 **(161)** AB,AB P(c);rep. 20.00

088-Men of Iron by Howard Pyle
10/51 **(89)** HD,LDr,GS,Original . . 125.00
01/60 **(154)** HD,LDr,GS,P(c);rep . . 20.00

089-Crime and Punishment by Fedor Dostoevsky
11/51 **(89)** RP,AB P(c),Original . . 125.00
09/59 **(152)** RP,AB P(c);rep. 25.00

090-Green Mansions by William Henry Hudson
12/51 **(89)** AB,AB P(c),Original . . 125.00
01/59 **(148)** AB,New LbC P(c);rep. 30.00
1962 **(165)** AB,LbC P(c);rep 18.00

091-The Call of the Wild by Jack London
01/52 **(92)** MDb,P(c),Original. . . . 100.00
10/53 **(112)** MDb,P(c);rep 20.00
03/55**(125)**MDb,P(c),'PictureProgress' Onn. Back(c);rep 20.00
09/56 **(134)** MDb,P(c);rep 20.00
03/58 **(143)** MDb,P(c);rep 18.00
1962 **(165)** MDb,P(c);rep. 18.00

092-The Courtship of Miles Standish by Henry Wadsworth Longfellow
02/52 **(92)** AB,AB P(c),Original . . 100.00
1962 **(165)** AB,AB P(c);rep 20.00

093-Pudd'nhead Wilson by Mark Twain
03/52 **(94)** HcK,HcK P(c),Original 100.00
1962 **(165)** HcK,GMc New P(c);rep 25.00

094-David Balfour by Robert Louis Stevenson
04/52 **(94)** RP,P(c),Original 125.00

095-All Quiet on the Western Front by Erich Maria Remarque
05/52 **(96)** MDb,P(c),Original. . . . 200.00
05/52 **(99)** MDb,P(c),Original. 85.00

096-Daniel Boone by John Bakeless
06/52 **(97)** AB,P(c),Original 100.00
03/54 **(117)** AB,P(c);rep. 20.00
09/55 **(128)** AB,P(c);rep. 20.00
05/56 **(132)** AB,P(c);rep. 20.00
—— **(134)** AB,P(c),'Story of Jesus'on Back(c);rep. 20.00
09/60 **(158)** AB,P(c);rep. 20.00

Classics Illustrated #105
© Gilberton Publications

Classics Illustrated #109
© Gilberton Publications

Classics Illustrated #120
© Gilberton Publications

097-King Solomon's Mines by H. Rider Haggard
07/52 **(96)** HcK,P(c),Original 100.00
04/54 **(118)** HcK,P(c);rep. 20.00
03/56 **(131)** HcK,P(c);rep. 20.00
09/51 **(141)** HcK,P(c);rep. 20.00
09/60 **(158)** HcK,P(c);rep. 18.00

098-The Red Badge of Courage by Stephen Crane
08/52 **(98)** MDb,GS,P(c),Original. 100.00
04/54 **(118)** MDb,GS,P(c);rep 20.00
05/56 **(132)** MDb,GS,P(c);rep 20.00
01/58 **(142)** MDb,GS,P(c);rep 20.00
09/59 **(152)** MDb,GS,P(c);rep 20.00
03/61 **(161)** MDb,GS,P(c);rep 20.00

099-Hamlet by William Shakespeare
09/52 **(98)** AB,P(c),Original 100.00
07/54 **(121)** AB,P(c);rep. 20.00
11/57 **(141)** AB,P(c);rep. 20.00
09/60 **(158)** AB,P(c);rep. 18.00

100-Mutiny on the Bounty by Charles Nordhoff
10/52 **(100)** MsW,HcK P(c),Orig. . 100.00
03/54 **(117)** MsW,HcK P(c);rep . . . 20.00
05/56 **(132)** MsW,HcK P(c);rep . . . 20.00
01/58 **(142)** MsW,HcK P(c);rep . . . 20.00
03/60 **(155)** MsW,HcK P(c);rep . . . 18.00

101-William Tell by Frederick Schiller
11/52 **(101)** MDb,HcK P(c),Orig. . 100.00
04/54 **(118)** MDb,HcK P(c);rep . . . 20.00
11/57 **(141)** MDb,HcK P(c);rep . . . 20.00
09/60 **(158)** MDb,HcK P(c);rep . . . 18.00

102-The White Company by Sir Arthur Conan Doyle
12/52 **(101)** AB,P(c),Original 150.00
1962 **(165)** AB,P(c);rep 35.00

103-Men Against the Sea by Charles Nordhoff
01/53 **(104)** RP,HcK P(c),Original 100.00
12/53 **(114)** RP,HcK P(c);rep 30.00
03/56 **(131)** RP,New P(c);rep. 35.00
03/59 **(149)** RP,P(c);rep. 30.00
09/60 **(158)** RP,P(c);rep. 38.00

104-Bring 'Em Back Alive by Frank Buck & Edward Anthony
02/53 **(105)** HcK,HcK P(c)Original100.00
04/54 **(118)** HcK,HcK P(c);rep. . . . 20.00
07/56 **(133)** HcK,HcK P(c);rep. . . . 20.00
05/59 **(150)** HcK,HcK P(c);rep. . . . 18.00
09/60 **(158)** HcK,HcK P(c);rep. . . . 18.00

105-From the Earth to the Moon by Jules Verne
03/53 **(106)** AB,P(c),Original 100.00
04/54 **(118)** AB,P(c);rep 20.00
03/56 **(132)** AB,P(c);rep 20.00
11/57 **(141)** AB,P(c);rep 20.00
09/58 **(146)** AB,P(c);rep 20.00
05/60 **(156)** AB,P(c);rep 20.00

106-Buffalo Bill by William F. Cody
04/53 **(107)** MDb,P(c),Original. . . 100.00
04/54 **(118)** MDb,P(c);rep 20.00
03/56 **(132)** MDb,P(c);rep 20.00
01/58 **(142)** MDb,P(c);rep 20.00
03/61 **(161)** MDb,P(c);rep 18.00

107-King of the Khyber Rifles by Talbot Mundy
05/53 **(108)** SMz,P(c),Original . . . 100.00
04/54 **(118)** SMz,P(c);rep. 20.00
09/58 **(146)** SMz,P(c);rep 20.00
09/60 **(158)** SMz,P(c);rep 18.00

108-Knights of the Round Table by Howard Pyle?
06/53 **(108)** AB,P(c),Original 100.00
06/53 **(109)** AB,P(c),Original 70.00
03/54 **(117)** AB,P(c);rep 20.00
11/59 **(153)** AB,P(c);rep 18.00
1962 **(165)** AB,P(c);rep 18.00

109-Pitcairn's Island by Charles Nordhoff
07/53 **(110)** RP,P(c),Original 100.00
1962 **(165)** RP,P(c);rep 20.00

110-A Study in Scarlet by Sir Arthur Conan Doyle
08/53 **(111)** SMz,P(c),Original . . . 200.00
1962 **(165)** SMz,P(c);rep 100.00

111-The Talisman by Sir Walter Scott
09/53 **(112)** HcK,HcK P(c),
Original 100.00
1962 **(165)** HcK,HcK P(c);rep 20.00

112-Adventures of Kit Carson by John S. C. Abbott
10/53 **(113)** RP,P(c),Original 100.00
11/55 **(129)** RP,P(c);rep 20.00
11/57 **(141)** RP,P(c);rep 20.00
09/59 **(152)** RP,P(c);rep 18.00
03/61 **(161)** RP,P(c);rep 18.00

113-The Forty-Five Guardsmen by Alexandre Dumas
11/53 **(114)** MDb,P(c),Original . . . 150.00

114-The Red Rover by James Fenimore Cooper
12/53 **(115)** PrC,JP P(c),Original . 150.00

115-How I Found Livingston by Sir Henry Stanley
01/54 **(116)** SF&ST,P(c),Original . 200.00

116-The Bottle Imp by Robert Louis Stevenson
02/54 **(117)** LC,P(c),Original 200.00

117-Captains Courageous by Rudyard Kipling
03/54 **(118)** PrC,P(c),Original . . . 200.00

118-Rob Roy by Sir Walter Scott
04/54 **(119)** RP,WIP,P(c),Original. 200.00

119-Solders of Fortune by Richard Harding Davis
05/54 **(120)** KS,P(c),Original 150.00

120-The Hurricane by Charles Nordhoff
1954 **(121)** LC,LC P(c),Original . . 150.00

121-Wild Bill Hickok
07/54 **(122)** MI,ST,P(c),Original . . 125.00
05/56 **(132)** MI,ST,P(c);rep 20.00
11/57 **(141)** MI,ST,P(c);rep. 20.00
01/60 **(154)** MI,ST,P(c);rep 20.00

122-The Mutineers by Charles Boardman Hawes
09/54 **(123)** PrC,P(c),Original . . . 150.00
01/57 **(136)** PrC,P(c);rep 20.00
09/58 **(146)** PrC,P(c);rep 20.00
09/60 **(158)** PrC,P(c);rep 18.00

123-Fang and Claw by Frank Buck
11/54 **(124)** LnS,P(c),Original . . . 125.00
07/56 **(133)** LnS,P(c);rep 20.00
03/58 **(143)** LnS,P(c);rep 20.00
01/60 **(154)** LnS,P(c);rep 18.00

124-The War of the Worlds by H. G. Wells
01/55 **(125)** LC,LC P(c),Original . 200.00
03/56 **(131)** LC,LC P(c);rep 20.00
11/57 **(141)** LC,LC P(c);rep 20.00
01/59 **(148)** LC,LC P(c);rep 20.00
05/60 **(156)** LC,LC P(c);rep 25.00
1962 **(165)** LC,LC P(c);rep 20.00

125-The Ox Bow Incident by Walter Van Tilberg Clark
03/55 **(—-)** NN,P(c),Original 125.00
03/58 **(143)** NN,P(c);rep 20.00
09/59 **(152)** NN,P(c);rep 20.00

Classics Illustrated #130
© Gilberton Publications

Classics Illustrated #141
© Gilberton Publications

Classics Illustrated #156
© Gilberton Publications

03/61 **(149)** NN,P(c);rep 20.00

126-The Downfall
by Emile Zola
05/55 **(—)** LC,LC P(c),Original,' Picture Progress'Replaces Reorder List. 125.00

127-The King of the Mountains
by Edmond About
07/55 **(128)** NN,P(c),Original 150.00

128-Macbeth
by William Shakespeare
09/55 **(128)** AB,P(c),Original 125.00
03/58 **(143)** AB,P(c);rep 20.00
09/60 **(158)** AB,P(c);rep 20.00

129-Davy Crockett
Author Unknown
11/55 **(129)** LC,P(c),Original 200.00

130-Caesar's Conquests
by Julius Caesar
01/56 **(130)** JO,P(c),Original 125.00
01/58 **(142)** JO,P(c);rep 20.00
09/59 **(152)** JO,P(c);rep 20.00
03/61 **(149)** JO,P(c);rep 20.00

131-The Covered Wagon
by Emerson Hough
03/56 **(131)** NN,P(c),Original 125.00
03/58 **(143)** NN,P(c);rep 20.00
09/59 **(152)** NN,P(c);rep 20.00
09/60 **(158)** NN,P(c);rep 20.00

132-The Dark Frigate
by Charles Boardman Hawes
05/56 **(132)** EW&RWb,P(c),Orig. . 125.00
05/59 **(150)** EW&RWb,P(c);rep . . . 20.00

133-The Time Machine
by H. G. Wells
07/56 **(132)** LC,P(c),Original 175.00
01/58 **(142)** LC,P(c);rep 20.00
09/59 **(152)** LC,P(c);rep 20.00
09/60 **(158)** LC,P(c);rep 20.00

134-Romeo and Juliet
by William Shakespeare
09/56 **(134)** GE,P(c),Original 125.00
03/61 **(161)** GE,P(c);rep 20.00

135-Waterloo
by Emile Erckmann & Alexandre Chatrian
11/56 (135) Grl,AB P(c),Original . 125.00
11/59 **(153)** Grl,AB P(c);rep. 20.00

136-Lord Jim
by Joseph Conrad
01/57 **(136)** GE,P(c),Original 150.00

137-The Little Savage
by Captain Frederick Marryat
03/57 **(136)** GE,P(c),Original 125.00
01/59 **(148)** GE,P(c);rep 20.00
05/60 **(156)** GE,P(c);rep 20.00

138-A Journey to the Center of the Earth
by Jules Verne
05/57 **(136)** NN,P(c),Original 175.00
09/58 **(146)** NN,P(c);rep 20.00
05/60 **(156)** NN,P(c);rep 20.00
09/60 **(158)** NN,P(c);rep 20.00

139-In the Reign of Terror
by George Alfred Henty
07/57 **(139)** GE,P(c),Original 125.00
01/60 **(154)** GE,P(c);rep 20.00

140-On Jungle Trails
by Frank Buck
09/57 **(140)** NN,P(c),Original 125.00
05/59 **(150)** NN,P(c);rep 20.00
01/61 **(160)** NN,P(c);rep 20.00

141-Castle Dangerous
by Sir Walter Scott
11/57 **(141)** StC,P(c),Original. . . . 150.00
09/59 **(152)** StC,P(c);rep 20.00

142-Abraham Lincoln
by Benjamin Thomas
01/58 **(142)** NN,P(c),Original 150.00
01/60 **(154)** NN,P(c);rep 20.00
09/60 **(158)** NN,P(c);rep 20.00

143-Kim
by Rudyard Kipling
03/58 **(143)** JO,P(c)Original. 125.00

144-The First Men in the Moon
by H. G. Wells
05/58 **(143)** GWb,AW,AT,RKr, GMC P(c), Original 175.00
11/59 **(153)** GWb,AW,AT,RKr, GMC, P(c); rep 20.00
03/61 **(161)** GWb,AW,AT,RKr, GMC, P(c); rep 18.00

145-The Crisis
by Winston Churchill
07/58 **(143)** GE,P(c),Original 125.00
05/60 **(156)** GE,P(c);rep 20.00

146-With Fire and Sword
by Henryk Sienkiewicz
09/58 **(143)** GWb,P(c),Original . . 125.00
05/60 **(156)** GWb,P(c);rep 25.00

147-Ben-Hur
by Lew Wallace
11/58 **(147)** JO,P(c),Original 125.00
11/59 **(153)** JO,P(c);rep 65.00
09/60 **(158)** JO,P(c);rep 20.00

148-The Buckaneer
by Lyle Saxon
01/59 **(148)** GE&RJ,NS P(c),orig. 125.00
—— **(568)** GE&RJ,NS P(c),Juniors List Only;rep 20.00

149-Off on a Comet
by Jules Verne
03/59 **(149)** GMc,P(c),Original. . . 125.00
03/60 **(155)** GMc,P(c);rep 20.00
03/61 **(149)** GMc,P(c);rep 20.00

150-The Virginian
by Owen Winster
05/59 **(150)** NN,DrG P(c),Original 200.00
1961 **(164)** NN,DrG P(c);rep 30.00

151-Won by the Sword
by George Alfred Henty
07/59 **(150)** JTg,P(c),Original . . . 125.00
1961 **(164)** JTg,P(c);rep. 25.00

152-Wild Animals I Have Known
by Ernest Thompson Seton
09/59 **(152)** LbC,LbC P(c), Original 125.00
03/61 **(149)** LbC,LbC P(c),P(c);rep 20.00

153-The Invisible Man
by H. G. Wells
11/59 **(153)** NN,GB P(c),Original. 150.00
03/61 **(149)** NN,GB P(c);rep 20.00

154-The Conspiracy of Pontiac
by Francis Parkman
01/60 **(154)** GMc,GMc P(c), Original 125.00

155-The Lion of the North
by George Alfred Henty
03/60 **(154)** NN,GMc P(c),Original125.00

156-The Conquest of Mexico
by Bernal Diaz Del Castillo
05/60 **(156)** BPr,BPr P(c),Original 125.00

157-Lives of the Hunted
by Ernest Thompson Seton
07/60 **(156)** NN,LbC P(c),Original 150.00

158-The Conspirators
by Alexandre Dumas
09/60 **(156)** GMc,GMc P(c), Original 150.00

159-The Octopus
by Frank Norris
11/60 **(159)** GM&GE,LbC P(c), Original 150.00

All comics prices listed are for *Near Mint* condition.

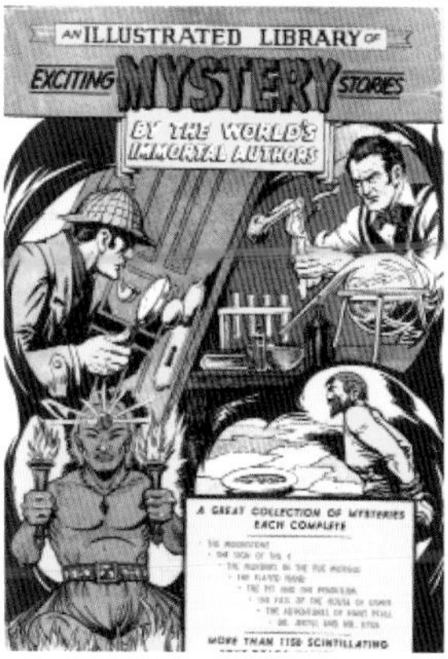

Classics Illustrated Giants-Exciting Mystery Stories © Gilberton Publ.

Classics Illustrated Junior #513 © Gilberton Publications

Classics Illustrated Special United Nations © Gilberton Publ.

160-The Food of the Gods by H.G. Wells
01/61 **(159)** TyT,GMc P(c), Original 150.00
01/61 **(160)** TyT,GMc P(c),Original; Same Except For the HRN# . . 60.00

161-Cleopatra by H. Rider Haggard
03/61 **(161)** NN,Pch P(c),Original 125.00

162-Robur the Conqueror by Jules Verne
05/61 **(162)** GM&DPn,CJ P(c), Original 125.00

163-Master of the World by Jules Verne
07/61 **(163)** GM,P(c),Original. . . . 125.00

164-The Cossack Chief by Nicolai Gogol
1961 **(164)** SyM,P(c),Original . . . 125.00

165-The Queen's Necklace by Alexandre Dumas
01/62 **(164)** GM,P(c),Original. . . . 125.00

166-Tigers and Traitors by Jules Verne
05/62 **(165)** NN,P(c),Original 150.00

167-Faust by Johann Wolfgang von Goethe
08/62 **(165)** NN,NN P(c),Original. 200.00

CLASSICS ILLUSTRATED GIANTS

Gilberton Publications, 1949

An Illustrated Library of Great Adventure Stories -(reps. of Issues 6,7,8,10) 2,000.00
An Illustrated Library of Exciting Mystery Stories -(reps. of Issues 30,21,40,13) 2,100.00
An Illustrated Library of Great Indian Stories -(reps. of Issues 4,17,22,37) 2,000.00

CLASSICS ILLUSTRATED JUNIOR

Gilberton Publications, Oct., 1953

501-Snow White and the Seven Dwarfs 150.00
502-The Ugly Duckling 100.00
503-Cinderella 75.00
504-The Pied Piper 75.00
505-The Sleeping Beauty 75.00
506-The Three Little Pigs 75.00
507-Jack and the Beanstalk 75.00
508-Goldilocks & the Three Bears. 75.00
509-Beauty and the Beast. 75.00
510-Little Red Riding Hood 75.00
511-Puss-N-Boots 75.00
512-Rumpelstiltskin 75.00
513-Pinocchio 75.00
514-The Steadfast Tin Soldier . . . 100.00
515-Johnny Appleseed 75.00
516-Aladdin and His Lamp 75.00
517-The Emperor's New Clothes . 75.00
518-The Golden Goose 75.00
519-Paul Bunyan 75.00
520-Thumbelina 75.00
521-King of the Golden River 75.00
522-The Nightingale. 75.00
523-The Gallant Tailor 75.00
524-The Wild Swans 75.00
525-The Little Mermaid 75.00
526-The Frog Prince 75.00
527-The Golden-Haired Giant 75.00
528-The Penny Prince 75.00
529-The Magic Servants 75.00
530-The Golden Bird 75.00
531-Rapunzel. 75.00
532-The Dancing Princesses. 75.00
533-The Magic Fountain 75.00
534-The Golden Touch 75.00
535-The Wizard of Oz 100.00
536-The Chimney Sweep 75.00
537-The Three Fairies 75.00
538-Silly Hans 75.00
539-The Enchanted Fish 75.00
540-The Tinder-Box 75.00
541-Snow White and Rose Red . . 75.00
542-The Donkey's Tail 75.00
543-The House in the Woods 75.00
544-The Golden Fleece 75.00
545-The Glass Mountain 75.00
546-The Elves and the Shoemaker 75.00
547-The Wishing Table 75.00
548-The Magic Pitcher. 75.00
549-Simple Kate 75.00
550-The Singing Donkey 75.00
551-The Queen Bee 75.00
552-The Three Little Dwarfs 75.00
553-King Thrushbeard 75.00
554-The Enchanted Deer 75.00
555-The Three Golden Apples. . . . 75.00
556-The Elf Mound 75.00
557-Silly Willy. 75.00
558-The Magic Dish,LbC(c). 75.00
559-The Japanese Lantern,LbC(c) 90.00
560-The Doll Princess,LbC(c) 90.00
561-Hans Humdrum,LbC(c). 75.00
562-The Enchanted Pony,LbC(c) . 90.00
563-The Wishing Well,LbC(c) 75.00
564-The Salt Mountain,LbC(c). . . . 75.00
565-The Silly Princess,LbC(c) 75.00
566-Clumsy Hans,LbC(c). 75.00
567-The Bearskin Soldier,LbC(c). . 75.00
568-The Happy Hedgehog,LbC(c). 75.00
569-The Three Giants 75.00
570-The Pearl Princess 75.00
571-How Fire Came to the Indians 75.00
572-The Drummer Boy 75.00
573-The Crystal Ball 75.00
574-Brightboots 75.00
575-The Fearless Prince 75.00
576-The Princess Who Saw Everything 90.00
577-The Runaway Dumpling 100.00

CLASSICS ILLLUSTRATED SPECIAL ISSUE

Gilberton Publications Dec., 1955–July, 1962

N# United Nations 400.00
129-The Story of Jesus,Jesus on Mountain(c) 150.00
129a-Three Camels(c). 150.00
129b-Mountain(c),HRN to 161 . . 125.00
129c-Mountain(c) (1968) 100.00
132A-The Story of America 125.00
135A-The Ten Commandments. . 125.00
138A-Adventures in Science 125.00
138Aa-HRN to 149 . . . . 100.00
138Ab-rep.,12/61 . . . . 100.00
141A-GE,The Rough Rider 125.00
144A-RC,GE,Blazing the Trails . . 125.00
147A-RC,GE,Crossing the Rockies 125.00
150A-Grl,Royal Canadian Police. 125.00
153A-GE,Men, Guns, & Cattle. . . 125.00
156A-GE,GM,The Atomic Age . . . 125.00
159A-GE,GM,Rockets, Jets and Missiles 125.00
162A-RC,GE,War Between the States 165.00
165A-RC/GE,JK,Grl,To the Stars. 125.00
166A-RC/GE,JK,Grl,World War II 150.00
167A-RC/GE,JK,Prehistoric World 150.00
167Aa-HRN to 167. . . . . 110.00

Clown Comics #3
© Harvey Publications

Clue Comics #15
© Hillman Periodicals

Colossus Comics #1
© Sun Publications

CLAY CODY, GUNSLINGER
Better Publications, 1957

1 Western hero . . . 100.00

CLEAN FUN, STARRING 'SHOOGAFOOTS JONES'
Specialty Book Co., 1945

N# . . . 200.00

CLIMAX!
Gilmor Magazines, 1955

1 Mystery . . . 200.00
2 . . . 150.00

CLOAK AND DAGGER
Approved Comics (Ziff-Davis), Fall, 1952

1 NS(c),Al Kennedy of the Secret Service . . . 400.00

CLOWN COMICS
Harvey Publications, 1945

N# . . . 300.00
2 . . . 200.00
3 . . . 200.00

CLUBHOUSE RASCALS
Sussex Publ. Co. 1956

1 Humor . . . 125.00
2 . . . 100.00

CLUB "16"
Famous Funnies, 1948

1 Teen-age . . . 140.00
2 thru 4 . . . @100.00

CLUE COMICS
Hillman Periodicals, 1943

1 O:Boy King,Nightmare,Micro-Face, Twilight,Zippo. . . . 3,000.00
2 . . . 2,000.00
3 Boy King V:The Crane . . . 1,500.00
4 V:The Crane . . . 1,200.00
5 V:The Crane . . . 1,200.00
6 Hells Kitchen . . . 750.00
7 V:Dr. Plasma,Torture(c) . . . 750.00
8 RP,A:The Gold Mummy King . . . 700.00
9 I:Paris . . . 700.00
10 O:Gun Master . . . 700.00
11 A:Gun Master . . . 700.00
12 O:Rackman . . . 700.00
2-1 S&K,O:Nightro,A:Iron Lady. 1,300.00
2-2 S&K,Bondage(c) . . . 1,800.00
2-3 S&K . . . 1,300.00

Becomes:

REAL CLUE CRIME STORIES
June, 1947

2-4 DBw,S&K,True Story of Ma Barker . . . 1,300.00
2-5 S&K, Newface surgery(c) . . 1,000.00
2-6 S&K, Breakout (c) . . . 1,000.00
2-7 S&K, Stick up (c) . . . 1,000.00
2-8 Kidnapping (c) . . . 250.00
2-9 DBa,Boxing fix (c) . . . 250.00
2-10 DBa,Murder (c) . . . 250.00
2-11 Attempted bankrobbery (c) . 250.00
2-12 Murder (c) . . . 250.00
3-1 thru 3-12 . . . @250.00
4-1 thru 4-12 . . . @250.00
5-1 thru 5-12 . . . @200.00
6-1 thru 6-12 . . . @200.00
6-10 Bondage(c) . . . 250.00
7-1 thru 7-12 . . . @175.00
8-1 thru 8-5, May, 1953 . . . @175.00

THE CLUTCHING HAND
American Comics, 1954

1 Horror . . . 500.00

CLYDE BEATTY
Commodore Productions, 1953

1 Photo(c) . . . 400.00

C-M-O COMICS
Comic Corp. of America (Centaur), May, 1942

1 Invisible Terror . . . 2,500.00
2 Super Ann . . . 2,000.00

COCOMALT BIG BOOK OF COMICS
Harry A. Chesler, 1938

1 BoW,PGv,FGu,JCo,(Give away) Little Nemo . . . 4,000.00

CODY OF THE PONY EXPRESS
See: BULLS-EYE

CODY OF THE PONY EXPRESS
Fox Features Syndicate, 1950

1 Western . . . 300.00
2 . . . 250.00
3 . . . 250.00

COLOSSAL FEATURES MAGAZINE
Fox Features Syndicate, 1950

1 (33) Cody of the Pony Express 300.00
2 (34) Cody of the Pony Express 300.00
3 Crime . . . 300.00

COLOSSUS COMICS
Sun Publications March, 1940

1 A:Colossus . . . 10,000.00

COLT .45
Dell Publishing Co., 1958

1 Ph(c) all . . . 300.00
2 . . . 260.00
3 . . . 250.00
4 . . . 250.00
5 . . . 250.00
6 ATh . . . 275.00
7 . . . 250.00
8 . . . 250.00
9 . . . 250.00

COLUMBIA COMICS
William H. Wise Co., 1944

1 Joe Palooka,Charlie Chan . . . 450.00

COMBAT
Marvel Atlas, June, 1952

1 JMn,War Stories, Bare Bayonets . . . 350.00
2 RH, Break Thru,(Dedicated to US Infantry) . . . 250.00
3 JMn(c) . . . 200.00
4 BK . . . 225.00
5 thru 10 . . . @200.00
11 April, 1953 . . . 250.00

COMBAT CASEY
See: WAR COMBAT

Combat Kelly and the Deadly Dozen #12 © Marvel Comics Group

Comedy Comics #6 © Marvel Comics Group

Comic Cavalcade #6 © DC Comics

COMBAT KELLY AND THE DEADLY DOZEN

Marvel Atlas, Nov., 1951

1 RH,Korean War Stories 350.00
2 Big Push 200.00
3 The Volunteer 175.00
4 JMn,V:Communists 175.00
5 JMn,OW,V:Communists. 175.00
6 V:Communists 175.00
7 JMn,V:Communists 175.00
8 JMn,Death to the Reds 175.00
9 . . . . 175.00
10 JMn(c). 175.00
11 . . . . 150.00
12 thru 16. . . . . @150.00
17 A:Combat Casey. 175.00
18 A:Battle Brady. 125.00
19 V:Communists. 125.00
20 V:Communists 125.00
21 Transvestite Cover 75.00
22 thru 40 . . . . @100.00
41 thru 44 Aug., 1957 . . . . @100.00

COMEDY COMICS

Marvel Timely, 1942

9 . . . . 3,600.00
10 . . . . 2,800.00
11 . . . . 675.00
12 . . . . 250.00
13 Funny animal 250.00
14 Super Rabbit. 700.00
15 . . . . 200.00
16 . . . . 200.00
17 . . . . 200.00
18 . . . . 200.00
19 . . . . 200.00
20 . . . . 200.00
21 thru 32 . . . . @150.00
33 HK 200.00
34 BW 300.00
Becomes:

MARGIE COMICS

Marvel Comics, 1946

35 thru 39 Glamour Girl . . . . . . @250.00
40 . . . . 200.00
41 thru 49 . . . . @225.00
Becomes:

RENO BROWNE

Marvel Comics, 1950

50 Photo(c); Western babe 400.00
51 Photo(c); 350.00
52 Photo(c); 350.00

COMEDY COMICS

Marvel Animirth 1948–49

1 HK, Romance,F:Hedy, Millie,
Tessie 400.00
2 . . . . 200.00
3 . . . . 200.00
4 HK 225.00
5 . . . . 150.00
6 . . . . 150.00
7 . . . . 150.00
8 . . . . 150.00
9 . . . . 150.00
10 . . . . 150.00

COMIC ALBUM

Dell Publishing Co., March-May, 1958

1 Donald Duck 175.00
2 Bugs Bunny 125.00
3 Donald Duck 150.00
4 Tom & Jerry 125.00
5 Woody Woodpecker. 125.00
6 Bugs Bunny 125.00
7 Popeye. 150.00
8 Tom & Jerry 125.00
9 Woody Woodpecker. 125.00
10 Bugs Bunny 125.00
11 Popeye 160.00
12 Tom & Jerry 100.00
13 Woody Woodpecker 100.00
14 Bugs Bunny 100.00
15 Popeye 125.00
16 Flintstones. 150.00
17 Space Mouse 125.00
18 3 Stooges,Ph(c) 150.00

COMIC BOOKS

Metropolitan Printing Co. 1950

1 Boots & Saddles 125.00
1 Green Lama-The Green Jet . . 500.00
1 My Pal Dizzy 100.00
1 Talullah. 150.00
1 New World 100.00

COMIC CAPERS

Marvel Comics, 1944

1 Funny animal, Super Rabbit . . 300.00
2 . . . . 200.00
3 . . . . 150.00
4 . . . . 150.00
5 . . . . 150.00
6 . . . . 150.00

COMIC CAVALCADE

DC Comics, 1942–43

1 Green Lantern, Flash,
Wildcat, Wonder Woman,
Black Pirate 15,000.00
2 ShM,B:Mutt & Jeff. 4,000.00
3 ShM,B:HotHarrigan,Sorcerer 2,700.00
4 Gay Ghost, A:Scribby,
A:Red Tornado 2,500.00
5 Gr.Lantern,Flash,W.Woman . 2,400.00
6 Flash,W.Woman,Gr.Lantern . 2,000.00
7 A:Red Tornado, E:Scribby . . 2,000.00
8 Flash,W.Woman,Gr.Lantern . 2,000.00
9 Flash,W.Woman,Gr.Lantern . 2,000.00
10 Flash,W.Woman,Gr.Lantern. 2,000.00
11 Flash,W.Woman,Gr.Lantern. 1,400.00
12 E:Red, White & Blue 1,400.00
13 A:Solomon Grundy. 2,500.00
14 Flash,W.Woman,Gr.Lantern. 1,400.00
15 B:Johnny Peril 1,400.00
16 Flash,W.Woman,Gr.Lantern. 1,800.00
17 Flash,W.Woman,Gr.Lantern. 1,500.00
18 Flash,W.Woman,Gr.Lantern. 1,500.00
19 Flash,W.Woman,Gr.Lantern. 1,500.00
20 Flash,W.Woman,Gr.Lantern. 1,500.00
21 Flash,W.Woman,Gr.Lantern. 1,500.00
22 A:Atom 1,500.00
23 A:Atom 1,500.00
24 A:Solomon Grundy. 2,200.00
25 A:Black Canary 2,000.00
26 ATh, E:Mutt & Jeff 2,000.00
27 ATh,ATh(c) 2,000.00
28 ATh E:Flash, Wonder Woman
Green Lantern 2,000.00
29 E:Johnny Peril 1,800.00
30 RG,B:Fox & Crow 700.00
31 thru 39 RG . . . . @500.00
40 RG,ShM. 300.00
41 thru 49 RG,ShM . . . . @275.00
50 thru 62 RG,ShM . . . . @350.00
63 RG,ShM, July, 1954 . . . . 600.00

COMIC COMICS

Fawcett Publications, 1946

1 Captain Kidd 350.00
2 BW. 400.00
3 BW. 400.00
4 BW. 400.00
5 BW. 400.00
6 BW. 400.00
7 BW. 400.00
8 BW. 400.00
9 BW. 400.00
10 BW 400.00

Comics on Parade #5
© United Features Syndicate

Comics on Parade #47
© United Features Syndicate

Commander Battle and the Atomic Submarine #7 © American Comics

COMIC LAND
Fact and Fiction, 1946

1 Sandusky and the Senator . . . 350.00

COMICS, THE
Dell Publishing Co., March, 1937

1 I:Tom Mix & Arizona Kid 3,500.00
2 A:Tom Mix & Tom Beaty 2,500.00
3 A:Alley Oop 2,000.00
4 same 2,000.00
5 same 2,000.00
6 thru 11 same . . . . @2,000.00

THE COMICS CALENDAR
True Comics Press, 1946

1 . . . . 750.00

COMICS DIGEST
Parents Magazine Institute, 1942

1 True adventure. 250.00

COMICS FOR KIDS
Marvel Timely, 1945

1 Funny animal 300.00
2 . . . . 300.00

COMICS MAGAZINE
See: FUNNY PAGES

COMICS NOVEL
Fawcett Publications, 1947

1 Anarcho Dictator of Death 500.00

COMICS ON PARADE
United Features Syndicate, April, 1938–Feb., 1955

1 B:Tarzan,Captain and the Kids, Little Mary, Mixup,Abbie & Slats, Broncho Bill,Li'l Abner 6,000.00
2 Circus Parade of all 3,000.00
3 . . . . 2,500.00
4 On Rocket. 2,000.00
5 All at the Store 2,000.00
6 All at Picnic 1,500.00
7 Li'l Abner(c). 1,500.00
8 same 1,500.00
9 same 1,500.00
10 same 1,500.00
11 same 1,200.00
12 same 1,200.00
13 same 1,200.00
14 Abbie n' Slats (c) 1,200.00
15 Li'l Abner(c) 1,200.00
16 Abbie n' Slats(c). 1,200.00
17 Tarzan,Abbie n' Slats(c). . . . 1,300.00
18 Li'l Abner(c) 1,200.00
19 same 1,200.00
20 same 1,200.00
21 Li'l Abner(c) 1,000.00
22 Tail Spin Tommy(c). 1,000.00
23 Abbie n' Slats(c). 1,000.00
24 Tail Spin Tommy(c). 1,000.00
25 Li'l Abner(c) 1,000.00
26 Abbie n' Slats(c). 1,000.00
27 Li'l Abner(c) 1,000.00
28 Tail Spin Tommy(c). 1,000.00
29 Abbie n' Slats(c). 1,000.00
30 Li'l Abner(c). 600.00
31 The Captain & the Kids(c) . . . 400.00
32 Nancy and Fritzi Ritz(c) 350.00
33 Li'l Abner(c). 450.00
34 The Captain & the Kids(c) . . . 350.00
35 Nancy and Fritzi Ritz(c) 350.00
36 Li'l Abner(c). 450.00
37 The Captain & the Kids(c) . . . 350.00
38 Nancy and Fritzi Ritz(c) 300.00
39 Li'l Abner(c). 450.00
40 The Captain & the Kids(c) . . . 350.00
41 Nancy and Fritzi Ritz(c) 250.00
42 Li'l Abner(c). 450.00
43 The Captain & the Kids(c) . . . 350.00
44 Nancy and Fritzi Ritz(c) 250.00
45 Li'l Abner(c). 350.00
46 The Captain & the Kids(c) . . . 250.00
47 Nancy and Fritzi Ritz(c) 250.00
48 Li'l Abner(c). 350.00
49 The Captain & the Kids(c) . . . 250.00
50 Nancy and Fritzi Ritz(c) 250.00
51 Li'l Abner(c). 350.00
52 The Captain & the Kids(c) . . . 250.00
53 Nancy and Fritzi Ritz(c) 250.00
54 Li'l Abner(c). 350.00
55 Nancy and Fritzi Ritz(c) 250.00
56 The Captain & the Kids(c) . . . 250.00
57 Nancy and Fritzi Ritz(c) 250.00
58 Li'l Abner(c). 350.00
59 The Captain & the Kids(c) . . . 250.00
60 thru 76 Nancy & Fritzi Ritz(c) . . . . @200.00
77 Nancy & Sluggo(c) 150.00
78 thru 104 Nancy & Sluggo(c) @150.00

COMICS REVUE
St. John Publ. Co., 1947

1 Ella Cinders and Blackie 250.00
2 Hap Hopper 200.00
3 Iron Vic. 200.00
4 Eva Cinders 200.00
5 Gordo. 200.00

COMMANDER BATTLE AND THE ATOMIC SUBMARINE
American Comics Group, 1954

1 3-D(c) 1,300.00
2 . . . . 750.00
3 H-Bomb-3-D type. 800.00
4 . . . . 750.00
5 . . . . 750.00
6 . . . . 750.00
7 . . . . 750.00

COMMANDO ADVENTURES
Marvel Atlas, June, 1957

1 Seek, Find and Destroy 300.00
2 MD, Hit 'em and Hit 'em Hard, Aug.,1957 . . . . 150.00

COMPLETE BOOK OF COMICS AND FUNNIES
William H. Wise & Co., 1945

1 Wonderman-Magnet 700.00

COMPLETE BOOK OF TRUE CRIME COMICS
William H. Wise & Co., 1945

1 rep. Crime Does Not Pay . . . 2,000.00

COMPLETE COMICS
See: AMAZING COMICS

COMPLETE LOVE MAGAZINE
Ace Periodicals, 1951–56
(Formerly a pulp magazine)

1 (26/2. . . . . 150.00
2 (26/3) 100.00
3 thru 8 (27/1–27/6) . . . . @100.00
9 & 10 (28/1–28/2) 100.00

Complete Mystery #4
© Marvel Comics Group

Contact Comics #12
© Aviation Press

Cookie #9
© American Comics Group

11 thru 16 (29/1–29/6) . . . . @100.00
17 thru 22 (30/1–30/6) . . . . @100.00
23 thru 28 (31/1–31/6) . . . . @100.00
29 thru 32 (32/1–32/4) . . . . @100.00

COMPLETE MYSTERY
Marvel, Aug., 1948

1 Seven Dead Men 600.00
2 Jigsaw of Doom 450.00
3 Fear in the Night 450.00
4 A Squealer Dies Fast 450.00

Becomes:

TRUE COMPLETE MYSTERY
Marvel, 1949

5 Rice Mancini, The Deadly Dude 300.00
6 Ph(c),Frame-up that Failed . . . 250.00
7 Ph(c),Caught 250.00
8 Ph(c),The Downfall of Mr. Anderson, Oct., 1949 . . . . . . 250.00

CONFESSIONS ILLUSTRATED
E.C. Comics, 1956

1WW,JO,JCr,JKa,Adult romance 350.00
2 JCr,RC,JKa,JO 300.00

CONFESSIONS OF LOVE
Artful Publications, April, 1950

1 . . . . 300.00
2 July, 1950 . . . . 200.00

CONFESSIONS OF LOVE
Star Publications, July, 1952

11 AW,LbC(c)Intimate Secrets of Daring Romance 250.00
12 AW,LbC(c),I Couldn't Say No 250.00
13 AW,LbC(c),Heart Break 250.00
14 AW,LbC(c),My Fateful Love . 200.00
4 JyD,AW,LbC(c),The Longing Heart 200.00
5 AW,LbC(c),I Wanted Love 200.00
6 AW,LbC(c),My Jealous Heart. . 200.00

Becomes:

CONFESSIONS OF ROMANCE
Nov., 1953

7 LbC(c)Too Good 250.00
8 AW,LbC(c),I Lied About Love . 200.00
9 WW,AW,LbC(c),I Paid Love's Price 250.00
10 JyD,AW,LbC(c),My Heart Cries for Love 200.00
11 JyD,AW,LbC(c),Intimate Confessions, Nov., 1954 . . . . 200.00

CONFESSIONS OF LOVELORN
See: LOVELORN

CONGO BILL
DC Comics, 1954–56

1 . . . . 2,000.00
2 thru 7 . . . . @1,500.00

CONQUEROR COMICS
Albrecht Publications, Winter, 1945

1 . . . . 250.00

CONQUEST
Famous Funnies, 1955

1 Historical adventure 100.00

CONTACT COMICS
Aviation Press, July, 1944

N# LbC(c),B:Black Venus, Golden Eagle 900.00
2 LbC(c),Peace Jet 700.00
3 LbC(c),LbC,E:Flamingo 650.00
4 LbC(c),LbC 600.00
5 LbC(c),A:Phantom Flyer 650.00
6 LbC(c),HK 750.00
7 LbC(c),Flying Tigers 600.00
8 LbC(c),Peace Jet 600.00
9 LbC(c),LbC,A:Marine Flyers . . 600.00
10 LbC(c),A:Bombers of the AAF 600.00
11 LbC(c),HK,AF,Salutes Naval Aviation 700.00
12 LbC(c),A:Sky Rangers, Air Kids, May, 1946 . . . . 1,300.00

COO COO COMICS
Nedor/Animated Cartoons (Standard), Oct., 1942

1 O&I:Super Mouse 500.00
2 . . . . 250.00
3 . . . . 200.00
4 . . . . 225.00
5 . . . . 225.00
6 thru 10 . . . . @150.00
11 thru 33 . . . . @150.00
34 thru 40 FF illustration . . . . . @250.00
41 FF 400.00
42 FF 350.00
43 FF illustration 250.00
44 FF illustration 250.00
45 FF illustration 250.00
46 FF illustration 250.00
47 FF 350.00
48 FF illustration 250.00
49 FF illustration 250.00
50 FF illustration 250.00
51 thru 61 . . . . @125.00
62 April, 1952 . . . . 100.00

"COOKIE"
Michel Publ./Regis Publ. (American Comics Group) April, 1946

1 . . . . 350.00
2 . . . . 250.00
3 thru 5 . . . . @200.00
6 thru 20 . . . . @150.00
21 thru 30 . . . . @100.00
31 thru 54 . . . . @100.00
55 Aug., 1955 . . . . 100.00

COSMO CAT
Fox Features Syndicate, 1946

1 . . . . 325.00
2 . . . . 200.00
3 O:Cosmo Cat 225.00
4 thru 10 . . . . @150.00

COSMO THE MERRY MARTIAN
Radio Comics/Archie Publ., 1958

1 Funny alien 250.00
2 . . . . 200.00
3 . . . . 200.00
4 . . . . 200.00
5 . . . . 200.00
6 . . . . 200.00

COURAGE COMICS
J. Edward Slavin, 1945

1 . . . . 250.00
2 Boxing (c) 250.00
77 Naval rescue, PT99 (c) 250.00

Young Men #25
© Marvel Comics Group

Cowgirl Romances #12
© Fiction House

Crack Comics #14
© Comic Magazines

COWBOY ACTION
See: WESTERN THRILLERS

COWBOY COMICS
See: STAR RANGER

COWBOY LOVE
Fawcett Publications, 1949

1 Photo(c), Western romance. . . 300.00
2 Photo(c). 100.00
3 Photo(c). 100.00
4 Photo(c). 100.00
5 Photo(c). 100.00
6 Photo(c). 100.00
7 GE,AW,Photo(c). 150.00
8 thru 11 Photo(c) . . . . @100.00

COWBOY ROMANCES
Marvel, Oct., 1949

1 Ph(c),Outlaw and the Lady . . . 275.00
2 Ph(c),William Holden/Mona Freeman,Streets of Laredo . . 250.00
3 Phc,Romance in Roaring Valley 150.00

Becomes:

YOUNG MEN
Marvel, 1950

4 A Kid Names Shorty. 250.00
5 Jaws of Death 200.00
6 Man-Size 200.00
7 The Last Laugh 200.00
8 Adventure stories continued . . 200.00
9 Draft Dodging story 200.00
10 JMn,US Draft Story. 200.00
11 Adventure stories continued . . 200.00
12 JMn,B:On the Battlefield, inc.Spearhead 200.00
13 RH,Break-through. 200.00
14 GC,RH,Fox Hole. 200.00
15 GC,JMn,Battlefield stories cont.. . . . . 200.00
16 Sniper Patrol. 200.00
17 Battlefield stories cont, ... 200.00
18 BEv,Warlord 200.00
19 BEv 200.00
20 BEv,E:On the Battlefield 200.00
21 B:Flash Foster and his High Gear Hot Shots 200.00
22 Screaming Tires 200.00
23 E:Flash Foster and his High Gear Hot Shots 200.00
24 BEv,B:Capt. America,Human Torch,Sub-Mariner,O:Capt. America,Red Skull 3,600.00
25 BEv,JR, Human Torch,Capt. America,Sub-Mariner 1,500.00
26 BEv,Human Torch, Capt. America,Sub Mariner 1,500.00
27 Bev, Human Torch/Toro V:Hypnotist 1,400.00
28 E:Human Torch, Capt.America, Sub Mariner,June, 1954 . . . 1,400.00

COWBOYS 'N' INJUNS
Compix (M.E. Enterprises), 1946-47

1 Funny Animal Western 300.00
2 thru 5 . . . . @250.00
6 thru 8 See: *A-1 Comics*, #23,#41,#48

COWBOY WESTERN/ COMICS/HEROES
See: YELLOWJACKET

COWGIRL ROMANCES
Fiction House Magazine, 1952

1 The Range of Singing Guns . . 450.00
2 The Lady of Lawless Range . . 225.00
3 Daughter of the Devil's Band. 200.00
4 Bride Wore Buckskin 200.00
5 Taming of Lone-Star Lou 200.00
6 Rose of Mustang Mesa 175.00
7 Nobody Loves a Gun Man. . . . 175.00
8 Wild Beauty 175.00
9 Gun-Feud Sweethearts 175.00
10 JKa,AW,No Girl of Stampede Valley. 375.00
11 Love is Where You Find It. . . . 175.00
12 Dec., 1952 . . . . 175.00

COWGIRL ROMANCES
See: DARING MYSTERY

COW PUNCHER
Avon Periodicals/ Realistic Publ., Jan., 1947

1 JKu 500.00
2 JKu,JKa(c),Bondage (c) 400.00
3 AU(c) 350.00
4 . . . . 350.00
5 . . . . 350.00
6 WJo(c),Drug story 400.00
7 . . . . 350.00
1 JKu 350.00

CRACK COMICS
Comic Magazines (Quality Comics Group) 1940

1 LF,O:Black Condor,Madame Fatal, Red Torpedo, Rock Bradden, Space Legion, B:The Clock,Wizard Wells . 9,000.00
2 Black Condor (c) 4,000.00
3 The Clock (c) 3,000.00
4 Black Condor (c) 2,700.00
5 LF,The Clock (c) 2,000.00
6 PG,Black Condor (c) 1,800.00
7 Clock (c) 1,800.00
8 Black Condor (c) 1,800.00
9 Clock (c) 1,800.00
10 Black Condor (c) 1,800.00
11 LF,PG,Clock (c) 1,500.00
12 LF,PG,Black Condor (c) 1,500.00
13 LF,PG,Clock (c) 1,500.00
14 AMc,LF,PG,Clack Condor(c) 1,500.00
15 AMc,LF,PG,Clock (c) 1,500.00
16 AMc,LF,PG,Black Condor(c) 1,500.00
17 FGu,AMc,LF,PG,Clock (c) . . 1,500.00
18 AMc,LF,PG,Black Condor(c) 1,500.00
19 AMc,LF,PG,Clock (c) 1,500.00
20 AMc,LF,PG,BlackCondor(c) 1,500.00
21 AMc,LF,PG,same 1,200.00
22 LF,PG,same 1,200.00
23 AMc,LF,PG,same 1,200.00
24 AMc,LF,PG,same 1,200.00
25 AMc,same 1,000.00
26 AMc,same 1,000.00
27 AMc,I&O:Captain Triumph . . 1,800.00
28 Captain Triumph (c). 1,000.00
29 A:Spade the Ruthless 1,000.00
30 I:Biff 800.00
31 Helps Spade Dig His Own Grave. 500.00
32 Newspaper (c) 500.00
33 V:Men of Darkness 500.00
34 . . . . 500.00
35 V:The Man Who Conquered Flame. 500.00
36 Good Neighbor Tour 500.00
37 V:The Tyrant of Toar Valley. . . 500.00
38 Castle of Shadows 500.00
39 V:Crime over the City 500.00
40 Thrilling Murder Mystery 350.00
41 . . . . 350.00

Crack Western #63
© Comic Magazines

Crackajack Funnies #1
© Dell Publishing Co.

Crash Comics #1
© Tem Publishing Co.

42 All that Glitters is Not Gold . . . 350.00
43 Smashes the Evil Spell of Silent . . . 350.00
44 V:Silver Tip . . . 350.00
45 V:King-The Jack of all Trades. 350.00
46 V:Mr. Weary . . . 350.00
47 V:Hypnotic Eyes Khor. . . 400.00
48 Murder in the Sky . . . 400.00
49 . . . 400.00
50 A Key to Trouble . . . 400.00
51 V:Werewolf . . . 400.00
52 V:Porcupine . . . 400.00
53 V:Man Who Robbed the Dead 400.00
54 Shoulders the Troubles of the World . . . 400.00
55 Brain against Brawn . . . 400.00
56 Gossip leads to Murder . . . 400.00
57 V:Sitok–Green God of Evil . . . 400.00
58 V:Targets. . . 300.00
59 A Cargo of Mystery . . . 300.00
60 Trouble is no Picnic . . . 300.00
61 V:Mr. Pointer-Finger of Fear . . 300.00
62 V:The Vanishing Vandals . . . 300.00

Becomes:

CRACK WESTERN

Nov., 1949–May, 1951

63 PG, I&O:Two-Gun Lil, B:Frontier Marshal,Arizona Ames, . . . 350.00
64 RC,Arizona AmesV:Two-Legged Coyote . . . 225.00
65 RC,Ames Tramples on Trouble . . . 225.00
66 Arizona Ames Arizona Raines, Tim Holt,Ph(c) . . . 150.00
67 RC, Ph(c),Randolph Scott . . . 225.00
68 Ph(c) . . . 150.00
69 RC. . . 150.00
70 O&I:Whip and Diablo . . . 175.00
71 Bob Allen, Marshall,RC(c). . . 200.00
72 RC,Tim Holt,Ph(c). . . 150.00
73 Tim Holt,Ph(c). . . 100.00
74 RC(c). . . 150.00
75 RC(c). . . 150.00
76 RC(c),Stage Coach to Oblivion . . . 150.00
77 RC(c),Comanche Terror . . . 150.00
78 RC(c),Killers of Laurel Ridge . 150.00
79 RC(c),Fires of Revenge . . . 150.00
80 RC(c),Mexican Massacre . . . 150.00
81 RC(c),Secrets of Terror Canyon . . . 150.00
82 The Killer with a Thousand Faces. . . 125.00
83 Rattlesnake Pete's Revenge . 125.00
84 PG(c),Revolt at Broke Creek . 125.00

CRACKAJACK FUNNIES

Dell Publishing Co., 1938

1 AMc,A:Dan Dunn,The Nebbs, Don Winslow . . . 4,000.00
2 AMc,same. . . 2,000.00
3 AMc,same. . . 1,500.00
4 AMc,same. . . 1,200.00
5 AMc,Naked Women(c) . . . 1,400.00
6 AMc,same. . . 1,100.00
7 AMc,same. . . 1,100.00
8 AMc,same. . . 1,100.00
9 AMc,A:Red Ryder. . . 2,300.00
10 AMc,A:Red Ryder. . . 900.00
11 AMc,A:Red Ryder . . . 800.00
12 AMc,A:Red Ryder. . . 800.00
13 AMc,A:Red Ryder. . . 800.00
14 AMc,A:Red Ryder. . . 800.00
15 AMc,A:Tarzan . . . 900.00
16 AMc. . . 750.00
17 AMc. . . 750.00
18 AMc,A:Stratosphere Jim . . . 750.00
19 AMc. . . 750.00
20 AMc. . . 750.00
21 AMc. . . 750.00
22 AMc. . . 750.00
23 AMc,A:Ellery Queen . . . 750.00
24 AMc. . . 750.00
25 AMc,I:The Owl . . . 1,500.00
26 AMc . . . 1,000.00
27 AMc . . . 1,000.00
28 AMc,A:The Owl . . . 1,000.00
29 AMc,A:Ellery Queen. . . 1,000.00
30 AMc,A:Tarzan. . . 1,000.00
31 AMc,A:Tarzan. . . 1,000.00
32 AMc,O:Owl Girl . . . 1,100.00
33 AMc,A:Tarzan . . . 900.00
34 AMc,same. . . 900.00
35 AMc,same. . . 900.00
36 AMc,same. . . 900.00
37 AMc. . . 900.00
38 AMc. . . 900.00
39 AMc,I:Andy Panada . . . 1,100.00
40 AMc,A:Owl(c) . . . 750.00
41 AMc. . . 750.00
42 AMc. . . 750.00
43 AMc,Terry & The Pirates, A:Owl(c). . . 700.00

CRACKED

Major Magazines, 1958

1 AW. . . 300.00
2 . . . 250.00
3 . . . 250.00
4 . . . 250.00
5 . . . 250.00
6 . . . 250.00
7 thru 10 . . . @200.00
11 thru 20. . . @150.00

CRASH COMICS

Tem Publishing Co., May, 1940

1 S&K,O:Strongman, B:Blue Streak, Perfect Human, Shangra . . 6,000.00
2 S&K . . . 3,500.00
3 S&K . . . 2,500.00
4 S&K,O&I:Catman . . . 6,000.00
5 S&K, Nov., 1940 . . . 2,500.00

CRAZY

Marvel Atlas, Dec., 1953

1 JMn,BEv,satire, Frank N. Steins Castle . . . 450.00
2 JMn,BEv,Beast from 1000 Fathoms. . . 300.00
3 JMn,BEv,RH,Madame Knock-wurst's Whacks Museum. . . 250.00
4 JMn,BEv,DAv,I Love Lucy satire . . . 250.00
5 JMn,BEv,Censorship satire . . . 250.00
6 JMn,BEv,MD,satire . . . 300.00
7 JMn,BEv,RH,satire,July, 1954 250.00

CRIME AND JUSTICE

Capitol Stories/ Charlton Comics 1951–55

1 . . . 400.00
2 . . . 250.00
3 . . . 200.00
4 . . . 200.00
5 . . . 200.00
6 Negligee. . . 250.00
7 . . . 200.00
8 . . . 200.00
9 . . . 350.00
10 . . . 175.00
11 thru 14 . . . @250.00
15 Negligee . . . 250.00
16 . . . 200.00
17 . . . 200.00
18 SD . . . 300.00
19 thru 21 . . . @200.00

Becomes:

BADGE OF JUSTICE

Charlton Comics, 1955

22 (1) . . . 200.00
23 (2). . . 150.00

Crime and Punishment #10
© Lev Gleason Publications

Crime Detective Vol. 3 #1
© Hillman Publications

Crime Exposed #2
© Marvel Comics Group

24 (3) 150.00
25 (4) 150.00
Revived as:

CRIME AND JUSTICE
Charlton Comics, 1955
23 thru 26 . . . . @150.00

CRIME AND PUNISHMENT
Lev Gleason Publications, April, 1948
1 CBi(c),Mr.Crime(c) 450.00
2 CBi(c) 250.00
3 CBi(c),BF 275.00
4 CBi(c),BF 200.00
5 CBi(c) 200.00
6 thru 10 CBi(c) . . . . @125.00
11 thru 15 CBi(c) . . . . @100.00
16 thru 27 CBi(c) . . . . @100.00
28 thru 38 . . . . @100.00
39 Drug issue 125.00
40 thru 44 . . . . @100.00
45 Drug issue 100.00
46 thru 58 . . . . @100.00
59 . . . . 350.00
60 thru 65 . . . . @100.00
66 ATh 450.00
67 Drug Storm 425.00
68 ATh(c) 350.00
69 Drug issue 125.00
74 Aug., 1955 . . . . 100.00

CRIME CAN'T WIN
See: KRAZY COMICS

CRIME CASES COMICS
Marvel Atlas, 1950–52
(Formerly: WILLIE COMICS)
(See: IDEAL)
1 (24) Police 250.00
2 (25) 200.00
3 (26) 150.00
4 (27) 150.00
5 . . . . 150.00
6 . . . . 150.00
7 . . . . 150.00
8 . . . . 150.00
9 . . . . 150.00
10 . . . . 150.00
11 . . . . 150.00
12 . . . . 150.00

CRIME CLINIC
Approved Publ.
(Ziff-Davis), 1951
1 (10) F:Dr. Tom Rogers 350.00
2 (11) 250.00
3 . . . . 250.00
4 . . . . 250.00
5 . . . . 250.00

CRIME DETECTOR
Timor Publications, 1954
1 . . . . 300.00
2 . . . . 250.00
3 . . . . 225.00
4 . . . . 225.00
5 . . . . 250.00

CRIME DETECTIVE COMICS
Hillman Publications, March–April, 1948
1 BF(c),A:Invisible 6 . . . . 400.00
2 Jewel Robbery (c) 250.00
3 Stolen Cash (c) 200.00
4 Crime Boss Murder (c) 200.00
5 BK,Maestro (c) 200.00
6 AMc,Gorilla (c) 150.00
7 GMc,Wedding (c) 150.00
8 . . . . 150.00
9 Safe Robbery (c) (a classic) . . 500.00
10 . . . . 150.00
11 BP 150.00
12 BK 150.00
2-1 Bluebird Captured 200.00
2-2 . . . . 150.00
2-3 . . . . 150.00
2-4 BK 175.00
2-5 . . . . 150.00
2-6 . . . . 150.00
2-7 BK,GMc 175.00
2-8 . . . . 150.00
2-9 . . . . 150.00
2-10 . . . . 150.00
2-11 . . . . 150.00
2-12 . . . . 150.00
3-1 Drug Story 150.00
3-2 thru 3-7 . . . . @150.00
3-8 May/June, 1953 . . . . 100.00

CRIME DOES NOT PAY
See: SILVER STREAK COMICS

CRIME EXPOSED
Marvel Atlas Comics, 1948–52
1 . . . . 400.00
2 . . . . 200.00
3 GT 150.00
4 GT 150.00
5 thru 7 . . . . @150.00
8 MMe(c) 175.00
9 . . . . 150.00
10 . . . . 150.00
11 JeR 175.00
12 BK,JeR 200.00
13 BK 200.00
14 . . . . 125.00

CRIMEFIGHTERS
Marvel, April, 1948–Nov., 1949
1 Police Stories 350.00
2 Jewelry Robbery 200.00
3 The Nine Who Were Doomed, addiction 225.00
4 Human Beast at Bay 150.00
5 V:Gangsters 150.00
6 Pickpockets 150.00
7 True Cases, Crime Can't Win . 150.00
8 True Cases, Crime Can't Win . 150.00
9 Ph(c),It Happened at Night . . . 150.00
10 Ph(c),Killer at Large 150.00
Becomes:

CRIME FIGHTERS ALWAYS WIN
Marvel Atlas, 1954–1955
11 JMn,V:Gangsters 175.00
12 V:Gangsters 150.00
13 Clay Pidgeon 150.00

CRIME-FIGHTING DETECTIVE
See: CRIMINALS ON THE RUN

CRIME FILES
Standard Comics, 1952
5 ATh 300.00
6 . . . . 200.00

CRIME ILLUSTRATED
E.C. Comics, Nov.–Dec., 1955
1 Grl,RC,GE,JO 400.00
2 Grl,RC,JCr,JDa,JO 300.00

 All comics prices listed are for *Near Mint* condition.

Crime(s) Incorporated #1 (12)
© Fox Features Syndicate

Crime Mysteries #7
© Ribage Publishing

Tales From the Crypt #26
© E.C. Comics

CRIME INCORPORATED

Fox Features Syndicate, 1950
(Formerly: WESTERN THRILLERS; MY PAST CONFESSIONS)

1 (12) Crimes Incorporated 300.00
2 . . . . . 225.00
3 . . . . . 225.00

CRIME MUST LOSE!

Marvel Atlas, 1950

4 . . . . . 300.00
5 . . . . . 200.00
6 . . . . . 200.00
7 . . . . . 200.00
8 . . . . . 200.00
9 JeR 225.00
10 . . . . . 200.00
11 . . . . . 200.00
12 . . . . . 200.00

CRIME MUST PAY THE PENALTY

Ace Magazines, 1948–56

1 "True cases of actual crimes" . 550.00
2 Violent 350.00
3 . . . . . 300.00
4 . . . . . 300.00
5 . . . . . 200.00
6 . . . . . 200.00
7 . . . . . 200.00
8 Transvestite 300.00
9 . . . . . 200.00
10 . . . . . 200.00
11 thru 19 . . . . . @200.00
20 Drugs 250.00
21 thru 30 . . . . . @200.00
31 thru 48 . . . . . @200.00

CRIME MUST STOP

Hillman Periodicals, Oct., 1952

1 BK 1,000.00

CRIME MYSTERIES

Ribage Publishing Corp., May, 1952

1 Transvestism,Bondage(c) . . . 1,000.00
2 A:Manhunter, Lance Storm, Drug 750.00
3 FF-one page, A:Dr. Foo 500.00
4 A:Queenie Star, BondageStar . 750.00
5 Claws of the Green Girl 400.00
6 . . . . . 400.00
7 Sons of Satan 400.00
8 Death Stalks the Crown, Bondage(c) 400.00
9 You are the Murderer 375.00
10 The Hoax of the Death 375.00
11 The Strangler 375.00
12 Bondage(c) 450.00
13 AT,6 lives for one 500.00
14 Painted in Blood 375.00
15 Feast of the Dead,Acid Face . 650.00
Becomes:

SECRET MYSTERIES

Nov., 1954

16 Hiding Place,Horror 400.00
17 The Deadly Diamond,Horror . . 300.00
18 Horror 350.00
19 Horror,July, 1955 . . . . . 350.00

INTERNATIONAL COMICS

E.C. Publ. Co., Spring, 1947

1 KS,I:Manhattan's Files 1,000.00
2 KS,A: Van Manhattan & Madelon 750.00
3 KS,same 600.00
4 KS,same 600.00
5 I:International Crime-Busting Patrol 600.00
Becomes:

INTERNATIONAL CRIME PATROL

Spring, 1948

6 A:Moon Girl & The Prince . . 1,000.00
Becomes:

CRIME PATROL

Summer, 1948

7 SMo,A:Capt. Crime Jr.,Field Marshall of Murder 1,200.00
8 JCr,State Prison (c) 1,000.00
9 AF,JCr,Bank Robbery 1,000.00
10 AF,JCr,Wanted:James Dore. 1,000.00
11 AF,JCr 1,000.00
12 AF,Grl,JCr,Interrogation(c) . . 1,000.00
13 AF,JCr 1,000.00
14 AF,JCr,Smugglers (c) 1,000.00
15 AF,JCr,Crypt of Terror 6,000.00
16 AF,JCr,Crypt of Terror 3,500.00
Becomes:

CRYPT OF TERROR

E.C. Comics, April, 1950

17 JCr(a&c),AF,'Werewolf Strikes Again' 5,000.00
18 JCr(a&c),AF,WW,HK 'The Living Corpse' 3,000.00
19 JCr(a&c),AF,Grl, 'Voodoo Drums' 2,900.00
Becomes:

TALES FROM THE CRYPT

Oct., 1950

20 JCr(a&c),AF,GI,JKa 'Day of Death' 3,200.00
21 AF(a&c),WW,HK,GI,'Cooper Dies in the Electric Chair . . 3,000.00
22 AF, JCr(c) 2,200.00
23 AF(a&c),JCr,JDa,Grl 'Locked in a Mausoleum' . . 1,500.00
24 AF(c),WW,JDa,JCr,Grl 'Danger...Quicksand' 1,500.00
25 AF(c),WW,JDa,JKa,Grl 'Mataud Waxworks' 1,500.00
26 WW(c),JDa,Grl, 'Scared Graveyard' 1,200.00
27 JKa, WW(c), Guillotine (c) . . 1,200.00
28 AF(c),JDa,JKa,Grl,JO 'Buried Alive' 1,200.00
29 JDa(a&c),JKa,Grl,JO 'Coffin Burier' 1,200.00
30 JDa(a&c),JO,JKa,Grl 'Underwater Death' 1,200.00
31 JDa(a&c),JKa,Grl,AW 'Hand Chopper' 1,500.00
32 JDa(a&c),GE,Grl,'Woman Crushed by Elephant' 1,500.00
33 JDa(a&c),GE,JKa,Grl,'Lower Berth',O:Crypt Keeper 1,500.00
34 JDa(a&c),JKa,GE,Grl,'Jack the Ripper,'RayBradbury adapt. 1,200.00
35 JDa(a&c),JKa,JO,Grl, 'Werewolf' 1,400.00
36 JDa(a&c),JKa,GE,Grl, Ray Bradbury adaptation 900.00
37 JDa(c),JO,BE 900.00
38 JDa(c),BE,RC,Grl,'Axe Man' . 900.00
39 JDa(a&c),JKa,JO,Grl,'Children in the Graveyard' 900.00
40 JDa(a&c),GE,BK,Grl, 'Underwater Monster' 1,500.00
41 JDa(a&c),JKa,GE,Grl, 'Knife Thrower' 1,500.00
42 JDa(c),JO,Vampire (c) 1,500.00
43 JDa(c),JO,GE 1,500.00

Crime Reporter #3
© St. John Publishing Co.

Crime SuspenStories #19
© E.C. Comics

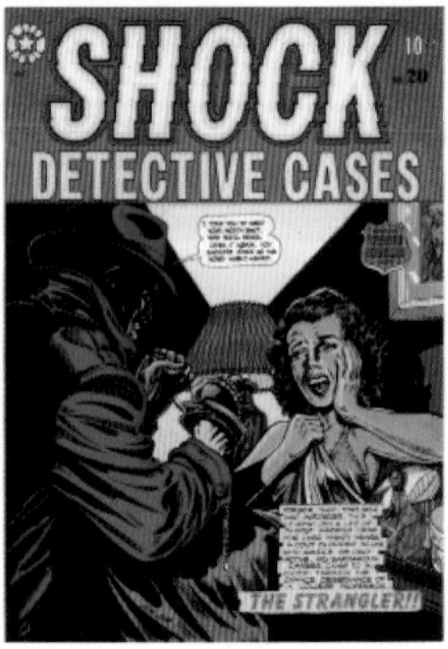

Shock Detective Cases #20
© Star Publications

44 JO,RC,Guillotine (c). 1,400.00
45 JDa(a&c),JKa,BK,GI,'Rat Takes Over His Life' 1,400.00
46 JDa(a&c),GE,JO,GI,Werewolf man being hunted,Feb.'55 . 1,400.00

CRIME REPORTER

St. John Publishing Co., Aug., 1948

1 Death Makes a Deadline . . . 2,000.00
2 GT,MB(c),Matinee Murders . 2,200.00
3 GT,MB(c),Dec., 1948 . . . . . . 1,800.00

CRIMES BY WOMEN

Fox Features Syndicate, June, 1948

1 Bonnie Parker 2,000.00
2 Vicious Female 1,300.00
3 Prison Break (c) 1,200.00
4 Murder (c) 1,200.00
5 . . . . 1,200.00
6 Girl Fight (c) 1,200.00
7 . . . . 900.00
8 . . . . 900.00
9 . . . . 900.00
10 Girl Fight (c) 800.00
11 . . . . 800.00
12 . . . . 800.00
13 ACME Jewelry Robbery (c) . . 800.00
14 Prison break (c) 800.00
15 Aug., 1951. . . . . 800.00

CRIME SMASHER

Fawcett Publications, Summer, 1948

1 The Unlucky Rabbit's Foot . . . 700.00

CRIME SMASHERS

Ribage Publishing Corp., Oct., 1950

1 Girl Rape. 1,500.00
2 JKu,A:Sally the Sleuth, Dan Turner, Girl Friday, Rat Hale . 800.00
3 MFa 600.00
4 Zak(c) 600.00
5 WW 1,000.00
6 . . . . 500.00
7 Bondage (c),Drugs. 600.00
8 . . . . 500.00
9 Bondage (c). 600.00
10 . . . . 500.00
11 . . . . 500.00
12 FF, Eye Injury 600.00
13 . . . . 600.00
14 & 15. . . . . @500.00

CRIMES ON THE WATERFRONT

See: FAMOUS GANGSTERS

CRIME SUSPENSTORIES

L.L. Publishing Co. (E.C. Comics), Oct.–Nov., 1950

1a JCr,Grl 2,700.00
1 JCr,WW,Grl 2,000.00
2 JCr,JKa,Grl 1,500.00
3 JCr,WW,Grl,Poe Story. 900.00
4 JCr,Gln,Grl,JDa 900.00
5 JCr,JKa,Grl,JDa. 900.00
6 JCr,JDa,Grl 600.00
7 JCr,Grl 600.00
8 JCr,Grl 600.00
9 JCr,Grl 600.00
10 JCr,Grl. 600.00
11 JCr,Grl. 500.00
12 JCr,Grl. 500.00
13 JCr,AW 550.00
14 JCr 500.00
15 JCr,Old Witch 500.00
16 JCr,AW 600.00
17 JCr,FF,AW, Ray Bradbury . . 1,300.00
18 JCr,RC,BE. 550.00
19 JCr,RC,GE,AF(c) 550.00
20 RC,JCr, Hanging (c) 600.00
21 JCr 500.00
22 RC,JO,JCr(c), Severed head (c). 600.00
23 JKa,RC,GE 550.00
24 BK,RC,JO 500.00
25 JKa,(c),RC 600.00
26 JKa,(c),RC,JO. 700.00
27 JKa,(c),GE,Grl,March, 1955 . . 500.00

CRIMINALS ON THE RUN

Premium Group of Comics, Aug., 1948

4-1 LbC(c) 500.00
4-2 LbC(c), A:Young King Cole . 400.00
4-3 LbC(c), Rip Roaring Action in Alps 400.00
4-4 LbC(c), Shark (c) 400.00
4-5 AMc 400.00
4-6 LbC,Dr. Doom 400.00
4-7 LbC 900.00
5-1 LbC 350.00
5-2 LbC 350.00
10 LbC 350.00

Becomes:

CRIME-FIGHTING DETECTIVE

April–May, 1950

11 LbC, Brodie Gang Captured . . 350.00
12 LbC(c), Jail Break Genius . . . 300.00
13 . . . . 250.00
14 LbC(c), A Night of Horror 300.00
15 LbC(c). 300.00
16 LbC(c), Wanton Murder 300.00
17 LbC(c), The Framer was Framed. 300.00
18 LbC(c), A Web of Evil 300.00
19 LbC(c), Lesson of the Law . . . 300.00

Becomes:

SHOCK DETECTIVE CASES

Star Publications, Sept., 1952

20 LbC(c), The Strangler 400.00
21 LbC(c), Death Ride. 400.00

Becomes:

SPOOK DETECTIVE CASES

Jan., 1953

22 Headless Horror 500.00

Becomes:

SPOOK SUSPENSE AND MYSTERY

23 LbC,Weird Picture of Murder . 350.00
24 LbC(c),Mummy's Case 400.00
25 LbC(c),Horror Beyond Door . . 350.00
26 LbC(c),JyD,Face of Death . . . 350.00
27 LbC(c),Ship of the Dead. 350.00
28 LbC(c),JyD,Creeping Death . . 350.00
29 LbC(c),Solo for Death. 350.00
30 LbC(c),JyD,Nightmare, Oct.,1954. . . . . 350.00

CROWN COMICS

Golfing/McCombs Publ., Winter 1944

1 Edgar Allen Poe adapt. 700.00
2 MB,I:Mickey Magic 500.00
3 MB,Jungle adventure (c) 500.00
4 MB(c),A:Voodah. 550.00
5 MB(c),Jungle Adventure (c) . . 550.00

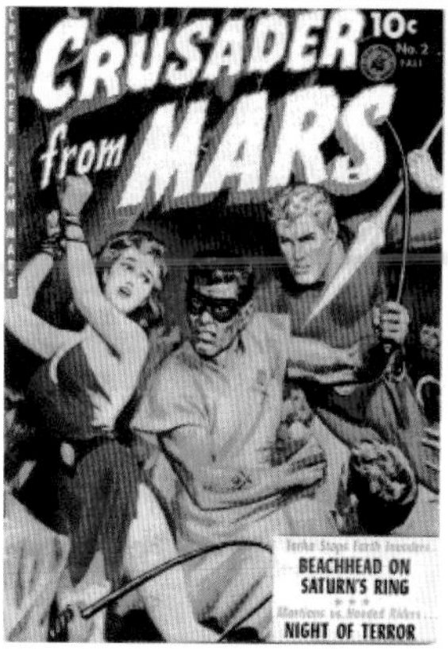

Crusader From Mars #2
© Ziff-Davis

Dagar Desert Hawk #14
© Fox Features Syndicate

Dagwood #28
© Harvey Publications

6 MB(c),Jungle Adventure (c) . . 550.00
7 JKa,AF,MB(c),Race Car (c) . . 550.00
8 MB 500.00
9 . . . . 300.00
10 Plane crash (c),A:Voodah 300.00
11 LSt,A:Voodah 250.00
12 LSt,AF,Master Marvin 250.00
13 LSt,AF,A:Voodah. 250.00
14 A:Voodah. 275.00
15 FBe,A:Voodah. 250.00
16 FBe,A:Voodah,Jungle
Adventure(c) 250.00
17 FBe,A:Voodah. 250.00
18 FBe,A:Voodah. 250.00
19 BP,A:Voodah,July, 1949 . . . . . 250.00

CRUSADER FROM MARS

Approved Publ. (Ziff-Davis), Jan.–March, 1952

1 Mission Thru Space, Death in
the Sai 1,300.00
2 Beachhead on Saturn's Ring,
Bondage(c),Fall, 1952 . . . . 1,000.00

CRYIN' LION, THE

William H. Wise Co., Fall, 1944

1 Funny Animal. 500.00
2 A. Hitler 300.00
3 Spring, 1945 . . . . 250.00

CRYPT OF TERROR
See: CRIME PATROL

CUPID

Marvel, Dec., 1949–March, 1950

1 Ph(c),Cora Dod's Amazing
Decision. 350.00
2 Ph(c),BP,Bettie Page 500.00

CURLY KAYOE COMICS

United Features Syndicate, 1946–50

1 Boxing 300.00
2 . . . . 250.00
3 . . . . 200.00
4 . . . . 200.00
5 . . . . 200.00
6 . . . . 200.00
7 . . . . 200.00
8 . . . . 200.00
1a United Presents ..... (1948) . . 200.00

CUTIE PIE

Junior Reader's Guild (Lev Gleason), 1955–56

1 . . . . 150.00
2 thru 5 . . . . @100.00

CYCLONE COMICS

Bibara Publ. Co., June, 1940

1 O:Tornado Tom 3,000.00
2 . . . . 2,500.00
3 . . . . 2,000.00
4 Voltron. 1,500.00
5 A:Mr. Q,Oct., 1940 . . . . 1,600.00

DAFFY

Dell Publishing Co., March, 1953

(1) *see Dell Four Color #457*
(2) *see Dell Four Color #536*
(3) *see Dell Four Color #615*
4 thru 7 . . . . @150.00
8 thru 11 . . . . @100.00
12 thru 17. . . . . @100.00
Becomes:

DAFFY DUCK

July, 1959

18 . . . . 100.00
19 . . . . 100.00
20 . . . . 100.00
21 thru 30. . . . . @100.00

DAFFY TUNES COMICS

Four Star Publications, 1947

12 Funny Animal 150.00

ALL GREAT COMICS

Fox Features Syndicate, Oct., 1947

12 A:Brenda Starr 1,500.00
13 JKa,O:Dagar, Desert Hawk . 1,800.00
Becomes:

DAGAR, DESERT HAWK

Feb., 1948

14 JKa,Monster of Mura 1,500.00
15 JKa,Curse of the Lost
Pharaoh 1,000.00
16 JKa,Wretched Antmen 900.00
19 Pyramid of Doom 800.00
20 . . . . 800.00
21 JKa(c),The Ghost of Fate 850.00
22 . . . . 800.00
23 Bondage (c) 850.00
Becomes:

CAPTAIN KIDD

June, 1949

24 Blackbeard the Pirate 300.00
25 Sorceress of the Deep 300.00
Becomes:

MY SECRET STORY

Oct., 1949

26 He Wanted More Than Love. . 300.00
27 My Husband Hated Me. 250.00
28 I Become a Marked Women . . 250.00
29 My Forbidden Rapture,
April, 1950 . . . . 250.00

DAGWOOD

Harvey Publications, 1950

1 . . . . 300.00
2 . . . . 200.00
3 . . . . 175.00
4 . . . . 175.00
5 . . . . 175.00
6 thru 10 . . . . @175.00
11 thru 20. . . . . @150.00
21 thru 30. . . . . @125.00
31 thru 50. . . . . @100.00
51 thru 70. . . . . @100.00
71 thru 109. . . . . @75.00
110 thru 140 . . . . @75.00

DAISY AND HER PUPS

Harvey Publications, 1951–1954

1 (21) F:Blondie & Dagwood's
dog. 150.00
2 (22). 110.00
3 (23). 110.00
4 (24). 110.00
5 (25). 110.00
6 (26). 110.00
7 (27). 110.00
8 . . . . 100.00
9 . . . . 100.00
10 . . . . 100.00
11 . . . . 100.00
12 . . . . 100.00
13 . . . . 100.00
14 . . . . 100.00
15 . . . . 100.00
16 . . . . 100.00
17 . . . . 100.00
18 . . . . 100.00

Dale Evans Comics #4
© DC Comics

Nature Boy #5
© Charlton Comics

Daredevil #11
© Lev Gleason

DAISY COMICS
Eastern Color Printing Co., 1936

N# 750.00

DAISY HANDBOOK
Daisy Manufacturing Co., 1946

1 Buck Rogers, Red Ryder. 475.00
2 Capt. Marvel 475.00
N# (1955). 400.00

DALE EVANS COMICS
DC Comics, 1948–52

1 Ph(c),ATh,B:Sierra Smith . . . 2,700.00
2 Ph(c),ATh 1,300.00
3 ATh. 800.00
4 . . . . 425.00
5 . . . . 425.00
6 thru 11 . . . . @425.00
12 thru 20. . . . . @325.00
21 thru 24. . . . . @300.00

DANDY COMICS
E.C. Comics 1947–48

1 Funny Animal. 450.00
2 . . . . 325.00
3 thru 7 . . . . @250.00

DANGER
Comic Media, 1953–54

1 DH(c&a). 300.00
2 PMo 150.00
3 PMo 150.00
4 Marijuana (c) & story 200.00
5 PMo 150.00
6 Drug 175.00
7 . . . . 150.00
8 Torture (c) 225.00
9 thru 11 . . . . 150.00

Charlton Comics, 1955

12 . . . . 150.00
13 and 14. . . . . @125.00
Becomes:

JIM BOWIE

15 thru 19. . . . . @100.00

DANGER AND ADVENTURE
See: THIS MAGAZINE IS HAUNTED

DANGER IS OUR BUSINESS
Toby Press/ I.W. Enterprises, 1953

1 AW,FF,Men Who Defy Death
for a Living. 750.00
2 Death Crowds the Cockpit . . . 300.00
3 Killer Mountain 250.00
4 . . . . 250.00
5 thru 9 . . . . @200.00
10 June, 1955 . . . . 250.00

DANGER TRAIL
DC Comics, July-Aug., 1950

1 CI,ATh,I:King For A Day 1,700.00
2 ATh 1,200.00
3 ATh 1,400.00
4 ATh 1,200.00
5 March-April, 1951 . . . . 1,200.00

DAN'L BOONE
Sussex Publ. Co. 1955–57

1 F:Dan'l Boone Greatest
Frontiersman 200.00
2 . . . . 150.00
3 . . . . 100.00
4 . . . . 100.00
5 . . . . 100.00
6 thru 8 . . . . @100.00

DANNY BLAZE
Charlton Comics, 1955

1 . . . . 150.00
2 . . . . 125.00
Becomes:

NATURE BOY

3 JB,O:Blue Beetle 300.00
4 . . . . 125.00
5 Feb., 1957 . . . . 100.00

DAREDEVIL COMICS
Lev Gleason Publications, July, 1941

1 Daredevil Battles Hitler, A:Silver
Streak, Lance Hale, Dickey Dean,
Cloud Curtis,V:The Claw,
O:Hitler 25,000.00
2 I:The Pioneer, Champion of
American,B:London,Pat
Patriot,Pirate Prince 5,000.00
3 CBi(c),O:Thirteen 3,000.00
4 CBi(c),Death is the Referee . 2,500.00
5 CBi(c),I:Sniffer&Jinx, Claw
V:Ghost,Lottery of Doom . . 2,000.00
6 CBi(c) 1,700.00
7 CBi(c), What Ghastly Sight Lies
within the Mysterious Trunk 1,600.00
8 V:Nazis (c), E:Nightro 1,500.00
9 V:Double 1,500.00
10 America will Remember
Pearl Harbor. 1,500.00
11 Bondage (c), E:Pat
Patriot, London. 1,700.00
12 BW,CBi(c), O:The Law. 2,200.00
13 BW,I:Little Wise Guys 1,700.00
14 BW,CBi(c) 1,200.00
15 BW,CBi(c), D:Meatball. 1,400.00
16 BW,CBi(c) 1,100.00
17 BW,CBi(c), Into the Valley
of Death 1,100.00
18 BW,CBi(c), O:Daredevil,
double length story. 2,000.00
19 BW,CBi(c), Buried Alive 900.00
20 BW,CBi(c), Boxing (c) 900.00
21 CBi(c), Can Little Wise Guys
Survive Blast of Dynamite? 1,500.00
22 CBi(c) 750.00
23 CBi(c), I:Pshyco 750.00
24 CBi(c), Punch and Judy
Murders 750.00
25 CBi(c), Baseball (c) 750.00
26 CBi(c) 700.00
27 CBi(c), Bondage (c) 750.00
28 CBi(c) 700.00
29 CBi(c) 700.00
30 CBi(c), Ann Hubbard White
1922-1943 . . . . 700.00
31 CBi(c), D:The Claw 1,400.00
32 V:Blackmarketeers 500.00
33 CBi(c) 500.00
34 CBi(c) 500.00
35 B:Two Daredevil stories
every issue 550.00
36 CBi(c) 550.00
37 CBi(c) 550.00
38 CBi(c), O:Daredevil. 800.00
39 CBi(c) 500.00
40 CBi(c) 500.00
41 . . . . 500.00
42 thru 50 CBi(c) . . . . @500.00
51 CBi(c) 350.00
52 CBi(c),Football (c). 400.00
53 thru 57. . . . . @350.00
58 Football (c) 400.00
59 . . . . 350.00
60 . . . . 350.00
61 thru 68 . . . . @350.00

Daring Mystery Comics #2
© Marvel Comics Group

Daring Comics #12
© Marvel Comics Group

Dark Mysteries #23
© Merit Publications

69 E:Daredevil 350.00
70 . . . . 250.00
71 thru 78 . . . . @150.00
79 B:Daredevil 250.00
80 . . . . 275.00
81 . . . . 150.00
82 . . . . 150.00
83 thru 99 . . . . @150.00
100 . . . . 175.00
101 thru 133 . . . . @150.00
134 Sept., 1956 . . . . 150.00

DARING CONFESSIONS
See: YOUTHFUL HEART

DARING LOVE
Gilmore Magazines, 1953
1 SD,1st work 800.00
Becomes:

RADIANT LOVE
Gilmore Magazines, 1953–54
2 . . . . 150.00
3 . . . . 125.00
4 . . . . 125.00
5 . . . . 125.00
6 . . . . 125.00

DARLING LOVE
See: YOUTHFUL ROMANCES

DARING MYSTERY COMICS
Marvel Timely, Jan., 1940
1 ASh(c),JSm,O:Fiery Mask, A:Monako John Steele,Doc Doyle, Flash FosterBarney Mullen, Sea Rover, Bondage (c) . . 50,000.00
2 ASh(c),JSm,O:Phantom Bullet A:Zephyr Jones & K4,Laughing Mask Mr.E,B:Trojak 30,000.00
3 ASh(c),JSm,A:Phantom Reporter,Marvex,Breeze Barton, B:Purple Mask . . 12,000.00
4 ASh(c),A:G-Man Ace,K4, Monako,Marvex,E:Purple Mask,B:Whirlwind Carter . . 8,000.00
5 ASh(c),JSm,B:Falcon,A:Fiery Mask,K4, Little Hercules, Bondage(c) 8,000.00
6 S&K,O:Marvel Boy,A:Fiery Mask, Flying Fame,Dynaman, Stuporman,E:Trojak 10,000.00
7 ASh(c),S&K,O:Blue Diamond, A:The Fin, Challenger,Captain Daring, Silver Scorpion, Thunderer 8,000.00
8 S&K,O:Citizen V,A:Thunderer, Fin Silver Scorpion,Captain Daring Blue Diamond 7,000.00
Becomes:

DARING COMICS
Marvel, 1944
9 ASh(c),B:Human Torch,Toro, Sub Mariner 3,000.00
10 ASh(c),A;The Angel 2,600.00
11 ASh(c),A:The Destroyer 2,600.00
12 E:Human Torch,Toro,Sub-Mariner, Fall, 1945 . . . . 2,600.00
Becomes:

JEANIE COMICS
Marvel, 1947
13 B:Jeanie,Queen of the Teens Mitzi,Willie 300.00
14 Baseball(c) 250.00
15 Schoolbus(c) 250.00
16 Swimsuit(c) 275.00
17 HK,Fancy Dress Party(c), Hey Look 225.00
18 HK,Jeanie's Date(c), Hey Look 200.00
19 Ice-Boat(c),Hey Look 225.00
20 Jukebox(c) 200.00
21 . . . . 200.00
22 HK,Hey Look 225.00
23 thru 25 . . . . @200.00
26 . . . . 200.00
27 E:Jeanie,Queen of Teens 200.00
Becomes:

COWGIRL ROMANCES
Marvel, 1950
28 Ph(c),Mona Freeman/MacDonald Carey,Copper Canyon 300.00

DARK MYSTERIES
Merit Publications, June–July, 1951
1 WW(a&c), Curse of the Sea Witch 1,500.00
2 WW(a&c), Vampire Fangs of Doom 1,200.00
3 Terror of the Unwilling Witch 800.00
4 Corpse that Came Alive 800.00
5 Horror of the Ghostly Crew . . . 650.00
6 If the Noose Fits Wear It! 650.00
7 Terror of the Cards of Death . . 650.00
8 Terror of the Ghostly Trail 650.00
9 Witch's Feast at Dawn 650.00
10 Terror of the Burning Witch . . . 650.00
11 The River of Blood 600.00
12 Horror of the Talking Dead . . . 600.00
13 Terror of the Hungry Cats 600.00
14 Horror of the Fingers of Doom 650.00
15 Terror of the Vampires Teeth . . 550.00
16 Horror of the Walking Dead . . 550.00
17 Terror of the Mask of Death . . 550.00
18 Terror of the Burning Corpse . 550.00
19 The Rack of Terror 750.00
20 Burning Executioner 650.00
21 The Sinister Secret 500.00
22 The Hand of Destiny 500.00
23 The Mardenburg Curse 350.00
24 Give A Man Enough Rope, July, 1955 . . . . 350.00

DARK SHADOWS
Steinway Publications/Ajax 1957–58
1 . . . . 350.00
2 . . . . 300.00
3 . . . . 300.00

DARLING LOVE
Archie-Close-up Publ., 1949
1 Photo(c) 250.00
2 Photo(c) 150.00
3 Photo(c) 125.00
4 Photo(c) 125.00
5 Photo(c) 125.00
6 Photo(c) 125.00
7 . . . . 125.00
8 . . . . 125.00
9 BK 150.00
10 . . . . 125.00
11 . . . . 125.00

DARLING ROMANCE
Archie Close-Up Publ., 1949
1 Photo(c) 350.00
2 . . . . 200.00
3 . . . . 150.00
4 . . . . 150.00
5 . . . . 150.00
6 . . . . 150.00
7 . . . . 150.00

A Date With Judy #7
© DC Comics

A Date With Judy #10
© DC Comics

Dear Lonely Heart #1
© Artful Publications

DATE WITH DANGER
Visual Editions (Standard Comics), 1952

5 Secret Agent	200.00
6 Atom Bomb	250.00

A DATE WITH JUDY
DC Comics, 1947

1 Teen-age	500.00
2	350.00
3	300.00
4	300.00
5	300.00
6	300.00
7	300.00
8	300.00
9	300.00
10	300.00
11 thru 20	@250.00
21 thru 30	@150.00
31 thru 50	@125.00
51 thru 78	@125.00
79 MD	150.00

A DATE WITH MILLIE
Marvel Atlas, Oct., 1956 [1st Series]

1	400.00
2	250.00
3 thru 7	@200.00

Marvel, [2nd Series], Oct., 1959

1	250.00
2 thru 7	@200.00

A DATE WITH PATSY
Marvel, Sept., 1957

1 A:Patsy Walker	150.00

DAVY CROCKETT
Avon Periodicals, 1951

1	250.00

FRONTIER FIGHTER
Charlton Comics, 1955

1 JK,Davy Crocket-Buffalo Bill	250.00
2 JK	150.00

Becomes:

DAVY CROCKETT
Charlton Comics, 1956

3 thru 7 JK	@150.00
8 Jan., 1957 JK	125.00

Becomes:

KID MONTANA
Charlton Comics, 1957

9	125.00
10	110.00
11	100.00
12	100.00
13 AW	100.00
14 thru 20	@100.00
21 thru 35	@75.00
36 thru 49	@75.00
50 March, 1965	75.00

DC SHOWCASE
See: SHOWCASE

DEAD END CRIME STORIES
Kirby Publishing Co., April, 1949

N# BP	750.00

DEAD-EYE WESTERN COMICS
Hillman Periodicals Nov.–Dec., 1948

1 BK	300.00
2	250.00
3	200.00
4 thru 12	@150.00
2-1	125.00
2-2	125.00
2-3	150.00
2-4	150.00
2-5 thru 2-12	@125.00
3-1	125.00

DEADWOOD GULCH
Dell Publishing Co., 1931

1	750.00

DEAR BEATRICE FAIRFAX
Best Books (Standard Comics), Nov., 1950

5	300.00
6 thru 9	@200.00

DEAR HEART
See: LONELY HEART

DEAR LONELY HEART
Artful Publications, March, 1951

1	300.00
2	200.00
3 MB,Jungle Girl	350.00
4	150.00
5 thru 8	@125.00

DEAR LONELY HEARTS
Comic Media, Aug., 1953

1 Six Months to Live	200.00
2 Date Hungry, Price of Passion	150.00
3 thru 8	@200.00

DEARLY BELOVED
Approved Comics (Ziff-Davis), Fall, 1952

1 Ph(c)	200.00

DEATH VALLEY
Comic Media/ Charlton Comics, 1953

1 Cowboys & Indians	200.00
2 DH(c)	150.00
3 PMo	125.00
4	125.00
5 PMo	125.00
6	125.00
7	125.00
8 BW	125.00
9	125.00

Becomes:

FRONTIER SCOUT DANIEL BOONE
Charlton Comics

10	150.00
11 thru 13	@100.00

DEBBIE DEAN, CAREER GIRL
Civil Service Publishing, April, 1945

1	300.00
2	250.00

Dell Giant Editions, Lone Ranger Western Treasury #1 © Dell Publ. Co.

Dell Giant Comics #37 © Dell Publishing Co.

Dennis the Menace #23 © Pines Publications

DELLA VISION

Marvel Atlas, April, 1955

1 The Television Queen 250.00
2 . . . . 200.00
3 . . . . 200.00

Becomes:

PATTY POWERS

Marvel, 1955

4 . . . . 200.00
5 & 6 . . . . @100.00
7 Oct., 1956 . . . . 100.00

DELL GIANT EDITIONS

Dell Publishing Co., 1952-58

Abe Lincoln Life Story 175.00
Cadet Gray of West Point 175.00
Golden West Rodeo Treasury . . . 200.00
Life Stories of American Presidents 165.00
Lone Ranger Golden West 400.00
Lone Ranger Movie Story 800.00
Lone Ranger Western Treasury('53) 400.00
Lone Ranger Western Treasury('54) 500.00
Moses & Ten Commandments. . . 150.00
Nancy & Sluggo Travel Time 200.00
Pogo Parade 750.00
Raggedy Ann & Andy. 350.00
Santa Claus Funnies 200.00
Tarzan's Jungle Annual #1. . . . . . 350.00
Tarzan's Jungle Annual #2. . . . . . 225.00
Tarzan's Jungle Annual #3. . . . . . 200.00
Tarzan's Jungle Annual #4. . . . . . 200.00
Tarzan's Jungle Annual #5. . . . . . 200.00
Tarzan's Jungle Annual #6. . . . . . 200.00
Tarzan's Jungle Annual #7. . . . . . 200.00
Treasury of Dogs 175.00
Treasury of Horses 175.00
Universal Presents-Dracula-The Mummy & Other Stories. 500.00
Western Roundup #1. . . . . 600.00
Western Roundup #2. . . . . 350.00
Western Roundup #3. . . . . 275.00
Western Roundup #4 thru #5. . @250.00
Western Roundup #6 thru #10. @250.00
Western Roundup #11 thru #17 @225.00
Western Roundup #18. . . . . 225.00
Western Roundup #19 thru #25@180.00
Woody Woodpecker Back to School #1 (1952). 300.00
Woody Woodpecker Back to School #2 (1953). 250.00
Woody Woodpecker Back to School #3 (1954). 250.00
Woody Woodpecker Back to School #4 (1955). 250.00
Woody Woodpecker County Fair #5 (1956) 250.00
Woody Woodpecker Back to School #6 (1957). 275.00
Woody Woodpecker County Fair #2 (1958) 250.00

Also See: Bugs Bunny; Marge's Little Lulu; Tom and Jerry, and Walt Disney Dell Giant Editions

DELL GIANT COMICS

Dell Publishing Co., Sept., 1959

21 M.G.M. Tom & Jerry Picnic Time 250.00
22 W.Disney's Huey, Dewey & Louie Back to School (Oct 1959) . . 250.00
23 Marge's Little Lulu & Tubby Halloween Fun 250.00
24 Woody Woodpeckers Family Fun. 225.00
25 Tarzan's Jungle World. 250.00
26 W.Disney's Christmas Parade,CB. 600.00
27 W.Disney's Man in Space (1960). 300.00
28 Bugs Bunny's Winter Fun 250.00
29 Marge's Little Lulu & Tubby in Hawaii. 300.00
30 W.Disney's DisneylandU.S.A.. 400.00
31 Huckleberry Hound Summer Fun 300.00
32 Bugs Bunny Beach Party 250.00
33 W.Disney's Daisy Duck & Uncle Scrooge Picnic Time . . 350.00
34 Nancy&SluggoSummerCamp. 250.00
35 W.Disney's Huey, Dewey & Louie Back to School 400.00
36 Marge's Little Lulu & Witch Hazel Halloween Fun 275.00
37 Tarzan, King of the Jungle . . . 250.00
38 W.Disney's Uncle Donald and his Nephews Family Fun . . . 350.00
39 W.Disney's Merry Christmas. . 350.00
40 Woody Woodpecker Christmas Parade 175.00
41 Yogi Bear's Winter Sports. . . . 275.00
42 Marge's Little Lulu & Tubby in Australia 300.00
43 Mighty Mouse in OuterSpace . 500.00
44 Around the World with Huckleberry & His Friends . . 300.00
45 Nancy&SluggoSummerCamp. 150.00
46 Bugs Bunny Beach Party 175.00
47 W.Disney's Mickey and Donald in Vacationland 300.00
48 The Flintstones #1 (Bedrock Bedlam) 500.00
49 W.Disney's Huey, Dewey & Louie Back to School 300.00
50 Marge's Little Lulu & Witch Hazel Trick 'N' Treat . . 275.00
51 Tarzan, King of the Jungle . . . 200.00
52 W.Disney's Uncle Donald & his Nephews Dude Ranch . . 300.00
53 W.Disney's Donald Duck Merry Christmas 300.00
54 Woody Woodpecker Christmas Party. 200.00
55 W.Disney's Daisy Duck & Uncle Scrooge Show Boat (1961). . 300.00

DELL JUNIOR TREASURY

Dell Publishing Co., June, 1955

1 Alice in Wonderland. 150.00
2 Aladdin 125.00
3 Gulliver's Travels 100.00
4 Adventures of Mr. Frog 125.00
5 Wizard of Oz 125.00
6 Heidi. 135.00
7 Santa & the Angel 135.00
8 Raggedy Ann 135.00
9 Clementina the Flying Pig 125.00
10 Adventures of Tom Sawyer. . . 125.00

DENNIS THE MENACE

Visual Editions/Literary Ent. (Standard, Pines), Aug., 1953

1 . . . . 1,200.00
2 . . . . 500.00
3 . . . . 300.00
4 . . . . 300.00
5 thru 10 . . . . @200.00
11 thru 20 . . . . @175.00
21 thru 31 . . . . @150.00

Hallden (Fawcett Publications)

32 thru 40. . . . . @125.00
41 thru 50. . . . . @125.00
51 thru 60. . . . . @100.00
61 thru 70. . . . . @100.00
71 thru 90. . . . . @100.00
91 thru 140. . . . . @50.00
141 thru 166. . . . . @35.00

Desperado #1
© Lev Gleason Publications

Detective Comics #7
© DC Comics

Detective Comics #92
© DC Comics

DENNIS THE MENACE GIANTS [VARIOUS SUBTITLES]

Fawcett, 1955–69

N# Vacation Special . . . 300.00
N# Christmas . . . 250.00
2 thru 10 . . . @200.00
11 thru 20 . . . @150.00
21 thru 30 . . . @100.00
31 thru 40 . . . @75.00
41 thru 75 . . . @75.00

DESPERADO

Lev Gleason Publications, June, 1948

1 CBi(c) . . . 300.00
2 CBi(c) . . . 200.00
3 CBi(c) . . . 250.00
4 CBi(c) . . . 150.00
5 CBi(c) . . . 150.00
6 CBi(c) . . . 150.00
7 CBi(c) . . . 150.00
8 CBi(c) . . . 150.00
Becomes:

BLACK DIAMOND WESTERN

March, 1949

9 CBi(c) . . . 300.00
10 CBi(c) . . . 200.00
11 CBi(c) . . . 150.00
12 CBi(c) . . . 150.00
13 CBi(c) . . . 150.00
14 CBi(c) . . . 150.00
15 CBi(c) . . . 150.00
16 thru 28 BW,Big Bang Buster @150.00
29 thru 40 . . . @175.00
41 thru 50 . . . @125.00
51 thru 52 3-D Luse . . . @250.00
53 thru 60 . . . @100.00

DETECTIVE COMICS

DC Comics, March, 1937

1 I:Slam Bradley . . . 100,000.00
2 JoS . . . 35,000.00
3 JoS . . . 25,000.00
4 JoS . . . 12,000.00
5 JoS . . . 10,000.00
6 JoS . . . 8,000.00
7 JoS . . . 7,500.00
8 JoS,Mr. Chang(c) . . . 12,000.00
9 JoS . . . 7,500.00
10 . . . 7,500.00
11 . . . 6,500.00
12 . . . 6,500.00
13 . . . 6,500.00
14 . . . 6,500.00
15 . . . 6,500.00
16 . . . 6,500.00
17 I:Fu Manchu . . . 6,500.00
18 Fu Manchu(c) . . . 10,000.00
19 . . . 6,500.00
20 I:Crimson Avenger . . . 9,000.00
21 . . . 5,000.00
22 . . . 6,500.00
23 . . . 5,000.00
24 . . . 5,000.00
25 . . . 5,000.00
26 . . . 5,000.00
27 BK,I:Batman . . . 475,000.00
28 BK,V:Frenchy Blake . . . 45,000.00
29 BK,I:Doctor Death . . . 65,000.00
30 BK,V:Dr. Death . . . 15,000.00
31 BK,I:Monk . . . 65,000.00
32 BK,V:Monk . . . 13,000.00
33 O:Batman,V:Scarlet Horde 75,000.00
34 V:Due D'Orterre . . . 9,000.00
35 V:Sheldon Lenox . . . 22,000.00
36 I:Hugo Strange . . . 16,000.00
37 V:Count Grutt, last Batman solo . . . 15,000.00
38 I:Robin, the Boy Wonder . 100,000.00
39 V:Green Dragon . . . 14,000.00
40 I:Clayface (Basil Karlo) . . . 15,000.00
41 V:Graves . . . 8,000.00
42 V:Pierre Antal . . . 6,500.00
43 V:Harliss Greer . . . 6,500.00
44 Robin Dream Story . . . 6,500.00
45 V:Joker . . . 8,500.00
46 V:Hugo Strange . . . 6,000.00
47 Meets Harvey Midas . . . 6,000.00
48 Meets Henry Lewis . . . 6,000.00
49 V:Clayface . . . 6,000.00
50 V:Three Devils . . . 6,000.00
51 V:Mindy Gang . . . 5,000.00
52 V:Loo Chung . . . 5,000.00
53 V:Toothy Hare Gang . . . 5,000.00
54 V:Hook Morgan . . . 5,000.00
55 V:Dr. Death . . . 5,000.00
56 V:Mad Mack . . . 5,000.00
57 Meet Richard Sneed . . . 5,000.00
58 I:Penguin . . . 9,000.00
59 V:Penguin . . . 4,000.00
60 V:Joker,I:Air Wave . . . 3,500.00
61 The Three Racketeers . . . 3,000.00
62 V:Joker . . . 5,000.00
63 I:Mr. Baffle . . . 3,000.00
64 I:Boy Commandos,V:Joker . 8,000.00
65 Meet Tom Bolton . . . 6,000.00
66 I:Two-Face . . . 8,000.00
67 V:Penguin . . . 5,000.00
68 V:Two-Face . . . 3,500.00
69 V:Joker . . . 3,500.00
70 Meet the Amazing Carlo . . . 2,500.00
71 V:Joker . . . 2,700.00
72 V:Larry the Judge . . . 2,200.00
73 V:Scarecrow . . . 2,600.00
74 I:Tweedledum&Tweedledee. 2,500.00
75 V:Robber Baron . . . 2,500.00
76 V:Joker . . . 2,800.00
77 V:Dr. Matthew Thorne . . . 2,600.00
78 V:Baron Von Luger . . . 2,600.00
79 Destiny's Auction . . . 2,600.00
80 V:Two-Face . . . 2,700.00
81 I:Cavalier . . . 1,700.00
82 V:Blackee Blondeen . . . 1,700.00
83 V:Dr. Goodwin . . . 1,800.00
84 V:Ivan Krafft . . . 1,700.00
85 V:Joker . . . 2,200.00
86 V:Gentleman Jim Jewell . . . 1,700.00
87 V:Penguin . . . 1,800.00
88 V:Big Hearted John . . . 1,700.00
89 V:Cavalier . . . 1,700.00
90 V:Capt. Ben . . . 1,700.00
91 V:Joker . . . 2,700.00
92 V:Braing Bulow . . . 1,600.00
93 V:Tiger Ragland . . . 1,600.00
94 V:Lefty Goran . . . 1,600.00
95 V:The Blaze . . . 1,600.00
96 F:Alfred . . . 1,600.00
97 V:Nick Petri . . . 1,600.00
98 Meets Casper Thurbridge . . 1,600.00
99 V:Penguin . . . 1,600.00
100 V:Digger . . . 1,600.00
101 V:Joe Bart . . . 1,600.00
102 V:Joker . . . 1,600.00
103 Meet Dean Gray . . . 1,600.00
104 V:Fat Frank Gang . . . 1,600.00
105 V:Simon Gurlan . . . 1,600.00
106 V:Todd Torrey . . . 1,600.00
107 V:Bugs Scarpis . . . 1,600.00
108 Meet Ed Gregory . . . 1,600.00
109 V:Joker . . . 5,000.00
110 V:Prof. Moriarty . . . 2,000.00
111 Coaltown, USA . . . 2,000.00
112 Case Without A Crime . . . 2,000.00
113 V:Blackhand . . . 2,000.00
114 V:Joker . . . 2,000.00
115 V:Basil Grimes . . . 2,000.00
116 A:Carter Nichols, Robin Hood . . . 2,000.00
117 Steeplejack's Slowdown . . . 2,000.00
118 V:Joker . . . 2,500.00
119 V:Wiley Derek . . . 1,500.00

Detective Comics #122
© DC Comics

Detective Comics #167
© DC Comics

Detective Comics #233
© DC Comics

120 V:Penguin 3,000.00
121 F:Commissioner Gordon . . 1,500.00
122 V:Catwoman 3,000.00
123 V:Shiner 1,300.00
124 V:Joker. 1,600.00
125 V:Thinker 1,200.00
126 V:Penguin 1,200.00
127 V:Dr. Agar. 1,200.00
128 V:Joker. 1,600.00
129 V:Diamond Dan Mob 1,500.00
130 . . . . 1,500.00
131 V:Trigger Joe 1,500.00
132 V:Human Key. 1,500.00
133 Meets Arthur Loom 1,500.00
134 V:Penguin 1,500.00
135 A:Baron Frankenstein,
Carter Nichols. 1,500.00
136 A:Carter Nichols. 1,500.00
137 V:Joker. 1,700.00
138 V:Joker,O:Robotman 1,900.00
139 V:Nick Bailey 1,400.00
140 I:Riddler 7,500.00
141 V:Blackie Nason. 1,400.00
142 V:Riddler 2,000.00
143 V:Pied Piper. 1,200.00
144 A:Kay Kyser (radio
personality). 1,200.00
145 V:Yellow Mask Mob 1,200.00
146 V:J.J. Jason 1,200.00
147 V:Tiger Shark 1,200.00
148 V:Prof. Zero 1,200.00
149 V:Joker. 1,500.00
150 V:Dr. Paul Visio 1,200.00
151 I&O:Pow Wow Smith 1,400.00
152 V:Goblin 1,200.00
153 V:Slits Danton 1,400.00
154 V:Hatch Marlin 1,200.00
155 A:Vicki Vale 1,200.00
156 The Batmobile of 1950 . . . 1,200.00
157 V:Bart Gillis 1,200.00
158 V:Dr. Doom 1,200.00
159 V:T. Worthington Chubb. . . 1,200.00
160 V:Globe-Trotter 1,200.00
161 V:Bill Waters 1,200.00
162 Batman on Railroad. 1,200.00
163 V:Slippery Jim Elgin. 1,200.00
164 Bat-signal story 1,200.00
165 The Strange Costumes
of Batman. 1,200.00
166 Meets John Gillen 1,200.00
167 A:Carter Nichols, Cleopatra 1,200.00
168 O:Joker 7,000.00
169 V:Squint Tolmar 1,200.00
170 Batman Teams with Navy
and Coast Guard 1,200.00
171 V:Penguin 1,400.00
172 V:Paul Gregorian 1,100.00
173 V:Killer Moth. 1,100.00
174 V:Dagger 1,100.00
175 V:Kangaroo Kiley 1,100.00
176 V:Mr. Velvet 1,100.00
177 Bat-Cave Story. 1,000.00
178 V:Baron Swane 1,000.00
179 Mayor Bruce Wayne 1,000.00
180 V:Joker. 1,000.00
181 V:Human Magnet. 1,000.00
182 V:Maestro Dorn 1,000.00
183 V:John Cook 1,000.00
184 I:Firefly(Garfield Lynns) . . . 1,000.00
185 Secrets of Batman's
Utility Belt 1,000.00
186 The Flying Bat-Cave 1,000.00
187 V:Two-Face 1,000.00
188 V:William Milden 1,000.00
189 V:Styx. 1,000.00
190 Meets Dr. Sampson,
O:Batman 1,200.00
191 V:Executioner. 1,000.00
192 V: Nails Riley 1,000.00
193 V:Joker. 1,000.00
194 V:Sammy Sabre. 1,000.00
195 Meets Hugo Marmon 1,000.00
196 V:Frank Lumardi 1,000.00
197 V:Wrecker 1,000.00
198 Batman in Scotland 1,000.00
199 V:Jack Baker 1,000.00
200 V:Brand Keldon 1,000.00
201 Meet Human Target 1,000.00
202 V:Jolly Roger 1,000.00
203 V:Catwoman 1,000.00
204 V:Odo Neral 1,000.00
205 O:Bat-Cave 1,000.00
206 V:Trapper 1,000.00
207 Meets Merko the Great . . . 1,000.00
208 V:Groff 1,000.00
209 V:Inventor. 1,000.00
210 V:Brain Hobson 1,000.00
211 V:Catwoman. 1,000.00
212 Meets Jonathan Bard. 1,000.00
213 O:Mirror-Man 1,000.00
214 The Batman Encyclopedia. 1,000.00
215 I:Ranger, Legionairy, Gaucho &
Musketeer,A:Knight & Squire
(See: World's Finest 89) 900.00
216 A:Brane Taylor 900.00
217 Meets Barney Barrows 900.00
218 V:Dr. Richard Marston 900.00
219 V:Marty Mantee. 900.00
220 A:Roger Bacon, historical
scientist/philosopher 900.00
221 V:Paul King 900.00
222 V:'Big Jim' Jarrell 900.00
223 V:'Blast' Varner 900.00
224. . . . . 900.00
225 I&O:Martian Manhunter
(J'onn J'onzz). 10,000.00
226 O:Robin's costume,
A:J'onn J'onzz 2,500.00
227 A:Roy Raymond, J'onn
J'onzz 1,000.00
228 A:Roy Raymond, J'onn
J'onzz 1,000.00
229 A:Roy Raymond, J'onn
J'onzz 1,000.00
230 A:Martian Manhunter,
I:Mad Hatter 1,100.00
231 A:Batman,Jr.,Roy Raymond
J'onn J'onzz. 750.00
232 A:J'onn J'onzz. 750.00
233 I&O:Batwoman. 2,400.00
234 V:Jay Caird 750.00
235 O:Batman's Costume. 1,100.00
236 V:Wallace Walby 1,000.00
237 F:Robin 750.00
238 V:Checkmate(villain) 750.00
239 Batman robot story 750.00
240 V:Burt Weaver. 750.00
241 The Rainbow Batman 750.00
242 Batcave story 600.00
243 V:Jay Vanney 600.00
244 O:Batarang 600.00
245 F:Comm.Gordon 600.00
246. . . . . 600.00
247 I:Professor Milo. 600.00
248. . . . . 600.00
249 V:Collector 600.00
250 V:John Stannor 600.00
251 V:Brand Ballard. 600.00
252 Batman in a movie 600.00
253 I:Terrible Trio. 600.00
254 A:Bathound 600.00
255 V:Fingers Nolan 600.00
256 Batman outer-space story. . . 600.00
257 Batman sci-fi story 600.00
258 Batman robot story 600.00
259 I:Calendar Man 600.00
260 Batman outer space story. . . 600.00
261 I:Dr. Double X 400.00
262 V:Jackal-Head. 400.00
263 V:The Professor 400.00
264. . . . . 400.00
265 O:Batman retold 600.00
266 V:Astro 400.00
267 I&O:Bat-Mite 600.00
268 V:'Big Joe' Foster 400.00
269 V:Director 400.00
270 Batman sci-fi story 400.00

Detective Picture Stories #5
© Comics Magazine Co.

Diary Loves #2
© Quality Comics Group

Dick Cole #8
© Star Publications

271 V:Crimson Knight,O:Martian Manhunter(retold) 400.00
272 V:Crystal Creature 400.00
273 A:Dragon Society 350.00
274 V:Nails Lewin 350.00
275 A:Zebra-Man 350.00
276 A:Batmite. 350.00
277 Batman Monster story. 350.00
278 A:Professor Simms 350.00
279 Batman robot story 350.00
280 A:Atomic Man 350.00
281 Batman robot story 300.00
282 Batman sci-fi story 300.00
283 V:Phantom of Gotham City. . 300.00
284 V:Hal Durgan 300.00
285 V:Harbin 300.00
286 A:Batwoman 300.00
287 A:Bathound 300.00
288 V:Multicreature 300.00
289 A:Bat-Mite 300.00
290 Batman's robot story. 300.00
291 Batman sci-fi story 300.00
292 Last Roy Raymond 300.00
293 A:Aquaman,J'onn J'onzz . . . 300.00
294 V:Elemental Men, A:Aquaman 300.00
295 A:Aquaman 300.00
296 A:Aquaman 300.00
297 A:Aquaman 300.00
298 I:Clayface(Matt Hagen). 550.00
299 Batman sci-fi stories 300.00
300 I:Mr.Polka-dot,E:Aquaman . . 250.00

DETECTIVE DAN, SECRET OP, 48

Humor Publ. Co., 1933

N# 10"x13", 36 pg. b&w 25,000.00

DETECTIVE EYE

Centaur Publications, Nov., 1940

1 B:Air Man, The Eye Sees, A:Masked Marvel 3,500.00
2 O:Don Rance, Mysticape, Dec., 1940 . . . . 2,500.00

DETECTIVE PICTURE STORIES

Comics Magazine Co., Dec., 1936

1 The Phantom Killer 7,000.00
2 . . . . 3,500.00
3 . . . . 2,500.00
4 WE, Muss Em Up 2,200.00
5 Trouble, April, 1937. . . . . 2,700.00

DEVIL-DOG DUGAN

Marvel Atlas, July, 1956

1 War Stories 200.00
2 JSe(c) 200.00
3 . . . . 150.00

Becomes:

TALE OF THE MARINES

4 BP,War Stories 150.00

Becomes:

MARINES AT WAR

5 War Stories 150.00
6 . . . . 150.00
7 The Big Push, Aug., 1957 . . . . 150.00

DEVIL DOGS

Street & Smith Publ., 1942

1 U.S. Marines 600.00

DEXTER COMICS

Dearfield Publications, Summer, 1948–July, 1949

1 . . . . 250.00
2 . . . . 200.00
3 thru 5 . . . . @150.00

DEXTER THE DEMON
See: MELVIN THE MONSTER

DIARY CONFESSIONS
See: TENDER ROMANCE

DIARY LOVES

Comic Magazines (Quality Comics Group) Sept., 1949

1 BWa Love Diary. 250.00
2 BWa 225.00
3 . . . . 150.00
4 RC 175.00
5 . . . . 125.00
6 . . . . 125.00
7 . . . . 125.00
8 BWa 150.00
9 BWa 150.00
10 BWa 150.00
11 . . . . 125.00
12 . . . . 125.00
13 . . . . 125.00
14 . . . . 125.00
15 BWa 150.00
16 BWa 150.00
17 thru 20. . . . . @125.00
21 BWa 150.00
22 thru 31. . . . . @100.00

Becomes:

G.I. SWEETHEARTS

June, 1953

32 Love Under Fire 150.00
33 thru 35. . . . . @125.00
36 Lend Lease Love Affair. 125.00
37 thru 45. . . . . @125.00

Becomes:

GIRLS IN LOVE

Sept., 1955

46 Somewhere I'll Find You. 150.00
47 thru 56 . . . . @125.00
57 MB(a&c), Can Love Really Change Him, Dec., 1956. . . . 150.00

DIARY SECRETS
See: TEEN-AGE DIARY SECRETS

DICK COLE

Curtis Publ./ Star Publications, Dec.–Jan., 1949

1 LbC(a&c),CS,All sports(c) 400.00
2 LbC 250.00
3 LbC(a&c) 275.00
4 LbC(a&c),Rowing (c) 275.00
5 LbC(a&c) 275.00
6 LbC(a&c), Rodeo (c) 275.00
7 LbC(a&c) 250.00
8 LbC(a&c), Football (c) 250.00
9 LbC(a&c), Basketball (c) 250.00
10 Joe Louis 300.00

Becomes:

SPORTS THRILLS

Nov., 1950–Nov., 1951

11 Ted Williams & Ty Cobb 450.00
12 LbC, Joe DiMaggio & Phil Rizzuto, Boxing (c) 400.00
13 LbC(c),Basketball (c) 350.00
14 LbC(c),Baseball (c). 375.00

 All comics prices listed are for *Near Mint* condition.

Dick Tracy Monthly #1
© Dell Publishing Co.

Dick Tracy Comics Monthly #38
© Harvey Publications

Dick Tracy Comics Monthly #85
© Harvey Publications

15 LbC(c),Baseball (c). 375.00

DICKIE DARE

Eastern Color Printing Co., 1941–42

1 BEv(c),M.Caniff 1,500.00
2 . . . . 750.00
3 . . . . 750.00
4 H. Scorcery Smith 800.00

DICK TRACY MONTHLY

Dell Publishing Co., Jan., 1948

1 ChG,AAv,Dick Tracy & the Mad Doctor'. 700.00
2 ChG,A:MarySteele,BorisArson 375.00
3 ChG,A:Spaldoni,Big Boy 375.00
4 ChG,A:Alderman Zeld 375.00
5 ChG,A:Spaldoni,Mrs.Spaldoni . 350.00
6 ChG,A:Steve the Tramp 350.00
7 ChG,A:Boris Arson,Mary Steele 350.00
8 ChG,A:Boris & Zora Arson . . . 350.00
9 ChG,A:Chief Yellowpony 350.00
10 ChG,A:Cutie Diamond. 350.00
11 ChG,A:Toby Townly, Bookie Joe. 275.00
12 ChG,A:Toby Townly, Bookie Joe. 275.00
13 ChG,A:Toby Townly, Blake . . . 300.00
14 ChG,A:Mayor Waite Wright. . . 250.00
15 ChG,A:Bowman Basil 250.00
16 ChG,A:Maw,'Muscle' & 'Cut' Famon 250.00
17 ChG,A:Jim Trailer, Mary Steele 250.00
18 ChG,A:Lips Manlis, Anthel Jones 250.00
19 I:Sparkle Plenty. 300.00
20 'Black Cat Mystery'. 275.00
21 'Tracy Meets Number One'. . . 275.00
22 'Tracy and the Alibi Maker' . . . 225.00
23 'Dick Tracy Meets Jukebox' . . 225.00
24 'Dick Tracy and Bubbles' 225.00

Becomes:

DICK TRACY COMICS MONTHLY

Harvey, May, 1950

25 ChG,A:Flattop 300.00
26 ChG,A:Vitamin Flintheart. 200.00
27 ChG,'Flattop Escapes Prision' 200.00
28 ChG,'Case o/t Torture Chamber'. 200.00
29 ChG,A:Brow,Gravel Gertie . . . 250.00
30 ChG,'Blackmail Racket'. 200.00
31 ChG,A:Snowflake Falls 175.00
32 ChG,A:Shaky,Snowflake Falls 175.00
33 ChG,'Strange Case of Measles' 225.00
34 ChG,A:Measles,Paprika 200.00
35 ChG,'Case of Stolen $50,000'. 200.00
36 ChG,'Case of the Runaway Blonde' 225.00
37 ChG,'Case of Stolen Money'. . 200.00
38 ChG,A:Breathless Mahoney . . 200.00
39 ChG,A:Itchy,B.O.Plenty. 200.00
40 ChG,'Case of Atomic Killer'. . . 200.00
41 ChG,Pt.1'Murder by Mail' 175.00
42 ChG,Pt.2'Murder by Mail' 175.00
43 ChG,'Case of the Underworld Brat' 175.00
44 ChG,'Case of the Mouthwash Murder' 175.00
45 ChG,'Case of the Evil Eyes' . . 175.00
46 ChG,'Case of the Camera Killers' 175.00
47 ChG,'Case of the Bloodthirsty Blonde'. 175.00
48 ChG,'Case of the Murderous Minstrel'. 175.00
49 ChG,Pt.1 'Killer Who Returned From the Dead 175.00
50 ChG,Pt.2 'Killer Who Returned From the Dead' . . . 175.00
51 ChG, 'Case of the High Tension Hijackers'. 150.00
52 ChG, 'Case of the Pipe-Stem Killer. 150.00
53 ChG,Pt.1 'Dick Tracy Meets the Murderous Midget'. 150.00
54 ChG,Pt.2 'Dick Tracy Meets the Murderous Midget'. 150.00
55 ChG,Pt.3 'Dick Tracy Meets the Murderous Midget' 150.00
56 ChG,'Case of the Teleguard Terror' 150.00
57 ChG,Pt.1 'Case of the Ice Cold Killer' 175.00
58 ChG,Pt.2 'Case of the Ice Cold Killer' 150.00
59 ChG,Pt.1 'Case of the Million Dollar Murder' 150.00
60 ChG,Pt.2 'Case of the Million Dollar Murder' 150.00
61 ChG,'Case of the Murderers Mask' 150.00
62 ChG,Pt.1 'Case of the White Rat Robbers' 150.00
63 ChG,Pt.2 'Case of the White Rat Robbers' 150.00
64 ChG,Pt.1 'Case of the Interrupted Honeymoon' 150.00
65 ChG,Pt.2 'Case of the Interrupted Honeymoon' 150.00
66 ChG,Pt.1 'Case of the Killer's Revenge' 150.00
67 ChG,Pt.2 'Case of the Killer's Revenge' 150.00
68 ChG,Pt.1'Case o/t TV Terror' . 150.00
69 ChG,Pt.2'Case o/t TV Terror' . 150.00
70 ChG,Pt.3'Case o/t TV Terror' . 135.00
71 ChG,A:Mrs. Forchune,Opal. . . 135.00
72 ChG,A:Empty Wiliams,Bonny . 135.00
73 ChG,A:Bonny Braids 135.00
74 ChG,A:Mr. & Mrs. Fortson Knox 135.00
75 ChG,A:Crewy Lou, Sphinx . . . 135.00
76 ChG,A:Diet Smith,Brainerd . . . 135.00
77 ChG,A:Crewy Lou, Bonny Braids 135.00
78 ChG,A:Spinner Records 135.00
79 ChG,A:Model Jones, Larry Jones 135.00
80 ChG,A:Tonsils,Dot View 135.00
81 ChG,A:Edward Moppet,Tonsils 135.00
82 ChG,A:Dot View,Mr. Crime . . . 135.00
83 ChG,A:RifleRuby,NewsuitNan. 135.00
84 ChG,A:Mr.Crime,NewsuitNan . 135.00
85 ChG,A:NewsuitNan, Mrs.Lava 135.00
86 ChG,A:Mr. Crime,Odds Zonn . 135.00
87 ChG,A:Odds Zonn,Wingy 135.00
88 ChG,A:Odds Zonn,Wingy 135.00
89 ChG,Pt.1'Canhead' 135.00
90 ChG,Pt.2'Canhead' 135.00
91 ChG,Pt.3'Canhead' 135.00
92 ChG,Pt.4'Canhead' 135.00
93 ChG,Pt.5'Canhead' 135.00
94 ChG,Pt.6'Canhead' 135.00
95 ChG,A:Mrs. Green,Dewdrop . . 135.00
96 ChG,A:Dewdrop,Sticks 135.00
97 ChG,A:Dewdrop,Sticks 135.00
98 ChG,A:Open-Mind Monty, Sticks 135.00
99 ChG,A:Open-Mind Monty, Sticks 150.00
100 ChG,A:Half-Pint,Dewdrop . . . 175.00
101 ChG,A:Open-Mind Monty . . . 135.00
102 ChG,A:Rainbow Reiley, Wingy. 135.00
103 ChG,A:Happy,Rughead. 135.00
104 ChG,A:Rainbow Reiley, Happy 135.00

Dick Tracy Comics Monthly #129
© Harvey Publications

Dixie Dugan #6
© Publication Enterprises

Doc Savage Comics #5
© Street & Smith Publications

105 ChG,A:Happy,Rughead. 135.00
106 ChG,A:Fence,Corny,Happy. . 135.00
107 ChG,A:Rainbow Reiley 135.00
108 ChG,A:Rughead,Corny, Fence. 135.00
109 ChG,A:Rughead,Mimi,Herky. 135.00
110 ChG,A:Vitamin Flintheart. . . . 135.00
111 ChG,A:Shoulders,Roach 135.00
112 ChG,A:Brilliant,Diet Smith . . . 135.00
113 ChG,A:Snowflake Falls 135.00
114 ChG,A:'Sketch'Paree, ... 135.00
115 ChG,A:Rod & Nylon Hoze. . . 135.00
116 ChG,A:Empty Williams 135.00
117 ChG,A:Spinner Records 135.00
118 ChG,A:Sleet. 135.00
119 ChG,A:Coffyhead 135.00
120 ChG,'Case Against Mumbles Quartet' 135.00
121 ChG,'Case of the Wild Boys'. 135.00
122 ChG,'Case of the Poisoned Pellet'. 135.00
123 ChG,'Case of the Deadly Treasure Hunt'. 135.00
124 ChG,'Case of Oodles Hears Only Evil'. 135.00
125 ChG,'Case of the Desparate Widow' 135.00
126 ChG,'Case of Oodles' Hideout'. 135.00
127 ChG,'Case Against Joe Period' 135.00
128 ChG,'Case Against Juvenile Delinquent'. 135.00
129 ChG,'Case of Son of Flattop' 135.00
130 ChG,'Case of Great Gang Roundup'. 135.00
131 ChG,'Strange Case of Flattop's Conscience' 135.00
132 ChG,'Case of Flattop's Big Show' 135.00
133 ChG,'Dick Tracy Follows Trail of Jewel Thief Gang' 135.00
134 ChG,'Last Stand of Jewel Thieves'. 135.00
135 ChG,'Case of the Rooftop Sniper' 135.00
136 ChG,'Mystery of the Iron Room'. 135.00
137 ChG,'Law Versus Dick Tracy' 135.00
138 ChG,'Mystery of Mary X'. . . . 135.00
139 ChG,'Yogee the Merciless' . . 135.00
140 ChG,'The Tunnel Trap' 135.00
141 ChG,'Case of Wormy & His Deadly Wagon' 135.00
142 ChG,'Case of the Killer's Revenge' 135.00
143 ChG,'Strange Case of Measles' 135.00
144 ChG,'Strange Case of Shoulders' 135.00
145 ChG,'Case of the Fiendish Photographers'; April, 1961 . . 135.00

DICK WINGATE OF THE U.S. NAVY

Superior Publ./ Toby Press, 1951

N# 200.00
N# reprint. 150.00

DILLY

Lev Gleason Publications, 1953

1 High School Humor 125.00
2 . . . . 100.00
3 . . . . 100.00

DIME COMICS

Newsbook Publ. Corp., 1945

1 LbC,A:Silver Streak 1,200.00

DING DONG

Compix (Magazine Enterprises), 1947

1 (fa). 300.00
2 (fa). 150.00
3 thru 5 (fa). . . . . @100.00

DINKY DUCK

St. John Publ. Co./Pines, Nov., 1951

1 . . . . 150.00
2 . . . . 125.00
3 thru 10 . . . . @100.00
11 thru 15 . . . . @100.00
16 thru 18. . . . . @75.00
19 Summer, 1958 . . . . 75.00

DIPPY DUCK

Marvel Atlas, 1957

1 Funny animal. 100.00

DIXIE DUGAN

Columbia Publ./ Publication Enterprises, July, 1942

1 Boxing (c),Joe Palooka 500.00
2 . . . . 300.00
3 . . . . 200.00
4 . . . . 150.00
5 . . . . @150.00
6 thru 12 . . . . @100.00
13 1949 . . . . 100.00

DIZZY DAMES

B&M Distribution Co. (American Comics), Sept.–Oct., 1952

1 . . . . 200.00
2 . . . . 125.00
3 . . . . 100.00
4 . . . . 100.00
5 . . . . 100.00
6 July–Aug., 1953 . . . . 100.00

DIZZY DON COMICS

Howard Publications/ Dizzy Dean Ent., 1943

1 B&W interior. 300.00
2 B&W Interior 200.00
3 B&W Interior 150.00
4 B&W Interior 150.00
5 thru 21 . . . . @150.00
22 Oct., 1946 . . . . 300.00
1a thru 3a. . . . . @350.00

DIZZY DUCK

See: BARNYARD COMICS

DOC CARTER V.D. COMICS

Health Publ. Inst., 1949

N# 350.00
N# 250.00

DOC SAVAGE COMICS

Street & Smith Publ., May, 1940

1 B:Doc Savage, Capt. Fury, Danny Garrett, Mark Mallory, Whisperer, Capt. Death, Treasure Island, A: The Magician . . . 7,500.00
2 O:Ajax,The Sun Man,E:The Whisperer. 2,500.00
3 Artic Ice Wastes 1,700.00
4 E:Treasure Island, Saves U.S. Navy 1,400.00
5 O:Astron, the Crocodile Queen, Sacred Ruby 1,100.00

Do-Do #1
© Nationwide Publishers

Doll Man #42
© Quality Comics Group

Donald and Mickey Merry Christmas
N# (#6) © Walt Disney

6 E: Capt. Fury, O:Red Falcon, Murderous Peace Clan 850.00
7 V:Zoombas 850.00
8 Finds the Long Lost Treasure . 850.00
9 Smashes Japan's Secret Oil Supply 850.00
10 O:Thunder Bolt, The Living Dead A:Lord Manhattan 850.00
11 V:Giants of Destruction 700.00
12 Saves Merchant Fleet from Complete Destruction 700.00
2-1 The Living Evil 700.00
2-2 V:Beggar King 700.00
2-3 .... 700.00
2-4 Fight to Death 700.00
2-5 Saves Panama Canal from Blood Raider 700.00
2-6 .... 700.00
2-7 V:Black Knight 700.00
2-8 Oct., 1943 .... 700.00

DR. ANTHONY KING HOLLYWOOD LOVE DOCTOR

Harvey, Publ., 1952

1 .... 250.00
2 .... 200.00
3 .... 200.00
4 BP,May, 1954.............. 200.00

DO-DO

Nationwide Publishers, 1950

1 Funny Animal Circus Humor .. 300.00
2 .... 150.00
3 .... 150.00
4 .... 150.00
5 thru 7 .... @150.00

DODO AND THE FROG
See: FUNNY STUFF

DOGFACE DOOLEY
See: A-1 COMICS

DOLL MAN

Comic Favorites (Quality Comics Group), Fall, 1941–Oct., 1953

1 RC,B:Doll Man & Justine Wright 5,000.00
2 B:Dragon 1,800.00
3 Five stories 1,500.00
4 Dolls of Death, Wanted: The Doll Man 1,300.00
5 RC,Four stories 1,100.00
6 Buy War Stamps (c) 750.00
7 Four stories 750.00
8 BWa,Three stories,A:Torchy . 2,200.00
9 Torchy 750.00
10 RC,V:Murder Marionettes, Grim, The Good Sport...... 600.00
11 Shocks Crime Square in the Eye 600.00
12 Torchy 600.00
13 RC,Blows Crime Sky High ... 600.00
14 Spotlight on Comics 600.00
15 Faces Danger............. 600.00
16 Torchy 550.00
17 Deals Out Punishment for Crime.................. 550.00
18 Redskins Scalp Crime 550.00
19 Fitted for a Cement Coffin ... 550.00
20 Destroys the Black Heart of Nemo Black............. 550.00
21 Problem of a Poison Pistol ... 500.00
22 V:Tom Thumb 500.00
23 V:Minstrel, Musician of Menace 500.00
24 V:Elixir of Youth........... 500.00
25 V:Thrawn, Lord of Lightning .. 500.00
26 V:Sultan of Satarr & Wonderous Runt 500.00
27 Space Conquest 500.00
28 V:The Flame 500.00
29 V:Queen MAB............. 500.00
30 V:Lord Damion 500.00
31 I:Elmo, the Wonder Dog 400.00
32 A:Jeb Rivers 400.00
33 & 34.................. @400.00
35 Prophet of Doom........... 400.00
36 Death Trap in the Deep 400.00
37 V:The Skull,B:Doll Girl, Bondage(c) 550.00
38 The Cult of Death 400.00
39 V:The Death Drug, Narcotics . 400.00
40 Giants of Crime 400.00
41 The Headless Horseman 250.00
42 Tale of the Mind Monster 250.00
43 The Thing that Kills......... 250.00
44 V:Radioactive Man 250.00
45 What was in the Doom Box? . 250.00
46 Monster from Tomorrow 250.00
47 V:Mad Hypnotist 250.00

DOLLY

Approved Comics/ Ziff-Davis Publ. Co., 1951

1 (10) Adventures in Toy Land .. 125.00

DOLLY DILL

Marvel, 1945

1 Newsstand 250.00

FAMOUS GANG, BOOK OF COMICS

Firestone Tire & Rubber Co., 1942

N# Porky Pig,Bugs Bunny 1,200.00

Becomes:

DONALD AND MICKEY MERRY CHRISTMAS

N# (2),CB, 1943............ 1,000.00
N# (3),CB, 1944 .... 900.00
N# (4),CB, 1945............ 1,400.00
N# (5),CB, 1946............ 1,000.00
N# (6),CB, 1947............ 1,000.00
N# (7),CB, 1948............ 1,000.00
N# (8),CB, 1949 .... 900.00

DONALD DUCK

Whitman

W.Disney's Donald Duck ('35) . 6,000.00
W.Disney's Donald Duck ('36) . 5,000.00
W.Disney's Donald Duck ('38) . 5,000.00

DONALD DUCK ALBUM

Dell Publishing Co., May-July, 1959

1 CB(c).................... 200.00
2 .... 150.00

DONALD DUCK GIVEAWAYS

Donald Duck Surprise Party (Icy Frost Ice Cream 1948)WK . 4,000.00
Donald Duck (Xmas Giveaway 1944) 1,500.00
Donald Duck Tells About Kites (P.G.&E., Florida 1954).... 4,000.00
Donald Duck Tells About Kites (S.C.Edison 1954) 3,500.00
Donald Duck and the Boys (Whitman 1948) 1,200.00

Donald Duck #30
© Walt Disney

Don Winslow of the Navy #36
© Fawcett Publications

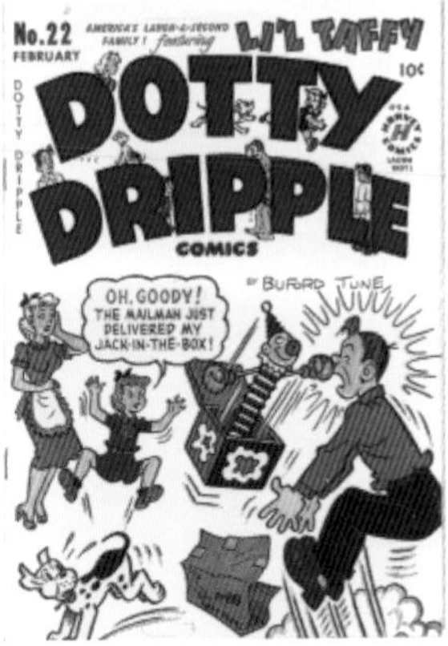

Dotty Dripple #22
© Harvey Publications

Donald Ducks Atom Bomb
(Cherrios 1947) 1,200.00

(WALT DISNEY'S) DONALD DUCK
Dell Publishing Co., Nov., 1952

(#1-#25) See *Dell Four Color*
26 CB;"Trick or Treat" (1952). . . . 800.00
27 CB(c);"Flying Horse"('53) 350.00
28 CB(c); Robert the Robot 300.00
29 CB(c). 300.00
30 CB(c). 300.00
31 thru 39. . . . . @200.00
40 . . . . 175.00
41 . . . . 175.00
42 . . . . 175.00
43 . . . . 175.00
44. . . . . 175.00
45 CB. 350.00
46 CB; "Secret of Hondorica" . . . 500.00
47 thru 51. . . . . @200.00
52 CB; "Lost Peg-Leg Mine" 350.00
53 . . . . 200.00
54 CB; "Forbidden Valley" 500.00
55 thru 59. . . . . @175.00
60 CB; "Donald Duck & the
Titanic Ants". 350.00
61 thru 67. . . . . @150.00
68 CB. 300.00
69 thru 78. . . . . @150.00
79 CB (1 page) 200.00
80 . . . . 125.00
81 CB (1 page) 150.00
82 . . . . 125.00
83 . . . . 125.00
84 . . . . 125.00

DON FORTUNE MAGAZINE
Don Fortune Publ. Co., Aug., 1946

1 CCB 400.00
2 CCB 250.00
3 CCB,Bondage(c) 225.00
4 CCB 200.00
5 CCB 200.00
6 CCB, Jan., 1947 . . . . 200.00

DON NEWCOMBE
Fawcett Publications, 1950

1 Baseball Star 650.00

DON WINSLOW OF THE NAVY
Fawcett Publ./ Charlton Comics, Feb., 1943

1 Captain Marvel (c) 2,000.00
2 Nips the Nipponese in
the Solomons 850.00
3 Single-Handed invasion of
the Philippines 600.00
4 Undermines the Nazis! 500.00
5 Stolen Battleship Mystery 500.00
6 War Stamps for Victory (c) . . . 500.00
7 Coast Guard 400.00
8 U.S. Marines 400.00
9 Fighting Marines 400.00
10 Fighting Seabees 400.00
11 . . . . 350.00
12 Tuned for Death 350.00
13 Hirohito's Hospitality 350.00
14 Catapults against the Axis . . . 350.00
15 Fighting Merchant Marine. . . . 300.00
16 V:The Most Diabolical Villain
of all Time 300.00
17 Buy War Stamps (c) 300.00
18 The First Underwater Convoy. 300.00
19 Bonape Excersion. 300.00
20 The Nazi Prison Ship 300.00
21 Prisoner of the Nazis 225.00
22 Suicide Football 225.00
23 Peril on the High Seas 225.00
24 Adventures on the High Seas. 225.00
25 Shanghaied Red Cross Ship . 225.00
26 V:The Scorpion 225.00
27 Buy War Stamps. 225.00
28 . . . . 225.00
29 Invitation to Trouble 225.00
30 . . . . 225.00
31 Man or Myth? 150.00
32 Return of the Renegade 150.00
33 Service Ribbons 150.00
34 Log Book. 150.00
35 . . . . 150.00
36 V:Octopus 150.00
37 V: Sea Serpent 150.00
38 Climbs Mt. Everest 150.00
39 Scorpion's Death Ledger 150.00
40 Kick Off! 150.00
41 Rides the Skis! 125.00
42 Amazon Island 125.00
43 Ghastly Doll Murder Case . . . 125.00
44 The Scorpions Web 125.00
45 V:Highwaymen of the Seas . . 125.00
46 Renegades Jailbreak 125.00
47 The Artic Expedition 125.00
48 Maelstrom of the Deep 125.00
49 The Vanishing Ship! 125.00
50 V:The Snake 125.00
51 A:Singapore Sal 125.00
52 Ghost of the Fishing Ships . . . 125.00
53 . . . . 125.00
54 . . . . 125.00
55 . . . . 125.00
56 Far East 125.00
57 A:Singapore Sal 125.00
58 . . . . 125.00
59 . . . . 125.00
60 thru 63. . . . . @125.00
64 MB. 125.00
65 Ph(c) 200.00
66 Ph(c) 200.00
67 Ph(c) 200.00
68 Ph(c) 200.00
69 Ph(c), Jaws of Destruction . . . 200.00
70 . . . . 125.00
71 . . . . 125.00
72 . . . . 125.00
73 Sept., 1955 . . . . 125.00

DOPEY DUCK COMICS
Marvel Timely, Fall, 1945

1 A:Casper Cat,Krazy Krow 250.00
2 A:Casper Cat,Krazy Krow 225.00
Becomes:

WACKY DUCK
Marvel, 1946

3 Paperchase(c) 225.00
4 Wacky Duck(c) 200.00
5 Duck & Devil(c) 175.00
6 Cliffhanger(c) 175.00
1 Baketball(c) 125.00
2 Traffic Light(c) 125.00
Becomes:

JUSTICE COMICS

DOROTHY LAMOUR
See: JUNGLE LIL

DOTTY
See: FOUR TEENERS

DOTTY DRIPPLE
Magazine Enterprises/ Harvey Publications, 1946

1 . . . . 150.00
2 . . . . 125.00

 All comics prices listed are for *Near Mint* condition.

Double Comics 1942 (#3)
© Elliot Publications

Dudley #2
© Prize Publications

Durango Kid #17
© Magazine Enterprises

3 thru 10 . . . . @100.00
11 thru 20 . . . . @100.00
21 thru 23 . . . . @75.00
24 June, 1952 . . . . 75.00
Becomes:

HORACE & DOTTY DRIPPLE
Aug., 1952

25 thru 42 . . . . @75.00
43 Oct., 1955 . . . . 75.00

DOUBLE ACTION COMICS
DC Comics, Jan., 1940

2 Pre-Hero DC 27,000.00

DOUBLE COMICS
Elliot Publications

1 ('40),Masked Marvel 4,000.00
2 ('41),Tornado Tim 3,000.00
3 ('42) 2,500.00
4 ('43) 2,000.00
5 ('44) 2,000.00

DOUBLE LIFE OF PRIVATE STRONG
Archie Publications, 1959

1 JSm/JK,I:Lancelot Strong/ Shield, The Fly 850.00
2 JSm/JK,GT A:Fly 550.00

DOUBLE TALK
Feature Publications

1 Anti-communist 150.00

DOUBLE TROUBLE
St. John Publishing Co., 1957

1 Funny kids 125.00

DOUBLE UP
Elliot Publications, 1941

1 . . . . 2,000.00

DOVER THE BIRD
Famous Funnies Publ. 1955

1 Funny animal 100.00

DOWN WITH CRIME
Fawcett Publications, Nov., 1951

1 A:Desarro 650.00
2 BP, A:Scanlon Gang 400.00
3 H-is for Heroin 375.00
4 BP, A:Desarro 350.00
5 No Jail Can Hold Me 400.00
6 The Puncture-Proof Assassin . 400.00
7 The Payoff, Nov., 1952 . . . . . . 400.00

DO YOU BELIEVE IN NIGHTMARES
St. John Publ. Co., 1957

1 SD 900.00
2 DAy 500.00

DREAM BOOK OF LOVE, and DREAM BOOK OF ROMANCE
See: A-1 COMICS

DUDLEY
Prize Publications, Nov.–Dec., 1952

1 . . . . 175.00
2 . . . . 125.00
3 March–April, 1950 . . . . 100.00

DUMBO WEEKLY
The Walt Disney Co., 1942

1 Gas giveaways 2,100.00
2 . . . . 1,500.00
3 . . . . 1,500.00
4 thru 16 . . . . @1,500.00

DO YOU BELIEVE IN NIGHTMARES?
St. John Publishing Co., 1957–58

1 SD 650.00
2 DAy 400.00

DURANGO KID
Magazine Enterprises, Oct.–Nov., 1949

1 FF, Charles Starrett photo (c) B:Durango Kid & Raider . . 1,200.00
2 FF, Charles Starrett Ph(c) 700.00
3 FF, Charles Starrett Ph(c) 600.00
4 FF, Charles Starrett Ph(c), Two-Timing Guns 500.00
5 FF, Charles Starrett Ph(c), Tracks Across the Trail 500.00
6 FF 300.00
7 FF,Atomic(c) 350.00
8 FF 300.00
9 FF 300.00
10 FF 300.00
11 FF 250.00
12 FF 250.00
13 FF 250.00
14 thru 16 FF . . . . @250.00
17 O:Durango Kid 300.00
18 FMe,DAy(c) 200.00
19 FMe,FGu 175.00
20 FMe,FGu 175.00
21 FMe,FGu 175.00
22 FMe,FGu 200.00
23 FMe,FGu,I:Red Scorpion 200.00
24 thru 30 FMe,FGu . . . . @200.00
31 FMe,FGu 200.00
32 thru 40 FGu . . . . @200.00
41 FGu,Oct., 1941 . . . . 200.00

DYNAMIC COMICS
Dynamic Publications (Harry 'A' Chesler), Oct., 1941

1 EK,O:Major Victory, Dynamic Man, Hale the Magician, A:Black Cobra 3,500.00
2 O:Dynamic Boy & Lady Satan,I:Green Knight, Lance Cooper 2,500.00
3 GT 2,200.00
8 Horror (c) 2,500.00
9 MRa,GT,B:Mr.E 2,500.00
10 . . . . 1,500.00
11 GT 1,350.00
12 GT 1,200.00
13 GT 1,300.00
14 . . . . 1,200.00
15 Sky Chief 1,200.00
16 GT,Bondage(c),Marijuana . . 1,500.00
17 . . . . 1,700.00
18 Ric 1,000.00
19 A:Dynamic Man 1,000.00
20 same,Nude Woman 2,000.00
21 same,Dinosaur(c) 1,000.00
22 same 1,000.00
23 A:Yankee Girl,1.0948 . . . . . . 1,000.00

Dynamite #1
© Comic Media

Eerie #4
© Avon Periodicals

Ellery Queen #1
© Superior Comics

DYNAMITE
Comic Media/Allen Hardy Publ., May, 1953

1 DH(c),A:Danger#6 . . . 400.00
2 . . . 200.00
3 PMo(a&c),B:Johnny Dynamite,Drug. . . . 300.00
4 PMo(a&c),Prostitution . . . 350.00
5 PMo(a&c) . . . 200.00
6 PMo(a&c). . . . 200.00
7 PMo(a&c) . . . 200.00
8 PMo(a&c) . . . 200.00
9 PMo(a&c) . . . 200.00

Becomes:

JOHNNY DYNAMITE
Charlton Comics, June, 1955

10 PMo(c) . . . 150.00
11 . . . 125.00
12 . . . 125.00

Becomes:

FOREIGN INTRIGUES
1956

13 A:Johnny Dynamite. . . . 150.00
14 same. . . . 125.00
15 same. . . . 125.00

Becomes:

BATTLEFIELD ACTION
Nov., 1957

16 . . . 150.00
17 . . . 100.00
18 . . . 100.00
19 . . . 100.00
20 . . . 100.00
21 thru 30. . . . @100.00

EAGLE, THE
Fox Features Syndicate, July, 1941

1 B:The Eagle,A:Rex Dexter of Mars . . . 4,000.00
2 B:Spider Queen . . . 2,000.00
3 B:Joe Spook . . . 1,800.00
4 Jan., 1942 . . . 1,800.00

EAGLE
Rural Home Publ., Feb.–March, 1945

1 LbC . . . 800.00
2 LbC,April–May, 1945 . . . 500.00

EAT RIGHT TO WORK AND WIN
Swift Co., 1942

N# Flash Gordon,Popeye . . . 750.00

EDDIE STANKY
Fawcett Publications, 1951

N# New York Giants . . . 450.00

EERIE
Avon Periodicals, May–June, 1951– Aug.–Sept., 1954

1 JKa,Horror from the Pit, Bondage(c) . . . 5,500.00
2,WW(a&c), Chamber of Death 1,000.00
3 WW(a&c),JKa,JO Monster of the Storm . . . 1,100.00
4 WW(c),Phantom of Reality . 1,000.00
5 WW(c), Operation Horror . . . 900.00
6 Devil Keeps a Date . . . 450.00
7 WW(c),JKa,JO,Blood for the Vampire . . . 700.00
8 EK, Song of the Undead . . . 400.00
9 JKa, Hands of Death . . . 400.00
10 Castle of Terror. . . . 400.00
11 Anatomical Monster . . . 400.00
12 Dracula . . . 500.00
13 . . . 400.00
14 Master of the Dead. . . . 400.00
15 Reprint #1 . . . 300.00
16 WW, Chamber of Death . . . 300.00
17 WW(c),JO,JKa,. . . . 350.00

EERIE ADVENTURES
Approved Comics (Ziff-Davis), Winter, 1951

1 BP,JKa,Bondage . . . 500.00

EGBERT
Arnold Publications/ Comic Magazine, Spring, 1946

1 I:Egbert & The Count . . . 400.00
2 . . . 250.00
3 . . . 200.00
4 . . . 200.00
5 . . . 200.00
6 . . . 250.00
7 thru 10 . . . @200.00
11 thru 17. . . . @150.00
18 1950 . . . 150.00

EH!
Charlton Comics, Dec., 1953–Nov., 1954

1 DAy(c),DG,Atomic Mouse . . . 400.00
2 DAy(c) . . . 250.00
3 DAy(c) . . . 225.00
4 DAy(c),Sexual . . . 250.00
5 DAy(c) . . . 225.00
6 DAy(c),Sexual . . . 250.00
7 DAy(c) . . . 225.00

EL BOMBO COMICS
Frances M. McQueeny, 1945

1 . . . 175.00

ELLA CINDERS
St. John Publishing Co. 1948

1 . . . 250.00
2 . . . 150.00
3 . . . 100.00
4 . . . 100.00
5 . . . 100.00

ELLERY QUEEN
Superior Comics, May–Nov., 1949

1 LbC(c),JKa,Horror . . . 700.00
2 . . . 500.00
3 Drug issue . . . 600.00
4 The Crooked Mile . . . 500.00

ELLERY QUEEN
Approved Comics (Ziff-Davis), Jan.–March, 1952

1 NS(c),The Corpse the Killed . . 600.00
2 NS,Killer's Revenge, Summer, 1952 . . . 500.00

ELMO COMICS
St. John Publishing Co., 1948

1 . . . 200.00

ELSIE THE COW
D.S. Publishing Co., Oct.–Nov., 1949

1 P(c) . . . 450.00
2 Bondage(c) . . . 300.00
3 July–Aug., 1950 . . . 200.00

Exciting Comics #1
© Standard Comics

Exciting Comics #33
© Standard Comics

Exciting Comics #59
© Standard Comics

ENCHANTING LOVE

Kirby Publishing Co.
Oct., 1949

1 Branded Guilty, Ph(c) 150.00
2 Ph(c),BP 100.00
3 Ph(c),Utter Defeat was Our
Victory; Jimmy Stewart 150.00
4 thru 6 . . . . @100.00

ERNIE COMICS
See: SCREAM COMICS

ESCAPE FROM FEAR

Planned Parenthood
of America, 1956

1 . . . . 150.00
2 (1962) 100.00

ETTA KETT

Best Books, Inc.
(Standard Comics),
Dec., 1948

11 . . . . 150.00
12 . . . . 100.00
13 . . . . 100.00
14 Sept., 1949 . . . . 100.00

EVA THE IMP

Red Top Comic/Decker, 1957

1 . . . . 100.00
2 . . . . 100.00

EVERYTHING HAPPENS TO HARVEY

DC Comics, 1953–54

1 Teen-age humor. 300.00
2 . . . . 175.00
3 . . . . 125.00
4 . . . . 125.00
5 . . . . 125.00
6 . . . . 125.00
7 . . . . 125.00

EXCITING COMICS

Better Publ./Visual Editions
(Standard Comics),
April, 1940

1 O:Mask, Jim Hatfield,
Dan Williams 7,000.00
2 B:Sphinx 4,000.00
3 V;Robot 3,000.00
4 V:Sea Monster 2,500.00
5 V:Gargoyle 2,500.00
6 . . . . 2,500.00
7 AS(c) 2,000.00
8 . . . . 2,000.00
9 O:Black Terror & Tim,
Bondage(c) 17,000.00
10 A:Black Terror 5,000.00
11 same 3,000.00
12 Bondage(c) 2,800.00
13 Bondage(c) 2,800.00
14 O:Sphinx 2,500.00
15 O:Liberator. 2,600.00
16 Black Terror 2,400.00
17 same 2,400.00
18 same 2,400.00
19 same 2,400.00
20 E:Mask,Bondage(c) 2,200.00
21 A:Liberator 2,200.00
22 O:The Eaglet,B:American
Eagle 2,200.00
23 Black Terror 1,800.00
24 Black Terror 1,800.00
25 Bondage(c) 1,800.00
26 ASh(c) 1,800.00
27 ASh(c) 1,800.00
28 ASh(c),B:Crime Crusader . . 2,000.00
29 ASh(c) 1,800.00
30 ASh(c),Bondage(c). 2,000.00
31 ASh(c) 1,500.00
32 ASh(c) 1,500.00
33 ASh(c) 1,500.00
34 ASh(c) 1,500.00
35 ASh(c),E:Liberator 1,500.00
36 ASh(c) 1,500.00
37 ASh(c) 1,500.00
38 ASh(c) 1,500.00
39 ASh(c)O:Kara, Jungle
Princess 3,400.00
40 ASh(c) 3,000.00
41 ASh(c) 3,000.00
42 ASh(c),B:Scarab 3,000.00
43 ASh(c) 1,200.00
44 ASh(c) 1,200.00
45 ASh(c),V:Robot 1,200.00
46 ASh(c) 1,200.00
47 ASh(c) 1,200.00
48 ASh(c) 1,200.00
49 ASh(c),E:Kara &
American Eagle 1,200.00
50 ASh(c),E:American Eagle . . 1,200.00
51 ASh(c),B:Miss Masque 1,500.00
52 ASh(c),Miss Masque 1,000.00
53 ASh(c),Miss Masque 1,000.00
54 ASh(c),E:Miss Masque 1,000.00
55 ASh(c),O&B:Judy o/t Jungle 1,000.00
56 ASh(c) 1,000.00
57 ASh(c) 1,000.00
58 ASh(c) 1,000.00
59 ASh(c),FF,Bondage(c) 1,200.00
60 ASh(c),The Mystery Rider . 1,000.00
61 ASh(c) 1,000.00
62 ASh(c),CQ 1,000.00
63 ASh(c) 1,000.00
64 ASh(c) 1,000.00
65 ASh(c),CQ 1,000.00
66 . . . . 1,000.00
67 GT 1,000.00
68 . . . . 1,000.00
69 Sept., 1949 . . . . 1,000.00

EXCITING ROMANCES

Fawcett Publications, 1949

1 Ph(c) 200.00
2 . . . . 150.00
3 . . . . 150.00
4 Ph(c) 150.00
5 thru 14 . . . . @100.00

EXCITING WAR

Visual Editions
(Standard Comics), 1952

5 Korean war 150.00
6 . . . . 100.00
7 . . . . 100.00
8 ATh. 125.00

EXOTIC ROMANCE
See: TRUE WAR ROMANCES

EXPLOITS OF DANIEL BOONE

Comic Magazines
(Quality Comics Group), 1955

1 Frontier hero 350.00
2 . . . . 200.00
3 . . . . 175.00
4 thru 6 . . . . @175.00

EXPLORER JOE

Approved Comics
(Ziff-Davis), Winter, 1951

1 NS,The Fire Opal
of Madagscar 150.00
2 BK, Oct.–Nov., 1952 . . . . 165.00

Ex

Exposed #6
© D.S. Publishing

Fairy Tales #10
© Ziff-Davis Publications

Famous Crimes #3
© Fox Features Syndicate

EXPOSED

D.S. Publishing Co., March–April, 1948

1 Corpses Cash and Carry 275.00
2 Giggling Killer 350.00
3 One Bloody Night 150.00
4 JO,Deadly Dummy 150.00
5 Body on the Beach 150.00
6 Fatal Masquerade 450.00
7 The Midnight Guest 450.00
8 Grl,The Secret in the Snow . . 450.00
9 The Gypsy Baron, July–Aug., 1949 . . . . 450.00

EXTRA COMICS

Magazine Enterprises, 1947

1 . . . . 750.00

EXTRA!

E.C. Comics, March–April, 1955

1 JCr,RC,JSe 400.00
2 JCr,RC,JSe 300.00
3 JCr,RC,JSe 300.00
4 JCr,RC,JSe 300.00
5 Nov.–Dec., 1955 . . . . 300.00

FACE, THE

Publication Enterprises (Columbia Comics), 1942

1 MBi(c),The Face 2,000.00
2 MBi(c) 1,500.00

Becomes:

TONY TRENT

1948

3 MBi,A:The Face 350.00
4 1949 . . . . 300.00

FAIRY TALE PARADE

Dell Publishing Co., 1942

1 WK,Giant 2,500.00
2 WK,Flying Horse 1,500.00
3 WK 1,000.00
4 WK 900.00
5 WK 900.00
6 WK 600.00
7 WK 600.00
8 WK 600.00
9 WK,Reluctant Dragon 600.00

FAIRY TALES

Approved Comics (Ziff-Davis), 1951

10 . . . . 350.00
11 . . . . 300.00

FAITHFUL

Marvel, Nov., 1949

1 Ph(c),I Take This Man 200.00
2 Ph(c),Love Thief,Feb.,1950 . . . 200.00

FALLING IN LOVE

Arleigh Publ./ National Periodical Publ., 1955

1 . . . . 475.00
2 . . . . 250.00
3 . . . . 150.00
4 . . . . 150.00
5 . . . . 150.00
6 . . . . 150.00
7 . . . . 150.00
8 . . . . 150.00
9 . . . . 150.00
10 . . . . 150.00
11 thru 20 . . . . @125.00
21 thru 47 . . . . @100.00

FAMILY FUNNIES

Harvey Publications, 1950

1 Mandrake 200.00
2 Flash Gordon 150.00
3 . . . . 125.00
4 Flash Gordon 125.00
5 Flash Gordon 125.00
6 . . . . 125.00
7 Flash Gordon 125.00
8 . . . . 125.00

Becomes:

TINY TOT FUNNIES

Harvey Publications, 1951

9 Dagwood (c),Flash Gordon . . . 150.00

Becomes:

JUNIOR FUNNIES

Harvey Publications, 1951–52

10 Blondie, Popeye 100.00
11 . . . . 100.00
12 . . . . 100.00
13 . . . . 100.00

FAMOUS COMICS

Whitman Publ. Co., 1934

1 3"x8", three per box 1,200.00
2 . . . . 1,000.00
3 . . . . 1,000.00

FAMOUS COMICS

Zain-Eppy Publ.

N# Joe Palooka 600.00

FAMOUS CRIMES

Fox Features Syndicate, June, 1948

1 Cold Blooded Killer 700.00
2 Near Nudity (c) 550.00
3 Crime Never Pays 650.00
4 . . . . 300.00
5 . . . . 300.00
6 . . . . 300.00
7 Drug issue 550.00
8 thru 19 . . . . @300.00
20 Aug., 1951 . . . . 250.00
51 1952 . . . . 200.00

FAMOUS FAIRY TALES

K.K. Publication Co., 1942

N# WK, Giveaway 500.00
N# WK, Giveaway 400.00
N# WK, Giveaway 400.00

FAMOUS FEATURE STORIES

Dell Publishing Co., 1938

1A:Tarzan, Terry and the Pirates Dick Tracy,Smilin' Jack 2,500.00

FAMOUS FUNNIES

Eastern Color Printing Co., 1933

N# A Carnival of Comics 30,000.00
N# Feb., 1934, 1st 10-cent comic 50,000.00
1 July, 1934 . . . . 35,000.00
2 . . . . 15,000.00
3 B:Buck Rogers 12,000.00
4 Football (c) 5,000.00
5 Christmas 4,500.00
6 . . . . 3,000.00
7 . . . . 3,000.00
8 . . . . 3,000.00
9 . . . . 3,000.00

Famous Funnies #17
© Eastern Color Printing

Famous Funnies #209
© Eastern Color Printing

Famous Stars #5
© Ziff-Davis Publications

10 . . . . 3,000.00
11 Four pages of Buck Rogers. 1,500.00
12 Four pages of Buck Rogers. 1,500.00
13 . . . . 1,200.00
14 . . . . 1,200.00
15 Football (c). 1,200.00
16 . . . . 1,200.00
17 Christmas (c) 1,200.00
18 Four pages of Buck Rogers. 1,500.00
19 . . . . 1,200.00
20 . . . . 1,200.00
21 Baseball. 1,100.00
22 Buck Rogers 1,300.00
23 . . . . 1,100.00
24 B: War on Crime 1,100.00
25 . . . . 1,100.00
26 . . . . 1,100.00
27 G-Men (c). 1,100.00
28 . . . . 1,100.00
29 Christmas. 1,100.00
30 . . . . 1,100.00
31 . . . . 800.00
32 Phantom Magician. 1,000.00
33 A:Baby Face Nelson &
John Dillinger. 800.00
34 . . . . 800.00
35 Buck Rogers 900.00
36 . . . . 800.00
37 . . . . 800.00
38 Portrait,Buck Rogers. . . . 900.00
39 . . . . 800.00
40 . . . . 800.00
41 thru 50. . . . . @700.00
51 thru 57. . . . . @600.00
58 Baseball (c). 600.00
59 . . . . 600.00
60 . . . . 600.00
61 . . . . 500.00
62 . . . . 500.00
63 . . . . 500.00
64 . . . . 500.00
65 JK 500.00
66 . . . . 500.00
67 . . . . 500.00
68 JK 500.00
69 . . . . 500.00
70 . . . . 500.00
71 BEv 400.00
72 BEv,B:Speed Spaulding . . . 400.00
73 BEv 400.00
74 BEv 400.00
75 BEv 400.00
76 BEv 400.00
77 BEv,Merry Christmas (c). . . 400.00
78 BEv 400.00
79 BEv 400.00
80 BEv,Buck Rogers 400.00
81 O:Invisible Scarlet O'Neil . . . 300.00
82 Buck Rogers (c) 400.00
83 Dickie Dare 250.00
84 Scotty Smith 250.00
85 Eagle Scout,Roy Rogers . . . 250.00
86 Moon Monsters 250.00
87 Scarlet O'Neil 250.00
88 Dickie Dare 250.00
89 O:Fearless Flint 250.00
90 Bondage (c) 350.00
91 . . . . 250.00
92 . . . . 250.00
93 . . . . 250.00
94 War Bonds 300.00
95 Invisible Scarlet O'Neil . . . 200.00
96 . . . . 200.00
97 War Bonds Promo 200.00
98 . . . . 200.00
99 . . . . 200.00
100 Anniversary issue 200.00
101 thru 110. . . . . @200.00
111 thru 130 . . . . @125.00
131 thru 150. . . . . @100.00
151 thru 162. . . . . @100.00
163 Valentine's Day (c) . . . 100.00
164 . . . . 100.00
165 . . . . 100.00
166 . . . . 100.00
167 . . . . 100.00
168 . . . . 100.00
169 AW 125.00
170 AW 125.00
171 thru 190. . . . . @150.00
191 thru 203. . . . . @125.00
204 War (c) 100.00
205 thru 208. . . . . @100.00
209 FF(c),Buck Rogers. 3,000.00
210 FF(c),Buck Rogers. 3,000.00
211 FF(c),Buck Rogers. 3,000.00
212 FF(c),Buck Rogers. 3,000.00
213 FF(c),Buck Rogers. 3,000.00
214 FF(c),Buck Rogers. 3,000.00
215 FF(c),Buck Rogers. 3,000.00
216 FF(c),Buck Rogers. 3,000.00
217 . . . . 100.00
218 July, 1955 . . . . 100.00

FAMOUS GANG, BOOK OF COMICS
See: DONALD AND MICKEY MERRY CHRISTMAS

FAMOUS GANGSTERS
Avon Periodicals, 1951

1 Al Capone, Dillinger,
Luciano & Shultz 500.00
2 WW(c),Dillinger Machine-
Gun Killer 450.00
3 Lucky Luciano & Murder Inc. . . 450.00

Becomes:

CRIME ON THE WATERFRONT
May, 1952

4 Underworld Gangsters who
Control the Shipment of
Drugs! 400.00

FAMOUS STARS
Ziff-Davis Publ. Co., 1950

1 OW,Shelley Winter,Susan
Peters & Shirley Temple . . 1,000.00
2 BEv,Betty Hutton, Bing Crosby 750.00
3 OW,Judy Garland, Alan Ladd . 800.00
4 RC,Jolson, Bob Mitchum 750.00
5 BK,Elizabeth Taylor,
Esther Williams 900.00
6 Gene Kelly, Spring, 1952 . . . . 700.00

FAMOUS STORIES
Dell Publishing Co., 1942

1 Treasure Island 375.00
2 Tom Sawyer 350.00

FAMOUS WESTERN BADMEN
See: REDSKIN

FANTASTIC
See: CAPTAIN SCIENCE

FANTASTIC COMICS
Fox Features Syndicate, 1939

1 LF(c),I&O:Samson,B:Star
Dust, Super Wizard, Space
Smith & Capt. Kid. 9,000.00
2 BP,LF(c),Samson Destroyed the
Battery & Routed the Foe. . 4,500.00
3 BP,LF(c),Slays the Iron
Monster. 12,000.00
4 GT,LF(c),Demolishes the
Closing Torture Walls 3,000.00

Fa

Fantastic Comics #23
© Fox Features Syndicate

Fast Fiction #4
© Seaboard Publications

Gunfighter #8
© E.C. Comics

5 GT,LF(c),Crumbles the Mighty War Machine. 2,700.00
6 JSm(c),Bondage(c) 2,500.00
7 JSm(c) 2,500.00
8 GT,Destroys the Mask of Fire,Bondage(c) 2,000.00
9 Mighty Muscles saved the Drowning Girl 2,000.00
10 I&O:David. 2,000.00
11 Wrecks the Torture Machine to save his fellow American 1,800.00
12 Heaved the Huge Ship high into the Air 1,800.00
13 Samson(c) 1,800.00
14 Samson(c) 1,800.00
15 Samson(c) 1,800.00
16 E:Stardust 1,800.00
17 Samson(c) 1,800.00
18 I:Black Fury & Chuck. 1,800.00
19 Samson(c) 1,700.00
20 Samson(c) 1,700.00
21 B&I: The Banshee,Hitler(c) . 2,000.00
22 Hittler & Samson(c) 1,800.00
23 O:The Gladiator, Hitler (c) Nov., 1941 . . . . 2,000.00

FANTASTIC FEARS
Farrell Publications (Ajax), 1953
(Formerly: CAPTAIN JET)

1 (7) Tales of Stalking Terror. . . . 650.00
2 (8) 400.00
3 . . . . 325.00
4 . . . . 325.00
5 SD,1st art 1,100.00
6 Decapitation. 700.00
7 . . . . 300.00
8 Decapitation. 500.00
9 . . . . 300.00

Becomes:

FANTASTIC COMICS
Ajax, 1954

10 Tales of Enchantment 250.00
11 Amazing Adventures 275.00

FANTASTIC WORLDS
Visual Editions (Standard Comics), 1952–53

5 ATh,Triumph Over Terror, Sci-fi 400.00
6 ATh,The Cosmic Terror 350.00
7 The Asteroid God. 250.00

FANTOMAN
See: AMAZING ADVENTURE FUNNIES

FARGO KID
See: JUSTICE TRAPS OF THE GUILTY

THE FARMER'S DAUGHTER
Trojan Magazines/ Stanhall Publ., 1954

1 Sexy humor, nudity 350.00
2 . . . . 200.00
3 . . . . 200.00
4 . . . . 200.00

FAST FICTION
Seaboard Publ., Oct., 1949

1 Scarlet Pimpernel 500.00
2 HcK,Captain Blood 400.00
3 She 500.00
4 The 39 Steps 350.00
5 HcK,Beau Geste 350.00

Becomes:

STORIES BY FAMOUS AUTHORS ILLUSTRATED
Famous Author Illustrated, Aug., 1950

1a Scarlet Pimpernel 400.00
2a Captain Blood 400.00
3a She 500.00
4a The 39 Steps 325.00
5a Beau Geste 300.00
6 HcK,MacBeth. 325.00
7 HcK,Window 275.00
8 HcK,Hamlet 300.00
9 Nicholas Nickleby 275.00
10 HcK,Romeo & Juliet 275.00
11 GS,Ben Hur. 290.00
12 GS,La Svengali. 275.00
13 HcK,Scaramouche 275.00

FAT AND SLAT JOKE BOOK
William H. Wise, 1944

N# 500.00

FAT AND SLAT
Fables Publ., Inc. (E.C. Comics), 1947

1 I&O:Voltage, Man of Lightning. 400.00
2 . . . . 275.00
3 . . . . 275.00
4 . . . . 275.00

Becomes:

GUNFIGHTER
Fables Publ., Inc. (E.C. Comics), 1948–50

5 JCr(c),Wild West 700.00
6 Grl,JCr(c),Moon Girl 500.00
7 AF,Grl. 500.00
8 AF,Grl. 500.00
9 AF,Grl. 500.00
10 JCr,AF,Grl 500.00
11 AF,Grl 500.00
12 Grl. 500.00
13 JCr,WW,Grl. 550.00
14 JCr,WW,Grl,Bondage 550.00

Becomes:

HAUNT OF FEAR

FAUNTLEROY COMICS
Close-Up Publ. (Archie Publ.) 1950–52

1 F:Super Duck. 150.00
2 . . . . 100.00
3 . . . . 100.00

FAVORITE COMICS
1934

1 Giveaways,Nebbs,Joe Palooka. 1,500.00
2 same. 1,000.00
3 same. 1,000.00

FAWCETT FUNNY ANIMALS
Fawcett Publications, Dec., 1942

1 I:Hoppy the Marvel Bunny, Captain Marvel (c) 1,200.00
2 X-Mas Issue 600.00
3 Spirit of '43 . . . . 500.00
4 and 5 . . . . @500.00
6 Buy War Bonds and Stamps . . 400.00
7 . . . . 400.00
8 Flag (c). 400.00

Fawcett Funny Animals #31
© Fawcett Publications

Feature Books #6
© David McKay Publications

Feature Funnies #10
© Harry A. Chesler Publications

9 and 10 . . . . @400.00
11 thru 20 . . . . @250.00
21 thru 30 . . . . @200.00
31 thru 40 . . . . @200.00
41 thru 83 . . . . @150.00

Charlton Comics

84 . . . . 150.00
85 thru 91 Feb., 1956. . . . . @100.00

FAWCETT MINIATURES

Fawcett Publ.
(Wheaties Giveaways), 1946

1 Capt. Marvel 250.00
2 Capt. Marvel 250.00
3 Capt. Marvel Jr. 250.00
4 Delecta of the Planets 400.00

FAWCETT MOVIE COMICS

Fawcett Publications, 1949

N# Dakota Lil 375.00
N#a Copper Canyon 300.00
N# Destination the Moon 1,100.00
N# Montana 300.00
N# Pioneer Marshal 300.00
N# Powder River Rustlers 450.00
N# Singing Guns 275.00
7 Gunmen of Abilene 325.00
8 King of the Bull Whip 425.00
9 BP,The Old Frontier 300.00
10 The Missourians 300.00
11 The Thundering Trail 400.00
12 Rustlers on Horseback 325.00
13 Warpath. 250.00
14 Last Outpost,RonaldReagan . 550.00
15 The Man from Planet-X 3,000.00
16 10 Tall Men 200.00
17 Rose Cimarron 150.00
18 The Brigand 175.00
19 Carbine Williams. 175.00
20 Ivanhoe, Dec., 1952 . . . . 300.00

FEATURE BOOKS

David McKay Publications, May, 1937

N# Dick Tracy 10,000.00
N# Popeye. 9,000.00
1 Zane Grey's King of the
Royal Mounted 800.00
2 Popeye 1,200.00
3 Popeye and the "Jeep" 1,000.00
4 Dick Tracy 2,000.00
5 Popeye and his Poppa 1,000.00
6 Dick Tracy 1,200.00
7 Little Orphan Annie 1,400.00
8 Secret Agent X-9 . . . . 750.00
9 Tracy & the Famon Boys . . . 1,200.00
10 Popeye & Susan 1,000.00
11 Annie Rooney 350.00
12 Blondie. 1,100.00
13 Inspector Wade. 325.00
14 Popeye in Wild Oats 1,200.00
15 Barney Baxter in the Air 500.00
16 Red Eagle. 400.00
17 Gang Busters 900.00
18 Mandrake the Magician 850.00
19 Mandrake 850.00
20 The Phantom 1,200.00
21 Lone Ranger 1,100.00
22 The Phantom 900.00
23 Mandrake in Teibe Castle. . . . 850.00
24 Lone Ranger 1,100.00
25 Flash Gordon on the
Planet Mongo. 1,500.00
26 Prince Valiant. 1,300.00
27 Blondie 250.00
28 Blondie and Dagwood. 250.00
29 Blondie at the Home
Sweet Home 250.00
30 Katzenjammer Kids 250.00
31 Blondie Keeps the Home
Fires Burning. 250.00
32 Katzenjammer Kids. 200.00
33 Romance of Flying 200.00
34 Blondie Home is Our Castle . . 250.00
35 Katzenjammer Kids. 200.00
36 Blondie on the Home Front. . . 225.00
37 Katzenjammer Kids. 250.00
38 Blondie the ModelHomemaker 225.00
39 The Phantom 700.00
40 Blondie 225.00
41 Katzenjammer Kids. 250.00
42 Blondie in Home-Spun Yarns . 225.00
43 Blondie Home-Cooked Scraps 225.00
44 Katzenjammer Kids in
Monkey Business 250.00
45 Blondie in Home of the Free
and the Brave 225.00
46 Mandrake in Fire World 500.00
47 Blondie in Eaten Out of
House and Home 225.00
48 The Maltese Falcon 1,200.00
49 Perry Mason - The Case of
the Lucky Legs 350.00
50 The Shoplifters Shoe,
P. Mason 350.00
51 Rip Kirby - Mystery of
the Mangler 350.00
52 Mandrake in the Land of X . . . 450.00
53 Phantom in Safari Suspense . 500.00
54 Rip Kirby - Case of the
Master Menace 425.00
55 Mandrake in 5-Numbers
Treasue Hunt. 450.00
56 Phantom Destroys the
Sky Band. 500.00
57 Phantom in the Blue Gang,
1948. 500.00

FEATURE FILMS

DC Comics, 1950

1 Captain China. 1,200.00
2 Riding High, Bing Crosby . . 1,200.00
3 The Eagle and the Hawk . . . 1,100.00
4 Fancy Pants, Bob Hope 1,400.00

FEATURE FUNNIES

Harry A. Chesler Publ./
Comic Favorites, Oct., 1937

1 RuG(a&c),A:Joe Palooka,
Mickey Finn, Bungles, Dixie
Dugan, Big Top, Strange as
It Seems, Off the Record . . 3,500.00
2 A: The Hawk 1,600.00
3 WE,Joe Palooka,The Clock . 1,200.00
4 RuG,WE,RuG(c),JoePalooka 1,200.00
5 WE, Joe Palooka drawing . . 1,200.00
6 WE, Joe Palooka (c) 1,200.00
7 WE,LLe, Gallant Knight story
by Vernon Henkel 1,000.00
8 WE 1,000.00
9 WE, Joe Palooka story 1,200.00
10 WE,Micky Finn(c). 1,000.00
11 WE,LLe,The Bungles(c). . . . 1,000.00
12 WE, Joe Palooka(c). 1,000.00
13 WE,LLe, World Series(c) . . . 1,100.00
14 WE,Ned Brant(c). 800.00
15 WE,Joe Palooka(c) 900.00
16 Mickey Finn(c) 800.00
17 WE 800.00
18 Joe Palooka (c). 900.00
19 WE,LLe,Mickey Finn(c). 800.00
20 WE,LLe 800.00

Becomes:

FEATURE COMICS

Quality Comics Group, June. 1939–May, 1950

21 Joe Palooka(c). 1,200.00
22 LLe(c),Mickey Finn(c) 700.00
23 B:Charlie Chan 700.00
24 AlA,Joe Palooka(c) 700.00
25 AlA,The Clock(c) 700.00

Feature Comics #36
© Quality Comics Group

Feature Presentation #2 (#6)
© Fox Features Syndicate

Felix the Cat #11
© Dell Publishing Co.

26 AIA,The Bundles(c) 700.00
27 WE,AIA,I:Doll Man 6,500.00
28 LF,AIA,The Clock(c) 2,500.00
29 LF,AIA,The Clock(c) 1,400.00
30 LF,AIA,Doll Man(c) 1,400.00
31 LF,AIA,Mickey Finn(c) 1,700.00
32 PGv,LF,GFx,Doll Man(c) 900.00
33 PGv,LF,GFx,Bundles(c) 750.00
34 PGv,LF,GFx,Doll Man(c) 900.00
35 PGv,LF,GFx,Bundles(c) 750.00
36 PGv,LF,GFx,Doll Man(c) 900.00
37 PGv,LF,GFx,Bundles(c) 750.00
38 PGv,GFx,Doll Man(c) 650.00
39 PGv,GFx,Bundles(c) 650.00
40 PGv,GFx,WE(c),Doll Man(c) . 650.00
41 PGv,GFx,WE(c),Bundles(c) . . 500.00
42 GFx,Doll Man(c) 500.00
43 RC,GFx,Bundles(c) 425.00
44 RC,GFx,Doll Man(c) 500.00
45 RC,GFx,Bundles(c) 400.00
46 RC,PGv,GFx,Doll Man(c) 600.00
47 RC,GFx,Bundles(c) 400.00
48 RC,GFx,Doll Man(c) 600.00
49 RC,GFx,Bundles(c) 400.00
50 RC,GFx,Doll Man(c) 600.00
51 RC,GFx,Bundles(c) 400.00
52 RC,GFx,Doll Man(c) 500.00
53 RC,GFx,Bundles(c) 325.00
54 RC,GFx,Doll Man(c) 500.00
55 RC,GFx,Bundles(c) 325.00
56 RC,GFx,Doll Man(c) 500.00
57 RC,GFx,Bundles(c) 325.00
58 RC,GFx,Doll Man (c) 500.00
59 RC,GFx,Mickey Finn(c) 325.00
60 RC,GFx,Doll Man(c) 500.00
61 RC,GFx,Bundles(c) 350.00
62 RC,GFx,Doll Man(c) 500.00
63 RC,GFx,Bundles(c) 350.00
64 BP,GFx,Doll Man(c) 600.00
65 BP,GFx(c),Bundles(c) 300.00
66 BP,GFx,Doll Man(c) 400.00
67 BP 300.00
68 BP,Doll Man vs.Bearded
Lady 700.00
69 BP,GFx(c),Devil (c) 300.00
70 BP,Doll Man(c) 700.00
71 BP,GFx(c) 300.00
72 BP,Doll Man(c) 500.00
73 BP,GFx(c),Bundles(c) 250.00
74 Doll Man(c) 500.00
75 GFx(c) 300.00
76 GFx(c) 300.00
77 Doll Man (c) until #140 . . . . . . 400.00
78 Knows no Fear but the
Knife Does 300.00
79 Little Luck God 300.00
80 . . . . 300.00
81 Wanted for Murder 250.00
82 V:Shawunkas the Shaman . . . 250.00
83 V:Mechanical Man 250.00
84 V:Masked Rider, Death
Goes to the Rodeo 250.00
85 V:King of Beasts 250.00
86 Is He A Killer? 250.00
87 The Maze of Murder 250.00
88 V:The Phantom Killer 250.00
89 Crook's Goose 250.00
90 V:Whispering Corpse 250.00
91 V:The Undertaker 250.00
92 V:The Image 250.00
93 . . . . 250.00
94 V:The Undertaker 250.00
95 Flatten's the Peacock's Pride . 250.00
96 Doll Man Proves
Justice is Blind 250.00
97 V:Peacock 250.00
98 V:Master Diablo 250.00
99 On the Warpath Again! 250.00
100 Crushes the City of Crime . . 300.00
101 Land of the Midget Men! 200.00
102 The Angle 200.00
103 V:The Queen of Ants 200.00
104 V:The Botanist 200.00
105 Dream of Death 200.00
106 V:The Sword Fish 200.00
107 Hand of Horror! 200.00
108 V:Cateye 200.00
109 V:The Brain 200.00
110 V:Fat Cat 200.00
111 V:The Undertaker 200.00
112 I:Mr. Curio & His Miniatures . 200.00
113 V:Highwayman 200.00
114 V:Tom Thumb 200.00
115 V:The Sphinx 200.00
116 V:Elbows 200.00
117 Polka Dot on the Spot 200.00
118 thru 144 . . . . @ 200.00

A FEATURE PRESENTATION

Fox Features Syndicate, 1950

1 (5) The Black Tarantula 700.00
2 (6) WW,Moby Dick 600.00
3 Jungle Thrills, bondage 500.00

FEDERAL MEN COMICS

Gerard Publ. Co., 1942

2 S&S,Spanking 800.00

FELIX THE CAT

Dell Publishing Co., Feb.–March, 1948

1 . . . . 450.00
2 . . . . 300.00
3 . . . . 200.00
4 . . . . 200.00
5 . . . . 200.00
6 . . . . 175.00
7 . . . . 175.00
8 . . . . 175.00
9 . . . . 175.00
10 . . . . 175.00
11 thru 19 . . . . @150.00

Toby Press

20 thru 30 . . . . @350.00
31 . . . . 150.00
32 . . . . 350.00
33 . . . . 350.00
34 & 35 . . . . 150.00
36 . . . . 300.00
37 Giant, Christmas(c) 750.00
38 thru 60 . . . . @300.00
61 . . . . 275.00

Harvey

62 thru 80 . . . . @125.00
81 thru 99 . . . . @100.00
100 . . . . 125.00
101 thru 118 . . . . @100.00
Spec., 100 pgs, 1952 . . . . 350.00
Summer Ann., 100 pgs. 1953 . . . 500.00
Winter Ann.,#2 100 pgs, 1954. . . 500.00

FELIX AND HIS FRIENDS

Toby, 1953

1 F:Felix the Cat 350.00
2 . . . . 400.00
3 . . . . 400.00

FELIX'S NEPHEWS INKY & DINKY

Harvey Publications, 1957

1 . . . . 150.00
2 . . . . 100.00
3 . . . . 100.00
4 thru 7 . . . . @100.00

FERDINAND THE BULL

Dell Publishing Co., 1938

1 . . . . 500.00

Fight Against Crime #10
© Story Comics

Fight Comics #24
© Fiction House Magazines

Fight Comics #49
© Fiction House Magazines

FIGHT AGAINST CRIME
Story Comics, May, 1951

1 Scorpion of Crime Inspector "Brains" Carroway 700.00
2 Ganglands Double Cross 400.00
3 Killer Dolan's Double Cross . . 300.00
4 Hopped Up Killers - The Con's Slaughter,Drug issue . 400.00
5 FF,Horror o/t Avenging Corpse 400.00
6 Terror of the Crazy Killer 250.00
7 . . . . 250.00
8 Killer with the Two-Bladed Knife 250.00
9 Rats Die by Gas,Horror 600.00
10 Horror of the Con's Revenge . 600.00
11 Case of the Crazy Killer 600.00
12 Horror,Drug issue 700.00
13 The Bloodless Killer 600.00
14 Electric Chair (c) 700.00
15 . . . . 600.00
16 RA,Bondage(c) 700.00
17 Knife in Neck(c) 700.00
18 Attempted Hanging (c) 700.00
19 Bondage(c) 700.00
20 Severed Head (c) 1,000.00
21 . . . . 500.00

Becomes:

FIGHT AGAINST THE GUILTY
Dec., 1954

22 RA,Electric Chair 500.00
23 March, 1955 . . . . 350.00

FIGHT COMICS
(Fiction House Magazines), Jan., 1940

1 LF,GT,WE(c),O:Spy Fighter . 7,000.00
2 GT,WE(c),Joe Lewis 3,000.00
3 WE(c),GT,B:Rip Regan, The Powerman 2,600.00
4 GT,LF(c) 2,500.00
5 WE(c) 2,500.00
6 GT,BP(c) 1,500.00
7 GT,BP(c),Powerman-Blood Money 1,500.00
8 GT,Chip Collins-Lair of the Vulture 1,500.00
9 GT,Chip Collins-Prey of the War Eagle 1,500.00
10 GT,Wolves of the Yukon . . . 1,500.00
11 . . . . 1,200.00
12 RA,Powerman-Monster of Madness 1,600.00
13 Shark Broodie-Legion of Satan 1,200.00
14 Shark Broodie-Lagoon of Death 1,200.00
15 Super-American-Hordes of the Secret Dicator. 1,500.00
16 B:Capt. Fight, Swastika Plague 1,500.00
17 Super-American-Blaster of the Pig-Boat Pirates 1,500.00
18 Shark Broodie-Plague of the Yellow Devils 1,500.00
19 E:Capt. Fight 1,500.00
20 . . . . 1,100.00
21 Rip Carson-Hell's Sky-Riders . 900.00
22 Rip Carson-Sky Devil's Mission 900.00
23 Rip Carson-Angels of Vengeance. 900.00
24 Baynonets for the Banzai Breed! Bondage(c) 1,500.00
25 Rip Carson-Samurai Showdown 1,000.00
26 Rip Carson-Fury of the Sky-Brigade 1,000.00
27 War-Loot for the Mikado Bondage(c). 2,000.00
28 Rip Carson. 1,000.00
29 Rip Carson-Charge of the Lost Region 1,000.00
30 Rip Carson-Jeep-Raiders of the Torture Jungle 1,000.00
31 Gangway for the Gyrenes, Decapitation (c) 1,500.00
32 Vengeance of the Hun-Hunters,Bondage(c) 1,500.00
33 B:Tiger Girl 750.00
34 Bondage(c) 1,000.00
35 MB. 750.00
36 MB. 750.00
37 MB. 750.00
38 MB,Bondage(c) 1,000.00
39 MB,Senorita Rio-Slave Brand of the Spider Cult. 750.00
40 MB,Bondage (c) 1,000.00
41 MB,Bondage (c). 1,000.00
42 MB. 600.00
43 MB,Senorita Rio-The Fire-Brides of the Lost Atlantis, Bondage(c) 500.00
44 MB,R:Capt. Fight 600.00
45 MB,Tonight Don Diablo Rides. 600.00
46 MB. 600.00
47 MB,SenoritaRio-Horror's Hacienda 600.00
48 MB. 600.00
49 MB,JKa,B:Tiger Girl(c) 600.00
50 MB. 600.00
51 MB,O:Tiger Girl. 800.00
52 MB,Winged Demons of Doom 375.00
53 MB,Shadowland Shrine 375.00
54 MB,Flee the Cobra Fury 375.00
55 MB,Jungle Juggernaut 375.00
56 MB. 375.00
57 MB,Jewels of Jeopardy. 375.00
58 MB. 375.00
59 MB,Vampires ofCrystalCavern 375.00
60 MB,Kraal of DeadlyDiamonds 375.00
61 MB,Seekers of the Sphinx, O:Tiger Girl 750.00
62 MB,Graveyard of the Tree Tribe 500.00
63 MB. 500.00
64 MB,DawnBeast from Karama-Zan! 500.00
65 Beware the Congo Girl 350.00
66 Man or Ape! 350.00
67 Head-Hunters of Taboo Trek . 350.00
68 Fangs of Dr. Voodoo. 350.00
69 Cage of the Congo Fury 350.00
70 Kraal of Traitor Tusks 350.00
71 Captives for the Golden Crocodile 350.00
72 Land of the Lost Safaris 350.00
73 War-Gods of the Jungle 350.00
74 Advengers of the Jungle 350.00
75 Perils of Momba-Kzar 350.00
76 Kraal of Zombi-Zaro 350.00
77 Slave-Queen of the Ape Man . 350.00
78 Great Congo Diamond Robbery. 500.00
79 A:Space Rangers 600.00
80 . . . . 300.00
81 E:Tiger Girl(c) 300.00
82 RipCarson-CommandoStrike . 300.00
83 NobodyLoves a Minesweeper 300.00
84 Rip Carson-Suicide Patrol . . . 300.00
85 . . . . 300.00
86 GE,Tigerman,Summer,1954 . . 350.00

FIGHT FOR LOVE
United Features Syndicate, 1952

N# Romance. 125.00

FIGHTIN' AIR FORCE
Charlton Comics, 1956–60

3 . . . . 150.00
4 . . . . 100.00

Fighting American #2
© Prize Publications

Fighting Undersea Commandos #1
© Avon Periodicals

Firehair Comics #1
© Fiction House

5 .... 100.00
6 .... 100.00
7 .... 100.00
8 .... 100.00
9 .... 100.00
10 .... 100.00
11 giant 125.00
12 US,Russia Nuclear attack.... 200.00
13 thru 20 .... @100.00
21 thru 30 .... @100.00

FIGHTING AMERICAN

Headline Publications (Prize), April–May, 1954

1 S&K,O:Fighting American & Speedboy 2,500.00
2 S&K(a&c) 1,200.00
3 S&K(a&c) 850.00
4 S&K(a&c) 850.00
5 S&K(a&c) 850.00
6 S&K(a&c),O:Fighting American 800.00
7 S&K(a&c), April–May, 1955 .. 700.00

FIGHTING FRONTS!

Harvey Publications, 1952–53

1 War 200.00
2 BP,violence 250.00
3 BP 150.00
4 .... 125.00
5 .... 125.00

FIGHTING DAVY CROCKETT

See: KIT CARSON

FIGHTING INDIANS OF THE WILD WEST

Avon Periodicals, March, 1952

1 EK,EL,Geronimo, Crazy Horse, Chief Victorio 200.00
2 EK,Same, Nov., 1952 .... 150.00

FIGHTING LEATHERNECKS

Toby Press, Feb., 1952

1 JkS,Duke's Diary 150.00
2 .... 125.00
3 .... 100.00

4 .... 100.00
5 .... 100.00
6 Dec., 1952 .... 100.00

THE FIGHTING MAN

Excellent Publications (Ajax/Farrell), 1952–53

1 War 150.00
2 .... 125.00
3 .... 100.00
4 .... 100.00
5 .... 100.00
6 .... 100.00
7 .... 100.00
8 .... 100.00
Ann.#1 (1952) 300.00

FIGHTIN' TEXAN

See: TEXAN, THE

FIGHTING UNDERSEA COMMANDOS

Avon Periodicals, 1952–53

1 Navy Frogmen............. 175.00
2 .... 125.00
3 .... 100.00
4 BK 110.00
5 .... 100.00

FIGHTING WAR STORIES

Men's Publications, 1952

1 .... 150.00
2 .... 100.00
3 .... 100.00
4 .... 100.00
5 .... 100.00

FIGHTING YANK

Nedor Publ./Better Publ. (Standard Comics) Sept., 1942

1 JaB,B:Fighting Yank, A:Wonder Man, Mystico, bondage (c). 6,000.00
2 JaB 3,200.00
3 Shark, bondage (c)........ 3,000.00
4 ASh(c), bondage (c) 3,000.00
5 ASh(c) 1,600.00
6 ASh(c) 1,600.00
7 ASh(c),Bomb(c) 1,500.00
8 ASh(c), bondage(c)........ 1,600.00
9 ASh(c) 1,500.00
10 ASh(c),bondage-torture(c) .. 1,600.00
11 ASh(c), A:Grim Reaper, bondage (c) 1,500.00
12 ASh(c), Hirohito bondage (c) 1,500.00
13 ASh(c),kid bondage,snake(c)1,500.00
14 ASh(c) 1,000.00
15 ASh(c),bondage-torture(c) .. 1,500.00
16 ASh(c),................. 1,000.00
17 ASh(c),bondage(c)........ 1,500.00
18 ASh(c), A:American Eagle .. 1,200.00
19 ASh(c) 1,000.00
20 ASh(c) Shark 1,000.00
21 ASh(c) A:Kara,Jungle Princess 1,000.00
22 ASh(c) A:Miss Masque-(c) story 1,400.00
23 ASh(c) Klu Klux Klan parody (c).............. 1,900.00
24 ASh(c),A:Miss Masque 800.00
25 ASh(c),JRo,MMe,A:Cavalier 1,500.00
26 ASh(c),JRo,MMe,A:Cavalier .. 800.00
27 ASh(c),JRo,MMe,A:Cavalier .. 800.00
28 ASh(c),JRo,MMe,AW A:Cavalier.............. 1,000.00
29 ASh(c),JRo,MMe,Aug., 1949 1,000.00

FILM FUNNIES

Marvel Chipiden Publ., 1949–50

1 Funny animal.............. 200.00
2 .... 150.00

FILM STAR ROMANCES

Star Publications, 1950

1 LbC(c), Rudy Valentino story . 650.00
2 Liz Taylor & Robert Taylor, photo (c) 700.00
3 May–June, 1950, photo(c).... 350.00

FIREHAIR COMICS

Flying Stories, Inc. (Fiction House Magazine), Winter, 1948–Spring, 1952

1 I:Firehair, Riders on the Pony Express 750.00
2 Bride of the Outlaw Guns 400.00
3 Kiss of the Six-Gun Siren! ... 350.00
4 .... 350.00
5 .... 350.00
6 .... 325.00
7 War Drums at Buffalo Bend .. 250.00
8 Raid on the Red Arrows 250.00
9 French Flags and Tomahawks 250.00
10 Slave Maiden of the Crees... 250.00
11 Wolves of the Overland Trail.. 250.00

 All comics prices listed are for *Near Mint* condition.

First Love Illustrated #67
© Harvey Publications

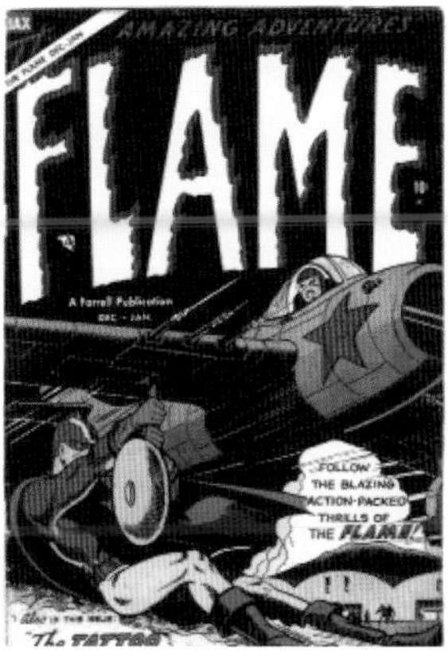

The Flame #1 (#5)
© Ajax/Farrell

Flash Comics #17
© DC Comics

FIRST KISS

Charlton Comics, 1957

1 . . . . 125.00
2 thru 5 . . . . @100.00
6 thru 10 . . . . @100.00
11 thru 40 . . . . @50.00

FIRST LOVE ILLUSTRATED

Harvey Publications, 1949–58

1 . . . . 250.00
2 . . . . 175.00
3 . . . . 150.00
4 . . . . 150.00
5 thru 10 . . . . @150.00
11 thru 30 . . . . @100.00
31 thru 34 . . . . @100.00
35 . . . . 250.00
36 "Love Slaves" Communism . . 200.00
37 thru 49 . . . . @75.00
50 thru 66 . . . . @75.00
67 thru 70 JK(c) . . . . @100.00
71 thru 88 . . . . @50.00

FIRST ROMANCE MAGAZINE

(Home Comics (Harvey Publications), 1949

1 BP,True love stories. 250.00
2 BP 150.00
3 BP 125.00
4 BP 125.00
5 BP 125.00
6 . . . . 100.00
7 . . . . 100.00
8 BP 100.00
9 BP 100.00
10 BP. 100.00
11 thru 20 BP (in many) . . . . . @100.00
21 thru 40 . . . . @75.00
41 thru 43 JK(c) . . . . @ 100.00
44 thru 52 BP(in many). . . . . . @ 100.00

5 CENT COMICS

Fawcett Publications, 1940

1 B&W, I:Dan Dare, very rare 10,000.00

FLAME, THE

Fox Feature Syndicate, Summer, 1940

1 LF,O:The Flame 7,000.00
2 GT,LF,Wing Turner 3,000.00
3 BP,Wonderworld 2,500.00
4 . . . . 2,500.00
5 GT 2,500.00
6 GT 2,500.00
7 A:The Yank 2,500.00
8 The Finger of the Frozen Death!, Jan., 1942 . . . . 2,500.00

FLAME, THE

Ajax/Farrell, 1954–55

1 (#5) superhero,O:Flame 600.00
2 . . . . 350.00
3 . . . . 350.00

FLAMING LOVE

Comic Magazines (Quality Comics Group), Dec., 1949

1 BWa,BWa(c),The Temptress I Feared in His Arms 500.00
2 Torrid Tales of Turbulent Passion 250.00
3 BWa,RC,My Heart's at Sea . . 300.00
4 One Women Who Made a Mockery of Love, Ph(c) 250.00
5 Bridge of Longing, Ph(c) 250.00
6 Men Both Loved & Feared Me, Oct., 1950 . . . . 250.00

FLAMING WESTERN ROMANCES

Star Publ., 1950

3 LbC,Robert Taylor Photo(c). . . 500.00

FLASH COMICS

DC Comics, Jan., 1940

1 SMo,SMo(c),O:Flash,Hawkman,The Whip & Johnny Thunder,B:Cliff Cornwall,Minute Movies . 150,000.00
2 B:Rod Rain 25,000.00
3 SMo,SMo(c),B:The King. . . 15,000.00
4 SMo,SMo(c),F:The Whip . . 12,000.00
5 SMo,SMo(c),F:The King . . . 10,000.00
6 F:Flash 15,000.00
7 Hawkman(c) 12,000.00
8 Male bondage(c). 6,500.00
9 Hawkman(c) 7,000.00
10 SMo,SMo(c),Flash(c). 7,000.00
11 SMo,SMo(c). 5,500.00
12 SMo,SMo(c),B:Les Watts. . . 5,500.00
13 SMo,SMo(c). 5,500.00
14 SMo,SMo(c). 6,000.00
15 SMo,SMo(c). 6,000.00
16 SMo,SMo(c). 6,000.00
17 SMo,SMo(c),E:CliffCornwall 6,000.00
18 SMo,SMo(c). 6,000.00
19 SMo,SMo(c). 6,000.00
20 SMo,SMo(c). 6,000.00
21 SMo(c). 7,000.00
22 SMo,SMo(c). 6,000.00
23 SMo,SMo(c). 6,000.00
24 SMo,SMo(c),Flash V:Spider-Men of Mars,A:Hawkgirl . . . 7,000.00
25 SMo,SMo(c). 4,000.00
26 SMo,SMo(c). 4,000.00
27 SMo,SMo(c). 4,000.00
28 SMo,SMo(c),Flash goes to Hollywood. 4,000.00
29 SMo,SMo(c). 4,000.00
30 SMo,SMo(c),Flash inAdventure of the Curiosity Ray!. 4,000.00
31 SMo,SMo(c),Hawkman(c) . . 4,000.00
32 SMo,SM(c),Flash inAdventure of the Fictious Villians. 4,000.00
33 SMo,SMo(c). 4,000.00
34 SMo,SMo(c),Flash in The Robbers of the Round Table 4,000.00
35 SMo,SMo(c). 4,000.00
36 SMo,SMo(c),F:Flash,Mystery of Doll Who Walks Like a Man 4,000.00
37 SMo,SMo(c). 3,500.00
38 SMo,SMo(c). 3,200.00
39 SMo,SMo(c). 3,200.00
40 SMo,SMo(c),F:Flash, Man Who Could Read Man's Souls!. . 4,000.00
41 SMo,SMo(c). 4,000.00
42 SMo,SMo(c),Flash V:The Gangsters Baby!. 4,000.00
43 SMo,SMo(c). 4,000.00
44 SMo,SMo(c),Flash V:The Liars Club 4,000.00
45 SMo,SMo(c),F:Hawkman,Big Butch Makes Hall of Fame. 4,000.00
46 SMo,SMo(c). 4,000.00
47 SMo,SMo(c),Hawkman in Crime Canned for the Duration. . . 2,500.00
48 SMo,SMo(c). 2,500.00
49 SMo,SMo(c). 2,500.00
50 SMo,SMo(c),Hawkman, Tale of the 1,000 Dollar Bill 2,500.00
51 SMo,SMo(c). 2,500.00
52 SMo,SMo(c),Flash, Machine that Thinks Like a Man. . . . 2,500.00
53 SMo,SMo(c),Hawkman, Simple Simon Met the Hawkman . . 2,500.00
54 SMo,SMo(c),Flash, Mysterious Bottle from the Sea 2,500.00

Flash Comics #83
© DC Comics

The Flash #113
© DC Comics

Flash Gordon #2
© Dell Publishing Co.

55 SMo,SMo(c),Hawkman, Riddle of the Stolen Statuette! 2,500.00
56 SMo,SMo(c). 2,500.00
57 SMo,SMo(c),Hawkman, Adventure of the Gangster & the Ghost 2,500.00
58 SMo,SMo(c),Merman meets the Flash. 2,500.00
59 SMo,SMo(c),Hawkman V:Pied Piper 2,500.00
60 SMo,SMo(c),Flash V:The Wind Master. 2,500.00
61 SMo,SMo(c),Hawkman V:The Beanstalk 2,500.00
62 JKu,Flash in High Jinks on the Rinks 3,000.00
63 JKu(c),Hawkman in The Tale of the Mystic Urn. 2,400.00
64 . . . . 2,400.00
65 JKu(c),Hawkman in Return of the Simple Simon 2,400.00
66 . . . . 2,400.00
67 JKu(c). 2,400.00
68 Flash in The Radio that Ran Wild. 2,400.00
69 . . . . 2,400.00
70 JKu(c). 2,400.00
71 JKu(c),Hawkman in Battle of the Birdmen 2,400.00
72 JKu. 2,400.00
73 JKu(c). 2,400.00
74 JKu(c). 2,400.00
75 JKu(c),Hawkman in Magic at the Mardi Gras 2,400.00
76 A:Worry Wart 2,400.00
77 Hawkman in The Case of the Curious Casket. 2,400.00
78 . . . . 2,400.00
79 Hawkman in The Battle of the Birds 2,400.00
80 Flash in The Story of the Boy Genius. 2,400.00
81 JKu(c),Hawkman's Voyage to Venus 2,400.00
82 A:Walter Jordan 2,400.00
83 JKu,JKu(c),Hawkman in Destined for Disaster 2,500.00
84 Flash V:The Changeling . . . 2,500.00
85 JKu,JKu(c),Hawkman in Hollywood. 2,500.00
86 JKu,1st Black Canary,Flash V:Stone Age Menace 8,000.00
87 Hawkman meets the Foil . . . 3,200.00
88 JKu,Flash in The Case of the Vanished Year! 3,200.00
89 I:The Thorn 4,500.00
90 Flash in Nine Empty Uniforms 3,200.00
91 Hawkman V:The Phantom Menace. 4,000.00
92 1st full-length Black Canary story 10,000.00
93 Flash V:Violin of Villainy . . . 4,000.00
94 JKu(c). 4,000.00
95 . . . . 4,000.00
96 . . . . 4,000.00
97 Flash in The Dream that Didn't Vanish 4,000.00
98 JKu(c),Hawkman in Crime Costume! 4,000.00
99 Flash in The Star Prize of the Year 4,000.00
100 Hawkman in The Human -Fly Bandits! 6,500.00
101 . . . . 5,500.00
102 Hawkman in The Flying Darkness 5,500.00
103 . . . . 6,500.00
104 JKu,Hawkman in Flaming Darkness' Feb., 1949 . . . . 20,000.00

Revived as:

FLASH, THE

DC Comics, Feb.–March, 1959

105 CI,O:Flash,I:Mirror Master. 17,000.00
106 CI,I&O:Gorilla Grodd, O:Pied Piper 5,000.00
107 CI,A:Grodd. 3,000.00
108 CI,A:Grodd. 2,200.00
109 CI,A:Mirror Master 2,000.00
110 CI,MA,I:Kid Flash, Weather Wizard 4,000.00
111 CI,A:Kid Flash,The Invasion Of the Cloud Creatures . . . 1,300.00
112 CI,I&O:Elongated Man, A:Kid Flash 1,500.00
113 CI,I&O:Trickster 1,300.00
114 CI,A:Captain Cold 900.00
115 CI,A:Grodd 800.00
116 CI,A:Kid Flash,The Man Who Stole Central City 800.00
117 CI,MA,I:Capt.Boomerang . . 1,000.00
118 CI,MA 700.00
119 CI,W:Elongated Man. 700.00
120 CI,A:Kid Flash,Land of Golden Giants 700.00
121 CI,A:Trickster 600.00
122 CI,I&O:The Top. 600.00
123 I:Earth 2,R:G.A.Flash. 3,500.00
124 CI,A:Capt.Boomerang. 450.00
125 CI,A:Kid Flash,The Conquerors of Time. 450.00
126 CI,A:Mirror Master 450.00
127 CI,A:Grodd 450.00
128 CI,O:Abra Kadabra 450.00
129 CI,A:Capt.Cold,Trickster,A:Gold. Age Flash,C:JLA (flashback). 700.00
130 CI,A:Mirror Master, Weather Wizard. 400.00
Ann.#1 O:ElongatedMan, G.Grodd 800.00

FLASH GORDON

Harvey Publications, Oct., 1950

1 AR,Bondage(c) 600.00
2 AR 300.00
3 AR Bondage(c) 400.00
4 AR, April, 1951 . . . . 275.00

FLASH GORDON

Dell Publishing Co., 1953

2 . . . . 200.00
See also FOUR COLOR

FLAT TOP

Magazine Publ., 1953–55

1 Teen-age 125.00
2 . . . . 100.00
3 . . . . 100.00
4 . . . . 100.00
5 . . . . 100.00
6 . . . . 100.00
7 . . . . 100.00

FLIP

Harvey Publications, April, 1954

1 HN 275.00
2 HN,BP,June, 1954 . . . . 275.00

FLIPPITY & FLOP

DC Comics, 1952

1 Funny animal. 325.00
2 . . . . 175.00
3 . . . . 150.00
4 . . . . 150.00
5 . . . . 150.00
6 . . . . 100.00
7 . . . . 100.00
8 . . . . 100.00
9 . . . . 100.00

The Flying A's Range Rider #11
© Dell Publishing Co.

Forbidden Love #1
© Quality Comics Group

Forbidden Worlds #1
© American Comics Group

10 ... 100.00
11 thru 20 ... @125.00
21 thru 47 ... @100.00

FLY BOY

Approved Comics (Ziff-Davis) Spring, 1952

1 NS(c),Angels without Wings ... 300.00
2 NS(c),Flyboy's Flame-Out, Oct.–Nov., 1952 ... 200.00

FLYING ACES

Key Publications, 1955–56

1 War ... 125.00
2 ... 100.00
3 ... 100.00
4 ... 100.00
5 ... 100.00

FLYING A'S RANGE RIDER, THE

Dell Publishing Co., June–Aug., 1953

(1) = *Dell Four Color #404*
2 Ph(c) all ... 200.00
3 ... 150.00
4 ... 125.00
5 ... 125.00
6 ... 125.00
7 ... 125.00
8 ... 125.00
9 ... 125.00
10 ... 125.00
11 ... 100.00
12 ... 100.00
13 ... 100.00
14 ... 100.00
15 ... 100.00
16 ... 100.00
17 ATh ... 150.00
19 ... 100.00
20 ... 100.00
21 ... 100.00
22 ... 100.00
23 ... 100.00
24 ... 100.00

FLYING CADET

Flying Cadet Publ. Co., 1943

1 Aviation for student Airmen ... 200.00
2 ... 150.00
3 Photo(c) ... 125.00
4 Photo(c) ... 125.00
5 Photo(c) ... 125.00
6a Photo(c) ... 125.00
6b Photo(c) ... 125.00
7 Photo(c) ... 125.00
8 Photo(c) ... 125.00
9 Photo(c) ... 125.00
10 ... 100.00
11 ... 100.00
12 ... 100.00
13 ... 100.00
14 ... 100.00
15 ... 100.00
16 ... 100.00
17 nudity-woman ... 300.00

FLYIN' JENNY

Pentagon Publ. Co, 1946

N# ... 300.00
2 ... 350.00

FLYING MODELS

Health-Knowledge Publications, 1954

1 ... 200.00

FOODINI

Continental Publications, March, 1950

1 TV Puppet ... 275.00
2 Jingle Dingle ... 150.00
3 ... 100.00
4 Aug., 1950 ... 100.00

FOOTBALL THRILLS

Approved Comics (Ziff-Davis), Fall-Winter, 1952

1 BP,NS(c),Red Grange story ... 350.00
2 NS(c),Bronko Nagurski, Spring,1952 ... 250.00

FORBIDDEN LOVE

Comic Magazine (Quality Comics Group), March, 1950

1 RC,Ph(c),Heartbreak Road ... 1,000.00
2 Ph(c),I Loved a Gigolo ... 800.00
3 Kissless Bride ... 500.00
4 BWa,Brimstone Kisses, Sept., 1950 ... 500.00

FORBIDDEN WORLDS

American Comics Group, July–Aug., 1951

1 AW,FF ... 2,500.00
2 ... 1,200.00
3 AW,WW,JD ... 1,400.00
4 Werewolf (c) ... 750.00
5 AW ... 850.00
6 AW,King Kong (c) ... 750.00
7 ... 500.00
8 ... 500.00
9 Atomic Bomb ... 600.00
10 JyD ... 375.00
11 The Mummy's Treasure ... 275.00
12 Chest of Death ... 275.00
13 Invasion from Hades ... 275.00
14 Million-Year Monster ... 275.00
15 The Vampire Cat ... 275.00
16 The Doll ... 275.00
17 ... 275.00
18 The Mummy ... 275.00
19 Pirate and the Voodoo Queen 275.00
20 Terror Island ... 275.00
21 The Ant Master ... 250.00
22 The Cursed Casket ... 250.00
23 Nightmare for Two ... 250.00
24 ... 250.00
25 Hallahan's Head ... 250.00
26 The Champ ... 250.00
27 SMo,The Thing with the Golden Hair ... 250.00
28 Portrait of Carlotta ... 250.00
29 The Frogman ... 250.00
30 The Things on the Beach ... 250.00
31 SMo,The Circle of the Doomed ... 225.00
32 The Invasion of the Dead Things ... 225.00
33 ... 225.00
34 Atomic Bomb ... 300.00
35 Comics Code ... 250.00
36 thru 62 ... @150.00
63 AW ... 150.00
64 ... 100.00
65 ... 100.00
66 ... 100.00
67 ... 100.00
68 OW(c) ... 100.00
69 AW ... 150.00
70 ... 100.00
71 ... 100.00
72 ... 100.00
73 OW,I:Herbie ... 475.00
74 ... 100.00
75 JB ... 100.00

Forbidden Worlds #103
© American Comics Group

Four Color, 1st Series #4
© Walt Disney Co.

Four Color, 2nd Series #69
© Oskar Lebeck

76 AW . . . 150.00
77 . . . 100.00
78 AW,OW(c) . . . 125.00
79 thru 85 JB . . . @100.00
86 Flying Saucer . . . 110.00
87 . . . 100.00
88 . . . 100.00
89 . . . 100.00
90 . . . 100.00
91 . . . 100.00
92 . . . 100.00
93 . . . 100.00
94 OW(c),A:Herbie . . . 150.00
95 . . . 100.00
96 AW . . . 125.00
97 thru 115 . . . @100.00
116 OW(c)A:Herbie . . . 110.00
117 . . . 100.00
118 . . . 100.00
119 . . . 100.00
120 thru 124 . . . @100.00
125 I:O:Magic Man . . . 100.00
126 A:Magic Man . . . 100.00
127 same . . . 100.00
128 same . . . 100.00
129 same . . . 100.00
130 same . . . 100.00
131 same . . . 100.00
132 same . . . 100.00
133 I:O:Dragona . . . 100.00
134 A:Magic Man . . . 100.00
135 A:Magic Man . . . 100.00
136 A:Nemesis . . . 100.00
137 A:Magic Man . . . 100.00
138 A:Magic Man . . . 100.00
139 A:Magic Man . . . 100.00
140 SD,A:Mark Midnight . . . 125.00
141 thru 145 . . . @100.00

FOREIGN INTRIGUES
See: DYNAMITE

FOUR COLOR
Dell Publishing Co., 1939

N# Dick Tracy . . . 10,000.00
N# Don Winslow of the Navy . 2,500.00
N# Myra North . . . 1,300.00
4 Disney's Donald Duck (1940) . . . 25,000.00
5 Smilin' Jack . . . 1,000.00
6 Dick Tracy . . . 2,300.00
7 Gang Busters . . . 600.00
8 Dick Tracy . . . 1,200.00
9 Terry and the Pirates . . . 1,000.00
10 Smilin' Jack . . . 900.00
11 Smitty . . . 600.00
12 Little Orphan Annie . . . 750.00
13 Walt Disney's Reluctant Dragon (1941) . . . 3,000.00
14 Moon Mullins . . . 600.00
15 Tillie the Toiler . . . 600.00
16 W.Disney's Mickey Mouse Outwits the Phantom Blob (1941) . 25,000.00
17 W.Disney's Dumbo the Flying Elephant (1941) . . . 5,000.00
18 Jiggs and Maggie . . . 600.00
19 Barney Google and Snuffy Smith . . . 600.00
20 Tiny Tim . . . 500.00
21 Dick Tracy . . . 1,000.00
22 Don Winslow . . . 550.00
23 Gang Busters . . . 500.00
24 Captain Easy . . . 700.00
25 Popeye . . . 1,200.00

[Second Series, 1942]

1 Little Joe . . . 1,000.00
2 Harold Teen . . . 500.00
3 Alley Oop . . . 900.00
4 Smilin' Jack . . . 700.00
5 Raggedy Ann and Andy . . . 900.00
6 Smitty . . . 350.00
7 Smokey Stover . . . 500.00
8 Tillie the Toiler . . . 400.00
9 Donald Duck finds Pirate Gold! . . . 20,000.00
10 Flash Gordon . . . 1,600.00
11 Wash Tubs . . . 500.00
12 Bambi . . . 1,200.00
13 Mr. District Attorney . . . 500.00
14 Smilin' Jack . . . 600.00
15 Felix the Cat . . . 1,200.00
16 Porky Pig . . . 1,500.00
17 Popeye . . . 800.00
18 Little Orphan Annie's Junior Commandos . . . 650.00
19 W.Disney's Thumper meets the Seven Dwarfs . . . 1,200.00
20 Barney Baxter . . . 500.00
21 Oswald the Rabbit . . . 800.00
22 Tillie the Toiler . . . 300.00
23 Raggedy Ann and Andy . . . 600.00
24 Gang Busters . . . 500.00
25 Andy Panda . . . 900.00
26 Popeye . . . 800.00
27 Mickey Mouse and the Seven Colored Terror . . . 2,500.00
28 Wash Tubbs . . . 375.00
29 CB,Donald Duck and the Mummy's Ring . . . 12,000.00
30 Bambi's Children . . . 900.00
31 Moon Mullins . . . 300.00
32 Smitty . . . 250.00
33 Bugs Bunny . . . 1,800.00
34 Dick Tracy . . . 700.00
35 Smokey Stover . . . 275.00
36 Smilin' Jack . . . 400.00
37 Bringing Up Father . . . 350.00
38 Roy Rogers . . . 4,000.00
39 Oswald the Rabbit . . . 650.00
40 Barney Google and Snuffy Smith . . . 375.00
41 WK,Mother Goose . . . 375.00
42 Tiny Tim . . . 300.00
43 Popeye . . . 550.00
44 Terry and the Pirates . . . 600.00
45 Raggedy Ann . . . 550.00
46 Felix the Cat and the Haunted House . . . 700.00
47 Gene Autry . . . 750.00
48 CB,Porky Pig of the Mounties . . . 2,000.00
49 W.Disney's Snow White and the Seven Dwarfs . . . 1,400.00
50 WK,Fairy Tale Parade . . . 450.00
51 Bugs Bunny Finds the Lost Treasure . . . 600.00
52 Little Orphan Annie . . . 500.00
53 Wash Tubbs . . . 250.00
54 Andy Panda . . . 500.00
55 Tillie the Toiler . . . 250.00
56 Dick Tracy . . . 600.00
57 Gene Autry . . . 700.00
58 Smilin' Jack . . . 400.00
59 WK,Mother Goose . . . 350.00
60 Tiny Folks Funnies . . . 275.00
61 Santa Claus Funnies . . . 400.00
62 CB,Donald Duck in Frozen Gold . . . 3,000.00
63 Roy Rogers-photo (c) . . . 900.00
64 Smokey Stover . . . 225.00
65 Smitty . . . 225.00
66 Gene Autry . . . 700.00
67 Oswald the Rabbit . . . 300.00
68 WK,Mother Goose . . . 300.00
69 WK,Fairy Tale Parade . . . 400.00
70 Popeye and Wimpy . . . 450.00
71 WK,Walt Disney's Three Caballeros . . . 1,300.00
72 Raggedy Ann . . . 450.00
73 The Grumps . . . 250.00
74 Marge's Little Lulu . . . 1,800.00
75 Gene Autry and the Wildcat . . 500.00
76 Little Orphan Annie . . . 400.00
77 Felix the Cat . . . 600.00
78 Porky Pig & the Bandit Twins . 700.00

 All comics prices listed are for *Near Mint* condition.

Four Color, 2nd Series #118
© Lone Ranger, Inc.

Four Color, 2nd Series #155
© King Features

Four Color, 2nd Series #182
© Warner Bros.

79 Mickey Mouse in the Riddle
of the Red Hat 2,000.00
80 Smilin' Jack 300.00
81 Moon Mullins. 200.00
82 Lone Ranger. 750.00
83 Gene Autry in Outlaw Trail . . . 500.00
84 Flash Gordon 750.00
85 Andy Panda and the
Mad Dog Mystery 300.00
86 Roy Rogers-photo (c) 600.00
87 WK,DNo(c),Fairy Tale Parade 400.00
88 Bugs Bunny 375.00
89 Tillie the Toiler. 250.00
90 WK,Christmas with
Mother Goose 300.00
91 WK,Santa Claus Funnies 300.00
92 WK,W.Disney's Pinocchio . . 1,000.00
93 Gene Autry 500.00
94 Winnie Winkle. 200.00
95 Roy Rogers,Ph(c) 600.00
96 Dick Tracy. 500.00
97 Marge's Little Lulu. 900.00
98 Lone Ranger. 600.00
99 Smitty 200.00
100 Gene Autry Comics-photo(c) 500.00
101 Terry and the Pirates 500.00
102 WK,Oswald the Rabbit 250.00
103 WK,Easter with
Mother Goose 300.00
104 WK,Fairy Tale Parade. 325.00
105 WK,Albert the Alligator. . . . 1,200.00
106 Tillie the Toiler. 200.00
107 Little Orphan Annie 350.00
108 Donald Duck in the
Terror of the River 2,600.00
109 Roy Rogers Comics 500.00
110 Marge's Little Lulu 600.00
111 Captain Easy. 250.00
112 Porky Pig's Adventure in
Gopher Gulch 600.00
113 Popeye 250.00
114 WK,Fairy Tale Parade 325.00
115 Marge's Little Lulu. 550.00
116 Mickey Mouse and the
House of Many Mysteries . . . 600.00
117 Roy Rogers Comics, Ph(c) . . 350.00
118 Lone Ranger. 500.00
119 Felix the Cat 550.00
120 Marge's Little Lulu 500.00
121 Fairy Tale Parade 225.00
122 Henry 250.00
123 Bugs Bunny's Dangerous
Venture 275.00
124 Roy Rogers Comics,Ph(c) . . 350.00
125 Lone Ranger. 350.00
126 WK,Christmas with
Mother Goose 250.00
127 Popeye 250.00
128 WK,Santa Claus Funnies . . . 250.00
129 W.Disney's Uncle Remus
& His Tales of Brer Rabbit. . . 500.00
130 Andy Panda 200.00
131 Marge's Little Lulu. 500.00
132 Tillie the Toiler. 200.00
133 Dick Tracy. 350.00
134 Tarzan and the Devil Ogre. 1,100.00
135 Felix the Cat 400.00
136 Lone Ranger. 375.00
137 Roy Rogers Comics 375.00
138 Smitty 175.00
139 Marge's Little Lulu. 500.00
140 WK,Easter with
Mother Goose 250.00
141 Mickey Mouse and the
Submarine Pirates. 500.00
142 Bugs Bunny and the
Haunted Mountain 250.00
143 Oswald the Rabbit & the
Prehistoric Egg 175.00
144 Poy Rogers Comics,Ph(c) . . 350.00
145 Popeye 250.00
146 Marge's Little Lulu. 475.00
147 W.Disney's Donald Duck
in Volcano Valley 1,800.00
148 WK,Albert the Alligator
and Pogo Possum. 950.00
149 Smilin' Jack. 175.00
150 Tillie the Toiler 150.00
151 Lone Ranger. 325.00
152 Little Orphan Annie 250.00
153 Roy Rogers Comics 325.00
154 Andy Panda 200.00
155 Henry 200.00
156 Porky Pig and the Phantom . 600.00
157 W.Disney's Mickey Mouse
and the Beanstalk 500.00
158 Marge's Little Lulu. 500.00
159 CB,W.Disney's Donald Duck
in the Ghost of the Grotto. . 3,000.00
160 Roy Rogers Comics,Ph(c) . . 350.00
161 Tarzan & the Fires of Tohr . . 900.00
162 Felix the Cat 300.00
163 Dick Tracy. 300.00
164 Bugs Bunny Finds the
Frozen Kingdom 275.00
165 Marge's Little Lulu. 500.00
166 Roy Rogers Comics,Ph(c) . . 325.00
167 Lone Ranger. 325.00
168 Popeye 250.00
169 Woody Woodpecker,Drug . . . 400.00
170 W.Disney's Mickey Mouse
on Spook's Island 350.00
171 Charlie McCarthy 450.00
172 WK,Christmas with
Mother Goose 250.00
173 Flash Gordon 300.00
174 Winnie Winkle. 150.00
175 WK,Santa Claus Funnies . . . 250.00
176 Tillie the Toiler. 150.00
177 Roy Rogers Comics,Ph(c) . . 325.00
178 CB,W.Disney's Donald
Duck Christmas on Bear
Mountain. 2,400.00
179 WK,Uncle Wiggily 275.00
180 Ozark the Ike 200.00
181 W.Disney's Mickey Mouse
in Jungle Magic 500.00
182 Porky Pig in Never-
Never Land 600.00
183 Oswald the Rabbit 175.00
184 Tillie the Toiler. 175.00
185 WK,Easter with
Mother Goose 250.00
186 W.Disney's Bambi. 300.00
187 Bugs Bunny and the
Dreadful Bunny 200.00
188 Woody Woodpecker 200.00
189 W.Disney's Donald Duck in
The Old Castle's Secret . . . 1,500.00
190 Flash Gordon 350.00
191 Porky Pig to the Rescue. . . . 500.00
192 WK,The Brownies. 250.00
193 Tom and Jerry. 350.00
194 W.Disney's Mickey Mouse
in the World Under the Sea. . 500.00
195 Tillie the Toiler. 125.00
196 Charlie McCarthy in The
Haunted Hide-Out 300.00
197 Spirit of the Border 200.00
198 Andy Panda 200.00
199 W.Disney's Donald Duck in
Sheriff of Bullet Valley 1,600.00
200 Bugs Bunny, Super Sleuth . . 225.00
201 WK,Christmas with
Mother Goose 200.00
202 Woody Woodpecker 150.00
203 CB,W.Disney's Donald Duck in
The Golden Christmas Tree 1,400.00
204 Flash Gordon 250.00
205 WK,Santa Claus Funnies . . . 275.00
206 Little Orphan Funnies 200.00
207 King of the Royal Mounted . . 250.00
208 W.Disney's Brer Rabbit
Does It Again. 200.00
209 Harold Teen 100.00
210 Tippe and Cap Stubbs 100.00
211 Little Beaver 150.00
212 Dr. Bobbs 75.00

Four Color, 2nd Series #239
© Western Printing

Four Color, 2nd Series #287
© Gene Autry

Four Color, 2nd Series #300
© Walt Disney Co.

Fo

213 Tillie the Toiler 125.00
214 W.Disney's Mickey Mouse
and his Sky Adventure 400.00
215 Sparkle Plenty 200.00
216 Andy Panda and the
Police Pup 150.00
217 Bugs Bunny in Court Jester . 200.00
218 W.Disney's 3 Little Pigs 225.00
219 Swee'pea 150.00
220 WK,Easter with
Mother Goose 200.00
221 WK,Uncle Wiggly 175.00
222 West of the Pecos 125.00
223 CB,W.Disney's Donald Duck in
Lost in the Andes 1,600.00
224 Little Iodine 200.00
225 Oswald the Rabbit 125.00
226 Porky Pig and Spoofy 400.00
227 W.Disney's Seven Dwarfs . . . 225.00
228 The Mark of Zorro 400.00
229 Smokey Stover 125.00
230 Sunset Press 125.00
231 W.Disney's Mickey Mouse
and the Rajah's Treasure . . . 400.00
232 Woody Woodpecker 125.00
233 Bugs Bunny 200.00
234 W.Disney's Dumbo in Sky
Voyage 250.00
235 Tiny Tim 75.00
236 Heritage of the Desert 125.00
237 Tillie the Toiler 125.00
238 CB,W.Disney's Donald Duck
in Voodoo Hoodoo 1,300.00
239 Adventure Bound 90.00
240 Andy Panda 125.00
241 Porky Pig 300.00
242 Tippie and Cap Stubbs 90.00
243 W.Disney's Thumper
Follows His Nose 200.00
244 WK,The Brownies 175.00
245 Dick's Adventures in
Dreamland 100.00
246 Thunder Mountain 75.00
247 Flash Gordon 500.00
248 W.Disney's Mickey Mouse
and the Black Sorcerer 275.00
249 Woody Woodpecker 150.00
250 Bugs Bunny in
Diamond Daze 200.00
251 Hubert at Camp Moonbeam . 100.00
252 W.Disney's Pinocchio 225.00
253 WK,Christmas with
Mother Goose 225.00
254 WK,Santa Claus Funnies,
A:Pogo 250.00
255 The Ranger 100.00
256 CB,W.Disney's Donald Duck in
Luck of the North 1,000.00
257 Little Iodine 150.00
258 Andy Panda and the
Ballon Race 150.00
259 Santa and the Angel 100.00
260 Porky Pig, Hero of the
Wild West 250.00
261 W.Disney's Mickey Mouse
and the Missing Key 300.00
262 Raggedy Ann and Andy 150.00
263 CB,W.Disney's Donald Duck in
Land of the Totem Poles . . 1,000.00
264 Woody Woodpecker in
the Magic Lantern 150.00
265 King of the Royal Mountain . 150.00
266 Bugs Bunny on the Isle of
Hercules 175.00
267 Little Beaver 300.00
268 W.Disney's Mickey Mouse's
Surprise Visitor 300.00
269 Johnny Mack Brown,Ph(c) . . 400.00
270 Drift Fence 100.00
271 Porky Pig 250.00
272 W.Disney's Cinderella 200.00
273 Oswald the Rabbit 100.00
274 Bugs Bunny 150.00
275 CB,W.Disney's Donald Duck
in Ancient Persia 900.00
276 Uncle Wiggly 150.00
277 PorkyPig in DesertAdventure 250.00
278 Bill Elliot Comics,Ph(c) 250.00
279 W.Disney's Mickey Mouse &
Pluto Battle the Giant Ants . . 300.00
280 Andy Panda in the Isle
of the Mechanical Men 150.00
281 Bugs Bunny in The Great
Circus Mystery 175.00
282 CB,W.Disney's Donald Duck in
The Pixilated Parrot 900.00
283 King of the Royal Mounted . . 150.00
284 Porky Pig in the Kingdom
of Nowhere 250.00
285 Bozo the Clown 350.00
286 W.Disney's Mickey Mouse
and the Uninvited Guest 300.00
287 Gene Autry's Champion in the
Ghost of BlackMountain,Ph(c)200.00
288 Woody Woodpecker 150.00
289 BugsBunny in IndianTrouble . 175.00
290 The Chief 125.00
291 CB,W.Disney's Donald Duck in
The Magic Hourglass 900.00
292 The Cisco Kid Comics 450.00
293 WK,The Brownies 175.00
294 Little Beaver 75.00
295 Porky Pig in President Pig . . 250.00
296 W.Disney's Mickey Mouse
Private Eye for Hire 200.00
297 Andy Panda in The
Haunted Inn 150.00
298 Bugs Bunny in Sheik
for a Day 175.00
299 Buck Jones & the Iron Trail . 250.00
300 CB,W.Disney's Donald Duck in
Big-Top Bedlam 900.00
301 The Mysterious Rider 100.00
302 Santa Claus Funnies 100.00
303 Porky Pig in The Land of
the Monstrous Flies 200.00
304 W.Disney's Mickey Mouse
in Tom-Tom Island 250.00
305 Woody Woodpecker 100.00
306 Raggedy Ann 100.00
307 Bugs Bunny in Lumber
Jack Rabbit 150.00
308 CB,W.Disney's Donald Duck in
Dangerous Disguise 800.00
309 Dollface and Her Gang 100.00
310 King of the Royal Mounted . 125.00
311 Porky Pig in Midget Horses
of Hidden Valley 200.00
312 Tonto 200.00
313 W.Disney's Mickey Mouse in
the Mystery of the Double-
Cross Ranch 250.00
314 Ambush 75.00
315 Oswald Rabbit 100.00
316 Rex Allen,Ph(c) 250.00
317 Bugs Bunny in Hare Today
Gone Tomorrow 150.00
318 CB,W.Disney's Donald Duck in
No Such Varmint 800.00
319 Gene Autry's Champion 100.00
320 Uncle Wiggly 150.00
321 Little Scouts 75.00
322 Porky Pig in Roaring Rockies 150.00
323 Susie Q. Smith 75.00
324 I Met a Handsome Cowboy . 150.00
325 W.Disney's Mickey Mouse
in the Haunted Castle 250.00
326 Andy Panda 75.00
327 Bugs Bunny and the
Rajah's Treasure 150.00
328 CB,W.Disney's Donald Duck
in Old California 850.00
329 Roy Roger's Trigger,Ph(c) . . 275.00
330 Porky Pig meets the
Bristled Bruiser 150.00
331 Disney's Alice in
Wonderland 275.00
332 Little Beaver 75.00

Four Color, 2nd Series #375
© Edgar Rice Burroughs, Inc.

Four Color, 2nd Series #387
© Walt Disney Co.

Four Color, 2nd Series #421
© Videofeatures

333 Wilderness Trek 75.00
334 W.Disney's Mickey Mouse
and Yukon Gold. 250.00
335 Francis the Famous
Talking Mule 200.00
336 Woody Woodpecker 100.00
337 The Brownies 100.00
338 Bugs Bunny and the
Rocking Horse Thieves 200.00
339 W.Disney's Donald Duck
and the Magic Fountain. 400.00
340 King of the Royal Mountain . 150.00
341 W.Disney's Unbirthday Party
with Alice in Wonderland 275.00
342 Porky Pig the Lucky
Peppermint Mine 150.00
343 W.Disney's Mickey Mouse in
Ruby Eye of Homar-Guy-Am 150.00
344 Sergeant Preston from
Challenge of the Yukon 250.00
345 Andy Panda in Scotland Yard 100.00
346 Hideout 100.00
347 Bugs Bunny the Frigid Hare . 150.00
348 CB,W.Disney's Donald Duck
The Crocodile Collector. 600.00
349 Uncle Wiggly. 125.00
350 Woody Woodpecker 100.00
351 Porky Pig and the Grand
Canyon Giant 150.00
352 W.Disney's Mickey Mouse
Mystery of Painted Valley . . . 200.00
353 CB(c),W.Disney'sDuckAlbum 300.00
354 Raggedy Ann & Andy 100.00
355 Bugs Bunny Hot-Rod Hair . . 150.00
356 CB(c),W.Disney's Donald
Duck in Rags to Riches. 500.00
357 Comeback. 75.00
358 Andy Panada 100.00
359 Frosty the Snowman. 150.00
360 Porky Pig in Tree Fortune . . 100.00
361 Santa Claus Funnies 100.00
362 W.Disney's Mickey Mouse &
the Smuggled Diamonds. . . . 250.00
363 King of the Royal Mounted . . 125.00
364 Woody Woodpecker 90.00
365 The Brownies 90.00
366 Bugs Bunny Uncle
Buckskin Comes to Town . . . 150.00
367 CB,W.Disney's Donald Duck in
A Christmas for Shacktown . . 900.00
368 Bob Clampett's
Beany and Cecil 500.00
369 Lone Ranger's Famous
Horse Hi-Yo Silver. 175.00
370 Porky Pig in Trouble
in the Big Trees 150.00
371 W.Disney's Mickey Mouse
the Inca Idol Case 200.00
372 Riders of the Purple Sage . . . 75.00
373 Sergeant Preston 150.00
374 Woody Woodpecker 75.00
375 John Carter of Mars 600.00
376 Bugs Bunny 200.00
377 Susie Q. Smith 75.00
378 Tom Corbett, Space Cadet . . 325.00
379 W.Disney's Donald Duck in
Southern Hospitality 300.00
380 Raggedy Ann & Andy 100.00
381 Marge's Tubby 350.00
382 W.Disney's Show White and
the Seven Dwarfs 200.00
383 Andy Panda 75.00
384 King of the Royal Mounted . . 100.00
385 Porky Pig 100.00
386 CB,W.Disney's Uncle Scrooge
in Only A Poor Old Man . . . 2,700.00
387 W.Disney's Mickey Mouse
in High Tibet 200.00
388 Oswald the Rabbit 100.00
389 Andy Hardy Comics 75.00
390 Woody Woodpecker 75.00
391 Uncle Wiggly. 125.00
392 Hi-Yo Silver. 100.00
393 Bugs Bunny 150.00
394 CB(c),W.Disney's Donald Duck
in Malayalaya 500.00
395 Forlorn River. 75.00
396 Tales of the Texas Rangers,
Ph(c) 200.00
397 Sergeant Preston o/t Yukon . 150.00
398 The Brownies 75.00
399 Porky Pig in the Lost
Gold Mine 100.00
400 AMc,Tom Corbett 200.00
401 W.Disney's Mickey Mouse &
Goofy's Mechanical Wizard. . 150.00
402 Mary Jane and Sniffles 100.00
403 W.Disney's Li'l Bad Wolf. . . . 150.00
404 The Ranger Rider,Ph(c) 200.00
405 Woody Woodpecker 75.00
406 Tweety and Sylvester 125.00
407 Bugs Bunny, Foreign-
Legion Hare. 125.00
408 CB,W.Disney's Donald Duck
and the Golden Helmet 750.00
409 Andy Panda 75.00
410 Porky Pig in the
Water Wizard. 100.00
411 W.Disney's Mickey Mouse
and the Old Sea Dog. 150.00
412 Nevada 75.00
413 Disney's Robin Hood(movie),
Ph(c) 200.00
414 Bob Clampett's Beany
and Cecil 250.00
415 Rootie Kazootie 175.00
416 Woody Woodpecker 75.00
417 Double Trouble with Goober. . 75.00
418 Rusty Riley 75.00
419 Sergeant Preston 150.00
420 Bugs Bunny 125.00
421 AMc,Tom Corbett 175.00
422 CB,W.Disney's Donald Duck
and the Gilded Man. 750.00
423 Rhubarb 100.00
424 Flash Gordon 175.00
425 Zorro 200.00
426 Porky Pig 100.00
427 W.Disney's Mickey Mouse &
the Wonderful Whizzix. 150.00
428 Uncle Wiggily 100.00
429 W.Disney's Pluto in
Why Dogs Leave Home 200.00
430 Marge's Tubby 200.00
431 Woody Woodpecker 100.00
432 Bugs Bunny and the
Rabbit Olympics 125.00
433 Wildfire 75.00
434 Rin Tin Tin,Ph(c). 250.00
435 Frosty the Snowman. 100.00
436 The Brownies 75.00
437 John Carter of Mars 400.00
438 W.Disney's Annie
Oakley (TV) 275.00
439 Little Hiawatha 100.00
440 Black Beauty 75.00
441 Fearless Fagan. 75.00
442 W.Disney's Peter Pan 175.00
443 Ben Bowie and His
Mountain Men 125.00
444 Marge's Tubby 200.00
445 Charlie McCarthy 100.00
446 Captain Hook and Peter Pan 150.00
447 Andy Hardy Comics 75.00
448 Beany and Cecil 275.00
449 Tappan's Burro 75.00
450 CB(c),W.Disney's Duck
Album 200.00
451 Rusty Riley 65.00
452 Raggedy Ann and Andy 100.00
453 Susie Q. Smith 65.00
454 Krazy Kat Comics 65.00
455 Johnny Mack Brown Comics,
Ph(c) 125.00
456 W.Disney's Uncle Scrooge
Back to the Klondike 1,500.00
457 Daffy 150.00
458 Oswald the Rabbit 75.00

Four Color, 2nd Series #460
© Dell Publishing Co.

Four Color, 2nd Series #520
© S. Slesinger

Four Color, 2nd Series #541
© Johnny Mack Brown

459 Rootie Kazootie 150.00
460 Buck Jones 175.00
461 Marge's Tubby 175.00
462 Little Scouts 50.00
463 Petunia 75.00
464 Bozo 150.00
465 Francis the Talking Mule 100.00
466 Rhubarb, the Millionaire Cat . . 75.00
467 Desert Gold 75.00
468 W.Disney's Goofy 300.00
469 Beetle Bailey 175.00
470 Elmer Fudd 100.00
471 Double Trouble with Goober . . 40.00
472 Wild Bill Elliot,Ph(c). 150.00
473 W.Disney's Li'l Bad Wolf 75.00
474 Mary Jane and Sniffles 125.00
475 M.G.M.'s the Two
Mouseketeers 125.00
476 Rin Tin Tin,Ph(c) 150.00
477 Bob Clampett's Beany and
Cecil. 275.00
478 Charlie McCarthy 100.00
479 Queen o/t West Dale Evans . 400.00
480 Andy Hardy Comics 50.00
481 Annie Oakley and Tagg. 150.00
482 Brownies 75.00
483 Little Beaver 75.00
484 River Feud 75.00
485 The Little People. 125.00
486 Rusty Riley 75.00
487 Mowgli, the Jungle Book. . . . 100.00
488 John Carter of Mars 350.00
489 Tweety and Sylvester 100.00
490 Jungle Jim 125.00
491 EK,Silvertip 150.00
492 W.Disney's Duck Album 150.00
493 Johnny Mack Brown,Ph(c) . . 125.00
494 The Little King. 175.00
495 CB, W.Disney's Uncle
Scrooge 1,000.00
496 The Green Hornet. 900.00
497 Zorro, (Sword of). 225.00
498 Bugs Bunny's Album. 100.00
499 M.G.M.'s Spike and Tyke 90.00
500 Buck Jones 100.00
501 Francis the Famous
Talking Mule 90.00
502 Rootie Kazootie 135.00
503 Uncle Wiggily 90.00
504 Krazy Kat 75.00
505 W.Disney's the Sword and
the Rose (TV),Ph(c) 150.00
506 The Little Scouts 40.00
507 Oswald the Rabbit 75.00
508 Bozo 150.00
509 W.Disney's Pluto. 100.00
510 Son of Black Beauty 60.00
511 EK,Outlaw Trail 75.00
512 Flash Gordon 125.00
513 Ben Bowie and His
Mountain Men 60.00
514 Frosty the Snowman. 100.00
515 Andy Hardy 50.00
516 Double Trouble With Goober . 40.00
517 Walt Disney's Chip 'N' Dale . 200.00
518 Rivets 50.00
519 Steve Canyon 150.00
520 Wild Bill Elliot,Ph(c). 125.00
521 Beetle Bailey. 100.00
522 The Brownies 75.00
523 Rin Tin Tin,Ph(c) 150.00
524 Tweety and Sylvester 90.00
525 Santa Claus Funnies 100.00
526 Napoleon. 50.00
527 Charlie McCarthy 100.00
528 Queen o/t West Dale Evans,
Ph(c) 200.00
529 Little Beaver 75.00
530 Bob Clampett's Beany
and Cecil 275.00
531 W.Disney's Duck Album 150.00
532 The Rustlers 60.00
533 Raggedy Ann and Andy 100.00
534 EK,Western Marshal. 125.00
535 I Love Lucy,Ph(c). 1,000.00
536 Daffy 100.00
537 Stormy, the Thoroughbred . . . 75.00
538 EK,The Mask of Zorro 250.00
539 Ben and Me 75.00
540 Knights of the Round Table,
Ph(c) 150.00
541 Johnny Mack Brown,Ph(c) . . 125.00
542 Super Circus Featuring
Mary Hartline 125.00
543 Uncle Wiggly. 100.00
544 W.Disney's Rob Roy(Movie),
Ph(c) 150.00
545 The Wonderful Adventures
of Pinocchio. 150.00
546 Buck Jones 100.00
547 Francis the Famous
Talking Mule 90.00
548 Krazy Kat 75.00
549 Oswald the Rabbit 75.00
550 The Little Scouts 40.00
551 Bozo 150.00
552 Beetle Bailey. 100.00
553 Susie Q. Smith 50.00
554 Rusty Riley 60.00
555 Range War 60.00
556 Double Trouble with Goober. . 40.00
557 Ben Bowie and His
Mountain Men 60.00
558 Elmer Fudd 75.00
559 I Love Lucy,Ph(c) 600.00
560 W.Disney's Duck Album 150.00
561 Mr. Magoo. 200.00
562 W.Disney's Goofy 150.00
563 Rhubarb, the Millionaire Cat. 100.00
564 W.Disney's Li'l Bad Wolf. . . . 100.00
565 Jungle Jim. 75.00
566 Son of Black Beauty 60.00
567 BF,Prince Valiant,Ph(c) 250.00
568 Gypsy Cat. 90.00
569 Priscilla's Pop 75.00
570 Bob Clampett's Beany
and Cecil 275.00
571 Charlie McCarthy 100.00
572 EK,Silvertip 90.00
573 The Little People. 100.00
574 The Hand of Zorro 225.00
575 Annie and Oakley and Tagg,
Ph(c) 175.00
576 Angel. 40.00
577 M.G.M.'s Spike and Tyke 60.00
578 Steve Canyon 90.00
579 Francis the Talking Mule. 75.00
580 Six Gun Ranch 75.00
581 Chip 'N' Dale. 100.00
582 Mowgli, the Jungle Book. . . . 100.00
583 The Lost Wagon Train 75.00
584 Johnny Mack Brown,Ph(c) . . 125.00
585 Bugs Bunny's Album. 100.00
586 W.Disney's Duck Album 160.00
587 The Little Scouts. 50.00
588 MB,King Richard and the
Crusaders,Ph(c) 175.00
589 Buck Jones 100.00
590 Hansel and Gretel. 125.00
591 EK,Western Marshal. 100.00
592 Super Circus. 125.00
593 Oswald the Rabbit 60.00
594 Bozo 160.00
595 Pluto 75.00
596 Turok, Son of Stone. 1,000.00
597 The Little King. 100.00
598 Captain Davy Jones 90.00
599 Ben Bowie and His
Mountain Men 75.00
600 Daisy Duck's Diary 150.00
601 Frosty the Snowman. 100.00
602 Mr. Magoo and the Gerald
McBoing-Boing 225.00
603 M.G.M.'s The Two
Mouseketeers 90.00
604 Shadow on the Trail 75.00
605 The Brownies 75.00

Four Color, 2nd Series #610
© Dell Publishing Co.

Four Color, 2nd Series #671
© Walt Disney Co.

Four Color, 2nd Series #716
© Walt Disney Co.

606 Sir Lancelot ... 150.00
607 Santa Claus Funnies ... 100.00
608 EK,Silver Tip ... 75.00
609 The Littlest Outlaw,Ph(c) ... 125.00
610 Drum Beat,Ph(c) ... 175.00
611 W.Disney's Duck Album ... 150.00
612 Little Beaver ... 65.00
613 EK,Western Marshal ... 100.00
614 W.Disney's 20,000 Leagues Under the Sea (Movie) ... 200.00
615 Daffy ... 100.00
616 To The Last Man ... 75.00
617 The Quest of Zorro ... 225.00
618 Johnny Mack Brown,Ph(c) ... 125.00
619 Krazy Kat ... 65.00
620 Mowgli, Jungle Book ... 90.00
621 Francis the Famous Talking Mule ... 65.00
622 Beetle Bailey ... 100.00
623 Oswald the Rabbit ... 65.00
624 Treasure Island,Ph(c) ... 150.00
625 Beaver Valley ... 125.00
626 Ben Bowie and His Mountain Men ... 65.00
627 Goofy ... 150.00
628 Elmer Fudd ... 65.00
629 Lady & The Tramp with Jock 150.00
630 Priscilla's Pop ... 65.00
631 W.Disney's Davy Crockett Indian Fighter (TV),Ph(c) ... 350.00
632 Fighting Caravans ... 65.00
633 The Little People ... 65.00
634 Lady and the Tramp Album ... 100.00
635 Bob Clampett's Beany and Cecil ... 300.00
636 Chip 'N' Dale ... 100.00
637 EK,Silvertip ... 75.00
638 M.G.M.'s Spike and Tyke ... 50.00
639 W.Disney's Davy Crockett at the Alamo (TV),Ph(c) ... 275.00
640 EK,Western Marshal ... 100.00
641 Steve Canyon ... 110.00
642 M.G.M.'s The Two Mouseketeers ... 75.00
643 Wild Bill Elliott,Ph(c) ... 65.00
644 Sir Walter Raleigh,Ph(c) ... 125.00
645 Johnny Mack Brown,Ph(c) ... 125.00
646 Dotty Dripple and Taffy ... 60.00
647 Bugs Bunny's Album ... 100.00
648 Jace Pearson of the Texas Rangers,Ph(c) ... 100.00
649 Duck Album ... 100.00
650 BF,Prince Valiant ... 125.00
651 EK,King Colt ... 60.00
652 Buck Jones ... 60.00
653 Smokey the Bear ... 200.00
654 Pluto ... 75.00
655 Francis the Famous Talking Mule ... 75.00
656 Turok, Son of Stone ... 550.00
657 Ben Bowie and His Mountain Men ... 60.00
658 Goofy ... 150.00
659 Daisy Duck's Diary ... 125.00
660 Little Beaver ... 65.00
661 Frosty the Snowman ... 100.00
662 Zoo Parade ... 100.00
663 Winky Dink ... 150.00
664 W.Disney's Davy Crockett in the Great Keelboat Race (TV),Ph(c) ... 300.00
665 The African Lion ... 100.00
666 Santa Claus Funnies ... 100.00
667 EK,Silvertip and the Stolen Stallion ... 100.00
668 W.Disney's Dumbo ... 325.00
668a W.Disney's Dumbo ... 300.00
669 W.Disney's Robin Hood (Movie),Ph(c) ... 100.00
670 M.G.M.'s Mouse Musketeers . 75.00
671 W.Disney's Davey Crockett & the River Pirates(TV),Ph(c) .. 275.00
672 Quentin Durward,Ph(c) ... 125.00
673 Buffalo Bill Jr.,Ph(c) ... 125.00
674 The Little Rascals ... 125.00
675 EK,Steve Donovan,Ph(c) ... 150.00
676 Will-Yum! ... 50.00
677 Little King ... 100.00
678 The Last Hunt,Ph(c) ... 150.00
679 Gunsmoke ... 350.00
680 Out Our Way with the Worry Wart ... 50.00
681 Forever, Darling,Lucile Ball Ph(c) ... 225.00
682 When Knighthood Was in Flower,Ph(c) ... 150.00
683 Hi and Lois ... 60.00
684 SB,Helen of Troy,Ph(c) ... 200.00
685 Johnny Mack Brown,Ph(c) .. 150.00
686 Duck Album ... 150.00
687 The Indian Fighter,Ph(c) ... 150.00
688 SB,Alexander the Great, Ph(c) ... 150.00
689 Elmer Fudd ... 60.00
690 The Conqueror, John Wayne Ph(c) ... 300.00
691 Dotty Dripple and Taffy ... 50.00
692 The Little People ... 60.00
693 W.Disney's Brer Rabbit Song of the South ... 175.00
694 Super Circus,Ph(c) ... 125.00
695 Little Beaver ... 60.00
696 Krazy Kat ... 60.00
697 Oswald the Rabbit ... 60.00
698 Francis the Famous Talking Mule ... 60.00
699 BA,Prince Valiant ... 150.00
700 Water Birds and the Olympic Elk ... 100.00
701 Jimmy Cricket ... 150.00
702 The Goofy Success Story ... 135.00
703 Scamp ... 175.00
704 Priscilla's Pop ... 60.00
705 Brave Eagle,Ph(c) ... 125.00
706 Bongo and Lumpjaw ... 100.00
707 Corky and White Shadow, Ph(c) ... 135.00
708 Smokey the Bear ... 100.00
709 The Searchers,John Wayne Ph(c) ... 450.00
710 Francis the Famous Talking Mule ... 60.00
711 M.G.M.'s Mouse Musketeers .. 50.00
712 The Great Locomotive Chase, Ph(c) ... 135.00
713 The Animal World ... 60.00
714 W.Disney's Spin & Marty (TV) ... 250.00
715 Timmy ... 60.00
716 Man in Space ... 150.00
717 Moby Dick,Ph(c) ... 150.00
718 Dotty Dripple and Taffy ... 50.00
719 BF,Prince Valiant ... 125.00
720 Gunsmoke,Ph(c) ... 175.00
721 Captain Kangaroo,Ph(c) ... 300.00
722 Johnny Mack Brown,Ph(c) .. 125.00
723 EK,Santiago ... 175.00
724 Bugs Bunny's Album ... 75.00
725 Elmer Fudd ... 50.00
726 Duck Album ... 100.00
727 The Nature of Things ... 110.00
728 M.G.M.'s Mouse Musketeers . 50.00
729 Bob Son of Battle ... 60.00
730 Smokey Stover ... 75.00
731 EK,Silvertip and The Fighting Four ... 75.00
732 Zorro, (the Challenge of) ... 250.00
733 Buck Rogers ... 65.00
734 Cheyenne,C.Walker Ph(c) .. 300.00
735 Crusader Rabbit ... 550.00
736 Pluto ... 75.00
737 Steve Canyon ... 100.00
738 Westward Ho, the Wagons, Ph(c) ... 200.00
739 MD,Bounty Guns ... 75.00
740 Chilly Willy ... 100.00
741 The Fastest Gun Alive,Ph(c). 150.00
742 Buffalo Bill Jr.,Ph(c) ... 100.00

Four Color, 2nd Series #760
© Walt Disney Co.

Four Color, 2nd Series #811
© Dell Publishing Co.

Four Color, 2nd Series #866
© Walt Disney Co.

743 Daisy Duck's Diary 110.00
744 Little Beaver 65.00
745 Francis the Famous Talking Mule 65.00
746 Dotty Dripple and Taffy 50.00
747 Goofy 135.00
748 Frosty the Snowman. 100.00
749 Secrets of Life,Ph(c) 100.00
750 The Great Cat 125.00
751 Our Miss Brooks,Ph(c) 150.00
752 Mandrake, the Magician 175.00
753 Walt Scott's Little People 75.00
754 Smokey the Bear 100.00
755 The Littlest Snowman 75.00
756 Santa Claus Funnies 100.00
757 The True Story of Jesse James,Ph(c) 175.00
758 Bear Country. 100.00
759 Circus Boy,Ph(c). 250.00
760 W.Disney's Hardy Boys(TV) . 250.00
761 Howdy Doody 250.00
762 SB,The Sharkfighters,Ph(c) . 150.00
763 GrandmaDuck'sFarmFriends 150.00
764 M.G.M.'s Mouse Musketeers . 50.00
765 Will-Yum!. 50.00
766 Buffalo Bill,Ph(c) 100.00
767 Spin and Marty 175.00
768 EK,Steve Donovan, Western Marshal,Ph(c) 125.00
769 Gunsmoke. 200.00
770 Brave Eagle,Ph(c) 65.00
771 MD,Brand of Empire 65.00
772 Cheyenne,C.Walker Ph(c) . . 150.00
773 The Brave One,Ph(c) 100.00
774 Hi and Lois 50.00
775 SB,Sir Lancelot and Brian,Ph(c). 175.00
776 Johnny Mack Brown,Ph(c) . . 125.00
777 Scamp. 135.00
778 The Little Rascals 100.00
779 Lee Hunter, Indian Fighter . . 100.00
780 Captain Kangaroo,Ph(c) 250.00
781 Fury,Ph(c) 150.00
782 Duck Album. 100.00
783 Elmer Fudd 50.00
784 Around the World in 80 Days,Ph(c). 125.00
785 Circus Boys,Ph(c). 250.00
786 Cinderella 125.00
787 Little Hiawatha 100.00
788 BF,Prince Valiant. 125.00
789 EK,Silvertip-Valley Thieves . . 100.00
790 ATh,The Wings of Eagles, J.Wayne Ph(c) 300.00
791 The 77th Bengal Lancers, Ph(c) 150.00
792 Oswald the Rabbit 65.00
793 Morty Meekle 50.00
794 SB,The Count of Monte Cristo 150.00
795 Jiminy Cricket 125.00
796 Ludwig Bemelman's Madeleine and Genevieve. . . . 60.00
797 Gunsmoke,Ph(c). 175.00
798 Buffalo Bill,Ph(c) 100.00
799 Priscilla's Pop 60.00
800 The Buccaneers,Ph(c) 150.00
801 Dotty Dripple and Taffy 50.00
802 Goofy 150.00
803 Cheyenne,C.Walker Ph(c) . . 150.00
804 Steve Canyon 100.00
805 Crusader Rabbit 450.00
806 Scamp. 125.00
807 MB,Savage Range 65.00
808 Spin and Marty,Ph(c) 175.00
809 The Little People. 75.00
810 Francis the Famous Talking Mule 65.00
811 Howdy Doody 200.00
812 The Big Land,A.Ladd Ph(c) . 200.00
813 Circus Boy,Ph(c). 225.00
814 Covered Wagon,A:Mickey Mouse 125.00
815 Dragoon Wells Massacre . . . 150.00
816 Brave Eagle,Ph(c). 65.00
817 Little Beaver 65.00
818 Smokey the Bear 100.00
819 Mickey Mouse in Magicland . 100.00
820 The Oklahoman,Ph(c). 175.00
821 Wringle Wrangle,Ph(c) 150.00
822 ATh,W.Disney's Paul Revere's Ride (TV) 175.00
823 Timmy 50.00
824 The Pride and the Passion, Ph(c) 150.00
825 The Little Rascals 100.00
826 Spin and Marty and Annette, Ph(c) 400.00
827 Smokey Stover 90.00
828 Buffalo Bill, Jr,Ph(c). 90.00
829 Tales of the Pony Express, Ph(c) 90.00
830 The Hardy Boys,Ph(c) 175.00
831 No Sleep 'Til Dawn,Ph(c) . . . 125.00
832 Lolly and Pepper. 65.00
833 Scamp. 125.00
834 Johnny Mack Brown,Ph(c) . . 125.00
835 Silvertip- The Fake Rider 90.00
836 Man in Fight 135.00
837 All-American Athlete Cotton Woods 55.00
838 Bugs Bunny's Life Story Album 75.00
839 The Vigilantes 125.00
840 Duck Album 100.00
841 Elmer Fudd 50.00
842 The Nature of Things 100.00
843 The First Americans 150.00
844 Gunsmoke,Ph(c). 150.00
845 ATh,The Land Unknown 225.00
846 ATh,Gun Glory 175.00
847 Perri 90.00
848 Marauder's Moon 55.00
849 BF,Prince Valiant. 125.00
850 Buck Jones 60.00
851 The Story of Mankind, V.Price Ph(c) 135.00
852 Chilly Willy 65.00
853 Pluto 75.00
854 Hunchback of Notre Dame, Ph(c) 225.00
855 Broken Arrow,Ph(c). 100.00
856 Buffalo Bill, Jr.,Ph(c) 100.00
857 The Goofy Adventure Story . 150.00
858 Daisy Duck's Diary 90.00
859 Topper and Neil. 80.00
860 Wyatt Earp,Ph(c) 175.00
861 Frosty the Snowman. 75.00
862 Truth About Mother Goose . . 135.00
863 Francis the Famous Talking Mule 60.00
864 The Littlest Snowman 75.00
865 Andy Burnett,Ph(c) 175.00
866 Mars and Beyond 150.00
867 Santa Claus Funnies 100.00
868 The Little People. 90.00
869 Old Yeller,Ph(c) 110.00
870 Little Beaver 65.00
871 Curly Kayoe 50.00
872 Captain Kangaroo,Ph(c) 235.00
873 Grandma Duck's Farm Friends. 90.00
874 Old Ironsides. 125.00
875 Trumpets West 60.00
876 Tales of Wells Fargo,Ph(c) . . 175.00
877 ATh,Frontier Doctor,Ph(c) . . . 175.00
878 Peanuts. 275.00
879 Brave Eagle,Ph(c). 60.00
880 MD,Steve Donovan,Ph(c) 75.00
881 The Captain and the Kids 60.00
882 ATh,W.DisneyPresentsZorro. 275.00
883 The Little Rascals 100.00
884 Hawkeye and the Last of the Mohicans,Ph(c) 135.00
885 Fury,Ph(c) 125.00
886 Bongo and Lumpjaw. 90.00
887 The Hardy Boys,Ph(c) 175.00

Four Color, 2nd Series #924
© Dell Publishing Co.

Four Color, 2nd Series #964
© Walt Disney Co.

Four Color, 2nd Series #1010
© Walt Disney Co.

888 Elmer Fudd 50.00
889 ATh,W.Disney's Clint
& Mac(TV),Ph(c) 225.00
890 Wyatt Earp,Ph(c) 135.00
891 Light in the Forest,
C.Parker Ph(c). 135.00
892 Maverick,J.Garner Ph(c). . . . 450.00
893 Jim Bowie,Ph(c) 100.00
894 Oswald the Rabbit 60.00
895 Wagon Train,Ph(c) 200.00
896 Adventures of Tinker Bell . . . 150.00
897 Jiminy Cricket 125.00
898 EK,Silvertip 90.00
899 Goofy 100.00
900 BF,Prince Valiant 125.00
901 Little Hiawatha 90.00
902 Will-Yum!. 60.00
903 Dotty Dripple and Taffy 50.00
904 Lee Hunter, Indian Fighter . . . 60.00
905 W.Disney's Annette (TV),
Ph(c) 500.00
906 Francis the Famous
Talking Mule 60.00
907 Ath,Sugarfoot,Ph(c). 235.00
908 The Little People
and the Giant. 75.00
909 Smitty 60.00
910 ATh,The Vikings,
K.Douglas Ph(c) 150.00
911 The Gray Ghost,Ph(c). 150.00
912 Leave it to Beaver,Ph(c) 300.00
913 The Left-Handed Gun,
Paul Newman Ph(c) 175.00
914 ATh,No Time for Sergeants,
Ph(c) 175.00
915 Casey Jones,Ph(c) 100.00
916 Red Ryder Ranch Comics . . . 90.00
917 The Life of Riley,Ph(c) 225.00
918 Beep Beep, the Roadrunner. 200.00
919 Boots and Saddles,Ph(c) . . . 135.00
920 Ath,Zorro,Ph(c) 225.00
921 Wyatt Earp.Ph(c) 135.00
922 Johnny Mack Brown,Ph(c) . . 135.00
923 Timmy 50.00
924 Colt .45,Ph(c) 175.00
925 Last of the Fast Guns,Ph(c) . 135.00
926 Peter Pan 75.00
927 SB,Top Gun 60.00
928 Sea Hunt,L.Bridges Ph(c). . . 225.00
929 Brave Eagle,Ph(c). 60.00
930 Maverick,J. Garner Ph(c) . . . 200.00
931 Have Gun, Will Travel,Ph(c) . 250.00
932 Smokey the Bear 100.00
933 ATh,W.Disney's Zorro 225.00
934 Restless Gun 225.00
935 King of the Royal Mounted . . . 65.00
936 The Little Rascals 100.00
937 Ruff and Ready. 225.00
938 Elmer Fudd 60.00
939 Steve Canyon 90.00
940 Lolly and Pepper 50.00
941 Pluto 60.00
942 Pony Express 90.00
943 White Wilderness 125.00
944 SB,7th Voyage of Sinbad . . . 250.00
945 Maverick,J.Garner Ph(c). . . . 250.00
946 The Big Country,Ph(c) 150.00
947 Broken Arrow,Ph(c). 90.00
948 Daisy Duck's Diary 90.00
949 High Adventure,Ph(c) 90.00
950 Frosty the Snowman 75.00
951 ATh,Lennon Sisters
Life Story,Ph(c) 250.00
952 Goofy 90.00
953 Francis the Famous
Talking Mule 60.00
954 Man in Space 135.00
955 Hi and Lois 50.00
956 Ricky Nelson,Ph(c). 350.00
957 Buffalo Bee 175.00
958 Santa Claus Funnies 90.00
959 Christmas Stories 75.00
960 ATh,W.Disney's Zorro 225.00
961 Jace Pearson's Tales of
Texas Rangers,Ph(c). 90.00
962 Maverick,J.Garner Ph(c). . . . 200.00
963 Johnny Mack Brown,Ph(c) . . 125.00
964 The Hardy Boys,Ph(c) 175.00
965 GrandmaDuck'sFarmFriends . 90.00
966 Tonka,Ph(c). 150.00
967 Chilly Willy 60.00
968 Tales of Wells Fargo,Ph(c) . . 150.00
969 Peanuts. 200.00
970 Lawman,Ph(c). 225.00
971 Wagon Train,Ph(c) 125.00
972 Tom Thumb. 175.00
973 SleepingBeauty & the Prince 200.00
974 The Little Rascals 125.00
975 Fury,Ph(c). 125.00
976 ATh,W.Disney's Zorro,Ph(c) . 200.00
977 Elmer Fudd 50.00
978 Lolly and Pepper. 50.00
979 Oswald the Rabbit 60.00
980 Maverick,J.Garner Ph(c). . . . 200.00
981 Ruff and Ready. 150.00
982 The New Adventures of
Tinker Bell 150.00
983 Have Gun, Will Travel,Ph(c). 175.00
984 Sleeping Beauty's Fairy
Godmothers. 165.00
985 Shaggy Dog,Ph(c) 150.00
986 Restless Gun,Ph(c). 150.00
987 Goofy 90.00
988 Little Hiawatha 90.00
989 Jimmy Cricket 125.00
990 Huckleberry Hound 235.00
991 Francis the Famous
Talking Mule 60.00
992 ATh,Sugarfoot,Ph(c) 200.00
993 Jim Bowie,Ph(c) 90.00
994 Sea HuntL.Bridges Ph(c) . . . 150.00
995 Donald Duck Album 125.00
996 Nevada 60.00
997 Walt Disney Presents,Ph(c) . 150.00
998 Ricky Nelson,Ph(c). 350.00
999 Leave It To Beaver,Ph(c) . . . 300.00
1000 The Gray Ghost,Ph(c). 150.00
1001 Lowell Thomas' High
Adventure,Ph(c). 90.00
1002 Buffalo Bee 125.00
1003 ATh,W.Disney's Zorro,Ph(c) 200.00
1004 Colt .45,Ph(c) 150.00
1005 Maverick,J.Garner Ph(c). . . 200.00
1006 SB,Hercules 175.00
1007 John Paul Jones,Ph(c) 90.00
1008 Beep, Beep, the
Road Runner. 90.00
1009 CB,The Rifleman,Ph(c) . . . 450.00
1010 Grandma Duck's Farm
Friends. 225.00
1011 Buckskin,Ph(c) 150.00
1012 Last Train from Gun
Hill,Ph(c) 155.00
1013 Bat Masterson,Ph(c). 225.00
1014 ATh,The Lennon Sisters,
Ph(c) 250.00
1015 Peanuts. 200.00
1016 Smokey the Bear 75.00
1017 Chilly Willy 60.00
1018 Rio Bravo,J.Wayne Ph(c) . . 400.00
1019 Wagoon Train,Ph(c) 125.00
1020 Jungle 60.00
1021 Jace Pearson's Tales of
the Texas Rangers,Ph(c). 90.00
1022 Timmy. 50.00
1023 Tales of Wells Fargo,Ph(c) . 150.00
1024 ATh,Darby O'Gill and
the Little People,Ph(c). 175.00
1025 CB,W.Disney's Vacation in
Disneyland. 350.00
1026 Spin and Marty,Ph(c) 135.00
1027 The Texan,Ph(c) 150.00
1028 Rawhide,
Clint Eastwood Ph(c). 425.00
1029 Boots and Saddles,Ph(c) . . 100.00
1030 Spanky and Alfalfa, the
Little Rascals 100.00
1031 Fury,Ph(c) 125.00

Four Color, 2nd Series #1043
© Dell Publishing Co.

Four Color, 2nd Series #1097
© Columbia Broadcasting System

Four Color, 2nd Series #1166
© P. A. T. Ward

1032 Elmer Fudd 50.00
1033 Steve Canyon,Ph(c) 90.00
1034 Nancy and Sluggo
Summer Camp 75.00
1035 Lawman,Ph(c). 135.00
1036 The Big Circus,Ph(c). 125.00
1037 Zorro,Ph(c) 275.00
1038 Ruff and Ready. 150.00
1039 Pluto 75.00
1040 Quick Draw McGraw 250.00
1041 ATh,Sea Hunt,
L.Bridges Ph(c) 150.00
1042 The Three Chipmunks 125.00
1043 The Three Stooges,Ph(c) . . 400.00
1044 Have Gun,Will Travel,Ph(c) 165.00
1045 Restless Gun,Ph(c). 150.00
1046 Beep Beep, the
Road Runner. 100.00
1047 CB,W.Disney's
GyroGearloose 300.00
1048 The Horse Soldiers
J.Wayne Ph(c). 250.00
1049 Don't Give Up the Ship
J.Lewis Ph(c). 150.00
1050 Huckleberry Hound 150.00
1051 Donald in Mathmagic Land. 150.00
1052 RsM,Ben-Hur 175.00
1053 Goofy 90.00
1054 Huckleberry Hound
Winter Fun. 150.00
1055 CB,Daisy Duck's Diary 175.00
1056 Yellowstone Kelly,
C.Walker Ph(c) 120.00
1057 Mickey Mouse Album 100.00
1058 Colt .45,Ph(c) 175.00
1059 Sugarfoot 155.00
1060 Journey to the Center of the
Earth, P.Boone Ph(c) 225.00
1061 Buffalo Bill. 125.00
1062 Christmas Stories 75.00
1063 Santa Claus Funnies 90.00
1064 Bugs Bunny's Merry
Christmas 90.00
1065 Frosty the Snowman. 75.00
1066 ATh,77 Sunset Strip,Ph(c). . 225.00
1067 Yogi Bear 200.00
1068 Francis the Famous
Talking Mule 60.00
1069 ATh,The FBI Story,Ph(c) . . . 175.00
1070 Soloman and Sheba,Ph(c) . 160.00
1071 ATh,TheRealMcCoys,Ph(c). 175.00
1072 Blythe 90.00
1073 CB,Grandma Duck's Farm
Friends. 235.00
1074 Chilly Willy 60.00
1075 Tales of Wells Fargo,Ph(c) . 150.00
1076 MSy,The Rebel,Ph(c) 175.00
1077 SB,The Deputy,
H.Fonda Ph(c). 225.00
1078 The Three Stooges,Ph(c) . . 225.00
1079 The Little Rascals 100.00
1080 Fury,Ph(c) 125.00
1081 Elmer Fudd 50.00
1082 Spin and Marty 150.00
1083 Men into Space,Ph(c) 150.00
1084 Speedy Gonzales 90.00
1085 ATh,The Time Machine. . . . 300.00
1086 Lolly and Pepper. 50.00
1087 Peter Gunn,Ph(c) 175.00
1088 A Dog of Flanders,Ph(c) 90.00
1089 Restless Gun,Ph(c). 150.00
1090 Francis the Famous
Talking Mule 60.00
1091 Jacky's Diary. 90.00
1092 Toby Tyler,Ph(c) 125.00
1093 MacKenzie's Raiders,Ph(c) 125.00
1094 Goofy 90.00
1095 CB,W.Disney's
GyroGearloose 170.00
1096 The Texan,Ph(c) 150.00
1097 Rawhide,C.Eastwood Ph(c) 275.00
1098 Sugarfoot,Ph(c). 150.00
1099 CB(c),Donald Duck Album . 150.00
1100 W.Disney's Annette's
Life Story (TV),Ph(c) 400.00
1101 Robert Louis Stevenson's
Kidnapped,Ph(c) 125.00
1102 Wanted: Dead or Alive,
Ph(c) 225.00
1103 Leave It To Beaver,Ph(c). . . 275.00
1104 Yogi Bear Goes to College . 150.00
1105 ATh,Gale Storm,Ph(c) 225.00
1106 ATh,77 Sunset Strip,Ph(c). . 175.00
1107 Buckskin,Ph(c) 125.00
1108 The Troubleshooters,Ph(c) . . 90.00
1109 This Is Your Life, Donald
Duck,O:Donald Duck. 250.00
1110 Bonanza,Ph(c) 600.00
1111 Shotgun Slade. 125.00
1112 Pixie and Dixie
and Mr. Jinks 150.00
1113 Tales of Wells Fargo,Ph(c) . 165.00
1114 Huckleberry Finn,Ph(c) 90.00
1115 Ricky Nelson,Ph(c) 275.00
1116 Boots and Saddles,Ph(c) . . . 90.00
1117 Boy and the Pirate,Ph(c). . . 125.00
1118 Sword and the Dragon,Ph(c)135.00
1119 Smokey and the Bear
Nature Stories 65.00
1120 Dinosaurus,Ph(c) 150.00
1121 RC,GE,HerculesUnchained 175.00
1122 Chilly Willy. 60.00
1123 Tombstone Territory,Ph(c) . . 175.00
1124 Whirlybirds,Ph(c). 165.00
1125 GK,RH,Laramie,Ph(c) 175.00
1126 Sundance,Ph(c) 125.00
1127 The Three Stooges,Ph(c) . . 225.00
1128 Rocky and His Friends 600.00
1129 Pollyanna,H.Mills Ph(c). . . . 135.00
1130 SB,The Deputy,
H.Fonda Ph(c) 175.00
1131 Elmer Fudd 50.00
1132 Space Mouse 75.00
1133 Fury,Ph(c) 125.00
1134 ATh,Real McCoys,Ph(c) . . . 175.00
1135 M.G.M.'s Mouse Musketeers. 90.00
1136 Jungle Cat,Ph(c). 120.00
1137 The Little Rascals 90.00
1138 The Rebel,Ph(c) 165.00
1139 SB,Spartacus,Ph(c). 225.00
1140 Donald Duck Album 150.00
1141 Huckleberry Hound for
President 150.00
1142 Johnny Ringo,Ph(c) 135.00
1143 Pluto 60.00
1144 The Story of Ruth,Ph(c) . . . 150.00
1145 GK,The Lost World,Ph(c) . . 175.00
1146 Restless Gun,Ph(c). 135.00
1147 Sugarfoot,Ph(c). 150.00
1148 I aim at the Stars,Ph(c) 135.00
1149 Goofy. 90.00
1150 CB,Daisy Duck's Diary 200.00
1151 Mickey Mouse Album 60.00
1152 Rocky and His Friends 400.00
1153 Frosty the Snowman. 90.00
1154 Santa Claus Funnies. 175.00
1155 North to Alaska 275.00
1156 Walt Disney Swiss
Family Robinson 135.00
1157 Master of the World. 90.00
1158 Three Worlds of Gulliver . . . 125.00
1159 ATh,77 Sunset Strip 170.00
1160 Rawhide 250.00
1161 CB,Grandma Duck's
Farm Friends. 225.00
1162 Yogi Bera joins the Marines 135.00
1163 Daniel Boone 90.00
1164 Wanted: Dead or Alive 175.00
1165 Ellery Queen 200.00
1166 Rocky and His Friends 375.00
1167 Tales of Wells Fargo,Ph(c) . 135.00
1168 The Detectives,
R.Taylor Ph(c) 175.00
1169 New Adventures of
Sherlock Holmes 275.00
1170 The Three Stooges,Ph(c) . . 225.00
1171 Elmer Fudd 50.00
1172 Fury,Ph(c) 125.00

 All comics prices listed are for *Near Mint* condition.

Four Color, 2nd Series #1191
© Gomalco Productions

Four Color, 2nd Series #1237
© Dell Publishing Co.

Four Color, 2nd Series #1275
© P. A. T. Ward

1173 The Twilight Zone 400.00
1174 The Little Rascals 75.00
1175 M.G.M.'s Mouse Musketeers. 45.00
1176 Dondi,Ph(c). 75.00
1177 Chilly Willy. 60.00
1178 Ten Who Dared. 135.00
1179 The Swamp Fox,
L.Nielson Ph(c) 150.00
1180 The Danny Thomas Show . 275.00
1181 Texas John Slaughter,Ph(c) 135.00
1182 Donald Duck Album 100.00
1183 101 Dalmatians. 175.00
1184 CB,W.Disney's
Gyro Gearloose. 165.00
1185 Sweetie Pie. 75.00
1186 JDa,Yak Yak 145.00
1187 The Three Stooges,Ph(c) . . 200.00
1188 Atlantis the Lost
Continent,Ph(c) 200.00
1189 Greyfriars Bobby,Ph(c) 135.00
1190 CB(c),Donald and
the Wheel 135.00
1191 Leave It to Beaver,Ph(c) . . . 250.00
1192 Rocky Nelson,Ph(c) 265.00
1193 The Real McCoys,Ph(c) . . . 150.00
1194 Pepe,Ph(c) 50.00
1195 National Velvet,Ph(c) 125.00
1196 Pixie and Dixie
and Mr. Jinks 90.00
1197 The Aquanauts,Ph(c) 135.00
1198 Donald in Mathmagic Land . 125.00
1199 Absent-Minded Professor,
Ph(c) 150.00
1200 Hennessey,Ph(c) 125.00
1201 Goofy 90.00
1202 Rawhide,C.Eastwood Ph(c) 275.00
1203 Pinocchio 100.00
1204 Scamp. 65.00
1205 David & Goliath,Ph(c). 125.00
1206 Lolly and Pepper. 40.00
1207 MSy,The Rebel,Ph(c) 150.00
1208 Rocky and His Friends 375.00
1209 Sugarfoot,Ph(c). 150.00
1210 The Parent Trap,
H.Mills Ph(c) 175.00
1211 RsM,77 Sunset Strip,Ph(c) . 150.00
1212 Chilly Willy 60.00
1213 Mysterious Island,Ph(c) . . . 150.00
1214 Smokey the Bear 65.00
1215 Tales of Wells Fargo,Ph(c) . 135.00
1216 Whirlybirds,Ph(c). 135.00
1218 Fury,Ph(c) 125.00
1219 The Detectives,
Robert Taylor Ph(c) 150.00
1220 Gunslinger,Ph(c) 150.00
1221 Bonanza,Ph(c) 300.00
1222 Elmer Fudd 50.00
1223 GK,Laramie,Ph(c) 125.00
1224 The Little Rascals 75.00
1225 The Deputy,H.Fonda Ph(c). 175.00
1226 Nikki, Wild Dog of the North . 90.00
1227 Morgan the Pirate,Ph(c) . . . 135.00
1229 Thief of Bagdad,Ph(c). 125.00
1230 Voyage to the Bottom
of the Sea,Ph(c) 200.00
1231 Danger Man,Ph(c) 200.00
1232 On the Double. 75.00
1233 Tammy Tell Me True 125.00
1234 The Phantom Planet. 135.00
1235 Mister Magoo 150.00
1236 King of Kings,Ph(c). 135.00
1237 ATh,The Untouchables,
Ph(c) 375.00
1238 Deputy Dawg 200.00
1239 CB(c),Donald Duck Album . 150.00
1240 The Detectives,
R.Taylor Ph(c) 150.00
1241 Sweetie Pies. 50.00
1242 King Leonardo and
His Short Subjects. 225.00
1243 Ellery Queen. 150.00
1244 Space Mouse 75.00
1245 New Adventures of
Sherlock Holmes 250.00
1246 Mickey Mouse Album 100.00
1247 Daisy Duck's Diary 125.00
1248 Pluto 60.00
1249 The Danny Thomas Show,
Ph(c) 275.00
1250 Four Horseman of the
Apocalypse,Ph(c) 125.00
1251 Everything's Ducky 85.00
1252 The Andy Griffith Show,
Ph(c) 600.00
1253 Spaceman. 135.00
1254 'Diver Dan' 90.00
1255 The Wonders of Aladdin . . . 125.00
1256 Kona, Monarch of
Monster Isle. 135.00
1257 Car 54, Where Are You?,
Ph(c) 150.00
1258 GE,The Frogmen 135.00
1259 El Cid,Ph(c). 135.00
1260 The Horsemasters,Ph(c) . . 225.00
1261 Rawhide,C.Eastwood Ph(c) 250.00
1262 The Rebel,Ph(c) 150.00
1263 RsM,77 Sunset Strip,Ph(c) . 150.00
1264 Pixie & Dixie & Mr.Jinks . . . 100.00
1265 The Real McCoys,Ph(c) . . . 150.00
1266 M.G.M.'s Spike and Tyke . . . 50.00
1267 CB,GyroGearloose 125.00
1268 Oswald the Rabbit 60.00
1269 Rawhide,C.Eastwood Ph(c) 250.00
1270 Bullwinkle and Rocky 350.00
1271 Yogi Bear Birthday Party. . . . 90.00
1272 Frosty the Snowman. 90.00
1273 Hans Brinker,Ph(c) 100.00
1274 Santa Claus Funnies 75.00
1275 Rocky and His Friends 375.00
1276 Dondi. 45.00
1278 King Leonardo and
His Short Subjects. 225.00
1279 Grandma Duck's Farm
Friends. 75.00
1280 Hennessey,Ph(c) 110.00
1281 Chilly Willy 60.00
1282 Babes in Toyland,Ph(c). . . . 225.00
1283 Bonanza,Ph(c) 300.00
1284 RH,Laramie,Ph(c). 125.00
1285 Leave It to Beaver,Ph(c). . . 275.00
1286 The Untouchables,Ph(c). . . 275.00
1287 Man from Wells Fargo,Ph(c)100.00
1288 RC,GE,The Twilight Zone. . 225.00
1289 Ellery Queen. 150.00
1290 M.G.M.'s Mouse
Musketeers 45.00
1291 RsM,77 Sunset Strip,Ph(c) . 150.00
1293 Elmer Fudd 50.00
1294 Ripcord 125.00
1295 Mr. Ed, the Talking Horse,
Ph(c) 225.00
1296 Fury,Ph(c) 125.00
1297 Spanky, Alfalfa and the
Little Rascals. 75.00
1298 The Hathaways,Ph(c) 75.00
1299 Deputy Dawg 200.00
1300 The Comancheros 275.00
1301 Adventures in Paradise . . . 100.00
1302 JohnnyJason,TeenReporter . 50.00
1303 Lad: A Dog,Ph(c). 65.00
1304 Nellie the Nurse 125.00
1305 Mister Magoo 150.00
1306 Target: The Corruptors,
Ph(c) 100.00
1307 Margie. 90.00
1308 Tales of the Wizard of Oz . . 200.00
1309 BK,87th Precinct,Ph(c) 175.00
1310 Huck and Yogi Winter
Sports 150.00
1311 Rocky and His Friends 375.00
1312 National Velvet,Ph(c) 60.00
1313 Moon Pilot.Ph(c) 135.00
1328 GE,The Underwater
City,Ph(c). 125.00
1330 GK,Brain Boy 225.00
1332 Bachelor Father 135.00
1333 Short Ribs. 90.00
1335 Aggie Mack 60.00

Fo

Four Favorites #18
© Ace Magazines

Foremost Boys #39
© Star Publications

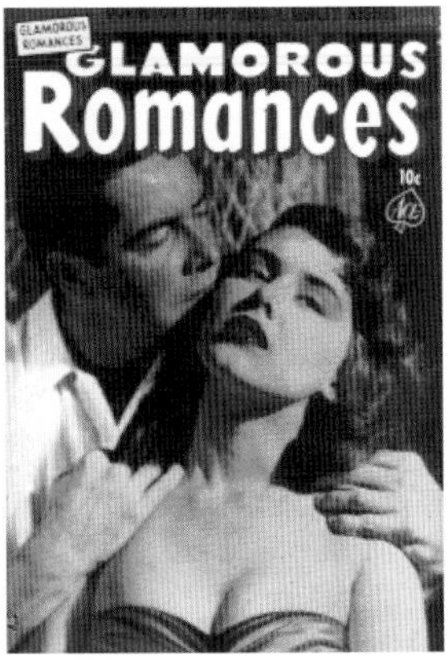

Glamorous Romances #67
© Ace Magazines

1336 On Stage 75.00
1337 Dr. Kildare,Ph(c) 150.00
1341 The Andy Griffith Show, Ph(c) 575.00
1348 JDa,Yak Yak 150.00
1349 Yogi Berra Visits the U.N. . . 175.00
1350 Commanche,Ph(c) 90.00
1354 Calvin and the Colonel 150.00

FOUR FAVORITES

Ace Magazines, Sept., 1941

1 B:Vulcan, Lash Lighting, Magno the Magnetic Man, Raven, Flag (c),Hitler 3,000.00
2 A: Black Ace 1,400.00
3 E:Vulcan 1,200.00
4 E:Raven,B:Unknown Soldiers 1,000.00
5 B:Captain Courageous 1,000.00
6 A: The Flag, B: Mr. Risk 900.00
7 JM 900.00
8 . . . . 900.00
9 RP,HK 1,000.00
10 HK 1,200.00
11 HK,LbC,UnKnown Soldier . . 1,500.00
12 LbC 800.00
13 LbC 700.00
14 Fer 700.00
15 Fer. 700.00
16 Bondage(c) 800.00
17 Magno Lighting 700.00
18 Magno Lighting 700.00
19 RP(a&c) 400.00
20 RP(a&c) 400.00
21 RP(a&c) 400.00
22 RP(c). 350.00
23 RP(c). 350.00
24 RP(c). 350.00
25 RP(c). 350.00
26 RP(c). 350.00
27 RP(c). 300.00
28 . . . . 300.00
29 . . . . 300.00
30 thru 32 . . . . @250.00

4MOST

Novelty Publ./Star Publ., Winter 1941

1 The Target, The Cadet 2,500.00
2 The Target. 1,500.00
3 Dan'l Flannel, Flag(c) 700.00
4 Dr. Seuss (1pg.). 700.00
2-1 . . . . 400.00
2-2 . . . . 400.00
2-3 . . . . 400.00
2-4 Hitler,Tojo,Mussolini (c) 600.00
3-1 . . . . 300.00
3-2 . . . . 300.00
3-3 . . . . 300.00
3-4 . . . . 300.00
4-1 . . . . 250.00
4-2 Walter Johnson(c) 250.00
4-3 . . . . 250.00
4-4 . . . . 250.00
5-1 The Target, Football(c) 200.00
5-2 . . . . 200.00
5-3 . . . . 200.00
5-4 Football(c) 200.00
6-1 Skiing(c). 200.00
6-2 LbC(c) 500.00
6-3 Tennis(c) 200.00
6-4 Football(c) 200.00
6-5 . . . . 300.00
7-1 Basketball(c) 200.00
7-2 LbC(c) 500.00
7-3 . . . . 250.00
7-4 LbC(c) 500.00
7-5 . . . . 250.00
7-6 LbC(c) 500.00
Becomes:

FOREMOST BOYS

Jan., 1949

8-1 . . . . 250.00
8-2 LbC(c),Surfing(c) 500.00
8-3 LbC(c) 500.00
8-4 LbC 500.00
8-5 LbC(c) 500.00
8-6 LbC 500.00
38 LbC(c), Johnny Weismuller. . . 500.00
39 LbC(c), Johnny Weismuller. . . 500.00
40 LbC(c), White Rider 500.00
Becomes:

THRILLING CRIME CASES

FOUR TEENERS

A.A. Wyn, Inc. (Ace Magazines), 1948
34 . . . . 125.00
Becomes:

DOTTY

A.A. Wyn, Inc (Ace Magazines), 1948

35 Teen-age. 150.00
36 . . . . 100.00
37 Transvestism. 250.00
38 thru 40. . . . . @100.00
Becomes:

GLAMOROUS ROMANCES

A.A. Wyn, Inc. (Ace Magazines), 1949–56

41 Dotty 150.00
42 thru 68 . . . . @100.00
69 thru 72 Photo(c) . . . . @100.00
73 JbC 150.00
74 thru 90 Photo(c) . . . . @100.00

FOX AND THE CROW

DC Comics, Dec.–Jan., 1951

1 . . . . 1,450.00
2 . . . . 675.00
3 . . . . 400.00
4 . . . . 400.00
5 . . . . 400.00
6 thru 10 . . . . @300.00
11 thru 20 . . . . @225.00
21 thru 40 . . . . @150.00
41 thru 60 . . . . @125.00
61 thru 80 . . . . @100.00
81 thru 94 . . . . @100.00
95 . . . . 125.00
96 thru 99. . . . . @75.00
100 . . . . 75.00
101 thru 108 . . . . @75.00

FOX GIANTS

Fox Features Syndicate 1944–50

Over 40 different "titles" consisting of four remainder comics, rebound
Romance or western titles 400 to 500.00
Crime or jungle titles. . . . . 500 to 750.00

FOXHOLE

Mainline Publ., 1954

1 JK. 575.00
2 JK. 400.00
3 JK(c) 225.00
4 JK(c) 225.00

Charlton Comics, 1955–56

5 JK(c) 350.00
6 JK. 350.00
7 . . . . 150.00

FOXY FAGAN

Dearfield Publ. Co., 1946–48

1 . . . . 200.00
2 . . . . 150.00
3 . . . . 125.00
4 . . . . 125.00

Frankenstein Comics #26
© Prize Publications

Freedom Train N#
© Street & Smith Publications

Frisky Fables #40
© Star Publications

5 . . . . 125.00
6 Rocket 125.00
7 . . . . 125.00

FRANK BUCK
Fox Features Syndicate, 1950

1 (70) WW. 400.00
2 (71) WW. 225.00
3 . . . . 150.00

FRANKENSTEIN COMICS
Crestwood Publications (Prize Publ.), Summer, 1945

1 B:Frankenstein,DBr(a&c) . . . 2,000.00
2 DBr(a&c) 1,000.00
3 DBr(a&c) 750.00
4 DBr(a&c) 750.00
5 DBr(a&c) 750.00
6 DBr(a&c),S&K 600.00
7 DBr(a&c),S&K 600.00
8 DBr(a&c),S&K 600.00
9 DBr(a&c),S&K 600.00
10 DBr(a&c),S&K. 600.00
11 DBr(a&c)A:Boris Karloff 500.00
12 DBr(a&c). 500.00
13 DBr(a&c). 500.00
14 DBr(a&c). 500.00
15 DBr(a&c). 500.00
16 DBr(a&c). 500.00
17 DBr(a&c). 500.00
18 DBr,B:Horror 750.00
19 DBr 400.00
3-4 DBr. 350.00
3-5 DBr. 350.00
3-6 DBr. 350.00
4-1 thru 4-6 DBr . . . . @350.00
5-1 thru 5-4 DBr . . . . @350.00
5-5 DBr, Oct.–Nov., 1954 . . . . . . 350.00

FRANKIE
See: ANIMATED MOVIE-TUNES

FRANKIE & LANA
See: ANIMATED MOVIE-TUNES

FRANKIE FUDDLE
See: ANIMATED MOVIE TUNES

FRANK LUTHER'S SILLY PILLY COMICS
Children's Comics, 1949

1 Radio characters 150.00

FRANK MERRIWELL AT YALE
Charlton Comics, 1955–56

1 . . . . 125.00
2 thru 4 . . . . @100.00

FRECKLES AND HIS FRIENDS
Visual Editions (Standard Comics), 1947–49

5 . . . . 150.00
6 . . . . 100.00
7 . . . . 100.00
8 . . . . 100.00
9 . . . . 100.00
10 . . . . 100.00
11 Lingerie 250.00
12. . . . . 100.00

FRECKLES AND HIS FRIENDS
Argo Publ., 1955

1 . . . . 125.00
2 . . . . 100.00
3 . . . . 100.00
4 . . . . 100.00

FREEDOM TRAIN
Street & Smith Publications

1 BP 250.00

FRIENDLY GHOST CASPER, THE
Harvey Publications, 1958

1 . . . . 500.00
2 . . . . 200.00
3 thru 10 . . . . @150.00
11 thru 20. . . . . @125.00
21 thru 30. . . . . @100.00
31 thru 50. . . . . @100.00
51 thru 100. . . . . @75.00
101 thru 159. . . . . @50.00
160 thru 163 52 pgs. . . . . @30.00
164 thru 253. . . . . @30.00

FRISKY ANIMALS ON PARADE
Ajax-Farrell Publ., 1957

1 LbC(c) 250.00
2 . . . . 125.00
3 LbC(c) 250.00

FRISKY FABLES
Novelty Press/Premium Group/ Star Publ., Spring, 1945

1 AFa 250.00
2 AFa 150.00
3 AFa 150.00
4 AFa 125.00
5 AFa 125.00
6 AFa 125.00
7 AFa,Flag (c). 150.00
2-1 AFa,Rainbow(c). 150.00
2-2 AFa 135.00
2-3 AFa 135.00
2-4 AFa 135.00
2-5 AFa 135.00
2-6 AFa 135.00
2-7 AFa 135.00
2-8 AFa,Halloween (c). 135.00
2-9 AFa,Thanksgiving(c) 125.00
2-10 AFa,Christmas (c) 135.00
2-11 AFa. 135.00
2-12 AFa,Valentine's Day (c) 125.00
3-1 AFa 125.00
3-2 AFa 125.00
3-3 AFa 135.00
3-4 AFa 125.00
3-5 AFa 125.00
3-6 AFa 125.00
3-7 AFa 125.00
3-8 AFa,Turkey (c). 125.00
3-9 AFa 125.00
3-10 AFa 125.00
3-11 AFa,1948(c). 125.00
3-12 AFa 125.00
4-1 thru 4-7 AFa . . . . @125.00
5-1 AFa 125.00
5-2 AFa 125.00
5-3 . . . . 125.00
5-4 Star Publications 125.00
39 LbC(c). 250.00
40 LbC(c), Christmas 250.00
41 LbC(c). 250.00
42 LbC(c). 250.00
43 LbC(c). 100.00
Becomes:

Frisky Animals #52
© Star Publications

From Here to Insanity #11
© Charlton Comics

Frontline Combat #13
© E.C. Comics

FRISKY ANIMALS
Star Publications Jan., 1951

44 LbC, Super Cat 250.00
45 LbC 350.00
46 LbC,Baseball 250.00
47 LbC 250.00
48 LbC 250.00
49 LbC 250.00
50 LbC 250.00
51 LbC(c) 250.00
52 LbC(c), Christmas 275.00
53 LbC(c) 250.00
54 LbC(c),Supercat(c) 250.00
55 LbC(c),same 250.00
56 LbC(c),same 250.00
57 LbC(c),same 250.00
58 LbC(c),same,July, 1954 . . . . . 250.00

FRITZI RITZ
United Features Syndicate/ St. John Publications, Fall, 1948

N# Special issue 250.00
2 . . . . . 150.00
3 . . . . . 125.00
4 and 5 . . . . . @125.00
6 A:Abbie & Slats 150.00
7 . . . . . 125.00

Becomes:

UNITED COMICS
United Features, 1950

8 thru 26 Bushmiller(c) . . . . . @125.00

Becomes:

FRITZI RITZ
United Features, 1953

27 thru 59 . . . . . @125.00

FROGMAN COMICS
Hillman Periodicals, Jan.–Feb., 1952–May, 1953

1 . . . . . 200.00
2 . . . . . 150.00
3 . . . . . 150.00
4 MMe 150.00
5 BK,AT 150.00
6 thru 11 . . . . . @100.00

FROM HERE TO INSANITY
Charlton Comics, 1955

8 . . . . . 200.00
9 . . . . . 150.00
10 SD(c) 250.00
11 JK 250.00
12 JK 250.00
3-1 . . . . . 350.00

FRONTIER FIGHTER
See: DAVY CROCKETT

FRONTIER FIGHTERS
DC Comics, 1955–56

1 JKu,Davy Crocket, Buffalo Bill . 750.00
2 JKu 500.00
3 thru 8 JKu . . . . . @475.00

FRONTIER ROMANCES
Avon Periodicals, Nov.–Dec., 1949

1 She Learned to Ride and Shoot, and Kissing Came Natural . . 600.00
2 Bronc-Busters Sweetheart, Jan.–Feb., 1950 . . . . . 450.00

FRONTIER SCOUT DANIEL BOONE
See: DEATH VALLEY

FRONTIER TRAIL
See: RIDER, THE

FRONTIER WESTERN
Marvel, Feb., 1956

1 RH, ... 300.00
2 AW,GT,GC,JMn 200.00
3 MD 200.00
4 MD,Ringo Kid 150.00
5 RC,DW,JDa 200.00
6 AW,GC 175.00
7 JR,JMn 150.00
8 RC,DW 150.00
9 JMn 150.00
10 SC,Aug., 1957 . . . . . 150.00

FRONTLINE COMBAT
Tiny Tot Publications (E.C. Comics), , July–Aug., 1951

1 HK(c),WW, JSe,JDa,Hanhung Changjn (c) 1,500.00
2 HK(c),WW,Tank Battle (c) 600.00
3 HK(c),WW,Naval Battleship fire (c) 900.00
4 HK(c),WW, Bazooka (c) 700.00
5 HK(c),JSe 900.00
6 HK(c),WW,JSe 500.00
7 HK(c),WW,JSe,Document of the Action at Iwo Jima 500.00
8 HK(c),WW,ATh 500.00
9 HK(c),WW,JSe,Civil War iss. . 500.00
10 GE,HK(c),WW, Crying Child (c) 400.00
11 GE 300.00
12 GE,Air Force issue 300.00
13 JSe,GE,WW(c), Bi-Planes (c) 300.00
14 JKu,GE,WW(c) 300.00
15 JSe,GE,WW(c), Jan., 1954 . . 300.00

FRONT PAGE COMIC BOOK
Front Page Comics, 1945

1 JKu,BP,BF(c),I:Man in Black . . 500.00

FUGITIVES FROM JUSTICE
St. John Publishing Co., Feb., 1952

1 . . . . . 250.00
2 MB, Killer Boomerang 300.00
3 GT 250.00
4 . . . . . 200.00
5 Bondage (c), Oct., 1952 . . . . . 275.00

FULL OF FUN
Decker Publications (Red Top), 1957

1 . . . . . 125.00
2 . . . . . 100.00

FUN COMICS
See: HOLIDAY COMICS

FUNLAND
Approved Comics (Ziff-Davis), 1949

N# 225.00

FUNLAND COMICS
Croyden Publ., 1945

1 Funny Animal 600.00

 All comics prices listed are for *Near Mint* condition.

The Funnies 2nd Series #1
© Dell Publishing Co.

New Funnies #84
© Dell Publishing Co.

Funny Films #11
© American Comics Group

FUNNIES, THE (1ST SERIES)

Dell Publishing Co., 1929-30

1 B:Foxy Grandpa, Sniffy. 3,000.00
2 thru 21. . . . . @1,000.00
N#(22) 800.00
N#(23) thru (36) . . . . @800.00

FUNNIES, THE (2ND SERIES)

Dell Publishing Co., Oct., 1936

1 Tailspin Tommy,Mutt & Jeff, Capt. Easy,D.Dixon 6,000.00
2 Scribbly. 3,000.00
3 . . . . 2,500.00
4 Christmas issue 2,000.00
5 . . . . 2,000.00
6 thru 10. . . . . @1,500.00
11 thru 22 . . . . 1,200.00
23 thru 29 . . . . @1,000.00
30 B:John Carter of Mars 3,500.00
31 inc. Dick Tracy 1,500.00
32 . . . . 1,500.00
33 . . . . 1,500.00
34 . . . . 1,500.00
35 John Carter (c). 1,500.00
36 John Carter (c). 1,500.00
37 John Carter (c). 1,500.00
38 Rex King of the Deep (c) . . . 1,500.00
39 Rex King (c). 1,500.00
40 John Carter (c). 1,500.00
41 Sky Ranger (c). 1,500.00
42 Rex King (c). 1,500.00
43 Rex King (c). 1,500.00
44 Rex King (c). 1,500.00
45 I&O:Phantasmo:Master of the World 1,600.00
46 Phantasmo (c) 900.00
47 Phantasmo (c) 800.00
48 Phantasmo (c) 800.00
49 Phantasmo (c) 800.00
50 Phantasmo (c) 800.00
51 Phantasmo (c) 800.00
52 Phantasmo (c) 750.00
53 Phantasmo (c) 750.00
54 Phantasmo (c) 750.00
55 Phantasmo (c) 750.00
56 Phantasmo (c) E:John Carter 750.00
57 I&O:Captain Midnight. 6,000.00
58 Captain Midnight (c). 1,800.00
59 Captain Midnight (c). 1,800.00
60 Captain Midnight (c). 1,800.00
61 Captain Midnight (c). 1,500.00
62 Captain Midnight (c). 1,200.00
63 Captain Midnight (c). 1,200.00
64 B: Woody Woodpecker 1,650.00

Becomes:

NEW FUNNIES

Dell Publishing Co. July, 1942

65 Andy Panda, Raggedy Ann & Andy, Peter Rabbit 1,600.00
66 same. 750.00
67 Felix the Cat 750.00
68 . . . . 750.00
69 WK, The Brownies 750.00
70 . . . . 750.00
71 . . . . 500.00
72 WK 500.00
73 . . . . 500.00
74 . . . . 500.00
75 WK,Brownies 500.00
76 CB,Andy Panda, Woody Woodpecker 2,000.00
77 same. 500.00
78 Andy Panda 500.00
79 . . . . 350.00
80 . . . . 350.00
81 . . . . 350.00
82 WK,Brownies 400.00
83 WK,Brownies 400.00
84 WK,Brownies 400.00
85 WK,Brownies 400.00
86 . . . . 300.00
87 Woody Woodpecker 250.00
88 same. 250.00
89 same. 250.00
90 same. 250.00
91 thru 99. . . . . @200.00
100 . . . . 175.00
101 thru 110. . . . . @150.00
111 thru 118 . . . . @150.00
119 Christmas 150.00
120 thru 142. . . . . @150.00
143 Christmas (c) 150.00
144 thru 149. . . . . @150.00
150 thru 154. . . . . @100.00
155 Christmas (c) 150.00
156 thru 167. . . . . @100.00
168 Christmas (c) 150.00
169 thru 181. . . . . @100.00
182 I&O:Knothead & Splinter. . . . 100.00
183 thru 200. . . . . @100.00
201 thru 240 . . . . @100.00
241 thru 288. . . . . @75.00

THE FUNNIES ANNUAL

Avon Periodicals, 1959

1 Best newspaper strips 600.00

FUNNIES ON PARADE

Eastern Color Printing Co., 1933

N# Mutt & Jeff, Joe Palooka. . 18,000.00

FUNNY BONE

LaSalle Publishing Co., 1944

N# 350.00

FUNNY BOOK

Funny Book Publ. Corp., (Parents Magazine) Dec., 1952

1 Alec, the Funny Bunny, Alice in Wonderland 200.00
2 Gulliver in Giant-Land 150.00
3 . . . . 125.00
4 Adventures of Robin Hood . . . 100.00
5 . . . . 100.00
6 . . . . 100.00
7 . . . . 100.00
8 . . . . 100.00
9 . . . . 100.00

FUNNY FABLES

Decker Publ. (Red Top Comics), 1957

1 . . . . 125.00
2 . . . . 100.00

FUNNY FILMS

Best Syndicated Features (American Comics Group), Sept.–Oct., 1949

1 B:Puss An' Boots, Blunderbunny 225.00
2 . . . . 100.00
3 . . . . 125.00
4 . . . . 100.00
5 . . . . 100.00
6 . . . . 100.00
7 . . . . 100.00
8 . . . . 100.00
9 . . . . 100.00
10 . . . . 100.00
11 thru 20. . . . . @100.00
21 thru 28. . . . . @100.00
29 May–June, 1954 . . . . 100.00

Funny Folks #10
© DC Comics

Funny Pages #36
© Comics Magazine

Funny Stuff #7
© DC Comics

FUNNY FOLKS
DC Comics, 1946–1950

1 Nutsy Squirrel	500.00
2	250.00
3	175.00
4 1st Nutsy Squirrel(c)	175.00
5 HK	175.00
6	125.00
7	125.00
8	125.00
9	125.00
10	125.00
11 thru 20	@125.00
21 thru 26	@125.00

Becomes:

HOLLYWOOD FUNNY FOLKES
DC Comics, 1950–54

27	150.00
28 thru 40	@125.00
41 thru 60	@100.00

FUNNY FROLICS
Marvel, Summer, 1945

1 Shardy Fox,KrazyKroid,(fa)	250.00
2	150.00
3	100.00
4	100.00
5 HK	125.00

FUNNY FUNNIES
Nedor Publ. Co., April, 1943

1 Funny Animals	225.00

COMICS MAGAZINE
Comics Magazine/Centaur, May, 1936

1 S&S, Dr. Mystic	17,000.00
2 S&S, Federal Agent	4,000.00
3	3,000.00
4	3,000.00
5	3,000.00

Becomes:

FUNNY PAGES
Nov., 1936

6 I:The Clock,1st masked hero	3,500.00
7 WE	1,500.00
8 WE	1,500.00
9	1,500.00
10 WE	1,500.00
11	1,500.00
12	1,000.00
13 FGu,BoW	1,000.00
14 JCo,FGu,BoW	1,000.00
15 JCo.	1,000.00
16 JCo,FGu.	1,000.00
17 Centaur	1,500.00
18	1,000.00
19	1,000.00
20	1,000.00
21 B:The Arrow	5,000.00
22 BEv,GFx	2,500.00
23	2,500.00
24 BKa,B.Wayne prototype	2,800.00
25 JCo.	2,000.00
26	2,000.00
27	2,000.00
28	2,000.00
29 JCo,BoW	2,000.00
30 BoW,The Arrow(c)	4,000.00
31	4,000.00
32 JCo,BoW	2,000.00
33 JCo,BoW,The Arrow(c)	3,000.00
34 JCo,The Arrow(c)	4,000.00
35 BoW,The Arrow(c)	4,000.00
36 Mad Ming (c)	2,000.00
37 JCo,Mad Ming (c)	2,000.00
38 Mad Ming(c)	2,000.00
39 The Arrow(c)	3,000.00
40 BoW,The Arrow(c)	3,000.00
41 BoW,The Arrow(c)	3,000.00
42 BoW,The Arrow(c)	3,000.00

FUNNY PICTURE STORIES
Comics Magazine/Centaur Publ., Nov., 1936

1 B:The Clock	4,500.00
2 The Spinner Talks	1,600.00
3 Tyrant Gold	1,000.00
4 WE,The Brothers Three	1,000.00
5 Timber Terror	1,000.00
6 War in Asia (c)	1,000.00
7 Racist Humor (c)	1,000.00
Vol 2	
#1(10)	700.00
#2 (11) BoW	700.00
#3 (12)BoW	600.00
#4 (13) Christmas (c)	700.00
#5 (14) BoW	600.00
#6 (15) Centaur	1,000.00
#7 (16)	550.00
#8 (17)	550.00
#9 (18)	550.00
#10 (19)	550.00
#11 (20)	550.00
Vol 3	
#1	550.00
#2	550.00
#3	550.00

Becomes:

COMIC PAGES
July, 1939

4 BoW	800.00
5	600.00
6	600.00

FUNNYMAN
Magazine Enterprises of Canada, Dec., 1947

1 S&K(a&c)	600.00
2 S&K(a&c)	325.00
3 S&K(a&c)	250.00
4 S&K(a&c)	250.00
5 S&K(a&c)	250.00
6 S&K(a&c), Aug., 1948	250.00

FUNNY STUFF
DC Comics, Summer, 1944

1 B:3 Mouseketeers Terrific Whatzit	1,800.00
2	800.00
3	500.00
4	500.00
5	500.00
6 thru 10	@300.00
11 thru 20	@250.00
21	175.00
22 C:Superman	600.00
23 thru 30	@200.00
31 thru 78	@150.00
79 July-Aug., 1954	150.00

Becomes:

DODO AND THE FROG
DC Comics, 1954

80 F:Doodles Duck	250.00
81	150.00
82	150.00
83 thru 91	@150.00
92 scarce	200.00

FUNNY TUNES
Marvel Timely, 1944–46 (KRAZY KOMICS spinoff)

16 Animated Funny Comic-Tunes	250.00
17	200.00
18	200.00
19	200.00

 All comics prices listed are for *Near Mint* condition.

Funny Tunes #22
© Marvel Comics Group

Gabby Hayes Western #18
© Fawcett Publications

Gang Busters #1
© DC Comics

20 . . . 200.00
21 . . . 200.00
22 . . . 200.00
23 HK . . . 200.00
Becomes:

OSCAR

FUNNY TUNES

Avon Periodicals, July, 1953

1 (fa),Space Mouse, Peter Rabbit Merry Mouse,Cicero the Cat . 150.00
2 same . . . 100.00
3 same . . . 100.00
Becomes:

SPACE COMICS

Avon Periodicals, March–April, 1954

4 (fa),F:Space Mouse . . . 125.00
5 (fa),F:Space Mouse . . . 100.00

FUNNY WORLD

Marbak Press, 1947–48

1 . . . 150.00
2 . . . 125.00
3 . . . 125.00

FUN TIME

Ace Periodicals, 1953

N# Funny animal . . . 200.00
2 . . . 160.00
3 . . . 160.00
4 . . . 160.00

FUTURE COMICS

David McKay Publications, June, 1940

1 Lone Ranger,Phantom . . . 4,000.00
2 Lone Ranger . . . 2,000.00
3 Lone Ranger . . . 1,600.00
4 Lone Ranger,Sept., 1940 . . . 1,500.00

FUTURE WORLD COMICS

George W. Dougherty, Summer, 1946

1 . . . 600.00
2 Fall, 1946 . . . 500.00

GABBY

Comic Favorites (Quality Comics Group), 1953 (KEN SHANNON spinoff)

1 (11) teen-age . . . 150.00
2 . . . 100.00
3 . . . 100.00
4 . . . 100.00
5 . . . 100.00
6 . . . 100.00
7 . . . 100.00
8 . . . 100.00
9 . . . 100.00

GABBY HAYES WESTERN

Fawcett Publ., Nov., 1948

1 Ph(c) . . . 650.00
2 Ph(c) . . . 300.00
3 The Rage of the Purple Sage, Ph(c) . . . 200.00
4 Ph(c) . . . 200.00
5 Ph(c) . . . 175.00
6 Ph(c) . . . 175.00
7 Ph(c) . . . 150.00
8 Ph(c) . . . 150.00
9 Ph(c),V:The Kangaroo Crook . 150.00
10 Ph(c) . . . 150.00
11 Ph(c), Chariot Race . . . 150.00
12 V:Beaver Ben, The Biting Bandit,Ph(c) . . . 125.00
13 thru 15 . . . @125.00
16 . . . 125.00
17 . . . 125.00
18 thru 20 . . . @125.00
21 thru 50 . . . @125.00

Charlton Comics

51 . . . 125.00
52 thru 59 Dec., 1954 . . . @75.00

GAGS

United Features Syndicate, 1937

1 Jokes and Cartoons . . . 300.00

GANDY GOOSE

St. John Publ. Co., 1953

1 Funny animal . . . 150.00
2 . . . 125.00
3 . . . 125.00
4 . . . 125.00

Pines, 1956–58

5 . . . 100.00
6 . . . 100.00

GANG BUSTERS

DC Comics, 1947–58

1 . . . 1,200.00
2 . . . 500.00
3 . . . 400.00
4 . . . 400.00
5 . . . 400.00
6 . . . 400.00
7 . . . 400.00
8 . . . 400.00
9 Ph(c) . . . 275.00
10 Ph(c) . . . 275.00
11 Ph(c) . . . 225.00
12 Ph(c) . . . 225.00
13 Ph(c) . . . 225.00
14 Ph(c),FF . . . 500.00
15 . . . 200.00
16 . . . 200.00
17 . . . 500.00
18 . . . 175.00
19 . . . 175.00
20 . . . 175.00
21 thru 25 . . . @150.00
26 JK . . . 150.00
27 thru 40 . . . @150.00
41 thru 44 . . . @125.00
45 Comics Code . . . 125.00
46 thru 50 . . . @125.00
51 MD . . . 125.00
52 thru 67 . . . @125.00

GANGSTERS AND GUN MOLLS

Realistic Comics (Avon), Sept., 1951

1 WW,A:Big Jim Colosimo, Evelyn Ellis . . . 600.00
2 JKa, A:Bonnie Parker, The Kissing Bandit . . . 500.00
3 EK, A:Juanita Perez, Crimes Homicide Squad . . . 400.00
4 A:Mara Hite, Elkins Boys, June, 1952 . . . 350.00

GANGSTERS CAN'T WIN

D.S. Publishing Co., Feb.–March, 1948

1 Shot Cop (c) . . . 400.00
2 A:Eddie Bentz . . . 200.00

Gay Comics #20
© Marvel Comics Group

Gene Autry Comics #62
© Dell Publishing Co.

Georgie Comics #3
© Marvel Comics Group

3 Twin Trouble Trigger Man 175.00
4 Suicide on SoundStageSeven 225.00
5 Trail of Terror 175.00
6 Mystery at the Circus 175.00
7 Talisman Trail 150.00
8 . . . . 150.00
9 Suprise at Buoy 13,
June–July, 1949 . . . . 150.00

GANG WORLD

Literary Enterprises (Standard Comics), Oct., 1952

5 Bondage (c) 350.00
6 Mob Payoff, Jan., 1953 . . . . . 150.00

GASOLINE ALLEY

Star Publications, Oct., 1950

1 . . . . 250.00
2 LBc 275.00
3 LBc(c), April, 1950 . . . . 250.00

GAY COMICS

Marvel Timely, 1944

1 BW,Guys and gals humor 600.00
18 BW 375.00
19 BW 300.00
20 BW 300.00
21 BW 300.00
22 BW 300.00
23 BW 300.00
24 BW,HK,Hey Look 300.00
25 BW 300.00
26 BW 300.00
27 BW 300.00
28 BW 300.00
29 BW,HK,Hey Look 300.00
30 HK,Hey Look. 200.00
31 HK,Hey Look. 200.00
32 . . . . 100.00
33 HK,Hey Look. 200.00
34 HK,Hey Look. 200.00
35 thru 40 . . . . @100.00

Becomes:

HONEYMOON

Marvel Comics, 1950

41 Photo(c) 125.00

GEM COMICS

Spotlight Publ. April, 1945

1 A:Steve Strong,Bondage(c) . . 600.00

GENE AUTRY COMICS

Fawcett Publications, Jan., 1942

1 The Mark of Cloven Hoof . 12,000.00
2 . . . . 2,200.00
3 Secret o/t Aztec Treasure . . 1,600.00
4 . . . . 1,400.00
5 Mystery of Paint Rock
Canyon 1,400.00
6 Outlaw Round-up 1,300.00
7 Border Bullets 1,300.00
8 Blazing Guns 1,300.00
9 Range Robbers 1,300.00
10 Fightin' Buckaroo, Danger's
Trail, Sept., 1943 . . . . 1,300.00
11 . . . . 1,200.00
12 . . . . 1,200.00

GENE AUTRY COMICS

Dell Publishing Co., May/June, 1946

1 . . . . 1,000.00
2 Ph(c) 600.00
3 Ph(c) 400.00
4 Ph(c),I:Flap Jack 400.00
5 Ph(c), all. 400.00
6 thru 10 . . . . @300.00
11 thru 19 . . . . @300.00
20 . . . . 275.00
21 thru 29. . . . . @200.00
30 thru 40, B:Giants . . . . @175.00
41 thru 56 E:Giants . . . . @150.00
57 . . . . 150.00
58 Christmas (c) 125.00
59 thru 66. . . . . @125.00
67 thru 80, B:Giant. . . . . @125.00
81 thru 90, E:Giant. . . . . @100.00
91 thru 93. . . . . @100.00
94 Christmas (c) 100.00
95 thru 99. . . . . @100.00
100 . . . . 150.00
101 thru 111 . . . . @125.00
112 thru 121 . . . . @125.00

GENE AUTRY'S CHAMPION

Dell Publishing Co., Aug., 1950

(1) *see Dell Four Color #287*
(2) *see Dell Four Color #319*
3 . . . . 150.00
4 thru 19 . . . . @125.00

GEORGE PAL'S PUPPETOON'S

Fawcett Publications, Dec., 1945

1 Captain Marvel (c) 700.00
2 . . . . 400.00
3 . . . . 300.00
4 thru 17 . . . . @250.00
18 Dec., 1947 . . . . 200.00

GEORGIE COMICS

Marvel, Spring, 1945

1 Georgie stories begin 275.00
2 Pet Shop (c) 150.00
3 Georgie/Judy(c) 125.00
4 Wedding Dress(c) 125.00
5 Monty/Policeman(c) 125.00
6 Classroom(c) 125.00
7 Fishing(c) 135.00
8 Soda Jerk(c) 135.00
9 Georgie/Judy(c),HK,Hey Look 135.00
10 Georgie/Girls(c),HK,Hey Look 135.00
11 Table Tennis(c),A:Margie,Millie 100.00
12 Camping(c). 100.00
13 Life Guard(c),HK,Hey Look. . . 150.00
14 Classroom(c),HK,Hey Look . . 150.00
15 Winter Sports(c) 100.00
16 . . . . 100.00
17 HK,Hey Look. 150.00
18 . . . . 100.00
19 Baseball(c) 100.00

Becomes:

GEORGIE & JUDY COMICS

20 . . . . 125.00
21 . . . . 100.00

Becomes:

GEORGIE COMICS

22 Georgie comics 100.00
23 . . . . 100.00
24 . . . . 100.00
25 Driben painted (c). 125.00
26 thru 28. . . . . @100.00
29 . . . . 125.00
30 thru 38. . . . . @100.00
39 Oct., 1952. . . . . 100.00

GENERAL DOUGLAS MACARTHUR

Fox Features Syndicate, 1950

N# True life story 250.00

Geronimo #1
© Avon Periodicals

Giant Comics Editions #4
© St. John Publications

G. I. Combat #15
© Quality Comics Group

GERALD McBOING-BOING AND THE NEARSIGHTED MR. MAGOO

Dell Publishing Co., Aug.–Oct., 1952

1 . . . . 225.00
2 thru 5 . . . . @175.00

GERONIMO

Avon Periodicals, 1950

1 Massacre at San Pedro Pass . 200.00
2 EK(c), Murderous Battle at Kiskayah 150.00
3 EK(c) 150.00
4 EK(c),Apache Death Trap, Feb., 1952 . . . . 125.00

GET LOST

Mikeross Publications, Feb.–March, 1954

1 . . . . 350.00
2 . . . . 225.00
3 June–July, 1954 . . . . 200.00

GHOST

Fiction House Magazine, Winter, 1951–Summer, 1954

1 The Banshee Bells 1,500.00
2 I Woke In Terror 900.00
3 The Haunted Hand of X 800.00
4 Flee the Mad Furies 350.00
5 The Hex of Ruby Eye 800.00
6 The Sleepers in the Crypt 800.00
7 When Dead Rogues Ride 800.00
8 Curse of the Mist-Thing 800.00
9 It Crawls by Night, Bondage(c). 1,000.00
10 Halfway to Hades 800.00
11 GE, The Witch's Doll. 800.00

GHOST BREAKERS

Street & Smith Publ., 1948

1 BP(a&c), A:Dr. Neff 1,000.00
2 BP(a&c), Breaks the Voodoo Hoodoo,Dec., 1948 . . . . 800.00

GHOSTLY WEIRD STORIES

See: BLUE BOLT

GHOST RIDER

See: A-1 COMICS

GIANT BOY BOOK OF COMICS

Newsbook Publ. (Lev Gleason), 1945

1 A:Crime Buster & Young Robin Hood 1,200.00

GIANT COMICS

Charlton Comics Summer, 1957

1 A:Atomic Mouse,Hoppy 250.00
2 A:Atomic Mouse. 200.00
3 . . . . 200.00

GIANT COMICS EDITION

St. John Publ., 1948

1 Mighty Mouse 650.00
2 Abbie and Slats 325.00
3 Terry Toons 500.00
4 Crime Comics 750.00
5 MB, Police Case Book 750.00
6 MB(a&c), Western Picture Story 650.00
7 Mopsy 400.00
8 Adventures of Mighty Mouse . . 450.00
9 JKu,MB,Romance & Confession Stories,Ph(c) 750.00
10 Terry Toons 450.00
11 MB(a&c),JKu,Western Picture Stories 650.00
12 MB(a&c),Diary Secrets, Prostitute 1,500.00
13 MB,JKu, Romances 650.00
14 Mighty Mouse Album 450.00
15 MB(c),Romance 750.00
16 Little Audrey 450.00
N#, Mighty Mouse Album 450.00

GIANT COMICS EDITION

United Features Syndicate, 1945

1 A:Abbie & Slats, Jim Hardy, Ella Cinders,Iron Vic 500.00
2 Elmo, Jim Hardy, Abbie & Slats, 1945 . . . . 350.00

G.I. COMBAT

Quality Comics Group, 1952

1 RC(c), Beyond the Call of Duty 900.00
2 RC(c), Operation Massacre . . 400.00
3 An Indestructible Marine 375.00
4 Bridge to Blood Hill 375.00
5 Hell Breaks loose on Suicide Hill. 375.00
6 Beachhead Inferno 300.00
7 Fire Power Assault 250.00
8 RC(c),Death-trap Hill 250.00
9 Devil Riders 250.00
10 RC(c), Two-Ton Booby Trap . . 350.00
11 Hell's Heroes. 225.00
12 Hand Grenade Hero 225.00
13 Commando Assault. 225.00
14 Spear Head Assault 225.00
15 Vengeance Assault 225.00
16 Trapped Under Fire. 200.00
17 Attack on Death Mountain. . . . 200.00
18 Red Battle Ground 200.00
19 Death on Helicopter Hill 200.00
20 Doomed Legion-Death Trap . 200.00
21 Red Sneak Attack 175.00
22 Vengeance Raid 175.00
23 No Grandstand in Hell 175.00
24 Operation Steel Trap,Comics Code. 175.00
25 Charge of the Commie Brigade 175.00
26 Red Guerrilla Trap 175.00
27 Trapped Behind Commie Lines 175.00
28 Atomic Battleground 175.00
29 Patrol Ambush 175.00
30 Operation Booby Trap 175.00
31 Human Fly on Heartbreak Hill 175.00
32 Atomic Rocket Assault 200.00
33 Bridge to Oblivion 175.00
34 RC,Desperate Mission 200.00
35 Doom Patrol 175.00
36 Fire Power Assault 175.00
37 Attack at Dawn 175.00
38 Get That Tank 175.00
39 Mystery of No Man's Land . . . 175.00
40 Maneuver Battleground 175.00
41 Trumpet of Doom 175.00
42 March of Doom 175.00
43 Operation Showdown 175.00

DC Comics, Jan., 1957

44 RH,JKu,The Eagle and the Wolves. 900.00
45 RH,JKu,Fireworks Hill. 400.00

G.I. Combat #56
© DC Comics

Giggle Comics #49
© American Comics Group

G.I. Joe #11
© Ziff-Davis Publication Co.

46 JKu,The Long Walk To Wansan . . . 350.00
47 RH, The Walking Weapon . . . 350.00
48 No Fence For A Jet . . . 350.00
49 Frying Pan Seat . . . 350.00
50 Foxhole Pilot . . . 350.00
51 RH,The Walking Grenade . . . 350.00
52 JKu,JKu(c),Call For A Tank . . . 250.00
53 JKu,The Paper Trap . . . 250.00
54 RH,JKu,Sky Tank . . . 250.00
55 Call For A Gunner . . . 250.00
56 JKu,JKu(c),The D.I.-And the Sand Fleas . . . 350.00
57 RH,Live Wire For Easy . . . 300.00
58 JKu(c),Flying Saddle . . . 300.00
59 JKu,Hot Corner . . . 250.00
60 RH,Bazooka Crossroads . . . 250.00
61 JKu(c),The Big Run . . . 225.00
62 RH,JKu,Drop An Inch . . . 225.00
63 MD,JKu(c),Last Stand . . . 225.00
64 MD,RH,JKu,JKu(c),The Silent Jet . . . 225.00
65 JKu,Battle Parade . . . 225.00
66 MD,The Eagle of Easy Company . . . 300.00
67 JKu(c),I:Tank Killer . . . 300.00
68 JKu,RH,The Rock . . . 1,000.00
69 JKu,RH,The Steel Ribbon . . . 200.00
70 JKu,Bull's-Eye Bridge . . . 200.00
71 MD,JKu(c),Last Stand . . . 200.00
72 MD,JKu(c),Ground Fire . . . 200.00
73 RH,JKu(c),Window War . . . 200.00
74 RH,A Flag For Joey . . . 200.00
75 RH,Dogtag Hill . . . 250.00
76 MD,RH,JKu,Bazooka For A Mouse . . . 250.00
77 RH,JKu,H-Hour For A Gunner 250.00
78 MD,RH,JKu(c),Who Cares About The Infantry . . . 250.00
79 JKu,RH,Big Gun-Little Gun . . . 250.00
80 JKu,RH(c),Flying Horsemen . . 250.00
81 Jump For Glory . . . 200.00
82 IN,Get Off My Back . . . 200.00
83 Too Tired To Fight . . . 200.00
84 JKu(c),Dog Company Is Holding . . . 180.00
85 IN,JKu(c),The T.N.T. Trio . . . 180.00
86 JKu,RH(c),Not Return . . . 180.00
87 RH(c),I:Haunted Tank . . . 900.00
88 RH,JKu(c),Haunted Tank Vs. Ghost Tank . . . 325.00
89 JA,RH,IN,Tank With Wings . . . 200.00
90 JA,IN,RH,Tank Raiders . . . 200.00
91 IN,RH,Tank and the Turtle . . . 200.00
92 JA,IN,The Tank of Doom . . . 200.00
93 RH(c),JA,No-Return Mission . 200.00
94 IN,RH(c),Haunted Tank Vs. The Killer Tank . . . 200.00
95 JA,RH(c),The Ghost of the Haunted Tank . . . 200.00
96 JA,RH(c),The Lonesome Tank 200.00
97 IN,RH(c),The Decoy Tank . . . 200.00
98 JA,RH(c),Trap of Dragon's Teeth . . . 200.00
99 JA,JKu,RH(c),Battle of the Thirsty Tanks . . . 200.00
100 JA,JKu,Return of the Ghost Tank . . . 200.00

GIFT COMICS

Fawcett Publications, March, 1942

1 A:Captain Marvel, Bulletman, Golden Arrow,Ibis, the Invincible, Spy Smasher . . . 4,000.00
2 . . . 2,500.00
3 . . . 1,800.00
4 A:Marvel Family, 1949 . . . 1,500.00

GIGGLE COMICS

Creston Publ./ American Comics Group, Oct., 1943

1 (fa)same . . . 400.00
2 KHu . . . 250.00
3 KHu . . . 225.00
4 KHu . . . 200.00
5 KHu . . . 200.00
6 KHu . . . 150.00
7 KHu . . . 150.00
8 KHu . . . 150.00
9 I:Super Katt . . . 175.00
10 KHu . . . 125.00
11 thru 20 KHu . . . @125.00
21 thru 30 KHu . . . @125.00
31 thru 40 KHu . . . @100.00
41 thru 94 KHu . . . @100.00
95 A:Spencer Spook . . . 100.00
96 KHu . . . 100.00
97 KHu . . . 100.00
98 KHu . . . 100.00
99 KHu . . . 100.00
100 and 101 March–April,1955 @100.00

G.I. IN BATTLE

Ajax/Farrell, 1952

1 War stories . . . 150.00
2 . . . 100.00
3 . . . 100.00
4 . . . 100.00
5 . . . 100.00
6 . . . 100.00
7 . . . 100.00
8 . . . 100.00
9 . . . 100.00
Ann #1 100 pgs. (1952) . . . 300.00

Ajax, 1957

1 . . . 125.00
2 . . . 100.00
3 thru 6 . . . @100.00

G.I. JANE

Stanhall Publ., May, 1953

1 . . . 150.00
2 thru 6 . . . @125.00
7 thru 9 . . . @100.00
10 Dec., 1954 . . . 100.00

G.I. JOE

Ziff-Davis Publication Co., 1950

10 NS(c),Red Devils of Korea, V:Seoul City Lou . . . 175.00
11 NS(c),The Guerrilla's Lair . . . 125.00
12 NS(c) . . . 125.00
13 NS(c),Attack at Dawn . . . 125.00
14 NS(c),Temple of Terror, A:Peanuts the Great . . . 135.00
2-6 It's a Foot Soldiers Job, I:Frankie of the Pump . . . 125.00
2-7 BP,NS(c),The Rout at Sugar Creek . . . 125.00
8 BP,NS(c),Waldo'sSqueezeBox 125.00
9 NS(c),Dear John . . . 125.00
10 NS(c),Joe Flies the Payroll . . 125.00
11 NS(c),For the Love of Benny . 125.00
12 NS(c),Patch work Quilt . . . 125.00
13 NS(c) . . . 125.00
14 NS(c),The Wedding Ring . . . 125.00
15 The Lacrosse Whoopee . . . 125.00
16 Mamie's Mortar . . . 125.00
17 A Time for Waiting . . . 125.00
18 Giant . . . 275.00
19 Old Army Game..Buck Passer 125.00
20 General Confusion . . . 125.00
21 Save 'Im for Brooklyn . . . 125.00
22 Portrait of a Lady . . . 125.00
23 Take Care of My Little Wagon 125.00
24 Operation 'Operation' . . . 125.00
25 The Two-Leaf Clover . . . 125.00
26 NS(c),Nobody Flies Alone Mud & Wings . . . 125.00

Girl Confessions #13
© Marvel Comics Group

Girls' Love Stories #17
© DC Comics

Golden Arrow #1
© Fawcett Publications

27 'Dear Son...Come Home' 125.00
28 They Alway's Come Back
Bondage (c). 125.00
29 What a Picnic 100.00
30 NS(c),The One-Sleeved
Kimono 125.00
31 NS(c),Get a Horse 100.00
32 thru 47. . . . . @100.00
48 Atom Bomb 125.00
49 thru 51 June, 1957 . . . . @100.00

GINGER

Close-Up Publ.
(Archie Publications),
Jan., 1951

1 GFs 200.00
2 . . . . 150.00
3 . . . . 125.00
4 . . . . 125.00
5 . . . . 100.00
6 . . . . 100.00
7 thru 9 . . . . @125.00
10 A:Katy Keene,Summer,1954. . 150.00

GIRL COMICS

Marvel Atlas, Nov., 1949

1 Ph(c),True love stories,I Could
Escape From Love 250.00
2 Ph(c),JKu,Blind Date 135.00
3 BEv,Ph(c),Liz Taylor 300.00
4 PH(c),Borrowed Love 100.00
5 Love stories 100.00
6 same 100.00
7 same 100.00
8 same 100.00
9 same 100.00
10 The Deadly Double-Cross . . . 100.00
11 Love stories. 100.00
12 BK,The Dark Hallway 125.00
Becomes:

GIRL CONFESSIONS

Marvel, 1952

13 . . . . 150.00
14 . . . . 125.00
15 . . . . 125.00
16 BEv 150.00
17 BEv 150.00
18 BEv 150.00
19 . . . . 110.00
20 . . . . 110.00
21 thru 34 . . . . @100.00
35 Aug., 1954. . . . . 100.00

GIRLS IN LOVE

Fawcett Publications,
May, 1950

1 . . . . 125.00
2 Ph(c),July, 1950 . . . . 100.00

GIRLS IN LOVE
See: DIARY LOVES

GIRLS' LIFE

Marvel Atlas, Jan., 1954

1 . . . . 150.00
2 . . . . 125.00
3 . . . . 100.00
4 . . . . 100.00
5 . . . . 100.00
6 November, 1954 . . . . 100.00

GIRLS' LOVE STORIES

DC Comics, 1949

1 ATh,EK,Romance 700.00
2 EK 375.00
3 . . . . 250.00
4 . . . . 250.00
5 . . . . 250.00
6 . . . . 250.00
7 CI 250.00
8 . . . . 250.00
9 . . . . 250.00
10 . . . . 250.00
11 thru 20 . . . . @200.00
21 EK. 150.00
22 thru 83 . . . . @100.00

GIRLS' ROMANCES

DC Comics, 1950

1 Ph(c) 700.00
2 ATh,Ph(c). 375.00
3 Ph(c) 275.00
4 Ph(c) 250.00
5 Ph(c) 250.00
6 Ph(c) 250.00
7 . . . . 250.00
8 . . . . 250.00
9 . . . . 250.00
10 . . . . 250.00
11 . . . . 175.00
12 . . . . 175.00
13 ATh(c) 200.00
14 thru 20. . . . . @175.00
21 thru 31 . . . . @150.00

32 thru 50 . . . . @125.00
51 thru 80 . . . . @100.00

G.I. SWEETHEARTS
See: DIARY LOVES

G.I. TALES
See: SERGEANT BARNEY BARKER

G.I. WAR BRIDES

Superior Publ. Ltd.,
April, 1954

1 . . . . 150.00
2 . . . . 125.00
3 thru 7 . . . . @100.00
8 June, 1955 . . . . 100.00

GLAMOROUS ROMANCES
See: FOUR TEENERS

GOING STEADY
See: TEEN-AGE TEMPTATIONS

GOLDEN ARROW

Fawcett Publications,
Spring, 1942

1 B:Golden Arrow 1,100.00
2 . . . . 550.00
3 . . . . 400.00
4 . . . . 375.00
5 Spring, 1947 . . . . 375.00
6 BK 400.00
6a 1944 Well Known Comics
(Giveaway) 450.00

GOLDEN LAD

Spark Publications,
July, 1945–June, 1946

1 MMe(a&c),A:Kid Wizards,
Swift Arrow,B:Golden Ladd. 1,200.00
2 MMe(a&c) 600.00
3 MMe(a&c) 600.00
4 MMe(a&c), The Menace of
the Minstrel 600.00
5 MMe(a&c),O:Golden Girl 600.00

Goofy Comics #7
© Standard Comics

Green Giant Comics #1
© Pelican Publications

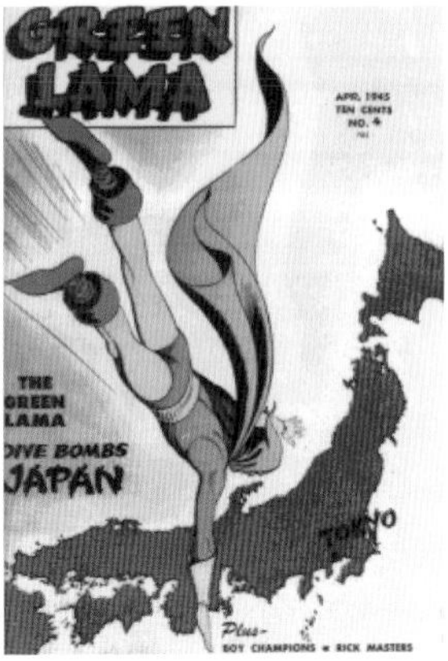

Green Lama #4
© Prize Publications

GOLDEN WEST LOVE

Kirby Publishing Co., Sept.–Oct., 1949

1 BP,I Rode Heartbreak Hill, Ph(c) 250.00
2 BP 175.00
3 BP,Ph(c) 175.00
4 BP,April, 1950 . . . . 175.00

GOLD MEDAL COMICS

Cambridge House, 1945

N# Captain Truth 600.00

GOOFY COMICS

Nedor Publ. Co./ Animated Cartoons (Standard Comics), June, 1943

1 (fa) 500.00
2 . . . . 300.00
3 VP 250.00
4 VP 225.00
5 VP 225.00
6 thru 10 VP . . . . @225.00
11 thru 15 . . . . @200.00
15 thru 19 . . . . @200.00
20 thru 35 FF . . . . @150.00
36 thru 48 . . . . @125.00

GREAT AMERICAN COMICS PRESENTS– THE SECRET VOICE

4 Star Publ., 1944

1 Hitler,Secret Weapon 700.00

GREAT COMICS

Novak Publ. Co., 1945

1 LbC(c) 650.00

GREAT COMICS

Great Comics Publications, Nov., 1941

1 I:The Great Zorro 2,000.00
2 Buck Johnson 1,000.00
3 The Lost City, Jan., 1942 . . . 4,000.00

GREAT EXPLOITS

Decker Publ./Red Top, 1957

91 BK, Rep. Daring Adventure . . 125.00

GREAT LOVER ROMANCES

Toby Press, March, 1951

1 Jon Juan,A:Dr. King 200.00
2 Hollywood Girl 100.00
3 Love in a Taxi 125.00
4 The Experimental Kiss 125.00
5 After the Honeymoon 125.00
6 HK,The Kid Sister Falls in Love 150.00
7 Man Crazy 125.00
8 Stand-in Boyfriend 125.00
9 The Cheat 125.00
10 Heart Breaker 125.00
11 . . . . 125.00
12 . . . . 125.00
13 Powerhouse of Deceit 125.00
14 . . . . 125.00
15 Ph(c),Still Undecided, Liz Taylor 200.00
16 thru 21 . . . . @100.00
22 May, 1955 . . . . 100.00

GREAT WESTERN

See: A-1 COMICS

GREEN GIANT COMICS

Pelican Publications, 1941

1 Black Arrow, Dr. Nerod O:Colossus 17,000.00

GREEN HORNET COMICS

Helnit Publ. Co./ Family Comics (Harvey Publ.), Dec., 1940

1 B:Green Hornet,P(c) 10,000.00
2 . . . . 3,500.00
3 BWh(c) 2,500.00
4 BWh(c) 2,000.00
5 BWh(c) 2,000.00
6 . . . . 2,000.00
7 BP, O:Zebra, B:Robin Hood & Spirit of 76 . . . . . . 1,800.00
8 BP,Bondage (c) 2,200.00
9 BP,JK(c),Behind the (c) 1,800.00
10 BP 2,000.00
11 Who is Mr. Q? 1,500.00
12 BP,A:Mr.Q 1,800.00
13 Hitler (c) 2,200.00
14 BP,Spirit of 76-Twinkle Twins, Bondage(c) 1,500.00
15 ASh(c),Nazi Ghost Ship 1,500.00
16 BP,Prisoner of War 1,500.00
17 BP,ASh(c),Nazis' Last Stand 1,500.00
18 BP,ASh(c),Jap's Treacherous Plot,Bondage (c) 1,500.00
19 BP,ASh(c),Clash with the Rampaging Japs 1,500.00
20 BP,ASh(c),Tojo's Propaganda Hoax 2,200.00
21 BP,ASh(c),Unwelcome Cargo 1,200.00
22 ASh(c),Rendezvous with Jap Saboteurs 600.00
23 BF,ASh(c),Jap's Diabolical Plot #B2978 . . . . 1,200.00
24 BF,Science Fiction (c) 1,500.00
25 thru 29 . . . . @1,200.00
30 BP,JKu,AAv 1,200.00
31 BP,JKu 1,200.00
32 BP,JKu 1,000.00
33 BP,JKu,AAv 1,000.00
34 BP,JKu 1,000.00
35 BP,JKu 1,000.00
36 BP,JKu,Bondage (c) 1,500.00
37 BP,JKu,AAv,S&K 1,000.00
38 BP,JKu 1,000.00
39 S&K,AAv 1,400.00
40 thru 45 . . . . @900.00
46 Drug 1,100.00
47 AAv,Sept., 1949 . . . . 800.00

GREEN LAMA

Spark Publications/Prize Publ., Dec., 1944

1 I:Green Lama, Lt. Hercules & Boy Champions 2,500.00
2 MRa,Forward to Victory in 1945 . . . . 2,000.00
3 MRa,The Riddles of Toys . . 1,500.00
4 MRa,Dive Bombs Japan . . . 1,400.00
5 MRa(a&c),Fights for the Four Freedoms 1,400.00
6 MRa,Smashes a Plot against America 1,400.00
7 MRa,Merry X-Mas 1,000.00
8 MRa,Smashes Toy Master of Crime, March, 1946 . . . . 1,000.00

GREEN LANTERN

DC Comics, Autumn, 1941

1 O:Green Lantern, V:Master of Light, Arson in the Slums . 55,000.00
2 V:Baldy,Tycoon's Legacy . . 10,000.00
3 War cover 7,500.00

 All comics prices listed are for *Near Mint* condition.

Green Lantern #13
© DC Comics

The Green Mask Volume 2, #4
© Fox Features Syndicate

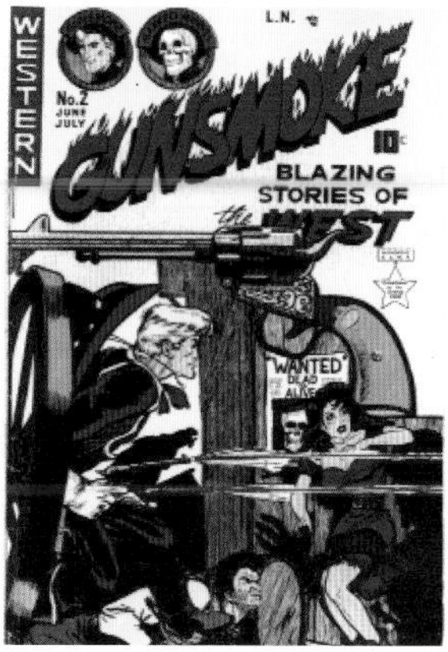

Gunsmoke #2
© Western Comics

4 Doiby and Green Lantern join the Army. 6,000.00
5 V:Nazis and Black Prophet,A:General Prophet 4,000.00
6 V:Nordo & Hordes of War Hungy Henchmen,Exhile of Exiles, A:Shiloh 3,000.00
7 The Wizard of Odds 3,100.00
8 The Lady and Her Jewels, A:Hop Harrigan. 3,000.00
9 V:The Whistler, The School for Vandals 2,500.00
10 V:Vandal Savage,The Man Who Wanted the World,O:Vandal Savage 2,500.00
11 The Distardly Designs of Doiby Dickles' Pals. 1,900.00
12 O:The Gambler 1,900.00
13 A:Angela Van Enters 1,900.00
14 Case of the Crooked Cook . 1,900.00
15 V:Albert Zero, One...Two... Three...Stop Thinking 1,900.00
16 V:The Lizard. 1,900.00
17 V:Kid Triangle, Reward for Green Lantern 1,900.00
18 V:The Dandy,The Connoisseur of Crime, X-mas(c). 2,200.00
19 V:Harpies, Sing a Song of Disaster A:Fate. 1,800.00
20 A:Gambler 1,800.00
21 V:The Woodman,The Good Humor Man. 1,500.00
22 A:Dapper Dan Crocker. 1,500.00
23 Doiby Dickles Movie Ajax Pictures 1,500.00
24 A:Mike Mattson,OnceA Cop. 1,500.00
25 The Diamond Magnet 1,500.00
26 The Scourge of the Sea. . . . 1,500.00
27 V:Sky Pirate. 1,500.00
28 The Tricks of the Sports Master 1,500.00
29 Meets the Challenge of the Harlequin 1,500.00
30 I:Streak the Wonder Dog . . . 1,500.00
31 The Terror of the Talismans. 1,300.00
32 The Case of the Astonishing Juggler 1,300.00
33 Crime Goes West 1,300.00
34 Streak meets the Princess. . 1,300.00
35 V:Three-in-One Criminal . . . 1,300.00
36 The Mystery of the Missing Messenger 1,700.00
37 A:Sargon 1,700.00
38 DoublePlay,May-June,1949. 1,700.00

GREEN MASK, THE

Fox Features Syndicate, Summer, 1940

1 LF(c),O:Green Mask & Domino 6,500.00
2 A:Zanzibar 2,200.00
3 BP 1,500.00
4 B:Navy Jones 1,200.00
5 . . . . 1,000.00
6 B:Nightbird,E:Navy Jones, Bondage (c) 900.00
7 B:Timothy Smith & The Tumbler 800.00
8 JSs 750.00
9 E:Nightbird, Death Wields a Scalpel! 750.00
10 . . . . 500.00
11 The Banshee of Dead Man's Hill. 500.00
2-1 Election of Skulls 400.00
2-2 Pigeons of Death 400.00
2-3 Wandering Gold Brick 350.00
2-4 Time on His Hands 350.00
2-5 JFe,SFd 450.00
2-6 Adventure of the Disappearing Trains, Oct.–Nov., 1946. . . . . 450.00

GUMPS, THE

Dell Publishing Co., 1945

1 . . . . 300.00
2 . . . . 250.00
3 thru 5 . . . . @200.00

GUNHAWK, THE
See: BLAZE CARSON

GUNFIGHTER
See: FAT AND SLAT

GUNSLINGER
See: TEX DAWSON, GUNSLINGER

GUNS AGAINST GANGSTERS

Curtis Publ./Novelty Press, Sept.–Oct., 1948

1 LbC(a&c),B:Toni Gayle 500.00
2 LbC(a&c) 350.00
3 LbC(a&c) 300.00
4 LbC(a&c) 300.00
5 LbC(a&c) 300.00
6 LbC(a&c),Shark 300.00
2-1 LbC(a&c),Sept.–Oct., 1949 . 300.00

GUNSMOKE

Western Comics, Inc., April–May, 1949

1 GrI(a&c),Gunsmoke & Masked Marvel,Bondage (c) 500.00
2 GrI(a&c) 350.00
3 GrI(a&c) 275.00
4 GrI(c),Bondage(c) 250.00
5 GrI(c) 250.00
6 . . . . 225.00
7 . . . . 150.00
8 . . . . 150.00
9 . . . . 150.00
10. . . . . 150.00
11 thru 15. . . . . @125.00
16 Jan., 1952. . . . . 125.00

GUNSMOKE

Dell Publishing Co., 1956

1 J.Arness Ph(c) all 300.00
2 . . . . 175.00
3 . . . . 175.00
4 . . . . 175.00
5 . . . . 175.00
6 . . . . 150.00
7 . . . . 150.00
8 . . . . 155.00
9 . . . . 155.00
10 AW,RC 165.00
11 . . . . 155.00
12 AW 165.00
13 thru 27. . . . . @125.00

GUNSMOKE TRAIL

Four Star Comic. Corp (Ajax/Farrell), 1957

1 Western action. 125.00
2 . . . . 100.00
3 . . . . 100.00
4 . . . . 100.00

GUNSMOKE WESTERN
See: ALL WINNERS COMICS

Ha Ha Comics #53
© American Comics Group

Hans Christian Andersen N#
© Ziff-Davis Publications

Harvey Comic Hits #51
© Harvey Publications

HA HA COMICS

Creston Publ. (American Comics Group), Oct., 1943

1 Funny Animal, all 350.00
2 . . . . 200.00
3 . . . . 150.00
4 . . . . 150.00
5 . . . . 150.00
6 thru 10 . . . . @125.00
11 . . . . 100.00
12 thru 15 KHu . . . . @100.00
16 thru 20 KHu . . . . @100.00
21 thru 30 KHu . . . . @100.00
31 thru 101 . . . . @100.00
102 Feb.–March, 1955 . . . . 100.00

MISTER RISK

Humor Publ., Oct., 1950

1 (7) B:Mr. Risk 200.00
2 . . . . 200.00

Becomes:

MEN AGAINST CRIME

Ace Magazines, Feb., 1951

3 A:Mr. Risk, Case of the Carnival Killer 200.00
4 Murder-And the Crowd Roars 150.00
5 . . . . 150.00
6 . . . . 150.00
7 Get Them! 150.00

Becomes:

HAND OF FATE

Ace Magazines, Dec., 1951

8 . . . . 600.00
9 LC 400.00
10 LC 400.00
11 Genie(c) 300.00
12 . . . . 275.00
13 Hanging(c) 500.00
14 . . . . 275.00
15 . . . . 275.00
16 . . . . 275.00
17 . . . . 275.00
18 . . . . 275.00
19 Drug issue,Quicksand(c) 400.00
20 . . . . 300.00
21 Drug issue 400.00
22 . . . . 300.00
23 Graveyard(c) 400.00
24 LC,Electric Chair 500.00
25 Nov., 1954 . . . . 250.00
25a Dec., 1954 . . . . 275.00

HANGMAN COMICS
See: LAUGH COMICS

HANK

Pentagon Publications, 1946

N# War stories 200.00

HANS CHRISTIAN ANDERSEN

Ziff-Davis Publications, 1953

N# Movie comic 200.00

HAP HAZARD COMICS

A.A. Wyn/Red Seal Publ./ Readers Research, Summer, 1944

1 Funny Teen 300.00
2 Dog Show 250.00
3 Sgr, ... 200.00
4 Sgr, ... 200.00
5 thru 10 Sgr, ... @200.00
11 thru 13 Sgr, ... @150.00
14 AF(c) 175.00
15 . . . . 150.00
16 thru 24 . . . . @150.00

Becomes:

REAL LOVE

April, 1949

25 Dangerous Dates 250.00
26 . . . . 200.00
27 LbC(c), Revenge Conquest . . 275.00
28 thru 40 . . . . @150.00
41 thru 66 . . . . @125.00
67 Comics code 100.00
68 thru 76, Nov., 1956 . . . . @100.00

HAPPY COMICS

Nedor Publications/ Animated Cartoons, Aug., 1943

1 Funny Animal in all 400.00
2 . . . . 300.00
3 . . . . 200.00
4 . . . . 200.00
5 thru 10 . . . . @200.00
11 thru 20 . . . . @150.00
21 thru 31 . . . . @150.00
32 FF 350.00
33 FF 500.00
34 thru 37 FF . . . . @200.00
38 thru 40 . . . . @100.00

Becomes:

HAPPY RABBIT

Standard Comics, Feb., 1951

41 Funny Animal in all 125.00
42 thru 50 . . . . @100.00

HAPPY HOULIHANS
See: SADDLE JUSTICE

HAPPY JACK

Decker Publ. (Red Top), 1957

1 . . . . 100.00
2 . . . . 100.00

HARVEY COMIC HITS

Harvey Publications, Oct., 1951 (Formerly: JOE PALOOKA)

51 Phantom 400.00
52 Steve Canyon's Air Power . . . 200.00
53 Mandrake 300.00
54 Tim Tyler's Tales of Jungle Terror 175.00
55 Love Stories of Mary Worth . . 125.00
56 Phantom, Bondage (c) 400.00
57 AR,Kidnap Racket 250.00
58 Girls in White 150.00
59 Tales of the Invisible 200.00
60 Paramount Animated Comics 600.00
61 Casper the Friendly Ghost . . . 750.00
62 Paramount Animated Comics, April, 1953 . . . . 225.00

HARVEY COMICS LIBRARY

Harvey Publications, 1952

1 Teen-age dope slaves 1,500.00
2 Sparkle Plenty 275.00

HARVEY HITS

Harvey Publications, 1957

1 The Phantom 400.00
2 Rags Rabbit 60.00
3 Richie Rich 2,000.00
4 Little Dot's Uncles 250.00
5 Stevie Mazie's Boy Friend 50.00
6 JK(c),BP,The Phantom 300.00
7 Wendy the Witch 500.00
8 Sad Sack's Army Life 100.00
9 Richie Rich's Golden Deeds . . 700.00

Harvey Hits #48
© Harvey Publications

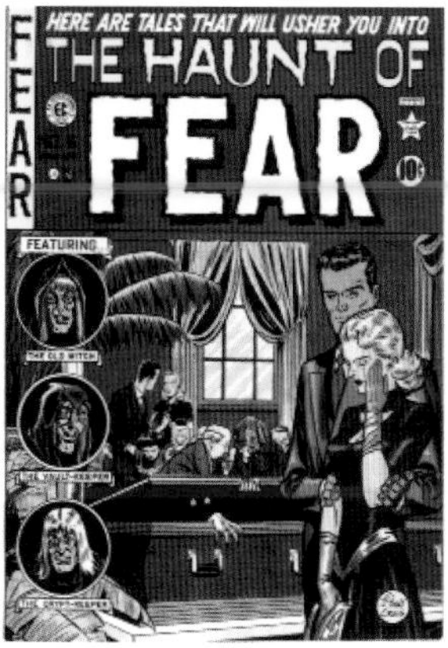

Haunt of Fear #6
© E.C. Comics

Headline Comics #23
© Prize Publications

10 Little Lotta 175.00
11 Little Audrey Summer Fun . . . 150.00
12 The Phantom 300.00
13 Little Dot's Uncles 100.00
14 Herman & Katnip 50.00
15 The Phantom 300.00
16 Wendy the Witch 300.00
17 Sad Sack's Army Life 75.00
18 Buzzy & the Crow 50.00
19 Little Audrey 75.00
20 Casper & Spooky 100.00
21 Wendy the Witch 250.00
22 Sad Sack's Army Life 75.00
23 Wendy the Witch 250.00
24 Little Dot's Uncles 150.00
25 Herman & Katnip 50.00
26 The Phantom 250.00
27 Wendy the Good Little Witch . 300.00
28 Sad Sack's Army Life 50.00
29 Harvey-Toon 75.00
30 Wendy the Witch 200.00
31 Herman & Katnip 40.00
32 Sad Sack's Army Life 50.00
33 Wendy the Witch 200.00
34 Harvey-Toon 50.00
35 Funday Funnies 40.00
36 The Phantom 200.00
37 Casper & Nightmare 75.00
38 Harvey-Toon 50.00
39 Sad Sack's Army Life 50.00
40 Funday Funnies 35.00
41 Herman & Katnip 35.00
42 Harvey-Toon 40.00
43 Sad Sack's Army Life 40.00
44 The Phantom 200.00
45 Casper & Nightmare 75.00
46 Harvey-Toon 40.00
47 Sad Sack's Army Life 40.00
48 The Phantom 200.00
49 Stumbo the Giant 150.00
50 Harvey-Toon 30.00

HAUNTED THRILLS

Four Star Publ.
(Ajax/Farrell), June, 1952

1 Ellery Queen 600.00
2 LbC,Ellery Queen 450.00
3 Drug Story 600.00
4 Ghouls Castle 350.00
5 Fatal Scapel 350.00
6 Pit of Horror 400.00
7 Trail to a Tomb 300.00
8 Vanishing Skull 300.00
9 Madness of Terror 300.00
10 . . . . 300.00

11 Nazi Concentration Camp 400.00
12 RWb 225.00
13 . . . . 225.00
14 RWb 250.00
15 The Devil Collects 225.00
16 . . . . 225.00
17 Mirror of Madness 225.00
18 No Place to Go,
Nov.–Dec., 1954 . . . . 250.00

HAUNT OF FEAR

Fables Publ. (E.C. Comics) ,
May–June, 1950

15 JCr(a&c),AF,WW 5,000.00
16 JCr(a&c),AF,WW 2,500.00
17 JCr(a&c),AF,WW,O:Crypt
of Terror,Vault of Horror
& Haunt of Fear 2,400.00
4 AF(c),WW,JDa 1,800.00
5 JCr(a&c),WW,JDa,Eye Injury 1,500.00
6 JCr(a&c),WW,JDa 1,200.00
7 JCr(a&c),WW,JDa 1,200.00
8 AF(c),JKa,JDa,
Shrunken Head 1,200.00
9 AF(c),JCr,JDa 1,200.00
10 AF(c),GrI,JDa 900.00
11 JKa,GrI,JDa 1,200.00
12 JCr,GrI,JDa 900.00
13 GrI,JDa 900.00
14 GrI(a&c),JDa,O:Old Witch . . 1,200.00
15 JDa 700.00
16 GrI(c),JDa,Ray Bradbury
adaptation 700.00
17 JDa,GrI(c),Classic
Ghastly (c) 700.00
18 JDa,GrI(c),JKa,Ray Bradbury
adaptation 700.00
19 JDa,Guillotine (c),
Bondage (c) 900.00
20 RC,JDa,GrI(a&c) 1,000.00
21 JDa,GrI(a&c) 1,000.00
22 JDa,GrI(a&c) 900.00
23 JDa,GrI(a&c) 900.00
22 JDa,GrI(a&c) 900.00
23 JDa,GrI(a&c) 900.00
24 JDa,GrI(a&c) 900.00
25 JDa,GrI(a&c) 900.00
26 RC,JDa,GrI(a&c) 1,000.00
27 JDa,GrI(a&c), Cannibalism . 1,000.00
28 Dec., 1954 . . . . 900.00

HAVE GUN, WILL TRAVEL

Dell Publishing Co., 1958

1 Richard Boone Ph(c) all 250.00

2 . . . . 200.00
3 . . . . 200.00
5 . . . . 150.00
6 . . . . 150.00
7 . . . . 150.00
8 thru 14 . . . . @150.00

HAWK, THE

Approved Comics
(Ziff-Davis), Winter, 1951

1 MA,The Law of the Colt,P(c) . 250.00
2 JKu,Iron Caravan of the
Mojave, P(c) 125.00
3 Leverett's Last Stand,P(c) 110.00
4 Killer's Town,P(c) 100.00
5 . . . . 100.00
6 . . . . 100.00
7 . . . . 100.00
8 MB(c),Dry River Rampage . . . 135.00
9 MB(a&c),JKu 135.00
10 MB(c) 135.00
11 MB(c) 135.00
12 MB(a&c), May, 1955 . . . . 135.00

HEADLINE COMICS

American Boys Comics/
Headline Publ. (Prize Publ.),
Feb., 1943

1 B:Jr. Rangers 1,000.00
2 JaB(a&c) 500.00
3 JaB(a&c) 450.00
4 . . . . 350.00
5 HcK 350.00
6 HcK 350.00
7 HcK,Jr. Rangers 350.00
8 HcK,Hitler (c) 900.00
9 HcK 350.00
10 HcK,Hitler story,Wizard(c) 400.00
11 . . . . 325.00
12 HcK,Heroes of Yesterday 325.00
13 HcK,A:Blue Streak 325.00
14 HcK,A:Blue Streak 325.00
15 HcK,A:Blue Streak 325.00
16 HcK,O:Atomic Man 450.00
17 Atomic Man(c) 250.00
18 Atomic Man(c) 250.00
19 S&K,Atomic Man(c) 500.00
20 Atomic Man(c) 250.00
21 E:Atomic Man 250.00
22 HcK 200.00
23 S&K(a&c),Valentines Day
Massacre 400.00
24 S&K(a&c),You Can't Forget
a Killer 400.00

Headline Comics #60
© Prize Publications

Heart Throbs #48
© DC Comics

Hedy Hollywood #40
© Marvel Comics Group

25 S&K(a&c),Crime Never Pays . 400.00
26 S&K(a&c),Crime Never Pays . 400.00
27 S&K(a&c),Crime Never Pays . 400.00
28 S&K(a&c),Crime Never Pays . 400.00
29 S&K(a&c),Crime Never Pays . 400.00
30 S&K(a&c),Crime Never Pays . 400.00
31 S&K(a&c),Crime Never Pays . 400.00
32 S&K(a&c),Crime Never Pays . 400.00
33 S&K(a&c),Police and FBI Heroes . . . 400.00
34 S&K(a&c),same . . . 400.00
35 S&K(a&c),same . . . 400.00
36 S&K,same,Ph(c) . . . 350.00
37 S&K,MvS,same,Ph(c) . . . 400.00
38 S&K,same,Ph(c) . . . 200.00
39 S&K,same,Ph(c) . . . 200.00
40 S&K,Ph(c)Violent Crime . . . 200.00
41 Ph(c),J.Edgar Hoover(c) . . . 200.00
42 Ph(c) . . . 150.00
43 Ph(c) . . . 150.00
44 MMe,MvS,WE,S&K . . . 300.00
45 JK . . . 250.00
46 . . . 200.00
47 . . . 200.00
48 . . . 200.00
49 MMe . . . 200.00
50 . . . 200.00
51 JK . . . 200.00
52 . . . 200.00
53 . . . 200.00
54 . . . 200.00
55 . . . 200.00
56 S&K . . . 275.00
57 . . . 150.00
58 . . . 150.00
59 . . . 150.00
60 MvS(c) . . . 150.00
61 MMe,MvS(c) . . . 150.00
62 MMe(a&c) . . . 150.00
63 MMe(a&c) . . . 150.00
64 MMe(a&c) . . . 150.00
65 MMe(a&c) . . . 150.00
66 MMe(a&c) . . . 150.00
67 MMe(a&c) . . . 150.00
68 MMe(a&c) . . . 150.00
69 MMe(a&c) . . . 150.00
70 MMe(a&c) . . . 150.00
71 MMe(a&c) . . . 150.00
72 MMe(a&c) . . . 150.00
73 MMe(a&c) . . . 150.00
74 MMe(a&c) . . . 150.00
75 MMe(a&c) . . . 150.00
76 MMe(a&c) . . . 150.00
77 MMe(a&c),Oct., 1956 . . . 150.00

HEART THROBS

Comics Magazines (Quality), Aug., 1949

1 BWa(c),PG,Spoiled Brat . . . 500.00
2 BWa(c),PG,Siren of the Tropics . . . 300.00
3 PG . . . 150.00
4 BWa(c),Greed Turned Me into a Scheming Vixen,Ph(c) . . . 200.00
5 Ph(c) . . . 150.00
6 BWa . . . 200.00
7 . . . 150.00
8 BWa . . . 250.00
9 I Hated Men,Ph(c) . . . 200.00
10 BWa,My Secret Fears . . . 275.00
11 . . . 150.00
12 . . . 150.00
13 . . . 150.00
14 BWa . . . 150.00
15 My Right to Happiness,Ph(c) . 200.00
16 . . . 125.00
17 . . . 125.00
18 . . . 125.00
19 . . . 125.00
20 . . . 125.00
21 BWa . . . 200.00
22 BWa . . . 200.00
23 BWa . . . 200.00
24 thru 30 . . . @125.00
31 thru 33 . . . @125.00
34 thru 39 . . . @125.00
40 BWa . . . 200.00
41 . . . 125.00
42 . . . 100.00
43 thru 46 . . . @125.00

DC Comics, 1957

47 . . . 350.00
48 . . . 150.00
49 . . . 125.00
50 thru 60 . . . @100.00
61 thru 74 . . . @100.00

HECKLE AND JECKLE

St. John Publ./Pines, Nov., 1951

1 Blue Ribbon Comics . . . 300.00
2 Blue Ribbon Comics . . . 150.00
3 . . . 125.00
4 . . . 125.00
5 . . . 125.00
6 . . . 125.00
7 . . . 125.00
8 . . . 100.00
9 . . . 100.00
10 . . . 100.00
11 . . . 100.00
12 . . . 100.00
13 . . . 100.00
14 . . . 100.00
15 . . . 125.00
16 thru 20 . . . @100.00
21 thru 33 . . . @100.00
34 June, 1959 . . . 100.00

HECTOR COMICS

Key Publications, 1953

1 Teen-age humor . . . 125.00
2 . . . 100.00
3 . . . 100.00

HEDY DEVINE COMICS

Marvel, Aug., 1947—Sept., 1952

22 I:Hedy Devine . . . 275.00
23 BW,Beauty and the Beach, HK,Hey Look . . . 200.00
24 High Jinx in Hollywood, HK, Hey Look . . . 200.00
25 Hedy/Bull(c),HK,Hey Look . . . 200.00
26 Skating(c),HK,Giggles&Grins . 225.00
27 Hedy at Show(c),HK,HeyLook 200.00
28 Hedy/Charlie(c),HK,HeyLook . 200.00
29 Tennis(c),HK,Hey Look . . . 200.00
30 . . . 150.00
31 thru 35 . . . @150.00

Becomes:

HEDY HOLLYWOOD

36 thru 50 . . . @150.00

HEDY WOLFE

Marvel Atlas, Aug., 1957

1 Patsy Walker's Rival . . . 125.00

HELLO PAL COMICS

Harvey Publications, Jan., 1943

1 B:Rocketman & Rocket Girl, Mickey Rooney, Ph(c) . . . 2,000.00
2 Charlie McCarthy, Ph(c) . . . 1,500.00
3 Bob Hope, Ph(c), May, 1943 1,700.00

HE-MAN

Approved Comics (Ziff-Davis)/Toby Press, 1952

1 "Real-Life Adventure" . . . 175.00
1a . . . 165.00
2a . . . 165.00

All comics prices listed are for *Near Mint* condition.

Henry #14
© Dell Publishing Co.

Heroic Comics #9
© Eastern Color Printing Co.

Heroic Comics #81
© Eastern Color Printing Co.

HENRY

Dell Publishing Co., Oct., 1946

1 . . . . 250.00
2 . . . . 150.00
3 thru 10 . . . . @150.00
11 thru 20 . . . . @125.00
21 thru 30 . . . . @125.00
31 thru 40 . . . . @100.00
41 thru 50 . . . . @75.00
51 thru 65 . . . . @75.00

HENRY ALDRICH COMICS

Dell Publishing Co., Aug.–Sept., 1950

1 . . . . 200.00
2 . . . . 150.00
3 . . . . 125.00
4 . . . . 125.00
5 . . . . 125.00
6 . . . . 100.00
7 . . . . 100.00
8 . . . . 100.00
9 . . . . 100.00
10 . . . . 100.00
11 thru 22 . . . . @100.00

HERE'S HOWIE COMICS

DC Comics, 1952–54

1 Teen-age humor 300.00
2 . . . . 200.00
3 . . . . 150.00
4 . . . . 150.00
5 Military humor 150.00
6 . . . . 125.00
7 . . . . 125.00
8 . . . . 125.00
9 . . . . 125.00
10 . . . . 125.00
11 . . . . 100.00
12 . . . . 100.00
13 . . . . 100.00
14 . . . . 100.00
15 . . . . 100.00
16 . . . . 100.00
17 . . . . 100.00
18 . . . . 100.00

HEROES OF THE WILD FRONTIER

See: BAFFLING MYSTERIES

HEROIC COMICS

Eastern Color Printing Co./ Famous Funnies Aug., 1940

1 BEv(a&c),O:Hydroman,Purple Zombie, B:Man of India . . . 3,000.00
2 BEv(a&c),B:Hydroman (c)s. . 1,500.00
3 BEv(a&c) 750.00
4 BEv(a&c) 750.00
5 BEv(a&c) 700.00
6 BEv(a&c) 650.00
7 BEv(a&c),O:Man O'Metal 750.00
8 BEv(a&c) 500.00
9 BEv 500.00
10 BEv 500.00
11 BEv,E:Hydroman (c)s 500.00
12 BEv,B&0:Music Master 550.00
13 BEv,RC,LF 500.00
14 BEv 550.00
15 BEv,I:Downbeat 550.00
16 BEv,BTh,CCB(c),A:Lieut Nininger, Major Heidger,Lieut Welch,B:P(c) 300.00
17 BEv,A:JohnJames Powers,Hewitt T.Wheless, Irving Strobing. . . 300.00
18 HcK,BEv,Pass the Ammunition 300.00
19 HcK,BEv,A:Barney Ross. 300.00
20 HcK,BEv 300.00
21 HcK,BEv 200.00
22 HcK,BEv,Howard Gilmore. . . . 200.00
23 HcK,BEv 200.00
24 HcK,BEv 200.00
25 HcK,BEv 200.00
26 HcK,BEv 200.00
27 HcK,BEv 200.00
28 HcK,BEv,E:Man O'Metal. 200.00
29 HcK,BEv,E:Hydroman. 200.00
30 BEv 200.00
31 BEv,CCB,Capt. Tootsie 125.00
32 ATh,CCB,WWII(c), Capt. Tootsie 150.00
33 ATh, ... 175.00
34 WWII(c) 125.00
35 Ath,B:Rescue(c) 175.00
36 HcK,ATh 150.00
37 same 75.00
38 ATh 150.00
39 HcK,ATh 125.00
40 ATh,Boxing 125.00
41 Grl(c),ATh 125.00
42 ATh 125.00
43 ATh 100.00
44 HcK,ATh 100.00
45 HcK 100.00
46 HcK 100.00
47 HcK 100.00
48 HcK 125.00
49 HcK 100.00
50 HcK 100.00
51 HcK,ATh,AW 150.00
52 HcK,AW 125.00
53 HcK 125.00
54 . . . . 125.00
55 ATh 125.00
56 ATh(c) 100.00
57 ATh(c) 100.00
58 ATh(c) 100.00
59 ATh(c) 100.00
60 ATh(c) 100.00
61 BEv(c) 100.00
62 BEv(c) 100.00
63 BEv(c) 100.00
64 GE,BEv(c) 100.00
65 HcK(c),FF,ATh,AW,GE 150.00
66 HcK(c),FF 125.00
67 HcK(c),FF,Korean War(c) 125.00
68 HcK(c),Korean War(c). 100.00
69 HcK(c),FF 150.00
70 HcK(c),FF,B:Korean War(c) . . 100.00
71 HcK(c),FF 100.00
72 HcK(c),FF 150.00
73 HcK(c),FF 100.00
74 HcK(c) 100.00
75 HcK(c),FF 100.00
76 thru 80 HcK,HcK(c). . . . . . . @100.00
81 FF,HcK(c) 100.00
82 FF,HcK(c) 100.00
83 FF,HcK(c) 100.00
84 HcK(c) 100.00
85 HcK(c) 100.00
86 FF,HcK(c) 120.00
87 FF,HcK(c) 120.00
88 HcK(c),E:Korean War (c)s . . . 100.00
89 HcK(c) 100.00
90 HcK(c) 100.00
91 HcK(c) 100.00
92 HcK(c) 100.00
93 HcK(c) 100.00
94 HcK(c) 120.00
95 HcK(c) 100.00
96 HcK(c) 100.00
97 HcK(c),E:P(c),June, 1955. . . . 100.00

HICKORY

Comic Magazine (Quality Comics Group), Oct., 1949

1 HSa, ... 200.00
2 HSa, ... 125.00
3 HSa, ... 100.00

Hi-School Romance #57
© Harvey Publications

Hit Comics #5
© Quality Comics Group

Hit Comics #58
© Quality Comics Group

Hi

4 HSa, ... 100.00
5 HSa, ... 100.00
6 HSa,Aug., 1950 . . . . 100.00

HIGH ADVENTURE
Decker Publ. (Red Top), 1957

1 BK 100.00

HI-HO COMICS
Four Star Publications, 1946

1 LbC(c) 600.00
2 LbC(c) 300.00
3 1946 . . . . 250.00

HI-JINX
B & I Publ. Co. (American Comics Group), July–Aug., 1947

1 (fa) all. 250.00
2 . . . . 175.00
3 . . . . 125.00
4 thru 7 . . . . @100.00
N# 150.00

HI-LITE COMICS
E.R. Ross Publ. Fall, 1945

1 . . . . 350.00

HILLBILLY COMICS
Charlton Comics, 1955

1 . . . . 125.00
2 thru 4 July 1956 . . . . @100.00

HI-SCHOOL ROMANCE
Harvey Publications, 1949–58

1 BP,Ph(c). 175.00
2 BP,Ph(c). 150.00
3 BP,Ph(c). 125.00
4 Ph(c) 125.00
5 BPPh(c) 125.00
6 . . . . 125.00
7 . . . . 125.00
8 BP 125.00
9 . . . . 125.00
10 Rare 150.00
11 thru 20 BP(in many) . . . . . . @100.00
21 thru 50 . . . . @100.00
51 thru 75 . . . . @75.00

HI-SPOT COMICS
See: RED RYDER COMICS

HIT COMICS
Comics Magazine (Quality Comics Group), July, 1940

1 LF(c),O:Neon,Hercules,I:The Red Bee, B:Bob & Swab, Blaze Barton Strange Twins,X-5 Super Agent Casey Jones,Jack & Jill . . . 9,500.00
2 GT,LF(c),B:Old Witch 3,500.00
3 GT,LF(c),E:Casey Jones. . . . 3,200.00
4 GT,LF(c),B:Super Agent & Betty Bates,E:X-5 . . . . 2,900.00
5 GT,LF(c),B:Red Bee (c) 8,000.00
6 GT,LF(c) 2,500.00
7 GT,LF(c),E:Red Bee (c) 2,500.00
8 GT,LF(c),B:Neon (c) 2,500.00
9 JCo,LF(c),E:Neon (c) 2,500.00
10 JCo,RC,LF(c),B:Hercules(c) 2,500.00
11 JCo,RC,LF(c),A:Hercules. . . 2,200.00
12 JCo,RC,LF(c),A:Hercules . . 2,200.00
13 JCo,RC,LF(c),A:Hercules . . 2,200.00
14 JCo,RC,LF(c),A:Hercules . . 2,200.00
15 JCo,RC,A:Hercules 1,500.00
16 JCo,RC,LF(c),A:Hercules . . 1,500.00
17 JCo,RC,LF(c),E:Hercules(c) 1,500.00
18 JCo,RC(a&c),O:Stormy Foster,B:Ghost of Flanders 1,600.00
19 JCo,RC(c),B:Stormy Foster(c). 1,300.00
20 JCo,RC(c),A:Stormy Foster . 1,400.00
21 JCo,RC(c) 1,350.00
22 JCo. 1,350.00
23 JCo,RC(a&c) 1,300.00
24 JCo,E:Stormy Foster (c) . . . 1,300.00
25 JCo,RP,O:Kid Eternity 2,500.00
26 JCo,RP,A:Black Hawk 1,400.00
27 JCo,RP,B:Kid Eternity (c)s . . . 700.00
28 JCo,RP,A:Her Highness 700.00
29 JCo,RP 700.00
30 JCo,RP,HK,V:Julius Caesar and his Legion of Warriors . . 600.00
31 JCo,RP 600.00
32 JCo,RP,V:Merlin the Wizard . . 350.00
33 JCo,RP 300.00
34 JCo,RP,E:Stormy Foster 300.00
35 JCo,Kid Eternity Accused of Murder. 300.00
36 JCo,The Witch's Curse 300.00
37 JCo,V:Mr. Silence 300.00
38 JCo 300.00
39 JCo,Runaway River Boat 300.00
40 PG,V:Monster from the Past . 300.00
41 PG,Did Kid Eternity Lose His Power? 250.00
42 PG,Kid Eternity Loses Killer Cronson 250.00
43 JCo,PG,V:Modern Bluebeard 250.00
44 JCo,PG,Trips up the Shoe . . . 250.00
45 JCo,PG,Pancho Villa against Don Pablo 250.00
46 JCo,V:Mr. Hardeel. 250.00
47 A Polished Diamond Can Be Rough on Rats 250.00
48 EhH,A Treasure Chest of Trouble 250.00
49 EhH,V:Monsters from the Mirror. 250.00
50 EhH,Heads for Trouble 250.00
51 EhH,Enters the Forgotten World 225.00
52 EhH,Heroes out of the Past . . 225.00
53 EhH,V:Mr. Puny 225.00
54 V:Ghost Town Killer. 225.00
55 V:The Brute. 225.00
56 V:Big Odds 225.00
57 Solves the Picture in a Frame 225.00
58 Destroys Oppression! 225.00
59 Battles Tomorrow's Crimes Today! 225.00
60 E:Kid Eternity (c)s, V:The Mummy 225.00
61 RC(a&c),I:Jeb Rivers 250.00
62 RC(c). 225.00
63 RC(c),A:Jeb Rivers 250.00
64 RC,A:Jeb Rivers 250.00
65 Bondage (c),RC,July, 1950. . . 275.00

HOLIDAY COMICS
Fawcett Publ., Nov., 1942

1 Captain Marvel (c) 2,100.00

HOLIDAY COMICS
Marvel Star, Jan., 1951

1 LbC(c),Christmas(c). 450.00
2 LbC(c),Easter Parade(c) 450.00
3 LbC(c),4th of July(c) 300.00
4 LbC(c),Summer Vacation. 275.00
5 LbC(c),Christmas(c). 275.00
6 LbC(c),Birthday(c) 275.00
7 LbC(c),Rodeo (c). 275.00
8 LbC(c),Xmas(c) Oct., 1952 . . . 275.00
Becomes:

FUN COMICS
Marvel Star, 1953

9 LbC 275.00

All comics prices listed are for *Near Mint* condition.

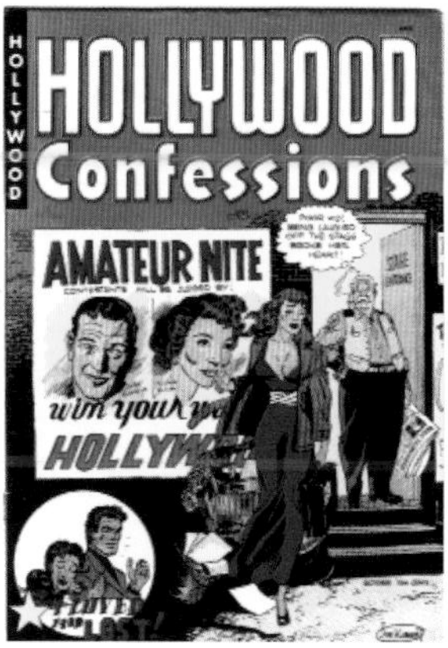

Hollywood Confessions #1
© St. John Publ. Co.

Holyoke One-Shot #3
© Holyoke Publ. Co.

Hoot Gibson Western #6
© Fox Features Syndicate

10 LbC 250.00
11 LbC 250.00
12 LbC 250.00
Becomes:

MIGHTY BEAR
Marvel Star, 1954

13 LbC 100.00
14 LbC 100.00
Becomes:

UNSANE
Marvel Star, 1954

15 . . . . 475.00

HOLLYWOOD COMICS
New Age Publishers, Winter, 1944

1 (fa) 200.00

HOLLYWOOD CONFESSIONS
St. John Publ. Co., Oct., 1949

1 JKu(a&c) 350.00
2 JKu(a&c), Dec., 1949 . . . . 400.00

HOLLYWOOD DIARY
Comics Magazine (Quality Comics), Dec., 1949

1 . . . . 250.00
2 Photo (c) 200.00
3 Photo (c) 150.00
4 . . . . 150.00
5 Photo (c), Aug., 1950 . . . . 150.00

HOLLYWOOD FILM STORIES
Feature Publications, (Prize) April, 1950

1 June Allison,Ph(c) 250.00
2 Lizabeth Scott,Ph(c) 150.00
3 Barbara Stanwick,Ph(c) 150.00
4 Beth Hutton, Aug., 1950 . . . . . 150.00

HOLLYWOOD FUNNY FOLKES
See: FUNNY FOLKES

HOLLYWOOD SECRETS
Comics Magazine (Quality Comics Group), Nov., 1949

1 BWa,BWa(c) 400.00
2 BWa,BWa(c),RC 300.00
3 Ph(c) 200.00
4 Ph(c),May, 1950 . . . . 200.00
5 Ph(c) 200.00
6 Ph(c) 200.00

HOLYOKE ONE-SHOT
Tem Publ. (Holyoke Publ. Co.), 1944

1 Grit Grady 300.00
2 Rusty Dugan 300.00
3 JK,Miss Victory,O:Cat Woman. 400.00
4 Mr. Miracle 250.00
5 U.S. Border Patrol 250.00
6 Capt. Fearless 250.00
7 Strong Man 300.00
8 Blue Streak 200.00
9 S&K, Citizen Smith 300.00
10 S&K, Capt. Stone 300.00

HOMER, THE HAPPY GHOST
Marvel, March, 1955

1 . . . . 250.00
2 . . . . 150.00
3 . . . . 125.00
4 thru 15 . . . . @125.00
16 thru 22 . . . . @100.00

HOMER HOOPER
Marvel Atlas, 1953

1 Teen-age romance humor 150.00
2 . . . . 100.00
3 . . . . 100.00
4 . . . . 100.00

HONEYMOON
See: GAY COMICS

HONEYMOON ROMANCE
Artful Publications (Digest Size), April, 1950

1 . . . . 450.00
2 July, 1950 . . . . 425.00

THE HOODED HORSEMAN
See: BLAZING WEST
Also: OUT OF THE NIGHT

HOORAY COMICS
Tendon Publishing Co., 1946

1 Funny animal 250.00

HOOT GIBSON WESTERN
Fox Features Syndicate, 1950
(Formerly: MY LOVE STORY)

1 (5) Ph(c). 350.00
2 (6) 325.00
3 WW 350.00

HOPALONG CASSIDY
Fawcett Publications, Feb., 1943

1 B:Hopalong Cassidy & Topper, Captain Marvel (c) 7,000.00
2 . . . . 1,000.00
3 Blazing Trails 600.00
4 5-full length story 500.00
5 Death in the Saddle, Ph(c) . . . 450.00
6 . . . . 450.00
7 . . . . 450.00
8 Phantom Stage Coach 450.00
9 The Last Stockade 450.00
10 4-spine tingling adventures. . . 450.00
11 Desperate Jetters! Ph(c). 300.00
12 The Mysterious Message 300.00
13 The Human Target, Ph(c) 300.00
14 Land of the Lawless, Ph(c). . . 300.00
15 Death holds the Reins, Ph(c) . 300.00
16 Webfoot's Revenge, Ph(c) . . . 300.00
17 The Hangman's Noose, Ph(c) 300.00
18 The Ghost of Dude Ranch, Ph(c) 300.00
19 A:William Boyd,Ph(c) 300.00
20 The Notorious Nellie Blaine!, B:P(c). 225.00
21 V:Arizona Kid 225.00
22 V:Arizona Kid 225.00
23 Hayride Horror 225.00
24 Twin River Giant 225.00
25 On the Trails of the Wild and Wooly West 225.00
26 thru 30. . . . . @200.00
31 52 pages. 150.00
32 36 pages. 150.00
33 52 pages. 150.00

Hopalong Cassidy #25
© Fawcett Publications

Hopalong Cassidy #86
© DC Comics

Hoppy the Marvel Bunny #1
© Fawcett Publications

34 52 pages 150.00
35 52 pages 150.00
36 36 pages 125.00
37 thru 40, 52 pages . . . . @150.00
40 36 pages 150.00
41 E:P(c) 150.00
42 B:Ph(c) 150.00
43 . . . . 150.00
44 . . . . 125.00
45 . . . . 135.00
46 thru 51 . . . . @125.00
52 . . . . 100.00
53 . . . . 125.00
54 . . . . 125.00
55 . . . . 100.00
56 . . . . 125.00
57 thru 70 . . . . @125.00
71 thru 84 . . . . @100.00
85 E:Ph(c),Jan., 1954 . . . . 125.00

HOPALONG CASSIDY

DC Comics, Feb., 1954

86 GC,Ph(c):William Boyd & Topper, Secret o/t Tattooed Burro . . . 500.00
87 GC,Ph(c),Tenderfoot Outlaw . . 250.00
88 Ph(c),GC,15 Robbers of Rimfire Ridge 175.00
89 GC,Ph(c),One-Day Boom Town 175.00
90 GC,Ph(c),Cowboy Clown Robberies 175.00
91 GC,Ph(c),The Riddle of the Roaring R Ranch 175.00
92 GC,Ph(c),Sky-RidingOutlaws . 150.00
93 GC,Ph(c),Silver Badge of Courage 150.00
94 GC,Ph(c),Mystery of the Masquerading Lion 150.00
95 GC,Ph(c),Showdown at the Post-Hole Bank 150.00
96 GC,Ph(c),Knights of the Range 150.00
97 GC,Ph(c),The Mystery of the Three-Eyed Cowboy 150.00
98 GC,Ph(c),Hopalong's Unlucky Day 150.00
99 GC,Ph(c),Partners in Peril . . . 150.00
100 GC,Ph(c),The Secrets of a Sheriff 175.00
101 GC,Ph(c),Way Out West Where The East Begins 125.00
102 GC,Ph(c),Secret of the Buffalo Hat 125.00
103 GC,Ph(c),The Train-Rustlers of Avalance Valley 125.00
104 GC,Ph(c),Secret of the Surrendering Outlaws 125.00
105 GC,Ph(c),Three Signs to Danger 125.00
106 GC,Ph(c),The Secret of the Stolen Signature 125.00
107 GC,Ph(c),The Mystery Trail to Stagecoach Town 125.00
108 GC,Ph(c),The Mystery Stage From Burro Bend 125.00
109 GC,The Big Gun on Saddletop Mountain 125.00
110 GC,The Dangerous Stunts of Hopalong Cassidy 100.00
111 GC,Sheriff Cassidy's Mystery Clue 100.00
112 GC,Treasure Trail to Thunderbolt Ridge 100.00
113 GC,The Shadow of the Toy Soldier 100.00
114 GC,Ambush at Natural Bridge 100.00
115 GC,The Empty-Handed Robberies 100.00
116 GC,Mystery of the Vanishing Cabin 100.00
117 GC,School for Sheriffs 100.00
118 GC,The Hero of Comanche Ridge 100.00
119 GC,The Dream Sheriff of Twin Rivers 100.00
120 GC,Salute to a Star-Wearer . 100.00
121 GC,The Secret of the Golden Caravan 100.00
122 GC,The Rocking Horse Bandits 100.00
123 GK,Mystery of the One-Dollar Bank Robbery . . . 100.00
124 GK,Mystery of the Double-X Brand 100.00
125 GK,Hopalong Cassidy's Secret Brother 100.00
126 GK,Trail of the Telltale Clues 100.00
127 GK,Hopalong Cassidy's Golden Riddle 100.00
128 GK,The House That Hated Outlaws 100.00
129 GK,Hopalong Cassidy's Indian Sign 100.00
130 GK,The Return of the Canine Sheriff 100.00
131 GK&GK(c),The Amazing Sheriff of Double Creek 100.00
132 GK,Track of the Invisible Indians 100.00
133 GK,Golden Trail to Danger . . 100.00
134 GK,Case of the Three Crack-Shots 100.00
135 GK,May-June, 1959 . . . . 100.00

HOPPY THE MARVEL BUNNY

Fawcett Publications, Dec., 1945

1 A:Marvel Bunny 650.00
2 . . . . 300.00
3 . . . . 250.00
4 . . . . 250.00
5 . . . . 250.00
6 thru 14 . . . . @200.00
15 Sept., 1947 . . . . 200.00

HORACE & DOTTY DRIPPLE

See: DOTTY DRIPPLE

HORRIFIC

Artful/Comic Media/ Harwell Publ./Mystery, Sept., 1952

1 Conductor in Flames(c) 700.00
2 Human Puppets(c) 400.00
3 DH(c),Bullet hole in head(c) 800.00
4 DH(c),head on a stick (c) 350.00
5 DH(c) 350.00
6 DH(c),Jack the Ripper 350.00
7 DH(c),Shrunken Skulls 350.00
8 DH(c),I:The Teller 400.00
9 DH(c),Claws of Horror, Wolves of Midnight 350.00
10 DH(c),The Teller-Four Eerie Tales of Horror 350.00
11 DH(c),A:Gary Ghoul,Freddie, Demon,Victor Vampire Walter Werewolf 300.00
12 DH(c),A:Gary Ghoul,Freddie Demon,Victor Vampire, Walter Werewolf 300.00
13 DH(c),A:Gary Ghoul,Freddie Demom,Victor Vampire, Walter Werewolf 300.00

Becomes:

TERRIFIC COMICS

Dec., 1954

14 Eye Injury 800.00

 All comics prices listed are for *Near Mint* condition.

Horrors #15
© Marvel Comics Group

Hot Rods and Racing Cars #9
© Charlton Comics

House of Mystery #8
© DC Comics

15 . . . . 400.00
16 B:Wonderboy 400.00
Becomes:

WONDERBOY

Ajax/Farrell Publ., May, 1955

17 The Enemy's Enemy. 600.00
18 Success is No Accident,
July, 1955 . . . . 500.00

HORROR FROM THE TOMB
See: MYSTERIOUS STORIES

HORRORS, THE

Marvel Star Publications, Jan., 1953–April, 1954

11 LbC(c),JyD,Horrors of War . . . 350.00
12 LbC(c),Horrors of War 350.00
13 LbC(c),Horrors of Mystery . . . 300.00
14 LbC(c),Horrors of the
Underworld 350.00
15 LbC(c),Horrors of the
Underworld 350.00

HORSE FEATHER COMICS

Lev Gleason Publications, Nov., 1947

1 BW 350.00
2 . . . . 250.00
3 . . . . 200.00
4 Summer, 1948 . . . . 200.00

HOT DOG
See: A-1 COMICS

HOT ROD AND SPEEDWAY COMICS

Hillman Periodicals Feb.–March, 1952

1 . . . . 350.00
2 BK 250.00
3 . . . . 200.00
4 . . . . 200.00
5 April–May, 1953 . . . . 200.00

HOT ROD COMICS

Fawcett Publications, Feb., 1952–53

N# BP,BP(c),F:Clint Curtis 600.00
2 BP,BP(c),Safety comes First . . 375.00
3 BP,BP(c),The Racing Game . . 200.00
4 BP,BP(c),Bonneville National
Championships 200.00
5 BP,BP(c), ... 200.00
6 BP,BP(c),Race to Death 200.00

HOT ROD KING

Approved Comics (Ziff-Davis), Fall, 1952

1 P(c) 300.00

HOT RODS AND RACING CARS

Motor Mag./ Charlton Comics, 1951

1 Speedy Davis. 350.00
2 . . . . 200.00
3 . . . . 150.00
4 . . . . 150.00
5 . . . . 150.00
6 . . . . 150.00
7 . . . . 150.00
8 . . . . 150.00
9 . . . . 150.00
10 . . . . 150.00
11 thru 20 . . . . @125.00
21 thru 70 . . . . @100.00

HOT STUFF, THE LITTLE DEVIL

Harvey Publications, 1957

1 . . . . 650.00
2 1st Stumbo the Giant 300.00
3 thru 5 . . . . @225.00
6 thru 10 . . . . @200.00
11 thru 20. . . . . @150.00
21 thru 40. . . . . @125.00
41 thru 60. . . . . @100.00

HOT STUFF SIZZLERS

Harvey Publications, 1960

1 F:Hot Stuff 225.00
2 . . . . 150.00
3 . . . . 125.00
4 . . . . 125.00
5 . . . . 125.00

6 . . . . 100.00
7 . . . . 100.00
8 . . . . 100.00
9 . . . . 100.00
10 . . . . 100.00
11 thru 15 . . . . @75.00

HOUSE OF MYSTERY

DC Comics, Dec.–Jan., 1952

1 I Fell In Love With
a Monster 3,500.00
2 The Mark of X. 1,500.00
3 The Dummy of Death 1,100.00
4 The Man With the Evil Eye . . . 750.00
5 The Man With the Strangler
Hands!. 750.00
6 The Monster in Clay! 650.00
7 Nine Lives of Alger Denham!. . 650.00
8 Tattoos of Doom 650.00
9 Secret of the Little Black Bag . 650.00
10 The Wishes of Doom 650.00
11 Deadly Game of G-H-O-S-T . . 550.00
12 The Devil's Chessboard 550.00
13 The Theater Of A
Thousand Thrills!. 550.00
14 The Deadly Dolls 550.00
15 The Man Who Could Change
the World 550.00
16 Dead Men Tell No Tales!. 450.00
17 Man With the X-Ray Eyes . . . 325.00
18 Dance of Doom. 325.00
19 The Strange Faces of Death. . 325.00
20 The Beast Of Bristol 325.00
21 Man Who Could See Death . . 325.00
22 The Phantom's Return 325.00
23 Stamps of Doom 325.00
24 Kill The Black Cat 325.00
25 The Man With Three Eyes!. . . 325.00
26 The Man with Magic Ears. . . . 300.00
27 Fate Held Four Aces! 300.00
28 The Wings Of Mr. Milo! 300.00
29 . . . . 300.00
30 . . . . 300.00
31 The Incredible Illusions! 300.00
32 Pied Piper of the Sea 300.00
33 Mr. Misfortune! 300.00
34 The Hundred Year Duel 300.00
35 . . . . 300.00
36 The Treasure of Montezuma! . 250.00
37 MD,The Statue That
Came to Life 250.00
38 The Voyage Of No Return . . . 250.00
39 . . . . 250.00
40 The Coins That Came To Life. 250.00
41 The Impossible Tricks! 250.00

House of Mystery #53
© DC Comics

House of Mystery #113
© DC Comics

House of Secrets #17
© DC Comics

Ho

42 The Stranger From Out There 250.00
43 . . . . 250.00
44 The Secret Of Hill 14 . . . . 250.00
45 . . . . 250.00
46 The Bird of Fate 250.00
47 The Robot Named Think. 250.00
48 The Man Marooned On Earth. 250.00
49 The Mysterious Mr. Omen . . . 250.00
50 . . . . 275.00
51 Man Who Stole Teardrops . . . 225.00
52 The Man With The Golden
Shoes 225.00
53 The Man Who Hated Mirrors . 225.00
54 The Woman Who Lived Twice 225.00
55 I Turned Back Time. 225.00
56 The Thing In The Black Box . . 225.00
57 The Untamed 225.00
58 . . . . 225.00
59 The Tomb Of Ramfis. 225.00
60 The Prisoner On Canvas 225.00
61 JK,Superstition Day 225.00
62 The Haunting Scarecrow 200.00
63 JK,The Lady & The Creature . 225.00
64 The Golden Doom 200.00
65 JK,The Magic Lantern. 275.00
66 JK,Sinister Shadow. 275.00
67 The Wizard of Water. 200.00
68 The Book That Bewitched. . . . 200.00
69 The Miniature Disasters 200.00
70 JK,The Man With Nine Lives . 200.00
71 Menace of the Mole Man 200.00
72 JK,Dark Journey. 200.00
73 Museum That Came to Life . . 200.00
74 Museum That Came To Life . . 200.00
75 Assignment Unknown! 200.00
76 JK,Prisoners Of The Tiny
Universe 200.00
77 The Eyes That Went Berserk . 175.00
78 JK(c),The 13th Hour 200.00
79 JK(c),The Fantastic Sky
Puzzle 200.00
80 Man With Countless Faces! . . 175.00
81 The Man Who Made Utopia . . 175.00
82 The Riddle of the Earth's
Second Moon 175.00
83 The Mystery of the
Martian Eye 175.00
84 JK,BK,100-Century Doom . . . 250.00
85 JK(c),Earth's Strangest
Salesman. 225.00
86 The Baffling Bargains 200.00
87 The Human Diamond 200.00
88 Return of the Animal Man. . . . 200.00
89 The Cosmic Plant! 200.00
90 The Invasion Of the Energy
Creatures! 200.00
91 DD&SMo(c),The Riddle of the
Alien Satellite. 200.00
92 DD(c),Menace of the
Golden Globule 200.00
93 NC(c),I Fought The
Molten Monster 200.00
94 DD&SMo(c),The Creature
In Echo Lake 200.00
95 The Wizard's Gift 200.00
96 The Amazing 70-Ton Man. . . . 200.00
97 The Alien Who Change
History 200.00
98 DD&SMo(c),The Midnight
Creature. 200.00
99 The Secret of the
Leopard God 200.00
100 The Beast Beneath Earth . . . 225.00
101 The Magnificent Monster . . . 175.00
102 Cellmate to a Monster 175.00
103 Hail the Conquering Aliens . . 175.00
104 I was the Seeing-Eye Man . . 175.00
105 Case of the Creature X-14 . . 175.00
106 Invaders from the Doomed
Dimension 175.00
107 Captives o/t Alien
Fisherman 175.00
108 RMo,Four Faces of Frank
Forbes 175.00
109 ATh,JKu,Secret of the Hybrid
Creatures. 175.00
110 Beast Who Stalked Through
Time. 175.00
111 Operation Beast Slayer. 175.00
112 Menace of Craven's
Creatures. 175.00
113 RMo,Prisoners of Beast
Asteroid 175.00
114 The Movies from Nowhere . . 175.00
115 Prisoner o/t Golden Mask . . . 175.00
116 RMo,Return of the
Barsfo Beast 175.00

HOUSE OF SECRETS

DC Comics, Nov.–Dec., 1956

1 MD,JM,The Hand of Doom. . 2,100.00
2 MMe,RMo,NC,Mask of Fear . . 700.00
3 JM,JK,MMe,The Three
Prophecies. 600.00
4 JM,JK,MMe,Master of
Unknown 500.00
5 MMe,The Man Who
Hated Fear 325.00
6 NC,MMe,Experiment 1000 . . . 325.00
7 RMo,Island o/t Enchantress . . 325.00
8 JK,RMo,The Electrified Man . . 350.00
9 JM,JSt,The Jigsaw Creatures . 275.00
10 JSt,NC,I was a Prisoner
of the Sea 275.00
11 KJ(c),NC,The Man who
Couldn't Stop Growing. 275.00
12 JK,The Hole in the Sky. 300.00
13 The Face in the Mist. 200.00
14 MMe,The Man who Stole Air . 200.00
15 The Creature in the Camera. . 200.00
16 NC,We Matched Wits with a
Gorilla Genius 175.00
17 DW,Lady in the Moon 175.00
18 MMe,The Fantastic
Typewriter 175.00
19 MMe,NC,Lair of the
Dragonfly. 175.00
20 Incredible Fireball Creatures. . 175.00
21 Girl from 50,000 Fathoms. . . . 175.00
22 MMe,Thing from Beyond 175.00
23 MMe,I&O:Mark Merlin. 200.00
24 NC,Mark Merlin story 175.00
25 MMe,Mark Merlin story 150.00
26 NC,MMe, Mark Merlin story . . 150.00
27 MMe,Mark Merlin 150.00
28 MMe,Mark Merlin 150.00
29 NC,MMe,Mark Merlin 150.00
30 JKu,MMe,Mark Merlin. 150.00
31 DD,MMe,RH,Mark Merlin 140.00
32 MMe,Mark Merlin 140.00
33 MMe,Mark Merlin 140.00
34 MMe,Mark Merlin 140.00
35 MMe,Mark Merlin 140.00
36 MMe,Mark Merlin 140.00
37 MMe,Mark Merlin 140.00
38 MMe,Mark Merlin 140.00
39 JKu,MMe,Mark Merlin. 140.00
40 NC,MMe,Mark Merlin 140.00
41 MMe,Mark Merlin 140.00
42 MMe,Mark Merlin 140.00
43 RMo,MMe,CI,Mark Merlin. . . . 140.00
44 MMe,Mark Merlin 140.00
45 MMe,Mark Merlin 140.00
46 MMe,Mark Merlin 140.00
47 MMe,Mark Merlin 140.00
48 ATh,MMe,Mark Merlin. 140.00
49 MMe,Mark Merlin 140.00
50 MMe,Mark Merlin 140.00
51 MMe,Mark Merlin 140.00
52 MMe,Mark Merlin 140.00
53 CI,Mark Merlin 140.00
54 RMo,MMe,Mark Merlin 140.00
55 MMe,Mark Merlin 140.00
56 MMe,Mark Merlin 140.00
57 MMe,Mark Merlin 140.00
58 MMe,O:Mark Merlin 140.00
59 MMe,Mark Merlin 140.00

Howdy Doody #1
© Dell Publishing Co.

Human Torch #12
© Marvel Comics Group

Humbug #2
© Harvey Kurtzman

60 MMe,Mark Merlin 140.00
61 I:Eclipso,A:Mark Merlin 250.00
62 MMe,Eclipso,Mark Merlin 140.00

HOWDY DOODY
Dell Publishing Co., Jan., 1950

1 Ph(c). 1,600.00
2 Ph(c) 750.00
3 Ph(c) 350.00
4 Ph(c) 350.00
5 Ph(c) 350.00
6 P(c) 400.00
7 thru 10 . . . . @250.00
11 & 12. . . . . @225.00
13 Christmas (c) 225.00
14 thru 20. . . . . @225.00
21 thru 38. . . . . @175.00

HOW STALIN HOPES WE WILL DESTROY AMERICA
Pictorial News, 1951

N# (Giveaway) 600.00

HOW TO SHOOT
Remington, 1952

N# (promotional) 100.00

HUCKLEBERRY HOUND
Dell Publishing Co., May-July, 1959

1 . . . . 200.00
2 . . . . 150.00
3 thru 7 . . . . @125.00
8 thru 10 . . . . @100.00
11 thru 17. . . . . @75.00

RED RAVEN COMICS
Marvel Timely Comics Aug., 1940

1 JK,O:Red Raven,I:Magar,A:Comet Pierce & Mercury,Human Top, Eternal Brain 25,000.00

Becomes:

HUMAN TORCH
Marvel Comcis, 1940–49

2 (#1)ASh(c),BEv,B:Sub-Mariner A:Fiery Mask,Falcon,Mantor, Microman 55,000.00
3 (#2)Ash(c),BEv,V:Sub-Mariner,Bondage(c) 10,000.00
4 (#3)ASh(c),BEv,O:Patriot . . . 7,500.00
5 (#4)V:Nazis,A:Patriot,Angel crossover 6,000.00
5a(#5)ASh(c),V:Sub-Mariner . . 9,000.00
6 ASh(c),Doom Dungeon. 4,500.00
7 ASh(c),V:Japanese 4,700.00
8 ASh(c),BW,V:Sub-Mariner . . 6,000.00
9 ASh(c),V:General Rommel . . 5,000.00
10 ASh(c),BW,V:Sub-Mariner . . 5,000.00
11 ASh(c),Nazi Oil Refinery . . . 3,000.00
12 ASh(c),V:Japanese, Bondage(c). 5,000.00
13 ASh(c),V:Japanese, Bondage(c). 3,000.00
14 ASh(c),V:Nazis. 3,000.00
15 ASh(c),Toro Trapped 3,000.00
16 ASh(c),V:Japanese 2,500.00
17 ASh(c),V:Japanese 2,500.00
18 ASh(c),V:Japanese, MacArthurs HQ. 2,500.00
19 ASh(c),Bondage(c). 2,700.00
20 ASh(c),Last War Issue 2,500.00
21 ASh(c),V:Organized Crime. . 2,500.00
22 ASh(c),V:Smugglers. 2,500.00
23 ASh(c),V:Giant Robot. 2,800.00
24 SSh(c),V:Mobsters. 4,000.00
25 The Masked Monster. 3,500.00
26 SSh(c),Her Diary of Terror . . 3,500.00
27 SSh(c),BEv,V:The Asbestos Lady. 3,500.00
28 BEv,The Twins Who Weren't 3,500.00
29 SSh(c),You'll Die Laughing . 3,500.00
30 SSh(c),BEv,The Stranger, A:Namora 2,500.00
31 A:Namora. 2,200.00
32 SSh(c),A:Sungirl,Namora. . . 1,300.00
33 Capt.America crossover . . . 2,500.00
34 The Flat of the Land 2,200.00
35 A;Captain America,Sungirl . . 2,500.00

Becomes:

LOVE TALES

Revived As:

HUMAN TORCH
Marvel Comics, 1954

36 A:Submariner. 2,000.00
37 BEv,A:Submariner 1,800.00
38 BEv,A:Submariner 1,800.00

HUMBUG
Harvey Kurtzman, 1957

1 JDa,WW,WE,End of the World 400.00
2 JDa,WE,Radiator. 200.00
3 JDa,WE 150.00
4 JDa,WE,Queen Victoria(c). . . . 150.00
5 JDa,WE 150.00
6 JDa,WE 150.00
7 JDa,WE,Sputnik(c). 175.00
8 JDa,WE,Elvis/George Washington(c) 150.00
9 JDa,WE 150.00
10 JDa,Magazine. 250.00
11 JDa,WE,HK,Magazine 200.00

HUMDINGER
Novelty Press/Premium Service, May–June, 1946

1 B:Jerkwater Line,Dink, Mickey Starlight 500.00
2 . . . . 300.00
3 . . . . 250.00
4 . . . . 250.00
5 . . . . 250.00
6 . . . . 250.00
2-1 . . . . 225.00
2-2 July–Aug., 1947 . . . . 225.00

HUMPHREY COMICS
Harvey Publications, Oct., 1948

1 BP,Joe Palooka 250.00
2 BP 150.00
3 BP 135.00
4 BP,A:Boy Heroes 150.00
5 BP 125.00
6 BP 125.00
7 BP,A:Little Dot 125.00
8 BP,O:Humphrey. 125.00
9 BP 100.00
10 BP. 100.00
11 thru 21. . . . . @100.00
22 April, 1952. . . . . 100.00

HUNTED
Fox Features Syndicate, 1950
(Formerly: MY LOVE MEMOIRS)

1 (13) Famous Crime Cases . . . 400.00
2 . . . . 200.00

HURRICANE COMICS
Cambridge House, 1945

1 F:Hurry Kane 350.00

Hyper Mystery Comics #1
© Hyper Publications

Ideal Comics #2
© Marvel Comics Group

I Love Lucy #4
© Dell Publishing Co.

HYPER MYSTERY COMICS

Hyper Publications, May, 1940

1 B:Hyper ... 3,000.00
2 June, 1940 ... 2,000.00

IBIS, THE INVINCIBLE

Fawcett Publications, Jan., 1942–Spring, 1948

1 MRa(c),O:Ibis ... 3,500.00
2 Bondage (c) ... 2,000.00
3 BW ... 1,500.00
4 BW,A:Mystic Snake People ... 900.00
5 BW,Bondage (c),The Devil's Ibistick ... 1,000.00
6 BW, The Book of Evil ... 1,000.00

IDEAL

Marvel Timely, July, 1948

1 Antony and Cleopatra ... 400.00
2 The Corpses of Dr.Sacotti ... 350.00
3 Joan of Arc ... 325.00
4 Richard the Lionhearted A:The Witness ... 500.00
5 Phc,Love and Romance ... 250.00

Becomes:

LOVE ROMANCES

6 Ph(c),I Loved a Scoundrel ... 250.00
7 Ph(c) ... 175.00
8 Ph(c) ... 200.00
9 thru 12 Ph(c) ... @150.00
13 thru 20 ... @150.00
21 BK ... 125.00
22 ... 125.00
23 ... 125.00
24 BK ... 125.00
25 ... 125.00
26 thru 35 ... @125.00
36 BK ... 125.00
37 ... 125.00
38 BK ... 150.00
39 thru 44 ... @125.00
45 MB ... 150.00
46 ... 150.00
47 ... 150.00
48 ... 125.00
49 ATh ... 150.00
50 ... 125.00
51 ... 125.00
52 ... 125.00
53 ATh ... 140.00
54 ... 125.00
55 ... 125.00
56 ... 125.00
57 MB ... 135.00
58 thru 74 ... @135.00
75 MB ... 135.00
76 ... 125.00
77 MB ... 135.00
78 ... 125.00
79 ... 125.00
80 RH(c) ... 125.00
81 ... 125.00
82 MB,JK(c) ... 150.00
83 JSe,JK(c) ... 150.00
84 JK ... 150.00
85 JK ... 150.00
86 thru 95 ... @100.00
96 JK ... 150.00
97 ... 150.00
98 JK ... 160.00
99 JK ... 160.00
100 thru 104 ... @160.00
105 JK ... 160.00
106 JK,July, 1963 ... 160.00

IDEAL COMICS

Marvel Timely, Fall, 1944

1 B:Super Rabbit,Giant Super Rabbit V:Axis(c) ... 275.00
2 Super Rabbit at Fair(c) ... 200.00
3 Beach Party(c) ... 200.00
4 How to Catch Robbers ... 200.00

Becomes:

WILLIE COMICS

Marvel, 1946

5 B:Willie,George,Margie,Nellie Football(c) ... 250.00
6 Record Player(c) ... 175.00
7 Soda Fountain(c),HK ... 175.00
8 Fancy Dress(c) ... 150.00
9 ... 150.00
10 HK,Hey Look ... 175.00
11 HK,Hey Look ... 175.00
12 ... 150.00
13 ... 150.00
14 ... 150.00
15 ... 150.00
16 thru 18 ... @150.00
19 ... 175.00
20 Li'L Willie Comics ... 150.00
21 Li'L Willie Comics ... 150.00
22 ... 150.00
23 May, 1950 ... 150.00

Becomes:

CRIME CASES

IDEAL ROMANCE
See: TENDER ROMANCE

IF THE DEVIL WOULD TALK

Catechetical Guild, 1950

N# Rare ... 1,000.00
N#, 1958 Very Rare ... 850.00

ILLUSTRATED STORIES OF THE OPERAS

B. Bailey Publ. Co., 1943

N# Faust ... 800.00
N# Aida ... 750.00
N# Carman ... 750.00
N# Rigoletto ... 750.00

I LOVED
See: ZOOT COMICS

I LOVE LUCY COMICS

Dell Publishing Co., 1954

(1) *see Dell Four Color #535*
(2) *see Dell Four Color #559*
3 Lucile Ball Ph(c) all ... 400.00
4 ... 350.00
5 ... 350.00
6 thru 10 ... @300.00
11 thru 20 ... @200.00
21 thru 35 ... @175.00

I LOVE YOU

Fawcett Publications, 1950

1 Photo(c) ... 175.00

I'M A COP
See: A-1 COMICS

IMPACT

E.C. Comics, March–April, 1955

1 RC,GE,BK,Grl ... 400.00
2 RC,JDu,Grl,BK,JO ... 300.00
3 JO,RC,JDU,Grl,JKa,BK ... 275.00
4 RC,JO,JDa,GE,Grl,BK ... 275.00
5 Nov.–Dec., 1955 ... 275.00

Indian Fighter #5
© Youthful Magazines

Indians #2
© Fiction House

Inside Crime #3
© Fox Features Syndicate

INCREDIBLE SCIENCE FANTASY
See: WEIRD SCIENCE

INCREDIBLE SCIENCE FICTION
E.C. Comics, July–Aug., 1955

30 JDa,BK,JO,WW . . . 800.00
31 AW,WW,BK . . . 750.00
32 AW,JDa,BK,JO . . . 750.00
33JDa,BK,JO,WW . . . 750.00

INDIAN BRAVES
See: BAFFLING MYSTERIES

INDIAN CHIEF
Dell Publishing Co., July–Sept., 1951

3 P(c) all . . . 150.00
4 . . . 125.00
5 . . . 125.00
6 A:White Eagle . . . 125.00
7 . . . 125.00
8 . . . 125.00
9 . . . 125.00
10 . . . 125.00
11 . . . 125.00
12 I:White Eagle . . . 135.00
13 thru 29 . . . @100.00
30 SB . . . 100.00
31 thru 33 SB . . . @100.00

INDIAN FIGHTER
Youthful Magazines, May, 1950

1 Revenge of Chief Crazy Horse . . . 250.00
2 Bondage (c) . . . 250.00
3 . . . 125.00
4 Cheyenne Warpath . . . 125.00
5 . . . 125.00
6 Davy Crockett in Death Stalks the Alamo . . . 125.00
7 Tom Horn-Bloodshed at Massacre Valley . . . 125.00
8 Tales of Wild Bill Hickory, Jan., 1952 . . . 125.00

INDIANS
Wings Publ. Co. (Fiction House), Spring, 1950

1 B:Long Bow, Manzar, White Indian & Orphan . . . 350.00
2 B:Starlight . . . 175.00
3 Longbow(c) . . . 150.00
4 Longbow(c) . . . 125.00
5 Manzar(c) . . . 150.00
6 Captive of the Semecas . . . 125.00
7 Longbow(c) . . . 125.00
8 A:Long Bow . . . 125.00
9 A:Long Bow . . . 125.00
10 Manzar(c) . . . 125.00
11 thru 16 . . . @100.00
17 Spring, 1953,Longbow(c) . . . 100.00

INDIANS ON THE WARPATH
St. John Publ. Co., 1950

N# MB(c) . . . 400.00

INDIAN WARRIORS
See: OUTLAWS, THE

INFORMER, THE
Feature Television Productions, April, 1954

1 MSy,The Greatest Social Menace of our Time! . . . 200.00
2 MSy . . . 150.00
3 MSy . . . 100.00
4 MSy . . . 100.00
5 Dec., 1954 . . . 100.00

IN LOVE
Mainline, Aug., 1954

1 S&K,Bride of the Star . . . 450.00
2 S&K,Marilyn's Men . . . 250.00
3 S&K . . . 250.00
4 S&K,Comics Code . . . 275.00
5 S&K(c) . . . 125.00
6 . . . 100.00

Becomes:

I LOVE YOU
Charlton Comics, Sept., 1955

7 JK(c),BP . . . 150.00
8 . . . 125.00
9 . . . 125.00
10 . . . 125.00
11 thru 16 . . . @100.00
17 Giant . . . 150.00
18 . . . 100.00
19 . . . 100.00
20 . . . 100.00
21 thru 50 . . . @75.00
51 thru 59 . . . @75.00
60 Elvis . . . 225.00
61 thru 100 . . . @75.00
101 thru 130 . . . @25.00

INSIDE CRIME
Hero Books/ Fox Feature Syndicate, 1950

1 . . . 325.00
2 . . . 275.00
N# . . . 700.00

INTERNATIONAL COMICS
See: CRIME PATROL

INTERNATIONAL CRIME PATROL
See: CRIME PATROL

INTIMATE
Charlton Comics, 1957

1 thru 3 . . . @100.00

Becomes:

TEEN-AGE LOVE

4 . . . 75.00
5 thru 9 . . . @50.00
10 thru 35 . . . @50.00
36 thru 96 . . . @50.00

INTIMATE CONFESSIONS
Fawcett Publ./ Realistic Comics, 1951

1a P(c) all, Unmarried Bride . . 1,000.00
1 EK,EK(c),Days of Temptation... Nights of Desire . . . 250.00
2 Doomed to Silence . . . 250.00
3 EK(c), The Only Man For Me . 175.00
3a Robert Briffault . . . 275.00
4 EK(c),Tormented Love . . . 250.00
5 Her Secret Sin . . . 250.00
6 Reckless Pick-up . . . 250.00
7 A Love Like Ours,Spanking . . . 275.00
8 Fatal Woman, March, 1953 . . 250.00

Intrigue #1
© Quality Comics Group

Is This Tomorrow #1
© Catechetical Guild

Jace Pearson of the Texas Rangers #8
© Dell Publishing Co.

INTIMATE LOVE

Standard Magazines, Jan., 1950

5 Wings on My Heart,Ph(c) 150.00
6 WE,JSe,Ph(c) 175.00
7 WE,JSe,Ph(c),I Toyed with Love 175.00
8 WE,JSe,Ph(c) 175.00
9 Ph(c) 100.00
10 Ph(c),My Hopeless Heart 175.00
11 . . . . 100.00
12 . . . . 100.00
13 thru 18. . . . . @100.00
19 ATh 125.00
20 . . . . 100.00
21 ATh 125.00
22 ATh 125.00
23 ATh 100.00
24 ATh 125.00
25 ATh 100.00
26 ATh 125.00
27 ATh 100.00
28 ATh,Aug., 1954 . . . . 100.00

INTIMATE SECRETS OF ROMANCE

Star Publications, Sept., 1953

1 LbC(c) 275.00
2 LbC(c) 250.00

INTRIGUE

Comics Magazine (Quality Comics Group), 1955

1 LbC,Ghost Ship 400.00

INVISIBLE SCARLET O'NEIL

Harvey Publications, Dec., 1950

1 . . . . 200.00
2 . . . . 150.00
3 April, 1951 . . . . 150.00

IRON VIC

United Features Syndicate/ St. John Publ. Co., 1940

1-shot 600.00

IS THIS TOMORROW?

Catechetical Guild, 1950

1 Communist threat 200.00
2 (1) Canada. 150.00
3 (1) America 200.00
4 (1) Turkey. 100.00
5 (1) Australia 150.00

IT REALLY HAPPENED

William H. Wise/ Visual Editions, 1945

1 Benjamin Franklin, Kit Carson 300.00
2 The Terrible Tiddlers 200.00
3 Maid of the Margiris 150.00
4 Chaplain Albert J. Hoffman . . . 150.00
5 AS(c),Monarchs of the Sea,Lou Gehrig, Amelia Earhart 275.00
6 AS(c),Ernie Pyle 150.00
7 FGu,Teddy Roosevelt,Jefferson Davis,Story of the Helicopter. 150.00
8 FGu,Man O' War,Roy Rogers . 250.00
9 AS(c),The Story of Old Ironsides 150.00
10 AS(c),Honus Wagner, The Story of Mark Twain. 200.00
11 AS(c),MB,Queen of the Spanish Main, Oct., 1947 . . . . 175.00

IT'S A DUCK'S LIFE

Marvel, Feb., 1950

1 F;Buck Duck,Super Rabbit . . . 150.00
2 . . . . 100.00
3 thru 11 . . . . @100.00

IT'S FUN TO STAY ALIVE

Nat.'l Auto Dealers Assoc., 1947

1 Bugs Bunny 250.00

IT'S GAMETIME

DC Comics, Sept.–Oct., 1955

1 . . . . 1,000.00
2 Dodo and the Frog. 700.00
3 . . . . 700.00
4 March-April, 1956 . . . . 700.00

IT'S LOVE, LOVE, LOVE

St. John Publishing Co., 1957

1 . . . . 100.00
2 . . . . 100.00

JACE PEARSON OF THE TEXAS RANGERS

Dell Publishing Co., May, 1952

(1) *see Dell Four Color #396*
2 Ph(c),Joel McRae 150.00
3 Ph(c),Joel McRae 150.00
4 Ph(c),Joel McRae 150.00
5 Ph(c),Joel McRae 150.00
6 Ph(c),Joel McRae 150.00
7 Ph(c),Joel McRae 150.00
8 Ph(c),Joel McRae 150.00
9 Ph(c),Joel McRae 150.00
(10) *see Dell Four Color #648*
Becomes:

TALES OF JACE PEARSON OF THE TEXAS RANGERS

Feb., 1955

11 . . . . 125.00
12 . . . . 125.00
13 . . . . 125.00
14 . . . . 125.00
15 ATh 150.00
16 ATh 150.00
17 thru 20. . . . . @100.00

JACK ARMSTRONG

Parents' Institute, Nov., 1947

1 Artic Mystery 600.00
2 Den of the Golden Dragon . . . 250.00
3 Lost Valley of Ice 200.00
4 Land of the Leopard Men 200.00
5 Fight against Racketeers of the Ring 200.00
6 . . . . 175.00
7 Baffling Mystery on the Diamond 175.00
8 . . . . 175.00
9 Mystery of the Midgets 175.00
10 Secret Cargo. 175.00
11 . . . . 175.00
12 Madman's Island, rare 200.00
13 Sept., 1949 . . . . 175.00

JACKIE GLEASON

St. John Publishing Co., Sept., 1955

1 Ph(c) 900.00
2 . . . . 550.00

Jackie Gleason and the Honeymooners #11 © DC Comics

Jamboree #1 © Round Publishing

Jesse James #7 © Avon Periodicals

3 . . . . 500.00
4 Dec., 1955 . . . . 500.00

JACKIE GLEASON AND THE HONEYMOONERS

DC Comics, June-July, 1956

1 Based on TV show 1,300.00
2 . . . . 700.00
3 . . . . 500.00
4 . . . . 500.00
5 . . . . 500.00
6 . . . . 500.00
7 . . . . 500.00
8 . . . . 500.00
9 . . . . 500.00
10 . . . . 500.00
11 . . . . 500.00
12 April-May, 1958 . . . . . . 850.00

JACKIE ROBINSON

Fawcett Publications, May, 1950

N# Ph(c) all issues. 1,800.00
2 . . . . 1,000.00
3 . . . . 900.00
4 . . . . 900.00
5 . . . . 900.00
6 May, 1952 . . . . 900.00

JACK IN THE BOX

See: YELLOW JACKET COMICS

JACKPOT COMICS

MLJ Magazines, Spring, 1941

1 CBi(c),B:Black Hood,Mr.Justice, Steel Sterling,Sgt.Boyle . . . 4,500.00
2 SCp(c), ... 2,000.00
3 Bondage (c) 1,800.00
4 First Archie 5,500.00
5 Hitler(c). 2,000.00
6 Son of the Skull v:Black Hood, Bondage(c) 1,800.00
7 Bondage (c) 1,800.00
8 Sal(c), ... 1,500.00
9 Sal(c), ... 1,500.00

Becomes:

JOLLY JINGLES

Summer, 1943

10 Super Duck,(fa). 450.00
11 Super Duck 225.00
12 Hitler parody (c),A:Woody Woodpecker 250.00
13 thru 15 Super Duck. . . . . . @150.00
16 Dec., 1944 . . . . 150.00

JACK THE GIANT KILLER

Bimfort & Co., Aug.–Sept., 1953

1 HcK,HcK(c) 250.00

JAMBOREE

Round Publishing Co., Feb., 1946

1 . . . . 250.00
2 March, 1946 . . . . 150.00

JANE ARDEN

St. John Publ. Co., March, 1948

1 . . . . 200.00
2 June, 1948 . . . . 150.00

JANN OF THE JUNGLE

See: JUNGLE TALES

JEANIE COMICS

See: DARING MYSTERY

JEEP COMICS

R.B. Leffingwell & Co., Winter, 1944

1 B;Captain Power 700.00
2 . . . . 400.00
3 LbC(c),March–April, 1948 . . . . 600.00

JEFF JORDAN, U.S. AGENT

D.S. Publ. Co., Dec., 1947

1 . . . . 250.00

JERRY DRUMMER

Charlton Comics, 1957

1 Revolutionary War. 100.00
2 . . . . 100.00

JESSE JAMES

Avon Periodicals/ Realistic Publ., Aug., 1950

1 JKu,The San Antonio Stage Robbery 250.00
2 JKu,The Daring Liberty Bank Robbery 175.00
3 JKu,The California Stagecoach Robberies 175.00
4 EK(c),Deadliest Deed! 100.00
5 JKu,WW,Great Prison Break . 175.00
6 JKu,Wanted Dead or Alive . . . 175.00
7 JKu,Six-Gun Slaughter at San Romano! 150.00
8 EK,Daring Train Robbery! 125.00
9 EK 100.00
10 thru 14 {Do not exist}
15 EK. 125.00
16 EK, Butch Cassidy 100.00
17 EK, Jessie James. 100.00
18 JKu 100.00
19 JKu 100.00
20 AW,FF,A:Chief Vic,Kit West . . 200.00
21 EK, Two Jessie James 100.00
22 EK,Chuck Wagon 100.00
23 EK. 100.00
24 EK,B:New McCarty. 100.00
25 EK. 100.00
26 EK. 100.00
27 EK,E:New McCarty. 100.00
28 Quantrells Raiders 100.00
29 Aug., 1956. . . . . 100.00

JEST

Harry 'A' Chesler, 1944

10 J. Rebel,Yankee Boy 350.00
11 1944,Little Nemo. 400.00

JET ACES

Real Adventure Publ. Co. (Fiction House), 1952

1 Set 'em up in MIG Alley 250.00
2 Kiss-Off for Moscow Molly . . . 150.00
3 Red Task Force Sighted 150.00
4 Death-Date at 40,000, 1953 . . 150.00

JET FIGHTERS

Standard Magazines, Nov., 1953

5 ATh,Korean War Stories 150.00
6 Circus Pilot 125.00
7 ATh, Iron Curtains for Ivan, March, 1953 . . . . 150.00

Jimmy Wakely #3
© DC Comics

Jingle Jangle Comics #6
© Eastern Color Printing

Joe Louis #2
© Fawcett Periodicals

JET POWERS
See: A-1 COMICS

JETTA OF THE 21st CENTURY
Standard Comics, Dec., 1952

5 Teen Stories 250.00
6 Robot (c) 250.00
7 April, 1953 . . . . 150.00

JIGGS AND MAGGIE
Best Books (Standard)/ Harvey Publ., June, 1949

11 . . . . 125.00
12 thru 21 . . . . @100.00
22 thru 25 . . . . @100.00
26 Part 3-D 250.00
27 Feb.–March, 1954 . . . . 100.00

JIM BOWIE
See: DANGER

JIM DANDY
Dandy Magazine (Lev Gleason), 1956

1 Teen-age humor 125.00
2 . . . . 100.00
3 . . . . 100.00

JIM HARDY
Spotlight Publ., 1944

N# Dynamite Jim,Mirror Man . . . 700.00

JIMMY OLSEN
See: SUPERMAN'S PAL JIMMY OLSEN

JIMMY WAKELY
DC Comics, Sept.–Oct., 1949

1 Ph(c),ATh,The Cowboy Swordsman 1,800.00
2 Ph(c),ATh,The Prize Pony 750.00
3 Ph(c),ATh,The Return of Tulsa Tom 650.00
4 Ph(c),ATh,FF,HK,Where There's Smoke There's Gunfire 625.00
5 ATh,The Return of the Conquistadores 500.00
6 ATh,Two Lives of Jimmy Wakely 500.00
7 The Secret of Hairpin Canyon . 500.00
8 ATh,The Lost City of Blue Valley 500.00
9 ATh,The Return of the Western Firebrands 350.00
10 ATh,Secret of Lantikin'sLight . 350.00
11 ATh,Trail o/a Thousand Hoofs. 350.00
12 ATh,JKU,The King of Sierra Valley 350.00
13 ATh,The Raiders of Treasure Mountain 350.00
14 ATh(c),JKu,The Badmen of Roaring Flame Valley 350.00
15 GK(c),Tommyguns on the Range 350.00
16 GK(c),The Bad Luck Boots . . . 300.00
17 GK(c),Terror atThunderBasin . 300.00
18 July-Aug., 1952 . . . . 350.00

JIM RAY'S AVIATION SKETCH BOOK
Vital Publishers, Feb., 1946

1 Radar, the Invisible eye 550.00
2 Gen.Hap Arnold, May, 1946 . . 350.00

JINGLE JANGLE COMICS
Eastern Color Printing Co., Feb., 1942

1 B:Benny Bear,Pie Face Prince, Jingle Jangle Tales,Hortense 700.00
2 GCn 350.00
3 GCn 300.00
4 GCn,Pie Face (c) 300.00
5 GCn,B:Pie Face 300.00
6 GCn, ... 250.00
7 . . . . 250.00
8 . . . . 250.00
9 . . . . 250.00
10 . . . . 250.00
11 . . . . 200.00
12 . . . . 200.00
13 . . . . 200.00
14 . . . . 200.00
15 E:Pie Face . . . . @200.00
16 thru 20 . . . . @175.00
21 thru 25 . . . . @150.00
26 thru 30 . . . . @150.00
31 thru 41 . . . . @100.00
42 Dec., 1949 . . . . 100.00

JING PALS
Victory Publ. Corp., Feb., 1946

1 Johnny Rabbit 250.00
2 . . . . 200.00
3 . . . . 200.00
4 Aug., 1948 . . . . 200.00

JOE COLLEGE
Hillman Periodicals, Fall, 1949

1 BP,DPr 150.00
2 BP, Winter, 1949 . . . . 125.00

JOE LOUIS
Fawcett Periodicals, Sept., 1950

1 Ph(c),Life Story 750.00
2 Ph(c),Nov., 1950 . . . . 500.00

JOE PALOOKA
Publication Enterprises (Columbia Comics Group) 1943

1 Lost in the Desert 1,200.00
2 Hitler (c) 850.00
3 KO's the Nazis! 700.00
4 Eiffel tower (c), 1944 . . . . 375.00

JOE PALOOKA
Harvey Publications, Nov., 1945–March, 1961

1 Joe Tells How He Became World Champ 600.00
2 Skiing (c) 300.00
3 . . . . 175.00
4 Welcome Home Pals! 175.00
5 S&K,The Great Carnival Murder Mystery 250.00
6 Classic Joe Palooka (c) 175.00
7 BP,V:Grumpopski 150.00
8 BP,Mystery of the Ghost Ship . 150.00
9 Drooten Island Mystery 150.00
10 BP 150.00
11 . . . . 100.00
12 BP,Boxing Course 100.00
13 . . . . 110.00
14 BP,Palooka's Toughest Fight. . 110.00
15 BP,O:Humphrey 175.00
16 BP,A:Humphrey 110.00
17 BP,I:Little Max,A:Humphrey . . 175.00
18 A:Little Max 110.00
19 BP,Freedom Train(c) 125.00

Joe Palooka #25
© Harvey Publications

Joe Yank #13
© Standard Comics

John Wayne Adventure Comics #2
© Toby Press

20 Punch Out(c) . . . 110.00
21 . . . 100.00
22 V:Assassin . . . 100.00
23 Big Bathing Beauty Issue . . . 100.00
24 . . . 100.00
25 . . . 100.00
26 BP,Big Prize Fight Robberies . 100.00
27 BP,Mystery of Bal Eagle Cabin,A:Little Max . . . 100.00
28 BP,Fights Out West, Babe Ruth . . . 100.00
29 BP,Joe Busts Crime Wide Open . . . 100.00
30 BP,V:Hoodlums, Nude Painting . . . 125.00
31 BP, Dizzy Dean . . . 125.00
32 BP,Fight Palooka Was Sure to Lose . . . 100.00
33 BP,Joe finds Ann . . . 100.00
34 BP,How to Box like a Champ . 100.00
35 BP,More Adventures of Little Max, Joe Louis . . . 125.00
36 BP . . . 100.00
37 BP,Joe as a Boy . . . 100.00
38 BP . . . 100.00
39 BP,Original Hillbillies with Big Leviticus . . . 100.00
40 BP,Joe's Toughest Fight . . . 100.00
41 BP,Humphrey's Grudge Fight . 100.00
42 BP . . . 100.00
43 BP . . . 100.00
44 BP,M:Ann Howe, Markies . . . 125.00
45 BP . . . 90.00
46 Champ of Champs . . . 90.00
47 BreathtakingUnderwaterBattle . 90.00
48 BP,Exciting Indian Adventure . . 90.00
49 BP . . . 90.00
50 BP,Bondage(c) . . . 90.00
51 BP, Babe Ruth . . . 90.00
52 BP,V:Balonki . . . 90.00
53 BP . . . 90.00
54 V:Bad Man Trigger McGehee . . 90.00
55 . . . 90.00
56 Foul Play on the High Seas . . . 90.00
57 Curtains for the Champ . . . 90.00
58 V:The Man-Eating Swamp Terror . . . 90.00
59 The Enemy Attacks . . . 90.00
60 Joe Fights Escaped Convict . . 90.00
61 . . . 90.00
62 S&K, Boy Explorers . . . 125.00
63 . . . 90.00
64 . . . 90.00
65 . . . 90.00
66 Drug . . . 125.00
67 Drug . . . 150.00
68 . . . 90.00
69 Torture . . . 150.00
70 BP, Vs. "Gooks" . . . 90.00
71 Bloody Bayonets . . . 90.00
72 Tank . . . 90.00
73 BP . . . 90.00
74 thru 115 . . . @90.00
116 thru 117 giants . . . @150.00
118 Giant, Jack Dempsey . . . @150.00
Giant 1 Body Building . . . 150.00
Giant 2 Fights His Way Back . . . 200.00
Giant 3 Visits Lost City . . . 125.00
Giant 4 All in Family . . . 150.00

JOE YANK

Visual Editions (Standard Comics), March, 1952

5 ATh,WE,Korean Jackpot! . . . 150.00
6 Bacon and Bullets, G.I.Renegade . . . 150.00
7 Two-Man War,A:Sgt. Glamour 100.00
8 ATh(c),Miss Foxhole of 1952, . 125.00
9 G.I.'s and Dolls,Colonel Blood 100.00
10 A Good Way to Die, A:General Joe . . . 100.00
11 . . . 100.00
12 RA . . . 100.00
13 . . . 100.00
14 . . . 100.00
15 . . . 100.00
16 July, 1954 . . . 100.00

JOHN HIX SCRAPBOOK

Eastern Color Printing Co., 1937

1 Strange as It Seems . . . 650.00
2 Strange as It Seems . . . 500.00

JOHNNY DANGER

Toby Press, Aug., 1954

1 Ph(c),Private Detective . . . 200.00

JOHNNY DYNAMITE
See: DYNAMITE

JOHNNY HAZARD

Best Books (Standard Comics), Aug., 1948

5 FR . . . 250.00
6 FR,FR(c) . . . 225.00
7 FR(c) . . . 200.00
8 FR,FR(c), May, 1949 . . . 200.00

JOHNNY LAW, SKY RANGER

Good Comics (Lev Gleason), April, 1955

1 . . . 125.00
2 . . . 100.00
3 . . . 100.00
4 Nov., 1955 . . . 100.00

JOHNNY MACK BROWN

Dell Publishing Co., 1950–52

1 *See: FOUR COLOR*
2 Western hero . . . 200.00
3 . . . 150.00
4 . . . 125.00
5 . . . 125.00
6 . . . 125.00
7 . . . 125.00
8 . . . 125.00
9 . . . 125.00
10 . . . 125.00

JOHN WAYNE ADVENTURE COMICS

Toby Press, Winter, 1949

1 Ph(c),The Mysterious Valley of Violence . . . 2,200.00
2 AW,FF,Ph(c) . . . 1,000.00
3 AW,FF,Flying Sheriff . . . 1,000.00
4 AW,FF,Double-Danger,Ph(c) 1,000.00
5 Volcano of Death,Ph(c) . . . 650.00
6 AW,FF,Caravan of Doom, Ph(c) . . . 800.00
7 AW,FF,Ph(c) . . . 700.00
8 AW,FF,Duel of Death,Ph(c) . . . 900.00
9 Ghost Guns,Ph(c) . . . 500.00
10 Dangerous Journey,Ph(c) . . . 450.00
11 Manhunt!,Ph(c) . . . 450.00
12 HK,Joins the Marines,Ph(c) . . 450.00
13 V:Frank Stacy . . . 400.00
14 Operation Peeping John . . . 400.00
15 Bridge Head . . . 400.00
16 AW,FF,Golden Double-Cross . 400.00
17 Murderer's Music . . . 400.00
18 AW,FF,Larson's Folly . . . 475.00
19 . . . 350.00
20 Whale (c) . . . 350.00
21 . . . 350.00
22 Flash Flood! . . . 350.00

Jo-Jo Comics #18
© Fox Features Syndicate

Joker Comics #4
© Marvel Comics Group

Adventures Into Terror #20
© Marvel Comics Group

Jo

23 Death on Two Wheels 350.00
24 Desert 350.00
25 AW,FF,Hondo!,Ph(c) 475.00
26 Ph(c) 400.00
27 Ph(c) 400.00
28 Dead Man's Boots! 400.00
29 AW,FF,Ph(c),Crash in California Desert 450.00
30 The Wild One, Ph(c) 400.00
31 AW,FF,May, 1955 . . . . 450.00

JO-JO COMICS
Fox Features Syndicate, Spring, 1946

N# (fa) JoJo 250.00
2 (fa) Electro 150.00
3 (fa) 150.00
4 (fa) 150.00
5 (fa) 150.00
6 (fa) 150.00
7 B:Jo-Jo Congo King 1,200.00
8 (7)B:Tanee,V:The Giant Queen 900.00
9 (8)The Mountain of Skulls 750.00
10 (9)Death of the Fanged Lady . 750.00
11 (10) 750.00
12 (11)Bondage(c), Water Warriors. 625.00
13 (12) Jade Juggernaut 600.00
14 The Leopards of Learda 600.00
15 The Flaming Fiend 600.00
16 Golden Gorilla,bondage(c) . . . 600.00
17 Stark-Mad Thespian, bondage(c) 675.00
18 The Death Traveler 600.00
19 Gladiator of Gore 600.00
20 . . . . 600.00
21 . . . . 600.00
22 . . . . 600.00
23 . . . . 600.00
24 . . . . 600.00
25 Bondage(c) 675.00
26 . . . . 600.00
27 . . . . 600.00
28 . . . . 600.00
29 July, 1949 . . . . 650.00

JOKER COMICS
Marvel Timely, April, 1942

1 BW,I&B:Powerhouse Pepper, A:Stuporman 5,000.00
2 BW,I:Tessie the Typist 2,000.00
3 BW,A:Tessie the Typist, Squat Car Squad 1,500.00
4 BW,Squat Car (c) 1,400.00
5 BW,same 1,400.00
6 BW, ... 1,000.00
7 BW 1,000.00
8 BW 1,000.00
9 BW 1,000.00
10 BW,Shooting Gallery (c) . . . 1,000.00
11 BW 1,000.00
12 BW 1,000.00
13 BW 1,000.00
14 BW 1,000.00
15 BW 1,000.00
16 BW 1,000.00
17 BW 1,000.00
18 BW 1,000.00
19 BW 1,000.00
20 BW 1,000.00
21 BW 1,000.00
22 BW 1,000.00
23 BW,HK,Hey Look 1,000.00
24 BW,HK,Laff Favorites 800.00
25 BW,HK,same 1,100.00
26 BW,HK,same 1,100.00
27 BW 1,100.00
28 . . . . 250.00
29 BW 1,100.00
30 BW 1,100.00
31 BW 1,100.00
32 B:Millie,Hedy 250.00
33 HK 275.00
34 . . . . 250.00
35 HK 275.00
36 HK 250.00
37 . . . . 250.00
38 . . . . 250.00
39 . . . . 250.00
40 . . . . 250.00
41 A:Nellie the Nurse 250.00
42 I:Patty Pin-up 275.00
Becomes:

ADVENTURES INTO TERROR
Marvel, 1950

43(1)AH,B:Horror Stories 900.00
44(2)AH,Won't You Step Into My Palor 600.00
3 GC,I Stalk By Night 400.00
4 DR,The Torture Room 400.00
5 GC,DR,The Hitchhiker 375.00
6 RH,The Dark Room 325.00
7 GT(c),BW,JMn,Where Monsters Dwell 750.00
8 JSt,Enter... the Lizard 400.00
9 RH(c),JSt,The Dark Dungeon 375.00
10 JMn,When the Vampire Calls . 375.00
11 JMn,JSt,Dead Man's Escape . 325.00
12 BK,Man Who Cried Ghost . . . 350.00
13 BEv(c),The Hands of Death . . 350.00
14 GC,GT,The Hands 300.00
15 Trapped by the Tarantula 300.00
16 RH(c),Her Name Is Death . . . 300.00
17 I Die Too Often,Bondage(c) . . 350.00
18 He's Trying To Kill Me 300.00
19 The Girl Who Couldn't Die . . . 275.00
20 . . . . 275.00
21 GC,JMn. 250.00
22 JMn 250.00
23 . . . . 250.00
24 MF,GC 250.00
25 MF 300.00
26 GC 250.00
27 . . . . 250.00
28 GC 250.00
29 GC,JMn 250.00
30 . . . . 250.00
31 May, 1954 . . . . 250.00

JOLLY JINGLES
See: JACKPOT

JONESY
Comic Favorites (Quality Comics Group), 1953–54

1 teen-age 125.00
2 . . . . 100.00
3 . . . . 100.00
4 . . . . 100.00
5 . . . . 100.00
6 . . . . 100.00
7 . . . . 100.00
8 . . . . 100.00

JON JUAN
Toby Press, 1950

1 ASh(c),Superlover 800.00

JOURNEY INTO FEAR
Superior Publications, May, 1951–Sept., 1954

1 MB,Preview of Chaos 1,000.00
2 Debt to the Devil 600.00
3 Midnight Prowler 500.00
4 Invisible Terror 500.00
5 Devil Cat 350.00

Journey Into Fear #6
© Superior Publications

Journey Into Mystery #72
© Marvel Comics Group

Jughead's Fantasy #3
© Archie Publications

6 Partners in Blood 350.00
7 The Werewolf Lurks 350.00
8 Bells of the Damned 350.00
9 Masked Death 350.00
10 Gallery of the Dead. 350.00
11 Beast of Bedlam 300.00
12 No Rest for the Dead 300.00
13 Cult of the Dead 300.00
14 Jury of the Undead 300.00
15 Corpse in Make-up 350.00
16 Death by Invitation 300.00
17 Deadline for Death 300.00
18 Here's to Horror 300.00
19 This Body is Mine! 300.00
20 Masters of the Dead 300.00
21 Horror in the Clock 300.00

JOURNEY INTO MYSTERY

Marvel, June, 1952

1 RH(c),B:Mystery/Horror stories 4,500.00
2 Don't Look 1,500.00
3 I Didn't See Anything 1,200.00
4 RH,BEv(c),I'm Drowning, Severed Hand (c) 1,200.00
5 RH,BEv(c),Fright 750.00
6 BEv(c),Till Death Do Us Part 750.00
7 BEv(c),Ghost Guard 750.00
8 He Who Hesitates 750.00
9 BEv(c),I Made A Monster 750.00
10 The Assassin of Paris 750.00
11 RH,GT,Meet the Dead. 700.00
12 A Night At Dragmoor Castle . . 600.00
13 The Living and the Dead 600.00
14 DAy,RH,The Man Who Owned A World 600.00
15 RH(c),Till Death Do Us Part . . 600.00
16 DW,Vampire Tale 600.00
17 SC,Midnight On Black Mountain 600.00
18 He Wouldn't Stay Dead. 600.00
19 JF,The Little Things. 600.00
20 BEv,BP,After Man, What. 600.00
21 JKu,The Man With No Past . . 600.00
22 Haunted House. 600.00
23 GC,Gone, But Not Forgotten . 450.00
24 The Locked Drawer 450.00
25 The Man Who Lost Himself . . 450.00
26 The Man From Out There. . . . 450.00
27 BP,JSe,Masterpiece 450.00
28 The Survivor 450.00
29 Three Frightened People 450.00
30 JO,The Lady Who Vanished. . 450.00
31 The Man Who Had No Fear . . 450.00
32 Elevator In The Sky 450.00
33 SD,AW,There'll Be Some Changes Made 500.00
34 BP,BK,The Of The Mystic Ring 450.00
35 LC,JF,Turn Back The Clock . . 450.00
36 I, The Pharaoh 450.00
37 BEv(c),The Volcano 450.00
38 SD,Those Who Vanish 450.00
39 BEv(c),DAy,WW,The Forbidden Room 450.00
40 BEv(c),JF,The Strange Secret Of Henry Hill 450.00
41 BEv(c),GM,RC,I Switched Bodies 400.00
42 BEv(c),GM,What Was Farley's Other Face. 400.00
43 AW,Ghost Ship 400.00
44 SD,JK,BEv 400.00
45 BEv,JO 375.00
46 . . . . 375.00
47 BEv 375.00
48 . . . . 375.00
49 . . . . 375.00
50 SD 375.00
51 SD,JK 400.00
52 JK 375.00
53 DH. 375.00
54 AW 400.00
55 . . . . 400.00
56 thru 61 SD,JK . . . . @350.00
62 SD,JK,I:Xemnu 600.00
63 SD,JK 500.00
64 SD,JK 500.00
65 SD,JK 500.00
66 Hulk Type 600.00
67 SD,JK 500.00
68 SD,JK 500.00
69 SD,JK 500.00
70 Sandman Type 550.00
71 JK,SD 500.00
72 JK,SD 500.00
73 JK,DH,Spider-Man type 700.00
74 . . . . 400.00
75 JK,DH 400.00
76 JK,DH 350.00
77 DH,SD,JK 350.00
78 DH,Dr.Strange Type 450.00
79 JK,DH,SD 400.00
80 JK,DH,SD 300.00
81 JK,DH,SD 300.00
82 JK,DH,SD 300.00
83 JK,SD,I&O:Thor. 9,500.00
84 JK,SD,DH,I:Executioner. . . . 2,500.00
85 JK,SD,I:Loki,Heimdall,Balder, Tyr,Odin,Asgard 1,500.00
86 JK,SD,DH,V:Tomorrow Man 1,000.00
87 JK,SD,V:Communists 650.00
88 JK,SD,V:Loki. 650.00
89 JK,SD,O:Thor(rep) 650.00
90 SD,I:Carbon Copy. 500.00
91 JSt,SD,I:Sandu 450.00
92 JSt,SD,V:Loki,I:Frigga. 450.00
93 DAy,JK,SD,I:Radioactive Man 500.00
94 JSt,SD,V:Loki 450.00
95 JSt,SD,I:Duplicator 450.00
96 JSt,SD,I:Merlin II. 450.00
97 JK,I:Lava Man,O:Odin 500.00
98 DH,JK,I&O:Cobra 350.00
99 DH,JK,I:Mr.Hyde,Surtur 350.00
100 DH,JK,V:Mr.Hyde 350.00

JOURNEY INTO UNKNOWN WORLDS

See: ALL WINNERS COMICS

JUDE, THE FORGOTTEN SAINT

Catechetical Guild, 1953

N# 100.00

JUDGE PARKER

Argo, Feb., 1956

1 . . . . 100.00
2 . . . . 100.00

JUDO JOE

Jay-Jay Corp., Aug., 1952

1 Drug. 250.00
2 . . . . 150.00
3 Drug, Dec., 1953 . . . . 200.00

JUDY CANOVA

See: ALL TOP COMICS

JUGHEAD'S FANTASY

Archie Publications, 1960

1 Sir Jugalot 275.00
2 Peter Goon 200.00
3 Superjughead 15000

Jughead's Folly #1
© Archie Publications

Jumbo Comics #26
© Fiction House

Jumbo Comics #80
© Fiction House

JUGHEAD'S FOLLY

Archie Publications, 1957

1 Jughead like Elvis 650.00

JUKE BOX

Famous Funnies, March, 1948

1 ATh(c),Spike Jones 500.00
2 Dinah Shore,Transvestitism. . . 500.00
3 Vic Damone, Peggie Lee. 250.00
4 Jimmy Durante. 250.00
5 . . . . 250.00
6 Jan., 1949,Desi Arnaz 300.00

JUMBO COMICS

Real Adventure Publ. Co. (Fiction House), Sept., 1938

1 LF,BKa,JK,WE(a&c),B:Sheena Queen of the Jungle,The Hawk The Hunchback 30,000.00
2 LF,JK,WE,BKa,BP, O:Sheena 10,000.00
3 JK,WE(a&c),BP,LF,BKa 6,000.00
4 WE(a&c),MMe,LF,BKa, O:The Hawk 5,800.00
5 WE(a&c),BP,BKa 5,000.00
6 WE(a&c),BP,BKa 4,500.00
7 WE,BKa,BP 4,400.00
8 LF(c),BP,BKa,World of Tommorow 4,400.00
9 LF(c),BP 3,500.00
10 WE,LF(c),BKa,Regular size issues begin 2,500.00
11 LF(c),WE&BP,War of the Emerald Gas 2,000.00
12 WE(c),WE&BP,Hawk in Buccaneer Vengeance,Bondage(c) . . . 2,500.00
13 WE(c),BP,Sheena in The Thundering Herds. 2,000.00
14 WE(c),LF,BP,Hawk in Siege of Thunder Isle,B:Lightning 2,100.00
15 BP(a&c),Sheena(c) 1,100.00
16 BP(a&c),The Lightning Strikes Twice 1,500.00
17 BP(c), B:Sheena covers and lead stories 1,100.00
18 BP 1,100.00
19 BP(c),BKa,Warriors of the Bush 1,100.00
20 BP,BKa,Spoilers of the Wild. 1,100.00
21 BP,BKa,Prey of the Giant Killers 800.00
22 BP,BKa,Victims of the Super-Ape,O:Hawk 900.00
23 BP,BKa,Swamp of the Green Terror 900.00
24 BP,BKa,Curse of the Black Venom 900.00
25 BP,BKa,Bait for the Beast. . . . 800.00
26 BP,BKa,Tiger-Man Terror 800.00
27 BP,BKa,Sabre-Tooth Terror. . . 800.00
28 BKa,RWd,The Devil of the Congo 800.00
29 BKa,RWd,Elephant-Scourge . 800.00
30 BKa,RWd,Slashing Fangs . . . 800.00
31 BKa,RWd,Voodoo Treasure of Black Slave Lake. 750.00
32 BKa,RWd,AB,Captives of the Gorilla-Men 750.00
33 BKa,RWd,AB,Stampede Tusks 750.00
34 BKa,RWd,AB,Claws of the Devil-Cat 750.00
35 BKa,RWd,AB,Hostage of the Devil Apes 750.00
36 BKa,RWd,AB,Voodoo Flames 750.00
37 BKa,RWd,AB,Congo Terror . . 750.00
38 BKa,RWd,AB,Death-Trap of the River Demons 750.00
39 BKa,RWd,AB,Cannibal Bait . . 750.00
40 BKa,RWd,AB, Assagai Poison 750.00
41 BKa,RWd,AB,Killer's Kraal, Bondage(c) 600.00
42 BKa,RWd,AB,Plague of Spotted Killers 600.00
43 BKa,RWd,AB,Beasts of the Devil Queen. 600.00
44 BKa,RWd,AB,Blood-Cult of K'Douma 600.00
45 BKa,RWd,AB,Fanged Keeper of the Fire-Gem 600.00
46 BKa,RWd,AB,Lair of the Armored Monsters. 600.00
47 BKa,RWd,AB,The Bantu Blood-Monster 600.00
48 BKa,RWd,AB,Red Meat for the Cat-Pack 600.00
49 BKa,RWd,AB,Empire of the Hairy Ones 600.00
50 BKa,RWd,AB,Eyrie of the Leopard Birds 600.00
51 BKa,RWd.AB,Monsters with Wings. 500.00
52 BKa,RWd,AB,Man-Eaters Paradise 500.00
53 RWd,AB,Slaves of the Blood Moon 500.00
54 RWd,AB,Congo Kill. 500.00
55 RWd,AB,Bait for the Silver King Cat. 500.00
56 RWd,AB,Sabre Monsters of the Aba-Zanzi,Bondage(c). . . 700.00
57 RWd,AB,Arena of Beasts 500.00
58 RWd,AB,Sky-Atlas of the Thunder-Birds 500.00
59 RWd,AB,Kraal of Shrunken Heads 500.00
60 RWd,AB,Land of the Stalking Death 400.00
61 RWd,AB,King-Beast of the Masai. 400.00
62 RWd,AB,Valley of Golden Death. 400.00
63 RWd,AB,The Dwarf Makers . . 400.00
64 RWd,The Slave-Brand of Ibn Ben Satan,Male Bondage . . . 600.00
65 RWd,The Man-Eaters of Linpopo 400.00
66 RWd,Valley of Monsters 400.00
67 RWd,Land of Feathered Evil . 400.00
68 RWd,Spear of Blood Ju-Ju . . . 400.00
69 RWd,AB,MB,Slaves for the White Sheik. 400.00
70 RWd,AB,MB,The Rogue Beast's Prey 400.00
71 RWd,AB,MB,The Serpent-God Speaks. 350.00
72 RWd,AB,MB,Curse of the Half-Dead 350.00
73 RWd,AB,MB,War Apes of the T'Kanis. 350.00
74 RWd,AB,MB,Drums of the Voodoo God 350.00
75 RWd,AB,MB,Terror Trail of the Devil's Horn 350.00
76 RWd,AB,MB,Fire Gems of Skull Valley 350.00
77 RWd,AB,MB,Blood Dragons from Fire Valley 350.00
78 RWd,AB,MB,Veldt of the Vampire Apes 350.00
79 RWd,AB,MB,Dancing Skeletons. 350.00
80 RWd,AB,MB,Banshee Cats 350.00
81 RWd,MB,AB,JKa,Heads for King' Hondo's Harem. 300.00
82 RWd,MB,AB,JKa,Ghost Riders of the Golden Tuskers 300.00
83 RWd,MB,AB,JKa,Charge of the Condo Juggernauts. 300.00
84 RWd,MB,AB,JKa,Valley of the Whispering Fangs 300.00

 All comics prices listed are for *Near Mint* condition.

Jumbo Comics #107
© Fiction House

Jumbo Comics #135
© Fiction House

Jungle Action #2
© Marvel Comics Group

85 RWd,MB,AB,JKa,Red Tusks of Zulu-Za'an 300.00
86 RWd,MB,AB,JKa,Witch-Maiden of the Burning Blade 300.00
87 RWd,AB,MB,JKa,Sargasso of Lost Safaris 300.00
88 RWd,AB,MB,JKa,Kill-Quest of the Ju-Ju Tusks 300.00
89 RWd,AB,MB,JKa,Ghost Slaves of Bwana Rojo 300.00
90 RWd,AB,MB,JKa,Death Kraal of the Mastadons 300.00
91 RWd,AB,MB,JKa,Spoor of the Sabre-Horn Tiger. 275.00
92 RWd,MB,JKa,Pied Piper of the Congo 275.00
93 RWd,MB,JKa,The Beasts that Dawn Begot 275.00
94 RWd,MB,JKa,Wheel of a Thousand Deaths 350.00
95 RWd,MB,JKa,Flame Dance of the Ju-Ju Witch 275.00
96 RWd,MB,JKa,Ghost Safari. 275.00
97 RWd,MB,JKa,Banshee Wail of the Undead,Bondage(c) . . 400.00
98 RWd,MB,JKa,Seekers of the Terror Fangs 300.00
99 RWd,MB,JKa,Shrine of the Seven Souls 300.00
100 RWd,MB,Slave Brand of Hassan Bey. 350.00
101 RWd,MB,Quest of the Two-Face Ju Ju. 300.00
102 RWd,MB,Viper Gods of Vengeance Veldt 300.00
103 RWd,MB,Blood for the Idol of Blades. 300.00
104 RWd,MB,Valley of Eternal Sleep 300.00
105 RWd,MB,Man Cubs from Momba-Zu 350.00
106 RWd,MB,The River of No-Return 350.00
107 RWd,MB,Vandals of the Veldt 300.00
108 RWd,MB,The Orphan of Vengeance Vale. 300.00
109 RWd,MB,The Pygmy's Hiss is Poison 300.00
110 RWd,MB,Death Guards the Congo Keep 300.00
111 RWd,MB,Beware of the Witch-Man's Brew 300.00
112 RWd,MB,The Blood-Mask from G'Shinis Grave 275.00
113 RWd,MB,The Mask's of Zombi-Zan 275.00
114 RWd,MB 275.00
115 RWd,MB,Svengali of the Apes 275.00
116 RWd,MB,The Vessel of Marbel Monsters 275.00
117 RWd,MB,Lair of the Half-Man King 275.00
118 RWd,MB,Quest of the Congo Dwarflings 275.00
119 RWd,MB,King Crocodile's Domain 275.00
120 RWd,MB,The Beast-Pack Howls the Moon 275.00
121 RWd,MB,The Kraal of Evil Ivory 275.00
122 RWd,MB,Castaways of the Congo 250.00
123 RWd,MB,. 250.00
124 RWd,MB,The Voodoo Beasts of Changra-Lo 250.00
125 RWd,MB,JKa(c),The Beast-Pack Strikes at Dawn 250.00
126 RWd,MB,JKa(c),Lair of the Swamp Beast 250.00
127 RWd,MB,JKa(c),The Phantom of Lost Lagoon. 250.00
128 RWd,MB,JKa(c),Mad Mistress of the Congo-Tuskers 250.00
129 RWd,MB,JKa(c),Slaves of King Simbas Kraal. 250.00
130 RWd,MB,JKa(c),Quest of the Pharaoh's Idol 250.00
131 RWd,JKa(c),Congo Giants at Bay 250.00
132 RWd,JKa(c),The Doom of the Devil's Gorge. 250.00
133 RWd,JKa(c),Blaze the Pitfall Trail 250.00
134 RWd,JKa(c),Catacombs of the Jackal-Men 250.00
135 RWd,JKa(c),The 40 Thieves of Ankar-Lo 250.00
136 RWd,JKa(c),The Perils of Paradise Lost 250.00
137 RWd,JKa(c),The Kraal of Missing Men 250.00
138 RWd,JKa(c),The Panthers of Kajo-Kazar. 250.00
139 RWd,JKa(c),Stampede of the Congo Lancers 250.00
140 RWd,JKa(c),The Moon Beasts from Vulture Valley . . 250.00
141 RWd,JKa(c),B:Long Bow 275.00
142 RWd,JKa(c),Man-Eaters of N'Gamba 250.00
143 RWd,JKa(c),The Curse of the Cannibal Drum 250.00
144 RWd,JKa(c),The Secrets of Killers Cave 250.00
145 RWd,JKa(c),Killers of the Crypt 250.00
146 RWd,JKa(c),Sinbad of the Lost Lagoon. 250.00
147 RWd,JKa(c),The Wizard of Gorilla Glade 250.00
148 RWd,JKa(c),Derelict of the Slave King 250.00
149 RWd,JKa(c),Lash Lord of the Elephants 250.00
150 RWd,JKa(c),Queen of the Pharaoh's Idol 250.00
151 RWd,The Voodoo Claws of Doomsday Trek 250.00
152 RWd,Red Blades of Africa . . 250.00
153 RWd,Lost Legions of the Nile 250.00
154 RWd,The Track of the Black Devil. 250.00
155 RWd,The Ghosts of Blow- Gun Trail 250.00
156 RWd,The Slave-Runners of Bambaru 250.00
157 RWd,Cave of the Golden Skull 250.00
158 RWd,Gun Trek to Panther Valley 250.00
159 RWd,A:Space Scout 225.00
160 RWd,Savage Cargo, E:Sheena covers 225.00
161 RWd,Dawns of the Pit 225.00
162 RWd,Hangman's Haunt 225.00
163 RWd,Cagliostro Cursed Thee 225.00
164 RWd,Death Bars the Door . . 225.00
165 RWd,Day off from a Corpse . 225.00
166 RWd,The Gallows Bird 225.00
167 RWd,Cult of the Clawmen, March, 1953 . . . . 225.00

JUNGLE ACTION

Marvel Atlas, Oct., 1954

1 JMn,JMn(c),B:Leopard Girl . . . 450.00
2 JMn,JMn(c) 475.00
3 JMn,JMn(c) 300.00
4 JMn,JMn(c) 300.00
5 JMn,JMn(c) 300.00
6 JMn,JMn(c),Aug., 1955 . . . . . 300.00

Jungle Comics #
© Fiction House

Jungle Comics #34
© Fiction House

Jungle Comics #68
© Fiction House

JUNGLE COMICS

Glen Kel Publ./Fiction House, Jan., 1940

1 HcK,DBr,LF(c),O:The White Panther,Kaanga,Tabu, B:The Jungle Boy,Camilla, all Kaanga covers & stories . . 7,000.00
2 HcK,DBr,WE(c),B:Fantomah 2,300.00
3 HcK,DBr,GT,The Crocodiles of Death River 1,900.00
4 HcK,DBr,Wambi in Thundering Herds. 1,700.00
5 WE(c),GT,HcK,DBr,Empire of the Ape Men. 1,900.00
6 WE(c),GT,DBr,HcK,Tigress of the Deep Jungle Swamp 1,200.00
7 BP(c),DBr,GT,HcK,Live Sacrifice,Bondage(c) 1,100.00
8 BP(c),GT,HcK,Safari into Shadowland 1,100.00
9 GT,HcK,Captive of the Voodoo Master 1,100.00
10 GT,HcK,BP,Lair of the Renegade Killer 1,100.00
11 GT,HcK,V:Beasts of Africa's Ancient Primieval Swamp Land 750.00
12 GT,HcK,The Devil's Death-Trap 750.00
13 GT(c),GT,HcK,Stalker of the Beasts 800.00
14 HcK,Vengeance of the Gorilla Hordes 750.00
15 HcK,Terror of the Voodoo Cauldron 750.00
16 HcK,Caveman Killers 750.00
17 HcK,Valley of the Killer-Birds . 750.00
18 HcK,Trap of the Tawny Killer, Bondage(c) 800.00
19 HcK,Revolt of the Man-Apes . 750.00
20 HcK,One-offering to Ju-Ju Demon 750.00
21 HcK,Monster of the Dismal Swamp, Bondage(c) 600.00
22 HcK,Lair o/t Winged Fiend . . . 550.00
23 HcK,Man-Eater Jaws 550.00
24 HcK,Battle of the Beasts. 550.00
25 HcK,Kaghis the Blood God, Bondage(c) 700.00
26 HcK,Gorillas of the Witch-Queen 550.00
27 HcK,Spore o/t Gold-Raiders . . 550.00
28 HcK,Vengeance of the Flame God, Bondage(c). 700.00
29 HcK,Juggernaut of Doom 550.00
30 HcK,Claws o/t Black Terror . . 550.00
31 HcK,Land of Shrunken Skulls. 500.00
32 HcK,Curse of the King-Beast . 500.00
33 HcK,Scaly Guardians of Massacre Pool,Bondage(c) . . 600.00
34 HcK,Bait of the Spotted Fury,Bondage(c) 600.00
35 HcK,Stampede of the Slave-Masters 500.00
36 HcK,GT,The Flame-Death of Ju Ju Mountain 500.00
37 HcK,GT,Scaly Sentinel of Taboo Swamp 500.00
38 HcK,GT,Duel of the Congo Destroyers 500.00
39 HcK,Land of Laughing Bones. 500.00
40 HcK,Killer Plague 500.00
41 Hck,The King Ape Feeds at Dawn 400.00
42 Hck,RC,Master of the Moon-Beasts 425.00
43 HcK,The White Shiek 400.00
44 HcK,Monster of the Boiling Pool 400.00
45 HcK,The Bone-Grinders of B'Zambi, Bondage(c). 500.00
46 HcK,Blood Raiders of Tree Trail 400.00
47 HcK,GT,Monsters of the Man Pool, Bondage(c). 500.00
48 HcK,GT,Strangest Congo Adventure 350.00
49 HcK,GT,Lair of the King -Serpent. 350.00
50 HcK,GT,Juggernaut of the Bush 350.00
51 HcK,GT,The Golden Lion of Genghis Kahn 350.00
52 HcK,Feast for the River Devils, Bondage(c) 500.00
53 HcK,GT,Slaves for Horrors Harem 375.00
54 HcK,GT,Blood Bride of the Crocodile 350.00
55 HcK,GT,The Tree Devil. 350.00
56 HcK,Bride for the Rainmaker Raj. 350.00
57 HcK,Fire Gems of T'ulaki 350.00
58 HcK,Land of the Cannibal God 350.00
59 HcK,Dwellers of the Mist Bondage(c) 450.00
60 HcK,Bush Devil's Spoor 400.00
61 HcK,Curse of the Blood Madness 400.00
62 Bondage(c). 450.00
63 HcK,Fire-Birds for the Cliff Dwellers 350.00
64 Valley of the Ju-Ju Idols 350.00
65 Shrine of the Seven Ju Jus, Bondage(c) 400.00
66 Spoor of the Purple Skulls . . . 350.00
67 Devil Beasts of the Golden Temple. 350.00
68 Satan's Safari 350.00
69 Brides for the Serpent King . . 350.00
70 Brides for the King Beast, Bondage(c) 400.00
71 Congo Prey,Bondage(c) 400.00
72 Blood-Brand o/t Veldt Cats . . . 350.00
73 The Killer of M'omba Raj, Bondage(c) 400.00
74 AgF,GoldenJaws, Bondage(c) 400.00
75 AgF,Congo Kill 350.00
76 AgF,Blood Thirst of the Golden Tusk 350.00
77 AgF,The Golden Gourds Shriek Blood,Bondage(c) . . . 400.00
78 AgF,Bondage(c) 400.00
79 AgF,Death has a Thousand Fangs 375.00
80 AgF,Salome of the Devil-Cats Bondage(c) 400.00
81 AgF,Colossus of the Congo . . 375.00
82 AgF,Blood Jewels of the Fire-Bird. 375.00
83 AgF,Vampire Veldt, Bondage(c) 400.00
84 AgF,Blood Spoor of the Faceless Monster 375.00
85 AgF,Brides for the Man-Apes Bondage(c) 400.00
86 AgF,Firegems of L'hama Lost, Bondage(c). 400.00
87 AgF,Horror Kraal of the Legless One,Bondage(c). . . . 400.00
88 AgF,Beyond the Ju-Ju Mists . . 375.00
89 AgF,Blood-Moon over the Whispering Veldt 350.00
90 AgF,The Skulls for the Altar of Doom,Bondage(c) . . 425.00
91 AgF,Monsters from the Mist Lands, Bondage(c) 425.00
92 AgF,Vendetta of the Tree Tribes 400.00
93 AgF,Witch Queen of the Hairy Ones 400.00
94 AgF,Terror Raid of the Congo Caesar 400.00
95 Agf,Flame-Tongues of the Sky Gods. 400.00

All comics prices listed are for *Near Mint* condition.

Jungle Comics #115
© Fiction House

Jungle Comics #146
© Fiction House

Jungle Jim #10
© Dell Publishing Co.

96 Agf,Phantom Guardians of the Enchanted Lake,Bondage(c). 400.00
97 AgF,Wizard of the Whirling Doom,Bondage(c) 375.00
98 AgF,Ten Tusks of Zulu Ivory . . 450.00
99 AgF,Cannibal Caravan, Bondage(c) 375.00
100 AgF,Hate has a Thousand Claws 375.00
101 AgF,The Blade of Buddha, Bondage(c) 375.00
102 AgF,Queen of the Amazon Lancers 350.00
103 AgF,The Phantoms of Lost Lagoon. 350.00
104 AgF 350.00
105 AgF,The Red Witch of Ubangi-Shan 350.00
106 AgF,Bondage(c) 375.00
107 Banshee Valley. 375.00
108 HcK,Merchants of Murder. . . 375.00
109 HcK,Caravan of the Golden Bones 350.00
110 HcK,Raid of the Fire-Fangs . 350.00
111 HcK,The Trek of the Terror-Paws 350.00
112 HcK,Morass of the Mammoths. 350.00
113 HcK,Two-Tusked Terror 350.00
114 HcK,Mad Jackals Hunt by Night 350.00
115 HcK,Treasure Trove in Vulture Sky 350.00
116 HcK,The Banshees of Voodoo Veldt 350.00
117 HcK,The Fangs of the Hooded Scorpion. 350.00
118 HcK,The Muffled Drums of Doom. 350.00
119 HcK,Fury of the Golden Doom. 350.00
120 HcK,Killer King Domain 350.00
121 HcK,Wolves of the Desert Night 350.00
122 HcK,The Veldt of Phantom Fangs. 350.00
123 HcK,The Ark of the Mist-Maids 350.00
124 HcK,The Trail of the Pharaoh's Eye. 350.00
125 HcK,Skulls for Sale on Dismal River 350.00
126 HcK,Safari Sinister 300.00
127 HcK,Bondage(c) 300.00
128 HcK,Dawn-Men of the Congo 300.00
129 HcK,The Captives of Crocodile Swamp 300.00
130 HcK,Phantoms of the Congo 300.00
131 HcK,Treasure-Tomb of the Ape-King 300.00
132 HcK,Bondage(c) 350.00
133 HcK,Scourge of the Sudan Bondage(c) 350.00
134 HcK,The Black Avengers of Kaffir Pass 300.00
135 HcK 300.00
136 HcK,The Death Kraals of Kongola 300.00
137 BWg(c),HcK,The Safari of Golden Ghosts 300.00
138 BWg(c),HcK,Track of the Black Terror Bondage(c) 350.00
139 BWg(c),HcK,Captain Kidd of the Congo 300.00
140 BWg(c),HcK,The Monsters of Kilimanjaro 300.00
141 BWg(c)HcK,The Death Hunt of the Man Cubs 300.00
142 BWg(c),Hck,Sheba of the Terror Claws,Bondage(c). . . . 350.00
143 BWg(c)Hck,The Moon of Devil Drums. 300.00
144 BWg(c)Hck,Quest of the Dragon's Claw 300.00
145 BWg(c)Hck,Spawn of the Devil's Moon 300.00
146 BWg(c),HcK,Orphans of the Congo 300.00
147 BWG(c),HcK,The Treasure of Tembo Wanculu. 300.00
148 BWg(c),HcK,Caged Beasts of Plunder-Men,Bondage(c) . 350.00
149 BWg(c),HcK 275.00
150 BWg(c),HcK,Rhino Rampage, Bondage(c) 350.00
151 BWg(c),HcK 275.00
152 BWg(c),HcK,The Rogue of Kopje Kull 275.00
153 BWg(c),HcK,The Wild Men of N'Gara. 275.00
154 BWg(c),HcK,The Fire Wizard 275.00
155 BWg(c),HcK,Swamp of the Shrieking Dead 275.00
156 BWg(c),HcK 275.00
157 BWg(c),HcK 275.00
158 BWg(c),HcK,A:Sheena 275.00
159 BWg(c),HcK,The Blow-Gun Kill 275.00
160 BWg,HcK,King Fang. 275.00
161 BWg(c),HcK,The Barbarizi Man-Eaters 275.00
162 BWg(c) 275.00
163 BWg(c),Jackals at the Kill, Summer,1954 . . . . 275.00

JUNGLE JIM

Best Books (Standard Comics), Jan., 1949

11 . . . . 125.00
12 Mystery Island. 100.00
13 Flowers of Peril. 100.00
14 . . . . 100.00
15 . . . . 100.00
16 . . . . 100.00
17 . . . . 100.00
18 . . . . 100.00
19 . . . . 100.00
20 1951 . . . . 100.00

JUNGLE JIM

Dell Publishing Co., Aug., 1953

(1) *see Dell Four Color #490*
(1) *see Dell Four Color #565*
3 P(c) all 125.00
4 . . . . 125.00
5 . . . . 125.00
6 . . . . 100.00
7 . . . . 100.00
8 thru 12 . . . . @100.00
13 'Mystery Island'. 100.00
14 'Flowers of Peril' 100.00
15 thru 20. . . . . @100.00

JUNGLE JO

Hero Books (Fox Features Syndicate), March, 1950

N# Congo King 550.00
1 WW,Mystery of Doc Jungle . . 600.00
2 Tangl 450.00
3 The Secret of Youth, Sept., 1950 . . . . 450.00

JUNGLE LIL

Hero Books, April, 1950

1 Betrayer of the Kombe Dead. . 500.00
Becomes:

DOROTHY LAMOUR

Fox Features Syndicate, June 1950

2 WW,Ph(c)The Lost Safari 500.00
3 WW,Ph(c), Aug., 1950 . . . . . . 300.00

Ju

Jungle Tales #2
© Marvel Comics Group

Junior Miss #27
© Marvel Comics Group

Justice Traps the Guilty #45
© Prize Publications

JUNGLE TALES

Marvel Atlas, Sept., 1954

1 B:Jann of the Jungle,Cliff Mason,Waku 450.00
2 GT,Jann Stories cont. 300.00
3 Cliff Mason,White Hunter, Waku Unknown Jungle 300.00
4 Cliff Mason,Waku,Unknown Jungle 300.00
5 RH(c),SSh,Cliff Mason,Waku, Unknown Jungle 300.00
6 DH,SSh,Cliff Mason,Waku, Unknown Jungle 300.00
7 DH,SSh,Cliff Mason,Waku, Unknown Jungle 300.00

Becomes:

JANN OF THE JUNGLE

Marvel, 1955

8 SH,SSh,The Jungle Outlaw. . . 400.00
9 With Fang and Talons 250.00
10 AW,The Jackal's Lair. 250.00
11 Bottomless Pit. 250.00
12 The Lost Safari 250.00
13 When the Trap Closed 250.00
14 V:Hunters 250.00
15 BEv(c),DH,V:Hunters 250.00
16 BEv(c),AW,JungleVengeance . 275.00
17 BEv(c),DH,AW,June, 1957 . . . 275.00

JUNGLE THRILLS

See: TERRORS OF THE JUNGLE

JUNIE PROM

Dearfield Publishing Co. Winter, 1947

1 Teenage Stories 150.00
2 . . . . 125.00
3 thru 5 . . . . @100.00
6 June, 1949 . . . . 100.00

JUNIOR COMICS

Fox Features Syndicate, Sept., 1947

9 AF(a&c) ,Teenage Stories. . . 1,200.00
10 AF(a&c) 1,000.00
11 AF(a&c) 1,000.00
12 AF(a&c) 1,000.00
13 AF(a&c) 1,000.00
14 AF(a&c) 1,000.00
15 AF(a&c) 1,000.00
16 AF(a&c),July,1948 . . . . 1,000.00

JUNIOR FUNNIES

See: FAMILY FUNNIES

JUNIOR HOOP COMICS

Stanmor Publications, Jan., 1952

1 . . . . 125.00
2 . . . . 100.00
3 July, 1952 . . . . 100.00

JUNIOR MISS

Marvel Timely, 1944, 1947–50

1 F:Frank Sinatra &June Allyson 350.00
24 . . . . 150.00
25 thru 38 Cindy . . . . @125.00
39 HK. 150.00

JUSTICE COMICS

Marvel Atlas, Fall, 1947

7(1) B:FBI in Action,Mystery of White Death. 350.00
8(2),HK,Crime is For Suckers . . . 250.00
9(3),FBI Raid 200.00
4 Bank Robbery 200.00
5 Subway(c) 175.00
6 E:FBI In Action 175.00
7 Symbolic(c) 175.00
8 Funeral(c) 175.00
9 B:True Cases Proving Crime Can't Win. 175.00
10 Ph(c),Bank Hold Up 175.00
11 Ph(c),Behind Bars. 175.00
12 Ph(c),The Crime of Martin Blaine 135.00
13 Ph(c),The Cautious Crook . . . 135.00
14 Ph(c) 135.00
15 Ph(c) 135.00
16 F:"Ears"Karpik-Mobster. 125.00
17 The Ragged Stranger 125.00
18 Criss-Cross 125.00
19 Death Of A Spy 125.00
20 Miami Mob 125.00
21 Trap. 125.00
22 The Big Break. 125.00
23 thru 40. . . . . @100.00
41 Electrocution cover 200.00
42 thru 51 . . . . @100.00
52 Flare Up 100.00

Becomes:

TALES OF JUSTICE

Marvel, May, 1955—Aug., 1957

53 BEv,Keeper Of The Keys 200.00
54 thru 57. . . . . @175.00
58 BK 150.00
59 BK 150.00
60 thru 63. . . . . @100.00
64 RC,DW,JSe. 125.00
65 RC. 125.00
66 JO,AT 125.00
67 DW 125.00

JUSTICE TRAPS THE GUILTY

Headline Publications, (Prize) Oct.–Nov., 1947

2-1 S&K(a&c),Electric chair (c) . 800.00
2 S&K(a&c) 450.00
3 S&K(a&c) 400.00
4 S&K(a&c),True Confession of a Girl Gangleader 400.00
5 S&K(a&c) 400.00
6 S&K(a&c) 400.00
7 S&K(a&c) 400.00
8 S&K(a&c) 400.00
9 S&K(a&c) 400.00
10 S&K(a&c) 400.00
11 S&K(a&c) 175.00
12 . . . . 125.00
13 . . . . 150.00
14 . . . . 125.00
15 . . . . 125.00
16 . . . . 125.00
17 . . . . 125.00
18 S&K(a&c) 150.00
19 S&K(a&c) 150.00
20 . . . . 150.00
21 S&K. 175.00
22 S&K(c). 175.00
23 S&K(c). 175.00
24 . . . . 100.00
25 . . . . 100.00
26 . . . . 100.00
27 S&K(c). 175.00
28 . . . . 100.00
29 . . . . 100.00
30 S&K. 150.00
31 thru 50. . . . . @100.00
51 thru 54. . . . . @100.00
55 . . . . 100.00
56 . . . . 100.00
57 . . . . 100.00
58 Drug 300.00
59 thru 92. . . . . @100.00

Ka'a'nga Comics #12
© Fiction House

Katy Keene #44
© Archie Publications

Katzenjammer Kids #20
© Standard Comics

Becomes:

FARGO KID

Headline Publications (Prize), June–July. 1958

93 AW,JSe,O:Kid Fargo 175.00
94 JSe 125.00
95 June–July, 1958,JSe 125.00

JUST MARRIED

Charlton Comics, 1958

1 . . . . 125.00
2 . . . . 125.00
3 . . . . 100.00
4 . . . . 100.00
5 . . . . 100.00
6 . . . . 100.00
7 . . . . 100.00
8 . . . . 100.00
9 . . . . 100.00
10 . . . . 100.00

KA'A'NGA COMICS

Glen-Kel Publ. (Fiction House), Spring, 1949–Summer, 1954

1 Phantoms of the Congo 700.00
2 V:The Jungle Octopus 350.00
3 . . . . 250.00
4 The Wizard Apes of Inkosi-Khan 235.00
5 A:Camilla 225.00
6 Captive of the Devil Apes 175.00
7 GT,Beast-Men of Mombassa . 200.00
8 The Congo Kill-Cry 175.00
9 Tabu-Wizard. 175.00
10 Stampede for Congo Gold . . . 175.00
11 Claws of the Roaring Congo. . 125.00
12 Bondage(c). 250.00
13 Death Web of the Amazons . . 125.00
14 Slave Galley of the Lost Nile Bondage(c). 250.00
15 Crocodile Moon,Bondage(c). . 250.00
16 Valley of Devil-Dwarfs,Sheena 150.00
17 Tembu of the Elephants 125.00
18 The Red Claw of Vengeance . 125.00
19 The Devil-Devil Trail 125.00
20 The Cult of the Killer Claws . . 125.00

KASCO COMICS

Kasco Grainfeed (Giveaway), 1945

1 BWo 300.00
2 1949,BWo 250.00

KATHY

Standard Comics, Sept., 1949

1 Teen-Age Stories 150.00
2 ASh 125.00
3 thru 6 . . . . @100.00
7 thru 17 . . . . @100.00

KATHY

Marvel Atlas, Oct., 1959—Feb., 1964

1 Teenage Tornado. 125.00
2 . . . . 100.00
3 thru 15 . . . . @75.00
16 thru 27. . . . . @60.00

KATY KEENE

Archie Publications/Close-Up Radio Comics, 1949

1 BWo 1,700.00
2 BWo 1,200.00
3 BWo 1,000.00
4 BWo 1,000.00
5 BWo 900.00
6 BWo 800.00
7 BWo 600.00
8 thru 12 BWo . . . . @500.00
13 thru 20 BWo . . . . @400.00
21 thru 29 BWo . . . . @300.00
30 thru 38 BWo . . . . @300.00
39 thru 62 BWo . . . . @300.00
Ann.#1. 1,200.00
Ann.#2 thru #6 . . . . @700.00

KATY KEENE FASHION BOOK MAGAZINE

Archie Publications, 1955

1 Woggon(a&c). 800.00
2 . . . . 500.00
3 thru 10 not published
11 thru 18. . . . . @300.00
19 . . . . 250.00
20 . . . . 250.00
21 . . . . 250.00
22 . . . . 250.00
23 Winter 1958-59. . . . . 250.00

KATY KEENE PINUP PARADE

Archie Publications, 1955

1 . . . . 750.00
2 . . . . 400.00
3 . . . . 350.00
4 . . . . 350.00
5 . . . . 350.00
6 . . . . 275.00
7 . . . . 275.00
8 . . . . 275.00
9 . . . . 275.00
10 Woggon art. 275.00
11 Story on comics. 350.00
12 . . . . 275.00
13 . . . . 275.00
14 . . . . 275.00
15 Sept., 1961 . . . . 500.00

KATZENJAMMER KIDS

David McKay Publ., 1947–50

1 . . . . 250.00
2 . . . . 125.00
3 . . . . 100.00
4 . . . . 100.00
5 . . . . 100.00
6 . . . . 100.00
7 . . . . 100.00
8 . . . . 100.00
9 . . . . 100.00
10 . . . . 100.00
11 . . . . 100.00

Standard Comics, 1950–53

12 thru 22 . . . . @100.00

Harvey Publ., 1953–54

22 thru 25 . . . . @100.00

KAYO

See: SCOOP COMICS

KEEN DETECTIVE FUNNIES

Centaur Publications, July, 1938

1-8 B:The Clock, ... 3,000.00
1-9 WE 1,200.00
1-10 . . . . 1,100.00
1-11 Dean Denton 1,100.00
2-1 The Eye Sees. 900.00
2-2 JCo 900.00
2-3 TNT. 900.00
2-4 Gabby Flynn 900.00
5 . . . . 1,000.00
6 . . . . 900.00
7 Masked Marvel 3,300.00

Keen Detective Funnies #8
© Centaur Publications

Kerry Drake Detective Cases #12
© Harvey Publications

Key Comics #4
© Consolidated Magazines

8 PGv,Gabby Flynn,Nudity
Expanded 16 pages 1,400.00
9 Dean Denton 1,000.00
10 . . . . 1,000.00
11 BEv,Sidekick 1,000.00
12 Masked Marvel(c) 1,200.00
3-1 Masked Marvel(c). 1,000.00
3-2 Masked Marvel(c). 1,000.00
3-3 BEv. 1,000.00
16 BEv 1,000.00
17 JSm 1,000.00
18 The Eye Sees,Bondage(c). . 1,200.00
19 LFe 950.00
20 BEv,The Eye Sees. 1,400.00
21 Masked Marvel(c). 950.00
22 Masked Marvel(c). 950.00
23 B:Airman 1,300.00
24 Airman 1,400.00

KEEN KOMICS

Centaur Publications, May, 1939

1 Teenage Stories 1,300.00
2 PGv,JaB,CBu,Cut Carson 800.00
3 JCo,Saddle Sniffl 800.00

KEEN TEENS

Life's Romances Publ./Leader/ Magazine Enterprises, 1945

N# P(c),Claire Voyant. 450.00
N# Ph(c),Van Johnson 350.00
3 Ph(c), ... 125.00
4 Ph(c),Glenn Ford 150.00
5 Ph(c),Perry Como 150.00
6 . . . . 125.00

KELLYS, THE

See: KID KOMICS

KEN MAYNARD WESTERN

Fawcett Publications, Sept., 1950–Feb., 1952

1 B:Ken Maynard & Tarzan (horse)
The Outlaw Treasure Trail . . 800.00
2 Invasion of the Badmen 500.00
3 Pied Piper of the West 350.00
4 Outlaw Hoax 350.00
5 Mystery of Badman City 350.00
6 Redwood Robbery 350.00
7 Seven Wonders of the West . . 350.00
8 Mighty Mountain Menace 350.00

KEN SHANNON

Quality Comics Group, Oct., 1951–April, 1953

1 RC, Evil Eye of Count Ducrie . 500.00
2 RC, Cut Rate Corpses 350.00
3 RC, Corpse that Wouldn't
Sleep 275.00
4 RC, Stone Hatchet Murder . . . 275.00
5 RC, Case of the Carney Killer 275.00
6 Weird Vampire Mob 275.00
7 RC,Ugliest Man in the World . 225.00
8 Chinatown Murders,Drug. 350.00
9 RC, Necklace of Blood 200.00
10 RC, Shadow of the Chair 200.00

KEN STUART

Publication Enterprises, 1949

1 . . . . 150.00

KENT BLAKE OF THE SECRET SERVICE

Marvel, May, 1951—July, 1953

1 U.S. Govt. Secret Agent
stories,Bondage cover 400.00
2 JSt,Drug issue,Man without
A Face 350.00
3 JMn,Trapped By The Chinese
Reds. 125.00
4 Secret Service Stories. 125.00
5 RH(c),Condemned To Death . . 125.00
6 Cases from Kent Blake files . . 125.00
7 RH(c),Behind Enemy Lines . . 125.00
8 GT,V:Communists 125.00
9 thru 14 . . . . @125.00

KERRY DRAKE DETECTIVE CASES

Life's Romances/M.E., 1944

(1) *see N# A-1 Comics*
2 A:The Faceless Horror 200.00
3 . . . . 150.00
4 A:Squirrel, Dr. Zero, Caresse . 150.00
5 Bondage (c) 500.00

Harvey Publ., Jan., 1952

6 A:Stitches 250.00
7 A:Shuteye 275.00
8 Bondage (c) 350.00
9 Drug 350.00
10 BP,A:Meatball,Drug. 350.00
11 BP,I:Kid Gloves 150.00
12 BP. 150.00
13 BP,A:Torso 125.00
14 BP,Bullseye Murder Syndicate 125.00
15 BP,Fake Mystic Racket. 125.00
16 BP,A:Vixen 100.00
17 BP,Case of the $50,000
Robbery. 100.00
18 BP,A:Vixen 100.00
19 BP,Case of the Dope
Smugglers 250.00
20 BP,Secret Treasury Agent. . . . 100.00
21 BP,Murder on Record 100.00
22 BP,Death Rides the Air Waves 100.00
23 BP,Blackmailer's Secret
Weapon 100.00
24 Blackmailer's Trap 100.00
25 Pretty Boy Killer 100.00
26 . . . . 100.00
27 . . . . 100.00
28 BP. 100.00
29 BP. 100.00
30 Mystery Mine,Bondage(c) . . . 250.00
31 . . . . 100.00
32 . . . . 100.00
33 Aug., 1952. . . . . 100.00

KEWPIES

Will Eisner Publications, Spring, 1949

1 . . . . 600.00

KEY COMICS

Consolidated Magazines Jan., 1944

1 B:The Key, Will-O-The-Wisp . . 550.00
2 . . . . 300.00
3 . . . . 250.00
4 WJo(c) O:John Quincy,
B:The Atom 275.00
5 HoK,Aug., 1946 . . . . 300.00

KEY RING COMICS

Dell Publishing Co., 1941

1 . . . . 250.00
(1) Radior. 300.00

KID CARROTS

St. John Publishing Co., 1953

1 Funny animal. 100.00

KID COLT OUTLAW

Marvel Atlas, Aug., 1948

1 B:Kid Colt,A:Two-Gun Kid . . 1,400.00
2 Gun-Fighter and the Girl 700.00

Kid Colt Outlaw #10
© Marvel Comics Group

Kid Eternity #1
© Comics Magazine

Kid Komics #8
© Marvel Comics Group

3 SSh,Colt-Quick Killers
For Hire 550.00
4 Wanted,A:Tex Taylor 550.00
5 Mystery of the Misssing
Mine,A:Blaze Carson. 550.00
6 A:Tex Taylor,Valley of
the Werewolf 350.00
7 B:Nimo the Lion 350.00
8 . . . . 350.00
9 . . . . 350.00
10 The Whip Strikes,E:Nimo
the Lion. 350.00
11 O:Kid Colt 400.00
12 . . . . 225.00
13 DRi 225.00
14 . . . . 225.00
15 Gun Whipped in ShotgunCity . 225.00
16 . . . . 225.00
17 . . . . 225.00
18 DRi 225.00
19 . . . . 200.00
20 The Outlaw 200.00
21 thru 30. . . . . @200.00
31 . . . . 200.00
32 . . . . 200.00
33 thru 45 A:Black Rider . . . . . @150.00
46 RH(c). 150.00
47 DW 150.00
48 RH(c),JKu 150.00
49 . . . . 150.00
50 . . . . 150.00
51 thru 56. . . . . @125.00
57 AW 125.00
58 AW 125.00
59 AW 125.00
60 AW 125.00
61 . . . . 100.00
62 . . . . 100.00
63 . . . . 100.00
64 RC. 110.00
65 RC. 110.00
66 AW 150.00
67 thru 78. . . . . @100.00
79 Origin Retold. 110.00
80 thru 86. . . . . @100.00
87 JDa(reprint) 110.00
88 AW 120.00
89 AW,Matt Slade 120.00
90 thru 99. . . . . @100.00
100 JK 120.00

KID COWBOY

Approved Comics/
St. John Publ. Co., 1950

1 B:Lucy Belle & Red Feather . . 200.00
2 Six-Gun Justice 150.00
3 Shadow on Hangman's Bridge 125.00
4 Red Feather V:Eagle of Doom 100.00
5 Killers on the Rampage 100.00
6 The Stovepipe Hat 100.00
7 Ghost Town of Twin Buttes . . . 100.00
8 Thundering Hoofs 100.00
9 Terror on the Salt Flats 100.00
10 Valley of Death 100.00
11 Vanished Herds,Bondage(c) . . 200.00
12 . . . . 100.00
13 . . . . 100.00
14 1954 . . . . 100.00

KIDDIE KARNIVAL

Approved Comics, 1952

N# 450.00

KIDDY KAPERS

Farrell Publ./Red Top/
Decker Publ., 1946

1 Funny animal, Little Bit 125.00
1a (1957) 100.00

KID ETERNITY

Comics Magazine,
Spring, 1946

1 . . . . 1,300.00
2 . . . . 500.00
3 Follow Him Out of This World . 550.00
4 Great Heroes of the Past 350.00
5 Don't Kid with Crime 300.00
6 Busy Battling Crime 300.00
7 Protects the World 300.00
8 Fly to the Rescue 300.00
9 Swoop Down on Crime 300.00
10 Golden Touch from Mr. Midas. 300.00
11 Aid the Living by Calling
the Dead 250.00
12 Finds Death 250.00
13 Invades General Poschka. . . . 250.00
14 Battles Double 250.00
15 A: Master Man. 250.00
16 Balance Scales of Justice. . . . 225.00
17 A:Baron Roxx 225.00
18 A:Man with Two Faces 225.00
Becomes:

BUCCANEERS

Quality Comics Group,
Jan., 1950

19 RC,Sword Fight(c) 700.00
20 RC,Treasure Chest 450.00
21 RC,Death Trap 500.00
22 A:Lady Dolores,Snuff,
Bondage(c) 400.00
23 RC,V:Treasure Hungry
Plunderers of the Sea 375.00
24 A:Adam Peril,Black Roger,
Eric Falcon 300.00
25 V:Clews 300.00
26 V:Admiral Blood 300.00
27 RC(a&c)May, 1951 . . . . 450.00

KID FROM DODGE CITY

Marvel Atlas, July, 1957—Sept., 1957

1 . . . . 150.00
2 . . . . 100.00

KID FROM TEXAS

Marvel Atlas, June, 1957—Aug., 1957

1 . . . . 125.00
2 . . . . 100.00

KID KOMICS

Marvel Timely, Feb., 1943

1 SSh(c),BW,O:Captain Wonder
& Tim Mulrooney I:Whitewash,
Knuckles,Trixie Trouble,
Pinto Pete Subbie. 7,500.00
2 AsH(c),F:Captain Wonder
Subbie, B:Young Allies,
B:Red Hawk,Tommy Tyme 3,500.00
3 ASh(c),AAv,SSh,A:The Vision
& Daredevils 3,000.00
4 ASh(c),B:Destroyer,A:Sub-Mariner,
E:Red Hawk,Tommy Tyme 2,200.00
5 ASh(c),V:Nazis 1,800.00
6 ASh(c),V:Japanese 1,800.00
7 ASh(c),B;Whizzer 1,600.00
8 ASh(c),V:Train Robbers 1,600.00
9 ASh(c),V:Elves 1,600.00
10 ASh(c),E:Young Allies,
The Destoyer,The Whizzer 1,600.00
Becomes:

KID MOVIE KOMICS

Marvel, 1946

11 F:Silly Seal,Ziggy Pig
HK,Hey Look 300.00
Becomes:

RUSTY COMICS

Marvel, 1947

12 F:Rusty,A:Mitzi 225.00
13 Do not Disturb(c). 125.00

The Killers #2
© Magazine Enterprises

The Kilroys #33
© American Comics

King Comics #19
© David McKay Publications

14 Beach(c),BW,HK,Hey Look. . . 250.00
15 Picnic(c),HK,Hey Look 175.00
16 Juniors Grades,HK,HeyLook . 175.00
17 John in Trouble,HK,HeyLook . 175.00
18 John Fired. 125.00
19 Fridge raid(c),HK 125.00
20 And Her Family,HK 200.00
21 And Her Family,HK 250.00
22 HK. 250.00
Becomes:

KELLYS, THE

Marvel, 1950

23 F:The Kelly Family(Pop, Mom,Mike,Pat & Goliath) . . . 125.00
24 Mike's Date,A;Margie 75.00
25 Wrestling(c). 75.00
Becomes:

SPY CASES

Marvel, 1950

26(#1) Spy stories 350.00
27(#2) BEv,Bondage(c) 300.00
28(#3) Sabotage,A:Douglas Grant Secret Agent. 175.00
4 The Secret Invasion 150.00
5 The Vengeance of Comrade de Casto 150.00
6 A:Secret Agent Doug Grant . . 150.00
7 GT,A:Doug Grant 150.00
8 Atom Bomb(c),Frozen Horror 250.00
9 Undeclared War 125.00
10 Battlefield Adventures. 125.00
11 Battlefield Adventures 125.00
12 Battlefield Adventures 125.00
13 Battlefield Adventures 125.00
14 Battlefield Adventures. 125.00
15 Doug Grant 125.00
16 Doug Grant 125.00
17 Doug Grant 125.00
18 Contact in Ankara 125.00
19 Final Issue,Oct., 1953. . . . . . . 125.00

KID MONTANA
See: DAVY CROCKETT

KID SLADE GUNFIGHTER
See: MATT SLADE

KID ZOO COMICS

Street & Smith Publ., 1948

1 (fa) 325.00

KILLERS, THE

Magazine Enterprises, 1947

1 LbC(c),Thou Shall Not Kill . . 1,500.00
2 Grl,OW,Assassins Mad Slayers of the East,Hanging(c),Drug 1,300.00

KILROYS, THE

B&L Publishing Co./ American Comics, June–July, 1947

1 Three Girls in Love(c) 300.00
2 Flat Tire(c) 150.00
3 Right to Swear(c) 125.00
4 Kissing Booth(c) 125.00
5 Skiing(c) 125.00
6 Prom(c) 100.00
7 To School 100.00
8 . . . . 100.00
9 . . . . 100.00
10 B:Solid Jackson solo. 100.00
11 . . . . 100.00
12 Life Guard(c). 100.00
13 thru 21. . . . . @100.00
22 thru 30. . . . . @100.00
31 thru 40. . . . . @100.00
41 thru 47. . . . . @100.00
48 3-D effect 200.00
49 3-D effect 200.00
50 thru 54, July, 1954. . . . . @100.00

KING COMICS

David McKay Publications, April, 1936 (all have Popeye covers)

1 AR,EC,B:Popeye,Flash Gordon,B: Henry,Mandrake 15,000.00
2 AR,EC,Flash Gordon 3,500.00
3 AR,EC,Flash Gordon 2,500.00
4 AR,EC,Flash Gordon 2,000.00
5 AR,EC,Flash Gordon 1,500.00
6 AR,EC,Flash Gordon 1,100.00
7 AR,EC,King Royal Mounties 1,050.00
8 AR,EC,Thanksgiving(c) 1,000.00
9 AR,EC,Christmas(c) 1,000.00
10 AR,EC,Flash Gordon 1,000.00
11 AR,EC,Flash Gordon 750.00
12 AR,EC,Flash Gordon 750.00
13 AR,EC,Flash Gordon 750.00
14 AR,EC,Flash Gordon 750.00
15 AR,EC,Flash Gordon 750.00
16 AR,EC,Flash Gordon 750.00
17 AR,EC,Flash Gordon 700.00
18 AR,EC,Flash Gordon 700.00
Covers say: "Starring Popeye"
19 AR,EC,Flash Gordon 700.00
20 AR,EC,Football(c). 700.00
21 AR,EC,Flash Gordon 600.00
22 AR,EC,Flash Gordon 600.00
23 AR,EC,Flash Gordon 600.00
24 AR,EC,Flash Gordon 600.00
25 AR,EC,Flash Gordon 600.00
26 AR,EC,Flash Gordon 550.00
27 AR,EC,Flash Gordon 550.00
28 AR,EC,Flash Gordon 550.00
29 AR,EC,Flash Gordon 550.00
30 AR,EC,Flash Gordon 550.00
31 AR,EC,Flash Gordon 550.00
32 AR,EC,Flash Gordon 550.00
33 AR,EC,Skiing(c) 550.00
34 AR,Ping Pong(c). 450.00
35 AR,Flash Gordon 450.00
36 AR,Flash Gordon 450.00
37 AR,Flash Gordon 450.00
38 AR,Flash Gordon 450.00
39 AR,Baseball(c) 450.00
40 AR,Flash Gordon 450.00
41 AR,Flash Gordon 400.00
42 AR,Flash Gordon 400.00
43 AR,Flash Gordon 400.00
44 AR,Popeye golf(c). 400.00
45 AR,Flash Gordon 400.00
46 AR,B:Little Lulu 400.00
47 AR,Flash Gordon 400.00
48 AR,Flash Gordon 400.00
49 AR,Weather Vane 400.00
50 AR,B:Love Ranger 400.00
51 AR,Flash Gordon 300.00
52 AR,Flash Gordon 300.00
53 AR,Flash Gordon 300.00
54 AR,Flash Gordon 300.00
55 AR,Magic Carpet. 300.00
56 AR,Flash Gordon 300.00
57 AR,Cows Over Moon(c) 300.00
58 AR,Flash Gordon 300.00
59 AR,Flash Gordon 300.00
60 AR,Flash Gordon 300.00
61 AR,B:Phantom,Baseball(c) . . . 300.00
62 AR,Flash Gordon 300.00
63 AR,Flash Gordon 200.00
64 AR,Flash Gordon 200.00
65 AR,Flash Gordon 200.00
66 AR,Flash Gordon 200.00
67 AR,Sweet Pea. 200.00
68 AR,Flash Gordon 200.00
69 AR,Flash Gordon 200.00
70 AR,Flash Gordon 200.00
71 AR,Flash Gordon 200.00
72 AR,Flash Gordon 200.00
73 AR,Flash Gordon 200.00

King Comics #127
© David McKay

Kit Carson #5
© Avon Periodicals

Krazy Komics #2
© Marvel Comics Group

74 AR,Flash Gordon 200.00
75 AR,Flash Godron 200.00
76 AR,Flag(c). 200.00
77 AR,Flash Gordon 200.00
78 AR,Popeye,Olive Oil(c) 200.00
79 AR,Sweet Pea. 200.00
80 AR,Wimpy(c). 200.00
81 AR,B:Blondie(c). 200.00
82 thru 91 AR . . . . @150.00
92 thru 98 AR . . . . @150.00
99 AR,Olive Oil(c) 150.00
100 . . . . 200.00
101 thru 116 AR . . . . @175.00
117 O:Phantom 200.00
118 Flash Gordon 175.00
119 Flash Gordon 150.00
120 Wimpy(c). 125.00
121 thru 140. . . . . @125.00
141 Flash Gordon 125.00
142 Flash Gordon 125.00
143 Flash Gordon 125.00
144 Flash Gordon 125.00
145 Prince Valiant 100.00
146 Prince Valiant 100.00
147 Prince Valiant 100.00
148 thru 154. . . . . @75.00
155 E:Flash Gordon. 75.00
156 Baseball(c) 75.00
157 thru 159. . . . . @75.00

KING OF THE ROYAL MOUNTED

Dell Publishing Co., Dec., 1948–1958

(1) *see Dell Four Color #207*
(2) *see Dell Four Color #265*
(3) *see Dell Four Color #283*
(4) *see Dell Four Color #310*
(5) *see Dell Four Color #340*
(6) *see Dell Four Color #363*
(7) *see Dell Four Color #384*
8 Zane Grey adapt. 150.00
9 . . . . 125.00
10 . . . . 125.00
11 thru 28 . . . . @100.00

KIT CARSON

Avon Periodicals, 1950

N# EK(c) Indian Scout 200.00
2 EK(c),Kit Carson's Revenge,
Doom Trail 150.00
3 EK(c),V:Comanche Raiders . . 100.00
4 . . . . 100.00
5 EK(c),Trail of Doom 100.00
6 EK(c) 100.00
7 EK(c) 100.00
8 EK(c) 100.00
Becomes:

FIGHTING DAVY CROCKETT

Oct.–Nov, 1955

9 EK(c) 100.00

KITTY

St. John Publishing Co., 1948

1 . . . . 150.00

KNOCK KNOCK

Whitman Publications, 1936

1 . . . . 200.00

KNOCKOUT ADVENTURES

Fiction House, 1953

1 Rep. Fight Comics #53 . . . . . . 150.00

KOKEY KOALA

Toby Press, 1952

1 . . . . 125.00

KOKO AND KOLA

Compix/Magazine Enterprises, Fall, 1946

1 (fa) 175.00
2 X-Mas Issue 150.00
3 . . . . 100.00
4 . . . . 100.00
5 . . . . 100.00
6 May, 1947 . . . . 100.00

KO KOMICS

Gerona Publications, Oct., 1945

1 . . . . 900.00

KOKONUT KOMICS

Gerona Publications, 1945

1 . . . . 150.00

KOMIC KARTOONS

Marvel Timely, 1945

1 Funny Animal. 225.00
2 . . . . 225.00

KOMIK PAGES

See: SCOOP COMICS

KRAZY KAT COMICS

Dell Publishing Co., May–June, 1951

1 . . . . 125.00
2 . . . . 100.00
3 . . . . 100.00
4 . . . . 100.00
5 . . . . 100.00

KRAZY KOMICS

Marvel Timely, July, 1942

1 B:Ziggy Pig,Silly Seal 750.00
2 Toughy Tomcat(c) 325.00
3 Toughy Tomcat/Bunny(c) 250.00
4 Toughy Tomcat/Ziggy(c) 250.00
5 Ziggy/Buzz Saw(c) 250.00
6 Toughy/Cannon(c) 250.00
7 Cigar Store Indian(c) 250.00
8 Toughy/Hammock(c) 250.00
9 Hitler(c) 275.00
10 Newspaper(c) 225.00
11 Canoe(c) 225.00
12 Circus(c) 300.00
13 Pirate Treasure(c). 200.00
14 Fishing(c) 200.00
15 Ski-Jump(c). 175.00
16 Airplane(c). 125.00
17 Street corner(c). 125.00
18 Mallet/Bell(c). 125.00
19 Bicycle(c) 125.00
20 Ziggy(c) 125.00
21 Toughy's date(c) 125.00
22 Crystal Ball(c) 125.00
23 Sharks in bathtub(c) 150.00
24 Baseball(c) 125.00
25 HK,Krazy Krow(c) 150.00
26 Super Rabbit(c). 125.00
Becomes:

CINDY COMICS

Marvel, 1947

27 HK,B:Margie,Oscar. 250.00
28 HK,Snow sled(c). 150.00
29 . . . . 150.00
30 . . . . 150.00
31 HK. 150.00
32 . . . . 100.00
33 A;Georgie 100.00
34 thru 40. . . . . @100.00
Becomes:

Krazy Krow #1
© Marvel Comics Group

Land of the Lost #3
© E.C. Comics

Lars of Mars #10
© Ziff-Davis Publishing Co.

CRIME CAN'T WIN

Marvel, 1950

41 Crime stories. 300.00
42 . . . . 175.00
43 GT,Horror story 250.00
4 thru 11 . . . . @150.00
12 Sept., 1953 . . . . 125.00

KRAZY KOMICS

Marvel Timely
[2nd Series], 1948

1 BW,HK,B:Eustice Hayseed . . . 600.00
2 BW,O:Powerhouse Pepper . . . 400.00

KRAZY KROW

Marvel, Summer, 1945

1 B:Krazy Krow 250.00
2 . . . . 150.00
3 Winter, 1945-46 . . . . 150.00

KRAZY LIFE
See: PHANTOM LADY

LABOR IS A PARTNER

Catechetical Guild
Educational Society, 1949

1 . . . . 250.00

LADY LUCK
See: SMASH

LAFFY-DAFFY COMICS

Rural Home Publ. Co.,
Feb., 1945

1 (fa) 150.00
2 . . . . 150.00

LANA

Marvel, Aug., 1948

1 F:Lana Lane The Show Girl,
A:Rusty,B:Millie 225.00
2 HK,Hey Look,A:Rusty 200.00
3 Show(c),B:Nellie 100.00
4 Ship(c) 100.00
5 Audition(c) 100.00
6 Stop sign(c) 100.00
7 Beach(c) 100.00
Becomes:

LITTLE LANA

Marvel, 1949

8 Little Lana(c) 100.00
9 Final Issue,March, 1950 . . . . . 100.00

LANCE O'CASEY

Fawcett, 1946–47

1 High Seas Adventure
from Whiz comics 400.00
2 thru 4 . . . . @250.00

LAND OF THE LOST

E.C. Comics,
July–Aug., 1946–Spring 1948

1 Radio show adapt. 400.00
2 . . . . 275.00
3 thru 9 . . . . @225.00

LARGE FEATURE COMICS

Dell Publishing Co., 1939

1 Dick Tracy vs. the Blank 2,100.00
2 Terry and the Pirates 1,100.00
3 Heigh-Yo Silver!
the Lone Ranger. 1,700.00
4 Dick Tracy gets his man 1,200.00
5 Tarzan of the Apes 2,000.00
6 Terry and the Pirates 1,200.00
7 Lone Ranger to the rescue. . 1,600.00
8 Dick Tracy, Racket Buster . . 1,200.00
9 King of the Royal Mounted . . . 700.00
10 Gang Busters 800.00
11 Dick Tracy, Mad Doc Hump . 1,200.00
12 Smilin' Jack. 750.00
13 Dick Tracy and Scottie
of Scotland Yard 1,200.00
14 Smilin' Jack helps G-Men 750.00
15 Dick Tracy and
the Kidnapped Princes 1,200.00
16 Donald Duck, 1st Daisy. . . . 9,000.00
17 Gang Busters 600.00
18 Phantasmo The Master
of the World 500.00
19 Walt Disney's Dumbo. 4,000.00
20 Donald Duck 10,000.00
21 Private Buck 150.00
22 Nuts and Jolts 150.00
23 The Nebbs 200.00
24 Popeye in 'Thimble Theatre'. . 900.00
25 Smilin'Jack 700.00
26 Smitty 300.00
27 Terry and the Pirates 750.00
28 Grin and Bear It 100.00
29 Moon Mullins. 300.00
30 Tillie the Toiler 275.00

[Series 2]

1 Peter Rabbit. 500.00
2 Winnie Winkle 250.00
3 Dick Tracy 1,000.00
4 Tiny Tim 300.00
5 Toots and Casper. 150.00
6 Terry and the Pirates 750.00
7 Pluto saves the Ship. 2,000.00
8 Bugs Bunny 2,000.00
9 Bringing Up Father 250.00
10 Popeye 650.00
11 Barney Google&SnuffySmith . 300.00
12 Private Buck 150.00
13 1001 Hours of Fun 200.00

LARRY DOBY, BASEBALL HERO

Fawcett Publications, 1950

1 Ph(c),BW 1,100.00

LARS OF MARS

Ziff-Davis Publishing Co.,
April–May, 1951

10 MA,'Terror from the Sky' . . . 1,100.00
11 GC, The Terror Weapon 900.00

LASH LARUE WESTERN

Fawcett Publications,
Summer, 1949

1 Ph(c),The Fatal Roundups . . 1,500.00
2 Ph(c),Perfect Hide Out 750.00
3 Ph(c),The Suspect. 600.00
4 Ph(c),Death on Stage 600.00
5 Ph(c),Rustler's Haven 600.00
6 Ph(c) 500.00
7 Ph(c),Shadow of the Noose. . . 425.00
8 Ph(c),Double Deadline. 425.00
9 Ph(c),Generals Last Stand . . . 425.00
10 Ph(c) 425.00
11 Ph(c) 350.00
12 thru 20 Ph(c) . . . . @300.00
21 thru 29 Ph(c) . . . . @250.00
30 thru 46 Ph(c). . . . . @225.00
46 Ph(c),Lost Chance 225.00

LASSIE

Dell Publishing Co.,
Oct.–Dec., 1950

1 Ph(c) all 250.00

Lassie
© Dell Publishing Co.

Laugh Comics #47
© Archie Publications

Laurel and Hardy #3
© St. John Publishing Co.

2 . . . . 150.00
3 . . . . 125.00
4 . . . . 125.00
5 . . . . 125.00
6 . . . . 125.00
7 . . . . 125.00
8 . . . . 125.00
9 . . . . 125.00
10 . . . . 125.00
11 . . . . 100.00
12 Rocky Langford. 100.00
13 . . . . 100.00
14 . . . . 100.00
15 I:Timbu 100.00
16 . . . . 100.00
17 . . . . 100.00
18 . . . . 100.00
19 . . . . 100.00
20 MB. 125.00
21 MB. 125.00
22 MB. 125.00
23 thru 38. . . . . @100.00
39 I:Timmy 100.00
40 thru 62. . . . . @100.00
63 E:Timmy 100.00
64 thru 70. . . . . @100.00

LATEST COMICS

Spotlight Publ./ Palace Promotions, March, 1945

1 Funny Animal-Super Duper . . . 250.00
2 . . . . 200.00

SPECIAL COMICS

MLJ Magazines, Winter, 1941

1 O:Boy Buddies & Hangman, D:The Comet 4,000.00

Becomes:

HANGMAN COMICS

Spring, 1942

2 B:Hangman & Boy Buddies . 2,700.00
3 V:Nazis (c),Bondage(c) 1,800.00
4 V:Nazis (c) 1,500.00
5 Bondage (c) 1,500.00
6 . . . . 1,500.00
7 BF,Graveyard (c) 1,500.00
8 BF 1,500.00

Becomes:

BLACK HOOD

Winter, 1943–44

9 BF, Hang Man. 1,500.00
10 BF,A:Dusty, the Boy Detective 800.00
11 Here lies the Black Hood 600.00
12 . . . . 500.00
13 EK(c). 500.00
14 EK(c). 500.00
15 EK. 500.00
16 EK(c). 500.00
17 Bondage (c) 650.00
18 . . . . 500.00
19 I.D. Revealed 700.00

Becomes:

LAUGH COMICS

Archie Comics, Fall, 1946

20 BWo,B:Archie,Katy Keene . . . 850.00
21 BWo 400.00
22 BWo 400.00
23 Bwo. 400.00
24 BWo,JK,Pipsy 425.00
25 BWo 400.00
26 BWo 225.00
27 BWo 225.00
28 BWo 225.00
29 BWo 225.00
30 BWo 225.00
31 thru 40 BWo . . . . @200.00
41 thru 50 BWo . . . . @175.00
51 thru 60 BWo . . . . @150.00
61 thru 80 BWo . . . . @150.00
81 thru 99 BWo . . . . @150.00
100 BWo 150.00
101 thru 126 BWo . . . . @125.00
127 A:Jaguar 150.00
128 A:The Fly. 150.00
129 A:The Fly. 150.00
130 A:Jaguar 150.00
131 A:Jaguar 150.00
132 A:The Fly. 150.00
133 A:Jaguar 150.00
134 A:The Fly. 150.00
135 A:Jaguar 150.00
136 A:Fly Girl 150.00
137 A:Fly Girl 150.00
138 A:The Fly. 150.00
139 A:The Fly. 150.00
140 A:Jaguar 150.00
141 A:Jaguar 150.00
142 . . . . 150.00
143 . . . . 150.00
144. . . . . 150.00

LAUGH COMIX

See: TOP-NOTCH COMICS

LAUREL AND HARDY

St. John Publishing Co., March, 1949

1 . . . . 900.00
2 . . . . 500.00
3 . . . . 350.00
26 Rep #1 . . . . 200.00
27 Rep #2 . . . . 200.00
28 Rep #3 . . . . 200.00

LAWBREAKERS

Law & Order Magazines (Charlton), March, 1951

1 . . . . 500.00
2 . . . . 250.00
3 . . . . 200.00
4 Drug. 300.00
5 . . . . 200.00
6 LM(c) 225.00
7 Drug. 300.00
8 . . . . 200.00
9 StC(c). 200.00

Becomes:

LAWBREAKERS SUSPENSE STORIES

Jan., 1953

10 StC(c) 500.00
11 LM(c),Negligee(c). 1,300.00
12 LM(c). 275.00
13 DG(c) 275.00
14 DG(c),Sharks 275.00
15 DG(c),Acid in Face(c). 750.00

Becomes:

STRANGE SUSPENSE STORIES

Jan., 1954

16 DG(c) 400.00
17 DG(c) 300.00
18 SD,SD(c). 450.00
19 SD,SD(c),Electric Chair 600.00
20 SD,SD(c) 500.00
21 SD,SD(c). 300.00
22 SD,SD(c). 450.00

Becomes:

THIS IS SUSPENSE

Feb., 1955

23 WW; Comics Code 325.00
24 GE,DG(c) 175.00
25 DG(c) 150.00
26 DG(c) 50.00

Becomes:

La

Lawbreakers Always Lose #2
© Marvel Comics Group

Leading Comics #9
© DC Comics

Leave It To Binky #1
© DC Comics

STRANGE SUSPENSE STORIES

Oct., 1955

27 . . . . 150.00
28 . . . . 125.00
29 . . . . 125.00
30 . . . . 125.00
31 SD 250.00
32 SD 250.00
33 SD 250.00
34 SD 600.00
35 SD 250.00
36 SD 250.00
37 SD 250.00
38 . . . . 125.00
39 SD 200.00
40 SD 225.00
41 SD 200.00
42 . . . . 100.00
43 . . . . 100.00
44 . . . . 100.00
45 . . . . 100.00
46 . . . . 100.00
47 SD 225.00
48 SD 225.00
49 . . . . 100.00
50 SD 225.00
51 SD 225.00
52 SD 225.00
53 SD 225.00
54 thru 60 . . . . @100.00
61 thru 74 . . . . @100.00
75 SD,SD(c), Captain Atom 200.00
77 Oct 1965 . . . . 125.00

LAWBREAKERS ALWAYS LOSE

Marvel Crime Bureau Stories, 1948–49

1 HK; FBI Reward Poster Photo Adam and Eve, HK,Giggles and Grins 500.00
2 FBI V:Fur Theives 250.00
3 . . . . 200.00
4 AyB(c),Vampire 200.00
5 AyB(c) 200.00
6 Anti Wertham Edition 225.00
7 Crime at Midnight 350.00
8 Prison Break 150.00
9 Ph(c),He Prowled at Night . . . 150.00
10 Phc(c),I Met My Murderer. . . . 150.00

LAW-CRIME

Essenkay Publications, April, 1948

1 LbC,LbC-(c);Raymond Hamilton Dies In The Chair 1,000.00
2 LbC,LbC-(c);Strangled Beauty Puzzles Police. 750.00
3 LbC,LbC-(c);Lipstick Slayer Sought; Aug., 1943 . . . . 900.00

LAWMAN

Dell Publishing Co., 1959

1 Ph(c) all 200.00
2 . . . . 100.00
3 ATh. 125.00
4 . . . . 100.00
5 . . . . 100.00
6 . . . . 100.00
7 . . . . 100.00
8 thru 11 . . . . @100.00

LEADING COMICS

DC Comics, Winter, 1941–42

1 O:Seven Soldiers of Victory, B:Crimson Avenger,Green Arrow & Speedy,Shining Knight, A:The Dummy 9,000.00
2 MMe,V:Black Star 4,000.00
3 V:Dr. Doome 3,000.00
4 Seven Steps to Conquest, V:The Sixth Sense 2,500.00
5 The Miracles that Money Couldn't Buy 2,500.00
6 Treasure that Time Forgot . . 2,000.00
7 The Wizard of Wisstark 2,000.00
8 Seven Soldiers Go back through the Centuries. 2,000.00
9 V:Mr. X,Chameleon of Crime 2,000.00
10 King of the Hundred Isles . . 2,000.00
11 The Hard Luck Hat! 1,400.00
12 The Million Dollar Challenge! 1,400.00
13 The Trophies of Crime 1,400.00
14 Bandits from the Book 1,400.00
15 (fa). 300.00
16 thru 22 (fa) . . . . @125.00
23 (fa),I:Peter Porkchops. 250.00
24 thru 30 (fa) . . . . @125.00
31 (fa). 100.00
32 (fa). 100.00
33 (fa). 100.00
34 thru 40 (fa) . . . . @100.00
41 (fa),Feb.–March, 1950 . . . . . . 100.00
Becomes:

LEADING SCREEN COMICS

DC Comics, 1950

42 thru 50 Funny Animal . . . . . @125.00
51 thru 60 . . . . @100.00
61 thru 70 . . . . @100.00
71 thru 77 . . . . @100.00

LEAVE IT TO BINKY

DC Comics, 1948

1ShM, teen-age 400.00
2 ShM 200.00
3 . . . . 135.00
4 . . . . 135.00
5 A:Superman 200.00
6 . . . . 125.00
7 . . . . 125.00
8 . . . . 125.00
9 . . . . 125.00
10 . . . . 125.00
11 thru 13 . . . . @100.00
14 ShM 125.00
15 thru 20 . . . . @90.00
21 thru 27 . . . . @100.00
28 MD 125.00
29 . . . . 100.00
30 . . . . 100.00
31 thru 60 . . . . @100.00

LEGENDS OF DANIEL BOONE, THE

DC Comics, Oct., 1955–Jan., 1957

1 . . . . 750.00
2 . . . . 550.00
3 thru 8 . . . . 450.00

LEROY

Visual Editions (Standard Comics), Nov., 1949

1 FunniestTeenager of them All . 150.00
2 . . . . 125.00
3 thru 6 . . . . @100.00

LET'S PRETEND

D.S. Publishing Company, May–June, 1950

1 From Radio Nursery Tales . . . 200.00
2 . . . . 150.00
3 Nov., 1950 . . . . 150.00

La

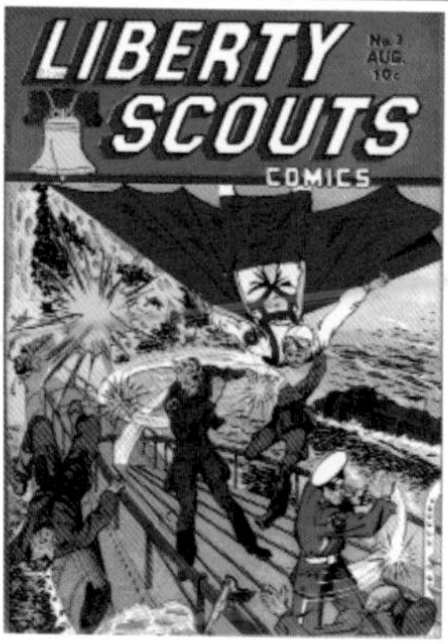

Liberty Scouts #3
© Comic Corp. of America

Life With Archie #1
© Archie Publications

Li'l Abner #68
© Harvey Publications

LET'S TAKE A TRIP
Pines Publ., 1958

1 . . . . 40.00

MISS LIBERTY
Burten Publishing, circa 1944

1 Reprints-Shield,Wizard 550.00

Becomes:

LIBERTY COMICS
Green Publishing, May, 1946

10 Reprints,Hangman 250.00
11 Wilbur in women's clothes . . . 225.00
12 Black Hood, Skull(c) 500.00
14 Patty of Airliner 150.00
15 Patty of Airliner 150.00

LIBERTY GUARDS
Chicago Mail Order (Comic Corp of America), Circa 1942

1 PG(c),Liberty Scouts 500.00

Becomes:

LIBERTY SCOUTS
June, 1941–Aug., 1941

PG(a&c)O:Fireman,Liberty Scouts 1,800.00
3 PG,PG(c),O:Sentinel 1,200.00

LIFE STORY
Fawcett Publications, April, 1949

1 Ph(c) 200.00
2 Ph(c) 150.00
3 Ph(c) 125.00
4 Ph(c) 125.00
5 Ph(c) 125.00
6 Ph(c) 125.00
7 Ph(c) 100.00
8 Ph(c) 100.00
9 Ph(c) 100.00
10 Ph(c) 100.00
11 . . . . . . 100.00
12 . . . . . . 100.00
13 WW, Drug 250.00
14 . . . . . . 100.00
15 . . . . . . 100.00
16 thru 21 . . . . . . @100.00
22 Drug 200.00
23 . . . . . . 100.00
24 . . . . . . 100.00
25 thru 35 . . . . . . @100.00
36 Drug 200.00
37 . . . . . . 100.00
38 . . . . . . 100.00
39 . . . . . . 100.00
40 . . . . . . 100.00
41 . . . . . . 100.00
42 . . . . . . 100.00
43 GE 125.00
44 . . . . . . 100.00
45 1952 . . . . . . 100.00

LIFE WITH ARCHIE
Archie Publications, 1958

1 . . . . . . 400.00
2 . . . . . . 200.00
3 . . . . . . 150.00
4 . . . . . . 150.00
5 . . . . . . 150.00
6 . . . . . . 125.00
7 . . . . . . 125.00
8 . . . . . . 125.00
9 . . . . . . 125.00
10 . . . . . . 125.00
11 thru 20 . . . . . . @100.00

LIFE WITH SNARKY PARKER
Fox Feature Syndicate, Aug., 1950

1 . . . . . . 300.00

SURE-FIRE
Ace Magazines, 1940

1 O:Flash Lightning 2,200.00
2 Whiz Wilson 1,100.00
3 The Raven,Sept., 1940 . . . . . . 800.00
3a Ace McCoy,Oct., 1940 . . . . . . 800.00

Becomes:

LIGHTNING COMICS
Dec., 1940

4 Sure-Fire Stories 1,700.00
5 JM 1,000.00
6 JM,Dr. Nemesis 1,000.00

Vol. 2

1 JM 750.00
2 JM,Flash Lightning 750.00
3 JM 750.00
4 JM 750.00
5 JM 750.00
6 JM, bondage(c) 900.00

Vol. 3

1 I:Lightning Girl 750.00

LINDA
Ajax/Farrell Publications, 1954

1 . . . . . . 200.00
2 Lingerie 150.00
3 . . . . . . 125.00
4 . . . . . . 125.00

LINDA
See: PHANTOM LADY

LI'L ABNER
Harvey Publications, Dec., 1947

61 BP,BW,Sadie Hawkins Day . . . 400.00
62 . . . . . . 250.00
63 . . . . . . 250.00
64 . . . . . . 250.00
65 BP 250.00
66 . . . . . . 200.00
67 . . . . . . 200.00
68 FearlessFosdick V:Any Face . 275.00
69 . . . . . . 275.00
70 . . . . . . 200.00

Toby Press

71 . . . . . . 175.00
72 . . . . . . 175.00
73 . . . . . . 175.00
74 . . . . . . 175.00
75 HK 200.00
76 . . . . . . 175.00
77 HK 200.00
78 HK 200.00
79 HK 200.00
80 . . . . . . 175.00
81 . . . . . . 150.00
82 . . . . . . 150.00
83 Baseball 175.00
84 . . . . . . 150.00
85 . . . . . . 150.00
86 HK 250.00
87 . . . . . . 150.00
88 . . . . . . 150.00
89 . . . . . . 150.00
90 . . . . . . 150.00
91 Rep. #77 . . . . . . 165.00
92 . . . . . . 150.00
93 Rep. #71 . . . . . . 165.00
94 . . . . . . 150.00
95 Fearless Fosdick 175.00
96 . . . . . . 150.00
97 Jan., 1955 . . . . . . 150.00

Little Al of the Secret Service #10
© Ziff Davis

Little Audrey #17
© St. John Publ. Co.

Little Dot #17
© Harvey Publications

LITTLE AL OF THE F.B.I.

Approved Comics (Ziff Davis), 1950

10	200.00
11	150.00

LITTLE AL OF THE SECRET SERVICE

Approved Comics (Ziff Davis), 1951

1	200.00
2	150.00
3	150.00

LITTLE AMBROSE

Archie Publications, 1958

1	150.00

LITTLE ANGEL

Standard Comics, 1954–59

5	125.00
6	100.00
7	100.00
8	100.00
9	100.00
10	100.00
11	100.00
12	100.00
13	100.00
14	100.00
15	100.00
16	100.00

LITTLE ARCHIE

Archie Publications, 1956

1	1,000.00
2	400.00
3	250.00
4	250.00
5	250.00
6 thru 10	@200.00
11 thru 20	@150.00
21 thru 30	@100.00

LITTLE ANNIE ROONEY

St. John Publishing Co./Standard, 1948

1	175.00
2	100.00
3	100.00

LITTLE ASPIRIN

Marvel Comics, 1949

1 HK	200.00
2 HK	125.00
3	100.00

LITTLE AUDREY

St. John Publ. Co./ Harvey Comics, April, 1948

1	550.00
2	300.00
3 thru 6	@175.00
7 thru 10	@150.00
11 thru 20	@125.00
21 thru 24	@100.00
25 B:Harvey Comics	200.00
26 A: Casper	150.00
27 A: Casper	150.00
28 A: Casper	150.00
29 thru 31	@125.00
32 A: Casper	125.00
33 A: Casper	125.00
34 A: Casper	125.00
35 A: Casper	125.00
36 thru 53	@100.00

LITTLE BEAVER

Dell Publishing Co., 1951

3	100.00
4	100.00
5	100.00
6	100.00
7	100.00
8	100.00

LITTLE BIT

Jubilee Publishing Company, March, 1949

1	150.00
2 June, 1949	125.00

LITTLE DOT

Harvey Publications, Sept., 1953

1 I: Richie Rich & Little Lotta	2,200.00
2	900.00
3	550.00
4	450.00
5 O:Dots on Little Dot's Dress	550.00
6 1st Richie Rich(c)	450.00
7	300.00
8	275.00
9	275.00
10	275.00
11 thru 20	@175.00
21 thru 30	@150.00
31 thru 39	@125.00
40 thru 50	@100.00
51 thru 60	@100.00
61 thru 70	@100.00
71 thru 80	@100.00
81 thru 100	@100.00
101 thru 130	@75.00
131 thru 140	@75.00
141 thru 145, 52 pages	@75.00
146 thru 163	@50.00

LITTLE EVA

St. John Publishing Co., May, 1952

1	200.00
2	150.00
3	125.00
4	125.00
5 thru 10	@100.00
11 thru 30	@100.00
31 Nov., 1956	100.00

LI'L GENIUS

Charlton Comics, 1955

1	125.00
2	100.00
3 thru 15	@100.00
16 Giants	125.00
17 Giants	125.00
18 Giants,100 pages	150.00
19 thru 40	@75.00
41 thru 54	@75.00
55 1965	75.00

LI'L GHOST

St. John Publishing/ Fago Magazine Co.

1	150.00
2a	100.00
3	100.00

LITTLE GIANT COMICS

Centaur Publications, July, 1938

1 PG, B&W with Color(c)	900.00
2 B&W with Color(c)	750.00
3 B&W with Color(c)	750.00
4 B&W with Color(c)	750.00

All comics prices listed are for *Near Mint* condition.

Little Iodine #13
© Dell Publishing Co.

Little Lotta #1
© Harvey Publications

Little Orphan Annie #1
© Dell Publishing Co.

LITTLE GIANT DETECTIVE FUNNIES

Centaur Publications, Oct., 1938–Jan., 1939

1 B&W 1,000.00
2 B&W 750.00
3 B&W 750.00
4 WE 750.00

LITTLE GIANT MOVIE FUNNIES

Centaur Publications, Aug., 1938

1 Ed Wheelan-a 1,000.00
2 Ed Wheelan-a, Oct., 1938 750.00

LITTLE GROUCHO

Reston Publ., Co. 1955

1 125.00
2 100.00

LITTLE IKE

St. John Publishing Co., April, 1953

1 125.00
2 100.00
3 100.00
4 Oct., 1953 100.00

LITTLE IODINE

Dell Publishing Co., April, 1949

1 175.00
2 125.00
3 125.00
4 125.00
5 125.00
6 thru 10 @100.00
11 thru 30 @100.00
31 thru 50 @100.00
51 thru 56 @100.00

LITTLE JACK FROST

Avon Periodicals, 1951

1 100.00

LI'L JINX

Archie Publications, 1956

11 150.00
12 125.00
13 125.00
14 125.00
15 125.00
16 125.00

LITTLE JOE

St. John Publishing Co., 1953

1 100.00

LITTLE LANA

See: LANA

LITTLE LENNY

Marvel Classic Detective, 1949

1 125.00
2 100.00
3 100.00

LITTLE LIZZIE

Marvel, June, 1949

1 Roller Skating(c) 150.00
2 Soda(c) 100.00
3 Movies(c) 100.00
4 Lizzie(c) 100.00
5 Lizzie/Swing(c) April,1950 100.00

Marvel, [2nd Series] Sept., 1953

1 100.00
2 75.00
3 Jan., 1954 75.00

LITTLE LOTTA

Harvey Publications, 1955

1 B:Richie Rich and Little Lotta 550.00
2 250.00
3 200.00
4 150.00
5 150.00
6 125.00
7 125.00
8 125.00
9 125.00
10 125.00
11 thru 20 @100.00
21 thru 40 @100.00
41 thru 60 @100.00
61 thru 80 @75.00
81 thru 99 @75.00
100 thru 103 52 pgs @75.00

LITTLE LULU

See: MARGE'S LITTLE LULU

LI'L MENACE

Fago Magazine Co., 1958

1 125.00
2 100.00

LITTLE MAX COMICS

Harvey Publications, Oct., 1949

1 I: Little Dot,Joe Palooka(c) 300.00
2 A: Little Dot,Joe Palooka(c) 250.00
3 A: Little Dot,Joe Palooka(c) 200.00
4 150.00
5 C: Little Dot 150.00
6 thru 10 @100.00
11 thru 22 @100.00
23 A: Little Dot 100.00
24 thru 37 @100.00
38 Rep. #20 100.00
39 thru 72 @100.00
73 A: Richie Rich; Nov.'61 100.00

LITTLE MISS MUFFET

Best Books (Standard Comics), Dec., 1948

11 Strip Reprints 150.00
12 Strip Reprints 125.00
13 Strip Reprints; Mar.'49 125.00

LITTLE MISS SUNBEAM COMICS

Magazine Enterprises, June–July, 1950

1 175.00
2 100.00
3 100.00
4 Dec.–Jan., 1951 100.00

LITTLE ORPHAN ANNIE

Dell Publishing Co., 1948

1 250.00
2 Orphan Annie and the Rescue 150.00
3 150.00

See also: *Four Color*

Li

The Living Bible #3
© Living Bible Corp.

Lone Ranger #28
© Dell Publishing Co.

The Lone Ranger's Companion Tonto
#7 © Dell Publishing Co.

Li

LI'L PAN

Fox Features Syndicate, Dec.–Jan., 1946-47

6 . . . . . 150.00
7 . . . . . 125.00
8 April–May, 1947 . . . . . 125.00

LITTLE ROQUEFORT

St. John Publishing Co., June,1952

1 . . . . . 125.00
2 . . . . . 100.00
3 thru 9 . . . . . @100.00

Pines

10 Summer 1958 . . . . . 100.00

LITTLE SCOUTS

Dell Publishing Co., March, 1951

(1) *see Dell Four Color #321*
2 . . . . . 125.00
3 . . . . . 100.00
4 . . . . . 100.00
5 . . . . . 100.00
6 . . . . . 100.00

LITTLEST SNOWMAN

Dell Publishing Co., Dec., 1956

1 . . . . . 100.00

LIVING BIBLE, THE

Living Bible Corp. Autumn, 1945

1 LbC-(c) Life of Paul 500.00
2 LbC-(c) Joseph &His Brethern. 400.00
3 LbC-(c) Chaplains At War 475.00

LOIS LANE
See: SUPERMAN'S GIRL FRIEND LOIS LANE

LONE EAGLE

Ajax/Farrell, April–May, 1954

1 . . . . . 200.00
2 . . . . . 150.00
3 Bondage(c) 250.00
4 Oct.–Nov., 1954 . . . . . 150.00

LONELY HEART

Excellent Publications (Ajax/Farrell), 1955

9 . . . . . 150.00
10 . . . . . 100.00
11 . . . . . 100.00
12 . . . . . 100.00
13 . . . . . 100.00
14 . . . . . 100.00

Becomes:

DEAR HEART

Ajax/Farrell Publ., 1956

15 . . . . . 100.00
16 . . . . . 100.00

LONE RANGER

Dell Publishing Co., Jan.–Feb., 1948

1 B:Lone Ranger & Tonto
B:Strip Reprint 1,400.00
2 . . . . . 600.00
3 . . . . . 400.00
4 . . . . . 400.00
5 . . . . . 400.00
6 . . . . . 350.00
7 . . . . . 350.00
8 O:Retold 400.00
9 . . . . . 350.00
10 . . . . . 350.00
11 B:Young Hawk 250.00
12 thru 20 . . . . . @250.00
21 . . . . . 200.00
22 . . . . . 200.00
23 O:Retold 275.00
24 thru 30 . . . . . @200.00
31 (1st Mask Logo) 250.00
32 thru 36 . . . . . @175.00
37 (E:Strip reprints) 150.00
38 thru 50 . . . . . @150.00
51 thru 75 . . . . . @150.00
76 thru 99 . . . . . @125.00
100 . . . . . 150.00
101 thru 111 . . . . . @150.00
112 B:Clayton Moore Ph(c) 350.00
113 thru 117 . . . . . @200.00
118 O:Lone Ranger & Tonto
retold, Anniv. issue 400.00
119 thru 144 . . . . . @200.00
145 final issue,May/July, 1962. . . 200.00

THE LONE RANGER'S COMPANION TONTO

Dell Publishing Co., Jan., 1951

(1) *see Dell Four Color #312*
2 P(c) all 200.00
3 . . . . . 150.00
4 . . . . . 125.00
5 . . . . . 125.00
6 thru 10 . . . . . @125.00
11 thru 20 . . . . . @100.00
21 thru 25 . . . . . @100.00
26 thru 33 . . . . . @100.00

THE LONE RANGER'S FAMOUS HORSE HI-YO SILVER

Dell Publishing Co., Jan., 1952

(1) *see Dell Four Color #369*
(1) *see Dell Four Color #392*
3 P(c) all 125.00
4 . . . . . 125.00
5 . . . . . 125.00
6 thru 10 . . . . . @125.00
11 thru 36 . . . . . @100.00

LONE RIDER

Farrell (Superior Comics), April, 1951

1 . . . . . 350.00
2 I&O: Golden Arrow; 52 pgs. . . 200.00
3 . . . . . 175.00
4 . . . . . 175.00
5 . . . . . 175.00
6 E: Golden Arrow 175.00
7 G.Arrow Becomes Swift Arrow 175.00
8 O: Swift Arrow 200.00
9 thru 14 . . . . . @100.00
15 O: Golden Arrow Rep. #2 . . . . 125.00
16 thru 19 . . . . . @100.00
20 . . . . . 100.00
21 3-D (c) 250.00
22 . . . . . 100.00
23 A: Apache Kid 100.00
24 . . . . . 100.00
25 . . . . . 100.00
26 July, 1955 . . . . . 100.00

LONG BOW

Real Adventures Publ. (Fiction House), Winter, 1950

1 . . . . . 200.00

 All comics prices listed are for *Near Mint* condition.

Looney Tunes and Merrie Melodies #24 © Warner Bros.

Looney Tunes #169 © Warner Bros.

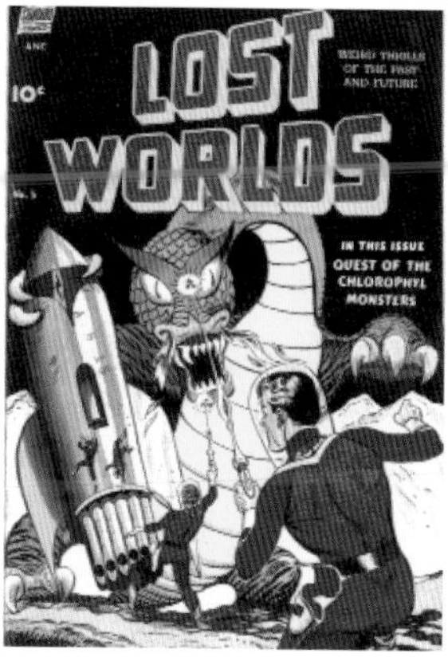

Lost Worlds #5 © Standard Comics

2 . . . . 125.00
3 'Red Arrows Means War' 125.00
4 'Trial of Tomahawk' 125.00
5 . . . . 125.00
6 'Rattlesnake Raiders' 100.00
7 . . . . 100.00
8 . . . . 100.00
9 Spring, 1953 . . . . 100.00

LONG JOHN SILVER AND THE PIRATES

See: TERRY AND THE PIRATES

LOONEY TUNES AND MERRIE MELODIES

Dell Publishing Co., 1941

1 B:&1st Comic App. Bugs Bunny Daffy Duck,Elmer Fudd . . 20,000.00
2 Bugs/Porky(c) 4,000.00
3 Bugs/Porky(c) B:WK, Kandi the Cave 3,000.00
4 Bugs/Porky(c),WK 3,000.00
5 Bugs/Porky(c),WK, A:Super Rabbit 2,500.00
6 Bugs/Porky/Elmer(c),E:WK, Kandi the Cave 2,200.00
7 Bugs/Porky(c) 1,500.00
8 Bugs/Porky swimming(c),F:WK, Kandi the Cave 2,000.00
9 Porky/Elmer car painted(c) . . 1,500.00
10 Porky/Bugs/Elmer Parade(c) 1,500.00
11 Bugs/Porky(c),F:WK, Kandi the Cave 1,500.00
12 Bugs/Porky rollerskating(c) . 1,100.00
13 Bugs/Porky(c) 1,100.00
14 Bugs/Porky(c) 1,100.00
15 Bugs/Porky X-Mas(c),F:WK Kandi the Cave 1,000.00
16 Bugs/Porky ice-skating(c) . . 1,000.00
17 Bugs/Petunia Valentines(c) . 1,000.00
18 Sgt.Bugs Marine(c) 1,000.00
19 Bugs/Painting(c) 1,000.00
20 Bugs/Porky/ElmerWarBonds(c), B:WK,Pat,Patsy&Pete 1,000.00
21 Bugs/Porky 4th July(c) 1,000.00
22 Porky(c) 1,000.00
23 Bugs/Porky Fishing(c) 1,000.00
24 Bugs/Porky Football(c) 1,000.00
25 Bugs/Porky/Petunia Halloween (c),E:WK,Pat, Patsy & Pete 1,000.00
26 Bugs Thanksgiving(c) 750.00
27 Bugs/Porky New Years(c) 750.00
28 Bugs/Porky Ice-Skating(c) . . . 750.00
29 Bugs Valentine(c) 750.00
30 Bugs(c) 750.00
31 Bugs(c) 600.00
32 Bugs/Porky Hot Dogs(c) 600.00
33 Bugs/Porky War Bonds(c) . . . 750.00
34 Bugs/Porky Fishing(c) 500.00
35 Bugs/Porky Swimming(c) 500.00
36 Bugs/Porky(c) 500.00
37 Bugs Halloween(c) 500.00
38 Bugs Thanksgiving(c) 500.00
39 Bugs X-Mas(c) 500.00
40 Bugs(c) 500.00
41 Bugs Washington's Birthday(c) 400.00
42 Bugs Magician(c) 400.00
43 Bugs Dream(c) 400.00
44 Bugs/Porky(c) 400.00
45 Bugs War Bonds(c) 400.00
46 Bugs/Porky(c) 400.00
47 Bugs Beach(c) 350.00
48 Bugs/Porky Picnic(c) 350.00
49 Bugs(c) 350.00
50 Bugs(c) 350.00
51 thru 60 . . . . @300.00
61 thru 80 . . . . @250.00
81 thru 86 . . . . @150.00
87 Bugs X-Mas(c) 175.00
88 thru 99 . . . . @150.00
100 . . . . 150.00
101 thru 110 . . . . @150.00
111 thru 125 . . . . @150.00
126 thru 150 . . . . @150.00
151 thru 165 . . . . @100.00

Becomes:

LOONEY TUNES

Aug., 1955

166 thru 200 . . . . @100.00
201 thru 245 . . . . @100.00
246 final issue,Sept.1962 . . . . . . 100.00

LORNA, THE JUNGLE GIRL

Marvel Atlas, 1953–57

1 Terrors of the Jungle,O:Lorna . 450.00
2 Headhunter's Strike I:Greg Knight 225.00
3 . . . . 200.00
4 . . . . 200.00
5 . . . . 200.00
6 RH(c),GT 150.00
7 RH(c) 150.00
8 Jungle Queen Strikes Again . . 150.00
9 . . . . 150.00
10 White Fang 150.00
11 Death From the Skies 150.00
12 Day of Doom 125.00
13 thru 17 . . . . @125.00
18 AW(c) 150.00
19 thru 26 . . . . @100.00

LOST WORLDS

Literary Enterprises (Standard Comics), Oct., 1952

5 ATh, Alice in Terrorland 600.00
6 ATh 450.00

LOVE ADVENTURES

Marvel Atlas, Oct., 1949

1 Ph(c) 250.00
2 BP,Ph(c),Tyrone Power/ Gene Tierney 225.00
3 thru 12 . . . . @150.00

Becomes:

ACTUAL CONFESSIONS

Marvel, 1952

13 . . . . 100.00
14 Dec., 1952 . . . . 100.00

LOVE AND MARRIAGE

Superior Comics Ltd., March, 1952

1 . . . . 150.00
2 . . . . 125.00
3 . . . . 100.00
4 . . . . 100.00
5 . . . . 100.00
6 . . . . 100.00
7 thru 15 . . . . @100.00
16 Sept., 1954 . . . . 100.00

LOVE AT FIRST SIGHT

Periodical House (Ace Magazines), Oct., 1949

1 P(c) 200.00
2 P(c) 150.00
3 . . . . 125.00
4 P(c) 125.00
5 thru 10 . . . . @125.00
11 thru 33 . . . . @125.00
34 1st Edition Under Code 100.00
35 thru 41 . . . . @100.00
42 1956 . . . . 100.00

Love Confessions #8
© Quality Comics Group

Love Lessions #1
© Harvey Publications

Love Letters #1
© Quality Comics Group

LOVE CLASSICS

Marvel Classic Detective, 1949

1 . . . . 160.00
2 . . . . 150.00

LOVE CONFESSIONS

Comics Magazine (Quality Comics Group), Oct., 1949

1 PG,BWa(c)& Some-a 400.00
2 PG,BWa(c) 300.00
3 . . . . 150.00
4 RC 175.00
5 BWa 200.00
6 Ph(c) 125.00
7 Ph(c) Van Johnson 125.00
8 BWa,Robert Mitchum 125.00
9 Ph(c)Jane Russell/Robert Mitchum 125.00
10 BWa 200.00
11 thru 18 Ph(c) . . . . @150.00
19 . . . . 150.00
20 BWa 175.00
21 . . . . 100.00
22 BWa 150.00
23 thru 28 . . . . @100.00
29 BWa 150.00
30 thru 38 . . . . @100.00
39 MB 150.00
40 thru 42 . . . . @100.00
43 1st Edition Under Code 100.00
44 . . . . 100.00
45 BWa(a) 150.00
46 . . . . 100.00
47 BWa(c) 150.00
48 . . . . 100.00
49 MB 150.00
50 thru 54 Dec., 1956 . . . . . . @100.00

LOVE DIARY

Our Publishing Co./Toytown, July, 1949–Oct., 1955

1 BK,Ph(c) 250.00
2 BK,Ph(c) 200.00
3 BK,Ph(c) 200.00
4 thru 9 Ph(c) . . . . @150.00
10 BEv, Ph(c) 150.00
11 thru 24 Ph(c) . . . . @125.00
25 . . . . 100.00
26 . . . . 100.00
27 Ph(c) 125.00
28 . . . . 100.00
29 Ph(c) 100.00
30 . . . . 100.00
31 JB(c) 100.00
32 thru 41 . . . . @100.00
42 MB(c) 100.00
43 thru 47 . . . . @100.00
48 1st Edition Under Code 100.00

LOVE DIARY

Quality Comics Group, Sept., 1949

1 BWa(c) 400.00

LOVE DIARY

Charlton Comics, 1958

1 . . . . 150.00
2 . . . . 125.00
3 . . . . 100.00
4 . . . . 100.00
5 . . . . 100.00
6 . . . . 100.00
7 . . . . 100.00
8 . . . . 100.00
9 . . . . 100.00
10 . . . . 100.00
11 thru 15 . . . . @100.00
16 thru 20 . . . . @100.00
21 thru 40 . . . . @75.00

LOVE DRAMAS

Marvel, Oct., 1949

1 Ph(c),JKa 200.00
2 Jan., 1950 . . . . 150.00

LOVE JOURNAL

Our Publishing Co., 1951–54

10 . . . . 150.00
11 . . . . 125.00
12 . . . . 125.00
13 . . . . 125.00
14 . . . . 125.00
15 . . . . 125.00
16 . . . . 125.00
17 . . . . 125.00
18 . . . . 125.00
19 . . . . 125.00
20 . . . . 125.00
21 thru 25 . . . . @125.00

LOVELAND

Marvel, 1949

1 Ph(c) 150.00
2 Ph(c) 150.00

LOVE LESSONS

Harvey Publications, Oct., 1949

1 Silver(c) 350.00
2 BP 250.00
3 Ph(c) 200.00
4 . . . . 200.00
5 June, 1950 . . . . 200.00

LOVE LETTERS

Comic Magazines (Quality Comics Group), Nov., 1949

1 PG,BWa(c) 350.00
2 PG,BWa(c) 300.00
3 PG,Ph(c) 250.00
4 BWa,Ph(c) 300.00
5 Ph(c) 150.00
6 Ph(c) 150.00
7 Ph(c) 150.00
8 Ph(c) 150.00
9 Ph(c) of Robert Mitchum 175.00
10 Ph(c) 150.00
11 BWa,Ph(c) Broadway Romances 200.00
12 Ph(c) 125.00
13 Ph(c) 125.00
14 Ph(c) 125.00
15 Ph(c) 125.00
16 Ph(c) of Anthony Quinn 200.00
17 BWa, Ph(c) of Jane Russell . . 200.00
18 thru 28 Ph(c) . . . . @125.00
29 . . . . 125.00
30 & 31 BWa . . . . @200.00

Becomes:

LOVE SECRETS

Aug., 1953

32 . . . . 200.00
33 . . . . 125.00
34 BWa 200.00
35 thru 39 . . . . @150.00
40 MB(c)1st Edition Under Code 125.00
41 thru 48 . . . . @100.00
49 MB 150.00
50 MB 150.00
51 MB(c) 150.00
52 thru 56 . . . . @100.00

LOVELORN

Best Syndicated/Michel Publ. (American Comics Group), Aug.–Sept., 1949

1 . . . . 200.00

All comics prices listed are for *Near Mint* condition.

Love Secrets #35
© Quality Comics Group

Love Mystery #2
© Fawcett Publications

Lovers' Lane #2
© Lev Gleason Publications

2	150.00
3 thru 10	@135.00
11 thru 17	@125.00
18 2pgs. MD-a	125.00
19	125.00
20	125.00
21 Prostitution Story	200.00
22 thru 50	@125.00
51 July, 1954, 3-D	250.00

Becomes:

CONFESSIONS OF THE LOVELORN

Aug., 1954

52 3-D	350.00
53	100.00
54 3-D	350.00
55	150.00
56 Communist Story	150.00
57 Comics Code	125.00
58 thru 90	@125.00
91 AW	150.00
92 thru 105	@100.00
106 P(c)	100.00
107 P(c)	100.00
108 thru 114	@100.00

LOVE MEMORIES

Fawcett Publications, Autumn, 1949

1 Ph(c)	175.00
2 Ph(c)	125.00
3 Ph(c)	125.00
4 Ph(c)	125.00

LOVE MYSTERY

Fawcett Publications, June, 1950

1 GE, Ph(c)	250.00
2 GE, Ph(c)	200.00
3 GE & BP, Ph(c); Oct., 1950	200.00

LOVE PROBLEMS AND ADVICE ILLUSTRATED

McCombs/Harvey Publications Home Comics, June, 1949

1 BP	250.00
2 BP	200.00
3	150.00
4	150.00
5 LEI(c)	125.00
6	125.00
7 BP	125.00
8 BP	125.00
9 BP	125.00
10 BP	125.00
11 BP	100.00
12 BP	100.00
13 BP	100.00
14 BP	100.00
15	100.00
16	100.00
17 thru 23 BP	@100.00
24 BP, Rape Scene	150.00
25 BP	100.00
26	100.00
27	100.00
28 BP	100.00
29 BP	100.00
30	100.00
31	100.00
32 Comics Code	100.00
33 BP	100.00
34	100.00
35	100.00
36	100.00
37	100.00
38 S&K (c)	100.00
39	100.00
40 BP	100.00
41 BP	100.00
42	100.00
43	100.00
44 March, 1957	100.00

LOVE ROMANCES

See: IDEAL

LOVERS

See: ALL-SELECT COMICS

LOVE SCANDALS

Comic Magazines (Quality Comics Group), Feb., 1950

1 BW(a&c)	300.00
2 PG-a, Ph(c)	125.00
3 PG-a, Ph(c)	125.00
4 BWa(a&c) 18Pgs.; GFx-a	250.00
5 Ph(c), Oct., 1950	125.00

LOVE SECRETS

Marvel, Oct., 1949

1	175.00
2 Jan., 1950	125.00

LOVE SECRETS

See: LOVE LETTERS

LOVERS LANE

Lev Gleason Publications, Oct., 1949

1 CBi (c),FGu-a	250.00
2 P(c)	150.00
3 P(c)	125.00
4 P(c)	125.00
5 P(c)	125.00
6 GT,P(c),	125.00
7 P(c),	125.00
8 P(c),	125.00
9 P(c),	125.00
10 P(c)	125.00
11 thru 19 P(c)	@100.00
20 Ph(c); FF 1 page Ad,	125.00
21 Ph(c)	100.00
22 Ph(c)	100.00
23	100.00
24	100.00
25	100.00
26 Ph(c)	100.00
27 Ph(c)	100.00
28 Ph(c)	100.00
29 thru 38	@100.00
39 Story Narrated by Frank Sinatra	150.00
40	100.00
41 June, 1954	100.00

LOVE STORIES OF MARY WORTH

Harvey Publications, Sept., 1949

1 Newspaper Reprints	150.00
2 Newspaper Reprints	125.00
3 Newspaper Reprints	100.00
4 Newspaper Reprints,	100.00
5 May, 1950	100.00

LOVE TALES

Marvel Atlas, 1949–56

(Formerly: The Human Torch)

36 Ph(c)	250.00
37	175.00
38	150.00
39 thru 41	@150.00
42 thru 44	@125.00
45 BP	150.00

Lucky Comics #5
© Consolidated Magazines

Meet Miss Pepper #6
© St. John Publishing Co.

Mad Magazine #45
© E.C. Comics

46 thru 51 . . . . @125.00
52 BK 150.00
53 thru 68 . . . . @125.00
69 BEv 150.00
70 thru 75 . . . . @100.00

LOVE TRAILS
Marvel Current Detective, 1949
1 western romance 175.00
2 . . . . 175.00

Lo

LUCKY COMICS
Consolidated Magazines, Jan., 1944–Summer 1946
1 Lucky Star 300.00
2 HcK(c) 200.00
3 . . . . 200.00
4 . . . . 200.00
5 Devil(c) 200.00

LUCKY DUCK
Standard Comics (Literary Enterprises), Jan.–Sept., 1953
5 IS(a&c) 125.00
6 IS(a&c) 100.00
7 IS(a&c). 100.00
8 IS(a&c) 100.00

LUCKY FIGHTS IT THROUGH
Educational Comics, 1949
N# HK-a, V.D. Prevention 1,500.00

LUCKY "7" COMICS
Howard Publications, 1944
1 Bondage(c) Pioneer 700.00

LUCKY STAR
Nationwide Publications, 1950
1 JDa,B:52 pages western 225.00
2 JDa 150.00
3 JDa 150.00
4 JDa 125.00
5 JDa 125.00
6 JDa 125.00
7 JDa 125.00
8 thru 13 . . . . @100.00
14 1955,E:52 pages western. . . . 100.00

LUCY, THE REAL GONE GAL
St. John Publishing Co., June, 1953
1 Negligee Panels,Teenage 300.00
2 . . . . 150.00
3 MD-a 125.00
4 Feb., 1954 . . . . 100.00
Becomes:

MEET MISS PEPPER
April, 1954
5 JKu-a 225.00
6 JKu (a&c), June,1954 . . . . 175.00

MAD
E.C. Comics, Oct.–Nov., 1952
1 JSe,HK(c),JDa,WW 15,000.00
2 JSe,JDa(c),JDa,WW. 4,500.00
3 JSe,HK(c),JDa,WW 2,700.00
4 JSe,HK(c),JDa-Flob Was
A Slob,JDa,WW 2,500.00
5 JSe,BE(c).JDa,WW 3,000.00
6 JSe,HK(c),Jda,WW. 1,500.00
7 HK(c),JDa,WW 1,500.00
8 HK(c),JDa,WW 1,500.00
9 JSe,HK(c),JDa,WW 1,500.00
10 JSe,HK(c),JDa,WW 1,600.00
11 BW,BW(c),JDa,WW,Life(c). . 1,500.00
12 BK,JDa,WW. 1,400.00
13 HK(c),JDa,WW,Red(c). 1,400.00
14 RH,HK(c),JDa,WW,
Mona Lisa(c). 1,400.00
15 JDa,WW,Alice in
Wonderland(c) 1,400.00
16 HK(c),JDa,WW,
Newspaper(c) 1,400.00
17 BK,BW,JDa,WW 1,400.00
18 HK(c),JDa,WW. 1,400.00
19 JDa,WW,Racing Form(c) . . . 1,000.00
20 JDa,WW,Composition(c) . . . 1,200.00
21 JDa,WW,1st A.E.Neuman(c) 1,500.00
22 BE,JDa,WW,Picasso(c) 1,500.00
23 Last Comic Format Edition,
JDa,WW Think(c) 1,000.00
24 BK,WW, HK Logo & Border;
1st Magazine Format 1,800.00
25 WW,AlJaffee Becomes Reg. 1,000.00
26 BK,WW,WW(c) 500.00
27 WWa,RH,JDa(c) 400.00
28 WW,BE(c),RH Back(c) 400.00
29 JKa,BW,WW,WW(c);
1st Don Martin Artwork 400.00
30 BE,WW,RC; 1st A.E.
Neuman(c) By Mingo 600.00
31 JDa,WW,BW,Mingo(c) 350.00
32 MD,JO 1st as reg.;Mingo(c);
WW-Back(c) 350.00
33 WWa,Mingo(c);JO-Back(c) . . . 350.00
34 WWa,Mingo(c);1st Berg
as Reg. 250.00
35 WW,RC,Mingo
Wraparound(c). 225.00
36 WW,BW,Mingo(c),JO,MD 200.00
37 WW,Mingo(c)JO,MD 200.00
38 WW,JO,MD 200.00
39 WW,JO,MD 200.00
40 WW,BW,JO,MD 200.00
41 WW,JO,MD 150.00
42 WW,JO,MD 150.00
43 WW,JO,MD 150.00
44 WW,JO,MD 150.00
45 WW,JO,MD 150.00
46 JO,MD. 150.00
47 JO,MD. 150.00
48 JO,MD. 150.00
49 JO,MD. 150.00
50 JO,MD. 150.00
51 JO,MD. 125.00
52 JO,MD. 125.00
53 JO,MD. 125.00
54 JO,MD. 125.00
55 JO,MD. 125.00
56 JO,MD. 125.00
57 JO,MD. 125.00
58 JO,MD. 125.00
59 WW,JO,MD 150.00
60 JO,MD. 150.00

MAD HATTER, THE
O.W. Comics, 1946
1 Freddy the Firefly 1,200.00
2 V:Humpty Dumpty 600.00

MADHOUSE
Ajax/Farrell Publ., 1954
1 . . . . 375.00
2 . . . . 200.00
3 . . . . 200.00
4 . . . . 300.00

Second Series, 1957
1 . . . . 150.00
2 . . . . 125.00
3 . . . . 125.00

 All comics prices listed are for *Near Mint* condition.

Magic Comics #1
© *David McKay Publications*

Magic Comics #54
© *David McKay Publications*

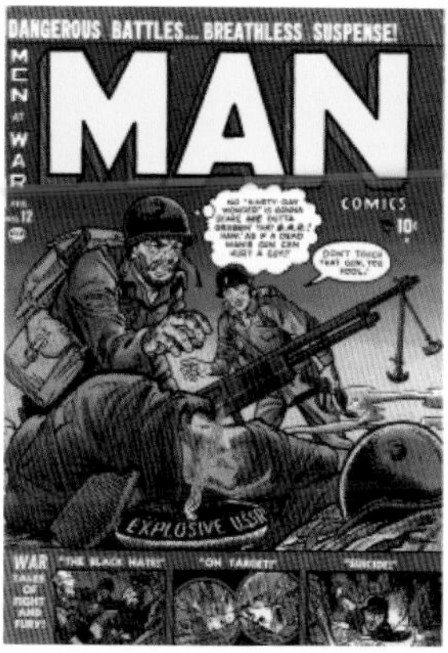

Man Comics #12
© *Marvel Comics Group*

MAGIC COMICS

David McKay Publications, Aug.,1939–Nov.-Dec., 1949

1 Mandrake the Magician, Henry, Popeye,Blondie, Barney Baxter, Secret Agent X-9, Bunky, Henry on(c) 3,800.00
2 Henry on(c). 1,400.00
3 Henry on(c) 1,000.00
4 Henry on(c),Mandrake-Logo . . 850.00
5 Henry on(c),Mandrake-Logo . . 750.00
6 Henry on(c),Mandrake-Logo . . 525.00
7 Henry on(c),Mandrake-Logo . . 525.00
8 B:Inspector Wade,Tippie 500.00
9 Henry-Mandrake Interact(c) . . 500.00
10 Henry-Mandrake Interact(c) . . 500.00
11 Henry-Mandrake Interact(c) . . 425.00
12 Mandrake on(c). 425.00
13 Mandrake on(c). 425.00
14 Mandrake on(c). 425.00
15 Mandrake on(c). 425.00
16 Mandrake on(c). 425.00
17 B:Lone Ranger 500.00
18 Mandrake/Robot on(c) 400.00
19 Mandrake on(c). 500.00
20 Mandrake on(c) 400.00
21 Mandrake on(c). 300.00
22 Mandrake on(c). 300.00
23 Mandrake on(c). 300.00
24 Mandrake on(c). 300.00
25 B:Blondie; Mandrake in Logo for Duration. 300.00
26 Blondie (c). 275.00
27 Blondie(c); HighSchoolHeroes 275.00
28 Blondie(c); HighSchoolHeroes 275.00
29 Blondie(c); HighSchoolHeroes 275.00
30 Blondie (c) 275.00
31 Blondie(c);High School Sports Page. 225.00
32 Blondie (c);Secret Agent X-9 . 225.00
33 C.Knight's-Romance of Flying 225.00
34 ClaytonKnight's-War in the Air 225.00
35 Blondie (c). 225.00
36 July'42; Patriotic-(c) 225.00
37 Blondie (c). 225.00
38 ClaytonKnight's-Flying Tigers . 225.00
39 Blondie (c). 225.00
40 Jimmie Doolittle bombs Tokyo 225.00
41 How German Became British Censor 200.00
42 Joe Musial's-Dollar-a-Dither . . 200.00
43 Clay Knight's-War in the Air . . 200.00
44 Flying Fortress in Action 200.00
45 Clayton Knight's-Gremlins . . . 200.00
46 Adventures of Aladdin Jr. 200.00
47 Secret Agent X-9. . . . . 200.00
48 General Arnold U.S.A.F. 200.00
49 Joe Musial's-Dollar-a-Dither . . 200.00
50 The Lone Ranger 200.00
51 Joe Musial's-Dollar-a-Dither . 150.00
52 C. Knights-Heroes on Wings . 150.00
53 C. Knights-Heroes on Wings . 150.00
54 High School Heroes 150.00
55 Blondie (c). 175.00
56 High School Heroes 150.00
57 Joe Musial's-Dollar-a-Dither . . 150.00
58 Private Breger Abroad 150.00
59 . . . . 150.00
60 . . . . 150.00
61 Joe Musial's-Dollar-a-Dither . . 125.00
62 . . . . 125.00
63 B:Buz Sawyer, Naval Pilot . . . 125.00
64 thru 70. . . . . @125.00
71 thru 80 . . . . @125.00
81 thru 90 . . . . @100.00
91 thru 99 . . . . @100.00
100 . . . . 125.00
101 thru 108. . . . . @100.00
108 Flash Gordon 125.00
109 Flash Gordon 125.00
110 thru 113 . . . . @125.00
114 The Lone Ranger 125.00
115 thru 119 . . . . @125.00
120 Secret Agent X-9 . . . . 150.00
121 Secret Agent X-9. . . . . 150.00
122 Secret Agent X-9. . . . . 150.00
123 Sec. Agent X-9 . . . . 150.00

MAJOR HOOPLE COMICS

Nedor Publications, 1942

1 Mary Worth,Phantom Soldier; Buy War Bonds On(c) 500.00

MAJOR INAPAK THE SPACE ACE

Magazine Enterprises, 1951

1 BP,Sci-Fi 200.00

MAJOR VICTORY COMICS

H. Clay Glover Svcs./ Harry A. Chestler, 1944

1 O:Major Victory,I:Spider Woman 850.00
2 A: Dynamic Boy 500.00
3 A: Rocket Boy 450.00

MAMMOTH COMICS

K.K. Publications, 1938

1 Alley Oop, Dick Tracy, etc. . . 3,000.00

MAN COMICS

Marvel Atlas, 1949–53

1 GT 350.00
2 GT 250.00
3 . . . . 200.00
4 . . . . 200.00
5 . . . . 200.00
6 . . . . 200.00
7 JeR 200.00
8 BEv 200.00
9 EC,TSe,War format begins . . . 150.00
10 JeR,MMe(c) 150.00
11 RH,TSe,MMe 150.00
12 . . . . 150.00
13 . . . . 150.00
14 GT,JeR 175.00
15 . . . . 150.00
16 . . . . 150.00
17 RH 175.00
18 . . . . 150.00
19 . . . . 150.00
20 . . . . 150.00
21 EC-RH. 175.00
22 BEv(c),BK 175.00
23 GT,JSt. 175.00
24 . . . . 150.00
25 BEv(c). 175.00
26 . . . . 150.00
27 . . . . 150.00
28 Where Mummies Prowl. 150.00

MANHUNT!

Magazine Enterprises, 1953

1 LbC,FGu,OW(c);B:Red Fox, Undercover Girl, Space Ace . 650.00
2 LbC,FGu,OW(c); Electrocution(c) 500.00
3 LbC,FGu,OW,OW(c) 400.00
4 LbC,FGu,OW,OW(c) 400.00
5 LbC,FGu,OW,OW(c) 400.00
6 LbC,OW,OW(c) 375.00
7 LbC,OW; E:Space Ace 350.00
8 LbC,OW,FGu(c);B:Trail Colt . . 350.00
9 LbC,OW 350.00
10 LbC,OW,OW(c),GwI 350.00
11 LbC,FF,OW;B:The Duke, Scotland Yard 500.00
12 LbC,OW 300.00
13 See: *A-1 Comics* #63
14 See: *A-1 Comics* #77

Man in Black #1
© Harvey Publications

March of Comics #25
© K. K. Publications

March of Comics #66
© K. K. Publications

MAN IN BLACK

Harvey Publications, 1957

1 BP . . . 200.00
2 BP . . . 150.00
3 BP . . . 150.00
4 BP, March, 1958 . . . 150.00

MAN OF WAR

Comic Corp. of America (Centaur Publ.), Nov., 1941

1 PG,PG(c);Flag(c);B:The Fire-Man,Man of War,The Sentinel, Liberty Guards,Vapoman . . 3,000.00
2 PG,PG(c);I: The Ferret . . . 2,500.00

MAN O'MARS

Fiction House/ I.W. Enterprises, 1953

1 MA, Space Rangers . . . 550.00
1 MA, Rep. Space Rangers . . . 100.00

MARCH OF COMICS

K.K. Publications/ Western Publ., 1946 (All were Giveaways)

N# WK back(c),Goldilocks . . . 325.00
N# WK,How Santa got His Red Suit . . . 325.00
N# WK,Our Gang . . . 450.00
N# CB,Donald Duck; 'Maharajah Donald' . . . 8,500.00
5 Andy Panda . . . 200.00
6 WK,Fairy Tales . . . 250.00
7 Oswald the Lucky Rabbit . . . 200.00
8 Mickey Mouse . . . 600.00
9 Gloomey Bunny . . . 125.00
10 Santa Claus . . . 125.00
11 Santa Claus. . . . 100.00
12 Santa's Toys . . . 100.00
13 Santa's Suprise . . . 100.00
14 Santa's Kitchen . . . 100.00
15 Hip-It-Ty Hop . . . 100.00
16 Woody Woodpecker . . . 150.00
17 Roy Rogers . . . 275.00
18 Fairy Tales . . . 125.00
19 Uncle Wiggily . . . 100.00
20 CB,Donald Duck . . . 5,000.00
21 Tom and Jerry . . . 125.00
22 Andy Panda . . . 100.00
23 Raggedy Ann and Andy . . . 150.00
24 Felix the Cat; By Otto Messmer . . . 250.00
25 Gene Autrey . . . 250.00
26 Our Gang . . . 275.00
27 Mickey Mouse . . . 450.00
28 Gene Autry . . . 250.00
29 Easter . . . 60.00
30 Santa . . . 50.00
31 Santa . . . 50.00
32 Does Not Exist
33 A Christmas Carol . . . 50.00
34 Woody Woodpecker . . . 125.00
35 Roy Rogers . . . 275.00
36 Felix the Cat . . . 225.00
37 Popeye . . . 150.00
38 Oswald the Lucky Rabbit . . . 90.00
39 Gene Autry . . . 250.00
40 Andy and Woody . . . 90.00
41 CB,DonaldDuck,SouthSeas. 4,500.00
42 Porky Pig . . . 100.00
43 Henry . . . 100.00
44 Bugs Bunny . . . 100.00
45 Mickey Mouse . . . 350.00
46 Tom and Jerry . . . 100.00
47 Roy Rogers . . . 250.00
48 Santa . . . 100.00
49 Santa . . . 100.00
50 Santa . . . 100.00
51 Felix the Cat . . . 175.00
52 Popeye . . . 150.00
53 Oswald the Lucky Rabbit . . . 100.00
54 Gene Autrey . . . 250.00
55 Andy and Woody . . . 100.00
56 CB back(c),Donald Duck . . . 350.00
57 Porky Pig . . . 100.00
58 Henry . . . 100.00
59 Bugs Bunny . . . 125.00
60 Mickey Mouse . . . 300.00
61 Tom and Jerry . . . 100.00
62 Roy Rogers . . . 250.00
63 Santa . . . 100.00
64 Santa . . . 100.00
65 Jingle Bells . . . 100.00
66 Popeye . . . 125.00
67 Oswald the Lucky Rabbit . . . 100.00
68 Roy Rogers . . . 225.00
69 Donald Duck . . . 300.00
70 Tom and Jerry . . . 100.00
71 Porky Pig . . . 100.00
72 Krazy Kat . . . 100.00
73 Roy Rogers . . . 200.00
74 Mickey Mouse . . . 300.00
75 Bugs Bunny . . . 100.00
76 Andy and Woody . . . 100.00
77 Roy Rogers . . . 175.00
78 Gene Autrey; last regular sized issue . . . 175.00
79 Andy Panda,5"x7" format . . . 100.00
80 Popeye . . . 100.00
81 Oswald the Lucky Rabbit . . . 75.00
82 Tarzan . . . 200.00
83 Bugs Bunny . . . 100.00
84 Henry . . . 100.00
85 Woody Woodpecker . . . 100.00
86 Roy Rogers . . . 150.00
87 Krazy Kat . . . 100.00
88 Tom and Jerry . . . 100.00
89 Porky Pig . . . 100.00
90 Gene Autrey . . . 125.00
91 Roy Rogers and Santa . . . 150.00
92 Christmas w/Santa . . . 75.00
93 Woody Woodpecker . . . 75.00
94 Indian Chief . . . 100.00
95 Oswald the Lucky Rabbit . . . 75.00
96 Popeye . . . 125.00
97 Bugs Bunny . . . 100.00
98 Tarzan,Lex Barker Ph(c) . . . 200.00
99 Porky Pig . . . 75.00
100 Roy Rogers . . . 125.00
101 Henry . . . 75.00
102 Tom Corbet,P(c) . . . 150.00
103 Tom and Jerry . . . 75.00
104 Gene Autrey . . . 100.00
105 Roy Rogers . . . 125.00
106 Santa's Helpers . . . 75.00
107 *Not Published*
108 Fun with Santa . . . 75.00
109 Woody Woodpecker . . . 75.00
110 Indian Chief . . . 75.00
111 Oswald the Lucky Rabbit . . . 75.00
112 Henry . . . 75.00
113 Porky Pig . . . 75.00
114 Tarzan,RsM . . . 175.00
115 Bugs Bunny . . . 75.00
116 Roy Rogers . . . 125.00
117 Popeye . . . 100.00
118 Flash Gordon, P(c) . . . 150.00
119 Tom and Jerry . . . 75.00
120 Gene Autrey . . . 100.00
121 Roy Rogers . . . 125.00
122 Santa's Suprise . . . 75.00
123 Santa's Christmas Book . . . 75.00
124 Woody Woodpecker . . . 75.00
125 Tarzan, Lex Barker Ph(c) . . . 175.00
126 Oswald the Lucky Rabbit . . . 75.00
127 Indian Chief . . . 100.00
128 Tom and Jerry . . . 75.00
129 Henry . . . 75.00
130 Porky Pig . . . 75.00
131 Roy Rogers . . . 125.00
132 Bugs Bunny . . . 75.00
133 Flash Gordon,Ph(c) . . . 125.00
134 Popeye . . . 100.00
135 Gene Autrey . . . 100.00
136 Roy Rogers . . . 100.00

 All comics prices listed are for *Near Mint* condition.

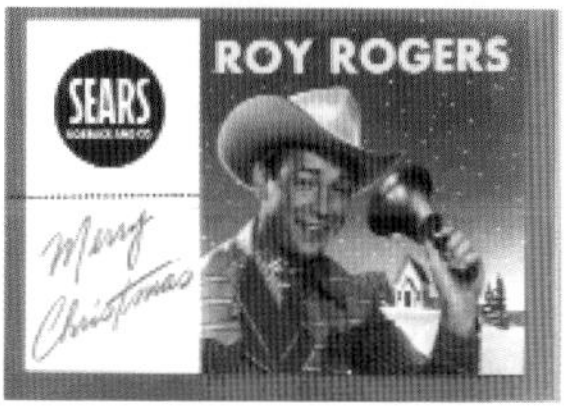

March of Comics #98 & #151
© Edgar Rice Burroughs. & Roy Rogers

March of Comics #205
© K. K. Publications

Marge's Little Lulu #28
© Dell Publishing Co.

137 Gifts from Santa . . . 50.00
138 Fun at Christmas . . . 50.00
139 Woody Woodpecker . . . 50.00
140 Indian Chief . . . 75.00
141 Oswald the Lucky Rabbit . . . 50.00
142 Flash Gordon . . . 100.00
143 Porky Pig . . . 50.00
144 RsM,Ph(c),Tarzan . . . 150.00
145 Tom and Jerry . . . 50.00
146 Roy Rogers,Ph(c) . . . 125.00
147 Henry . . . 50.00
148 Popeye . . . 100.00
149 Bugs Bunny . . . 50.00
150 Gene Autrey . . . 100.00
151 Roy Rogers . . . 100.00
152 The Night Before Christmas . . 50.00
153 Merry Christmas . . . 50.00
154 Tom and Jerry . . . 50.00
155 Tarzan,Ph(c) . . . 150.00
156 Oswald the Lucky Rabbit . . . 50.00
157 Popeye . . . 100.00
158 Woody Woodpecker . . . 50.00
159 Indian Chief . . . 100.00
160 Bugs Bunny . . . 50.00
161 Roy Rogers . . . 100.00
162 Henry . . . 50.00
163 Rin Tin Tin . . . 125.00
164 Porky Pig . . . 50.00
165 The Lone Ranger . . . 100.00
166 Santa & His Reindeer . . . 50.00
167 Roy Rogers and Santa . . . 100.00
168 Santa Claus' Workshop . . . 50.00
169 Popeye . . . 100.00
170 Indian Chief . . . 100.00
171 Oswald the Lucky Rabbit . . . 50.00
172 Tarzan . . . 175.00
173 Tom and Jerry . . . 50.00
174 The Lone Ranger . . . 125.00
175 Porky Pig . . . 50.00
176 Roy Rogers . . . 125.00
177 Woody Woodpecker . . . 50.00
178 Henry . . . 50.00
179 Bugs Bunny . . . 50.00
180 Rin Tin Tin . . . 100.00
181 Happy Holiday . . . 50.00
182 Happi Tim . . . 50.00
183 Welcome Santa . . . 50.00
184 Woody Woodpecker . . . 50.00
185 Tarzan, Ph(c) . . . 150.00
186 Oswald the Lucky Rabbit . . . 50.00
187 Indian Chief . . . 100.00
188 Bugs Bunny . . . 50.00
189 Henry . . . 50.00
190 Tom and Jerry . . . 50.00
191 Roy Rogers . . . 100.00
192 Porky Pig . . . 50.00
193 The Lone Ranger . . . 125.00
194 Popeye . . . 100.00
195 Rin Tin Tin . . . 150.00
196 *Not Published*
197 Santa is Coming . . . 50.00
198 Santa's Helper . . . 50.00
199 Huckleberry Hound . . . 150.00
200 Fury . . . 100.00
201 Bugs Bunny . . . 75.00
202 Space Explorer . . . 100.00
203 Woody Woodpecker . . . 50.00
204 Tarzan . . . 125.00
205 Mighty Mouse . . . 100.00
206 Roy Rogers,Ph(c) . . . 100.00
207 Tom and Jerry . . . 50.00
208 The Lone Ranger,Ph(c) . . . 150.00
209 Porky Pig . . . 50.00
210 Lassie . . . 100.00
211 *Not Published*
212 Christmas Eve . . . 50.00
213 Here Comes Santa . . . 50.00
214 Huckleberry Hound . . . 125.00
215 Hi Yo Silver . . . 125.00
216 Rocky & His Friends . . . 125.00
217 Lassie . . . 100.00
218 Porky Pig . . . 50.00
219 Journey to the Sun . . . 100.00
220 Bugs Bunny . . . 50.00
221 Roy and Dale,Ph(c) . . . 150.00
222 Woody Woodpecker . . . 50.00
223 Tarzan . . . 125.00
224 Tom and Jerry . . . 50.00
225 The Lone Ranger . . . 100.00
226 Christmas Treasury . . . 50.00
227 *Not Published*
228 Letters to Santa . . . 50.00
229 The Flintstones . . . 150.00
230 Lassie . . . 100.00
231 Bugs Bunny . . . 50.00
232 The Three Stooges . . . 275.00
233 Bullwinkle . . . 150.00
234 Smokey the Bear . . . 50.00
235 Huckleberry Hound . . . 100.00
236 Roy and Dale . . . 125.00
237 Mighty Mouse . . . 50.00
238 The Lone Ranger . . . 100.00
239 Woody Woodpecker . . . 50.00
240 Tarzan . . . 125.00
241 Santa Around the World . . . 50.00
242 Santa Toyland . . . 50.00
243 The Flintstones . . . 150.00
244 Mr.Ed,Ph(c) . . . 75.00
245 Bugs Bunny . . . 50.00
246 Popeye . . . 75.00
247 Mighty Mouse . . . 75.00
248 The Three Stooges . . . 250.00
249 Woody Woodpecker . . . 50.00
250 Roy and Dale . . . 125.00

MARCH OF CRIME
See: MY LOVE AFFAIR

MARGE'S LITTLE LULU
Dell Publishing Co., 1948

1 B:Lulu's Diary . . . 1,000.00
2 I:Gloria,Miss Feeny . . . 500.00
3 . . . 450.00
4 . . . 450.00
5 . . . 450.00
6 . . . 350.00
7 I:Annie,X-Mas (c) . . . 350.00
8 . . . 350.00
9 . . . 350.00
10 . . . 350.00
11 thru 18 . . . @300.00
19 I:Wilbur . . . 300.00
20 I:Mr.McNabbem . . . 300.00
21 thru 25 . . . @250.00
26 rep.Four Color#110 . . . 250.00
27 thru 29 . . . @250.00
30 Christmas (c) . . . 250.00
31 thru 34 . . . @225.00
35 B:Mumday Story . . . 225.00
36 thru 38 . . . @225.00
39 I:Witch Hazel . . . 250.00
40 Halloween (c) . . . 175.00
41 . . . 175.00
42 Christmas (c) . . . 175.00
43 Skiing (c) . . . 175.00
44 Valentines Day (c) . . . 175.00
45 2nd A:Witch Hazel . . . 175.00
46 thru 60 . . . @175.00
61 . . . 150.00
62 . . . 150.00
63 I:Chubby . . . 150.00
64 thru 67 . . . @150.00
68 I:Professor Cleff . . . 150.00
69 thru 77 . . . @150.00
78 Christmas (c) . . . 150.00
79 . . . 150.00
80 . . . 150.00
81 thru 89 . . . @125.00
90 Christmas (c) . . . 125.00
91 thru 99 . . . @125.00
100 . . . 150.00
101 thru 122 . . . @125.00
123 I:Fifi . . . 110.00
124 thru 164 . . . @100.00
165 giant sized . . . 200.00
166 giant sized . . . 200.00

Marmaduke Mouse #1
© Quality Comics Group

Marvel Mystery Comics #2
© Marvel Comics Group

Marvel Mystery Comics #33
© Marvel Comics Group

MARGE'S TUBBY

Dell Publishing Co., 1953

1 . . . . 350.00
2 . . . . 200.00
3 & 4 . . . . @175.00
5 thru 10 . . . . @135.00
11 thru 20 . . . . @125.00
21 thru 49 . . . . @100.00

MARGIE COMICS
See: COMEDY COMICS

MARINES AT WAR
See: DEVIL-DOG DUGAN

MARINES IN ACTION

Marvel Atlas, June, 1955

1 B:Rock Murdock,Boot Camp Brady 125.00
2 thru 13 . . . . @100.00
14 Sept., 1957 . . . . 100.00

MARINES IN BATTLE

Marvel Atlas, Aug., 1954

1 RH,B:Iron Mike McGraw 250.00
2 . . . . 150.00
3 thru 6 . . . . @125.00
7 thru 17 . . . . @125.00
18 thru 22 . . . . @100.00
23 . . . . 125.00
24 . . . . 100.00
25 Sept., 1958 . . . . 125.00

MARK TRAIL

Standard Magazines/ Fawcett/Pines, 1955

1 . . . . 125.00
5 . . . . 100.00
A1 . . . . 150.00

MARMADUKE MOUSE

Quality Comics Group (Arnold Publications), 1946

1 Funny Animal 250.00
2 Funny Animal 200.00
3 thru 8 Funny Animal . . . . . . @150.00
9 Funny Animal 100.00
10 Funny Animal 100.00
11 thru 20 Funny Animal . . . . . @100.00
21 thru 30 Funny Animal . . . . . . @75.00
31 thru 40 Funny Animal . . . . . . @75.00
41 thru 50 Funny Animal . . . . . . @75.00
51 thru 65 Funny Animal . . . . . . @75.00

MARTIN KANE

Hero Books (Fox Features Syndicate), June, 1950

1 WW,WW-(c) 350.00
2 WW,JO, Auguat, 1950 . . . . . . 250.00

MARVEL BOY
See: ASTONISHING

MARVEL COMICS

Marvel, Oct.-Nov., 1939

1 FP(c),BEv,CBu,O:Sub-Mariner I&B:The Angel,A:Human Torch, Ka-Zar,Jungle Terror, B:The Masked Raider . . 400,000.00

Becomes:

MARVEL MYSTERY COMICS

2 CSM(c),BEv,CBu,PGv, B:American, Ace,Human Torch,Sub-Mariner,Ka-Zar 50,000.00
3 ASh(c),BEv,CBu,PGv, E:American Ace 27,000.00
4 ASh(c),BEv,CBu,PGv, I&B:Electro,The Ferret, Mystery Detective 25,000.00
5 ASh(c),BEv,CBu,PGv, Human Torch(c) 45,000.00
6 ASh(c),BEv,CBu,PGv, Anglel(c) 15,000.00
7 ASh(c),BEv,CBu,PGv, Bondage(c) 15,000.00
8 ASh(c),BEv,CBu,PGv,Human TorchV:Sub-Mariner 18,000.00
9 ASh(c),BEv,CBu,PGv,Human Torch V:Sub-Mariner(c) . . 45,000.00
10 ASh(c),BEv,CBu,PGv,B:Terry Vance Boy Detective 16,000.00
11 ASh(c),BEv,CBu,PGv, Human Torch V:Nazis(c). . . 6,500.00
12 ASh(c),BEv,CBu, PGv,Angel(c) 7,000.00
13 ASh(c),BEv,CBu,PGv,S&K, I&B:The Vision 9,000.00
14 ASh(c),BEv,CBu,PGv,S&K, Sub-Mariner V:Nazis 4,800.00
15 ASh(c),BEv,CBu,PGv,S&K, Sub-Mariner(c) 4,800.00
16 ASh(c),BEv,CBu,PGv,S&K, HumanTorch/NaziAirbase. . 4,800.00
17 ASh(c),BEv,CBu,PGv,S&K Human Torch/Sub-Mariner 5,000.00
18 ASh(c),BEv,CBu,PGv,S&K, Human Torch & Toro(c) . . . 4,500.00
19 ASh(c),BEv,CBu,PGv,S&K, O:Toro,E:Electro 4,500.00
20 ASh(c),BEv,CBu,PGv,S&K, O:The Angel 4,500.00
21 ASh(c),BEv,CBu,PGv,S&K, I&B:The Patriot 4,500.00
22 ASh(c),BEv,CBu,PGv,S&K, AAv,Toro/Bomb(c). 4,000.00
23 ASh(c),BEv,CBu,PGv,S&K, O:Vision,E:The Angel 4,000.00
24 ASh(c),BEv,CBu,S&K, AAv,Human Torch(c). 4,000.00
25 BEv,CBu,S&K,ASh Nazi(c) . 4,000.00
26 ASh(c),BEv,CBu,S&K, Sub-Mariner(c) 3,500.00
27 ASh(c),BEv,CBu, S&K,E:Ka-Zar. 3,500.00
28 ASh(c),BEv,CBu,S&K,Bondage (c),B:Jimmy Jupiter 3,500.00
29 ASh(c),BEv,CBu,SSh, Bondage(c). 3,500.00
30 BEv,CBu,SSh,Pearl Harbor(c) 3,500.00
31 BEv,CBu,Human Torch(c) . . 4,200.00
32 CBu,I:The Boboes 3,500.00
33 ASh(c),CBu,SSh,Jap(c) 3,000.00
34 ASh(c),CBu,SSh,V:Hitler . . . 3,500.00
35 ASh(c),SSh,BeachAssault(c) 3,000.00
36 ASh(c),Nazi Invasion of NY . 3,000.00
37 SSh(c),Nazi(c) 3,000.00
38 SSh(c),Battlefield(c). 3,000.00
39 ASh(c),Nazis/U.S(c). 3,000.00
40 ASh(c),SSh,Zeppelin(c) . . . 3,000.00
41 ASh(c),Jap. Command(c) . . 2,700.00
42 ASh(c),Japanese Sub(c) . . . 2,700.00
43 ASh(c),SSh,Destroyed Bridge(c). 2,700.00
44 ASh(c),Nazi Super Plane(c). 2,700.00
45 ASh(c),SSh,Nazi(c) 2,700.00
46 ASh(c),Hitler Bondage(c). . . 2,700.00
47 ASh(c),Ruhr Valley Dam(c) . 2,700.00
48 ASh(c),E:Jimmy Jupiter, Vision,Allied Invasion(c) . . . 2,700.00
49 SSh(c),O:Miss America, Bondage(c) 3,000.00
50 ASh(c),Bondage(c),Miss Patriot 2,700.00
51 ASh(c),Nazi Torture(c) 2,500.00
52 ASh(c),Bondage(c). 2,500.00
53 ASh(c),Bondage(c). 2,500.00

All comics prices listed are for *Near Mint* condition.

Marvel Mystery Comics #67
© Marvel Comics Group

Marvel Tales #97
© Marvel Comics Group

The Marvel Family #1
© Fawcett Publications

54 ASh(c),Bondage(c). 2,500.00
55 ASh(c),Bondage(c). 2,500.00
56 ASh(c),Bondage(c). 2,500.00
57 ASh(c),Torture/Bondage(c) . 2,500.00
58 ASh(c),Torture(c) 2,500.00
59 ASh(c),Testing Room(c). . . . 2,500.00
60 ASh(c),Japanese Gun(c) . . 2,500.00
61 ASh(c),Torturer Chamber(c). 2,500.00
62 ASh(c),Violent(c) 2,500.00
63 ASh(c),Nazi High Command(c). 2,500.00
64 ASh(c),Last Nazi(c) 2,500.00
65 ASh(c),Bondage(c). 2,500.00
66 ASh(c),Last Japanese(c) . . . 2,500.00
67 ASh(c),Treasury raid(c) 2,500.00
68 ASh(c),Torture Chamber(c) . 3,600.00
69 ASh(c),Torture Chamber(c) . 2,500.00
70 Cops & Robbers(c) 2,500.00
71 ASh(c),Egyptian(c). 2,500.00
72 Police(c). 2,500.00
73 Werewolf Headlines(c). 2,500.00
74 ASh(c),Robbery(c),E:The Patriot 2,500.00
75 SSh,Tavern(c),B:YoungAllies 2,500.00
76 ASh(c),Shoot-out(c),B:Miss America 2,500.00
77 SSh,Human Torch/Sub-Mariner(c). 2,500.00
78 SSh,Safe Robbery(c). 2,500.00
79 SSh,Super Villians(c),E:The Angel 2,500.00
80 SSh,I:Capt.America (in Marvel) 3,000.00
81 SSh,Mystery o/t Crimson Terror 2,200.00
82 SSh,I:Sub-Mariner/Namora Team-up, O:Namora,A:Capt. America 4,500.00
83 SSh,The Photo Phantom, E;Young Allies. 1,800.00
84 SSh,BEv,B:Blonde Phantom 3,000.00
85 SSh,BEv,A:Blonde Phantom, E;Miss America. 2,000.00
86 BEv,Blonde Phantom ID Revealed,E:Bucky 1,800.00
87 SSh,BEv,I:Capt.America/Golden Girl Team-up. 3,200.00
88 SSh,BEv,E:Toro 1,800.00
89 SSh,BEv,AAv,I:Human Torch/ Sun Girl Team-up 1,800.00
90 BEv,Giant of the Mountains 1,800.00
91 BEv,I:Venus,E:Blonde Phantom,Sub-Mariner 1,800.00
92 BEv,How the Human Torch was Born,D:Professor Horton,I:The Witness,A:Capt.America. . . 5,500.00
92a Marvel #33(c)rare,reps. . . 40,000.00
Becomes:

MARVEL TALES

Marvel, Aug., 1949

93 The Ghoul Strikes 2,000.00
94 BEv,The Haunted Love 1,300.00
95 The Living Death. 900.00
96 MSy,SSh(c),Monster Returns . 900.00
97 DRi,MSy,The Wooden Horror 1,100.00
98 BEv,BK,MSy,The Curse of the Black Cat. 900.00
99 DRi,The Secret of the Wax Museum. 900.00
100 The Eyes of Doom 900.00
101 The Man Who Died Twice . . 900.00
102 BW,A Witch Among Us . . . 1,300.00
103 RA,A Touch of Death 1,000.00
104 RH(c),BW,BEv,The Thing in the Mirror 1,300.00
105 RH(c),GC,JSt,The Spider. . 1,000.00
106 RH(c),BK,BEv,In The Dead of the Night 750.00
107 GC,OW,BK,The Thing in the Sewer 750.00
108 RH(c),BEv,JR,Horror in the Moonlight. 500.00
109 BEv(c),Sight for Sore Eyes. . 500.00
110 RH,SSh,A Coffin for Carlos . 500.00
111 BEv,Horror Under the Earth . 500.00
112 The House That Death Built . 500.00
113 RH,Terror Tale. 500.00
114 BEv(c),GT,JM,2 for Zombie. . 500.00
115 The Man With No Face. 500.00
116 JSt. 500.00
117 BEv(c),GK,Terror in the North. 500.00
118 RH,DBr,GC,A World Goes Mad 500.00
119 RH,They Gave Him A Grave. 500.00
120 GC,Graveyard(c) 500.00
121 GC,Graveyard(c). 400.00
122 JKu,Missing One Body 400.00
123 No Way Out 400.00
124 He Waits at the Tombstone. . 400.00
125 JF,Horror House 400.00
126 DW,It Came From Nowhere . 375.00
127 BEv(c),GC,MD,Gone is the Gargoyle. 375.00
128 Emily,Flying Saucer(c) 375.00
129 You Can't Touch Bottom . . . 375.00
130 RH(c),JF,The Giant Killer . . . 375.00
131 GC,BEv,Five Fingers 375.00
132 . . . . 250.00
133 . . . . 250.00
134 BK,JKu,Flying Saucer(c). . . . 250.00
135 thru 143. . . . . @250.00
144 . . . . 265.00
145 . . . . 250.00
146 . . . . 200.00
147 . . . . 225.00
148 thru 151. . . . . @200.00
152 . . . . 225.00
153 . . . . 250.00
154 thru 158. . . . . @200.00
159 Aug., 1957. . . . . 225.00

MARVEL FAMILY, THE

Fawcett Publications, Dec., 1945–Jan., 1954

1 O:Captain Marvel,Captain Marvel Jr., Mary Marvel,Uncle Marvel; V:Black Adam 2,700.00
2 Uncle Marvel. 1,300.00
3 . . . . 900.00
4 The Witch's Tale 700.00
5 Civilization of a Prehistoric Race 600.00
6 . . . . 550.00
7 The Rock of Eternity 500.00
8 The Marvel Family Round Table 500.00
9 V: The Last Vikings 500.00
10 CCB(c),JaB,BTh,V:Sivana Family 500.00
11 V: The Well of Evil. 450.00
12 V: The Iron Horseman 450.00
13 BTh,CCB,PrC(c) 450.00
14 Captain Marvel Invalid 450.00
15 V: Mr. Triangle. 425.00
16 World's Mightiest Quarrell. . . . 425.00
17 . . . . 425.00
18 . . . . 425.00
19 V: The Monster Menace 425.00
20 The Marvel Family Feud 425.00
21 V: The Trio of Terror 400.00
22 V: The Triple Threat 400.00
23 March of Independence (c). . . 425.00
24 V: The Fighting Xergos. 400.00
25 Trial of the Marvel Family 400.00
26 V: Mr. Power 400.00
27 V: The Amoeba Men. 400.00
28 . . . . 400.00
29 V: The Monarch of Money . . . 400.00
30 A:World's Greatest Magician . 400.00
31 V:Sivana & The Great Hunger 350.00
32 The Marvel Family Goes Into Buisness. 350.00
33 I: The Hermit Family 350.00
34 V: Sivana's Miniature Menace 350.00

The Marvel Family #71
© Fawcett Publications

Mary Marvel Comics #25
© Fawcett Publications

Monte Hale Western #46
© Fawcett Publications

35 V: The Berzerk Machines 350.00
36 V: The Invaders From Infinity . 350.00
37 V: The Earth Changer. 350.00
38 V: Sivana's Instinct Exterminator Gun 350.00
39 The Legend of Atlantis 350.00
40 Seven Wonders of the Modern World 350.00
41 The Great Oxygen Theft. 350.00
42 V: The Endless Menace 300.00
43 . . . . 300.00
44 V: The Rust That Menaced the World. 300.00
45 The Hoax City. 300.00
46 The Day Civilization Vanished 300.00
47 V: The Interplanetary Thieves. 350.00
48 V: The Four Horsemen 300.00
49 ...Proves Human Hardness. . . 300.00
50 The Speech Scrambler Machine. 300.00
51 The Living Statues 325.00
52 The School of Witches 300.00
53 V:Man Who Changed World. . 300.00
54 . . . . 300.00
55 . . . . 300.00
56 The World's Mightiest Project. 300.00
57 . . . . 300.00
58 The Triple Time Plot 300.00
59 . . . . 300.00
60 . . . . 300.00
61 . . . . 300.00
62 . . . . 300.00
63 V: The Pirate Planet 300.00
64 . . . . 300.00
65 . . . . 300.00
66 The Miracle Stone. 300.00
67 . . . . 300.00
68 . . . . 300.00
69 V: The Menace of Old Age . . . 300.00
70 V: The Crusade of Evil 300.00
71 . . . . 300.00
72 . . . . 300.00
73 . . . . 300.00
74 . . . . 300.00
75 The Great Space Struggle . . . 300.00
76 . . . . 325.00
77 Anti-Communist. 400.00
78 V: The Red Vulture 300.00
79 Horror 250.00
80 . . . . 250.00
81 . . . . 250.00
82 . . . . 250.00
83 V: The Flying Skull 250.00
84 thru 87 . . . . @250.00
88 Jokes of Jeopardy. 250.00
89 And Then There Were None. . 250.00

MARVEL MYSTERY COMICS
See: MARVEL COMICS

MARVELS OF SCIENCE
Charlton Comics, 1946

1 1st Charlton Book; Atomic Bomb Story 400.00
2 . . . . 350.00
3 . . . . 350.00
4 President Truman(c); Jun.'6 . . 350.00

MARVEL TALES
See: MARVEL COMICS

MARVIN MOUSE
Marvel Atlas, Sept., 1957

1 BEv,F:Marvin Mouse 125.00

MARY MARVEL COMICS
Fawcett Publications, Dec., 1945

1 Intro: Mary Marvel. 2,700.00
2 . . . . 1,000.00
3 . . . . 750.00
4 On a Leave of Absence 700.00
5 Butterfly (c) Bullet Girl 500.00
6 A:Freckles,Teenager of Mischief 500.00
7 The Kingdom Undersea 500.00
8 Holiday Special Issue 500.00
9 Air Race (c) 450.00
10 A: Freckles 450.00
11 A: The Sad Dryads 300.00
12 Red Cross Appeal on(c) 300.00
13 Keep the Homefires Burning . 300.00
14 Meets Ghosts (c) 300.00
15 A: Freckles 300.00
16 The Jukebox Menace 275.00
17 Aunt Agatha's Adventures. . . . 275.00
18 . . . . 275.00
19 Witch (c) 275.00
20 . . . . 275.00
21 V: Dice Head. 225.00
22 The Silver Slippers 225.00
23 The Pendulum Strikes. 225.00
24 V: The Nightowl. 225.00
25 A: Freckles 225.00
26 A:Freckles dressed as Clown . 225.00
27 The Floating Oceanliner 225.00
28 Western, Sept., 1948 . . . . 225.00

Becomes:
MONTE HALE WESTERN
Fawcett Publications, Oct., 1948

29 Ph(c),B:Monte Hale & His Horse Pardner 650.00
30 Ph(c),B:Big Bow-Little Arrow; CCB,Captain Tootsie . 300.00
31 Ph(c),Giant 250.00
32 Ph(c),Giant 250.00
33 Ph(c),Giant 250.00
34 Ph(c),E:Big Bow-Little Arrow;B:Gabby Hayes,Giant . 250.00
35 Ph(c),Gabby Hayes, Giant . . . 250.00
36 Ph(c),Gabby Hayes, Giant . . . 250.00
37 Ph(c),Gabby Hayes 150.00
38 Ph(c),Gabby Hayes, Giant . . . 200.00
39 Ph(c);CCB, Captain Tootsie; Gabby Hayes, Giant 200.00
40 Ph(c),Gabby Hayes, Giant . . . 200.00
41 Ph(c),Gabby Hayes 150.00
42 Ph(c),Gabby Hayes, Giant . . . 175.00
43 Ph(c),Gabby Hayes, Giant . . . 175.00
44 Ph(c),Gabby Hayes, Giant . . . 175.00
45 Ph(c),Gabby Hayes 150.00
46 Ph(c),Gabby Hayes, Giant . . . 150.00
47 Ph(c),A:Big Bow-Little Arrow; Gabby Hayes, Giant 150.00
48 Ph(c),Gabby Hayes, Giant . . . 150.00
49 Ph(c),Gabby Hayes 150.00
50 Ph(c),Gabby Hayes, Giant . . . 150.00
51 Ph(c),Gabby Hayes, Giant . . . 135.00
52 Ph(c),Gabby Hayes, Giant . . . 135.00
53 Ph(c),A:Slim Pickens; Gabby Hayes. 125.00
54 Ph(c),Gabby Hayes, Giant . . . 135.00
55 Ph(c),Gabby Hayes, Giant . . . 135.00
56 Ph(c),Gabby Hayes, Giant . . . 125.00
57 Ph(c),Gabby Hayes 100.00
58 Ph(c),Gabby Hayes, Giant . . . 125.00
59 Ph(c),Gabby Hayes, Giant . . . 125.00
60 thru 79 Ph(c),Gabby Hayes @100.00
80 Ph(c),E: Gabby Hayes 100.00
81 Ph(c) 100.00
82 Final Ph(c) 125.00

Charlton Comics, Feb., 1955

83 R:G. Hayes Back B&W Ph(c) . 150.00
84 . . . . 100.00
85 . . . . 100.00
86 E: Gabby Hayes 100.00
87 . . . . 100.00
88 Jan., 1956. . . . . 100.00

Mask Comics #1
© Rural Home Publications

Master Comics #23
© Fawcett Publications

Master Comics #46
© Fawcett Publications

MARY WORTH
ARGO, 1956

1 . . . . 100.00

MASK COMICS
Rural Home Publications, Feb.–March, 1945

1 LbC,LbC-(c), Evil (c). 4,000.00
2 LbC-(c),A:Black Rider,The Collector The Boy Magician; Apr-May'45, Devil (c) 2,500.00

MASKED MARVEL
Centaur Publications, Sept., 1940

1 I: The Masked Marvel 2,400.00
2 PG, ... 1,500.00
3 Dec., 1940 . . . . 1,400.00

THE MASKED RAIDER
Charlton Comics, 1955

1 . . . . 150.00
2 . . . . 125.00
3 . . . . 100.00
4 . . . . 100.00
5 . . . . 100.00
6 . . . . 100.00
7 . . . . 100.00
8 Billy the Kid 100.00
9 . . . . 100.00
10 . . . . 100.00
11 thru 14 . . . . @100.00
15 AW 125.00
16 thru 30 . . . . @100.00

MASKED RANGER
Premier Magazines, April, 1954

1 FF,O&B:The Masked Ranger, Streak the Horse,The Crimson Avenger. 500.00
2 . . . . 175.00
3 . . . . 175.00
4 B: Jessie James,Billy the Kid, Wild Bill Hickok, Jim Bowie's Life Story 200.00
5 . . . . 200.00
6 . . . . 200.00
7 . . . . 200.00
8 . . . . 200.00
9 AT,E:All Features; A:Wyatt Earp Aug., 1955. . . . . 225.00

MASTER COMICS
Fawcett Publications, March, 1940

1-6 Oversized,7-Normal Format

1 O:Master Man; B:The Devil's Dagger, El Carin-Master of Magic, Rick O'Say, Morton Murch, White Rajah, Shipwreck Roberts, Frontier Marshall, Mr. Clue, Streak Sloan . . . 16,000.00
2 Master Man (c) 5,000.00
3 Master Man (c) Bondage . . . 4,600.00
4 Master Man (c) 4,500.00
5 Master Man (c) 4,500.00
6 E: All Above Features 4,600.00
7 B:Bulletman,Zorro,The Mystery Man, Lee Granger, Jungle King,Buck Jones 6,000.00
8 B:The Red Gaucho,Captain Venture, Planet Princess . . 3,600.00
9 Bulletman & Steam Roller . . 3,500.00
10 E: Lee Granger 5,500.00
11 O: Minute Man 5,500.00
12 Minute Man (c). 3,500.00
13 O:Bulletgirl; E:Red Gaucho . 4,000.00
14 B: The Companions Three. . 3,200.00
15 MRa, Bulletman & Girl (c) . . 3,200.00
16 MRa, Minute Man (c). 3,200.00
17 B:MRa on Bulletman 3,000.00
18 MRa, ... 3,000.00
19 MRa, Bulletman & Girl (c) . . 3,000.00
20 MRa,C:Cap.Marvel-Bulletman 3,000.00
21 MRa-(c),Capt. Marvel in Bulletman,I&O:Captain Nazi 9,000.00
22 MRa-(c),E:Mystery Man,Captain Venture; Bondage(c);Capt. Marvel Jr. X-Over In Bulletman; A:Capt. Nazi . . . 8,000.00
23 MRa(a&c),B:Capt. Marvel Jr. V:Capt. Nazi 5,000.00
24 MRa(a&c),Death By Radio . 3,000.00
25 MRa(a&c),The Jap Invasion 3,000.00
26 MRa(a&c),Capt. Marvel Jr. Avenges Pearl Harbor 3,000.00
27 MRa(a&c),V For Victory(c). . 3,000.00
28 MRa(a&c)Liberty Bell(c). . . . 3,000.00
29 MRa(a&c),Hitler & Hirohito(c). 3,200.00
30 MRa(a&c),Flag (c);Capt. Marvel Jr, V: Capt. Nazi . . 3,000.00
31 MRa(a&c),E:Companions Three,Capt.Marvel Jr, V:Mad Dr. Macabre 2,000.00
32 MRa(a&c),E: Buck Jones; CMJr Strikes Terror Castle . 2,000.00
33 MRa(a&c),B:Balbo the Boy Magician,Hopalong Cassidy2,000.00
34 MRa(a&c),Capt.Marvel Jr V: Capt.Nazi 2,500.00
35 MRa(a&c),CMJr Defies the Flame 2,000.00
36 MRa(a&c),Statue Of Liberty(c). 2,000.00
37 MRa(a&c),CMJr Blasts the Nazi Raiders. 1,800.00
38 MRa(a&c),CMJr V:the Japs . 1,800.00
39 MRa(a&c),CMJr Blasts Nazi Slave Ship 1,800.00
40 MRa(a&c),Flag (c) 1,800.00
41 MRa(a&c),Bulletman,Bulletgirl, CMJr X-over In Minuteman 1,800.00
42 MRa(a&c),CMJr V: Hitler's Dream Soldier 1,000.00
43 MRa(c),CMJr Battles For Stalingrad 1,000.00
44 MRa(c),CMJr In Crystal City of the Peculiar Penguins . . 1,000.00
45 MRa(c), ... 1,000.00
46 MRa(c) 1,000.00
47 MRa(c),A:Hitler; E: Balbo. . . 1,100.00
48 MRa(c),I:Bulletboy;Capt. Marvel A: in Minuteman . . . 1,200.00
49 MRa(c),E: Hopalong Cassidy, Minuteman 1,000.00
50 I&O: Radar,A:Capt. Marvel, B:Nyoka the Jungle Girl . . 1,000.00
51 MRa(c),CMJr V: Japanese . . . 750.00
52 MRa(c),CMJr & Radar Pitch War Stamps on (c). 750.00
53 CMJR V: Dr. Sivana 750.00
54 MRa(c),Capt.Marvel Jr Your Pin-Up Buddy 750.00
55 . . . . 750.00
56 MRa(c) 700.00
57 CMJr V: Dr. Sivana 700.00
58 MRa(a&c),. 700.00
59 MRa(c),A:The Upside Downies. 750.00
60 MRa(c) 750.00
61 CMJr Meets Uncle Marvel . . . 750.00
62 Uncle Sam on (c) 750.00
63 W/ Radar (c) 700.00
64 W/ Radar (c) 700.00
65 BTh(c),JkS 700.00
66 CMJr & Secret Of the Sphinx . 700.00
67 Knight (c) 700.00
68 CMJr in the Range of the Beasts 700.00
69 . . . . 700.00

Master Comics #77
© Fawcett Publications

Maverick #11
© Dell Publishing Co.

Meet Corliss Archer #3
© Fox Features Syndicate

70 . . . . 700.00
71 CMJr,V:Man in Metal Mask . . . 650.00
72 CMJr V: Sivana & The Whistle That Wouldn't Stop . . . 650.00
73 CMJr V: The Ghost of Evil . . . 650.00
74 CMJr & The Fountain of Age . 650.00
75 CMJr V: The Zombie Master. . 650.00
76 . . . . 650.00
77 BTh(c),BK,Pirate Treasure . . . 650.00
78 CMJr in Death on the Scenic Railway . . . 650.00
79 CMJr V: The Black Shroud . . . 650.00
80 CMJr-The Land of Backwards 650.00
81 CMJr & The Voyage 'Round the Horn. . . 450.00
82 CMJr,IN,Death at the Launching . . . 450.00
83 . . . . 450.00
84 BTh(c&a) CMJr V: The Human Magnet. . . 450.00
85 CMJr-Crime on the Campus . 300.00
86 CMJr & The City of Machines. 300.00
87 CMJr & The Root of Evil. . . . 300.00
88 CMJr V: The Wreckers; B: Hopalong Cassidy. . . 300.00
89 . . . . 300.00
90 CMJr V: The Caveman 300.00
91 CMJr V: The Blockmen. . . . 300.00
92 CMJr V: The Space Slavers . . 300.00
93 BK,CMJr,V:TheGrowingGiant . 300.00
94 E: Hopalong Cassidy 300.00
95 B: Tom Mix; CMJr Meets the Skyhawk . . . 300.00
96 CMJr Meets the World's Mightiest Horse . . . 300.00
97 CMJr Faces the Doubting Thomas . . . 300.00
98 KKK Type . . . 300.00
99 Witch (c) . . . 300.00
100 CMJr V: The Ghost Ship. . . . 350.00
101 thru 105 . . . @250.00
106 E: Bulletman . . . 250.00
107 CMJr Faces the Disappearance of the Statue of Liberty 300.00
108 . . . . 300.00
109 . . . . 300.00
110 CMJr & The Hidden Death . . 300.00
111 thru 122 . . . @300.00
123 CMJr V: The Flying Desperado. . . 300.00
124 . . . . 300.00
125 CMJr & The Bed of Mystery . 300.00
126 thru 131 . . . @300.00
132 V: Migs . . . 300.00
133 E: Tom Mix; April, 1953. . . . 350.00

Ma

MATT SLADE, GUNFIGHTER

Marvel Atlas, May, 1956

1 AW,AT,F:Matt Slade,Crimson Avenger . . . 225.00
2 AW,A:Crimson Avenger 175.00
3 A:Crimson Avenger 150.00
4 A:Crimson Avenger 125.00

Becomes:

KID SLADE GUNFIGHTER

5 F:Kid Slade . . . 125.00
6 . . . . 100.00
7 AW,Duel in the Night . . . 110.00
8 July, 1957 . . . 100.00

MAVERICK

Dell Publishing Co., 1958

1 Ph(c) Garner photos . . . 400.00
2 Ph(c) . . . 200.00
3 Ph(c) . . . 200.00
4 Ph(c) . . . 200.00
5 Ph(c) . . . 200.00
6 thru 14 Ph(c) last Garner. . . @150.00
15 thru 19 Ph(c) R. Moore . . . . @125.00

MAVERICK MARSHALL

Charlton Comics, 1958

1 . . . . 125.00
2 . . . . 100.00
3 . . . . 100.00
4 . . . . 100.00
5 . . . . 100.00
6 . . . . 100.00
7 May, 1960 . . . 100.00

MAZIE

Nationwide Publ./ Magazine Publ./ Harvey Publ., 1951–58

1 . . . . 150.00
2 . . . . 100.00
3 . . . . 100.00
4 . . . . 100.00
5 . . . . 100.00
6 . . . . 100.00
7 . . . . 100.00
8 . . . . 100.00
9 . . . . 100.00
10 . . . . 100.00
11 thru 20 . . . @100.00
21 thru 28 . . . @75.00

MD

E.C. Comics, April, 1955–Jan., 1956

1 RC,GE,Grl,JO,JCr(c). 600.00
2 thru 5 RC,GE,Grl,JO,JCr(c). @500.00

MEDAL OF HONOR COMICS

Stafford Publication, Spring, 1947

1 True Stories of Medal of Honor Recipients . . . 250.00

MEET CORLISS ARCHER

Fox Features Syndicate, March, 1948

1 AF,AF(c), Teenage 1,300.00
2 AF(c) . . . 750.00
3 . . . . 600.00

Becomes:

MY LIFE

Sept., 1948

4 JKa,AF, . . . 500.00
5 JKa, . . . 250.00
6 JKa,AF, . . . 275.00
7 WW,Watercolor & Ink Drawing on(c) . . . 300.00
8 . . . . 150.00
9 . . . . 150.00
10 WW, July, 1950. . . . 300.00

MEET MERTON

Toby Press, Dec., 1953

1 DBe,Teen Stories. . . . 125.00
2 DBe . . . 100.00
3 DBe . . . 100.00
4 DBe; June, 1954 . . . 100.00

MEET MISS BLISS

Marvel Atlas, 1955

1 . . . . 150.00
2 . . . . 100.00
3 . . . . 100.00
4 . . . . 100.00

MEET MISS PEPPER

See: LUCY THE REAL GONE GAL

 All comics prices listed are for *Near Mint* condition.

Menace #2
© Marvel Comics Group

MEET THE NEW POST GAZETTE SUNDAY FUNNIES

Pittsburg Post Gazette, 1949

N# One Shot Insert F: Several Syndicated Characters in Stories Exclusive to This Edition . . 7,000.00

MEL ALLEN SPORTS COMICS

Visual Editions, 1949

1 GT 250.00
2 Lou Gehrig 200.00

MELVIN THE MONSTER

Marvel Atlas, July, 1956

1 JMn 150.00
2 thru 6 . . . . @125.00
Becomes:

DEXTER THE DEMON

Marvel, Sept., 1957

7 . . . . 100.00

MENACE

Marvel Atlas, May, 1953

1 RH,BEv,GT,One Head Too Many 900.00
2 RH,BEv,GT,JSt,Burton'sBlood . 650.00
3 BEv,RH,JR,The Werewolf 450.00
4 BEv,RH,The Four Armed Man . 450.00
5 BEv,RH,GC,GT,I&O:Zombie . . 750.00
6 BEv,RH,JR,The Graymoor Ghost 450.00
7 JSt,RH,Fresh out of Flesh 350.00
8 RH,The Lizard Man 350.00
9 BEv,The Walking Dead 400.00
10 RH(c),Half Man,Half.... . . . . . . 350.00
11 JKz,JR,Locked In,May, 1954 . 350.00

MEN AGAINST CRIME
See: HAND OF FATE

MEN IN ACTION

Marvel Atlas, April, 1952

1 Sweating it Out 200.00
2 US Infantry stories 150.00
3 RH 100.00
4 War stories 100.00
5 JMn,Squad Charge 100.00

Mickey Finn #1
© Eastern Color Printing

6 War stories 100.00
7 RH(c),BK,No Risk Too Great . 150.00
8 JRo(c),They Strike By Night . . 100.00
9 SSh(c),Rangers Strike Back . . 100.00
Becomes:

BATTLE BRADY

10 SSh(c),F:Battle Brady 150.00
11 SSh(c) 100.00
12 SSh(c),Death to the Reds. . . . 100.00
13 . . . . 100.00
14 Final Issue,June, 1953 . . . . . . 100.00

MEN IN ACTION

Ajax/Farrell Publ., 1957

1 . . . . 125.00
2 . . . . 100.00
3 . . . . 100.00
4 . . . . 100.00
5 . . . . 100.00
6 . . . . 100.00

MEN OF COURAGE

Catechetical Guild

N# 100.00

MEN'S ADVENTURES
See: TRUE WESTERN

MERRY COMICS

Carlton Comics, 1945

N# A:Boogeyman 300.00

MERRY-GO-ROUND COMICS

LaSalle/Croyden/ Rotary Litho., 1944

1 LaSalle Publications Edition . . 200.00
1a 1946, Croyden Edition 100.00
1b Sept-Oct.'47,Rotary Litho Ed. 125.00
2 . . . . 125.00

MERRY MOUSE

Avon Periodicals, June, 1953

1 (fa),F. Carin (a&c) 150.00
2 (fa),F. Carin (a&c) 100.00
3 (fa),F. Carin (a&c) 100.00
4 (fa),F. Carin (a&c);Jan.'54 . . . . 100.00

Mickey Mouse #40
© Walt Disney

METEOR COMICS

Croyden Publications, Nov., 1945

1 Captain Wizard & Baldy Bean . 500.00

MICKEY FINN

Eastern Color/ Columbia Comics Group, 1942

1 . . . . 400.00
2 . . . . 300.00
3 A: Charlie Chan 250.00
4 . . . . 200.00
5 thru 9 . . . . @150.00
10 thru 15 . . . . @125.00

Mi

(WALT DISNEY'S) MICKEY MOUSE

Dell Publishing Co., Dec., 1952

#1-#27 Dell Four Color
28 . . . . 150.00
29 . . . . 125.00
30 . . . . 125.00
31 . . . . 125.00
32 thru 34 . . . . @125.00
35 thru 50 . . . . @125.00
51 thru 73 . . . . @100.00
74 . . . . 125.00
75 thru 99 . . . . @100.00
100 thru 105 rep. . . . . @125.00
106 thru 120 . . . . @150.00
121 thru 130 . . . . @100.00
131 thru 146 . . . . @30.00
147 rep,Phantom Fires 30.00
148 rep. 100.00
149 thru 158 . . . . @60.00
159 rep. 60.00
160 thru 170 . . . . @60.00
171 thru 199 . . . . @25.00
200 rep. 25.00
201 thru 218 . . . . @25.00

MICKEY MOUSE MAGAZINE

Kay Kamen, 1933

1 scarce 20,000.00
2 . . . . 5,000.00
3 thru 8 . . . . @4,000.00
9 . . . . 3,500.00

Mickey Mouse Magazine Vol. 1 #1
© Walt Disney (1935)

Mickey Mouse Magazine Vol 4 #7
© Walt Disney

Midget Comics #1
© St. John Publishing Co.

MICKEY MOUSE MAGAZINE

Kay Kamen, 1933–34

1 digest size (1933) 4,000.00
2 dairy give-away promo 2,000.00
3 dairy give-away promo 1,500.00
4 dairy give-away promo 1,500.00
5 dairy give-away promo 1,500.00
6 dairy give-away promo 1,500.00
7 dairy give-away promo 1,500.00
8 dairy give-away promo 1,500.00
9 dairy give-away promo 1,500.00
10 dairy give-away promo. 1,500.00
11 dairy give-away promo. 1,500.00
12 dairy give-away promo. 1,500.00

Volume II, 1934–35

1 dairy give-away promo 1,500.00
2 Christmas issue 1,500.00
3 dairy give-away promo 1,500.00
4 dairy give-away promo 1,500.00
5 1st Donald Duck as Sailor . . 5,000.00
6 dairy give-away promo 1,500.00
7 dairy give-away promo 1,500.00
8 dairy give-away promo 1,500.00
9 dairy give-away promo 1,500.00
10 dairy give-awaypromo 1,500.00
11 dairy give-awaypromo 1,500.00
12 dairy give-awaypromo 1,500.00

MICKEY MOUSE MAGAZINE

K.K. Pub./Westen Pub., 1935

1 (1935) 13¼"x10¼" 35,000.00
2 OM, new size 11½"x8½". . . . 6,000.00
3 OM 3,000.00
4 OM 3,000.00
5 (1936) Donald Duck solo . . . 5,000.00
6 Donald Duck editor. 4,500.00
7 . . . . 3,000.00
8 Donald Duck solo 4,500.00
9 1st Minnie & Minnie 4,500.00
10 . . . . 3,000.00
11 Mickey & Pluto 3,500.00
12 . . . . 3,000.00

Volume II

1 OM 2,500.00
2 OM 2,500.00
3 OM,Christmas issue, 100pg . 7,500.00
4 OM (1937) Roy Ranger adv.strip 2,000.00
5 Ted True strip 1,500.00
6 Mickey Mouse cut-outs. 1,500.00
7 Mickey Mouse cut-outs. 1,500.00
8 Mickey Mouse cut-outs. 1,500.00
9 Mickey Mouse cut-outs. 1,500.00
10 Full color 2,200.00
11 . . . . 1,500.00
12 Hiawatha 1,500.00
13 . . . . 1,500.00

Volume III

2 Big Bad Wolf (c) 1,700.00
3 CB,First Snow White 5,000.00
4 CB,(1938) Snow White. 3,000.00
5 Snow White (c) 3,000.00
6 Snow White ends 1,600.00
7 CB,7 Dwarfs Easter (c). 1,500.00
8 . . . . 1,400.00
9 CB,Dopey(c) 1,400.00
10 Goofy(c) 1,400.00
11 Mickey Mouse Sheriff. 1,400.00
12 CB,A:Snow White 1,400.00

Volume IV

1 OM,Practile Pig & Brave Little Tailor 1,500.00
2 I:Huey,Louis & Dewey(c) . . . 2,000.00
3 Ferdinand the Bull 1,500.00
4 (1939),B:Spotty. 1,400.00
5 Pluto solo 1,500.00
7 Ugly Duckling 1,500.00
7a Goofy & Wilber 1,500.00
8 Big Bad Wolf(c). 1,500.00
9 CB,The Pointer 1,500.00
10 CB,July 4th 1,700.00
11 Slick, oversize 1,500.00
12 CB,Donald's Penguin. 1,600.00

Volume V

1 Black Pete. 1,600.00
2 Goofy(c),I:Pinocchio 2,000.00
3 Pinocchio 2,200.00
4 (1940) 1,500.00
5 Jiminy Cricket(c). 1,500.00
6 Tugboat Mickey. 1,500.00
7 Huey, Louis & Dewey(c) 1,500.00
8 Figaro & Cleo 1,500.00
9 Donald(c),J.Cricket 1,700.00
10 July 4th 1,700.00
11 Mickey's Tailor 1,700.00
12 Change of comic format . . . 8,000.00
becomes:

WALT DISNEY COMICS & STORIES

MICKEY MOUSE

Whitman

904 W.Disney's Mickey Mouse and His Friends (1934). . . . 3,000.00
948 Disney'sMickeyMouse('34) 3,000.00

MIDGET COMICS

St. John Publishing Co., Feb., 1950

1 MB(c),Fighting Indian Stories . 200.00
2 April, 1950;Tex West-Cowboy Marshall 150.00

MIDNIGHT

Ajax/Farrell, 1957

1 Voodoo & Strange Fantasy . . . 175.00
2 . . . . 125.00

MIGHTY ATOM, THE

See: PIXIES

MIGHTY BEAR

See: HOLIDAY COMICS

MIGHTY MIDGET COMICS

4"x5" Format
Samuel E. Lowe & Co./ Fawcett, 1942-43

1 Bulletman. 500.00
2 Captain Marvel 500.00
3 Captain Marvel Jr. 500.00
4 Golden Arrow 400.00
5 Ibis the Invincible 500.00
6 Spy Smasher 450.00
7 Balbo, The Boy Magician 250.00
8 Bulletman 300.00
9 Commando Yank 200.00
10 Dr. Voltz, The Human Generator 250.00
11 Lance O'Casey 250.00
12 Leatherneck the Marine 250.00
13 Minute Man. 250.00
14 Mister Q 275.00
15 Mr. Scarlet & Pinky. 250.00
16 Pat Wilson & His Flying Fortress. 225.00
17 Phantom Eagle 250.00
18 State Trooper Stops Crime . . . 250.00
19 Tornado Tom 250.00

MIGHTY MOUSE

Marvel [1st Series], Fall, 1946

1 Terrytoons Presents 1,700.00

Mighty Mouse #28
© St. John Publishing Co.

Military Comics #7
© Quality Comics Group

Modern Comics #46
© Quality Comics Group

2 . . . . 750.00
3 . . . . 500.00
4 Summer, 1947 . . . . 500.00

St. John Publishing, Aug., 1947

5 . . . . 500.00
6 thru 10 . . . . @250.00
11 thru 20 . . . . @200.00
21 thru 25 . . . . @150.00
26 thru 30 . . . . @125.00
31 thru 34 . . . . @100.00
35 Flying Saucer 150.00
36 . . . . 100.00
37 . . . . 100.00
38 thru 45 Giant 100 pgs . . . . . @250.00
46 thru 66 . . . . @100.00
67 P(c),. 100.00

Pines

68 thru 81 Funny Animal . . . . . @100.00
82 Infinity (c) 100.00
83 June, 1959 . . . . 100.00

MIGHTY MOUSE ADVENTURES

See: ADVENTURES OF MIGHTY MOUSE

MIGHTY MOUSE ADVENTURE STORIES

St. John Publishing Co., 1953

N# 384 Pages,Rebound 600.00

MIKE BARNETT, MAN AGAINST CRIME

Fawcett Publications, Dec., 1951

1 The Mint of Dionysosi 250.00
2 Mystery of the Blue Madonna . 135.00
3 Revenge Holds the Torch 125.00
4 Special Delivery 125.00
5 Market For Morphine 150.00
6 Oct., 1952 . . . . 125.00

MILITARY COMICS

Comics Magazines (Quality Comics Group), Aug., 1941

1 JCo,CCu,FGu,BP,WE(c),O:Blackhawk, Miss America, Death Patrol, Blue Tracer; B:X of the Underground, Yankee Eagle,Q-Boat, Shot & Shell, Archie Atkins, Loops & Banks 20,000.00
2 JCo,FGu,BP,CCu,CCu(c),B: Secret War News 5,000.00
3 JCo,FGu,BP,AMc,CCu,CCu(c), I&O:Chop Chop 4,000.00
4 FGu,BP,AMc,CCu,CCu(c) . . 3,500.00
5 FGu,BP,AMc,CCu,CCu(c) B: The Sniper 3,000.00
6 FGu,BP,AMc,CCu,CCu(c) . . 2,600.00
7 FGu,BP,AMc,CCu,CCu(c) E:Death Patrol 2,600.00
8 FGu,BP,AMc,CCu,CCu(c) . . 2,600.00
9 FGu,BP,AMc,CCu,CCu(c), B: The Phantom Clipper . . 2,600.00
10 FGu,BP,CCu,AMc,WE(c) . . . 2,700.00
11 FGu,BP,CCu,AMc, WE(c),Flag(c) 2,500.00
12 FGu,BP,AMc,RC(a&c) 2,600.00
13 FGu,BP,AMc,RC(a&c),E:X of the Underground 2,500.00
14 FGu,AMc,RC(a&c),B:Private Dogtag 2,500.00
15 FGu,AMc,RC(a&c), ... 2,500.00
16 FGu,AMc,RC(a&c),E:The Phantom Clipper,Blue Tracer. 2,000.00
17 FGu,AMc,RC(a&c), B:P.T. Boat 2,000.00
18 FGu,AMc,RC(a&c), V: The Thunderer 2,000.00
19 FGu,RC(a&c), V:King Cobra 2,000.00
20 GFx,RC(a&c), Death Patrol 2,000.00
21 FGu,GFx 1,800.00
22 FGu,GFx 1,800.00
23 FGu,GFx 1,800.00
24 FGu,GFx,V: Man-Heavy Glasses. 1,800.00
25 FGu,GFx,V: Wang The Tiger 1,800.00
26 FGu,GFx,V: Skull. 1,500.00
27 FGu,JCo,R:The Death Patrol 1,500.00
28 FGu,JCo, Dungeon of Doom 1,500.00
29 FGu,JCo,V: Xanukhara 1,500.00
30 FGu,JCo,BWa(a&c),Blackhawk V: Dr. Koro 1,500.00
31 FGu,JCo,BWa,E:Death Patrol; I: Captain Hitsu 1,500.00
32 JCo,A: Captain Hitsu 1,400.00
33 W/ Civil War Veteran 1,400.00
34 A: Eve Rice 1,400.00
35 Shipwreck Island 1,400.00
36 Cult of the Wailing Tiger . . . 1,400.00
37 Pass of Bloody Peace 1,400.00
38 B.Hawk Faces Bloody Death 1,400.00
39 A: Kwan Yin 1,400.00
40 V: Ratru 1,300.00
41 W/ Chop Chop (c) 1,300.00
42 V: Jap Mata Hari 1,300.00
43 . . . . 1,300.00

Becomes:

MODERN COMICS

Nov., 1945

44 Duel of Honor. 1,200.00
45 V: Sakyo the Madman 750.00
46 RC, Soldiers of Fortune 750.00
47 RC,PG,V:Count Hokoy 750.00
48 RC,PG,V:Pirates of Perool . . . 750.00
49 RC,PG,I:Fear,Lady Adventuress. 750.00
50 RC,PG 750.00
51 RC,PG, Ancient City of Evil. . . 500.00
52 PG,BWa,V: The Vulture. 500.00
53 PG,BWa,B: Torchy 850.00
54 PG,RC,RC/CCu,BWa 500.00
55 PG,RC,RC/CCu,BWa 500.00
56 PG,RC/CCu,BWa 500.00
57 PG,RC/CCu,BWa 500.00
58 PG,RC,RC/CCu,BWa, V:The Grabber. 500.00
59 PG,RC,RC/CCu,BWa 500.00
60 PG,RC/CCu,BWa,RC(c), V:Green Plague. 500.00
61 PG,RC/CCu,BWa,RC(c) 475.00
62 PG,RC/CCu,BWa,RC(c) 475.00
63 PG,RC/CCu,BWa,RC(c) 450.00
64 PG,RC/CCu,BWa,RC(c) 450.00
65 PG,RC/CCu,BWa,RC(c) 450.00
66 PG,RC/CCu,BWa 450.00
67 PG,RC/CCu,BWa,RC(c) 450.00
68 PG,RC/CCu,BWa,RC(c); I:Madame Butterfly 450.00
69 PG,RC/CCu,BWa,RC(c) 450.00
70 PG,RC/CCu,BWa,RC(c) 450.00
71 PG,RC/CCu,BWa,RC(c) 450.00
72 PG,RC/CCu,BWa,RC(c) 450.00
73 PG,RC/CCu,BWa,RC(c) 450.00
74 PG,RC/CCu,BWa,RC(c) 450.00
75 PG,RC/CCu,BWa,RC(c) 450.00
76 PG,RC/CCu,BWa,RC(c) 450.00
77 PG,RC/CCu,BWa,RC(c) 450.00
78 PG,RC/CCu,BWa,JCo,RC(c) . 500.00
79 PG,RC/CCu,BWa,JCo,RC(c) . 450.00
80 PG,RC/CCu,BWa,JCo,RC(c) . 475.00
81 PG,RC/CCu,BWa,JCo,RC(c) . 475.00
82 PG,RC/CCu,BWa,JCo,RC(c) . 450.00
83 PG,RC/CCu.BWa,JCo,RC(c); E: Private Dogtag 450.00
84 PG,RC/CCu,BWa,RC(c) 450.00
85 PG,RC/CCu,BWa,RC(c) 450.00
86 PG,RC/CCu,BWa,RC(c) 450.00
87 PG,RC/CCu,BWa,RC(c) 450.00
88 PG,RC/CCu,BWa,RC(c) 450.00

Millie The Model #6
© Marvel Comics Group

Miss America Magazine #2
© Marvel Comics Group

Miss Fury Comics #6
© Marvel Comics Group

89 PG,RC/CCu,BWa,RC(c) 450.00
90 PG,RC/CCu,GFx,RC(c) 450.00
91 RC/CCu,GFx,RC(c) 450.00
92 RC/CCu,GFx,RC(c) 450.00
93 RC/CCu,GFx,RC(c) 450.00
94 RC/CCu,GFx,RC(c) 450.00
95 RC/CCu,GFx,RC(c) 450.00
96 RC/CCu,GFx,RC/CCu(c) 450.00
97 RC/CCu,GFx,RC/CCu(c) 450.00
98 RC/CCu,GFx,RC/CCu(c) 450.00
99 RC/CCu,GFx,JCo,RC/CCu(c). 450.00
100 GFx,JCo,RC/CCu(c). 475.00
101 GFx,JCo,RC/CCu(c). 450.00
102 GFx,JCo,WE,BWa,
RC/CCu(c). 600.00

MILLIE THE MODEL

Marvel, Winter, 1945

1 O:Millie the Model,
Bowling(c) 1,500.00
2 Totem Pole(c) 750.00
3 Anti-Noise(c) 500.00
4 Bathing Suit(c) 500.00
5 Blame it on Fame 500.00
6 Beauty and the Beast 500.00
7 Bathing Suit(c) 500.00
8 Fancy Dress(c),HK,Hey Look . 500.00
9 Paris(c),BW 600.00
10 Jewelry(c),HK,Hey Look 500.00
11 HK,Giggles and Grins 350.00
12 A;Rusty,Hedy Devine 250.00
13 A;Hedy Devine,HK,Hey Look . 275.00
14 HK,Hey Look. 275.00
15 HK,Hey Look. 250.00
16 HK,Hey Look. 250.00
17 thru 20. . . . . @275.00
21 thru 30. . . . . @225.00
31 thru 75. . . . . @225.00
76 thru 99. . . . . @150.00
100 . . . . 200.00
101 thru 126. . . . . @150.00
127 Millie/Clicker 165.00
128 A:Scarlet Mayfair. 125.00
129 The Truth about Agnes 125.00
130 thru 153. . . . . @125.00
154 B:New Millie 125.00
155 thru 206. . . . . @125.00
207 Dec., 1973 . . . . 125.00
Ann.#1 How Millie Became
a Model 450.00
Ann.#2 Millies Guide to
the World of Modeling 300.00
Ann.#3 Many Lives of Millie. 200.00
Ann.#4 Many Lives of Millie. 150.00

MILT GROSS FUNNIES

Milt Gross, Inc., Aug., 1947

1 Gag Oriented Caricature 225.00
2 Gag Oriented Caricature 150.00

MINUTE MAN

Fawcett Publications, Summer, 1941

1 V: The Nazis 3,000.00
2 V: The Mongol Horde 2,000.00
3 V: The Black Poet;Spr'42 . . 2,000.00

MIRACLE COMICS

E.C. Comics, Feb.,1940

1 B:Sky Wizard,Master of Space,
Dash Dixon,Man of Might,Dusty
Doyle,Pinkie Parker, The Kid
Cop,K-7 Secret Agent,Scorpion
& Blandu,Jungle Queen . . 2,500.00
2 . . . . 1,400.00
3 B:Bill Colt,The Ghost Rider . 1,400.00
4 A:The Veiled Prophet,
Bullet Bob; Mar'41 . . . . 1,100.00

MISS AMERICA COMICS

Marvel, 1944

1 Miss America(c),pin-ups . . . 2,200.00

MISS AMERICA MAGAZINE

Marvel, Nov., 1944—Nov., 1958

2 Ph(c),Miss America costume
I;Patsy Walker,Buzz Baxter,
Hedy Wolfe 1,700.00
3 Ph(c),A:Patsy Walker,Miss
America 650.00
4 Ph(c),Betty Page,A:Patsy
Walker,Miss America 650.00
5 Ph(c),A:Patsy Walker,Miss
America 650.00
6 Ph(c),A:Patsy Walker. 175.00
7 Patsy Walker stories 150.00
8 same 150.00
9 same 150.00
10 same 150.00
11 same 150.00
12 same 150.00
13 thru 18. . . . . @150.00
21 . . . . 175.00
22 thru 93. . . . . @100.00

MISS BEVERLY HILLS OF HOLLYWOOD

DC Comics, 1949–50

1 Alan Ladd. 800.00
2 William Holdon. 600.00
3 . . . . 500.00
4 . . . . 500.00
5 Bob Hope. 500.00
6 Lucile Ball 425.00
7 . . . . 425.00
8 Ronald Reagan 500.00
9 . . . . 425.00

MISS CAIRO JONES

Croyden Publishers, 1944

1 BO,Rep. Newspaper Strip . . . 250.00

MISS FURY COMICS

Marvel Timely, Winter, 1942-43

1 Newspaper strip reprints,
ASh(c) O:Miss Fury 5,500.00
2 V:Nazis(c) 2,500.00
3 Hitler/Nazi Flag(c) 2,000.00
4 ASh(c),Japanese(c) 1,500.00
5 ASh(c),Gangster(c) 1,300.00
6 ASh(c),Gangster(c). 1,200.00
7 Gangster(c) 1,100.00
8 Atom-Bomb Secrets(c)
Winter, 1946 . . . . 1,100.00

MISS LIBERTY

See: LIBERTY COMICS

MISS MELODY LANE OF BROADWAY

DC Comics, 1950

1 . . . . 800.00
2 . . . . 500.00
3 Ed Sullivan. 500.00

MR. ANTHONY'S LOVE CLINIC

Hillman Periodicals, 1945

1 Ph(c) 250.00
2 . . . . 150.00
3 . . . . 100.00
4 . . . . 100.00
5 Ph(c),Apr/May'50 . . . . 100.00

Mr. District Attorney #13
© DC Comics

Mister Mystery #14
© Aragon Publishing

Modern Love #3
© E. C. Comics

MR. DISTRICT ATTORNEY

DC Comics, Jan.–Feb., 1948

1 The Innocent Forger 1,400.00
2 The Richest Man In Prison . . . 600.00
3 The Honest Convicts 400.00
4 The Merchant of Death 400.00
5 The Booby-Trap Killer 400.00
6 The D.A. Meets Scotland Yard 350.00
7 The People vs. Killer Kane . . . 350.00
8 The Rise and Fall of 'Lucky' Lynn 350.00
9 The Case of the Living Counterfeit 350.00
10 The D.A. Takes a Vacation . . . 250.00
11 The Game That Has No Winners 250.00
12 Fake Accident Racket 250.00
13 The Execution of Caesar Larsen 250.00
14 The Innocent Man In Murderers' Row 250.00
15 Prison Train 250.00
16 The Wire Tap Crimes 250.00
17 The Bachelor of Crime 250.00
18 The Case of the Twelve O'Clock Killer 250.00
19 The Four King's Of Crime 250.00
20 You Catch a Killer 250.00
21 I Was A Killer's Bodyguard . . . 175.00
22 The Marksman of Crime 175.00
23 Diary of a Criminal 175.00
24 The Killer In The Iron Mask . . 175.00
25 I Hired My Killer 175.00
26 The Case of the Wanted Criminals 175.00
27 The Case of the Secret Six . . 175.00
28 Beware the Bogus Beggars . . 175.00
29 The Crimes of Mr. Jumbo 175.00
30 Man of a Thousand Faces . . . 175.00
31 The Hot Money Gang 175.00
32 The Case o/t Bad Luck Clues. 175.00
33 A Crime Is Born 175.00
34 The Amazing Crimes of Mr. X. 175.00
35 This Crime For Hire 175.00
36 The Chameleon of Crime 175.00
37 Miss Miller's Big Case 175.00
38 The Puzzle Shop For Crime . . 175.00
39 Man Who Killed Daredevils . . 175.00
40 The Human Vultures 175.00
41 The Great Token Take 175.00
42 Super-Market Sleuth 175.00
43 Hotel Detective 175.00
44 S.S. Justice,B:Comics Code. . 150.00
45 Miss Miller, Widow 150.00
46 Mr. District Attorney, Public Defender 150.00
47 The Missing Persons Racket . 150.00
48 Manhunt With the Mounties . . 150.00
49 The TV Dragnet 150.00
50 The Case of Frank Bragan, Little Shot 150.00
51 The Big Heist 150.00
52 Crooked Wheels of Fortune . . 150.00
53 The Courtroom Patrol 150.00
54 The Underworld Spy Squad . . 150.00
55 The Flying Saucer Mystery . . . 150.00
56 The Underworld Oracle 150.00
57 The Underworld Employment Agency 150.00
58 The Great Bomb Scare 150.00
59 Great Underworld Spy Plot . . . 150.00
60 The D.A.'s TV Rival 150.00
61 SMo(c),Architect of Crime 150.00
62 A-Bombs For Sale 150.00
63 The Flying Prison 150.00
64 SMo(c),The Underworld Treasure Hunt 150.00
65 SMo(c),World Wide Dragnet . . 150.00
66 SMo(c),The Secret of the D.A.'s Diary 150.00
67 Jan.–Feb., 1959 . . . . 150.00

MR. MUSCLES
See: THING, THE

MR. MUSCLES

Charlton Comics, 1956

22 . . . . 100.00
23 . . . . 75.00

MISTER MYSTERY

Media Publ./SPM Publ./ Aragon Publ., Sept., 1951

1 HK,RA,Horror 1,400.00
2 RA,RA(c) 800.00
3 RA(c) 800.00
4 Bondage(c) 900.00
5 Lingerie(c) 800.00
6 Bondage(c) 800.00
7 BW,Bondage(c);The Brain Bats of Venus 1,700.00
8 Lingerie(c) 750.00
9 HN 750.00
10 . . . . 750.00
11 BW,Robot Woman 1,100.00
12 Flaming Object to Eye (c) . . 1,600.00
13 . . . . 525.00
14 . . . . 525.00
15 The Coffin & Medusa's Head . 500.00
16 Bondage(c) 500.00
17 Severed Heads 500.00
18 BW,Bondage(c) 850.00
19 Reprints 500.00

MISTER RISK
See: HAND OF FATE

MISTER UNIVERSE

Mr. Publ./Media Publ./ Stanmore, July, 1951

1 . . . . 250.00
2 RA(c);Jungle That time Forgot 150.00
3 Marijuana Story 150.00
4 Mr. Universe Goes to War 125.00
5 Mr. Universe Goes to War; April, 1952 . . . . 125.00

MITZI COMICS

Marvel Timely, Spring, 1948

1 HK:Hey Look,Giggles and Grins 300.00

Becomes:

MITZI'S BOYFRIEND

2 F:Chip,Mitzi/Chip(c) 150.00
3 Chips adventures 125.00
4 thru 7 same . . . . @125.00

Becomes:

MITZI'S ROMANCES

8 Mitzi/Chip(c) 125.00
9 . . . . 100.00
10 Dec., 1949 . . . . 100.00

MODEL FUN

Harle Publications, 1954

2 . . . . 100.00
3 . . . . 75.00
4 . . . . 75.00
5 . . . . 75.00

MODERN COMICS
See: MILITARY COMICS

MODERN LOVE

Tiny Tot Comics (E.C. Comics), June–July, 1949

1 GrI,AF,Stolen Romance 900.00

Mo

Molly Manton's Romances #1
© Marvel Comics Group

Monster Crime #1
© Hillman Periodicals

Moon Girl #6
© E.C. Comics

2 Grl,JcR,AF(c),I Craved Excitement 600.00
3 AF(c);Our Families Clashed . . 500.00
4 AF(c);I Was a B Girl, panties . 700.00
5 RP,AF(c);Saved From Shame 700.00
6 AF(c);The Love That Might Have Been 700.00
7 Grl,WW,AF(c);They Won't Let Me Love Him 500.00
8 Grl,AF(c);Aug-Sept'50 . . . . . . 550.00

MOE & SHMOE COMICS
O.S. Publishing Co., Spring, 1948

1 Gag Oriented Caricature 100.00
2 Gag Oriented Caricature 60.00

MOLLY MANTON'S ROMANCES
Marvel, Sept., 1949

1 Ph(c),Dare Not Marry 175.00
2 Ph(c),Romances of 150.00

Becomes:

ROMANTIC AFFAIRS

3 Ph(c) 125.00

MOLLY O'DAY
Avon Periodicals, Feb., 1945

1 GT;The Enchanted Dagger . . . 700.00

THE MONKEY AND THE BEAR
Marvel Atlas, 1953

1 . . . . 100.00
2 . . . . 125.00

MONKEYSHINES COMICS
Publ. Specialists/Ace/ Summer, 1944

1 (fa),Several Short Features . . 150.00
2 (fa),Same Format Throughout Entire Run 125.00
3 thru 16 Funny Animal . . . . . @100.00

Ace

17 Funny Animal 125.00
18 thru 21 . . . . @100.00

Unity Publ.

22 (fa) 100.00
23 (fa) 100.00
24 (fa),AFa,AFa(c) 100.00
25 (fa) 100.00
26 (fa) 100.00
27 (fa),July, 1949 . . . . 100.00

MONSTER
Fiction House Magazines, 1953

1 Dr. Drew 750.00
2 . . . . 500.00

MONSTER CRIME COMICS
Hillman Periodicals, Oct., 1952

1 52 Pgs,15 Cent (c) Price . . . 1,400.00

MONSTERS ON THE PROWL
See: CHAMBER OF DARKNESS

MONTE HALL WESTERN
See: MARY MARVEL COMICS

MONTY HALL OF THE U.S. MARINES
Toby Press, Aug., 1951

1 JkS,:Monty Hall,Pin-Up Pete; (All Issues) 150.00
2 JkS 125.00
3 thru 5 JkS . . . . @100.00
6 JkS 100.00
7 JkS,The Fireball Express 100.00
8 JkS 100.00
9 JkS 100.00
10 The Vial of Death 100.00
11 Monju Island Prison Break . . . 100.00

MOON GIRL AND THE PRINCE
E.C. Comics, Autumn, 1947

1 JCr(c),O:Moon Girl 1,400.00

Becomes:

MOON GIRL
E.C. Comics, 1947

2 JCr(c),Battle of the Congo . . . 800.00
3 . . . . 750.00
4 V: A Vampire 750.00
5 1st E.C. Horror-Zombie Terror 1,500.00
6 . . . . 700.00

Becomes:

MOON GIRL FIGHTS CRIME
E.C. Comics, 1949

7 O:Star;The Fiend Who Fights With Fire 700.00
8 True Crime Feature 700.00

Becomes:

A MOON, A GIRL ...ROMANCE
Sept.–Oct., 1949

9 AF,Grl,AF(c),C:Moon Girl; Spanking Panels 1,000.00
10 AF,Grl,WW,AF(c),Suspicious of His Intentions 800.00
11 AF,Grl,WW,AF(c),Hearts Along the Ski Trail 800.00
12 AF,Grl,AF(c), March–April, 1950 . . . . 1,100.00

Becomes:

WEIRD FANTASY

MOON MULLINS
Michael Publ. (American Comics Group), 1948

1 . . . . 275.00
2 . . . . 150.00
3 . . . . 150.00
4 . . . . 150.00
5 . . . . 150.00
6 . . . . 150.00
7 . . . . 150.00
8 . . . . 150.00

MOPSY
St. John Publishing Co., Feb., 1948

1 Paper Dolls Enclosed 800.00
2 . . . . 550.00
3 . . . . 550.00
4 Paper Dolls Enclosed 550.00
5 Paper Dolls Enclosed 550.00

Motion Picture Comics #113
© Fawcett Publications

Movie Love #14
© Famous Funnies Publ.

Murder Incorporated #9
© Fox Features Syndicate

6 Paper Dolls Enclosed 550.00
7 . . . . 525.00
8 Paper Dolls Enclosed; Lingerie Panels 550.00
9 . . . . 500.00
10 . . . . 500.00
11 . . . . 500.00
12 . . . . 500.00
13 Paper Dolls Enclosed 500.00
14 thru 18 . . . . @500.00
19 Lingerie(c);Paper Dolls Enclosed 500.00

MORE FUN COMICS
See: NEW FUN COMICS

MORTIE
Magazine Publishers, Dec., 1952

1 ...Mazie's Friend 125.00
2 . . . . 100.00
3 . . . . 100.00

MOTION PICTURE COMICS
Fawcett Publications, Nov., 1950

101 Ph(c),Monte Hale's-Vanishing Westerner 450.00
102 Ph(c),Rocky Lane's-Code of the Silver Sage 400.00
103 Ph(c),Rocky Lane's-Covered Wagon Raid 400.00
104 BP,Ph(c),Rocky Lane's-Vigilante Hideout 400.00
105 BP,Ph(c),Audie Murphy's-Red Badge of Courage 500.00
106 Ph(c),George Montgomery's-The Texas Rangers 450.00
107 Ph(c),Rocky Lane's-Frisco Tornado 400.00
108 Ph(c),John Derek's-Mask of the Avenger 350.00
109 Ph(c),Rocky Lane's-Rough Rider of Durango 375.00
110 GE,Ph(c), When Worlds Collide 2,000.00
111 Ph(c),Lash LaRue's-The Vanishing Outpost 500.00
112 Ph(c),Jay Silverheels'-Brave Warrior 300.00
113 KS,Ph(c),George Murphy's-Walk East on Beacon 250.00
114 Ph(c),George Montgomery's-Cripple Creek;Jan, 1953 . . . . 250.00

MOTION PICTURES FUNNIES WEEKLY
1st Funnies Incorporated, 1939

1 BEv,1st Sub-Mariner 35,000.00
2 Cover Only 1,500.00
3 Cover Only 1,500.00
4 Cover Only 1,500.00

MOVIE COMICS
DC Comics, 1939

1 Gunga Din. 4,500.00
2 Stagecoach 3,000.00
3 East Side of Heaven. 2,500.00
4 Captain Fury,B:Oregon Trail . 1,800.00
5 Man in the Iron Mask 1,800.00
6 Phantom Creeps. 2,500.00

MOVIE COMICS
Fiction House Magazines, Dec., 1946

1 Big Town on(c) 700.00
2 MB,White Tie & Tails 500.00
3 MB,Andy Hardy Laugh Hit . . . 500.00
4 MB,Slave Girl 650.00

MOVIE LOVE
Famous Funnies Publ., Feb., 1950

1 Ph(c),Dick Powell(c) 200.00
2 Ph(c),Myrna Loy(c) 150.00
3 Ph(c),Cornell Wilde(c) 125.00
4 Ph(c),Paulette Goddard(c) . . . 125.00
5 Ph(c),Joan Fontaine(c) 125.00
6 Ph(c),Ricardo Montalban(c) . . 125.00
7 Ph(c),Fred Astaire(c) 150.00
8 AW,FF,Ph(c),Corinne Calvert(c) 600.00
9 Ph(c),John Lund(c) 125.00
10 Ph(c),Mona Freeman(c) 600.00
11 Ph(c),James Mason(c) 150.00
12 Ph(c),Jerry Lewis & Dean Martin(c). 200.00
13 Ph(c),Ronald Reagan(c). 200.00
14 Ph(c),Janet Leigh,Gene Kelly. 125.00
15 Ph(c),John Payne 125.00
16 Ph(c),Angela Lansbury 150.00
17 FF,Ph(c),Leslie Caron 150.00
18 Ph(c),Cornel Wilde 125.00
19 Ph(c),John Derek 125.00
20 Ph(c),Debbie Reynolds 150.00
21 Ph(c),Patricia Medina 125.00
22 Ph(c),John Payne 125.00

MOVIE THRILLERS
Magazine Enterprises 1949

1 Ph(c),Burt Lancaster's-Rope of Sand 375.00

MOVIE TUNES
See: ANIMATED MOVIE-TUNES

MUGGSY MOUSE
See: A-1 COMICS

MUGGY-DOO, BOY CAT
Stanhall Publications, July, 1953

1 . . . . 125.00
2 and 3 . . . . @100.00
4 Jan., 1954 . . . . 100.00

MURDER, INCORPORATED
Fox Features Incorporated, Jan., 1948–Aug., 1951

1 For Adults Only-on(c) 750.00
2 For Adults Only-on(c);Male Bondage(c),Electrocution sty 500.00
3 Dutch Schultz-Beast of Evil . . 275.00
4 The Ray Hamilton Case, Lingerie(c) 275.00
5 . . . . 275.00
6 . . . . 275.00
7 . . . . 275.00
8 . . . . 275.00
9 Bathrobe (c) 350.00
9a Lingerie (c) 350.00
10 . . . . 250.00
11 . . . . 250.00
12 . . . . 250.00
13 . . . . 275.00
14 Bill Hale-King o/t Murderers . . 250.00
15 . . . . 250.00
16(5),Second Series 200.00
17(2). 200.00
18(3), Bondage(c) w/Lingerie . . . 300.00

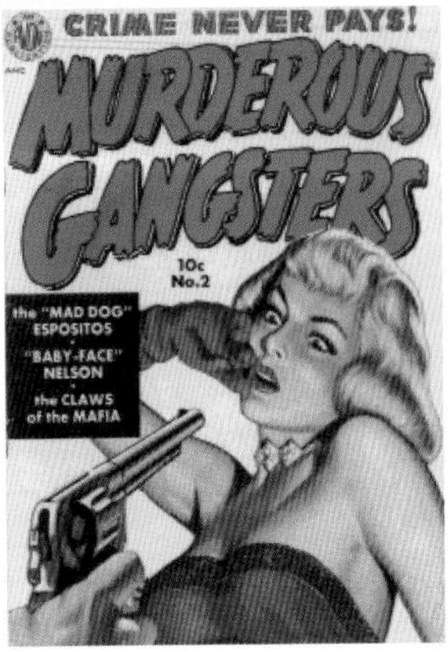

Murderous Gangsters #2
© Avon Periodicals

My Desire #4
© Fox Features Syndicate

My Greatest Adventure #10
© DC Comics

MURDEROUS GANGSTERS

Avon Periodicals/Realistic, July, 1951

1 WW,Pretty Boy Floyd, Leggs Diamond 550.00
2 WW,Baby Face Nelson,Mad Dog Esposito 350.00
3 P(c),Tony & Bud Fenner, Jed Hawkins 300.00
4 EK(c),Murder By Needle-Drug Story, June, 1952 . . . . . 400.00

MUTINY

Aragon Magazines, Oct., 1954

1 AH(c),Stormy Tales of the Seven Seas 200.00
2 AH(c) 150.00
3 Bondage(c),Feb., '55 . . . . 300.00

MUTT AND JEFF

DC Comics, 1939

1 . . . . 2,000.00
2 . . . . 900.00
3 Bucking Broncos 700.00
4 and 5 . . . . @600.00
6 thru 10 . . . . @350.00
11 thru 20 . . . . @250.00
21 thru 30 . . . . @225.00
31 thru 50 . . . . @200.00
51 thru 70 . . . . @150.00
71 thru 80 . . . . @125.00
81 thru 99 . . . . @100.00
100 . . . . 125.00
101 thru 103 . . . . @100.00
104 thru 148 . . . . @100.00

MY CONFESSIONS
See: WESTERN TRUE CRIME

MY DATE COMICS

Hillman Periodicals, July, 1944

1 S&K,S&K (c), Teenage 400.00
2 S&K,DB,S&K(c) 300.00
3 S&K,DB,S&K(c) 300.00
4 S&K,DB,S&K(c) 300.00

MY DESIRE

Fox Features Syndicate, Oct., 1949

1 Intimate Confessions 200.00
2 WW,They Called Me Wayward 200.00
3 I Hid My Lover 125.00
4 WW, April, 1950 . . . . 250.00

MY DIARY

Marvel, Dec., 1949–March, 1950

1 Ph(c),The Man I Love 175.00
2 Ph(c),I Was Anybody's Girl . . . 150.00

MY EXPERIENCE
See: ALL TOP

WESTERN LIFE ROMANCES

Marvel Comics, 1949

1 . . . . 225.00
2 . . . . 200.00

Becomes:

MY FRIEND IRMA

Marvel Atlas, 1950

3 . . . . 200.00
4 HK 225.00
5 HK 175.00
6 . . . . 125.00
7 HK 125.00
8 . . . . 125.00
9 Paper dolls 150.00
10 . . . . 125.00
11 . . . . 100.00
12 thru 22 . . . . @100.00
23 FF(one page) 125.00
24 thru 48 . . . . @100.00

MY GIRL PEARL

Marvel Atlas, 1955–61

1 . . . . 175.00
2 . . . . 150.00
3 . . . . 125.00
4 . . . . 125.00
5 . . . . 125.00
6 . . . . 125.00
7 . . . . 100.00
8 . . . . 100.00
9 . . . . 100.00
10 . . . . 100.00
11 . . . . 100.00

MY GREATEST ADVENTURE

DC Comics, Jan.–Feb., 1955

1 LSt,I Was King Of Danger Island 2,200.00
2 My Million Dollar Dive 900.00
3 I Found Captain Kidd's Treasure 600.00
4 I Had A Date With Doom 600.00
5 I Escaped From Castle Morte . 500.00
6 I Had To Spend A Million 500.00
7 I Was A Prisoner On Island X . 475.00
8 The Day They Stole My Face . 475.00
9 I Walked Through The Doors of Destiny 475.00
10 We Found A World Of Tiny Cavemen 475.00
11 LSt(c),My Friend, Madcap Manning 350.00
12 MMe(c),I Hunted Big Game in Outer Space 350.00
13 LSt(c),I Hunted Goliath The Robot 350.00
14 LSt,I Had the Midas Touch of Gold 350.00
15 JK, I Hunted the Worlds Wildest Animals 350.00
16 JK,I Died a Thousand Times . 350.00
17 JK,I Doomed the World 350.00
18 JK(c),We Discovered The Edge of the World 450.00
19 I Caught Earth's Strangest Criminal 350.00
20 JK,I Was Big-Game on Neptune 350.00
21 JK,We Were Doomed By The Metal-Eating Monster . . . 350.00
22 I Was Trapped In The Magic Mountains 325.00
23 I Was A Captive In Space Prison 325.00
24 NC(c),I Was The Robinson Crusoe of Space 325.00
25 I Led Earth's Strangest Safari! 325.00
26 NC(c),We Battled The Sand Creature 325.00
27 I Was the Earth's First Exile . . 325.00
28 I Stalked the Camouflage Creatures 325.00
29 I Tracked the Forbidden Powers 200.00
30 We Cruised Into the Supernatural! 200.00
31 I Was A Modern Hercules 175.00

My Greatest Adventure #57
© DC Comics

My Greatest Adventure #81
© DC Comics

My Love Affair #2
© Fox Features Syndicate

32 We Were Trapped In A Freak Valley! 175.00
33 I Was Pursued by the Elements 175.00
34 DD,We Unleashed The Cloud Creatures. 175.00
35 I Solved the Mystery of Volcano Valley 175.00
36 I Was Bewitched By Lady Doom. 175.00
37 DD&SMo(c),I Hunted the Legendary Creatures! 175.00
38 DD&SMo(c),I Was the Slave of the Dream-Master 175.00
39 DD&SMo(c),We were Trapped in the Valley of no Return . . . 175.00
40 We Battled the StormCreature 175.00
41 DD&SMo(c),I Was Tried by a Robot Court. 150.00
42 DD&SMo(c),My Brother Was a Robot 150.00
43 DD&SMo(c),I Fought the Sonar Creatures 150.00
44 DD&SMo(c),We Fought the Beasts of Petrified Island . . . 150.00
45 DD&SMo(c),We Battled the Black Narwahl 150.00
46 DD&SMo(c),We Were Prisoners of the Sundial of Doom 150.00
47 We Became Partners of the Beast Brigade 150.00
48 DD&SMo(c),I Was Marooned On Earth 150.00
49 DD&SMo(c),I Was An Ally Of A Criminal Creature 150.00
50 DD&SMo(c),I Fought the Idol King 150.00
51 DD&SMo(c),We Unleashed the Demon of the Dungeon. . 135.00
52 DD&SMo(c),I Was A Stand-In For an Alien. 135.00
53 DD&SMo(c),I, Creature Slayer 135.00
54 I Was Cursed With an Alien Pal 135.00
55 DD&SMo(c),I Became The Wonder-Man of Space. 135.00
56 DD&SMo(c),My Brother-The Alien. 135.00
57 DD&SMo(c),Don't Touch Me Or You'll Die. 135.00
58 DD&SMo(c),ATh,I was Trapped in the Land of L'Oz 150.00
59 DD&SMo(c),Listen Earth-I Am Still Alive 150.00
60 DD&SMo(c),ATh,I Lived in Two Worlds 150.00
61 DD&SMo(c),ATh,I Battled For the Doom-Stone 150.00
62 DD&SMo(c),I Fought For An Alien Enemy. 100.00
63 DD&SMo(c),We Braved the Trail of the Ancient Warrior . . 100.00
64 DD&SMo(c),They Crowned My Fiance Their King! 100.00
65 DD&SMo(c),I Lost the Life or Death Secret 100.00
66 DD&SMo(c),I Dueled with the Super Spirits 100.00
67 I Protected the Idols of Idoro! 100.00
68 DD&SMo(c),My Deadly Island of Space 100.00
69 DD&SMo(c),I Was A Courier From the Past 100.00
70 DD&SMo(c),We Tracked the Fabled Fish-Man! 100.00
71 We Dared to open the Door of Danger Dungeon 100.00
72 The Haunted Beach 100.00
73 I Defeiller Mountain. 100.00
74 GC(c),We Were Challenged By The River Spirit 100.00
75 GC(c),Castaway Cave-Men of 1950 . . . . 100.00
76 MMe(c),We Battled the Micro-Monster 100.00
77 ATh,We Found the Super-Tribes of Tomorrow 125.00
78 Destination-'Dead Man's Alley' 100.00
79 Countdown in Dinosaur Valley 100.00
80 BP,I:Doom Patrol 750.00
81 BP,ATh,I:Dr. Janus 250.00
82 BP,F:Doom Patrol 225.00
83 BP,F:Doom Patrol 225.00
84 BP,V:General Immortus 225.00
85 BP,ATh,F:Doom Patrol 225.00

MY GREAT LOVE

Fox Features Syndicate, Oct., 1949–Apr., 1950

1 Reunion In a Shack 175.00
2 My Crazy Dreams 100.00
3 He Was Ashamed of Me 100.00
4 My Two Wedding Rings 100.00

MY INTIMATE AFFAIR

Fox Features Syndicate, March, 1950

1 I Sold My Love 175.00
2 I Married a Jailbird;May'50 . . . 100.00

MY LIFE
See: MEET CORLISS ARCHER

MY LITTLE MARGIE

Charlton Comics, 1954–65

1 Ph(c) 400.00
2 Ph(c) 175.00
3 thru 8 . . . . @125.00
9 . . . . 110.00
10 . . . . 125.00
11 . . . . 100.00
12 . . . . 100.00
13 . . . . 100.00
14 thru 19. . . . . @100.00
20 Giant Size 125.00
21 thru 35. . . . . @100.00
36 thru 53. . . . . @100.00
54 Beatles (c). 225.00

MY LITTLE MARGIE'S BOY FRIEND

Charlton Comics, 1955–58

1 . . . . 200.00
2 . . . . 150.00
3 . . . . 100.00
4 . . . . 100.00
5 . . . . 100.00
6 . . . . 100.00
7 . . . . 100.00
8 . . . . 100.00
9 . . . . 100.00
10 . . . . 100.00
11 . . . . 100.00

MY LOVE

Marvel, July, 1949

1 Ph(c),One Heart to Give 175.00
2 Ph(c),Hate in My Heart 125.00
3 Ph(c), ... 125.00
4 Ph(c),Betty Page, April,1950 . . 400.00

MY LOVE AFFAIR

Fox Features Syndicate, July, 1949

1 Truck Driver's Sweetheart . . . 175.00
2 My Dreadful Secret 100.00
3 WW,I'll Make Him Marry Me . . 250.00
4 WW,They Called Me Wild 250.00
5 WW,Beauty Was My Bait 250.00
6 WW,The Man Downstairs 250.00

My Love Story #1
© Fox Features Syndicate

My Secret Life #24
© Fox Features Syndicate

My Secret Romance #2
© Fox Features Syndicate

Becomes:

MARCH OF CRIME

Fox Features Syndicate, 1950

1 (7) WW. 475.00
2 WW 450.00
3 . . . . 225.00

MY LOVE MEMORIES
See: WOMEN OUTLAWS

MY LOVE LIFE
See: ZEGRA, JUNGLE EMPRESS

MY LOVE STORY

Fox Features Syndicate, Sept., 1949

1 Men Gave Me Jewels 175.00
2 He Dared Me 100.00
3 WW,I Made Love a Plaything . 250.00
4 WW,I Tried to Be Good 250.00

MY PAST CONFESSIONS
See: WESTERN THRILLERS

MY PERSONAL PROBLEM

Ajax/Farrell Publ., 1955

1 . . . . 125.00
2 thru 4 . . . . @100.00

MY PRIVATE LIFE

Fox Features Syndicate, Feb., 1950

16 My Friendship Club Affair 150.00
17 My Guilty Kisses;April'50 . . . . 135.00

MY ROMANCE

Marvel, Sept., 1948

1 Romance Stories 175.00
2 . . . . 125.00
3 . . . . 125.00

Becomes:

MY OWN ROMANCE

4 Romance Stories Continue . . . 250.00
5 thru 10 . . . . @150.00
11 thru 20 . . . . @150.00
21 thru 50 . . . . @125.00
51 thru 54 . . . . @100.00
55 ATh 125.00
56 thru 60 . . . . @100.00
61 thru 70 . . . . @100.00
71 AW 125.00
72 thru 76 . . . . @100.00

Becomes:

TEENAGE ROMANCE

77 Romance Stories Continue . . . 100.00
78 thru 85 . . . . @100.00
86 March, 1962 . . . . 100.00

MY SECRET

Superior Comics, Aug., 1949

1 True Love Stories 150.00
2 I Was Guilty of Being a Cheating Wife 125.00
3 Was I His Second Love?; 125.00

Becomes:

OUR SECRET

Nov., 1949–June, 1950

4 JKa,She Loves Me,She Loves Me Not. 200.00
5 . . . . 125.00
6 . . . . 125.00
7 How Do You Fall In Love? 135.00
8 His Kiss Tore At My Heart 125.00

MY SECRET AFFAIR

Hero Books (Fox Features Syndicate), Dec., 1949

1 WW,SHn,My Stormy Love Affair 250.00
2 WW,I Loved a Weakling 250.00
3 WW, April, 1950 . . . . 250.00

MY SECRET CONFESSION

Sterling Comics, 1955

1 MSy 100.00

MY SECRET LIFE

Fox Features Syndicate, July, 1949

22 I Loved More Than Once 150.00
23 WW 250.00
24 Love Was a Habit 100.00
25 . . . . 100.00

Becomes:

ROMEO TUBBS

Dec., 1952

26 WW,That Lovable Teen-ager . 250.00

MY LOVE SECRET
See: PHANTOM LADY

MY SECRET MARRIAGE

Superior Comics, May, 1953

1 I Was a Cheat 150.00
2 . . . . 125.00
3 We Couldn't Wait 100.00
4 . . . . 100.00
5 . . . . 100.00
6 . . . . 100.00
7 thru 23 . . . . @100.00
24 1956 . . . . 100.00

MY SECRET ROMANCE

Hero Books (Fox Features Syndicate), Jan., 1950

1 WW,They Called Me 'That' Woman 250.00
2 WW,They Called Me Cheap . . 250.00

MY SECRET STORY
See: DAGAR, DESERT HAWK

MYSTERIES OF UNEXPLORED WORLDS/ SON OF VULCAN

Charlton Comics, 1956

1 . . . . 400.00
2 . . . . 175.00
3 SD,SD(c) 300.00
4 SD,Forbidden Room 350.00
5 SD,SD(c) 350.00
6 SD 350.00
7 SD, giant 375.00
8 SD 325.00
9 SD 325.00
10 SD,SD(c). 325.00
11 SD,SD(c). 325.00
12 SD,Charm Bracelet. 250.00
13 thru 18. . . . . @100.00
19 SD(c). 250.00

 All comics prices listed are for *Near Mint* condition.

Mysteries of Unexplored Worlds #20
© Charlton Comics

Mysterious Adventures #22
© Story Comics

Mystery in Space #11
© DC Comics

20 . . . . 100.00
21 thru 24 SD. . . . . @250.00
25 . . . . 100.00
26 SD. 250.00
27 thru 30. . . . . @100.00

MYSTERIES WEIRD AND STRANGE

Superior Comics/ Dynamic Publ., May, 1953

1 The Stolen Brain 500.00
2 The Screaming Room, Atomic Bomb. 350.00
3 SD,The Avenging Corpse 300.00
4 SD,Ghost on the Gallows 300.00
5 SD,Horror a la Mode 300.00
6 SD,Howling Horror 300.00
7 SD,Demon in Disguise 200.00
8 SD,The Devil's Birthmark 200.00
9 SD 200.00
10 SD. 300.00
11 SD 300.00

MYSTERIOUS ADVENTURES

Story Comics, March, 1951

1 WJo(c),Wild Terror of the Vampire Flag 900.00
2 Terror of the Ghoul's Corpse . 450.00
3 Terror of the Witche's Curse . . 400.00
4 The Little Coffin That Grew . . . 400.00
5 LC,Curse of the Jungle, Bondage(c) 450.00
6 LC,Ghostly Terror in the Cave 400.00
7 LC,Terror of the Ghostly Castle 500.00
8 Terror of the Flowers of Death. 650.00
9 The Ghostly Ghouls- Extreme Violence 450.00
10 Extreme Violence 400.00
11 The Trap of Terror. 450.00
12 SHn,Vultures of Death- Extreme Violence 450.00
13 Extreme Violence 450.00
14 Horror of the Flame Thrower Extreme Violence 450.00
15 DW,Ghoul Crazy. 500.00
16 Chilling Tales of Horror 500.00
17 DW,Bride of the Dead. 500.00
18 Extreme Violence 500.00
19 The Coffin 500.00
20 Horror o/t Avenging Corpse . . 500.00
21 Mother Ghoul's Nursery Tales, Bondage (c) 500.00
22 RA,Insane 400.00
23 RA,Extreme Violence 400.00
24 KS, ... 350.00
25 KS,Aug., 1955. . . . . 350.00

HORROR FROM THE TOMB

Premier Magazines, Sept., 1954

1 AT,GWb,The Corpse Returns . 500.00

Becomes:

MYSTERIOUS STORIES

Dec., 1954–Jan., 1955

2 GWb(c),Eternal Life 600.00
3 GWb,The Witch Doctor 350.00
4 That's the Spirit 325.00
5 King Barbarossa 325.00
6 GWb,Strangers in the Night. . . 350.00
7 KS,The Pipes of Pan;Dec'55. . 325.00

MYSTERIOUS TRAVELER COMICS

Trans-World Publications, Nov., 1948

1 BP,BP(c),Five Miles Down. . . . 700.00

MYSTERY COMICS

William H. Wise & Co., 1944

1 ASh(c),B:Brad Spencer-Wonderman, King of Futeria,The Magnet, Zudo-Jungle Boy,Silver Knight. . . 1,500.00
2 ASh(c),Bondage (c) 900.00
3 ASh(c),Robot(c),LanceLewis,B 800.00
4 ASh(c),E:All Features, KKK Type(c) 800.00

MYSTERY IN SPACE

DC Comics, April-May, 1951

1 Cl&FrG(c),FF,B:Knights of the Galaxy,Nine Worlds to Conquer 5,500.00
2 Cl(c),MA,A:Knights of the Galaxy, Jesse James-Highwayman of Space 2,500.00
3 Cl(c),A:Knights of the Galaxy, Duel of the Planets 1,500.00
4 Cl(c),S&K,MA,A:Knights of the Galaxy, Master of Doom. . . 1,400.00
5 Cl(c),A:Knights of the Galaxy, Outcast of the Lost World. . 1,400.00
6 Cl(c),A:Knights of the Galaxy, The Day the World Melted . 1,000.00
7 GK(c),ATh,A:Knights of the Galaxy, Challenge o/t Robot Knight 1,000.00
8 MA,It's a Women's World . . . 1,000.00
9 MA(c),The Seven Wonders of Space 900.00
10 MA(c),The Last Time I Saw Earth 900.00
11 GK(c),Unknown Spaceman. . . 750.00
12 MA,The Sword in the Sky. . . . 750.00
13 MA(c),MD,Signboard in Space. 750.00
14 MA,GK(c),Hollywood in Space. 750.00
15 MA(c),Doom from Station X . . 750.00
16 MA(c),Honeymoon in Space. . 750.00
17 MA(c),The Last Mile of Space. 750.00
18 MA(c),GK,Chain Gang of Space 750.00
19 MA(c),The Great Space-Train Robbery. 750.00
20 MA(c),The Man in the Martian Mask. 600.00
21 MA(c),Interplanetary Merry- Go-Round 600.00
22 MA(c),The Square Earth. 600.00
23 MA(c),Monkey-Rocket to Mars 600.00
24 MA(c),A:Space Cabby, Hitchhiker of Space 600.00
25 MA(c),Station Mars on the Air. 500.00
26 GK(c),Earth is the Target 500.00
27 The Human Fishbowl 500.00
28 The Radio Planet 500.00
29 GK(c),Space-Enemy Number One 500.00
30 GK(c),The Impossible World Named Earth. 500.00
31 GK(c),The Day the Earth Split in Two 475.00
32 GK(c),Riddle of the Vanishing Earthmen 475.00
33 The Wooden World War 475.00
34 GK(c),The Man Who Moved the World 475.00
35 The Counterfeit Earth 475.00
36 GK(c),Secret of the Moon Sphinx 475.00
37 GK(c),Secret of the Masked Martians. 475.00
38 GK(c),The Canals of Earth . . . 475.00
39 GK(c),Sorcerers of Space. . . . 475.00

Mystery in Space #48
© DC Comics

Mystery in Space #76
© DC Comics

Mystery Men Comics #3
© Fox Features Syndicate

40 GK(c),Riddle of the Runaway Earth 475.00
41 GK(c),The Miser of Space . . . 375.00
42 GK(c),The Secret of the Skyscraper Spaceship. 375.00
43 GK(c),Invaders From the Space Satellites. 375.00
44 GK(c),Amazing Space Flight of North America 375.00
45 GK(c),MA,Flying Saucers Over Mars 375.00
46 GK(c),MA,Mystery of the Moon Sniper 375.00
47 GK(c),MA,Interplanetary Tug of War 375.00
48 GK(c),MA,Secret of the Scarecrow World. 375.00
49 GK(c),The Sky-High Man 375.00
50 GK(c),The Runaway Space-Train 375.00
51 GK(c),MA,Battle of the Moon Monsters 375.00
52 GK(c),MSy,Mirror Menace of Mars 375.00
53 GK(c),B:Adam Strange stories, Menace o/t Robot Raiders . 3,500.00
54 GK(c),Invaders of the Underground World 850.00
55 GK(c),The Beast From the Runaway World 700.00
56 GK(c),The Menace of the Super-Atom 375.00
57 GK(c),Mystery of the Giant Footsteps 375.00
58 GK(c),Chariot in in the Sky . . . 375.00
59 GK(c),The Duel of the Two Adam Stranges 375.00
60 GK(c),The Attack of the Tentacle World. 375.00
61 CI&MA(c),Threat of the Tornado Tyrant. 300.00
62 CI&MA(c),The Beast with the Sizzling Blue Eyes. 300.00
63 The Weapon that Swallowed Men 300.00
64 The Radioactive Menace 300.00
65 Mechanical Masters of Rann 300.00
66 Space-Island of Peril. 300.00
67 Challenge of the Giant Fireflies 300.00
68 CI&MA(c),Fadeaway Doom . . 300.00
69 CI&MA(c),Menace of the Aqua-Ray Weapon 300.00
70 CI&MA(c),Vengeance of the Dust Devil 300.00
71 CI&MA(c),The Challenge of the Crystal Conquerors 300.00
72 The Multiple Menace Weapon 250.00
73 CI&MA(c),The Invisible Invaders of Rann. 250.00
74 CI&MA(c),The Spaceman Who Fought Himself 250.00
75 CI&MA(c),The Planet That Came to a Standstill 500.00
76 CI&MA(c),Challenge of the Rival Starman 250.00
77 CI&MA(c),Ray-Gun in the Sky 250.00
78 CI&MA(c),Shadow People of the Eclipse. 250.00
79 CI&MA(c),The Metal Conqueror of Rann 250.00
80 CI&MA(c),The Deadly Shadows of Adam Strange . . 250.00
81 CI&MA(c),The Cloud-Creature That Menaced Two Worlds . . 200.00
82 CI&MA(c),World War on Earth and Rann. 200.00
83 CI&MA(c),The Emotion-Master of Space 200.00
84 CI&MA(c),The Powerless Weapons of Adam Strange . . 200.00
85 CI&MA(c),Riddle of the Runaway Rockets 200.00
86 CI&MA(c),Attack of the Underworld Giants. 200.00
87 MA(c),The Super-Brain of Adam Strange,B:Hawkman . . 400.00
88 CI&MA(c),The Robot Wraith of Rann 300.00
89 MA(c),Siren o/t Space Ark . . . 275.00
90 CI&MA(c),Planets and Peril, E:Hawkman 275.00
91 CI&MA(c),Puzzle of the Perilous Prisons 150.00
92 DD&SMo(c),The Alien Invasion From Earth,B:Space Ranger . 150.00
93 DD&SMo(c),The Convict Twins of Space 150.00
94 DD&SMo(c),The Adam Strange Story. 150.00
95 The Hydra-Head From Outer Space 150.00
96 The Coins That Doomed Two Planets. 150.00
97 The Day Adam Strange Vanished 150.00
98 The Wizard of the Cosmos . . . 150.00
99 DD&SMo(c),The World-Destroyer From Space 150.00
100 DD&SMo(c),GK,The Death of Alanna 150.00
101 GK(c),The Valley of 1,000 Dooms 150.00
102 GK,The Robot World of Rann150.00
103 The Billion-Dollar Time-Capsule(Space Ranger),I:Ultra the Multi-Agent 150.00
104 thru 109. . . . . @125.00
110 Series ends, Sept., 1966 . . . 125.00

MYSTERY MEN COMICS

Fox Features Syndicate, Aug., 1939

1 GT,DBr,LF(c),Bondage(c);I:Blue Beetle,Green Mask,Rex Dexter of Mars,Zanzibar,Lt.Drake,D-13 Secret Agent,Chen Chang, Wing Turner,Capt. Denny 15,000.00
2 GT,BP,DBr,LF(c), Rex Dexter (c) 5,000.00
3 LF(c) 6,000.00
4 LF(c),B:Captain Savage 3,500.00
5 GT,BP,LF(c),Green Mask (c) 3,500.00
6 GT,BP 3,000.00
7 GT,BP,Bondage(c), Blue Beetle(c). 3,500.00
8 GT,BP,LF(c),Bondage(c), Blue Beetle. 3,200.00
9 GT,BP,DBr(c),B:The Moth. . . 1,500.00
10 GT,BP,JSm(c),A:Wing Turner; Bondage(c) 1,400.00
11 GT,BP,JSm(c),I:The Domino 1,400.00
12 GT,BP,JSm(c),BlueBeetle(c) 1,400.00
13 GT,I:The Lynx & Blackie . . . 1,000.00
14 GT,Male Bondage (c) 950.00
15 GT,Blue Beetle (c). 900.00
16 GT,Hypo(c),MaleBondage(c) . 950.00
17 GT,BP,Blue Beetle (c) 900.00
18 GT,Blue Beetle (c). 900.00
19 GT,I&B:Miss X 1,000.00
20 GT,DBr,Blue Beetle (c) 900.00
21 GT,E:Miss X 900.00
22 GT,CCu(c),Blue Beetle (c) . . . 900.00
23 GT,Blue Beetle (c). 900.00
24 GT,BP,DBr, Blue Beetle (c) . . . 900.00
25 GT,Bondage(c); A:Private O'Hara 950.00
26 GT,Bondage(c);B:The Wraith . 950.00
27 GT,Bondage(c),BlueBeetle(c) . 950.00
28 GT,Bondage(c);Satan's Private Needlewoman 950.00
29 GT,Bondage(c),Blue Beetle (c). 950.00
30 Holiday of Death 900.00
31 Bondage(c);Feb'42 . . . . 950.00

 All comics prices listed are for *Near Mint* condition.

Mystery Tales #6
© *Marvel Comics Group*

Mystic Comics #2
© *Marvel Comics Group*

Mystic #11
© *Marvel Comics Group*

MYSTERY TALES

Marvel Atlas, March, 1952

1 GC,Horror Strikes at Midnight 1,400.00
2 BK,BEv,OW,The Corpse is Mine 700.00
3 RH,GC,JM, Vampire Strikes . . 550.00
4 Funeral of Horror 550.00
5 Blackout at Midnight 550.00
6 A-Bomb Picture 550.00
7 JRo,The Ghost Hunter 550.00
8 BEv 550.00
9 BEv(c),the Man in the Morgue 550.00
10 BEV(c),GT,What Happened to Harry 550.00
11 BEv(c) 450.00
12 GT,MF 475.00
13 . . . . 450.00
14 BEv(c),GT 450.00
15 RH(c),EK 450.00
16 . . . . 450.00
17 RH(c) 450.00
18 AW,DAy,GC 475.00
19 . . . . 450.00
20 Electric Chair 450.00
21 JF,MF,BP,Decapitation 450.00
22 JF,MF 450.00
23 thru 27 . . . . @400.00
28 . . . . 350.00
29 thru 32 . . . . @375.00
33 BEv 350.00
34 . . . . 350.00
35 BEv,GC 350.00
36 . . . . 375.00
37 DW,BP,JR 350.00
38 BP 350.00
39 BK 375.00
40 JM 375.00
41 MD,BEv 350.00
42 JeR 350.00
41 GC 350.00
44 AW 350.00
45 SD 325.00
46 RC,SD,JP 325.00
47 DAy,BP 325.00
48 BEv 350.00
49 GM,AT,DAy 350.00
50 JO,AW,GM 325.00
51 DAy,JO 325.00
52 DAy 325.00
53 BEv 325.00
54 RC,Aug., 1957 . . . . 350.00

MYSTICAL TALES

Marvel Atlas, June, 1956

1 BEv,BP,JO,Say the Magical Words 600.00
2 BEv(c),JO,Black Blob 300.00
3 BEv(c),RC,Four Doors To 325.00
4 BEv(c).The Condemned 325.00
5 AW,Meeting at Midnight 350.00
6 BK,AT,He Hides in the Tower . 275.00
7 BEv,JF,JO,AT,FBe,The Haunted Tower 275.00
8 BK,SC, Stone Walls Can't Stop Him,Aug., 1957 . . . . . . 275.00

MYSTIC COMICS

Marvel Timely, March, 1940 [1st Series]

1 ASh(c),SSh,O;Blue Blaze,Dynamic, Man,Flexo,B:Dakor the Magician, A:Zephyr Jones,3X's, Deep Sea, Demon,bondage(c) 22,000.00
2 ASh(c),B:The Invisible Man Mastermind,Blue Blaze . . . 6,500.00
3 ASh(c),O:Hercules 4,500.00
4 ASh(c),O:Thin Man,Black Widow E:Hercules,Blue Blazes,Dynamic Man,Flexo,Invisible Man. . . 4,800.00
5 ASh(c)O:The Black Marvel, Blazing Skull,Super Slave Terror,Sub-Earth Man 4,500.00
6 ASh(c),O:The Challenger, B:The Destroyer 5,500.00
7 S&K(c),B:The Witness,O:Davey and the Demon,E;The Black Widow,Hitler(c) 5,500.00
8 Bondage(c) 3,000.00
9 MSy,DRi,Hitler/Bondage(c) . 3,000.00
10 E:Challenger,Terror 3,000.00

Marvel, [2nd Series] Oct., 1944

1 SSh,B:The Angel,Human Torch, Destroyer,Terry Vance, Tommy Tyme,Bondage(c) . 3,200.00
2 E:Human Torch,Terry Vance,Bondage(c) 1,600.00
3 E:The Angel,Tommy Tyme Bondage(c) 1,500.00
4 ASh(c),A:Young Allies Winter, 1944-45 . . . . 1,500.00

MYSTIC

Marvel, [3rd Series], March, 1951

1 MSy,Strange Tree 1,700.00
2 MSy,Dark Dungeon 900.00
3 GC,Jaws of Creeping Death . . 850.00
4 BW,MSy,The Den of the Devil Bird 1,500.00
5 MSy,Face 650.00
6 BW,She Wouldn't Stay Dead 1,500.00
7 GC,Untold Horror waits in the Tomb 650.00
8 DAy(c),BEv,GK,A Monster Among Us 650.00
9 BEv 650.00
10 GC 650.00
11 JR,The Black Gloves 600.00
12 GC 600.00
13 In the Dark 600.00
14 The Corpse and I 600.00
15 GT,JR,House of Horror 500.00
16 A Scream in the Dark 500.00
17 BEv,Behold the Vampire 500.00
18 BEv(c),The Russian Devil 500.00
19 Swamp Girl 500.00
20 RH(c) 500.00
21 BEv(c),GC 450.00
22 RH(c) 450.00
23 RH(c),RA,RMn,Chilling Tales . 450.00
24 GK,RMn,How Many Times Can You Die 450.00
25 RH(c),RA,E.C.Swipe 450.00
26 Severed Head(c) 450.00
27 Who Walks with a Zombie . . . 350.00
28 DW,RMn(c),Not Enough Dead 350.00
29 SMo,RMn(c),The Unseen 350.00
30 RH(c),DW 350.00
31 SC,JKz,RMn(c) 350.00
32 The Survivor 350.00
33 thru 36 . . . . @350.00
37 thru 51 . . . . @325.00
52 WW,RC 350.00
53 thru 57 . . . . @325.00
58 thru 60 . . . . @350.00
61 . . . . 325.00

MY STORY

See: ZAGO, JUNGLE PRINCE

MY TRUE LOVE

Fox Features Syndicate, 1949

65 . . . . 175.00
66 . . . . 125.00
67 WW 250.00
68 . . . . 125.00
69 PMo 150.00

Namora #1
© Marvel Comics Group

National Comics #33
© Quality Comics Group

Navy Combat #1
© Marvel Comics Group

NAMORA

Marvel, Fall, 1948–Dec., 1948

1 BEv,DR 3,500.00
2 BEv,A:Sub-Mariner,Blonde
Phantom 1,700.00
3 BEv,A:Sub-Mariner 1,900.00

NANCY AND SLUGGO
See: SPARKLER COMICS

NAPOLEON AND UNCLE ELBY

Eastern Color Printing, 1942

1 . . . . 600.00

NATIONAL COMICS

Comics Magazines (Quality Comics Group), July, 1940

1 GT,HcK,LF(c),B:Uncle Sam,
Wonder Boy,Merlin the Magician,
Cyclone, Kid Patrol,Sally O'Neil-
Police-woman, Pen Miller,
Prop Powers,PaulBunyan 10,000.00
2 WE,GT,HcK,LF&RC(c) 4,500.00
3 GT,HcK,LF,WE&RC(c) 3,000.00
4 GT,HcK,LF&RC(c),E:Cyclone;
Torpedo Islands of Death . . 3,400.00
5 GT,LF&RC(c),B:Quicksilver;
O:Uncle Sam 3,000.00
6 GT,LF&RC(c) 2,500.00
7 GT,LF&RC(c) 3,500.00
8 GT,LF&RC(c) 2,500.00
9 JCo,LF&RC(c) 2,500.00
10 RC,JCo,LF&RC(c) 2,500.00
11 RC,JCo,LF&RC(c) 2,500.00
12 RC,JCo,LF&RC(c) 1,800.00
13 RC,JCo,LF,LF&RC(c). 1,600.00
14 RC,JCo,LF,PG,LF&RC(c). . . 1,800.00
15 RC,JCo,LF,PG,LF&RC(c). . . 1,800.00
16 RC,JCo,LF,PG,LF&RC(c). . . 1,800.00
17 RC,JCo,LF,PG,LF&RC(c). . . 2,000.00
18 JCo,LF,PG,LF&RC(c),
Pearl Harbor 2,700.00
19 JCo,LF,PG,RC(c),The Black
Fog Mystery 2,000.00
20 JCo,LF,PG,LF&RC(c) 2,000.00
21 LF,JCo,PG,LF(c). 2,000.00
22 JCo,LF,PG,FGu,GFx,LF(c),
E:Jack & Jill,Pen Miller,
Paul Bunyan 2,000.00
23 JCo,PG,FGu,GFx,AMc,LF
& GFx(c),B:The Unknown,
Destroyer 171. . . . . 2,200.00
24 JCo,PG,RC,AMc,FGu,
GFx,RC(c) 2,200.00
25 AMc,RC,JCo,PG,FGu,
GFx,RC(c) 1,500.00
26 AMc,Jco,RC,PG,RC(c),
E:Prop Powers,WonderBoy 1,500.00
27 JCo,AMc 1,500.00
28 JCo,AMc 1,500.00
29 JCo,O:The Unknown;U.Sam
V:Dr. Dirge 1,600.00
30 JCo,RC(c) 1,200.00
31 JCo,RC(c) 1,400.00
32 JCo,RC(c) 1,400.00
33 JCo,GFx,RC(c),B:Chic Carter;
U.Sam V:Boss Spring. 1,400.00
34 JCo,GFx,U.Sam V:Big John
Fales. 1,400.00
35 JCo,GFx,E:Kid Patrol. 1,200.00
36 JCo. 1,200.00
37 JCo,FGu,A:The Vagabond. . 1,200.00
38 JCo,FGu,Boat of the Dead . 1,200.00
39 JCo,FGu,Hitler(c);U.Sam
V:The Black Market 1,700.00
40 JCo,FGu,U.Sam V:The
Syndicate of Crime 750.00
41 JCo,FGu 750.00
42 JCo,FGu,JCo(c),B:The Barker 600.00
43 JCo,FGu,JCo(c) 600.00
44 JCo,FGu 600.00
45 JCo,FGu,E:Merlin Magician . . 600.00
46 JCo,JCo(c),Murder is no Joke 600.00
47 JCo,JCo(c),E:Chic Carter 600.00
48 JCo,O:The Whistler 600.00
49 JCo,JCo(c),A Corpse
for a Cannonball 600.00
50 JCo,JCo(c),V:Rocks Myzer . . 600.00
51 JCo,BWa,JCo(c),
A:Sally O'Neil 700.00
52 JCo,A Carnival of Laughs 500.00
53 PG,V:Scramolo 500.00
54 PG,V:Raz-Ma-Taz 500.00
55 JCo,AMc,V:The Hawk. 500.00
56 GFx,JCo,AMc,V:The Grifter . . 500.00
57 GFx,JCo,AMc,V:Witch Doctor. 500.00
58 GFz,JCo,AMc,Talking Animals 500.00
59 GFx,JCo,AMc,V:The Birdman. 500.00
60 GFx,JCo,AMc,V:Big Ed Grew 500.00
61 GFx,AMc,Trouble Comes in
Small Packages. 400.00
62 GFx,AMc,V:Crocodile Man . . . 400.00
63 GFx,AMc,V:Bearded Lady . . . 400.00
64 GFx,V:The Human Fly 400.00
65 GFx,GFx(c)V:The King 400.00
66 GFx,GFx(c)V:The Man Who
Hates the Circus 400.00
67 GFx,Gfx(c),A:Quicksilver;
V:Ali Ben Riff Raff 400.00
68 GFx,GFx(c),V:Leo theLionMan 400.00
69 GFx,Gfx(c),A:Percy the
Powerful. 400.00
70 GFx,GFx(c),Barker Tires
of the Big Top 400.00
71 PG,GFx(c),V:SpellbinderSmith 400.00
72 PG,GFx(c),The Oldest Man
in the World 400.00
73 PG,GFx(c),V:A CountrySlicker 400.00
74 PG,GFx(c),V:Snake Oil Sam. . 400.00
75 PG,GFx(c),Barker Breakes the
Bank at Monte Marlo;Nov'49. 400.00

NATURE BOY
See: DANNY BLAZE

NAVY ACTION

Marvel, Aug., 1954

1 BP,US Navy War Stories 225.00
2 TLn,Navy(c) 125.00
3 BEv 100.00
4 and 5 . . . . @100.00
6 JH(c) 100.00
7 MD,JMn 100.00
8 JMn,GC. 100.00
9 thru 15 . . . . @100.00
16 BEv(c). 100.00
17 MD,BEv(c). 100.00
18 Aug., 1957. . . . . 100.00

NAVY COMBAT

Marvel Atlas, June, 1955

1 DH,JMn(c),B:Torpedo Taylor . . 225.00
2 DH 125.00
3 DH,BEv 100.00
4 DH 100.00
5 DH 100.00
6 JMn,A:Battleship Burke 100.00
7 thru 10 . . . . @100.00
11 MD,GC,JMn 100.00
12 RC. 125.00
13 GT. 100.00
14 AT,GT 100.00
15 GT. 100.00
16 . . . . 100.00
17 AW,AT,JMn 110.00
18 . . . . 100.00
19 . . . . 100.00
20 BEv,BP,AW,Oct., 1958 . . . . . . 110.00

Na

Negro Heroes #2
© National Urban League

Nellie the Nurse #1
© Marvel Comics Group

New Fun Comics #2
© DC Comics

NAVY HEROES
Almanac Publ. Co., 1945

1 Propaganda 135.00

NAVY PATROL
Key Publications, 1955

1 . . . . 125.00
2 . . . . 100.00
3 . . . . 100.00
4 . . . . 100.00

NAVY TALES
Marvel Atlas, Jan., 1957

1 BEv(c),BP,Torpedoes 175.00
2 AW,RC,JMn(c),One Hour to Live 175.00
3 JSe(c) 150.00
4 JSe(c),GC,JSt,RC,July, 1957 . 150.00

NAVY TASK FORCE
Stanmor Publ./ Aragon Publ., 1953

1 . . . . 150.00
2 . . . . 100.00
3 . . . . 100.00
4 . . . . 100.00
5 . . . . 100.00
6 . . . . 100.00
7 . . . . 100.00
8 . . . . 100.00

NEBBS, THE
Dell Publishing Co., 1941

1 rep. 250.00

NEGRO HEROES
National Urban League, 1947

1 . . . . 1,500.00
2 Jackie Robinson 2,000.00

NEGRO ROMANCE
Fawcett Publications, June, 1950

1 GE,Ph(c), Love's Decoy 1,600.00
2 GE,Ph(c), A Tragic Vow 1,200.00
3 GE,Ph(c), My Love Betrayed Me 1,200.00

Charlton Comics

4 Rep.FawcettEd.#2;May,1955 1,000.00

NELLIE THE NURSE
Marvel Atlas, 1945

1 Beach(c) 500.00
2 Nellie's Date(c) 250.00
3 Swimming Pool(c) 175.00
4 Roller Coaster(c) 175.00
5 Hospital(c),HK,Hey Look 175.00
6 Bedside Manner(c) 175.00
7 Comic book(c)A:Georgie 175.00
8 Hospital(c),A:Georgie 175.00
9 BW,Nellie/Swing(c)A:Millie . . . 175.00
10 Bathing Suit(c),A:Millie 175.00
11 HK,Hey Look 200.00
12 HK,Giggles 'n' Grins 175.00
13 HK 125.00
14 HK 150.00
15 HK 150.00
16 HK 150.00
17 HK.A:Annie Oakley 150.00
18 HK 150.00
19 . . . . 125.00
20 . . . . 125.00
21 . . . . 100.00
22 . . . . 100.00
23 . . . . 100.00
24 . . . . 100.00
25 . . . . 100.00
26 . . . . 100.00
27 . . . . 100.00
28 HK,Rusty Reprint 100.00
29 thru 35. . . . . @100.00
36 Oct., 1952 . . . . 100.00

NEW ADVENTURES OF CHARLIE CHAN
DC Comics, 1958

1 GK,SGe 900.00
2 . . . . 600.00
3 SGe 500.00
4 SGe 500.00
5 SGe 500.00
6 SGe 500.00

NEW BOOK OF COMICS
DC Comics, 1937

1 Dr.Occult. 20,000.00
2 Dr.Occult. 10,000.00

NEW COMICS
DC Comics, 1935

1 . . . . 30,000.00
2 . . . . 14,000.00
3 thru 6. . . . . @9,000.00
7 thru 11 . . . . @8,000.00

Becomes:

NEW ADVENTURE COMICS
DC Comics, Jan., 1937

12 S&S 7,500.00
13 thru 20 . . . . @6,000.00
21 . . . . 5,000.00
22 thru 31 . . . . @4,000.00

Becomes:

ADVENTURE COMICS

NEW FUN COMICS
DC Comics, Feb., 1935

1 B:Oswald the Rabbit, Jack Woods 60,000.00
2 . . . . 30,000.00
3 . . . . 15,000.00
4 . . . . 15,000.00
5 . . . . 15,000.00
6 S&S,B:Dr.Occult, Henri Duval. 30,000.00

Becomes:

MORE FUN COMICS
DC Comics, Jan., 1936

7 S&S,WK 17,000.00
8 S&S,WK 15,000.00
9 S&S,E:Henri Duval 18,000.00
10 S&S 10,000.00
11 S&S,B:Calling all Girls 10,000.00
12 S&S 10,000.00
13 S&S 10,000.00
14 S&S,Color,Dr.Occult. 19,000.00
15 S&S 10,000.00
16 S&S,Christmas(c) 10,000.00
17 S&S 9,000.00
18 S&S 3,500.00
19 S&S 3,500.00
20 HcK,S&S 3,500.00
21 S&S 3,800.00
22 S&S 3,800.00
23 S&S 3,800.00
24 S&S 3,800.00
25 S&S 3,500.00
26 S&S 3,200.00
27 S&S 3,200.00
28 S&S 3,000.00
29 S&S 3,000.00
30 S&S 3,000.00
31 S&S 3,200.00
32 S&S,E:Dr. Occult 3,000.00

More Fun #41
© DC Comics

More Fun #101
© DC Comics

Nickel Comics #6
© Fawcett Publications

33 . . . . 3,000.00
34 . . . . 3,000.00
35 . . . . 3,000.00
36 B:Masked Ranger 3,000.00
37 thru 40 . . . . @4,500.00
41 E:Masked Ranger 6,200.00
42 thru 50 . . . . @3,500.00
51 I:The Spectre 9,000.00
52 O:The Spectre,pt.1,
E:Wing Brady 135,000.00
53 O:The Spectre,pt.2,
B:Capt.Desmo 80,000.00
54 E:King Carter,Spectre(c) . . 25,000.00
55 I:Dr.Fate,E:Bulldog Martin,
Spectre(c). 30,000.00
56 B:Congo Bill,Dr.Fate(c) . . . 12,000.00
57 Spectre(c) 10,000.00
58 Spectre(c) 10,000.00
59 A:Spectre 10,000.00
60 Spectre(c) 10,000.00
61 Spectre(c) 10,000.00
62 Spectre(c) 7,000.00
63 Spectre(c),E:St.Bob Neal . . . 7,000.00
64 Spectre(c),B:Lance Larkin . . 7,000.00
65 Spectre(c) 7,000.00
66 Spectre(c) 7,000.00
67 Spectre(c),O:Dr. Fate,
E:Congo Bill,Biff Bronson. 12,000.00
68 Dr.Fate(c),B:Clip Carson . . . 7,000.00
69 Dr.Fate(c). 7,000.00
70 Dr.Fate(c),E:Lance Larkin . . 7,000.00
71 Dr.Fate(c),I:Johnny Quick . 10,000.00
72 Dr. Fate has Smaller Helmet,
E:Sgt. Carey,Sgt.O'Malley . 7,000.00
73 Dr.Fate(c),I:Aquaman,Green
Arrow,Speedy 27,000.00
74 Dr.Fate(c),A:Aquaman 7,500.00
75 Dr.Fate(c). 7,000.00
76 Dr.Fate(c),MMe,E:Clip Carson,
B:Johnny Quick 7,000.00
77 MMe,Green Arrow(c) 7,000.00
78 MMe,Green Arrow(c) 7,000.00
79 MMe,Green Arrow(c) 7,000.00
80 MMe,Green Arrow(c) 4,500.00
81 MMe,Green Arrow(c) 5,000.00
82 MMe,Green Arrow(c) 5,000.00
83 MMe,Green Arrow(c) 5,000.00
84 MMe,Green Arrow(c) 6,000.00
85 MMe,Green Arrow(c) 3,500.00
86 MMe. 3,500.00
87 MMe,E:Radio Squad 3,500.00
88 MMe,Green Arrow(c) 3,500.00
89 MMe,O:Gr.Arrow&Speedy . . 3,600.00
90 MMe,Green Arrow(c) 5,000.00
91 MMe,Green Arrow(c) 3,000.00
92 MMe,Green Arrow(c) 3,000.00
93 MMe,B:Dover & Clover 4,000.00
94 MMe,Green Arrow(c) 2,500.00
95 MMe,Green Arrow(c) 2,500.00
96 MMe,Green Arrow(c) 2,500.00
97 MMe,JKu,E:Johnny Quick . . 3,200.00
98 E:Dr. Fate. 3,700.00
99 Green Arrow(c) 3,500.00
100 Anniversary Issue 3,500.00
101 O&I:Superboy,
E:The Spectre. 17,000.00
102 A:Superboy 4,000.00
103 A:Superboy 3,500.00
104 Superboy(c). 3,000.00
105 Superboy(c). 3,000.00
106 . . . . 3,000.00
107 E:Superboy 3,000.00
108 A:Genius Jones,Genius
Meets Genius 800.00
109 A:Genius Jones, The
Disappearing Deposits 800.00
110 A:Genius Jones, Birds,
Brains and Burglary. 800.00
111 A:Genius Jones, Jeepers
Creepers 800.00
112 A:Genius Jones, The
Tell-Tale Tornado 800.00
113 A:Genius Jones, Clocks
and Shocks 800.00
114 A:Genius Jones, The
Milky Way 800.00
115 A:Genius Jones,Foolish
Questions 800.00
116 A:Genius Jones,Palette
For Plunder 800.00
117 A:Genius Jones,Battle of
the Pretzel Benders. 800.00
118 A:Genius Jones,The
Sinister Siren 800.00
119 A:Genius Jones,A
Perpetual Jackpot 800.00
120 A:Genius Jones,The Man
in the Moon 800.00
121 A:Genius Jones,The
Mayor Goes Haywire. 800.00
122 A:Genius Jones,When Thug-
Hood Was In Floor 800.00
123 A:Genius Jones,Hi Diddle Diddle,
the Cat and the Fiddle. 800.00
124 A:Genius Jones,
The Zany Zoo 800.00
125 Genius Jones,
Impossible But True 1,500.00
126 A:Genius Jones,The Case
of the Gravy Spots. 500.00
127 Nov.–Dec., 1947 . . . . 1,000.00

NEW FUNNIES
See: FUNNIES

NEW ROMANCES

Standard Comics, May, 1951

5 Ph(c), The Blame I Bore 175.00
6 Ph(c), No Wife Was I 150.00
7 Ph(c), My Runaway Heart,
Ray Miland 125.00
8 Ph(c) 125.00
9 Ph(c) 125.00
10 ATh,Ph(c) 150.00
11 ATh,Ph(c) of Elizabeth Taylor . 250.00
12 Ph(c). 125.00
13 Ph(c). 125.00
14 ATh,Ph(c) 150.00
15 Ph(c). 125.00
16 ATh,Ph(c) 150.00
17 Ath, ... 150.00
18 and 19. . . . . @125.00
20 GT, ... 125.00
21 April, 1954. . . . . 125.00

NEW YORK WORLD'S FAIR

DC Comics, 1939–40

1 1939 . . . . 30,000.00
2 1940 . . . . 17,000.00

NICKEL COMICS

Dell Publishing Co., 1938

1 Bobby & Chip 1,000.00

NICKEL COMICS

Fawcett Publications, May, 1940

1 JaB(c),O&I: Bulletman 6,000.00
2 JaB(c), ... 1,800.00
3 JaB(c), ... 1,400.00
4 JaB(c), B: Red Gaucho 1,300.00
5 CCB(c),Bondage(c) 1,300.00
6 and 7 CCB(c) . . . . @1,200.00
8 CCB(c),Aug. 23, 1940,
World's Fair 1,300.00

NICK HALIDAY

Argo, 1956

1 Strip reprints. 150.00

Nightmare #2
© Ziff-Davis Publishing Co.

Nutty Comics #6
© Harvey Publications

Nyoka The Jungle Girl #2
© Fawcett Publications

NIGHTMARE
See: WEIRD HORRORS

NIGHTMARE
Ziff-Davis Publishing Co., 1952
1 EK,GT,P(c),The Corpse That Wouldn't Stay Dead . . . 750.00
2 EK,P(c),Vampire Mermaid . . . 500.00

St. John Publishing Co.
3 EK,P(c),The Quivering Brain . 400.00
4 P(c),1953 . . . 350.00

NORTHWEST MOUNTIES
Jubilee Publications/ St. John Publ. Co., Oct., 1948
1 MB,BLb(c),Rose of the Yukon 600.00
2 MB,BLb(c),A:Ventrilo . . . 500.00
3 MB, Bondage(c) . . . 550.00
4 MB(c),A:Blue Monk,July'49 . . 450.00

NO TIME FOR SERGEANTS
Dell Publishing Co., 1958
1 Ph(c) . . . 175.00
2 Ph(c) . . . 100.00
3 Ph(c) . . . 100.00

NURSERY RHYMES
Ziff-Davis Publishing Co., 1950
1 How John Came Clean . . . 175.00
2 The Old Woman Who Lived in a Shoe . . . 175.00

NUTS!
Premere Comics Group, March, 1954
1 . . . 350.00
2 . . . 250.00
3 Mention of "Reefers" . . . 275.00
4 . . . 250.00
5 Captain Marvel Spoof;Nov.'54 250.00

NUTSY SQUIRREL
DC Comics, Sept.–Oct., 1954
61 SM . . . 125.00
62 thru 71 . . . @100.00
72 Nov., 1957 . . . 100.00

NUTTY COMICS
Harvey Publications, 1945
1 BW,Funny animal . . . 125.00
2 . . . 125.00
3 . . . 110.00
4 . . . 100.00
5 . . . 100.00
6 . . . 100.00
7 . . . 100.00
8 . . . 100.00

NUTTY COMICS
Fawcett Publications, Winter, 1946
1 (fa),F:Capt. Kid,Richard Richard, Joe Miller...Among others . . . 250.00

NUTTY LIFE
See: PHANTOM LADY

NYOKA THE JUNGLE GIRL
Fawcett Publications, Winter, 1945
1 Bondage(c);Partial Ph(c) of Kay Aldridge as Nyoka . . . 750.00
2 . . . 400.00
3 . . . 400.00
4 Bondage(c) . . . 500.00
5 Barbacosi Madness; Bondage(c) . . . 500.00
6 . . . 275.00
7 North Pole Jungle; Bondage(c) . . . 400.00
8 Bondage(c) . . . 400.00
9 . . . 225.00
10 . . . 225.00
11 Danger! Death! in an Unexplored Jungle . . . 225.00
12 . . . 200.00
13 The Human Leopards . . . 225.00
14 The Mad Witch Doctor; Bondage(c) . . . 400.00
15 Sacred Goat of Kristan . . . 200.00
16 BK,The Vultures of Kalahari . . 225.00
17 BK . . . 225.00
18 BK,The Art of Murder . . . 225.00
19 The Elephant Battle . . . 225.00
20 Explosive Volcano Action . . . 225.00
21 . . . 150.00
22 The Weird Monsters . . . 150.00
23 Danger in Duplicate . . . 150.00
24 The Human Jaguar; Bondage(c) . . . 400.00
25 Hand Colored Ph(c) . . . 135.00
26 A Jungle Stampede . . . 135.00
27 Adventure Laden . . . 135.00
28 The Human Statues of the Jungle . . . 135.00
29 Ph(c) . . . 135.00
30 Ph(c) . . . 135.00
31 thru 40 Ph(c) . . . @125.00
41 thru 50 Ph(c) . . . @135.00
51 thru 59 Ph(c) . . . @100.00
60 Ph(c) . . . 100.00
61 Ph(c),The Sacred Sword of the Jungle . . . 100.00
62 & 63 Ph(c) . . . @100.00
64 Ph(c), The Jungle Idol . . . 100.00
65 Ph(c) . . . 100.00
66 Ph(c) . . . 100.00
67 Ph(c), The Sky Man . . . 100.00
68 thru 74 Ph(c) . . . @100.00
75 Ph(c), The Jungle Myth of Terror . . . 100.00
76 Ph(c) . . . 100.00
77 Ph(c),The Phantoms of the Elephant Graveyard;Jun'53 . . 100.00

NYOKA, JUNGLE GIRL
Charlton Comics, 1955–57
14 . . . 125.00
15 . . . 100.00
16 . . . 100.00
17 . . . 100.00
18 . . . 100.00
19 . . . 100.00
20 . . . 100.00
21 . . . 100.00
22 . . . 100.00

OAKY DOAKS
Eastern Color Printing Co., July, 1942
1 Humor Oriented . . . 450.00

OBIE
Food Store Comics, 1953
1 . . . 100.00

OFFICIAL TRUE CRIME CASES
Marvel, Fall, 1947
24 (1)SSh(c),The Grinning Killer . 275.00

Okay Comics #1
© United Features Syndicate

Operation Peril #4
© American Comics Group

Oscar #5
© Marvel Comics Group

25 (2)She Made Me a Killer,HK. . 225.00
Becomes:

ALL-TRUE CRIME

Marvel, 1948

26 SSh(c),The True Story of Wilbur Underhill 400.00
27 Electric Chair(c),Robert Mais . 300.00
28 Cops V:Gangsters(c) 125.00
29 Cops V:Gangsters(c) 125.00
30 He Picked a Murderous Mind 125.00
31 Hitchiking Thugs(c). 125.00
32 Jewel Thieves(c). 125.00
33 The True Story of Dinton Phillips 125.00
34 Case of the Killers Revenge. . 125.00
35 Ph(c),Date with Danger 125.00
36 Ph(c) 125.00
37 Ph(c),Story of Robert Marone. 125.00
38 Murder Weapon,Nick Maxim . 125.00
39 Story of Vince Vanderee 125.00
40 . . . . 125.00
41 Lou 'Lucky' Raven 125.00
42 BK,Baby Face Nelson. 150.00
43 Doc Channing Paulson 125.00
44 Murder in the Big House. 125.00
45 While the City Sleeps 125.00
46 . . . . 125.00
47 Gangster Terry Craig 125.00
48 GT,They Vanish By Night 125.00
49 BK,Squeeze Play 150.00
50 Shoot to Kill. 125.00
51 Panic in the Big House 125.00
52 Prison Break, Sept., 1952. . . . 125.00

OH, BROTHER!

Stanhall Publications, Jan., 1953

1 Bill Williams-a 125.00
2 thru 5 . . . . @100.00

OKAY COMICS

United Features Syndicate, 1940

1 . . . . 600.00

OK COMICS

United Features Syndicate, July, 1940

1 B:Pal Peyton,Little Giant, Phantom Knight,Sunset Smith,Teller Twins, Don Ramon, Jerrry Sly,Kip Jaxon, Leatherneck,Ulysses 1,000.00
2 Oct., 1940 . . . . 1,100.00

OKLAHOMA KID

Ajax/Farrell Publ., 1957

1 . . . . 150.00
2 . . . . 125.00
3 . . . . 125.00
4 . . . . 125.00

100 PAGES OF COMICS

Dell Publishing Co., 1937

101 Alley Oop,OG,Wash Tubbs, Tom Mix,Dan Dunn. 2,000.00

ON THE AIR

NBC Network Comics, 1947

1 Giveaway, no cover 275.00

ON THE SPOT

Fawcett Publications, Autumn, 1948

N# Bondage(c),PrettyBoyFloyd . . 450.00

OPERATION PERIL

American Comics Group (Michel Publ.), Oct.–Nov., 1950

1 LSt,OW,OW(c),B:TyphoonTyler, DannyDanger,TimeTravellers 450.00
2 OW,OW(c),War (c). 275.00
3 OW,OW(c),Horror 250.00
4 OW,OW(c), Flying Saucers . . . 250.00
5 OW,OW(c), Science Fiction. . . 250.00
6 OW, Tyr. Rex 250.00
7 OW,OW(c),Sabretooth. 250.00
8 OW,OW(c) 225.00
9 OW,OW(c) 225.00
10 OW,OW(c),science fiction. . . . 225.00
11 OW,OW(c), War 225.00
12 OW,OW(c),E:Time Travellers . 225.00
13 OW,OW(c),War Stories 150.00
14 OW,OW(c),War Stories 150.00
15 OW,OW(c),War Stories 150.00
16 OW,OW(c),April–May,1953, War Stories 150.00

OSCAR COMICS

Marvel USA Comics, 1947–49 (FUNNY TUNES spin-off)

1 (24) 200.00
2 (25) BW,HK,Hey Look 250.00
3 . . . . 135.00
4 . . . . 135.00
5 . . . . 135.00
6 . . . . 135.00
7 . . . . 135.00
8 . . . . 135.00
9 . . . . 135.00
10 HK. 175.00
Becomes:

AWFUL OSCAR

Marvel USA Comics, 1949

11 . . . . 125.00
12 . . . . 125.00
Becomes:

OSCAR

13 . . . . 135.00

OUR ARMY AT WAR

DC Comics, Aug., 1952

1 CI(c),Dig Your FoxholeDeep. 2,800.00
2 CI(c),Champ 1,200.00
3 GK(c),No Exit. 850.00
4 IN(c),Last Man 700.00
5 IN(c),T.N.T. Bouquet 650.00
6 IN(c),Battle Flag. 650.00
7 IN(c),Dive Bomber 650.00
8 IN(c),One Man Army 650.00
9 GC(c),Undersea Raider. 650.00
10 IN(c),Soldiers on the High Wire. 650.00
11 IN(c),Scratch One Meatball. . . 650.00
12 IN(c),The Big Drop 500.00
13 BK(c),Ghost Ace 650.00
14 BK(c),Drummer of Waterloo . . 650.00
15 IN(c),Thunder in the Skies . . . 500.00
16 IN(c),A Million To One Shot . . 500.00
17 IN(c),The White Death 500.00
18 IN(c),Frontier Fighter 500.00
19 IN(c),The Big Ditch 500.00
20 IN(c),Abandon Ship 500.00
21 IN(c),Dairy of a Flattop 350.00
22 JGr(c),Ranger Raid. 350.00
23 IN(c),Jungle Navy 350.00
24 IN(c),Suprise Landing 350.00
25 JGr(c),Take 'Er Down 350.00
26 JGr(c),Sky Duel 350.00
27 IN(c),MD,Diary of a Frogman . 350.00
28 JGr(c),Detour-War 350.00
29 IN(c),Grounded Fighter. 350.00
30 JGr(c),Torpedo Raft 350.00
31 IN(c),Howitzer Hill. 350.00
32 JGr(c),Battle Mirror 350.00
33 JGr(c),Fighting Gunner. 350.00
34 JGr(c),Point-Blank War. 350.00
35 JGr(c),Frontline Tackle 350.00
36 JGr(c),Foxhole Mascot 350.00

Our Army at War #29
© DC Comics

Our Fighting Forces #2
© DC Comics

Our Fighting Forces #29
© DC Comics

37 JGr(c),Walking Battle Pin 350.00
38 JGr(c),Floating Pillbox 350.00
39 JGr(c),Trench Trap 350.00
40 RH(c),Tank Hunter 350.00
41 JGr(c),Jungle Target 350.00
42 IN(c),Shadow Targets 250.00
43 JGr(c),A Bridge For Billy 250.00
44 JGr(c),Thunder In The Desert 250.00
45 JGr(c),Diary of a Fighter Pilot. 250.00
46 JGr(c),Prize Package 250.00
47 JGr(c),Flying Jeep 250.00
48 JGr(c),Front Seat 250.00
49 JKu(c),Landing Postponed . . . 250.00
50 JGr(c),RH,Mop-Up Squad . . . 250.00
51 JGr(c),Battle Tag. 250.00
52 JGr(c),Pony Express Pilot. . . . 250.00
53 JGr(c),One Ringside-For War. 250.00
54 JKu(c),No-Man Secret 250.00
55 JGr(c),No Rest For A Raider. . 250.00
56 JKu(c),You're Next 250.00
57 JGr(c),Ten-Minute Break. 250.00
58 JKu(c),The Fighting SnowBird 250.00
59 JGr(c),The Mustang Had
My Number 250.00
60 JGr(c),Ranger Raid. 250.00
61 JGr(c),A Pigeon For Easy Co. 225.00
62 JKu(c),Trigger Man 225.00
63 JGr(c),The Big Toss 225.00
64 JKu(c),Tank Rider 225.00
65 JGr(c),Scramble-War Upstairs 225.00
66 RH(c),Gunner Wanted 225.00
67 JKu(c),MD,Boiling Point 225.00
68 JKu(c),MD,End of the Line . . . 225.00
69 JGr(c),Combat Cage. 225.00
70 JGr(c),Torpedo Tank 225.00
71 JGr(c),Flying Mosquitoes 225.00
72 JGr(c),No. 1 Pigeon 225.00
73 JKu(c),Shooting Gallery 225.00
74 JGr(c),Ace Without Guns 225.00
75 JGr(c),Blind Night Fighter. . . . 225.00
76 JKu(c),Clipped Hellcat 225.00
77 JGr(c),Jets Don't Dream. 225.00
78 IN(c),Battle Nurse 225.00
79 JGr(c),MD,What's the Price
of a B-17? 225.00
80 JGr(c),The Sparrow And
The...Hawk 225.00
81 JGr(c),Sgt. Rock in The
Rock of Easy Co. 4,000.00
82 JGr(c),MD,Gun Jockey 900.00
83 JGr(c),MD,B:Sgt.Rock Stories,
The Rock and the Wall. . . . 3,000.00
84 JKu(c),Laughter On
Snakehead Hill 450.00
85 JGr(c),Ice Cream Soldier 600.00
86 RH(c),Tank 711 . . . . 400.00
87 RH(c),Calling Easy Co. 400.00
88 JKu(c),The Hard Way 400.00
89 RH(c),No Shoot From Easy . . 400.00
90 JKu(c),3 Stripes Hill 400.00
91 JGr(c),No Answer from
Sarge 1,200.00
92 JGr(c),Luck of Easy 250.00
93 JGr(c),Deliver One Airfield . . . 250.00
94 JKu(c),Target-Easy Company. 250.00
95 JKu(c),Battle of the Stripes. . . 250.00
96 JGr(c),MD,Last Stand
For Easy 250.00
97 JKu(c),What Makes A
Sergeant Run? 250.00
98 JKu(c),Soldiers Never Die . . . 250.00
99 JKu(c),Easy's Hardest Battle . 250.00
100 JKu(c),No Exit For Easy 250.00

OUR FIGHTING FORCES

DC Comics, Oct.–Nov., 1954

1 IN,JGr(c),Human Booby Trap 1,800.00
2 RH,IN,IN(c),Mile-Long Step . . . 700.00
3 RA,JKu(c),Winter Ambush. . . . 550.00
4 RA,JGr(c),The Hot Seat 450.00
5 IN,RA,JGr(c),The Iron Punch . 450.00
6 IN,RA,JGr(c),The Sitting Tank . 375.00
7 RA,JKu,JGr(c),Battle Fist. 375.00
8 IN,RA,JGr(c),No War
For A Gunner. 375.00
9 JKu,RH,JGr(c),Crash-
Landing At Dawn 375.00
10 WW,RA,JGr(c),Grenade
Pitcher 375.00
11 JKu,JGr(c),Diary of a Sub. . . . 300.00
12 IN,JKu,JGr(c),Jump Seat 300.00
13 RA,JGr(c),Beach Party 300.00
14 JA,RA,IN,JGr(c),Unseen War . 300.00
15 RH,JKu,JGr(c),Target For
A Lame Duck. 300.00
16 RH,JGr(c),Night Fighter 300.00
17 RA,JGr(c),Anchored Frogman 300.00
18 RH,JKu,JGr(c),Cockpit Seat. . 300.00
19 RA,JKu(c),StraightenThatLine 300.00
20 RA,MD,JGr(c),The
Floating Pilot 350.00
21 RA,JKu(c),The Bouncing
Baby of Company B 200.00
22 JKu,RA,JGr(c),3 Doorways
To War 200.00
23 RA,IN,JA,JGr(c),Tin Fish Pilot 200.00
24 RA,RH,JGr(c),Frogman Duel . 200.00
25 RA,JKu(c),Dead End 200.00
26 IN,RH,JKu(c),Tag Day 200.00
27 MD,RA,JKu(c),TNT Escort . . . 200.00
28 RH,MD,JKu(c),AllQuiet atC.P. 200.00
29 JKu,JKu(c),Listen To A Jet . . . 200.00
30 IN,RA,JKu(c),Fort
For A Gunner. 200.00
31 MD,RA,JKu(c),Silent Sub 200.00
32 RH,MD,RH(c),PaperWorkWar 200.00
33 RH,JKu,JKu(c),Frogman
In A Net 200.00
34 JA,JGr,JKu(c),Calling U-217. . 200.00
35 JA,JGr,JKu(c),Mask of
a Frogman. 200.00
36 MD,JA,JKu(c),Steel Soldier . . 200.00
37 JA,JGr,JGr(c),Frogman
In A Bottle 200.00
38 RH,RA,JA,JGr(c),Sub Sinker . 200.00
39 JA,RH,RH(c),Last Torpedo . . . 200.00
40 JGr,JA,JKu,JKu(c),The
Silent Ones 200.00
41 JGr,RH,JA,JKu(c),Battle
Mustang. 250.00
42 RH,MD,JGr(c),Sorry-
Wrong Hill 175.00
43 MD,JKu,JGr(c),Inside Battle . . 175.00
44 MD,RH,RA,JGr(c),Big Job
For Baker. 175.00
45 RH,RA,JGr(c),B:Gunner and
Sarge, Mop-Up Squad. 600.00
46 RH,RA,JGr(c),Gunner's
Squad 250.00
47 RH,JKu(c),TNT Birthday. 175.00
48 JA,RH,JGr(c),A Statue
For Sarge 175.00
49 MD,RH,JGr(c),Blind Gunner. . 225.00
50 JA,RH,JGr(c),I:Pooch,My
Pal, The Pooch 175.00
51 RA,JA,RH(c),Underwater
Gunner. 150.00
52 MD,JKu,JKu(c),The Gunner
and the Nurse 125.00
53 JA,RA,JGr(c),An Egg
For Sarge 125.00
54 . . . . 125.00
55 MD,RH,JGr(c),The Last Patrol 125.00
56 RH,RA,JGr(c),Bridge of
Bullets 125.00
57 JA,IN,JGr(c),A Tank For Sarge 125.00
58 JA,JGr(c),Return of the Pooch 125.00
59 RH,JA,JGr(c),Pooch-Patrol
Leader 125.00
60 RH,JA,JGr(c),Tank Target. . . . 125.00
61 JA,JGr(c),Pass to Peril 125.00
62 JA,JGr(c),The Flying Pooch . . 125.00
63 JA,RH,JGr(c),Pooch-Tank
Hunter 125.00
64 JK,RH,JGr(c),A Lifeline
For Sarge 125.00
65 IN,JA,JGr(c),Dogtag Patrol. . . 125.00

Our Flag #2
© Ace Magazines

Tom and Jerry #72
© Dell Publishing Co.

Western Crime Cases #9
© Star Publications

66 JKu,JA,JGr(c),Trail of the Ghost Bomber 125.00
67 IN,JA,JGr(c),Purple Heart For Pooch 125.00
68 JA,JGr(c),Col. Hakawa's Birthday Party 125.00
69 JA,JKu,JGr(c), Destination Doom 125.00
70 JA,JKu(c),The Last Holdout . . 125.00

OUR FIGHTING MEN IN ACTION

Ajax/Farrell, 1957

1 . . . . 125.00
2 . . . . 100.00
3 . . . . 100.00
4 . . . . 100.00
5 . . . . 100.00
6 . . . . 100.00

OUR FLAG COMICS

Ace Magazines, Aug., 1941–April, 1942

1 MA,JM,B:Capt.Victory,Unknown Soldier,The Three Cheers . 3,700.00
2 JM,JM(c),O:The Flag 1,500.00
3 Tank Battle (c). 1,200.00
4 MA 1,200.00
5 I:Mr. Risk, Male Bondage . . . 1,400.00

OUR GANG COMICS

Dell Publishing Co., Sept.–Oct., 1942

1 WK,Barney Bear, Tom & Jerry 1,500.00
2 WK. 750.00
3 WK,Benny Burro 500.00
4 WK. 500.00
5 WK. 500.00
6 WK. 750.00
7 WK. 350.00
8 WK,CB,Benny Burro 900.00
9 WK,CB,Benny Burro 850.00
10 WK,CB,Benny Burro. 600.00
11 WK,I:Benny Bear 850.00
12 thru 20 WK . . . . @400.00
21 thru 29 WK . . . . @300.00
30 WK,Christmas(c). 250.00
31 thru 34 WK . . . . @250.00
35 WK,CB 200.00
36 WK,CB 200.00
37 thru 40 WK . . . . @125.00
41 thru 50 WK . . . . @125.00
51 thru 56 WK . . . . @125.00
57 . . . . 100.00
58 Our Gang 100.00
59 Our Gang 100.00
Becomes:

TOM AND JERRY

July, 1949

60 . . . . 175.00
61 . . . . 125.00
62 . . . . 100.00
63 . . . . 100.00
64 . . . . 100.00
65 . . . . 100.00
66 Christmas (c) 120.00
67 thru 70. . . . . @125.00
71 thru 76. . . . . @125.00
77 Christmas (c) 125.00
78 thru 80. . . . . @125.00
81 thru 89. . . . . @100.00
90 Christmas (c) 125.00
91 thru 99. . . . . @100.00
100 . . . . 125.00
101 thru 120. . . . . @100.00
121 thru 150. . . . . @100.00
151 thru 212. . . . . @100.00

OUR LOVE

Marvel, Sept., 1949

1 Ph(c),Guilt of Nancy Crane . . 175.00
2 Ph(c),My Kisses Were Cheap 125.00

OUR SECRET
See: MY SECRET

OUTER SPACE
See: CHARLIE CHAN

OUTLAW FIGHTERS

Marvel Atlas, Aug., 1954

1 GT,Western Tales 150.00
2 GT ,JMn(c). 100.00
3 . . . . 100.00
4 A;Patch Hawk 100.00
5 RH, Final Issue,April, 1955 . . . 100.00

OUTLAW KID

Marvel Atlas, Sept., 1954

1 SSh,DW,JMn(c),B&O:Outlaw Kid, A;Black Rider 350.00
2 DW,JMn(c),A:Black Rider 175.00
3 DW,AW,GWb,JMN(c) 175.00
4 DW(c),Death Rattle 150.00
5 JMn 150.00
6 JMn 150.00
7 JMn 150.00
8 AW,DW,JMn 150.00
9 . . . . 125.00
10 JSe 125.00
11 thru 17. . . . . @100.00
18 AW,JMn. 100.00
19 JSe,Sept., 1957 . . . . 100.00

OUTLAWS

D.S. Publishing Co., Feb.–March, 1948

1 HcK,Western Crime Stories . . 400.00
2 Grl,Doc Dawson's Dilema . . . 400.00
3 Cougar City Cleanup 175.00
4 JO,Death Stakes A Claim 200.00
5 RJ,RJ(c),Man Who Wanted Mexico 175.00
6 AMc,RJ,RJ(c),The Ghosts of Crackerbox Hill 175.00
7 Grl,Dynamite For Boss Cavitt . 300.00
8 Grl,The Gun & the Pen 300.00
9 FF,Shoot to Kill;June–July, 1949 . . . . 600.00

WHITE RIDER AND SUPER HORSE

Star Publications, Sept., 1950

1 LbC(c) 250.00
2 LbC(c) 200.00
3 LbC(c) 200.00
4 LbC(c) 200.00
5 LbC(c),Stampede of Hard Riding Thrills 225.00
6 LbC(c),Drums of the Sioux . . . 225.00
Becomes:

INDIAN WARRIORS

June, 1951

7 LbC(c),Winter on the Great Plains 250.00
8 LbC(c) 225.00
Becomes:

WESTERN CRIME CASES

Dec., 1951

9 LbC(c),The Card Sharp Killer . 250.00
Becomes:

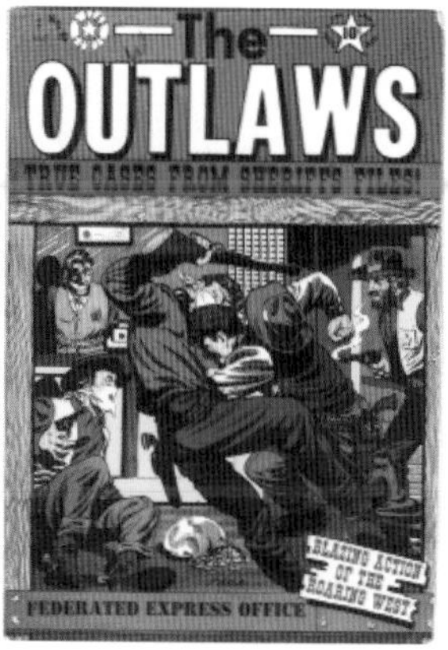

Outlaws #10
© Star Publications

Out of the Shadows #7
© Standard Comics

Oxydol-Dreft giveaways #3, #4 & #6
© Oxydol Dreft

OUTLAWS, THE

May, 1952

10 LbC(c),Federated Express . . . 250.00
11 LbC(c),Frontier Terror!!! 225.00
12 LbC(c),Ruthless Killer!!! 225.00
13 LbC(c),The Grim Avengers . . . 225.00
14 AF,JKa,LbC(c),Trouble in Dark Canyon,April, 1954 . . . . 225.00

OUTLAWS OF THE WEST
See: BULLS-EYE

OUT OF THE NIGHT

American Comics Group/ Best Synd. Feature, Feb.–March, 1952

1 AW 900.00
2 AW 600.00
3 . . . . 350.00
4 AW 500.00
5 . . . . 350.00
6 The Ghoul's Revenge 350.00
7 . . . . 350.00
8 The Frozen Ghost 350.00
9 Death Has Wings, Science Fiction 350.00
10 Ship of Death 350.00
11 . . . . 275.00
12 Music for the Dead 275.00
13 HN,From the Bottom of the Well 275.00
14 Out of the Screen 275.00
15 The Little Furry Thing 250.00
16 Nightmare From the Past 250.00
17 The Terror of the Labyrinth . . . 250.00

Becomes:

HOODED HORSEMAN

Dec., 1954–Jan., 1955

18 B: The Hooded Horseman . . . 125.00
19 The Horseman's Strangest Adventure 175.00
20 OW,O:Johnny Injun. 125.00
21 OW,OW(c). 175.00
22 OW 125.00
23 . . . . 125.00
24 . . . . 125.00
25 . . . . 100.00
26 O&I:Cowboy Sahib 125.00
27 Jan.–Feb., 1953 . . . . 110.00

OUT OF THE SHADOWS

Visual Editions (Standard Comics), July, 1952–Aug., 1954

5 ATh,GT,The Shoremouth Horror 750.00
6 ATh,JKz,Salesman of Death . . 500.00
7 JK,Plant of Death 350.00
8 Mask of Death 625.00
9 RC,Till Death Do Us Part 350.00
10 MSy,We Vowed,Till Death Do Us Part. 350.00
11 ATh,Fountain of Fear. 350.00
12 ATh,Hand of Death 500.00
13 MSy,The Cannibal 350.00
14 ATh,The Werewolf. 350.00

OUT OF THIS WORLD

Charlton Comics, 1956–59

1 . . . . 300.00
2 . . . . 150.00
3 SD 350.00
4 SD 350.00
5 SD 350.00
6 SD 350.00
7 SD,SD(c) 375.00
8 SD 300.00
9 SD 250.00
10 SD,Perfect Forcaster 250.00
11 SD 300.00
12 SD. 250.00
13 thru 15. . . . . @125.00
16 . . . . 325.00

OXYDOL-DREFT

Giveaways, 1950
The Set is More Valuable if the Original Envelope is Present

1 L'il Abner 150.00
2 Daisy Mae 150.00
3 Shmoo 175.00
4 AW&FF(c),John Wayne 150.00
5 Archie 175.00
6 Terry Toons Comics 150.00

OZARK IKE

Visual Editions (Standard Comics), 1948

11 . . . . 175.00
12 . . . . 100.00
13 . . . . 100.00
14 . . . . 100.00
15 . . . . 100.00
16 . . . . 100.00
17 . . . . 100.00
18 . . . . 100.00
19 . . . . 100.00
20 . . . . 100.00
21 thru 25 . . . . @100.00

OZZIE AND BABS

Fawcett Publications, Winter, 1946

1 Humor Oriented, Teenage 150.00
2 Humor Oriented 100.00
3 Humor Oriented 100.00
4 Humor Oriented 100.00
5 Humor Oriented 100.00
6 Humor Oriented 100.00
7 Humor Oriented 100.00
8 Humor Oriented 100.00
9 Humor Oriented 100.00
10 Humor Oriented 100.00
11 Humor Oriented 100.00
12 Humor Oriented 100.00
13 Humor Oriented;1949 . . . . 100.00

PAGEANT OF COMICS

St. John Publishing Co., Sept., 1947

1 Rep. Mopsy 250.00
2 Rep. Jane Arden,Crime Reporter. 250.00

PANHANDLE PETE AND JENNIFER

J. Charles Lave Publishing Co., July, 1951

1 (fa) 125.00
2 (fa) 100.00
3 (fa),Nov.'51 . . . . 100.00

PANIC

Tiny Tot Publications (E.C. Comics), March, 1954
"Humor in a Jugular Vein"

1 BE,JKa,JO,JDa,AF(c) 750.00
2 BE,JO,WW,JDa,A:Bomb 500.00
3 BE,JO,BW,WW,JDa,AF(c) . . . 400.00
4 BE,JO,WW,JDa,BW(c), Infinity(c) 400.00
5 BE,JO,WW,JDa,AF(c) 350.00
6 BE,JO,WW,JDa,Blank (c) 350.00
7 BE,JO,WW,JDa 350.00
8 BE,JO,WW,JDa,Eye Chart (c). 275.00

Paramount Animated Comics #8
© Harvey Publications

Parole Breakers #3
© Avon Periodicals

Patsy Walker #21
© Marvel Comics Group

9 BE,JO,WW,JDa,Ph(c), Confidential(c) 1,000.00
10 BE,JDa, Postal Package(c) . . 500.00
11 BE,WW,JDa,Wheaties parody as Weedies (c) 400.00
12 BE,WW,JDa,JDa(c); Dec.–Jan., 1955–56 . . . . 375.00

PARAMOUNT ANIMATED COMICS

Family Publications (Harvey Publ.), June, 1953

1 (fa),B:Baby Herman & Katnip, Baby Huey,Buzzy the Crow . 275.00
2 (fa) 125.00
3 (fa) 100.00
4 (fa) 100.00
5 (fa) 100.00
6 (fa) 100.00
7 (fa), Baby Huey (c) 250.00
8 (fa), Baby Huey (c) 100.00
9 (fa), Infinity(c),Baby Huey (c). . 100.00
10 thru 21 (fa),Baby Huey(c) . . @100.00
22 (fa), July, 1956, Baby Huey (c) 100.00

PAROLE BREAKERS

Avon Periodicals/Realistic, Dec., 1951–July, 1952

1 P(c),Hellen Willis,Gun Crazed Gun Moll 550.00
2 JKu,P(c),Vinnie Sherwood, The Racket King 400.00
3 EK(c),John "Slicer" Berry, Hatchetman of Crime 350.00

PAT BOONE

DC Comics, 1959

1 . . . . 600.00
2 Fabian, Paul Anka 450.00
3 . . . . 450.00
4 Bobby Darin, Johnny Mathis . . 450.00
5 Dick Clark, Frankie Avalon . . . 450.00

PATCHES

Rural Home Publ./ Patches Publ., March–April, 1945

1 LbC(c),Imagination In Bed(c). . 500.00
2 Dance (c). 200.00
3 Rocking Horse (c) 150.00
4 Music Band (c). 150.00
5 LbC(c),A:Danny Kaye,Football 250.00
6 A: Jackie Kelk 150.00
7 A: Hopalong Cassidy 225.00
8 A: Smiley Burnettte 150.00
9 BK,A: Senator Claghorn 150.00
10 A: Jack Carson 150.00
11 A: Red Skeleton; Dec'47. . . . . 200.00

PATSY & HEDY

Marvel Atlas, Feb., 1952

1 AJ(c),B:Patsy Walker & Hedy Wolfe 250.00
2 Skating(c) 175.00
3 Boyfriend Trouble 150.00
4 Swimsuit(c) 150.00
5 Patsy's Date(c) 150.00
6 Swimsuit/Picnic(c) 150.00
7 Double-Date(c) 150.00
8 AJ(c),The Dance 150.00
9 . . . . 150.00
10 . . . . 150.00
11 thru 25. . . . . @125.00
26 thru 50. . . . . @100.00
51 thru 60. . . . . @100.00
61 thru 109. . . . . @100.00
110 Feb., 1967 . . . . 100.00

PATSY & HER PALS

Marvel, May, 1953

1 MWs(c),F:Patsy Walker 225.00
2 MWs(c),Swimsuit(c) 125.00
3 MWs(c),Classroom(c) 100.00
4 MWs(c),Golfcourse(c) 100.00
5 MWs(c).Patsy/Buzz(c) 100.00
6 thru 10 . . . . @100.00
11 thru 28. . . . . @100.00
29 Aug., 1957. . . . . 100.00

PATSY WALKER

Marvel, 1945

1 F:Patsy Walker Adventures . . 650.00
2 Patsy/Car(c) 300.00
3 Skating(c) 225.00
4 Perfume(c) 225.00
5 Archery Lesson, Eye Injury(c) 225.00
6 Bus(c) 225.00
7 Charity Drive(c) 225.00
8 Organ Driver Monkey(c) 225.00
9 Date(c) 225.00
10 Skating(c),Wedding Bells, A:Millie. 225.00
11 Date with a Dream,A:Mitzi . . . 175.00
12 Love in Bloom,Artist(c), A:Rusty 175.00
13 Swimsuit(c),There Goes My Heart;HK,Hey Look 175.00
14 An Affair of the Heart, HK,Hey Look 175.00
15 Dance(c). 135.00
16 Skating(c) 150.00
17 Patsy's Diary(c),HK,Hey Look 225.00
18 Autograph(c). 200.00
19 HK,Hey Look. 200.00
20 HK,Hey Look 200.00
21 HK,Hey Look. 200.00
22 HK,Hey Look. 200.00
23 . . . . 150.00
24 . . . . 150.00
25 HK,Rusty. 200.00
26 . . . . 150.00
27 . . . . 150.00
28 . . . . 150.00
29 . . . . 150.00
30 HK,Egghead Double 150.00
31 . . . . 125.00
32 thru 56. . . . . @100.00
57 thru 58 AJ(c) . . . . @125.00
59 thru 99. . . . . @100.00
100 . . . . 100.00
Fashion Parade #1 . . . . 150.00

PAT THE BRAT

Radio Comics (Archie Publications), 1955–59

1 . . . . 175.00
2 . . . . 150.00
3 . . . . 125.00
4 . . . . 125.00
15 thru 20. . . . . @100.00
21 thru 33 . . . . @100.00

PATTY POWERS
See: DELLA VISION

PAUL TERRY'S COMICS
See: TERRY-TOONS COMICS

PAWNEE BILL

Story Comics, Feb.–July, 1951

1 A:Bat Masterson,Wyatt Earp, Indian Massacre at Devil's Gulch 125.00
2 Blood in Coffin Canyon 100.00

Pay-Off #1
© D.S. Publishing Co.

Pep Comics #17
© Archie Publications

The Perfect Crime #24
© Cross Publications

3 LC,O:Golden Warrior,Fiery Arrows at Apache Pass 100.00

PAY-OFF

D.S. Publishing Co., July–Aug., 1948– March–April, 1949

1 True Crime 1 & 2 . . . . . 300.00
2 The Pennsylvania Blue-Beard 175.00
3 The Forgetful Forger 150.00
4 RJ(c),Lady and the Jewels . . . 150.00
5 The Beautiful Embezzeler 150.00

PEANUTS

Dell Publishing Co., 1958

1 . . . . . 250.00
2 . . . . . 200.00
3 . . . . . 150.00
4 . . . . . 125.00
5 thru 13 . . . . . @100.00

PEDRO

Fox Features Syndicate, Jan., 1950

1 WW,WW(c),Humor Oriented . 250.00
2 Aug., 1950 . . . . . 175.00

PENNY

Avon Publications, 1947

1 The Slickest Chick of 'em All . 125.00
2 . . . . . 100.00
3 America's Teen-age Sweetheart 100.00
4 . . . . . 100.00
5 . . . . . 100.00
6 Perry Como Ph(c),Sept.– Oct., 1949 . . . . . 125.00

PEP COMICS

MJL Magazines/ Archie Publications, Jan., 1940

1 IN,JCo,MMe,IN(c),I:Shield, O:Comet,Queen of Diamonds, B:The Rocket,Press Guardian, Sergeant Boyle Chang,Bently of Scotland Yard 17,000.00
2 CBi,JCo,IN,IN(c),O:Rocket . . 4,500.00
3 JCo,IN,IN(c),Shield (c) 3,000.00
4 Cbi,JCo,MMe,IN,IN(c), C:Wizard(not Gareb) 2,400.00
5 Cbi,JCo,MMe,IN,IN(c), C:Wizard 2,400.00
6 IN,IN(c), Shield (c) 1,800.00
7 IN,IN(c),Bondage(c),Shield(c)1,800.00
8 JCo,IN, Shield (c) 1,800.00
9 IN, Shield (c) 1,800.00
10 IN,IN(c), Shield (c) 1,800.00
11 MMe,IN,IN(c),I:Dusty, Boy Detective 2,000.00
12 IN,IN(c),O:Fireball Bondage(c), E:Rocket, Queen of Diamonds 2,200.00
13 IN,IN(c),Bondage(c) 1,500.00
14 IN,IN(c) 1,500.00
15 IN,Bondage(c) 1,500.00
16 IN,O:Madam Satan 2,400.00
17 IN,IN(c),O:Hangman, D:Comet 6,000.00
18 IN,IN(c),Bondage(c) 1,500.00
19 IN 1,500.00
20 IN,IN(c),E:Fireball 1,500.00
21 IN,IN(c),Bondage(c), E: Madam Satan 1,500.00
22 IN,IN(c)I:Archie, Jughead, Betty 25,000.00
23 IN,IN(c) 2,200.00
24 IN,IN(c) 1,500.00
25 IN,IN(c) 1,500.00
26 IN,IN(c),I:Veronica 2,200.00
27 IN,IN(c),Bill of Rights (c) . . . 1,500.00
28 IN,IN(c), V:Capt. Swastika . . 1,500.00
29 ASh (c) 1,500.00
30 B:Capt.Commando 1,500.00
31 Bondage(c) 1,500.00
32 Bondage(c) 1,100.00
33 . . . . . 1,100.00
34 Bondage(c) 1,100.00
35 . . . . . 1,100.00
36 1st Archie(c) 2,500.00
37 Bondage(c) 750.00
38 ASh(c) 700.00
39 ASh(c), Human Shield 700.00
40 . . . . . 700.00
41 2nd Archie; I:Jughead 500.00
42 F:Archie & Jughead 500.00
43 F:Archie & Jughead 500.00
44 . . . . . 500.00
45 . . . . . 500.00
46 . . . . . 500.00
47 E:Hangman,Infinity(c) 500.00
48 B:Black Hood 500.00
49 . . . . . 500.00
50 . . . . . 500.00
51 . . . . . 350.00
52 B:Suzie 350.00
53 . . . . . 350.00
54 E:Captain Commando 350.00
55 . . . . . 350.00
56 thru 58 . . . . . @300.00
59 E:Suzie 300.00
60 B:Katy Keene 300.00
61 . . . . . 275.00
62 I L'il Jinx 275.00
63 . . . . . 275.00
64 . . . . . 275.00
65 E:Shield 275.00
66 thru 71 . . . . . @150.00
72 thru 80 . . . . . @125.00
81 thru 90 . . . . . @100.00
91 thru 99 . . . . . @100.00
100 . . . . . 150.00
101 thru 110 . . . . . @125.00
111 thru 120 . . . . . @100.00
121 thru 130 . . . . . @125.00
131 thru 140 . . . . . @100.00
141 thru 150 . . . . . @100.00
151 thru 160,A:Super Heroes . @100.00

PERFECT CRIME, THE

Cross Publications, Oct., 1949

1 BP,DW 400.00
2 BP 200.00
3 . . . . . 175.00
4 BP 175.00
5 DW 175.00
6 . . . . . 175.00
7 B:Steve Duncan 175.00
8 Drug Story 300.00
9 . . . . . 175.00
10 . . . . . 175.00
11 Bondage (c) 300.00
12 . . . . . 175.00
13 . . . . . 175.00
14 Poisoning (c) 350.00
15 'The Most Terrible Menace,' Drug 300.00
16 . . . . . 150.00
17 . . . . . 150.00
18 Drug (c) 400.00
19 . . . . . 150.00
20 thru 25 . . . . . @125.00
26 Drug w/ Hypodermic (c) 400.00
27 . . . . . 150.00
28 . . . . . 150.00
29 . . . . . 150.00
30 E:Steve Duncan, Rope Strangulation (c) 400.00
31 . . . . . 125.00
32 . . . . . 125.00
33 . . . . . 125.00

Perfect Love #3
© St. John Publ. Co.

Personal Love #32
© Famous Funnies

Phantom Lady #14
© Fox Features Syndicate

PERFECT LOVE

Approved Comics (Ziff-Davis)/ St. John Publ. Co., Aug.–Sept., 1951

1 (10),P(c),Our Kiss was a Prelude to Love Adrift 250.00
2 . . . . 150.00
3 P(c) 125.00
4 . . . . 100.00
5 . . . . 100.00
6 . . . . 100.00
7 . . . . 100.00
8 EK 125.00
9 EK,P(c) 100.00
10 Ph(c), Dec '53. . . . . 100.00

PERSONAL LOVE

Famous Funnies, Jan., 1950

1 Ph(c) Are You in Love 225.00
2 Ph(c) Serenade for Suzette Mario Lanzo. 125.00
3 Ph(c) 100.00
4 Ph(c) 100.00
5 Ph(c) 100.00
6 Ph(c) Be Mine Forever 110.00
7 Ph(c) You'll Always Be Mine, Robert Walker 110.00
8 EK,Ph(c),Esther Williams & Howard Keel 125.00
9 EK,Ph(c),Debra Paget & Louis Jordan 125.00
10 Ph(c),Loretta Young Joseph Cotton 100.00
11 ATh, Ph(c),Gene Tierney & Glenn Ford 150.00
12 Ph(c) Jane Greer & William Lundigan. 100.00
13 Ph(c) Debra Paget & Louis Jordan 100.00
14 Ph(c) Kirk Douglas & Patrice Wymore 110.00
15 Ph(c) Dale Robertson & Joanne Dru 100.00
16 Ph(c) Take Back Your Love . . 100.00
17 Ph(c) My Cruel Deception . . . 100.00
18 Ph(c) Gregory Peck & Susan Hayward. 125.00
19 Ph(c) Anthony Quinn. 125.00
20 Ph(c) The Couple in the Next Apartment, Bob Wagner 125.00
21 Ph(c) I'll Make You Care. 125.00
22 Ph(c) Doorway To Heartbreak 125.00
23 Ph(c) SaveMe from that Man . 125.00
24 FF, Ph(c) Tyrone Power 500.00
25 FF, Ph(c) The Dark Light 500.00
26 Ph(c) Love Needs A Break . . . 100.00
27 FF, Ph(c) Champ or Chump? . 500.00
28 FF, Ph(c) A Past to Forget . . . 500.00
29 Ph(c) Charlton Heston 125.00
30 Ph(c) The Lady is Lost 100.00
31 Ph(c) Marlon Brando. 125.00
32 FF, Ph(c) The Torment, Kirk Douglas 700.00
33 Ph(c) June, 1955 . . . . 100.00

PETER COTTONTAIL

Key Publications, Jan., 1954

1 No 3-D (fa). 100.00
1 Feb '54 3-D (fa) 250.00
2 Rep of 3-D #1,not in 3-D 100.00

PETER PANDA

DC Comics, Aug.–Sept., 1953

1 . . . . 500.00
2 . . . . 250.00
3 thru 9 . . . . @200.00
10 Aug.–Sept., 1958 . . . . 200.00

PETER PAUL'S 4 IN 1 JUMBO COMIC BOOK

Capitol Stories, 1953

1 F: Racket Squad in Action, Space Adventures,Crime & Justice,Space Western 500.00

PETER PENNY AND HIS MAGIC DOLLAR

American Bakers Assn., 1947

1 History from Colonial America to the 1950's 200.00
2 . . . . 125.00

PETER PIG

Literary Enterprises (Standard Comics), 1953

5 . . . . 100.00
6 . . . . 100.00

PETER PORKCHOPS

DC Comics, Nov.–Dec., 1949

1 . . . . 350.00
2 . . . . 175.00
3 thru 10 . . . . @125.00
11 thru 30 . . . . @100.00
31 thru 61 . . . . @100.00
62 Oct.–Dec., 1960 . . . . 100.00

PETER RABBIT

Avon Periodicals, 1947

1 HCa 450.00
2 HCa 275.00
3 HCa 250.00
4 HCa 250.00
5 HC 250.00
6 HCa 250.00
7 thru 10 . . . . @100.00
11 . . . . 100.00

PETE THE PANIC

Stanmor Publications, 1955

N# 100.00

KRAZY LIFE

Fox Features Syndicate, 1945

1 (fa) 100.00
Becomes:

NUTTY LIFE

Summer, 1946

2 (fa). 100.00
Becomes:

WOTALIFE

Fox Features Synd./ Green Publ., Aug.–Sept., 1946

3 (fa)B:L'il Pan,Cosmo Cat 150.00
4 . . . . 100.00
5 thru 11 . . . . @100.00
12 July, 1947 . . . . 100.00
9a rep (1959). 100.00
Becomes:

PHANTOM LADY

Fox Features Syndicate, Aug., 1947

13(#1) MB,MB(c) Knights of the Crooked Cross 6,000.00
14(#2) MB,MB(c) Scoundrels and Scandals 3,300.00
15 MB,MB(c) The Meanest Crook In the World 3,200.00
16 MB,MB(c) Claa Peete The Beautiful Beast, Negligee. . 3,200.00
17 MB.MB(c) The Soda Mint Killer, Bondage (c) 8,000.00

Pe

My Love Secret #26
© Fox Features Syndicate

Pictorial Romances #8
© St. John Publishing Co.

Picture News #1
© 299 Lafayette Street Corp.

18 MB,MB(c) The Case of Irene Shroeder 2,500.00
19 MB,MB(c) The Case of the Murderous Model 2,500.00
20 MB,MB(c) Ace of Spades. . . 2,000.00
21 MB,MB(c). 1,800.00
22 MB,JKa 1,800.00
23 MB,JKa Bondage (c) 2,000.00
Becomes:

MY LOVE SECRET

June, 1949

24 JKa, My Love Was For Sale . . 200.00
25 Second Hand Love 125.00
26 WW I Wanted Both Men 250.00
27 I Was a Love Cheat 100.00
28 WW, I Gave Him Love 250.00
29 . . . . 100.00
30 Ph(c) 100.00

LINDA

Ajax/Farrell, April–May, 1954

1 . . . . 175.00
2 Lingerie section 150.00
3 . . . . 100.00
4 Oct.–Nov.,1954 . . . . 100.00
Becomes:

PHANTOM LADY

Dec., 1954–Jan., 1955

5(1) MB 1,500.00
2 Last Pre-Code Edition 1,250.00
3 Comics Code 1,000.00
4 Red Rocket,June, 1955 . . . . 1,000.00

PHANTOM STRANGER

DC Comics, Aug.–Sept., 1952

1 . . . . 2,500.00
2 . . . . 1,500.00
3 thru 5. . . . . @1,200.00
6, June-July, 1953 . . . . 1,200.00

PHIL RIZZUTO

Fawcett Publications, 1951

Ph(c) The Sensational Story of The American Leagues MVP 950.00

PICTORIAL CONFESSIONS

St. John Publishing Co., Sept., 1949

1 MB,MB(c),I Threw Away My Reputation on a Worthless Love . . 350.00
2 MB,Ph(c) I Tried to be a Hollywood Glamour Girl 250.00
3 JKY,MB,MB(c),They Caught Me Cheating 300.00
Becomes:

PICTORIAL ROMANCES

Jan., 1950

4 Ph(c) MB, Trapped By Kisses I Couldn't Resist 350.00
5 MB,MB(c). 300.00
6 MB,MB(c) I Was Too Free With Boys 250.00
7 MB,MB(c) 250.00
8 MB,MB(c) I Made a Sinful Bargain 250.00
9 MB,MB(c) Dishonest Love. . . . 250.00
10 MB,MB(c) I Was The Other Woman 200.00
11 MB,MB(c) The Worst Mistake A Wife Can Make . . . 225.00
12 MB,MB(c) Love Urchin 200.00
13 MB,MB(c) Temptations of a Hatcheck Girl. 200.00
14 MB,MB(c) I Was A Gamblers Wife. 200.00
15 MB,MB(c) Wife Without Pride or Principles 200.00
16 MB,MB(c) The Truth of My Affair With a Farm Boy 200.00
17 MB,MB(c) True Confessions of a Girl in Love. 300.00
18 MB,MB(c) 300.00
20 MB,MB(c) 300.00
21 thru 23 MB,MB(c) . . . . @175.00
24 MB,MB(c) March,1954 . . . . . . 175.00

PICTORIAL LOVE STORIES

See: ZOO FUNNIES

PICTORIAL LOVE STORIES

St. John Publishing Co., Oct., 1952

1 MB,MB(c) I Lost My Head, My Heart and My Resistance . . . 350.00

PICTURE CRIMES

1937

1 . . . . 1,500.00

PICTURE NEWS

299 Lafayette Street Corp., Jan., 1946–Jan.-Feb., 1947

1 Will The Atom Blow The World Apart. 1,000.00
2 Meet America's 1st Girl Boxing Expert,Atomic Bomb 500.00
3 Hollywood's June Allison Shows You How to be Beautiful, Atomic Bomb. 400.00
4 Amazing Marine Who Became King of 10,000 Voodoos, Atomic Bomb. 450.00
5 G.I.Babies,Hank Greenberg. . . 400.00
6 Joe Louis(c) 450.00
7 Lovely Lady, Englands Future Queen 350.00
8 Champion of them All 350.00
9 Bikini Atom Bomb, Joe DiMaggio 400.00
10 Dick Quick, Ace Reporter, Atomic Bomb. 400.00

PICTURE PARADE

Gilberton Co., 1953

1 A-Bomb 300.00
2 . . . . 150.00
3 . . . . 150.00
4 Christmas issue 150.00
Becomes:

PICTURE PROGRESS

Gilberton Co., 1954

5 1953 News. 100.00
6 Birth of America 100.00
7 . . . . 100.00
8 Paul Revere. 100.00
9 Hawaiian Islands 100.00
10 Flight. 100.00
11 thru 20 . . . . @100.00

PICTURE SCOPE JUNGLE ADVENTURES

Star Publications, 1954

7 LbC(c) 650.00

PICTURE STORIES FROM AMERICAN HISTORY

E.C. Comics, 1946–47

1 . . . . 750.00
2 thru 4 . . . . @550.00

Pi

Picture Stories From Science #1
© Educational Comics

Piracy #6
© E.C. Comics

Planet Comics #39
© Fiction House Magazines

PICTURE STORIES FROM SCIENCE

Educational Comics, Spring, 1947

1 Understanding Air and Water . 500.00
2 Fall '47 Amazing Discoveries About Food & Health 400.00

PICTURE STORIES FROM THE BIBLE

DC Comics, Autumn, 1942–43

1 thru 4 Old Testament . . . . . . @700.00
1 thru 3 New Testament 900.00

PICTURE STORIES FROM WORLD HISTORY

E.C. Comics, Spring, 1947

1 Ancient World to the Fall of Rome 350.00
2 Europes Struggle for Civilization 300.00

Pi

PINHEAD AND FOODINI

Fawcett Publications, July, 1951–Jan., 1952

1 Ph(c) 350.00
2 Ph(c) 200.00
3 Ph(c) Too Many Pinheads 150.00
4 Foodini's Talking Camel. 150.00

PIN-UP PETE

Toby Publishers, 1952

1 Loves of a GI Casanova 250.00

PIONEER PICTURE STORIES

Street & Smith Publ., Dec., 1941

1 Red Warriors in Blackface 500.00
2 Life Story Of Errol Flynn 400.00
3 Success Stories of Brain Muscle in Action 300.00
4 Legless Ace & Boy Commando Raid Occupied France 300.00
5 How to Tell Uniform and Rank of Any Navy Man 300.00
6 General Jimmy Doolittle 350.00
7 Life Story of Admiral Halsey . . 350.00
8 Life Story of Timoshenko 300.00
9 Dec., '43,Man Who Conquered The Wild Frozen North 300.00

PIRACY

E.C. Comics, Oct.–Nov., 1954

1 WW,JDa,AW,WW(c),RC,AT . . 750.00
2 RC,JDa(c),WW,AW,AT. 600.00
3 RC,GE, RC(c),Grl 500.00
4 RC,GE,RC(c),Grl 450.00
5 RC,GE,BK(c),Grl 450.00
6 JDa,RC,GE,BK(c),Grl 450.00
7 Oct Nov GE(c),RC,GE,Grl . . . 450.00

PIRATES COMICS

Hillman Periodicals, Feb., 1950

1 . . . . 300.00
2 . . . . 200.00
3 . . . . 175.00
4 Aug–Sept., 1950 . . . . 175.00

PIXIES, THE

Magazine Enterprises, Winter, 1946

1 Mighty Atom. 200.00
2 . . . . 150.00
3 . . . . 150.00
4 . . . . 150.00
5 . . . . 150.00

Becomes:

MIGHTY ATOM, THE

1949

6 . . . . 150.00

PLANET COMICS

Love Romance Publ. (Fiction House Magazines), Jan., 1940–Winter, 1953

1 AB,DBr,HcK, Planet Comics, WE&LF,O:Aura,B:Flint Baker, Red Comet,Spurt Hammond, Capt. Nelson Cole 17,000.00
2 HcK,LF(c) 6,500.00
3 WE(c),HcK 4,000.00
4 HcK,B:Gale Allan and the Girl Squad 3,500.00
5 BP,HcK 3,200.00
6 BP,HcK,BP(c),The Ray Pirates of Venus 3,400.00
7 BP,AB,HcK,BP(c) B:Buzz Crandall Planet Payson . . . 3,000.00
8 BP,AB HcK 3,000.00
9 BP,AB,GT,HcK,B:Don Granville Cosmo Corrigan . 3,000.00
10 BP,AB,GT HcK 3,000.00
11 HcK, B:Crash Parker 3,000.00
12 Dri,B:Star Fighter 3,000.00
13 Dri,B:Reef Ryan. 2,000.00
14 Dri B:Norge Benson 2,000.00
15 B: Mars,God of War 3,900.00
16 Invasion From The Void. . . . 1,800.00
17 Warrior Maid of Mercury . . . 1,800.00
18 Bondage(c) 2,000.00
19 Monsters of the Inner World 1,800.00
20 RP, Winged Man Eaters of the Exile Star 1,800.00
21 RP,B:Lost World Hunt Bowman. 2,000.00
22 Inferno on the Fifth Moon . . 1,800.00
23 GT,Lizard Tyrant of the Twilight World 1,700.00
24 GT,Grl Raiders From The Red Moon 1,700.00
25 Grl,B:Norge Benson 1,700.00
26 Grl,B:The Space Rangers Bondage(c). 1,800.00
27 Grl, The Fire Eaters of Asteroid Z 1,500.00
28 Grl, Bondage (c) 2,200.00
29 Grl,Dragon Raiders of Aztla. 2,600.00
30 GT,Grl City of Lost Souls. . . 2,000.00
31 Grl,Fire Priests of Orbit6X . . 1,600.00
32 Slaver's Planetoid 1,700.00
33 MA 1,600.00
34 MA,Bondage 1,800.00
35 MA B:Mysta of The Moon . . 1,600.00
36 MA Collosus of the Blood Moon 1,600.00
37 MA, Behemoths of the Purple Void. 1,600.00
38 MA 1,500.00
39 MA.Death Webs Of Zenith 3 1,500.00
40 Chameleon Men from Galaxy 9 . . . . 1,500.00
41 MA,AgF,New O: Auro Bondage (c) 1,500.00
42 MA,AgF,E:Gale Allan 1,500.00
43 MA,AgF Death Rays From the Sun.. . . . . 1,500.00
44 MA,Bbl,B:Futura 1,500.00
45 Ma,Bbl,Her Evilness from Xanado. 1,500.00
46 MA,Bbl,GE The Mecho-Men From Mars 1,500.00
47 MA,Bbl,GE,The Great Green Spawn 1,200.00
48 MA,GE 1,200.00

All comics prices listed are for *Near Mint* condition.

Planet Comics #60
© Fiction House Magazines

Plastic Man #17
© Quality Comics Group

Playful Little Audrey #7
© Harvey Publications

49 MA,GE, Werewolves From Hydra Hell 1,200.00
50 MA,GE,The Things of Xeves 1,200.00
51 MA,GE, Mad Mute X-Adapts 1,000.00
52 GE,Mystery of the Time Chamber 1,000.00
53 MB,GE,Bondage(c) Dwarflings From Oceania . . 1,000.00
54 MB,GE,Robots From Inferno 1,000.00
55 MB,GE,Giants of the Golden Atom 1,000.00
56 MB,GE,Grl 900.00
57 MB,GE,Grl 900.00
58 MB,GE,Grl 900.00
59 MB,GE,Grl,LSe 900.00
60 GE,Grl,Vassals of Volta 900.00
61 GE,Grl, The Brute in the Bubble 800.00
62 GE,Musta,Moon Goddess . . . 800.00
63 GE,Paradise or Inferno 800.00
64 GE,Monkeys From the Blue . . 800.00
65 The Lost World 800.00
66 The Plague of the Locust Men 800.00
67 The Nymphs of Neptune 800.00
68 Synthoids of the 9th Moon . . . 800.00
69 The Mentalists of Mars 800.00
70 Cargo For Amazonia 800.00
71 Sandhogs of Mars 700.00
72 Last Ship to Paradise 700.00
73 The Martian Plague 700.00

PLASTIC MAN

Comics Magazines (Quality Comics Group), Summer, 1943–Nov., 1956

1 JCo(a&c)Game of Death . . . 6,000.00
2 JCo(a&c)The Gay Nineties Nightmare 2,500.00
3 JCo(a&c) 1,600.00
4 JCo(a&c) 1,500.00
5 JCo(a&c) 1,400.00
6 JCo(a&c) 1,500.00
7 JCo(a&c) 1,500.00
8 JCo(a&c) 1,500.00
9 JCo(a&c) 1,500.00
10 JCo(a&c) 1,500.00
11 JCo(a&c) 1,500.00
12 JCo(a&c),V:Spadehead 1,500.00
13 JCo(a&c),V:Mr.Hazard 1,500.00
14 JCo(a&c),Words,Symbol of Crime 1,500.00
15 JCo(a&c),V:BeauBrummel . . 1,500.00
16 JCo(a&c),Money Means Trouble 1,500.00
17 JCo(a&c),A:The Last Man on Earth 1,200.00
18 JCo(a&c),Goes Back to the Farm 1,200.00
19 JCo(a&c),V;Prehistoric Plunder 1,200.00
20 JCo(a&c),A:Sadly,Sadly 1,200.00
21 JCo(a&c),V:Crime Minded Mind Reader 800.00
22 JCo(a&c), Which Twin is the Phony 800.00
23 JCo(a&c),The Fountain of Age 800.00
24 JCo(a&c),The Black Box of Terror 800.00
25 JCo(a&c),A:Angus MacWhangus 800.00
26 JCo(a&c),On the Wrong Side of the Law? 800.00
27 JCo(a&c),V:The Leader 800.00
28 JCo(a&c),V:Shasta 800.00
29 JCo(a&c),V:Tricky Toledo 800.00
30 JCo(a&c),V:Weightless Wiggins 800.00
31 JCo(a&c),V:Raka the Witch Doctor 600.00
32 JCo(a&c),V:Mr.Fission 600.00
33 JCo(a&c),V:The Mad Professor 600.00
34 JCo(a&c),Smuggler'sHaven . . 600.00
35 JCo(a&c),V:The Hypnotist . . . 600.00
36 JCo(a&c),The Uranium Underground 600.00
37 JCo(a&c),V:Gigantic Ants 600.00
38 JCo(a&c),The Curse of Monk Mauley 600.00
39 JCo(a&c),The Stairway to Madness 600.00
40 JCo(a&c),The Ghoul of Ghost Swamp 600.00
41 JCo(a&c),The Beast with the Bloody Claws 500.00
42 JCo(a&c),The King of Thunderbolts 500.00
43 JCo(a&c),The Evil Terror 500.00
44 JCo(a&c),The Magic Cup 500.00
45 The Invisible Raiders 500.00
46 V:The Spider 500.00
47 The Fiend of a Thousand Faces 500.00
48 Killer Crossbones 500.00
49 JCo,The Weapon for Evil 500.00
50 V:Iron Fist 500.00
51 Incredible Sleep Weapon 500.00
52 V:Indestructible Wizard 500.00
53 V:Dazzia,Daughter of Darkness 500.00
54 V:Dr.Quomquat 500.00
55 The Man Below Zero 500.00
56 JCo, The Man Who Broke the Law of Gravity 500.00
57 The Chemist's Cauldron 500.00
58 JCo,The Amazing Duplicating Machine 500.00
59 JCo,V:The Super Spy 500.00
60 The Man in the Fiery Disguise 450.00
61 V:King of the Thunderbolts . . . 450.00
62 V:The Smokeweapon 450.00
63 V:Reflecto 450.00
64 The Invisible Raiders 450.00

PLAYFUL LITTLE AUDREY

Harvey Publications, 1957

1 . . . . 350.00
2 . . . . 200.00
3 . . . . 135.00
4 . . . . 135.00
5 . . . . 135.00
6 . . . . 100.00
7 . . . . 100.00
8 . . . . 100.00
9 . . . . 100.00
10 thru 30 . . . . @100.00

POCAHONTAS

Pocahontas Fuel Co., Oct., 1941

N# 350.00
2 . . . . 325.00

POCKET COMICS

Harvey Publications, Aug., 1941

1 100 pages,O:Black Cat,Spirit of '76,Red Blazer Phantom Sphinx & Zebra,B:Phantom Ranger,British Agent #99, Spin Hawkins,Satan 1,400.00
2 . . . . 900.00
3 . . . . 650.00
4 Jan.'42,All Features End 650.00

POGO POSSUM

Dell Publishing Co., 1941

1 WK,A:Swamp Land Band . . . 1,700.00
2 WK 1,000.00
3 WK 600.00

Police Against Crime #1
© Premier Magazines

Police Comics #29
© Quality Comics Group

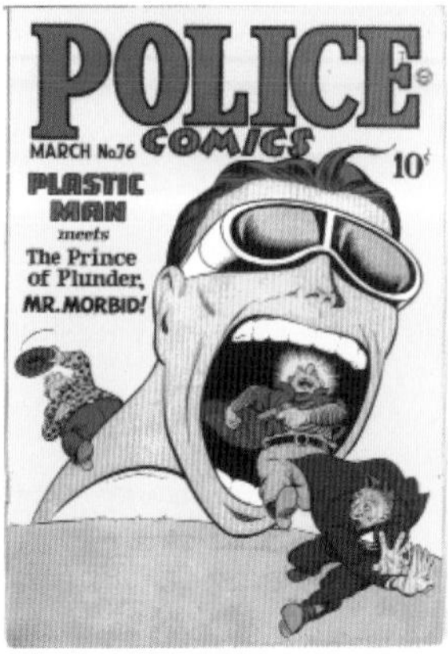

Police Comics #76
© Quality Comics Group

4 WK 600.00
5 WK 600.00
6 thru 10 WK . . . . @450.00
11 WK, Christmas (c) . . . . @400.00
12 thru 16 WK . . . . @500.00

POLICE ACTION

Marvel, Jan., 1954

1 JF,GC,JMn(c),Riot Squad 225.00
2 JF,Over the Wall 150.00
3 JMn 125.00
4 DAy 125.00
5 DAy,JMn. 125.00
6 . . . . 125.00
7 BPNov., 1954 . . . . 125.00

POLICE AGAINST CRIME

Premier Magazines, 1954

1 Knife in Face 300.00
2 . . . . 165.00
3 . . . . 125.00
4 thru 9 . . . . @125.00

Po

POLICE BADGE
See: SPY THRILLERS

POLICE BADGE #479

Marvel Atlas, 1955

5 . . . . 125.00

POLICE COMICS

Comic Magazines (Quality Comics Group), Aug., 1941

1 JCo,WE.PGv,RC,FGu,AB, GFx(a&c),B&O:Plastic Man The Human Bomb,#711,I&B, Chic Canter,The Firebrand Mouthpiece,Phantom Lady The Sword 11,000.00
2 JCo,PGv,WE,RC,FGu, GFx(a&c) 5,000.00
3 JCo,PGv,WE,RC,FGu, GFx(a&c) 3,000.00
4 JCo,GFx,PGv,WE,RC,FGu, GFx&WEC(c) 2,600.00
5 JCo,PGv,WE,RC,FGu, GFx(a&c) 2,500.00
6 JCo,PGv,WE,RC,FGu, GFx(a&c) 2,200.00
7 JCo,PGv,WE,RC,FGu, GFx(a&c) 2,200.00
8 JCo,PGv,WE,RC,FGu, GFx(a&c),B&O:Manhunter 2,500.00
9 JCo,PGv,WE,RC,FGu, GFx(a&c) 1,800.00
10 JCo,PGv,WE,RC,FGu, GFx(a&c) 1,700.00
11 JCo,PGv,WE,RC,FGu,GFx(a&c), B:Rep:Rep.Spirit Strips. . . . 3,000.00
12 JCo,GFx,PGv,WE,FGu,AB, RC(c) I:Ebony. 1,700.00
13 JCo,GFx,PGv,WE,FGu,AB,RC(c) E:Firebrand,I:Woozy Winks 1,700.00
14 JCo,PGv,WE,Jku,GFx(a&c). 1,500.00
15 JCo,PGv,WE,Jku,GFx(a&c) E#711,B:Destiny 1,500.00
16 JCo,PGv,WE,JKu. 1,500.00
17 PGv,WE,JKu,JCo(a&c) 1,500.00
18 PGv,WE,JCo(a&c) 1,500.00
19 PGv,WE,JCo(a&c) 1,500.00
20 PGv,WE,JCo(a&c),A:Jack Cole in Phantom Lady 1,500.00
21 PGv,WE,JCo(a&c) 1,400.00
22 PGv,WE,RP,JCo(a&c) The Eyes Have it 1,400.00
23 WE,RP,JCo(a&c),E:Phantom Lady 1,200.00
24 WE,HK,JCo(a&c),B:Flatfoot Burns 1,200.00
25 WE,HK,RP,JCo(a&c),The Bookstore Mysrery 1,200.00
26 WE,Hk,JCo(a&c)E:Flatfoot Burns 1,200.00
27 WE,JCo(a&c) 1,200.00
28 WE,JCo(a&c) 1,200.00
29 WE,JCo(a&c) 1,200.00
30 WE,JCo(a&c),A Slippery Racket 1,200.00
31 WE,JCo(a&c),Is Plastic Man Washed Up?. 1,100.00
32 WE,JCo(a&c),Fiesta Turns Into a Fracas 1,100.00
33 JCo,WE 1,100.00
34 WE,JCo(a&c) 1,100.00
35 WE,JCo(a&c) 1,100.00
36 WE,JCo(a&c),Rest In Peace 1,100.00
37 WE,PGv,JCo(a&c),Love Comes to Woozy 1,100.00
38 WE,PGv,JCo(a&c) 1,100.00
39 WE,PGv,JCo(a&c) 1,100.00
40 WE,PGv,JCo(a&c) 1,100.00
41 WE,PGv,JCo(a&c),E:Reps. of Spirit Strip 1,100.00
42 LF&WE,PGv,JCo(a&c), Woozy Cooks with Gas . . . 1,100.00
43 LF&WE,PGv,JCo(a&c). 1,100.00
44 PGv,LF,JCo(a&c) 1,100.00
45 PGv,LF,JCo(a&c) 1,100.00
46 PGv,LF,JCo(a&c) 1,100.00
47 PGv,LF,JCo(a&c),V:Dr.Slicer 1,100.00
48 PGv,LF,JCo(a&c),V:Big Beaver 1,100.00
49 PGv,LF,JCo(a&c),V:Thelma Twittle 1,100.00
50 PGv,LF,JCo(a&c) 1,100.00
51 PGv,LF,JCo(a&c),V:The Granite Lady 1,000.00
52 PGv,LF,JCo(a&c) 1,000.00
53 PGv,LF,JCo(a&c),V:Dr. Erudite 1,000.00
54 PGv,LF,JCo(a&c) 1,000.00
55 PGv,LF,JCo(a&c),V:The Sleepy Eyes 1,000.00
56 PGv,LF,JCo(a&c),V:The Yes Man 1,000.00
57 PGv,LF,JCo(a&c),V:Mr.Misfit 1,000.00
58 PGv,LF,JCo(a&c),E:The Human Bomb 1,000.00
59 PGv,LF,JCo(a&c),A:Mr. Happiness. 1,000.00
60 PGv,LF,JCo(a&c) 500.00
61 PGv,LF,JCo(a&c) 1,000.00
62 PGv,LF,JCo(a&c) 1,000.00
63 PGv,LF,JCo(a&c),V:The Crab 1,000.00
64 PGv,LF,HK,JCo(a&c) 1,000.00
65 PGv,LF,JCo(a&c) 1,000.00
66 PGv,LF,JCo(a&c) Love Can Mean Trouble 1,000.00
67 LF,JCo(a&c), V:The Gag Man 1,000.00
68 LF,JCo(a&c). 1,000.00
69 LF,JCo(a&c),V:Strecho. 1,000.00
70 LF,JCo(a&c). 1,000.00
71 LF,JCo(a&c) 600.00
72 LF,JCo(a&c),V:Mr.Cat 600.00
73 LF,JCo(a&c) 600.00
74 LF,JCo(a&c),V:Prof.Dimwit . . . 600.00
75 LF,JCo(a&c) 600.00
76 LF,JCo(a&c),V:Mr.Morbid 600.00
77 LF,JCo(a&c),V:Skull Face & Eloc 600.00
78 LF,JCo(a&c),A Hot Time In Dreamland. 600.00
79 LF,JCo(a&c),V:Eaglebeak. . . . 600.00
80 LF,JCo(a&c),V:Penetro 600.00
81 LF,JCo(a&c),V:A Gorilla 600.00
82 LF,JCo(a&c) 600.00
83 LF,JCo(a&c) 600.00
84 LF,JCo(a&c) 600.00
85 LF,JCo(a&c),V:Lucky 7 . . . . . . 600.00
86 LF,JCo(a&c),V:The Baker 600.00
87 LF,JCo(a&c) 600.00

Police Comics #115
© Quality Comics Group

Popeye #14
© Dell Publishing Co.

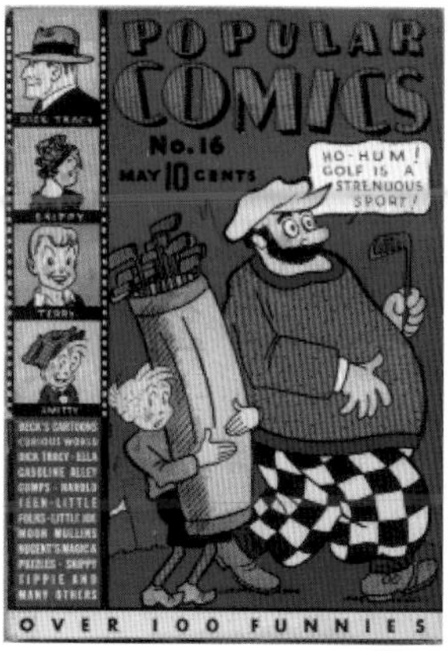

Popular Comics #16
© Dell Publishing Co.

88 LF,JCo(a&c),V:The Seen 600.00
89 JCo(a&c),V:The Vanishers . . . 550.00
90 LF,JCo(a&c),V:Capt.Rivers . . . 550.00
91 JCo(a&c),The Forest Primeval 600.00
92 LF,JCo(a&c),V:Closets Kennedy 600.00
93 JCo(a&c),V:The Twinning Terror 500.00
94 JCo(a&c),WE 800.00
95 JCo(a&c),WE,V:Scowls 800.00
96 JCo(a&c),WE,V:Black Widow . 800.00
97 JCo(a&c),WE,V:The Mime . . . 800.00
98 JCo(a&c),WE 800.00
99 JCo(a&c),WE 800.00
100 JCo(a&c) 1,000.00
101 JCo(a&c) 1,000.00
102 JCo(a&c),E:Plastic Man. . . 1,000.00
103 JCo,LF,B&I:Ken Shannon; Bondage(c) 550.00
104 The Handsome of Homocide 400.00
105 Invisible Hands of Murder. . . 400.00
106 Museum of Murder 400.00
107 Man with the Shrunken Head 400.00
108 The Headless Horse Player . 400.00
109 LF,Bondage(c),Blood on the Chinese Fan 400.00
110 Murder with a Bang. 400.00
111 Diana, Homocidal Huntress . 400.00
112 RC,The Corpse on the Sidewalk 450.00
113 RC(a&c), The Dead Man with the Size 13 Shoe 450.00
114 The Terrifying Secret of the Black Bear. 400.00
115 Don't Let Them Kill Me 400.00
116 Stage Was Set For Murder . . 400.00
117 Bullet Riddled Bookkeeper . . 400.00
118 Case of the Absent Corpse. . 400.00
119 A Fast & Bloody Buck 400.00
120 Death & The Derelict 400.00
121 Curse of the Clawed Killer . . 400.00
122 The Lonely Hearts Killer 400.00
123 Death Came Screaming 400.00
124 Masin Murder 400.00
125 Bondage(c),The Killer of King Arthur's Court 450.00
126 Hit & Run Murders 400.00
127 Oct'53,Death Drivers 400.00

POLICE LINE-UP

Avon Periodicals/ Realistic Comics, Aug., 1951

1 WW,P(c). 500.00
2 P(c),Drugs 400.00
3 JKu,EK,P(c) 250.00
4 July, '52;EK 250.00

POLICE TRAP

Mainline, Sept., 1954

1 S&K(c) 350.00
2 S&K(c) 200.00
3 S&K(c) 200.00
4 S&K(c) 200.00

Charlton Comics, July, 1955

5 S&K,S&K(c) 300.00
6 S&K,S&K(c) 300.00

Becomes:

PUBLIC DEFENDER IN ACTION

Charlton Comics, March, 1956

7 . . . . 125.00
8 and 9 . . . . @100.00
10 thru 12, ... @100.00

POLLY PIGTAILS

Parents' Magazine Institute, Jan., 1946

1 Ph(c) 150.00
2 Ph(c) 125.00
3 Ph(c) 100.00
4 Ph(c) 100.00
5 Ph(c) 100.00
6 Ph(c) 100.00
7 Ph(c) 100.00
8 . . . . 100.00
9 . . . . 100.00
10 . . . . 100.00
11 thru 22 . . . . @100.00
22 Ph(c) 100.00
23 Ph(c) 100.00
34 thru 43 . . . . @100.00

POPEYE

Dell Publishing Co., 1948

1 . . . . 450.00
2 . . . . 250.00
3 'Welcome to Ghost Island'. . . . 225.00
4 . . . . 225.00
5 . . . . 225.00
6 . . . . 225.00
7 . . . . 225.00
8 . . . . 225.00
9 . . . . 225.00
10 . . . . 225.00
11 . . . . 200.00
12 . . . . 200.00
13 . . . . 200.00
14 thru 20. . . . . @200.00
21 thru 30. . . . . @150.00
31 thru 40. . . . . @135.00
41 thru 45. . . . . @125.00
46 O:Swee' Pea. 150.00
47 thru 50. . . . . @125.00
51 thru 60. . . . . @100.00
61 thru 65. . . . . @100.00

POP-POP COMICS

R.B. Leffingwell Co., 1946

2 . . . . 150.00

POPSICLE PETE FUN BOOK

Joe Lowe Corp., 1947

N# 125.00

POPULAR COMICS

Dell Publishing Co., Feb., 1936

1 Dick Tracy, Little Orphan Annie 9,000.00
2 Terry Pirates 4,000.00
3 Terry,Annie,Dick Tracy 3,000.00
4 . . . . 2,000.00
5 B:Tom Mix 2,000.00
6 I:Scribbu 1,800.00
7 . . . . 1,500.00
8 Scribbu & Reg Fellers. 1,500.00
9 . . . . 1,500.00
10 Terry,Annie,Tracy 1,500.00
11 Terry,Annie,Tracy 1,000.00
12 Christmas(c). 1,000.00
13 Terry,Annie,Tracy 1,000.00
14 Terry,Annie,Tracy 1,000.00
15 Terry,Annie,Tracy 1,000.00
16 Terry,Annie,Tracy 1,000.00
17 Terry,Annie,Tracy 1,000.00
18 Terry,Annie,Tracy 1,000.00
19 Terry,Annie,Tracy 1,000.00
20 Terry,Annie,Tracy 1,000.00
21 Terry,Annie,Tracy 750.00
22 Terry,Annie,Tracy 750.00
23 Terry,Annie,Tracy 750.00
24 Terry,Annie,Tracy 750.00
25 Terry,Annie,Tracy 750.00
26 Terry,Annie,Tracy 750.00
27 E:Terry,Annie,Tracy. 750.00
28 A:Gene Autry. 550.00
29 . . . . 550.00
30 . . . . 550.00

Popular Comics #61
© Dell Publishing Co.

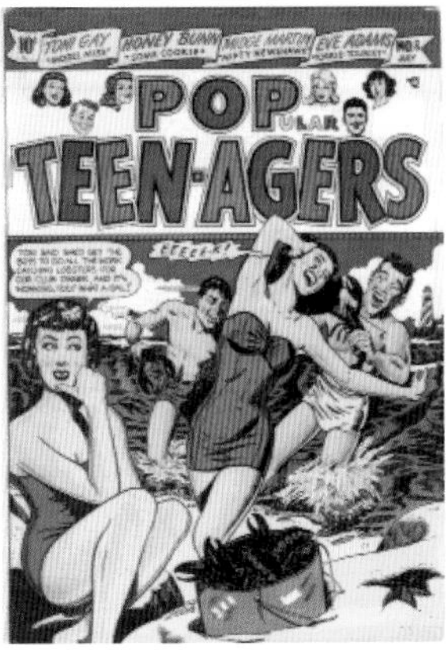

Popular Teen-Agers #8
© Star Publications

Powerhouse Pepper Comics #1
© Marvel Comics Group

31 A:Jim McCoy 550.00
32 A:Jim McCoy 550.00
33 . . . . . 550.00
34 . . . . . 550.00
35 Christmas(c),Tex Ritter 550.00
36 . . . . . 550.00
37 . . . . . 550.00
38 B:Gang Busters 600.00
39 . . . . . 550.00
40 . . . . . 550.00
41 . . . . . 550.00
42 . . . . . 550.00
43 F:Gang Busters 550.00
44 . . . . . 400.00
45 Tarzan(c) 400.00
46 O:Martan the Marvel Man 500.00
47 F:Martan the Marvel Man 350.00
48 F:Martan the Marvel Man 350.00
49 F:Martan the Marvel Man 350.00
50 . . . . . 350.00
51 B&O:Voice 350.00
52 A:Voice 350.00
53 F:The Voice 325.00
54 F:Gang Busters,A:Voice 325.00
55 F:Gang Busters 350.00
56 F:Gang Busters 325.00
57 F:The Marvel Man 325.00
58 F:The Marvel Man 325.00
59 F:The Marvel Man 325.00
60 O:Prof. Supermind 350.00
61 Prof. Supermind & Son 275.00
62 Supermind & Son 275.00
63 B:Smilin' Jack 275.00
64 Smilin'Jack,Supermind 275.00
65 Professor Supermind 275.00
66 . . . . . 275.00
67 Gasoline Alley 275.00
68 F:Smilin' Jack 275.00
69 F:Smilin' Jack 275.00
70 F:Smilin' Jack 275.00
71 F:Smilin' Jack 275.00
72 B:Owl,Terry & the Pirates 500.00
73 F:Terry and the Pirates 300.00
74 F:Smilin' Jack 300.00
75 F:Smilin'Jack,A:Owl 300.00
76 Captain Midnight 425.00
77 Captain Midnight 425.00
78 Captain Midnight 425.00
79 A:Owl 300.00
80 F:Smilin' Jack,A:Owl 300.00
81 F: Terry&thePirates,A:Owl 300.00
82 F:Smilin' Jack,A:Owl 300.00
83 F:Smilin' Jack,A:Owl 300.00
84 F:Smilin' Jack,A:Owl 300.00
85 F:ThreeLittleGremlins,A:Owl 300.00
86 F:Three Little Gremlins 200.00
87 F:Smilin' Jack 200.00
88 F:Smilin' Jack 200.00
89 F:Smokey Stover 200.00
90 F:Terry and the Pirates 200.00
91 F:Smokey Stover 200.00
92 F:Terry and the Pirates 200.00
93 F:Smilin' Jack 200.00
94 F:Terry and the Pirates 200.00
95 F:Smilin' Jack 200.00
96 F:Gang Busters 200.00
97 F:Smilin' Jack 200.00
98 B:Felix Cat 225.00
99 F:Bang Busters 200.00
100 . . . . . 250.00
101 thru 141 . . . . . @175.00
142 E:Terry & the Pirates 125.00
143 . . . . . 125.00
144 . . . . . 125.00
145 F:Harold Teen 125.00

POPULAR ROMANCES

Better Publications (Standard Comics), Dec., 1949

5 B:Ph(c) 150.00
6 Ph(c) 100.00
7 RP 100.00
8 Ph(c) 100.00
9 Ph(c) 100.00
10 WW 150.00
11 thru 16 . . . . . @100.00
17 WE 100.00
18 thru 21 . . . . . @100.00
22 thru 27 ATh,Ph(c) . . . . . @125.00

SCHOOL DAY ROMANCES

Star Publications, Nov.–Dec., 1949

1 LbC(c),Teen-Age 375.00
2 LbC(c) 350.00
3 LbC(c),Ph(c) 350.00
4 LbC(c),JyD,RonaldReagan . . . 400.00

Becomes:

POPULAR TEEN-AGERS

Sept., 1950

5 LbC(c),Toni Gay, Eve Adams . 400.00
6 LbC(c),Ginger Bunny, Midge Martin 350.00
7 LbC(c) 350.00
8 LbC(c) 350.00
9 LbC(c) Romances 250.00
10 LbC(c) Secrets of Love 225.00
11 LbC(c) Secrets of Love 225.00
12 LbC(c) Secrets of Love 225.00
13 LbC(c),JyD Secrets of Love . . 225.00
14 LbC,WW, Secrets of Love Spanking 300.00
15 LbC(c),JyD Secrets of Love . . 225.00
16 Secrets of Love 200.00
17 LbC(c),JyD Secrets of Love . . 200.00
18 LbC(c) Secrets of Love 200.00
19 LbC(c) Secrets of Love 200.00
20 LbC(c),JyD Secrets of Love . . 225.00
21 LbC(c),JyD Secrets of Love . . 225.00
22 LbC(c) Secrets of Love 200.00
23 LbC(c) Secrets of Love 200.00

POWER COMICS

Holyoke/Narrative Publ., 1944

1 LbC(c) 2,000.00
2 B:Dr.Mephisto,Hitler(c) 2,100.00
3 LbC(c) 2,400.00
4 LbC(c) 2,000.00

POWERHOUSE PEPPER COMICS

Marvel, 1943—Nov., 1948

1 BW,Movie Auditions(c) 2,500.00
2 BW,Dinner(c) 1,200.00
3 BW,Boxing Ring(c) 1,100.00
4 BW,Subway(c) 1,100.00
5 BW,Bankrobbers(c) 1,300.00

PRIDE OF THE YANKEES

Magazine Enterprises, 1949

1 N#,OW,Ph(c),The Life of Lou Gehrig 1,100.00

PRISON BREAK

Avon Periodicals/Realistic, Sept., 1951

1 WW(c),WW 550.00
2 WW(c),WW,JKu 400.00
3 JD,JO 300.00
4 EK 250.00
5 EK,CI 250.00

PRIVATE EYE

Marvel Atlas, Jan., 1951

1 . . . . . 250.00
2 . . . . . 175.00
3 GT 175.00
4 . . . . . 125.00
5 . . . . . 125.00

Po

Prize Comics #8
© Prize Publications

Prize Comics #51
© Prize Publications

Prize Comics Western #86
© Prize Comics

6 JSt 125.00
7 . . . . 125.00
8 March, 1952. . . . . 125.00

PRIZE COMICS

Feature Publications (Prize Publ.), March, 1940

1 O&B:Power Nelson,Jupiter. B:Ted O'Neil,Jaxon of the Jungle,Bucky Brady, Storm Curtis, Rocket(c) . . . 6,000.00
2 B:The Owl. 3,000.00
3 Power Nelson(c). 2,700.00
4 Power Nelson(c). 2,700.00
5 A:Dr.Dekkar. 2,400.00
6 A:Dr.Dekkar. 2,400.00
7 S&K,DBr,JK(c),O&B DR Frost, Frankenstein,B:GreenLama, Capt Gallant,Voodini Twist Turner 4,500.00
8 S&K,DBr 2,600.00
9 S&K,DBr,Black Owl(c) 2,500.00
10 DBr,Black Owl(c) 2,000.00
11 DBr,O:Bulldog Denny. 1,800.00
12 DBr. 1,800.00
13 DBr,O&B:Yank and Doodle,Bondage(c). 2,000.00
14 DBr,Black Owl(c) 1,800.00
15 DBr,Black Owl(c) 1,800.00
16 DBr,JaB,B:Spike Mason. . . . 1,800.00
17 DBr,Black Owl(c) 1,800.00
18 DBr,Black Owl(c) 1,800.00
19 DBr,Yank&Doodle(c) 1,800.00
20 DBr,Yank&Doodle(c) 1,800.00
21 DBr,JaB(c),Yank&Doodle(c). 1,500.00
22 DBr,Yank&Doodle(c) 1,500.00
23 DBr,Uncle Sam(c) 1,500.00
24 DBr,Abe Lincoln(c). 1,500.00
25 DBr,JaB,Yank&Doodle(c). . . 1,500.00
26 DBr,JaB,JaB(c),Liberty Bell(c) 1,500.00
27 DBr,Yank&Doodle(c) 1,000.00
28 DBr,Yank&Doodle(c). 900.00
29 DBr,JaB(c)Yank&Doodle(c). . . 900.00
30 DBr,Yank&Doodle(c) 1,000.00
31 DBr,Yank&Doodle(c). 900.00
32 DBr,Yank&Doodle(c). 900.00
33 DBr,Bondage(c),Yank & Doodle. 1,000.00
34 DBr,O:Airmale;New Black Owl 1,000.00
35 DBr,B:Flying Fist & Bingo 750.00
36 DBr,Yank&Doodle(c). 750.00
37 DBr,I:Stampy,Hitler(c) 800.00
38 DBr,B.Owl,Yank&Doodle(c) . . 750.00
39 DBr,B.Owl,Yank&Doodle(c) . . 750.00
40 DBr,B.Owl,Yank&Doodle(c) . . 750.00
41 DBr,B.Owl,Yank&Doodle(c) . . 750.00
42 DBr,B.Owl,Yank&Doodle(c) . . 500.00
43 DBr,B.Owl,Yank&Doodle(c) . . 500.00
44 DBr, B&I:Boom Boom Brannigan 500.00
45 DBr 500.00
46 DBr 500.00
47 DBr 500.00
48 DBr,B:Prince Ra;Bondage(c) . 600.00
49 DBr,Boom Boom(c). 500.00
50 DBr,Frankenstein(c) 500.00
51 DBr 500.00
52 DBr, B:Sir Prize. 500.00
53 DBr, The Man Who Could Read Features. 500.00
54 DBr 500.00
55 DBr,Yank&Doodle(c). 500.00
56 DBr,Boom Boom (c) 500.00
57 DBr,Santa Claus(c). 500.00
58 DBr,The Poisoned Punch 500.00
59 DBr,Boom Boom(c). 500.00
60 DBr,Sir Prise(c). 500.00
61 DBr,The Man wih the Fighting Feet 500.00
62 DBr,Hck(c),Yank&Doodle(c) . . 500.00
63 DBr,S&K,S&K(c),Boom Boom(c). 550.00
64 DBr,Blackowl Retires 400.00
65 DBr,DBr(c),Frankenstein. 400.00
66 DBr,DBr(c),Frankenstein. 400.00
67 DBr,B:Brothers in Crime 400.00
68 DBr,RP(c) 400.00

Becomes:

PRIZE COMICS WESTERN

Feature Publ., April–May, 1948

69 ACa(c),B:Dusty Ballew 150.00
70 ACa(c). 125.00
71 ACa(c). 125.00
72 ACa(c),JSe 125.00
73 ACa(c). 125.00
74 ACa(c). 125.00
75 JSe,S&K(c),6-Gun Showdown at Rattlesnake Gulch. 135.00
76 Ph(c),Randolph Scott 150.00
77 Ph(c),JSe,Streets of Laredo,movie. 135.00
78 Ph(c),JSe,HK,Bullet Code, movie 200.00
79 Ph(c),JSe,Stage to China, movie 200.00
80 Ph(c),Gunsmoke Justice. 150.00
81 Ph(c),The Man Who Shot Billy The Kid 150.00
82 Ph(c),MBi,JSe&BE,Death Draws a Circle. 150.00
83 JSe,S&K(c) 125.00
84 JSe 100.00
85 JSe,B:American Eagle 300.00
86 JSe 150.00
87 JSe&BE. 150.00
88 JSe&BE. 150.00
89 JSe&BE. 150.00
90 JSe&Be. 150.00
91 JSe&BE,JSe&BE(c) 150.00
92 JSe,JSe&BE(c). 150.00
93 JSe,JSe&BE(c), ... 150.00
94 JSe&BE,JSe&BE(c) 150.00
95 JSe,JSe&BE(c). 150.00
96 JSe,JSe&BE,JSe&BE(c). 150.00
97 JSe,JSe&BE,JSeBE(c) 150.00
98 JSe&BE,JSe&BE(c) 150.00
99 JSe&BE,JSe&BE(c) 150.00
100 JSe,JSe(c) 175.00
101 JSe 150.00
102 JSe 150.00
103 JSe 150.00
104 JSe 150.00
105 JSe 150.00
106 JSe 100.00
107 JSe 100.00
108 JSe 110.00
109 JSe&AW 125.00
110 JSe&BE. 125.00
111 JSe&BE. 125.00
112 . . . . 100.00
113 AW&JSe 125.00
114 MMe,B:The Drifter. 100.00
115 MMe 100.00
116 MMe 100.00
117 MMe 100.00
118 MMe,E:The Drifter. 100.00
119 Nov/Dec'56 . . . . 100.00

PRIZE MYSTERY

Key Publications, 1955

1 . . . . 125.00
2 and 3 . . . . @100.00

PSYCHOANALYSIS

E.C. Comics, March–April, 1955

1 JKa,JKa(c). 250.00
2 JKa,JKa(c). 200.00
3 JKa,JKa(c). 200.00
4 JKa,JKa(c) Sept.–Oct., 1955. . 200.00

Punch and Judy Comics #4
© Hillman Periodicals

Punch Comics #14
© Harry A Chesler

Race For the Moon #1
© Harvey Publications

PUBLIC DEFENDER IN ACTION
See: POLICE TRAP

PUBLIC ENEMIES
D.S. Publishing Co., 1948

1 AMc 300.00
2 AMc 250.00
3 AMc 200.00
4 AMc 200.00
5 AMc 200.00
6 AMc 150.00
7 AMc,Eye Injury. 200.00
8 . . . . 150.00
9 . . . . 150.00

PUDGY PIG
Charlton Comics, 1958

1 . . . . 125.00
2 . . . . 100.00

Pu

PUNCH AND JUDY COMICS
Hillman Periodicals, 1944

1 (fa) 300.00
2 . . . . 250.00
3 . . . . 200.00
4 thru 12 . . . . @175.00
2-1 . . . . 150.00
2-2 JK. 250.00
2-3 . . . . 150.00
2-4 . . . . 150.00
2-5 . . . . 150.00
2-6 . . . . 150.00
2-7 . . . . 150.00
2-8 . . . . 150.00
2-9 . . . . 150.00
2-10 JK. 250.00
2-11 JK. 250.00
2-12 JK. 250.00
3-1 JK. 250.00
3-2 . . . . 200.00
3-3 . . . . 100.00
3-4 . . . . 100.00
3-5 . . . . 100.00
3-6 . . . . 100.00
3-7 . . . . 100.00
3-8 . . . . 100.00
3-9 . . . . 100.00

PUNCH COMICS
Harry 'A' Chesler, Dec., 1941

1 B:Mr.E,The Sky Chief,Hale
the Magician,Kitty Kelly . . . 3,000.00
2 A:Capt.Glory 2,400.00
3-8 Do Not Exist
9 B:Rocket Man & Rocket
girl,Master Ken 2,400.00
10 JCo,A:Sky Chief. 1,700.00
11 JCo,O:Master Key,A:Little
Nemo 1,700.00
12 A:Rocket Boy,Capt.Glory . . . 4,000.00
13 Ric(c) 1,700.00
14 GT 1,200.00
15 FSm(c). 1,200.00
16 . . . . 1,200.00
17 . . . . 1,200.00
18 FSm(c),Bondage(c),Drug. . . 1,500.00
19 FSm(c). 1,200.00
20 Women semi-nude(c) 1,800.00
21 Drug 1,200.00
22 I:Baxter,Little Nemo 700.00
23 A:Little Nemo 700.00

PUPPET COMICS
Dougherty, Co., Spring, 1946

1 Funny Animal 125.00
2 . . . . 125.00

PURPLE CLAW, THE
Minoan Publishing Co./ Toby Press, Jan., 1953

1 O:Purple Claw 400.00
2 and 3 . . . . @250.00

PUZZLE FUN COMICS
George W. Dougherty Co., Spring, 1946

1 PGv 275.00
2 . . . . 200.00

QUEEN OF THE WEST, DALE EVANS
Dell Publishing Co., July, 1953

(1) *see Dell Four Color #479*
(1) *see Dell Four Color #528*
3 ATh, Ph(c) all 125.00
4 ATh,RsM. 110.00
5 RsM 100.00
6 RsM 100.00
7 RsM 100.00
8 RsM 100.00
9 RsM 100.00
10 RsM. 100.00
11 . . . . 75.00
12 RsM. 85.00
13 RsM. 85.00
14 RsM. 85.00
15 RsM. 85.00
16 RsM. 85.00
17 RsM. 85.00
18 RsM. 85.00
19 . . . . 75.00
20 RsM. 85.00
21 . . . . 75.00
22 RsM. 85.00

QUICK-TRIGGER WESTERN
See: WESTERN THRILLERS

RACE FOR THE MOON
Harvey Publications, 1958

1 BP 175.00
2 JK,AW,JK/AW(c) 300.00
3 JK,AW,JK/AW(c) 350.00

RACKET SQUAD IN ACTION
Capitol Stories/ Charlton Comics, May–June, 1952

1 Carnival(c) 350.00
2 . . . . 175.00
3 Roulette 175.00
4 FFr(c) 250.00
5 Just off the Boat 250.00
6 The Kidnap Racket 200.00
7 . . . . 150.00
8 . . . . 150.00
9 2 Fisted fix 150.00
10 Explosion Blast (c) 250.00
11 SD(a&c),Racing(c) 350.00
12 JoS,SD(c),Explosion(c). 900.00
13 JoS(c),The Notorious Modelling
Agency Racket,Acid 150.00
14 DG(c),Drug 200.00
15 Photo Extortion Racket. 150.00
16 thru 28 . . . . @150.00
29 March, 1958 . . . . 150.00

 All comics prices listed are for *Near Mint* condition.

Raggedy Ann and Andy #36
© Dell Publishing Co.

Range Romances #1
© Quality Comics

Rangers Comics #33
© Fiction House

RADIANT LOVE
See: DARING LOVE

RAGGEDY ANN AND ANDY
Dell Publishing Co., 1942

1 Billy & Bonnie Bee 600.00
2 . . . . 350.00
3 DNo,B:Egbert Elephant 350.00
4 DNo,WK 400.00
5 DNo 300.00
6 DNo 300.00
7 Little Black Sambo 300.00
8 . . . . 300.00
9 . . . . 300.00
10 . . . . 300.00
11 . . . . 250.00
12 . . . . 250.00
13 . . . . 250.00
14 . . . . 250.00
15 . . . . 250.00
16 thru 20 . . . . @250.00
21 Alice in Wonderland 300.00
22 thru 27 . . . . @200.00
28 WK 225.00
29 thru 39 . . . . @200.00

RAGS RABBIT
Harvey Publications, 1957

11 . . . . 120.00
12 . . . . 100.00
13 . . . . 100.00
14 . . . . 100.00
15 . . . . 100.00
16 . . . . 100.00
17 . . . . 100.00
18 . . . . 100.00

RALPH KINER HOME RUN KING
Fawcett Publications, 1950

1 N#, Life Story of the
Famous Pittsburgh Slugger . . 800.00

RAMAR OF THE JUNGLE
Toby Press/ Charlton Comics, 1954

1 Ph(c),TV Show 250.00
2 Ph(c) 200.00
3 . . . . 200.00
4 . . . . 200.00
5 Sept '56 . . . . 200.00

RANGE BUSTERS
Charlton Comics, 1955

8 . . . . 150.00
9 & 10 . . . . @100.00

RANGELAND LOVE
Marvel Comics, 1949

1 Robert Taylor 200.00
2 . . . . 150.00

RANGE ROMANCES
Comics Magazines (Quality Comics), Dec., 1949

1 PGv(a&c) 300.00
2 RC(a&c) 350.00
3 RC,Ph(c) 275.00
4 RC,Ph(c) 250.00
5 RC,PGv,Ph(c) 250.00

RANGERS OF FREEDOM
Flying Stories, Inc. (Fiction House), Oct., 1941

1 I:Ranger Girl & Rangers
of Freedom;V:Super-Brain . 5,000.00
2 V:Super -Brain 1,800.00
3 Bondage(c) The Headsman
of Hate 1,500.00
4 Hawaiian Inferno 1,200.00
5 RP,V:Super-Brain 1,200.00
6 RP,Bondage(c);Bugles
of the Damned 1,200.00
7 RP,Death to Tojo's Butchers . 1,000.00

Becomes:

RANGERS COMICS
Dec., 1942

8 RP,B:US Rangers 1,000.00
9 GT,BLb,Commando Steel
for Slant Eyes 1,000.00
10 BLb,Bondage (c) 1,100.00
11 Raiders of the
Purple Death 900.00
12 A:Commando Rangers 900.00
13 Grl,B:Commando Ranger . . 1,000.00
14 Grl,Bondage(c) 1,100.00
15 GT,Grl,Bondage(c) 1,100.00
16 Grl,GT;Burma Raid 650.00
17 GT,GT,Bondage(c),Raiders
of the Red Dawn 1,000.00
18 GT 650.00
19 GE,BLb,GT,Bondage(c) 1,100.00
20 GT 500.00
21 GT,Bondage(c) 650.00
22 GT,B&O:Firehair 500.00
23 GT,BLb,B:Kazanda 450.00
24 Bondage(c) 450.00
25 Bondage(c) 450.00
26 Angels From Hell 400.00
27 Bondage(c) 500.00
28 BLb,E:Kazanda;B&O Tiger
Man 450.00
29 Bondage(c) 500.00
30 BLb,B:Crusoe Island 450.00
31 BLb,Bondage(c) 400.00
32 BLb 400.00
33 BLb,Drug 550.00
34 BLb 300.00
35 Bl b,Bondage(c) 400.00
36 BLb,MB 300.00
37 BLb,Mb 350.00
38 BLb,MB,GE,Bondage(c) 400.00
39 BLb,GE 500.00
40 BLb,GE,BLb(c) 300.00
41 BLb,GE, L:Werewolf Hunter . . 300.00
42 BLb,GE 300.00
43 BLb,GE 300.00
44 BLb,GE 300.00
45 BLb,GEl 300.00
46 BLb,GE 300.00
47 BLb,JGr, Dr. Drew 300.00
48 BLb,JGr, L:Glory Forces 300.00
49 BLb,JGr 300.00
50 BLb,JGr,Bondage(c) 350.00
51 BLb,JGr 300.00
52 BLb,JGr,Bondage(c) 350.00
53 BLb,JGr,Prisoners of
Devil Pass 250.00
54 JGr,When The Wild
Commanches Ride 250.00
55 JGr,Massacre Guns at
Pawnee Pass 250.00
56 JGr, Gun Smuggler of
Apache Mesa 250.00
57 JGr,Redskins to the
Rescue 225.00
58 JGr,Brides of the
Buffalo Men 225.00
59 JGr,Plunder Portage 225.00
60 JGr, Buzzards of
Bushwack Trail 225.00
61 BWh(c)Devil Smoke at
Apache Basin 150.00
62 BWh(c)B:Cowboy Bob 150.00
63 BWh(c) 150.00
64 BWh(c)B:Suicide Smith 150.00

Ra

Rawhide Kid #1
© Marvel Comics Group

Real Heroes #1
© Parents' Magazine Institute

Real Life Comics #18
© Standard Publications

65 BWh(c):Wolves of the Overland Trail,Bondage(c) . . 165.00
66 BWh(c) 150.00
67 BWh(c)B:Space Rangers 150.00
68 BWh(c);Cargo for Coje 150.00
69 BWh(c);Great Red Death Ray 150.00

RAWHIDE KID

Marvel Atlas, March, 1955

1 JMn,B:Rawhide Kid & Randy, A:Wyatt Earp 1,200.00
2 JMn,Shoot-out(c) 500.00
3 V:Hustler 350.00
4 Rh(c) 350.00
5 GC,JMn 350.00
6 JMn,Six-Gun Lesson 250.00
7 AW 250.00
8 . . . . 250.00
9 . . . . 250.00
10 thru 16 Sept. 1957 . . . . @225.00
17 JK,O:Rawhide Kid; Aug. 1960 225.00
18 thru 20 . . . . @225.00
21 . . . . 225.00
22 . . . . 225.00
23 JK,O:Rawhide Kid Retold 300.00
24 thru 30 . . . . @200.00
31 JK,DAy,No Law in Mesa 200.00
32 JK,DAy,Beware of the Parker Brothers 200.00
33 JK(c),JDa,V:Jesse James. . . . 200.00
34 JDa,JK,V:Mister Lightning. . . . 200.00
35 JK(c),GC,JDa, I&D:The Raven 200.00

REAL ADVENTURE COMICS
See: ACTION ADVENTURE

REAL CLUE CRIME STORIES
See: CLUE COMICS

REAL EXPERIENCES
See: TESSIE THE TYPIST

REAL FACT COMICS

DC Comics, March-April, 1946

1 S&K,Harry Houdini story. . . . 1,000.00
2 S&K, Rin-Tin-Tin story 750.00
3 H.G. Wells story 600.00
4 Jimmy Stewart story,B:Just Imagine 650.00
5 Batman & Robin(c) 3,000.00
6 O:Tommy Tomorrow 2,400.00
7 The Flying White House 300.00
8 VF,A:Tommy Tomorrow. 1,200.00
9 S&K,Glen Miller story 500.00
10 MMe(s),The Vigilante 500.00
11 EK,How the G-Men Capture Public Enemies!. 300.00
12 How G-Men are Trained 300.00
13 Dale Evans story. 650.00
14 Will Rogers Story,Diary of Death. 400.00
15 A:The Master Magician-Thurston,A-Bomb 400.00
16 A:Four Reno Brothers, T.Tommorrow. 900.00
17 I Guard an Armored Car 400.00
18 The Mystery Man of Tombstone. 400.00
19 Weapon that Won the West . . 400.00
20 JKu,Daniel Boone 450.00
21 JKu,KitCarson,July-Aug.,1949 400.00

REAL FUNNIES

Nedor Publishing Co., Jan., 1943

1 (fa) 350.00
2 and 3 (fa) . . . . @200.00

REAL HEROES COMICS

Parents' Magazine Instituite, Sept., 1941

1 HcK,Franklin Roosevelt 500.00
2 J, Edgar Hoover. 300.00
3 General Wavell 250.00
4 Chiang Kai Shek, Churchill . . . 275.00
5 Stonewall Jackson 300.00
6 Lou Gehrig. 400.00
7 Chennault and his Flying Tigers 300.00
8 Admiral Nimitz 300.00
9 The Panda Man 250.00
10 Carl Akeley-Jungle Adventurer. 250.00
11 Wild Jack Howard 200.00
12 General Robert L Eichelberger 200.00
13 HcK,Victory at Climback 200.00
14 Pete Gray 200.00
15 Alexander Mackenzie 200.00
16 Balto of Nome Oct '46 . . . . . . 200.00

REAL LIFE STORY OF FESS PARKER

Dell Publishing Co., 1955

1 . . . . 125.00

REALISTIC ROMANCES

Avon Periodicals/ Realistic Comics, July–Aug., 1951

1 EK,Ph(c) 250.00
2 Ph(c) 150.00
3 P(c) 125.00
4 P(c) 125.00
5 . . . . 125.00
6 EK 150.00
7 GE, Avon (c) 150.00
8 EK 110.00
9 thru 14 . . . . @100.00
15 . . . . 100.00
16 EK,Drug 125.00
17 EK. 100.00

REAL LIFE COMICS

Visual Editions/Better/ Standard/Nedor, Sept., 1941

1 ASh(c),Lawrence of Arabia,Uncle Sam(c) 1,500.00
2 ASh(c),Liberty(c) 600.00
3 Adolph Hitler(c). 2,500.00
4 ASh(c)Robert Fulton, Charles DeGaulle, Old Glory. 400.00
5 ASh(c)Alexander the Great . . . 400.00
6 ASh(c)John Paul Jones,CDR . 350.00
7 ASh(c)Thomas Jefferson 350.00
8 Leonardo Da Vinci 350.00
9 US Coast Guard Issue. 350.00
10 Sir Hubert Wilkens 350.00
11 ASh(c),Odyssey on a Raft. . . . 300.00
12 ASh(c),ImpossibleLeatherneck 300.00
13 ASh(c)The Eternal Yank 300.00
14 ASh(c),Sir Isaac Newton. 300.00
15 ASh(c),William Tell 300.00
16 ASh(c),Marco Polo 300.00
17 ASh(c),Albert Einstein. 350.00
18 ASh(c),Ponce De Leon 300.00
19 ASh(c),The Fighting Seabees. 300.00
20 ASh(c),Joseph Pulitzer 300.00
21 ASh(c),Admiral Farragut 250.00
22 ASh(c),Thomas Paine. 250.00
23 ASh(c),Pedro Menendez 250.00
24 ASh(c),Babe Ruth 450.00
25 ASh(c),CQ,Marcus Whitman. . 250.00
26 ASh(c),CQ,Benvenuto Cellini . 250.00

Ra

Real Life Comics #57
© Standard Publications

Real West Romances #2
© Prize Publications

Red Dragon Comics #7
© Street & Smith

27 ASh(c),CQ,A-Bomb Story 350.00
28 ASh(c),CQ,Robert Blake. 250.00
29 ASh(c),CQ,Daniel DeFoe,
A-Bomb 300.00
30 ASh(c),CQ,Baron Robert Clive 250.00
31 ASh(c),CQ,Anthony Wayne . . 250.00
32 ASh(c),CQ,Frank Sinatra 275.00
33 ASh(c),CQ,Frederick Douglas 200.00
34 ASh(c),CQ,P Revere,J.Stewart 225.00
35 ASh(c),CQ,Rudyard Kipling . . 200.00
36 ASh(c),CQ,Story of the
Automobile. 200.00
37 ASh(c),CQ,Francis Manion,
Motion Picture, Bing Crosby . 200.00
38 ASh(c),CQ,Richard Henry
Dana 150.00
39 ASh(c),CQ,Samuel FB Morse. 150.00
40 FGu,CQ,ASh(c),Hans Christian
Anderson, Bob Feller. 250.00
41 CQ,Abe Lincoln,Jimmy Foxx . 200.00
42 Joseph Conrad,Fred Allen . . . 150.00
43 Louis Braille,O.W.Holmes 100.00
44 Citizens of Tomorrow 100.00
45 ASh(c),FrancoisVillon,
Olympics, Burl Ives 200.00
46 ASh(c),The Pony Express. . . . 200.00
47 ASh(c),Montezuma, Gershwin 200.00
48 ASh(c). 200.00
49 ASh(c),Gene Bearden,
Baseball. 200.00
50 FF,ASh(c),Lewis & Clark. 600.00
51 GE,ASh(c),Sam Houston 450.00
52 GE,FF,ASh(c),JSe&BE
Leif Erickson 650.00
53 GT,JSe&BE,Henry Wells &
William Fargo 300.00
54 GT,Alexander Graham Bell . . . 300.00
55 ASh(c),JSe&BE,The James
Brothers 300.00
56 JSe&BE. 300.00
57 JSe&BE. 300.00
58 JSe&BE,Jim Reaves. 350.00
59 FF,JSe&BE,Battle Orphan
Sept '52 . . . . 300.00

REAL LOVE
See: HAP HAZARD COMICS

REAL SCREEN COMICS
DC Comics, Spring, 1945

1 B:Fox & the Crow,Flippity
& Flop. 1,400.00
2 (fa) 650.00
3 (fa) 400.00
4 thru 7 (fa) . . . . @250.00
8 thru 11 (fa) . . . . @200.00
12 thru 20 (fa) . . . . @175.00
21 thru 30 (fa) . . . . @150.00
31 thru 40 (fa) . . . . @125.00
41 thru 128 (fa) . . . . @100.00

Becomes:

TV SCREEN CARTOONS

129 thru 137. . . . . @100.00
138 Jan.–Feb., 1961 . . . . 100.00

REAL LIFE SECRETS
Ace Books, 1949

1 . . . . 150.00

Becomes:

REAL SECRETS
Ace Periodicals, 1949

2 . . . . 125.00
3 thru 5 . . . . @100.00

REAL SPORTS COMICS
See: ALL SPORTS COMICS

REAL WESTERN HERO
See: WOW COMICS

REAL WEST ROMANCES
Crestwoood Publishing Co./ Prize Publ., April–May, 1949

1 S&K,Ph(c) 275.00
2 Ph(c),Spanking 150.00
3 JSe,BE,Ph(c) 150.00
4 S&K,JSe,BE,Ph(c) 250.00
5 S&K,MMe,JSe,Audie
Murphy Ph(c) 225.00
6 S&K,JSe,BE,Ph(c) 150.00

RECORD BOOK OF FAMOUS POLICE CASES
St. John Publishing Co., 1949

1 N#,JKu,MB(c) 450.00

RED ARROW
P.L. Publishing Co., May, 1951

1 Bondage(c) 550.00
2 . . . . 250.00
3 P(c) 250.00

RED BAND COMICS
Enwil Associates, Nov., 1944

1 The Bogeyman 500.00
2 O:Bogeyman,same(c)as#1 . . . 350.00
3 A:Captain Wizard. 300.00
4 May, '45,Repof#3,Same(c) . . . 300.00

RED CIRCLE COMICS
Enwil Associates (Rural Home Public), Jan., 1945

1 B:Red Riot,The Prankster 500.00
2 LSt,A:The Judge 400.00
3 LSt(A&c). 250.00
4 LSt(a&c) covers of #4
stapled over other comics . . . 250.00

TRAIL BLAZERS
Street & Smith Publ., Jan., 1942

1 Wright Brothers 400.00
2 Benjamin Franklin,Dodgers . . . 400.00
3 Red Barber,Yankees 500.00
4 Famous War song 250.00

Becomes:

RED DRAGON COMICS
Jan., 1943

5 JaB(c),B&O:Red Rover:
B:Capt.Jack Commando
Rex King&Jet,Minute Man . 1,500.00
6 O:Red Dragon. 3,000.00
7 The Curse of the
Boneless Men. 2,400.00
8 China V:Japan 1,000.00
9 The Reducing Ray,Jan '44 . . 1,000.00

(2nd Series) Nov., 1947

1 B:Red Dragon. 1,250.00
2 BP 900.00
3 BP,BP(c),I:Dr Neff 750.00
4 BP,BP(c) 1,000.00
5 MMe,BP,BP(c) 550.00
6 BP,BP(c) 550.00
7 MMe,BP,BP(c),May, 49 . . . . . . 550.00

REDDY KILOWATT
Educational Comics, 1958

N# 100.00
2 . . . . 150.00
3 . . . . 100.00

Red Rabbit #7
© J. Charles Lave Publ. Co.

Red Ryder Comics #89
© Dell Publishing Co.

Rex Dexter of Mars #1
© Fox Features Syndicate

RED MASK
See: TIM HOLT

RED RAVEN
See: HUMAN TORCH

RED RABBIT
**Dearfield/
J. Charles Lave Publ. Co.,
Jan., 1941**

1 (fa) 250.00
2 . . . . 150.00
3 . . . . 125.00
4 . . . . 125.00
5 . . . . 125.00
6 thru 10 . . . . @125.00
11 thru 22 . . . . @100.00

RED RYDER COMICS
**Hawley Publ./
Dell Publ. Co. 1940**

1 . . . . 4,000.00
Becomes:

HI-SPOT COMICS
Hawley Publications, 1940

2 Alley Oop, Capt. Easy. 1,700.00
Becomes:

RED RYDER COMICS
**Hawley Publ./Dell
Publ. Co., 1941**

3 Alley Oop, Capt. Easy. 2,000.00
4 . . . . 900.00
5 . . . . 900.00
6 . . . . 900.00
7 . . . . 700.00
8 . . . . 700.00
9 . . . . 700.00
10 . . . . 700.00
11 thru 20 . . . . @500.00
21 thru 30 . . . . @500.00
31 thru 40 . . . . @500.00
41 thru 50 . . . . @250.00
51 thru 60 . . . . @200.00
61 thru 70 . . . . @200.00
71 thru 80 . . . . @200.00
80 thru 99 . . . . @100.00
100 . . . . 150.00
101 thru 151 . . . . @100.00
Giant #1 . . . . 100.00
Giant #2 . . . . 100.00

RED SEAL COMICS
See: SCOOP

REDSKIN
**Youthful Magazines,
Sept., 1950**

1 Redskin,Bondage(c) 400.00
2 Apache Dance of Death. 125.00
3 Daniel Boone 100.00
4 Sitting Bull- Red Devil
of the Black Hills 100.00
5 . . . . 100.00
6 Geronimo- Terror of the
Desert,Bondage. 350.00
7 Firebrand of the Sioux 100.00
8 . . . . 100.00
9 . . . . 100.00
10 Dead Man's Magic 100.00
11 . . . . 100.00
12 Quanah Parker,Bondage(c) . . 300.00
Becomes:

FAMOUS WESTERN BADMEN
Dec., 1952

13 Redskin- Last of the
Comanches 150.00
14 . . . . 100.00
15 The Dalton Boys Apr '52. . . . . 100.00

RED WARRIOR
Marvel Atlas, Jan.–Dec., 1951

1 GT,Indian Tales 200.00
2 GT(c),The Trail of the Outcast 125.00
3 The Great Spirit Speaks 100.00
4 O:White Wing 100.00
5 . . . . 100.00
6 JMn(c) final issue. 100.00

REG'LAR FELLERS
**Visual Editions (Standard),
1947**

5 . . . . 100.00
6 . . . . 100.00

REMEMBER PEARL HARBOR
Street & Smith Publ., 1942

1 N# JaB,Battle of the
Pacific,Uncle Sam(c). 600.00

RENO BROWNE
See: COMEDY COMICS

RETURN OF THE OUTLAW
**Minoan Publishing Co.,
Feb., 1953**

1 Billy The Kid 150.00
2 . . . . 125.00
3 thru 11 . . . . @100.00

REVEALING ROMANCES
**A.A. Wyn
(Ace Magazines), Sept., 1949**

1 . . . . 135.00
2 . . . . 125.00
3 thru 6 . . . . @100.00

REX ALLEN COMICS
**Dell Publishing Co.,
Feb., 1951**

(1) *see Dell Four Color #316*
2 Western, Ph(c) all 175.00
3 thru 10 . . . . @125.00
11 thru 23. . . . . @100.00
24 ATh 110.00
25 thru 31. . . . . @100.00

REX DEXTER OF MARS
**Fox Features Syndicate,
Autumn, 1940**

1 DBr,DBr(c) Battle ofKooba . . 2,800.00

REX HART
See: BLAZE CARSON

REX MORGAN, M.D.
Argo Publications, 1950

1 . . . . 150.00
2 . . . . 100.00

RIBTICKLER
Fox Features Syndicate, 1945

1 . . . . 200.00
2 . . . . 150.00
3 Cosmo Cat. 125.00
4 thru 6 . . . . @100.00
7 Cosmo Cat. 100.00
8 thru 9 . . . . @100.00

 All comics prices listed are for *Near Mint* condition.

The Rifleman #2
© Dell Publishing Co

Rin Tin Tin #7
© Dell Publishing Co.

Rocket Ship X #1
© Fox Features Syndicate

RICKY

Visual Editions (Standard Comics), 1953

1 . . . . 100.00

THE RIDER

Four Star Comics (Ajax-Farrell Publ.), 1957

1 Swift Arrow. 150.00
2 thru 5 . . . . @100.00
Becomes:

FRONTIER TRAIL

Ajax-Farrell Publ., 1958

6 . . . . 100.00

RIFLEMAN, THE

Dell Publishing Co., 1959

1 Chuck Connors Ph(c) all 350.00
2 Ph(c) 200.00
3 ATh,Ph(c). 175.00
4 Ph(c) 165.00
5 Ph(c) 165.00
6 ATh 175.00
7 thru 10 Ph(c) . . . . @150.00
11 thru 20. . . . . @125.00

RINGO KID WESTERN

Marvel Atlas, Aug., 1954

1 JMn,JSt,O:Ringo Kid, B:Ringo Kid 350.00
2 JMn,I&O:Arab,A:Black Rider . 200.00
3 JMn 125.00
4 JMn 125.00
5 JMn 125.00
6 . . . . 125.00
7 . . . . 125.00
8 JSe. 125.00
9 . . . . 100.00
10 JSe(c),AW. 125.00
11 JSe(c) 100.00
12 JO 100.00
13 AW 125.00
14 thru 20. . . . . @100.00
21 Sept., 1957 . . . . 100.00

RIN TIN TIN

Dell Publishing Co., Nov., 1952

(1) *see Dell Four Color #434*
(1) *see Dell Four Color #476*
(1) *see Dell Four Color #523*
4 thru 10 Ph(c) all . . . . @100.00
11 thru 20 . . . . @125.00

RIOT

Marvel Atlas, 1954–56

1 RH,MMe,GC,BEv. 350.00
2 MMe,Li'l Abner. 275.00
3 MMe(c). 250.00
4 JSe,MMe,BEv,Marilyn Monroe 300.00
5 JSe,MMe,BEv,Marilyn Monroe 325.00
6 MMe,JSe 250.00

RIPLEY's BELIEVE IT OR NOT!

Harvey Publications, 1953–54

1 BP 150.00
2 Li'l Abner 125.00
3 . . . . 125.00
4 . . . . 125.00

RIVETS

Argo Publications, 1956

1 . . . . 125.00
2 . . . . 100.00
3 . . . . 100.00

ROBIN HOOD

Sussex Publ. Co (Magazine Enterprises), 1955

1 FBe 200.00
2 FBe 150.00
3 FBe 150.00
4 FBe 150.00
5 FBe 150.00
6 FBe,BP 150.00
Becomes:

ADVENTURES OF ROBIN HOOD

Magazine Enterprises, 1957

7 BP, Richard Green Ph(c) 200.00
8 Richard Green Ph(c) 200.00

ROBIN HOOD AND HIS MERRY MEN

See: THIS MAGAZINE IS HAUNTED

ROBIN HOOD TALES

Quality Comics Group, 1956

1 MB 400.00
2 MB 375.00
3 MB 375.00
4 MB 375.00
5 MB 375.00
6 MB 375.00

DC Comics, 1957–58

7 . . . . 450.00
8 thru 14 . . . . @400.00

ROCKET COMICS

Hillman Periodicals, March, 1940

1 O:Red Roberts;B:Rocket Riley,Phantom Ranger,Steel Shank,Buzzard Baynes,Lefty Larson,The Defender,Man with 1,000 Faces 4,500.00
2 . . . . 2,000.00
3 May, '40 E:All Features 2,500.00

ROCKET KELLY

Fox Features Syndicate, Autumn, 1945–Oct., Nov., 1946

N#. 400.00
1 . . . . 300.00
2 A:The Puppeteer 275.00
3 thru 6 . . . . @250.00

Ro

ROCKETMAN

Ajax/Farrell Publications, June, 1952

1 Space Stories of the Future . . . 500.00

ROCKET SHIP X

Fox Features Syndicate, Sept., 1951

1 . . . . 900.00
2 N# Variant of Original 500.00

ROCKY LANE WESTERN

Fawcett/Charlton Comics, May, 1949

1 Ph(c)B:Rocky Lane,Slim Pickins 1,400.00
2 Ph(c) 600.00
3 Ph(c) 500.00
4 Ph(c)CCB,Rail Riders Rampage,F Capt Tootsie. . . . 500.00

Rod Cameron Western #3
© Fawcett Publications

Romance Trail #1
© DC Comics

Romantic Adventures #2
© American Comics Group

5 Ph(c)The Missing Stagecoaches . . . 450.00
6 Ph(c)Ghost Town Showdown . 300.00
7 Ph(c)The Border Revolt . . . 350.00
8 Ph(c)The Sunset Feud . . . 350.00
9 Ph(c)Hermit of the Hills . . . 350.00
10 Ph(c)Badman's Reward . . . 300.00
11 Ph(c)Fool's Gold Fiasco . . . 250.00
12 Ph(c),CCB,Coyote Breed F:Capt Tootsie,Giant . . . 250.00
13 Ph(c),Giant . . . 250.00
14 Ph(c) . . . 200.00
15 Ph(c)B:Black Jacks Hitching Post,Giant . . . 225.00
16 Ph(c),Giant . . . 200.00
17 Ph(c),Giant . . . 200.00
18 Ph(c) . . . 225.00
19 Ph(c),Giant . . . 235.00
20 Ph(c)The Rodeo Rustler E:Slim Pickens . . . 235.00
21 Ph(c)B: Dee Dickens . . . 200.00
22 Ph(c) . . . 175.00
23 thru 30 . . . @200.00
31 thru 40 . . . @175.00
41 thru 55 . . . @175.00
56 thru 87 . . . @150.00

ROD CAMERON WESTERN
Fawcett Publications, Feb., 1950

1 Ph(c) . . . 750.00
2 Ph(c) . . . 350.00
3 Ph(c),Seven Cities of Cipiola . 300.00
4 Ph(c),Rip-Roaring Wild West . 250.00
5 Ph(c),Six Gun Sabotage . . . 250.00
6 Ph(c),Medicine Bead Murders 250.00
7 Ph(c),Wagon Train Of Death . 250.00
8 Ph(c),Bayou Badman . . . 250.00
9 Ph(c),Rustlers Ruse . . . 250.00
10 Ph(c),White Buffalo Trail . . . 250.00
11 Ph(c),Lead Poison . . . 225.00
12 Ph(c) . . . 225.00
13 Ph(c) . . . 225.00
14 Ph(c) . . . 225.00
15 Ph(c) . . . 225.00
16 thru 19 Ph(c) . . . @225.00
20 Phc(c),Great Army Hoax . . . 225.00

ROGER DODGER
Standard Comics, 1952

5 . . . 100.00

ROLY-POLY COMICS
Green Publishing Co., 1945

1 B:Red Rube&Steel Sterling . . 400.00
6 A:Blue Cycle . . . 250.00
10 A:Red Rube . . . 300.00
11 . . . 250.00
12 Black Hood . . . 250.00
13 . . . 250.00
14 A:Black Hood, Decapitation . . 450.00
15 A:Steel Fist;1946 . . . 400.00

ROMANCE AND CONFESSION STORIES
St. John Publishing Co., 1949

1 MB(c),MB . . . 500.00

ROMANCE DIARY
Marvel, Dec., 1949

1 . . . 150.00
2 March, 1950 . . . 125.00

THE ROMANCES OF NURSE HELEN GRANT
Marvel Atlas, 1957

1 . . . 100.00

ROMANCES OF THE WEST
Marvel, Nov., 1949

1 Ph(c),Calamity Jane, Sam Bass . . . 300.00
2 March, 1950 . . . 175.00

ROMANCE STORIES OF TRUE LOVE
See: TRUE LOVE PROBLEMS AND ADVICE ILLUSTRATED

ROMANCE TALES
Marvel, Oct., 1949
(no #1 thru 6)

7 . . . 150.00
8 . . . 100.00
9 March, 1950 . . . 100.00

ROMANCE TRAIL
DC Comics, 1949–50

1 EK,ATh . . . 800.00
2 EK . . . 400.00
3 EK,ATh . . . 425.00
4 ATh . . . 300.00
5 . . . 275.00
6 EK . . . 275.00

ROMANTIC ADVENTURES
B & I Publishing Co. (American Comics Group), 1949

1 . . . 200.00
2 . . . 150.00
3 thru 10 . . . @125.00
11 thru 20 . . . @125.00
20 thru 45 . . . @100.00
46 thru 50 3-D type . . . @75.00
51 thru 100 . . . @100.00

ROMANTIC AFFAIRS
See: MOLLY MANTON'S ROMANCES

ROMANTIC CONFESSIONS
Hillman Periodicals, 1949–53

1 . . . 175.00
2 . . . 125.00
3 . . . 150.00
4 . . . 125.00
5 . . . 125.00
6 . . . 125.00
7 . . . 125.00
8 . . . 125.00
9 . . . 125.00
10 . . . 125.00
11 . . . 125.00
12 . . . 125.00

Vol 2

1 . . . 150.00
2 . . . 150.00
3 BK . . . 150.00
4 thru 8 . . . @125.00
9 FF,AD . . . 125.00
10 thru 13 . . . @100.00

ROMANTIC HEARTS
Story Comics/Master Publ./Merrit Publ., 1951

1 . . . 200.00

 All comics prices listed are for *Near Mint* condition.

Romantic Love #1
© Avon Periodicals

Romantic Picture Novelettes #1
© Magazine Enterprises

Roundup #4
© D.S. Publishing Co.

2 . . . . 150.00
3 LC 125.00
4 LC 125.00
5 LC 125.00
6 LC 125.00
7 LC 125.00
8 LC 125.00
9 LC 125.00
10 LC 125.00
11 . . . . 150.00

Second Series, 1953
1 . . . . 125.00
2 thru 12 . . . . @125.00

ROMANTIC LOVE
Avon Periodicals/Realistic, Sept.–Oct., 1949
1 P(c) 275.00
2 P(c) 200.00
3 P(c) 200.00
4 Ph(c) 200.00
5 P(c) 200.00
6 Ph(c),Drug,Thrill Crazy 250.00
7 P(c) 200.00
8 P(c) 200.00
9 EK,P(c) 225.00
10 thru 11 P(c) . . . . @225.00
12 EK 225.00
20 . . . . 200.00
21 . . . . 200.00
22 EK 200.00
23 EK 200.00

ROMANTIC MARRIAGE
Ziff-Davis/ St. John Publishing Co., Nov.–Dec., 1950
1 Ph(c),Selfish Wife 250.00
2 P(c),Mother's Boy 150.00
3 P(c),Hen Peck House 135.00
4 P(c) 135.00
5 Ph(c) 135.00
6 Ph(c) 125.00
7 Ph(c) 125.00
8 P(c) 125.00
9 P(c) 125.00
10 P/PH(c) 250.00
11 . . . . 125.00
12 . . . . 125.00
13 Ph(c) 125.00
14 thru 20 . . . . @125.00
20 Ph(c) 125.00
21 . . . . 125.00
22 . . . . 125.00
23 MB 135.00
24 . . . . 125.00

ROMANTIC PICTURE NOVELETTES
Magazine Enterprises, 1946
1 Mary Worth Adventure 200.00

ROMANTIC SECRETS
Fawcett Publ./Charlton Comics, Sept., 1949
1 Ph(c) 250.00
2 MSy(c) 175.00
3 MSy(c) 175.00
4 GE 175.00
5 BP 150.00
6 . . . . 150.00
7 BP 150.00
8 . . . . 150.00
9 GE 150.00
10 BP 150.00
11 . . . . 125.00
12 BP 150.00
13 . . . . 125.00
14 . . . . 125.00
15 . . . . 125.00
16 BP,MSy 150.00
17 BP 150.00
18 . . . . 125.00
19 . . . . 125.00
20 BP,MBi 150.00
21 . . . . 125.00
22 . . . . 125.00
23 . . . . 125.00
24 GE 150.00
25 MSy 125.00
26 BP,MSy 125.00
27 MSy 125.00
28 . . . . 125.00
29 BP 125.00
30 thru 32 . . . . @125.00
33 MSy 125.00
34 BP 125.00
35 . . . . 125.00
36 BP 125.00
37 BP 125.00
38 thru 52 . . . . @100.00

ROMANTIC STORY
Fawcett Publ./Charlton Comics, Nov., 1949
1 Ph(c) 250.00
2 Ph(c) 200.00
3 Ph(c) 175.00
4 Ph(c) 175.00
5 Ph(c) 175.00
6 Ph(c) 175.00
7 BP,Ph(c) 150.00
8 BP,Ph(c) 150.00
9 Ph(c) 150.00
10 Ph(c) 150.00
11 Ph(c) 150.00
12 Ph(c) 150.00
13 Ph(c) 150.00
14 Ph(c) 150.00
15 GE,Ph(c) 200.00
16 BP,Ph(c) 125.00
17 Ph(c) 125.00
18 Ph(c) 125.00
19 Ph(c) 125.00
20 BP,Ph(c) 125.00
22 ATh,Ph(c) 125.00

Charlton Comics
23 . . . . 125.00
24 Ph(c) 100.00
25 thru 29 . . . . @100.00
30 BP 125.00
31 thru 39 . . . . @100.00

ROMANTIC WESTERN
Fawcett Publications, Winter, 1949
1 Ph(c) 300.00
2 Ph(c),AW,AMc 325.00
3 Ph(c) 250.00

ROMEO TUBBS
See: MY SECRET LIFE

ROOKIE COP
Charlton, 1955
27 . . . . 150.00
28 . . . . 100.00
29 . . . . 100.00
30 . . . . 100.00
31 thru 33 . . . . @100.00

ROUNDUP
D.S. Publishing Co., July–Aug., 1948
1 HcK 200.00
2 Drug 150.00
3 . . . . 125.00
4 . . . . 125.00
5 Male Bondage 135.00

Roy Rogers #83
© Dell Publishing Co.

Rugged Action #1
© Marvel Comics Group

Saddle Romances #10
© E.C. Comics

ROY CAMPANELLA, BASEBALL HERO
Fawcett Publications, 1950

N# Ph(c),Life Story of the Battling Dodgers Catcher . . 1,000.00

ROY ROGERS COMICS
Dell Publishing Co., 1948

1 photo (c) 1,500.00
2 . . . . 500.00
3 . . . . 350.00
4 . . . . 350.00
5 . . . . 350.00
6 thru 10 . . . . @250.00
11 thru 18 . . . . @225.00
19 Chuck Wagon Charlie 200.00
20 Trigger 200.00
21 thru 30 . . . . @200.00
31 thru 46 . . . . @150.00
47 thru 50 . . . . @125.00
51 thru 56 . . . . @110.00
57 Drug 125.00
58 Drug 135.00
59 thru 80 . . . . @125.00
81 thru 91 . . . . @100.00

Becomes:

ROY ROGERS AND TRIGGER
Aug., 1955

92 . . . . 100.00
93 . . . . 100.00
94 . . . . 100.00
95 . . . . 100.00
96 thru 99 . . . . @100.00
100 Trigger Returns 125.00
101 thru 118 . . . . @100.00
119 thru 125 ATn . . . . @150.00
126 thru 131 . . . . @120.00
132 Dale Evans 150.00
133 thru 144 RsM . . . . @110.00
145 . . . . 150.00

ROY ROGER'S TRIGGER
Dell Publishing Co., May, 1951

(1) *see Dell Four Color #329*
2 Ph(c) 250.00
3 P(c) 100.00
4 P(c) 100.00
5 P(c) 100.00
6 thru 17 P(c) . . . . @100.00

RUDOLPH THE RED–NOSED REINDEER
DC Comics, Dec., 1950

1950 . . . . 250.00
1951 thru 1954 . . . . @125.00
1955 thru 1962 Winter . . . . . . @100.00

RUFF AND READY
Dell Publishing Co., 1958

1 . . . . 200.00
2 . . . . 150.00
3 . . . . 150.00
4 thru 12 . . . . @100.00

RUGGED ACTION
Marvel Atlas, Dec., 1954

1 AyB,Man-Eater 150.00
2 JSe,DAy,JMn(c),Manta-Ray . . 100.00
3 DAy,JMn(c) 100.00
4 . . . . 100.00

Becomes:

STRANGE STORIES OF SUSPENSE

5 RH,JMn(c),Little Black Box . . . 500.00
6 BEv,The Illusion 300.00
7 JSe(c),BEv,Old John's House 325.00
8 AW,BP,Thumbs Down 325.00
9 BEv(c),Nightmare 350.00
10 RC,MME,AT 350.00
11 BEv(c) 225.00
12 AT 225.00
13 BEv,GM 225.00
14 AW 250.00
15 BK 250.00
16 MF,BP, Aug., 1957 . . . . 250.00

RULAH, JUNGLE GODDESS
See: ZOOT COMICS

RUSTY, BOY DETECTIVE
Good Comics/Lev Gleason Publ., 1955

1 . . . . 125.00
2 . . . . 100.00
3 . . . . 100.00
4 . . . . 100.00
5 . . . . 100.00

RUSTY COMICS
See: KID KOMICS

SAARI, THE JUNGLE GODDESS
P.L. Publishing Co., Nov., 1951

1 The Bantu Blood Curse 600.00

SABU, ELEPHANT BOY
Fox Features Syndicate, June, 1950

1(30) WW,Ph(c) 300.00
2 JKa,Ph(c),Aug.'50 . . . . 250.00

HAPPY HOULIHANS
Fables Publications (E.C. Comics), Autumn, 1947

1 O:Moon Girl 650.00
2 . . . . 350.00

Becomes:

SADDLE JUSTICE
Spring, 1948

3 HcK,JCr,AF 700.00
4 AF,JCr, Grl 600.00
5 AF,Grl, ... 500.00
6 AF,Grl 450.00
7 AF,Grl 450.00
8 AF,Grl, ... 500.00

Becomes:

SADDLE ROMANCES
Nov., 1949

9 Grl(c),Grl 600.00
10 AF(c),WW,Grl 550.00
11 AF(c),Grl 600.00

SAD SACK AND THE SARGE
Harvey Publications, 1957

1 . . . . 200.00
2 . . . . 150.00
3 . . . . 125.00
4 . . . . 125.00
5 . . . . 125.00
thru 10 . . . . @125.00
11 thru 20 . . . . @125.00
21 thru 40 . . . . @50.00
41 thru 50 . . . . @50.00

 All comics prices listed are for *Near Mint* condition.

Sad Sack Comics #10
© Harvey Publications

The Saint #9
© Avon Periodicals

Science Comics #1
© Fox Features Syndicate

SAD SACK COMICS
Harvey Publications, Sept., 1949

1 I:Little Dot. 900.00
2 Flying Fool 500.00
3 . . . . 400.00
4 . . . . 300.00
5 . . . . 300.00
6 thru 10 . . . . @300.00
11 thru 21 . . . . @200.00
22 Back in the Army Again, The Specialist 250.00
23 thru 50. . . . . @150.00
51 thru 100. . . . . @100.00

SAD SACK'S FUNNY FRIENDS
Harvey Publications, 1955

1 . . . . 150.00
2 . . . . 100.00
3 . . . . 100.00
4 . . . . 100.00
5 . . . . 100.00
6 thru 10 . . . . @100.00
11 thru 20 . . . . @75.00

SAD SACK LAUGH SPECIAL
Harvey Publications, 1958

1 . . . . 160.00
2 . . . . 120.00
3 . . . . 100.00
4 . . . . 100.00
5 . . . . 100.00
6 . . . . 100.00
7 . . . . 100.00
8 . . . . 100.00
9 . . . . 100.00
10 . . . . 100.00
11 thru 20 . . . . @100.00

SAINT, THE
Avon Periodicals, Aug., 1947

1 JKa,JKa(c),Bondage(c) 1,500.00
2 . . . . 1,000.00
3 Rolled Stocking Leg(c). 800.00
4 MB(c) Longerie 800.00
5 Spanking Panel 900.00
6 B:Miss Fury 900.00
7 WJo(c),Detective Cases(c) . . . 700.00
8 P(c),Detective Cases(c) 750.00
9 EK(c),The Notorious Murder Mob 750.00
10 WW,P(c),V:The Communist Menace 700.00
11 P(c),Wanted For Robbery. . . . 500.00
12 P(c),The Blowpipe Murders March, 1952 . . . . 500.00

SAM HILL PRIVATE EYE
Close-Up Publications, 1950

1 The Double Trouble Caper . . . 200.00
2 . . . . 150.00
3 . . . . 125.00
4 Negligee panels. 200.00
5 . . . . 100.00
6 . . . . 100.00
7 . . . . 100.00

SAMSON
Fox Features Syndicate, Autumn, 1940

1 BP,GT,A:Wing Turner 3,500.00
2 BP,A:Dr. Fung 1,400.00
3 JSh(c),A:Navy Jones 900.00
4 WE,B:Yarko 800.00
5 WE 750.00
6 WE,O:The Topper;Sept'41 . . . 750.00

SAMSON
Ajax Farrell Publ (Four Star), April, 1955

12 The Electric Curtain 350.00
13 Assignment Danger 300.00
14 The Red Raider;Aug'55 . . . . . 300.00

SANDS OF THE SOUTH PACIFIC
Toby Press, Jan., 1953

1 2-Fisted Romantic Adventure . 250.00

SANTA CLAUS FUNNIES
Dell Publishing Co., 1942

N# WK 600.00
2 WK. 400.00

SANTA CLAUS PARADE
Approved Comics (Ziff-Davis)/ St. John Publ., 1951

N# 350.00
2 . . . . 250.00
3 . . . . 225.00

SANTA'S CHRISTMAS COMICS
Best Books (Standard Comics), 1952

N# Dizzy Duck 225.00

SANTA'S FUN BOOK
Promotional Publ., 1951

N# 100.00

SANTA'S SECRET
Sam B. Anson, 1951

N# 100.00

SANTA'S TOYTOWN FUN BOOK
Promotional Publications, 1952

N# 100.00

SCHOOL DAY ROMANCES
See: POPULAR TEEN-AGERS

SCIENCE COMICS
Fox Features Syndicate, Feb., 1940

1 GT,LF(c),O&B:Electro,Perisphere Payne,The Eagle,Navy Jones; B:Marga,Cosmic Carson, Dr. Doom; Bondage(c) . . 10,000.00
2 GT,LF(c) 6,000.00
3 GT,LF(c),Dynamo 5,000.00
4 JK,Cosmic Carson 5,000.00
5 Giant Comiscope Offer Eagle(c) 2,500.00
6 Dynamop(c) 2,500.00
7 Bondage(c),Dynamo 2,700.00
8 Sept., 1940 Eagle(c). 2,500.00

SCIENCE COMICS
Humor Publications, Jan., 1946

1 RP(c),Story of the A-Bomb . . . 250.00
2 RP(c),How Museum Pieces Are Assembled 100.00
3 AF,RP(c),How Underwater Tunnels Are Made 175.00

Scoop Comics #8
© Harry A Chesler Jr.

Red Seal Comics #21
© Harry A Chesler, Jr.

Scribbly #4
© DC Comics

4 RP(c),Behind the Scenes at
A TV Broadcast 100.00
5 The Story of the World's
Bridges; Sept., 1946 . . . . . . 100.00

SCIENCE COMICS
Ziff-Davis Publ. Co.,
May, 1946

N# Used For A Mail Order
Test Market 500.00

SCIENCE COMICS
Export Publication Enterprises,
March, 1951

1 How to resurrect a dead rat. . . 125.00

SCOOP COMICS
Harry 'A' Chesler Jr.,
Nov., 1941

1 I&B:Rocketman&Rocketgirl;B:Dan
Hastings;O&B:Master Key . 1,800.00
2 A:Rocketboy,Eye Injury. 2,000.00
3 Partial rep. of #2 . . . . 900.00
4 thru 7 do not exist
8 1945 . . . . 600.00

Becomes:

SNAP
Harry 'A' Chesler Jr.,
1944

N# Humorous 150.00

Becomes:

KOMIK PAGES
Harry 'A' Chesler Jr.,
1944

1(10) JK,Duke of Darkness 350.00

Becomes:

BULLS-EYE
Harry 'A' Chesler Jr.,
1944

11 Green Knight, Skull (c) 550.00

Becomes:

KAYO
Harry 'A' Chesler Jr.,
1945

12 Green Knight. 200.00

Becomes:

CARNIVAL
Harry 'A' Chesler Jr., 1945

(13) Guardineer 225.00

Becomes:

RED SEAL COMICS
Harry 'A' Chesler, Jr./Superior,
Oct., 1945

14 GT,Bondage(c),Black Dwarf 1,000.00
15 GT,Torture 650.00
16 GT. 800.00
17 GT,Lady Satan,Sky Chief 700.00
18 Lady Satan,Sky Chief. 700.00
19 Lady Satan,Sky Chief. 600.00
20 Lady Satan,Sky Chief. 600.00
21 Lady Satan,Sky Chief. 550.00
22 Rocketman 450.00

SCOOTER COMICS
Rucker Publications, 1946

1 . . . . 200.00

SCOTLAND YARD
Charlton Comics, 1955

1 . . . . 165.00
2 . . . . 125.00
3 . . . . 125.00
4 . . . . 125.00

SCREAM COMICS
Humor Publ./Current Books
(Ace Magazines),
Autumn, 1944

1 . . . . 350.00
2 . . . . 250.00
3 thru 15 . . . . @200.00
16 I:Lily Belle 225.00
17 . . . . 200.00
18 Drug 400.00
19 . . . . 200.00

Becomes:

ANDY COMICS
June, 1948

20 Teenage 150.00
21 . . . . 150.00

Becomes:

ERNIE COMICS
Sept., 1948

22 Teenage 150.00
23 thru 25. . . . . @100.00

Becomes:

ALL LOVE ROMANCES
May, 1949

26 Ernie 125.00
27 LbC 250.00
28 thru 32. . . . . @100.00

SCRIBBLY
DC Comics, Aug.,
1948–Dec.–Jan., 1951–52

1 SM 1,000.00
2 . . . . 650.00
3 . . . . 500.00
4 . . . . 500.00
5 . . . . 500.00
6 thru 10 . . . . @350.00
11 thru 15. . . . . @300.00

(Capt. Silvers Log of...) SEA HOUND, THE
Avon Periodicals, 1945

N# The Esmerelda's Treasure . . 250.00
2 Adventures in Brazil 200.00
3 Louie the Llama. 150.00
4 In Greed & Vengence;
Jan-Feb, 1946. . . . . 150.00

SEA HUNT
Dell Publishing Co., 1958

1 L.BridgesPh(c) all 200.00
2 . . . . 150.00
3 ATh. 165.00
4 RsM 150.00
5 RsM 150.00
6 RsM 150.00
7 . . . . 125.00
8 RsM 150.00
9 RsM 150.00
10 RsM. 150.00
11 RsM. 150.00
12 . . . . 150.00
13 RsM. 150.00

SEARCH FOR LOVE
Best Syndicated Features
(American Comics), 1950

1 . . . . 125.00
2 . . . . 100.00

SECRET HEARTS
DC Comics, Sept.–Oct.,
1949–July, 1971

1 Make Believe Sweetheart 700.00
2 ATh,Love Is Not A Dream 350.00
3 Sing Me A Love Song 275.00
4 ATh. 275.00
5 ATh. 275.00
6 . . . . 275.00
7 . . . . 500.00

Sc

Secret Missions #1
© St. John Publishing Co.

Select Detective #1
© D.S. Publishing Co.

Sensation Comics #19
© DC Comics

8 thru 20 . . . . @175.00
21 thru 26. . . . . @150.00
27 B:Comics Code. 125.00
28 thru 30. . . . . @125.00
31 thru 70. . . . . @100.00
71 thru 75. . . . . @100.00

SECRET LOVE

Ajax/Farrell (Four Star Comic Corp.), 1955–57

1 . . . . 150.00
2 . . . . 125.00
3 . . . . 125.00

Second Series, Ajax, 1957

1 . . . . 150.00
2 . . . . 100.00
3 . . . . 100.00
4 . . . . 100.00
5 . . . . 100.00
6 . . . . 100.00

SECRET LOVES

Comics Magazines (Quality Comics), Nov., 1949

1 BWa(c). 300.00
2 BWa(c),Lingerie(c). 250.00
3 RC 200.00
4 . . . . 150.00
5 Boom Town Babe 200.00
6 . . . . 150.00

SECRET MISSIONS

St. John Publishing Co., 1950

1 JKu. 225.00

SECRET MYSTERIES

See: CRIME MYSTERIES

SECRET ROMANCES

Superior Publications, 1951

1 . . . . 175.00
2 . . . . 125.00
3 . . . . 125.00
4 . . . . 125.00
5 . . . . 125.00
6 . . . . 125.00
7 . . . . 125.00
8 . . . . 125.00
9 . . . . 125.00
10 . . . . 125.00
11 thru 18 . . . . @100.00
19 Lingerie. 200.00
20 . . . . 100.00
21 thru 27 . . . . @100.00

SECRET STORY ROMANCES

Marvel Atlas, 1953

1 BEv 175.00
2 . . . . 125.00
3 . . . . 100.00
4 . . . . 100.00
5 . . . . 100.00
6 . . . . 100.00
7 . . . . 100.00
8 . . . . 100.00
9 . . . . 100.00
10 ViC 100.00
11 thru 21 ViC (in many) . . . . . @100.00

SELECT DETECTIVE

D.S. Publishing Co., Aug.–Sept., 1948

1 MB,Exciting New Mystery
Cases 350.00
2 MB,AMc,Dead Men.... . . . . 200.00
3 Face in theFrame;Dec-Jan'48 . 175.00

SENSATIONAL POLICE CASES

Avon Periodicals, 1952

N# JKu,EK(c). 475.00
2 . . . . 200.00
3 . . . . 200.00
4 . . . . 200.00

SENSATION COMICS

DC Comics, 1942–52

1 I:Wonder Woman,Wildcat . . 60,000.00
2 I:Etta Candy & the Holiday
Girls, Dr. Poison 10,000.00
3 Diana Price joins Military
Intelligence 5,000.00
4 I:Baroness PaulaVonGunther 4,000.00
5 V:Axis Spies 3,500.00
6 Wonder Woman receives magic
lasso,V:Baroness Gunther . 3,500.00
7 V:Baroness Gunther 2,500.00
8 Meets Gloria Bullfinch. 2,500.00
9 A:The Real Diana Prince . . . 2,500.00
10 V:Ishti 2,500.00
11 I:Queen Desira. 2,500.00
12 V:Baroness Gunther 2,000.00
13 V:Olga,Hitler(c) 2,500.00
14 . . . . 2,000.00
15 V:Simon Slikery 2,000.00
16 V:Karl Schultz 2,000.00
17 V:Princess Yasmini 2,000.00
18 V:Quito. 2,000.00
19 Wonder Woman Goes
Berserk. 2,000.00
20 V:Stoffer 2,000.00
21 V:American Adolf 1,800.00
22 V:Cheetah 1,800.00
23 'War Laugh Mania'. 1,800.00
24 I:Wonder Woman's
Mental Radio 1,800.00
25 . . . . 1,800.00
26 A:Queen Hippolyte. 1,800.00
27 V:Ely Close 1,800.00
28 V:Mayor Prude. 1,800.00
29 V:Mimi Mendez 1,800.00
30 V:Anton Unreal. 1,800.00
31 Grow Down Land. 1,400.00
32 V:Crime Chief. 1,400.00
33 Meets Percy Pringle. 1,400.00
34 I:Sargon 1,500.00
35 V:Sontag Henya in Atlantis . 1,200.00
36 V:Bedwin Footh 1,200.00
37 A:Mala((1st app. All-Star #8) 1,200.00
38 V:The Gyp 1,200.00
39 V:Nero 1,200.00
40 I:Countess Draska Nishki . . 1,200.00
41 V:Creeper Jackson 1,100.00
42 V:Countess Nishki 1,100.00
43 Meets Joel Heyday 1,100.00
44 V:Lt. Sturm 1,100.00
45 V:Jose Perez 1,100.00
46 V:Lawbreakers Protective
League 1,100.00
47 V:Unknown. 1,100.00
48 V:Topso and Teena 1,100.00
49 V:Zavia. 1,100.00
50 V:'Ears' Fellock 1,100.00
51 V:Boss Brekel 1,000.00
52 Meets Prof. Toxino. 1,000.00
53 V:Wanta Wynn 1,000.00
54 V:Dr. Fiendo. 1,000.00
55 V:Bughumans 1,000.00
56 V:Dr. Novel. 1,000.00
57 V:Syonide. 1,000.00
58 Meets Olive Norton 1,000.00
59 V:Snow Man 750.00
60 V:Bifton Jones. 750.00
61 V:Bluff Robust. 750.00
62 V:Black Robert of Dogwood . . 750.00
63 V:Prof. Vibrate. 750.00
64 V:Cloudmen 750.00
65 V:Lim Slait. 800.00

Se

Sensation Comics #88
© DC Comics

Sensation Mystery #115
© DC Comics

Seven Seas Comics #4
© Universal Phoenix Features

66 V:Slick Skeener. 800.00
67 V:Daredevil Dix 800.00
68 Secret of the Menacing
Octopus 800.00
69 V:Darcy Wells 900.00
70 Unconquerable Woman of
Cocha Bamba 900.00
71 V:Queen Flaming 900.00
72 V:Blue Seal Gang 900.00
73 Wonder Woman time
travel story. 900.00
74 V:Spug Spangle 900.00
75 V:Shark 900.00
76 V:King Diamond 900.00
77 V:Boss Brekel 900.00
78 V:Furiosa. 900.00
79 Meets Leila and Solala 900.00
80 V:Don Enrago 900.00
81 V:Dr. Frenzi. 750.00
82 V:King Lunar. 600.00
83 V:Prowd 600.00
84 V:Duke Daxo. 600.00
85 Meets Leslie M. Gresham. . . . 600.00
86 Secret of the Amazing
Bracelets 600.00
87 In Twin Peaks(in Old West) . . 600.00
88 Wonder Woman in Holywood . 600.00
89 V:Abacus Rackeett Gang 600.00
90 The Secret of the Modern
Sphinx 600.00
91 . . . . 600.00
92 V:Duke of Deceptions. 600.00
93 V:Talbot 600.00
94 Girl Issue. 650.00
95 . . . . 750.00
96 . . . . 750.00
97 . . . . 750.00
98 Strange Mission 750.00
99 I:Astra 750.00
100 . . . . 800.00
101 Battle for the Atom World . . . 750.00
102 Queen of the South Seas . . . 750.00
103 V:Robot Archers 750.00
104 The End of Paradise
Island. 750.00
105 Secret of the Giant Forest . . 750.00
106 E:Wonder Woman. 750.00
107 ATh,Mystery issue 1,200.00
108 ATh,GK,I:Johnny Peril 1,000.00
109 Ath,GK,A:Johnny Peril 1,500.00

Becomes:

SENSATION MYSTERY

DC Comics, 1952–53

110 MA(c),B:Johnny Peril 800.00
111 GK,Spectre in the Flame. . . . 750.00
112 GK,Death Has 5 Guesses . . 750.00
113 GK, ... 750.00
114 GK,GC,The Haunted
Diamond 750.00
115 GK,The Phantom Castle. . . . 750.00
116 The Toy Assassins 750.00

SERGEANT BARNEY BARKER

Marvel, Aug., 1956

1 JSe,Comedy 250.00
2 JSe,Army Inspection(c) 150.00
3 JSe,Tank(c) 150.00

Becomes:

G.I. TALES

4 JSe,At Grips with the Enemy . 125.00
5 . . . . 100.00
6 JO,BP,GWb, July, 1957 . . . . . 100.00

SERGEANT BILKO

DC Comics, May-June, 1957

1 Based on TV show 1,000.00
2 . . . . 500.00
3 . . . . 400.00
4 . . . . 350.00
5 . . . . 350.00
6 thru 17 . . . . @300.00
18 March-April, 1960 . . . . 300.00

SERGEANT BILKO'S PVT. DOBERMAN

DC Comics, June-July, 1958

1 . . . . 550.00
2 . . . . 300.00
3 . . . . 225.00
4 . . . . 225.00
5 photo (c). 225.00
6 thru 10 . . . . @150.00
11 Feb.–March, 1960. . . . . 150.00

SERGEANT PRESTON OF THE YUKON

Dell Publishing Co., Aug., 1951

(1 thru 4) *see Dell Four Color #344; #373, 397, 419*
5 P(c) 150.00
6 Bondage, P(c) 200.00
7 thru 11 P(c) 150.00
12 P(c) 150.00
13 P(c),O:Sergeant Preston 200.00
14 thru 17 P(c) . . . . @150.00
18 Yukon King,P(c) 200.00
19 thru 29 Ph(c) . . . . @250.00

SEVEN SEAS COMICS

Universal Phoenix Features/ Leader Publ., April, 1946

1 MB,RWb(c),B:South Sea
Girl, Captain Cutlass 1,400.00
2 MB,RWb(c) 1,200.00
3 MB,AF,MB(c) 1,100.00
4 MB,MB(c) 1,200.00
5 MB,MB(c),Hangman's
Noose 1,100.00
6 MB,MB(c);1947 . . . . 1,000.00

SHADOW COMICS

Street & Smith Publ., March, 1940

1-1 P(c),B:Shadow,Doc Savage,
Bill Barnes,Nick Carter,
Frank Merriwell,Iron Munro 7,000.00
1-2 P(c),B: The Avenger 2,500.00
1-3 P(c),A: Norgill the
Magician 2,000.00
1-4 P(c),B:The Three
Musketeers. 1,500.00
1-5 P(c),E: Doc Savage 1,500.00
1-6 A: Captain Fury 1,200.00
1-7 O&B: The Wasp 1,300.00
1-8 A:Doc Savage 1,200.00
1-9 A:Norgill the Magician 1,200.00
1-10 O:Iron Ghost;B:The Dead
End Kids. 1,200.00
1-11 O:Hooded Wasp 1,200.00
1-12 Crime Does Not pay 1,100.00
2-1 . . . . 1,200.00
2-2 Shadow Becomes Invisible 1,700.00
2-3 O&B:Supersnipe;
F:Little Nemo 1,500.00
2-4 F:Little Nemo 1,200.00
2-5 V:The Ghost Faker 1,200.00
2-6 A:Blackstone the Magician 1,000.00
2-7 V:The White Dragon 1,000.00
2-8 A:Little Nemo 1,000.00
2-9 The Hand of Death 1,000.00
2-10 A:Beebo the WonderHorse 1,000.00
2-11 V:Devil Kyoti 1,000.00
2-12 V:Devil Kyoti 900.00
3-1 JaB(c),V:Devil Kyoti 900.00
3-2 Red Skeleton Life Story 900.00
3-3 V:Monstrodamus 900.00
3-4 V:Monstrodamus 900.00
3-5 V:Monstrodamus 900.00
3-6 V:Devil's of the Deep 900.00

All comics prices listed are for *Near Mint* condition.

Shadow Comics Vol. 4 #9
© Street & Smith Publications

Sheena, Queen of the Jungle #8
© Fiction House

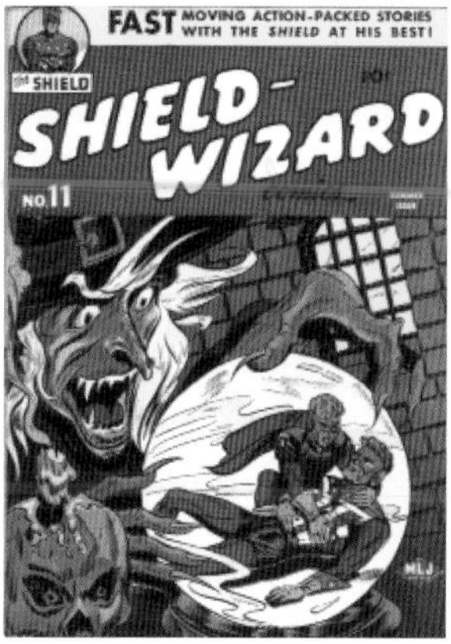

Shield-Wizard Comics #11
© MLJ Magazines

3-7 V: Monstrodamus 900.00
3-8 E: The Wasp 900.00
3-9 The Stolen Lighthouse 900.00
3-10 A:Doc Savage 900.00
3-11 P(c),V: Thade. 900.00
3-12 V: Thade 900.00
4-1 Red Cross Appeal on (c) . . . 800.00
4-2 V:The Brain of Nippon 800.00
4-3 Little Men in Space 800.00
4-4 ...Mystifies Berlin 800.00
4-5 ...Brings Terror to Tokio 800.00
4-6 V:The Tarantula 800.00
4-7 Crypt of the Seven Skulls . . . 800.00
4-8 V:the Indigo Mob 800.00
4-9 Ghost Guarded Treasure
of the Haunted Glen 800.00
4-10 V:The Hydra. 800.00
4-11 V:The Seven Sinners. 800.00
4-12 Club Curio. 1,000.00
5-1 A:Flatty Foote 1,000.00
5-2 Bells of Doom 1,000.00
5-3 The Circle of Death 1,000.00
5-4 The Empty Safe Riddle . . . 1,000.00
5-5 The Mighty Master Nomad . 1,200.00
5-6 ...Fights Piracy Among
the Golden Isles 750.00
5-7 V:The Talon 750.00
5-8 V:The Talon 750.00
5-9 V:The Talon 750.00
5-10 V:The Crime Master 750.00
5-11 The Clutch of the Talon 750.00
5-12 Most Dangerous Criminal . . 750.00
6-1 Double Z 600.00
6-2 Riddle of Prof.Mentalo 600.00
6-3 V:Judge Lawless 600.00
6-4 V:Dr. Zenith 600.00
6-5 . . . . 600.00
6-6 ...Invades the
Crucible of Death 600.00
6-7 Four Panel (c) 600.00
6-8 Crime Among the Aztecs . . . 600.00
6-9 I:Shadow Jr. 650.00
6-10 Devil's Passage. 600.00
6-11 The Black Pagoda 600.00
6-12 BP,BP(c),Atomic Bomb
Secrets Stolen 650.00
7-1 The Yellow Band 650.00
7-2 A:Shadow Jr. 650.00
7-3 BP,BP(c),Crime Under
the Border 800.00
7-4 BP,BP(c),One Tree Island,
Atomic Bomb. 900.00
7-5 A:Shadow Jr. 650.00
7-6 BP,BP(c),The Sacred Sword
of Sanjorojo 800.00
7-7 Crime K.O. 650.00
7-8 ...Raids Crime Harbor 650.00
7-9 BP.BP(c),Kilroy Was Here . . 800.00
7-10 BP,BP(c),The Riddle of
the Flying Saucer 1,000.00
7-11 BP,BP(c),Crime
Doesn't Pay. 800.00
7-12 BP,BP(c)Back From
the Grave. 800.00
8-1 BP,BP(c),Curse of the Cat . . 800.00
8-2 BP,BP(c),Decay,Vermin &
Murder in the Bayou 800.00
8-3 BP,BP(c),The Spider Boy . . . 800.00
8-4 BP,BP(c),Death Rises
Out of the Sea 800.00
8-5 BP,BP(c),Jekyll-
Hyde Murders 800.00
8-6 Secret of Valhalla Hall 800.00
8-7 BP,BP(c),Shadow in Danger 800.00
8-8 BP,BP(c),...Solves a
Twenty Year Old Crime 800.00
8-9 BP,BP(c),3-D Effect(c). 800.00
8-10 BP,BP(c),Up&Down(c). 800.00
8-11 BP,BP(c). 800.00
8-12 BP,BP(c),Arabs,Boat(c) 800.00
9-1 Airport(c) 800.00
9-2 BP,BP(c),Flying Cannon(c) . . 800.00
9-3 BP,BP(c),Shadow's Shadow . 800.00
9-4 BP,BP(c) 800.00
9-5 Death in the Stars;Aug'49 . . . 800.00

SHARP COMICS

H.C. Blackerby, Winter, 1945

1 O:Planetarian(c) 550.00
2 O:The Pioneer 400.00

SHEENA, QUEEN OF THE JUNGLE

Real Adventures (Fiction House) Spring, 1942–Winter, 1952

1 Blood Hunger 3,500.00
2 Black Orchid of Death 1,500.00
3 Harem Shackles 1,100.00
4 The Zebra Raiders 700.00
5 War of the Golden Apes 650.00
6 . . . . 625.00
7 They Claw By Night 600.00
8 The Congo Colossus 600.00
9 and 10 . . . . @550.00
11 Red Fangs of the Tree Tribe. . 550.00
12 . . . . 450.00
13 Veldt o/t Voo Doo Lions 450.00
14 The Hoo Doo Beasts of
Mozambique 450.00
15 . . . . 450.00
16 Black Ivory 450.00
17 Great Congo Treasure Trek . . 450.00
18 Doom of the Elephant Drum. . 450.00

SHERIFF OF TOMBSTONE

Charlton Comics, 1958–61

1 AW,JSe 150.00
2 thru 10 . . . . @100.00
11 thru 17 . . . . @75.00

SHERLOCK HOLMES

Charlton Comics, 1955

1 . . . . 500.00
2 . . . . 450.00

SHERRY THE SHOWGIRL

Marvel Atlas, 1956

1 . . . . 200.00
2 . . . . 135.00
3 . . . . 125.00
4 . . . . 125.00
5 thru 7 . . . . @125.00

SHIELD-WIZARD COMICS

MLJ Magazines, Summer, 1940

1 IN,EA,O:Shield 7,000.00
2 O:Shield;I:Roy 3,000.00
3 Roy,Child Bondage(c). 2,000.00
4 Shield,Roy,Wizard 1,800.00
5 B:Dusty-Boy Dectective,Child
Bondage 1,700.00
6 B:Roy the Super Boy,Child
Bondage 1,500.00
7 Shield(c),Roy Bondage(c) . . 1,600.00
8 Bondage(c) 1,500.00
9 Shield/Roy(c) 1,200.00
10 Shield/Roy(c) 1,200.00
11 Shield/Roy(c) 1,200.00
12 Shield/Roy(c) 1,200.00
13 Bondage (c);Spring'44 . . . . . 1,500.00

SHIP AHOY

Spotlight Publishers, Nov., 1944

1 LbC(c) 250.00

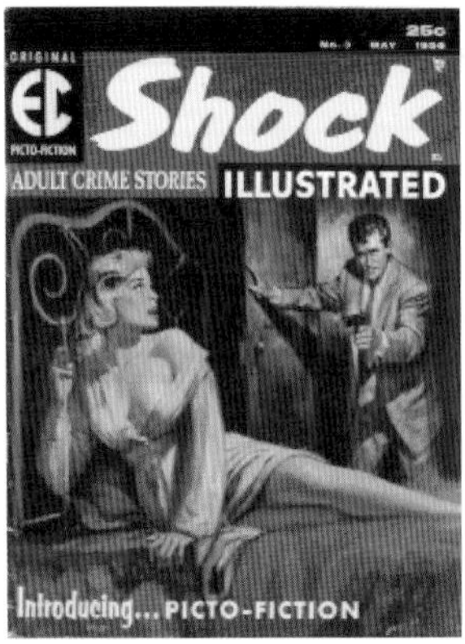

Shock Illustrated #3
© *E.C. Comics*

Showcase #17
© *DC Comics*

Silver Streak Comics #20
© *Lev Gleason*

SHOCK DETECTIVE CASE(S)
See: CRIMINALS ON THE RUN

SHOCK ILLUSTRATED
E.C. Comics, 1955
1 Drugs 300.00
2 AW,GI,RC. 200.00
3 RC. 4,000.00

SHOCK SUSPENSTORIES
Tiny Tot Comics (E.C. Comics), Feb.–March, 1952
1 JDa,JKa,AF(c),ElectricChair. 2,500.00
2 WW,JDa,GrI,JKa,WW(c). . . . 1,800.00
3 WW,JDa,JKa,WW(c). 1,200.00
4 WW,JDa,JKa,WW(c). 1,200.00
5 WW,JDa,JKa,WW(c), Hanging 1,400.00
6 WW,AF,JKa,WW(c), Bondage(c). 1,500.00
7 JKa,WW,GE,AF(c),Face Melting 1,500.00
8 JKa,AF,AW,GE,WW,AF(c) . . 1,100.00
9 JKa,AF,RC,WW,AF(c). 1,000.00
10 JKa,WW,RC,JKa(c),Drug. . . 1,000.00
11 JCr,JKa,WW,RC,JCr(c). 900.00
12 AF,JKa,WW,RC,AF(c) Drug(c) 1,000.00
13 JKa,WW,FF,JKa(c). 1,200.00
14 JKa,WW,BK,WW(c) 900.00
15 JKa,WW,RC,JDa(c) Strangulation 750.00
16 GE,RC,JKa,GE(c),Rape 750.00
17 GE,RC,JKa,GE(c). 600.00
18 GE,RC,JKa,GE(c);Jan'55 . . . . 600.00

SHOCKING MYSTERY CASES
See: THRILLING CRIME CASES

SHORTY SHINER
Dandy Comics, 1956
1 . . . . 125.00
2 . . . . 100.00
3 . . . . 100.00

SHOWCASE
DC Comics, 1956–70
1 F:Fire Fighters 5,500.00
2 JKu,F:Kings of Wild 1,600.00
3 F:Frogmen 1,500.00
4 CI,JKu,I&O:S.A. Flash (Barry Allen) 42,000.00
5 F:Manhunters 1,400.00
6 JK,I&O:Challengers of the Unknown. 6,000.00
7 JK,F:Challengers 2,800.00
8 CI,F:Flash,I:Capt.Cold 17,500.00
9 F:Lois Lane. 12,000.00
10 F:Lois Lane 4,600.00
11 JK(c),F:Challengers 2,500.00
12 JK(c),F:Challengers 2,500.00
13 CI,F:Flash,Mr.Element 6,500.00
14 CI,F:Flash,Mr.Element 6,800.00
15 I:Space Ranger 3,000.00
16 F:Space Ranger. 1,400.00
17 GK(c),I:Adam Strange 3,700.00
18 GK(c),F:Adam Strange 1,800.00
19 GK(c),F:Adam Strange 2,000.00
20 I:Rip Hunter 1,500.00
21 F:Rip Hunter 750.00
22 GK,I&O:S.A. Green Lantern (Hal Jordan) 7,200.00
23 GK,F:Green Lantern 2,400.00
24 GK,F:Green Lantern 2,400.00
25 JKu,F:Rip Hunter 500.00
26 JKu,F:Rip Hunter 500.00
27 RH,I:Sea Devils 1,300.00
28 RH,F:Sea Devils 600.00
29 RH,F:Sea Devils 600.00
30 O:Aquaman 1,200.00
31 GK(c),F:Aquaman. 600.00
32 F:Aquaman 600.00
33 F:Aquaman 650.00
34 GK,MA,I&O:S.A. Atom. 2,400.00
35 GK,MA,F:Atom. 1,200.00
36 GK,MA,F:Atom 900.00
37 RA,I:Metal Man 1,000.00
38 RA,F:Metal Man 650.00
39 RA,F:Metal Man 500.00
40 RA,F:Metal Man 425.00
41 & 42 F:Tommy Tomorrow . . @275.00
43 F:Dr.No(James Bond 007) . . . 675.00
44 F:Tommy Tomorrow 200.00
45 JKu,O:Sgt.Rock 450.00

SHOWGIRLS
Marvel Atlas, 1957
1 . . . . 150.00
2 . . . . 125.00

SILLY TUNES
Marvel Timely, 1945–47
1 Ziggy Pig 125.00
2 . . . . 125.00
3 . . . . 110.00
4 . . . . 110.00
5 . . . . 110.00
6 . . . . 110.00
7 . . . . 110.00

SILVER KID WESTERN
Key Publ./Stanmor Publ., 1954
1 . . . . 125.00
2 . . . . 100.00
3 . . . . 100.00
4 . . . . 100.00

SILVER STREAK COMICS
Your Guide/New Friday/ Comic House/Newsbrook Publications/Lev Gleason, Dec., 1939
1 JCo(a&c),I&B:The Claw,Red Reeves Capt.Fearless;B:Mr.Midnight,Wasp;A:Spiritman . . 16,500.00
2 JSm,JCo,JSm(c) 6,000.00
3 JaB(c),I&O:Silver Streak; B:Dickie Dean,Lance Hale, Ace Powers,Bill Wayne, Planet Patrol 5,000.00
4 JCo,JaB(c)B:Sky Wolf; N:Silver Streak,I:Lance Hale's Sidekick-Jackie 2,500.00
5 JCo(a&c),Dickie Dean V:The Raging Flood 3,000.00
6 JCo,JaB,JCo(a&c),O&I:Daredevil [Blue & Yellow Costume]; R:The Claw 21,000.00
7 JCo,N: Daredevil 15,000.00
8 JCo(a&c) 5,000.00
9 JCo,BoW(c) 3,000.00
10 BoW,BoW(c) 2,500.00
11 DRi(c) I:Mercury. 2,000.00
12 DRi(c). 1,500.00
13 JaB,JaB(c),O:Thun-Dohr . . . 1,500.00
14 JaB,JaB(c),A:Nazi Skull Men 1,500.00
15 JaB,DBr,JaB(c), B:Bingham Boys. 1,200.00
16 DBr,BoW(c),Hitler(c) 1,600.00
17 DBr,JaB(c),E:Daredevil 1,200.00
18 DBr,JaB(c),B:The Saint 1,100.00

Crime Does Not Pay #35
© Lev Gleason

Crime Does Not Pay #117
© Lev Gleason

Single Series #20
© United Features Syndicate

19 DBr,EA 900.00
20 BW,BEv,EA 900.00
21 BW,BEv 900.00
Becomes:

CRIME DOES NOT PAY

June, 1942

22(23) CBi(c),The Mad Musician & Tunes of Doom 3,500.00
23 CBi(c),John Dillinger-One Man Underworld 1,900.00
24 CBi(c),The Mystery of the Indian Dick 1,500.00
25 CBi(c),Dutch Shultz-King of the Underworld 800.00
26 CBi(c),Lucky Luciano-The Deadliest of Crime Rats 800.00
27 CBi(c),Pretty Boy Floyd 800.00
28 CBi(c), ... 800.00
29 CBi(c),Two-Gun Crowley-The Bad Kid with the Itchy Trigger Finger 750.00
30 CBi(c),"Monk"Eastman V:Thompson's Mob 750.00
31 CBi(c) The Million Dollar Bank Robbery 500.00
32 CBi(c),Seniorita of Sin 500.00
33 CBi(c),Meat Cleaver Murder . . 550.00
34 CBi(c),Elevator Shaft 500.00
35 CBi(c),Case o/t MissingToe . . 500.00
36 CBi(c) 450.00
37 CBi(c) 400.00
38 CBi(c) 400.00
39 FGu,CBi(c) 400.00
40 FGu,CBi(c) 450.00
41 FGu,RP,CBi(c),The Cocksure Counterfeiter 350.00
42 FGu,RP,CBi(c) 350.00
43 FGu,RP,CBi(c)Electrocution . . 500.00
44 FGu,CBi(c),The Most Shot At Gangster 250.00
45 FGu,CBi(c) 250.00
46 FGu,CBi(c),ChildKidnapping(c)300.00
47 FGu,CBi(c),ElectricChair. 400.00
48 FGu,CBi(c) 250.00
49 FGu,CBi(c) 250.00
50 FGu,CBi(c) 250.00
51 FGu,GT,CBi(c),1st Monthly. . . 225.00
52 FGu,GT,CBi(c) 225.00
53 FGu,CBi(c) 225.00
54 FGu,CBi(c) 225.00
55 FGu,CBi(c) 225.00
56 FGu,GT,CBi(c) 225.00
57 FGu,CBi(c) 225.00
58 FGu,CBi(c) 225.00
59 FGu,Cbi(c) 225.00
60 FGu,CBi(c) 225.00
61 FGu,GT,CBi(c) 225.00
62 FGu,CBi(c),Bondage(c) 225.00
63 FGu,GT,CBi(c) 200.00
64 FGu,GT,CBi(c) 200.00
65 FGu,CBi(c) 200.00
66 FGu,GT,CBi(c) 200.00
67 FGu,GT,CBi(c) 200.00
68 FGu,CBi(c) 200.00
69 FGu,CBi(c) 200.00
70 FGu,CBi(c) 200.00
71 FGu,CBi(c) 150.00
72 FGu,CBi(c) 150.00
73 FGu,CBi(c) 150.00
74 FGu,CBi(c) 150.00
75 FGu,CBi(c) 150.00
76 FGu,CBi(c) 150.00
77 FGu,CBi(c),Electrified Safe. . . 175.00
78 FGu,CBi(c) 150.00
79 FGu. 150.00
80 FGu. 150.00
81 FGu. 150.00
82 FGu. 150.00
83 FGu. 150.00
84 FGu. 150.00
85 FGu. 150.00
86 FGu. 150.00
87 FGu,P(c),The Rock-A-Bye Baby Murder 150.00
88 FGu,P(c),Death Carries Torch 150.00
89 FGu,BF,BF P(c),The Escort Murder Case 150.00
90 FGu,BF P(c),The Alhambra Club Murders. 150.00
91 FGu,AMc,BF P(c),Death Watches The Clock 150.00
92 BF,FGu,BF P(c) 150.00
93 BF,FGu,AMc,BF P(c) 150.00
94 BF,FGu,BF P(c) 150.00
95 FGu,AMc,BF P(c) 150.00
96 BF,FGu,BF P(c),The Case of the Movie Star's Double 150.00
97 FGu,BF P(c) 150.00
98 BF,FGu,BF P(c),Bondage(c). . 150.00
99 BF,FGu,BF P(c) 150.00
100 FGu,BF,AMc,P(c),The Case of the Jittery Patient 150.00
101 FGu,BF,AMc,P(c) 125.00
102 FGu,BF,AMc,BF P(c) 125.00
103 FGu,BF,AMc,BF P(c) 125.00
104 thru 110 FGu . . . . @125.00
111 thru 120 . . . . @125.00
121 thru 140. . . . . @100.00
141 JKu 100.00
142 JKu,CBi(c). 100.00
143 JKu,Comic Code. 100.00
144 I Helped Capture "Fat Face" George Klinerz 75.00
145 RP,Double Barrelled Menace . 75.00
146 BP,The Con & The Canary . . . 75.00
147 JKu,BP,A Long Shoe On the Highway;July, 1955 . . . . 125.00

SINGLE SERIES

United Features Syndicate, 1938

1 Captain & The Kids 1,200.00
2 Bronco Bill 650.00
3 Ella Cinders 500.00
4 Li'l Abner 1,000.00
5 Fritzi Ritz 300.00
6 Jim Hardy 500.00
7 Frankie Doodle 400.00
8 Peter Pat 400.00
9 Strange As it Seems 400.00
10 Little Mary Mixup. 400.00
11 Mr. & Mrs. Beans 400.00
12 Joe Jinx. 350.00
13 Looy Dot Dope 350.00
14 Billy Make Believe. 350.00
15 How It Began 400.00
16 Illustrated Gags. 250.00
17 Danny Dingle 300.00
18 Li'l Abner. 800.00
19 Broncho Bill. 550.00
20 Tarzan 1,500.00
21 Ella Cinders 400.00
22 Iron Vic 400.00
23 Tailspin Tommy 500.00
24 Alice In Wonderland 550.00
25 Abbie an' Slats 450.00
26 Little Mary Mixup. 400.00
27 Jim Hardy 400.00
28 Ella Cinders & Abbie AN' Slats 1942 . . . . 400.00

SIX GUN HEROES

Fawcett Publications, 1950

1 Rocky Lane,Hopalong Cassidy 600.00
2 . . . . 350.00
3 . . . . 250.00
4 . . . . 250.00
5 Lash Larue. 250.00
6 . . . . 175.00
7 . . . . 175.00
8 . . . . 175.00
9 . . . . 175.00
10 . . . . 175.00
11 thru 23 . . . . @125.00

Skeleton Hand #2
© American Comics Group

Slave Girl Comics #1
© Avon Periodicals

Smash Comics #17
© Comics Magazine, Inc.

Charlton Comics, 1954
24 . . . . 225.00
25 . . . . 125.00
26 thru 50 . . . . @100.00
51 thru 70 . . . . @100.00

SIX-GUN WESTERN
Marvel Atlas, Jan., 1957
1 JSe(c),RC,JR,Kid Yukon Gunslinger 225.00
2 SSh,AW,DAy,JO,His Guns Hang Low 150.00
3 AW,BP,DAy 150.00
4 JSe(c),JR,GWb 125.00

SKELETON HAND
American Comics Group, Sept.–Oct., 1952
1 . . . . 600.00
2 The Were-Serpent of Karnak. . 400.00
3 Waters of Doom 300.00
4 Black Dust 300.00
5 The Rise & Fall of the Bogey Man 300.00
6 July–Aug., 1953 . . . . 300.00

SKIPPY'S OWN BOOK OF COMICS
M.C. Gaines, 1934
N# 6,000.00

SKY BLAZERS
Hawley Publications, Sept., 1940
1 Flying Aces,Sky Pirates. 800.00
2 Nov., 1940 . . . . 600.00

SKYMAN
Columbia Comics Group, 1941
1 OW,OW(c),O:Skyman,Face . 1,600.00
2 OW,OW(c),Yankee Doodle . . . 800.00
3 OW,OW(c) 500.00
4 OW,OW(c),Statue of Liberty(c) 1948 . . . . 500.00

SKY PILOT
Ziff-Davis Publishing Co., 1950
10 NS, P(c),Lumber Pirates. 175.00
11 NS, P(c),The 2,00 Foot Drop; April–May, 1951. . . . . 150.00

SKY ROCKET
Home Guide Publ. (Harry 'A' Chesler), 1944
1 Alias the Dragon,Skyrocket . . . 400.00

SKY SHERIFF
D.S. Publishing, Summer, 1948
1 I:Breeze Lawson & the Prowl Plane Patrol 150.00

SLAM BANG COMICS
Fawcett Publications, Jan., 1940
1 B:Diamond Jack,Mark Swift, Lee Granger,Jungle King . . 5,000.00
2 F:Jim Dolan Two-Fisted Crime Buster 2,000.00
3 A: Eric the Talking Lion 3,500.00
4 F: Hurricane Hansen-Sea Adventurer 2,000.00
5 . . . . 2,000.00
6 I: Zoro the Mystery Man; Bondage(c) 2,000.00
7 Bondage(c);Sept., 1940 . . . . 2,000.00

SLAPSTICK COMICS
Comic Magazine Distrib., Inc., 1945
N# Humorous Parody 300.00

SLASH-D DOUBLECROSS
St. John Publishing Co., 1950
N# 250.00

SLAVE GIRL COMICS
Avon Periodicals, Feb., 1949
1 EL 1,250.00
2 EL 900.00

SLICK CHICK COMICS
Leader Enterprises, Inc., 1947
1 Teen-Aged Humor 125.00
2 Teen-Aged Humor 100.00
3 1947. . . . . 100.00

SLUGGER
Lev Gleason Publications, 1956
1 CBi(c). 100.00

SMASH COMICS
Comics Magazine, Inc. (Quality Comics Group), Aug., 1939
1 WE,O&B:Hugh Hazard, Bozo the Robot,Black X, Invisible Justice: B:Wings Wendall, Chic Carter 6,000.00
2 WE,A:Lone Star Rider 1,800.00
3 WE,B:Captain Cook, John Law 1,100.00
4 WE,PGv,B:Flash Fulton 1,000.00
5 WE,PGv,Bozo Robot 1,000.00
6 WE,PGv,GFx,Black X(c). . . . 1,000.00
7 WE,PGv,GFx,Wings Wendell(c) 900.00
8 WE,PGv,GFx,Bozo Robot 900.00
9 WE,PGv,GFx,Black X(c) 900.00
10 WE,PGv,GFx,Bozo Robot(c) . 900.00
11 WE,PGv,GFx,BP,Black X(c) . . 900.00
12 WE,PGv,GFx,BP,Bozo(c) 900.00
13 WE,PGv,GFx,AB,BP,B:Mango, Purple Trio,BlackX(c). 900.00
14 BP,LF,AB,PGv,I:The Ray . . . 4,500.00
15 BP,LF,AB,PGv,The Ram(c) . 2,000.00
16 BP,LF,AB,PGv,Bozo(c). 1,900.00
17 BP,LF,AB,PGv,JCo, The Ram(c) 1,900.00
18 BP,LF,AB,JCo,PGv, B&O:Midnight 2,500.00
19 BP,LF,AB,JCo,PGv,Bozo(c) . 1,400.00
20 BP,LF,AB,JCo,PGv, The Ram(c) 1,400.00
21 BP,LF,AB,JCo,PGv. 1,400.00
22 BP,LF,AB,JCo,PGv, B:The Jester. 1,400.00
23 BP,AB,JCo,RC,PGv, The Ram(c) 1,300.00
24 BP,AB,JCo,RC,PGv,A:Sword, E:ChicCarter, N:WingsWendall 1,300.00
25 AB,JCo,RC,PGv,O:Wildfire . 1,300.00
26 AB,JCo,RC,PGv,Bozo(c) . . . 1,200.00
27 AB,JCo,RC,PGv, The Ram(c) 1,200.00
28 AB,JCo,RC,PGv, 1st Midnight (c) 1,200.00
29 AB,JCo,Rc,PGv,B; Midnight(c) 1,200.00
30 AB,JCo,PGv. 1,200.00
31 AB,JCo,PGv. 1,000.00
32 AB,JCo,PGv. 1,000.00
33 AB,JCo,PGv,O:Marksman . . 1,100.00
34 AB,JCo,PGv. 1,000.00
35 AB,JCo,RC,PGv. 1,000.00

Smash Comics #60
© Comics Magazine, Inc.

Snappy Comics #1
© Cima Publications

Soldier Comics #4
© Fawcett Publications

36 AB,JCo,RC,PGv, E:Midnight(c) 1,000.00
37 AB,JCo,RC,PGv,Doc Wacky Becomes Fastest Human on Earth 1,000.00
38 JCo,RC,PGv,B:YankeeEagle 1,500.00
39 PGv,B:Midnight(c) 1,000.00
40 PGv,E:Ray 1,000.00
41 PGv. 800.00
42 PGv,B:Lady Luck 2,200.00
43 PGv,A:Lady Luck 900.00
44 PGv. 800.00
45 PGv,E:Midnight(c). 800.00
46 RC,Twelve Hours to Live 800.00
47 Wanted Midnight, Dead or Alive. 800.00
48 Midnight Meets the Menace from Mars 800.00
49 PGv,FGu,Mass of Muscle. . . . 800.00
50 I:Hyram the Hermit 800.00
51 A:Wild Bill Hiccup 500.00
52 PGv,FGu,Did Ancient Rome Fall, or was it Pushed? 500.00
53 Is ThereHonorAmongThieves. 400.00
54 A:Smear-Faced Schmaltz. . . . 450.00
55 Never Trouble Trouble until Trouble Troubles You 450.00
56 The Laughing Killer. 450.00
57 A Dummy that Turns Into A Curse 450.00
58 . . . . 450.00
59 A Corpse that Comes Alive. . . 450.00
60 The Swooner & the Trush. . . . 450.00
61 . . . . 400.00
62 V:The Lorelet 400.00
63 PGv 450.00
64 PGv,In Search of King Zoris . . 450.00
65 PGv,V:Cyanide Cindy 450.00
66 Under Circle's Spell 450.00
67 A Living Clue. 450.00
68 JCo,Atomic Dice 450.00
69 JCo,V:Sir Nuts 450.00
70 . . . . 450.00
71 . . . . 350.00
72 JCo,Angela,the Beautiful Bovine 350.00
73 . . . . 350.00
74 . . . . 350.00
75 The Revolution 350.00
76 Bowl Over Crime. 350.00
77 Who is Lilli Dilli? 350.00
78 JCo,Win Over Crime. 350.00
79 V:The Men From Mars 350.00
80 JCo,V:Big Hearted Bosco 350.00
81 V:Willie the Kid 350.00
82 V:Woodland Boy 350.00
83 JCo,Quizmaster 350.00
84 A Date With Father Time. 350.00
85 JCo,A Singing Swindle 350.00
Becomes:

LADY LUCK
Comics Magazine (Quality Comics), 1949

86 (1) 1,200.00
87 thru 90 . . . . @900.00

SMASH HITS SPORTS COMICS
Essankay Publications, Jan., 1949

1 LbC,LbC(c) 350.00

SMILEY BURNETTE WESTERN
Fawcett Publications, March, 1950

1 Ph(c),B:Red Eagle. 650.00
2 Ph(c) 500.00
3 Ph(c) 500.00
4 Ph(c) 500.00

SMILIN' JACK
Dell Publishing Co., 1948

1 . . . . 150.00
2 thru 8 . . . . @100.00

SMITTY
Dell Publishing Co., 1948

1 . . . . 150.00
2 . . . . 125.00
3 thru 7 . . . . @100.00

SNAP
See: SCOOP COMICS

SNAPPY COMICS
Cima Publications, (Prize), 1945

1 A:Animale 400.00

SNIFFY THE PUP
Animated Cartoons (Standard Comics), Nov., 1949

5 FF,Funny Animal 125.00
6 thru 9 Funny Animal . . . . . . @100.00
10 thru 17 Funny Animal . . . . . @100.00
18 Sept., 1953 . . . . 100.00

SOLDIER AND MARINE COMICS
Charlton Comics, 1954

11 . . . . 125.00
12 thru 15. . . . . @100.00
Vol 2 #9 . . . . 100.00

SOLDIER COMICS
Fawcett Publications, Jan., 1952

1 Fighting Yanks on Flaming Battlefronts 250.00
2 Blazing Battles Exploding with Combat 200.00
3 . . . . 150.00
4 A Blow for Freedom 150.00
5 Only The Dead Are Free 150.00
6 Blood & Guts 150.00
7 The Phantom Sub 150.00
8 More Plasma! 170.00
9 Red Artillery 150.00
10 . . . . 150.00
11 Sept., 1953 . . . . 150.00

SOLDIERS OF FORTUNE
Creston Publications (American Comics Group), Feb.–March, 1952

1 OW(c),B:Ace Carter, Crossbones, Lance Larson . 300.00
2 OW(c) 175.00
3 OW(c) 125.00
4 . . . . 125.00
5 OW(c) 125.00
6 OW(c),OW,Bondage(c) 250.00
7 . . . . 125.00
8 OW thru 10. . . . . @125.00
11 OW,Format Change to War . . 100.00
12 . . . . 100.00
13 OW,Feb.–March, 1953 . . . . . . 100.00

SON OF SINBAD
St. John Publishing Co., Feb., 1950

1 JKu,JKu(c),The Curse of the Caliph's Dancer 500.00

Space Action #2
© Ace Magazines

Space Detective #3
© Avon Periodicals

Space Worlds #6
© Marvel Comics Group

SORORITY SECRETS
Toby Press, 1954

1 . . . . 100.00

SPACE ACTION
Junior Books (Ace Magazines), June, 1952–Oct., 1952

1 Invaders from a Lost Galaxy 1,500.00
2 The Silicon Monster from Galaxy X 1,000.00
3 Attack on Ishtar. 1,000.00

SPACE ADVENTURES
Capitol Stories/ Charlton Comics, July, 1952

1 AFa&LM(c) 700.00
2 . . . . 325.00
3 DG(c) 250.00
4 DG(c) 250.00
5 StC(c) 250.00
6 StC(c),Two Worlds 225.00
7 DG(c),Transformation 250.00
8 DG(c),All For Love 225.00
9 DG(c) 225.00
10 SD,SD(c). 650.00
11 SD,JoS 750.00
12 SD(c). 800.00
13 A:Blue Beetle 250.00
14 A:Blue Beetle 250.00
15 Ph(c) of Rocky Jones 250.00
16 BKa,A:Rocky Jones 250.00
17 A:Rocky Jones 225.00
18 A:Rocky Jones 225.00
19 . . . . 200.00
20 First Trip to the Moon 350.00
21 War at Sea 200.00
22 Does Not Exist
23 SD,Space Trip to the Moon. . . 300.00
24 . . . . 225.00
25 Brontosaurus. 225.00
26 SD,Flying Saucers 300.00
27 SD,Flying Saucers 300.00
28 Moon Trap. 100.00
29 Captive From Space 100.00
30 Peril in the Sky 100.00
31 SD,SD(c),Enchanted Planet . . 250.00
32 SD,SD(c),Last Ship from Earth 250.00
33 Galactic Scourge, I&O:Captain Atom 650.00
34 SD,SD(c),A:Captain Atom. . . . 275.00
35 thru 40 SD,SD(c), A:Captain Atom . . . . @275.00

SPACE BUSTERS
Ziff-Davis Publishing Co., Spring, 1952

1 BK,NS(c),Ph(c),Charge of the Battle Women 1,200.00
2 EK,BK,MA,NS(c), Bondage(c),Ph(c) 800.00
3 Autumn, 1952 . . . . 750.00

SPACE COMICS
See: FUNNY TUNES

SPACE DETECTIVE
Avon Periodicals, July, 1951

1 WW,WW(c),Opium Smugglers of Venus 1,500.00
2 WW,WW(c),Batwomen of Mercury 1,200.00
3 EK(c),SeaNymphs ofNeptune 600.00
4 EK,Flame Women of Vulcan, Bondage(c) 650.00

SPACEMAN
Marvel Atlas, Sept., 1953

1 BEv(c),F:Speed Carter and the Space Sentinals. 900.00
2 JMn,Trapped in Space. 600.00
3 BEv(c),JMn,V:Ice Monster. . . . 450.00
4 JMn, A-Bomb 500.00
5 GT 450.00
6 JMn,Thing From Outer Space 450.00

SPACE MOUSE
Avon Periodicals, April, 1953

1 Funny Animal 150.00
2 Funny Animal. 125.00
3 thru 5 Funny Animal . . . . . . @100.00

SPACE PATROL
Approved Comics (Ziff-Davis), Summer, 1952

1 BK,NS,Ph(c), The Lady of Diamonds 1,400.00
2 BK,NS,Ph(c),Slave King of Pluto,Oct.–Nov., 1952 . . . . . 850.00

SPACE SQUADRON
Marvel Atlas, June, 1951

1 AyB,F:Capt. Jet Dixon,Blast, Dawn,Revere,Rusty Blake . . 900.00
2 GT(c),. 750.00
3 Planet of Madness,GT. 600.00
4 . . . . 600.00
5 AyB 600.00

Becomes:

SPACE WORLDS
Marvel, April, 1952

6 Midnight Horror 550.00

SPACE THRILLERS
Avon Periodicals, 1954

N# Contents May Vary. 1,500.00

SPACE WAR
Charlton Comics, 1959

1 . . . . 200.00
2 . . . . 100.00
3 . . . . 100.00
4 SD,SD(c) 200.00
5 SD,SD(c) 200.00
6 SD 200.00
7 . . . . 100.00
8 SD,SD(c) 200.00
9 . . . . 100.00
10 SD,SD(c). 200.00
11 . . . . 100.00
12 thru 15. . . . . @100.00
16 thru 27. . . . . @100.00

SPACE WESTERN COMICS
See: YELLOWJACKET COMICS

SPARKIE, RADIO PIXIE
Approved Publ. (Ziff-Davis), 1951

1 Radio Narration 350.00
2 . . . . 250.00

Becomes:

BIG JON AND SPARKIE
Approved Publ. (Ziff-Davis), 1952

3 . . . . 250.00
4 . . . . 250.00

 All comics prices listed are for *Near Mint* condition.

Sparkle Comics #2
© United Features Syndicate

Sparkler Comics #14
© United Features Syndicate

Sparkler Comics #120
© United Features Syndicate

SPARKLE COMICS

United Features Syndicate, 1948

1 Nancy, Li'l Abner 250.00
2 . . . . 150.00
3 . . . . 125.00
4 . . . . 125.00
5 . . . . 125.00
6 . . . . 125.00
7 . . . . 125.00
8 thru 10 . . . . @125.00
11 thru 20 . . . . @100.00
21 thru 32 . . . . @100.00
33 Peanuts. 125.00

SPARKLER COMICS

United Features Syndicate, July, 1940

1 Jim Handy 500.00
2 Frankie Doodle,Aug., 1940 . . . 400.00

SPARKLER COMICS

United Features Syndicate, July, 1941

1 BHg,O:Sparkman;B:Tarzan,Captain & the Kids,Ella Cinders,Danny Dingle,Dynamite Dunn, Nancy, Abbie an' Slats, Frankie Doodle,Broncho Bill 4,000.00
2 BHg, The Case of Poisoned Fruit 1,800.00
3 BHg 1,500.00
4 BHg,Case of Sparkman & the Firefly 1,500.00
5 BHg,Sparkman,Natch 1,200.00
6 BHg,Case of the Bronze Bees 1,200.00
7 BHg,Case of the Green Raiders 1,200.00
8 BHg,V:River Fiddler 1,200.00
9 BHg,N:Sparkman 1,200.00
10 BHg,B:Hap Hopper, Sparkman's ID revealed . . . 1,200.00
11 BHg,V:Japanese 900.00
12 BHg,Another N:Sparkman . . . 900.00
13 BHg,Hap Hopper Rides For Freedom 900.00
14 BHg,BHg(c),Tarzan V:Yellow Killer. 1,000.00
15 BHg. 700.00
16 BHg,Sparkman V:Japanese . . 700.00
17 BHg,Nancy(c) 700.00
18 BHg,Sparkman in Crete 700.00
19 BHg,I&B:Race Riley, Commandos 700.00
20 BHg,Nancy(c) 700.00
21 BHg,Tarzan(c). 750.00
22 BHg,Nancy(c) 600.00
23 BHg,Capt&Kids(c). 600.00
24 BHg,Nancy(c) 600.00
25 BHg,BHg(c),Tarzan(c). 750.00
26 BHg,Capt&Kids(c). 600.00
27 BHg,Nancy(c) 600.00
28 BHg,BHg(c),Tarzan(c). 750.00
29 BHg,Capt&Kids(c). 600.00
30 BHg,Nancy(c) 600.00
31 BHg,BHg(c),Tarzan(c). 750.00
32 BHg,Capt&Kids(c). 400.00
33 BHg,Nancy(c) 400.00
34 BHg,BHg(c),Tarzan(c). 750.00
35 BHg,Capt&Kids(c). 400.00
36 BHg,Nancy(c) 400.00
37 BHg,BHg(c),Tarzan(c). 750.00
38 BHg,Capt&Kids(c). 350.00
39 BHg,BHg(c),Tarzan(c). 800.00
40 BHg,Nancy(c) 350.00
41 BHg,Capt&Kids(c). 300.00
42 BHg,BHg,Tarzan(c). 500.00
43 BHg,Nancy(c) 300.00
44 BHg,Tarzan(c). 500.00
45 BHg,Capt&Kids(c). 300.00
46 BHg,Nancy(c) 300.00
47 BHg,Tarzan(c). 500.00
48 BHg,Nancy(c) 300.00
49 BHg,Capt&Kids(c). 300.00
50 BHg,BHg(c),Tarzan(c). 500.00
51 BHg,Capt&Kids(c). 300.00
52 BHg,Nancy(c) 300.00
53 BHg,BHg(c),Tarzan(c). 500.00
54 BHg,Capt&Kids(c). 250.00
55 BHg,Nancy(c) 250.00
56 BHg,Capt&Kids(c). 250.00
57 BHg,F:Li'l Abner 250.00
58 BHg,A:Fearless Fosdick 350.00
59 BHg,B:Li'l Abner 350.00
60 BHg,Nancy(c) 250.00
61 BHg,Capt&Kids(c). 250.00
62 BHg,Li'L Abner(c) 250.00
63 BHg,Capt&Kids(c). 250.00
64 BHg,Valentines (c) 250.00
65 BHg,Nancy(c) 250.00
66 BHg,Capt&Kids(c). 250.00
67 BHg,Nancy(c) 250.00
68 BHg, ... 250.00
69 BHg,B:Nancy (c). 250.00
70 BHg. 250.00
71 thru 80 BHg. . . . . @200.00
81 BHg,E:Nancy(c) 200.00
82 BHg. 200.00
83 BHg,Tarzan(c). 350.00
84 BHg. 175.00
85 BHg,E:Li'l Abner 175.00
86 BHg. 175.00
87 BHg,Nancy(c) 175.00
88 thru 96 BHg. . . . . @175.00
97 BHg,O:Lady Ruggles 350.00
98 BHg. 150.00
99 BHg,Nancy(c) 150.00
100 BHg,Nancy(c) 175.00
101 thru 107 BHg. . . . . @125.00
108 & 109 BHg,ATh. 200.00
110 BHg 125.00
111 BHg 125.00
112 BHg 125.00
113 BHg,ATh 200.00
114 thru 120 BHg. . . . . @150.00
Becomes:

NANCY AND SLUGGO

St. John/Dell Publ. 1955

121 . . . . 150.00
122 thru 130. . . . . @125.00
131 thru 145. . . . . @100.00

Dell Publishing Co., 1957

146 B:Peanuts 150.00
147 Peanuts. 125.00
148 Peanuts. 125.00
149 Peanuts. 125.00
150 thru 161. . . . . @125.00
162 thru 165. . . . . @200.00
166 thru 176 A:OONA . . . . @200.00
177 thru 180. . . . . @125.00
181 thru 187. . . . . @125.00

SPARKLING STARS

Holyoke Publishing Co., June, 1944

1 B:Hell's Angels,Ali Baba,FBI, Boxie Weaver,Petey & Pop . 350.00
2 Speed Spaulding 300.00
3 FBI 200.00
4 thru 12 . . . . @200.00
13 O&I:Jungo, The Man-Beast . . 225.00
14 thru 19. . . . . @200.00
20 I:Fangs the Wolfboy 200.00
21 thru 28. . . . . @200.00
29 Bondage(c) 350.00
30 thru 32. . . . . @150.00
33 March, 1948 . . . . 150.00

SPARKMAN

Frances M. McQueeny, 1944

1 O:Sparkman. 375.00

Sp

Special Edition Comics #1
© Fawcett Publications

A Spectacular Feature Magazine #11
© Fox Features Syndicate

Spellbound #11
© Marvel Comics Group

SPARKY WATTS

Columbia Comics Group, 1942

1 A:Skyman,Hitler(c) 1,500.00
2 . . . . 500.00
3 . . . . 400.00
4 O:Skyman 400.00
5 A:Skyman 350.00
6 . . . . 200.00
7 . . . . 200.00
8 . . . . 250.00
9 . . . . 200.00
10 1949 . . . . 200.00

[STEVE SAUNDERS] SPECIAL AGENT

Parents Magazine/ Commended Comics, Dec., 1947

1 J. Edgar Hoover, Ph(c) 250.00
2 . . . . 150.00
3 thru 7 . . . . @125.00
8 Sept., 1949 . . . . 125.00

SPECIAL COMICS
See: LAUGH COMICS

SPECIAL EDITION

DC Comics, 1944–45

(Reprint giveaways for U.S. Navy)

1 Action Comics #80,WB 750.00
2 Action Comics#81,WB 750.00
3 Superman #33 . . . . 750.00
4 Detective Comics#97. . . . . 750.00
5 Superman #34 . . . . 750.00
6 Action Comics #84,WB 750.00

SPECIAL EDITION COMICS

Fawcett Publications, Aug., 1940

1 CCB,CCB(c),F:Captain
Marvel 20,000.00

A SPECTACULAR FEATURE MAGAZINE

Fox Features Syndicate, 1950

1 (11) Samson and Delilah 350.00
Becomes:

SPECTACULAR FEATURES MAGAZINE

Fox Features Syndicate, 1950

2 (12) Iwo Jima 360.00
3 True Crime Cases 275.00

SPECTACULAR STORIES MAGAZINE

Hero Books (Fox Features Syndicate), 1950

3 Actual Crime Cases. 500.00
4 Sherlock Holmes 325.00

SPEED COMICS

Brookwood/Speed Publ. Harvey Publications, Oct., 1939

1 BP,B&O:Shock Gibson,B:Spike
Marlin,Biff Bannon 5,000.00
2 BP,B:Shock Gibson(c) 1,500.00
3 BP,GT 1,200.00
4 BP 1,000.00
5 BP,DBr 1,000.00
6 BP,GT 900.00
7 GT,JKu,Bondage, B:Mars
Mason 900.00
8 JKu 850.00
9 JKu 850.00
10 JKu,E:Shock Gibson(c). 850.00
11 JKu,E:Mars Mason 850.00
12 B:The Wasp 1,000.00
13 I:Captain Freedom;B:Girls
Commandos,Pat Parker . . . 1,100.00
14 AAv,Pocket sized-100pgs. . . 1,200.00
15 AAv,Pocket size 1,200.00
16 JKu,AAv,Pocket size 1,200.00
17 O:Black Cat 1,500.00
18 B:Capt.Freedom,Bondage(c) 1,200.00
19 S&K 1,000.00
20 S&K 1,000.00
21 JKu(c),Hitler & Tojo 1,400.00
22 JKu(c). 1,000.00
23 JKu(c),O:Girl Commandos. . 1,000.00
24 Hitler,Tojo & Mussilini(c). . . . 1,200.00
25 . . . . 1,000.00
26 GT,Flag (c),Black Cat. 1,000.00
27 GT,Black Cat 1,000.00
28 E:Capt Freedom 1,000.00
29 Case o/t Black Marketeers . 1,000.00
30 POW Death Chambers 1,000.00
31 ASh(c),Nazi Thrashing(c). . . 1,200.00
32 ASh(c) 1,100.00
33 ASh(c) 1,100.00
34 ASh(c) 1,100.00
35 ASh(c),BlackCat'sDeathTrap 1,150.00
36 ASh(c) 1,100.00
37 RP(c) 1,100.00
38 RP(c),War Bond Plea with Iwo
Jima flag allusion(c) 1,100.00
39 RP(c),B:Capt Freedom(c) . . 1,200.00
40 RP(c) 1,200.00
41 RP(c) 1,200.00
42 JKu,RP(c). 1,200.00
43 JKu,AAv,E:Capt Freedom(c) 1,250.00
44 BP,JKu,Four Kids on a raft,
Jan.–Feb., 1947 . . . . 1,300.00

SPEED SMITH THE HOT ROD KING

Ziff-Davis Publishing Co., Spring, 1952

1 INS,Ph(c),A:Roscoe
the Rascal 250.00

SPELLBOUND

Marvel Atlas, March, 1952

1 AyB(c),Step into my Coffin . . 1,200.00
2 BEv,RH,Horror Story,
A:Edgar A. Poe 700.00
3 RH(c),OW 600.00
4 RH,Decapitation story 600.00
5 AyB,BEv,JM,Its in the Bag. . . . 600.00
6 AyB,BK,The Man Who Couldn't
be Killed. 600.00
7 AyB,BEv,JMn,Don't Close
the Door. 500.00
8 BEv(c),RH,JSt,DAy,
The Operation 500.00
9 BEv(c),RH,The Death of
Agatha Slurl. 500.00
10 AyB,BEv,RH,JMn(c),The Living
Mummy 500.00
11 The Empty Coffin 400.00
12 RH,My Friend the Ghost. 400.00
13 JM,AyB,The Dead Men. 400.00
14 BEv(c),RH,JMn,Close Shave . 400.00
15 AyB,CI,Get Out of my
Graveyard 400.00
16 RH,BEv,JF,JSt,Behind
the Door. 400.00
17 BEv(c),GC,BK,Goodbye
Forever 400.00
18 BEv(c),JM 350.00
19 BEv(c),BP,Witch Doctor 350.00
20 RH(c),BP 350.00
21 RH(c). 325.00
22 . . . . 325.00

The Spirit 8/8/43
© Will Eisner

The Spirit #3
© Quality Comics Group

Spitfire Comics #2
© Harvey Publications

23 . . . . 325.00
24 JMn(c),JR 300.00
25 JO,AyB,Look Into My Eyes . . . 300.00
26 JR,AyB,Things in the Box 300.00
27 JMn,JR,AyB,Trap in the Mirage 300.00
28 BEv 300.00
29 JSe(c),SD 325.00
30 BEv(c) 300.00
31 . . . . 300.00
32 BP,AyB,Almost Human 300.00
33 AT 300.00
34 June, 1957 . . . . 300.00

SPIRIT, THE

Will Eisner (Weekly Coverless Comic Book), June, 1940

WE,O:SPirit 1,000.00
6/9/40 WE 600.00
6/16/40 WE,Black Queen . . . 300.00
6/23/40 WE,Mr Mystic 250.00
6/30/40 WE 250.00
7/7/40 WE,Black Queen 250.00
7/14/40 WE 200.00
7/21/40 WE 200.00
7/28/40 WE 200.00
8/4/40 WE 200.00
7/7/40-11/24/40,WE 165.00
11/10/40 WE,Black Queen . . 150.00
12/1/40 WE,Ellen Spanking(c) 225.00
12/8/40-12/29/40 . . . . 125.00
1941 WE Each 125.00
3/16 WE I:Silk Satin 200.00
6/15 WE I Twilight 125.00
6/22 WE Hitler 125.00
1942 WE Each 100.00
2-1 Duchess 125.00
2-15 . . . . 100.00
2-23 . . . . 150.00
1943 WE Each,LF,WE scripts . . . 100.00
1944 JCo,LF 100.00
1945 LF Each, ... 100.00
1946 WE Each 100.00
1/13 WE,O:The Spirit 125.00
1/20 WE,Satin 125.00
3/17 WE,I:Nylon 125.00
4/21 WE,I:Mr.Carrion 150.00
7/7 WE,I:Dulcet Tone&Skinny 125.00
10/6 WE,I:F:Gell 100.00
1947 WE Each 100.00
7/13.,WE,Hansel &Gretel . . . 125.00
7/20,WE,A:Bomb 125.00
9/28,WE,Flying Saucers 100.00
10/5,WE, Cinderella 125.00
12/7,WE,I:Power Puff 125.00
1948 WE Each 125.00
1/11,WE,Sparrow Fallon 125.00
1/25,WE,I:Last A Net 125.00
3/14,WE,A:Kretuama 125.00
4/4,WE,A:Wildrice 125.00
7/25,The Thing 100.00
8/22,Poe Tale,Horror 125.00
9/18, A:Lorelei 100.00
11/7,WE,A:Plaster of Paris . . 100.00
1949 WE Each 100.00
1/23 WE,I:Thorne 100.00
8/21 WE,I:Monica Veto 100.00
9/25 WE,A;Ice 100.00
12/4 WE,I:Flaxen 100.00
1950 WE Each 100.00
1/8 WE,I:Sand Saref 150.00
2/10, Horror Issue 100.00
1951 WE(Last WE 8/12/51) . . @100.00
Non-Eisners . . . . @25.00
1952 Non-Eisners . . . . @25.00
7/27 WW,Denny Colt 500.00
8/3 WW,Moon 500.00
8/10 WW.Moon 500.00
8/17 WW,WE,Heart 400.00
8/24 WW,Rescue 400.00
8/31 WW,Last Man 400.00
9/7 WW,Man Moon 550.00
9/14 WE 150.00
9/21 WE Space 350.00
9/28 WE Moon 400.00
10/5 WE Last Story 250.00

SPIRIT, THE

Quality Comics Group/ Vital Publ., 1944

N# Wanted Dead or Alive! . . . 1,000.00
N# ...in Crime Doesn't Pay,LF(c) 600.00
N# ...In Murder Runs Wild 500.00
4 ...Flirts with Death 400.00
5 ...Wanted Dead or Alive 350.00
6 ...Gives You Triple Value 300.00
7 ...Rocks the Underworld 300.00
8 ...Cracks Down on Crime,LF(c) 300.00
9 ...Throws Fear Into the Heart of Crime 300.00
10 ...Stalks Crime,RC(c) 300.00
11 ...America's Greatest Crime Buster 250.00
12 WE(c),...The Famous Outlaw Who Smashes Crime 400.00
13 WE(c),...and Ebony Cleans Out the Underworld;Bondage(c) . 400.00
14 WE(c) 400.00
15 WE(c),Bank Robber at Large . 400.00
16 WE(c),The Case of the Uncanny Cat 400.00
17 WE(c),The Organ Grinding Bank Robber 400.00
18 WE,WE(c),'The Bucket of Blood 450.00
19 WE,WE(c),'The Man Who Murdered the Spirit' 450.00
20 WE,WE(c),'The Vortex' 450.00
21 WE,WE(c),'P'Gell of Paris' . . . 450.00
22 WE(c),TheOctopus,Aug.1950 . 800.00

SPIRIT, THE

Fiction House Magazines, 1952

1 Curse of Claymore Castle . . . 500.00
2 WE,WE(c),Who Says Crime Doesn't Pay 450.00
3 WE/JGr(c),League of Lions . . 400.00
4 WE,WE&JGr(c),Last Prowl of Mr. Mephisto;Bondage (c) . . 450.00
5 WE,WE(c),Ph(c)1954 . . . . 450.00

SPIRITMAN

Will Eisner, 1944

1 3 Spirit Sections from 1944 Bound Together 250.00
2 LF, 2 Spirit Sections from 1944 Bound Together . . 200.00

SPITFIRE COMICS

Harvey Publ., Aug., 1941

1 MKd(c),100-pgs.,Pocket-size 1,000.00
2 100-pgs.,Pocket-size, Oct., 1941 . . . . 950.00

SPITFIRE

Malverne Herald/ Elliot Publ. Co., 1944

132 & 133. . . . . @300.00

SPOOK COMICS

Baily Publications, 1946

1 A:Mr. Lucifer 400.00

SPOOK DETECTIVE CASES

See: CRIMINALS ON THE RUN

Spooky #1
© *Harvey Publications*

Spotlight Comics #2
© *Harry A Chesler*

Spy Fighters #1
© *Marvel Comics Group*

SPOOK SUSPENSE MYSTERY
See: CRIMINALS ON THE RUN

SPOOKY
Harvey Publications, Nov., 1955

1 Funny Apparition 600.00
2 same 300.00
3 . . . . 200.00
4 . . . . 200.00
5 . . . . 200.00
6 thru 10 same . . . . @200.00
11 thru 20 same . . . . @150.00
21 thru 30 same . . . . @125.00
31 thru 40 same . . . . @125.00
41 thru 70 same . . . . @125.00
71 thru 90 same . . . . @100.00

SPOOKY MYSTERIES
Your Guide Publishing Co., 1946

1 Rib-Tickling Horror 250.00

SPORT COMICS
See: TRUE SPORT PICTURE STORIES

SPORTS STARS
Sport Stars, Inc. (Parents' Magazine), 1946

1 Johnny Weissmuller. 500.00
2 Baseball Greats 350.00
3 . . . . 275.00
4 . . . . 275.00

SPORT STARS
Marvel, Nov., 1949

1 The Life of Knute Rockne 600.00

Becomes:

SPORTS ACTION

2 BP(c),Life of George Gipp 550.00
3 BEv,Hack Wilson 300.00
4 Art Houtteman 250.00
5 Nile Kinnick 250.00
6 Warren Gun 250.00
7 Jim Konstanty 250.00
8 Ralph Kiner 275.00
9 Ed 'Strangler' Lewis 250.00
10 JMn,The Yella-Belly 250.00
11 The Killers 250.00
12 BEv,Man Behind the Mask . . . 250.00
13 BEv,Lew Andrews 260.00
14 MWs,Ken Roper,Sept.,1952 . . 260.00

SPORTS THRILLS
See: DICK COLE

SPOTLIGHT COMICS
Harry 'A' Chesler Jr. Publications, Nov., 1944

1 GT,GT(c),B:Veiled Avenger,
Black Dwarf,Barry Kuda 900.00
2 . . . . 750.00
3 1945,Eye Injury 800.00

SPOTTY THE PUP
Avon Periodicals, 1953

N# 125.00
3 . . . . 100.00

SPUNKY
Standard Comics, April, 1949

1 FF,Adventures of a Junior
Cowboy 125.00
2 FF 100.00
3 . . . . 100.00
4 . . . . 100.00
5 . . . . 100.00
6 . . . . 100.00
7 Nov., 1951 . . . . 100.00

SPUNKY THE SMILING SPOOK
Four Star Comic (Ajax/Farrell Publ.), 1957

1 rep. Frisky Fables 125.00
2 thru 4 . . . . @100.00

SPY AND COUNTERSPY
Best Syndicated Features (American Comics Group), Aug.–Sept., 1949

1 I&O:Jonathan Kent 350.00
2 . . . . 200.00

Becomes:

SPY-HUNTERS
Dec., 1949–Jan., 1950

3 Jonathan Kent 300.00
4 J.Kent. 150.00
5 J.Kent. 150.00
6 J.Kent. 150.00
7 OW(c),J.Kent 150.00
8 OW(c),J.Kent 150.00
9 OW(c),J.Kent 150.00
10 OW(c),J.Kent 150.00
11 . . . . 125.00
12 OW(c),MD 125.00
13 and 14 . . . . @125.00
15 OW(c) 125.00
16 AW 175.00
17 . . . . 100.00
18 War (c) 100.00
19 and 20 . . . . @100.00
21 B:War Content 100.00
22 . . . . 100.00
23 Torture 250.00
24 'BlackmailBrigade',July,1953 . 100.00

SPY CASES
See: KID KOMICS

SPY FIGHTERS
Marvel, March, 1951

1 GT 300.00
2 GT 150.00
3 . . . . 125.00
4 thru 13 . . . . @125.00
14 thru 15 July, 1953 . . . . @135.00

SPY SMASHER
Fawcett Publications, Autumn, 1941

1 B;Spy Smasher 6,000.00
2 MRa(c) 2,800.00
3 Bondage (c) 2,000.00
4 . . . . 1,800.00
5 MRa,Mt. Rushmore(c) 1,800.00
6 MRa(a&c),V:The Sharks
of Steel 1,500.00
7 MRa 1,500.00
8 AB 1,300.00
9 AB,Hitler,Tojo, Mussolini(c) . . 1,600.00
10 AB,Did Spy Smasher
Kill Hitler? 1,500.00
11 AB,Feb., 1943 . . . . 1,300.00

Sp

Spy Thrillers #1
© Marvel Comics Group

Starlet O'Hara in Hollywood #2
© Standard Comics

Stars and Stripes Comics #3
© Centaur Publications

SPY THRILLERS

Marvel Atlas, Nov., 1954

1 AyB(c),The Tickling Death 250.00
2 V:Communists 150.00
3 . . . . 100.00
4 . . . . 100.00

Becomes:

POLICE BADGE

5 Sept., 1955 . . . . 125.00

SQUEEKS

Lev Gleason Publications, Oct., 1953

1 CBi(c),(fa) 150.00
2 CBi(c),(fa) 100.00
3 CBi(c),(fa) 100.00
4 (fa) 100.00
5 (fa),Jan., 1954 . . . . 100.00

STAMPS COMICS

Youthful Magazines/Stamp Comics, Inc., Oct., 1951

1 HcK,Birth of Liberty 350.00
2 HcK,RP,Battle of White Plains 200.00
3 HcK,DW,RP,Iwo Jima 150.00
4 HcK,DW,RP 150.00
5 HcK,Von Hindenberg disaster . 175.00
6 HcK,The Immortal Chaplains. . 150.00
7 HcK,RKr,RP,B&O:Railroad . . . 250.00

Becomes:

THRILLING ADVENTURES IN STAMPS

Jan., 1953

8 HcK, 100 Pgs.. . . . . 1,000.00

STANLEY & HIS MONSTER

See: FOX AND THE CROW

STAR COMICS

Comic Magazines/Ultem Publ./Chesler Centaur Publications, Feb., 1937

1 B:Dan Hastings. 2,500.00
2 . . . . 1,100.00
3 . . . . 900.00
4 WMc(c) 900.00
5 WMc(c),A:Little Nemo 900.00
6 CBi(c),FGu 850.00
7 FGu 800.00
8 BoW,BoW(c),FGu,A:Little Nemo,Horror 850.00
9 FGu,CBi(c) 800.00
10 FGu,CBi(c),BoW,A:Impyk . . 1,100.00
11 FGu,BoW,JCo 850.00
12 FGu,BoW,B:Riders of the Golden West 750.00
13 FGu,BoW 750.00
14 FGu,GFx(c). 750.00
15 CBu,B:The Last Pirate 750.00
16 CBu,B:Phantom Rider 750.00
2-1 CBu,B:Phantom Rider(c) . . . 800.00
2-2 CBu,A:Diana Deane 750.00
2-3 GFx(c),CBu 700.00
2-4 CBu 700.00
2-5 CBu 700.00
2-6 CBu,E:Phantom Rider 700.00
2-7 CBu,Aug., 1939 . . . . 700.00

STARLET O'HARA IN HOLLYWOOD

Standard Comics, Dec., 1948

1 The Terrific Tee-Age Comic . . . 275.00
2 Her Romantic Adventures in Movie land 150.00
3 and 4, Sept., 1949 . . . . @125.00

STAR RANGER

Comics Magazines/Ultem/ Centaur Publ., Feb., 1937

1 FGu,I:Western Comic 2,500.00
2 . . . . 1,300.00
3 FGu 1,100.00
4 . . . . 1,100.00
5 . . . . 1,100.00
6 FGu 1,000.00
7 FGu 900.00
8 GFx,FGu,PGv,BoW 900.00
9 GFx,FGu,PGv,BoW 900.00
10 JCo,GFx,FGu,PGv,BoW . . . 1,300.00
11 . . . . 850.00
12 JCo(a&c),FGu,PGv. 850.00

Becomes:

COWBOY COMICS

July, 1938

13 FGu,PGv 1,000.00
14 FGu,PGv. 900.00

Becomes:

STAR RANGER FUNNIES

Oct., 1938

15 WE,PGv. 1,300.00
2-1(16) JCo(a&c) 1,000.00
2-2(17) PGv,JCo,A:Night Hawk . . 900.00
2-3(18) JCo,FGu 750.00
2-4(19) A:Kit Carson 750.00
2-5(20) Oct., 1939 . . . . 750.00

STARS AND STRIPES COMICS

Comic Corp of America (Centaur Publications), May, 1941

2 PGv,PGv(c),'Called to Colors', The Shark,The Voice 3,000.00
3 PGv,PGv(c),O:Dr.Synthe . . . 1,700.00
4 PGv,PGv(c),I:The Stars & Stripes 1,500.00
5 . . . . 1,000.00
6(5), Dec., 1941 . . . . 1,000.00

STAR SPANGLED COMICS

DC Comics, Oct., 1941

1 O:Tarantula,B:Captain X of the R.A.F.,Star Spangled Kid, Armstrong of the Army 7,500.00
2 V:Dr. Weerd 3,000.00
3 . . . . 2,500.00
4 V:The Needle 2,500.00
5 V:Dr. Weerd 2,500.00
6 E:Armstrong 1,700.00
7 S&K,O&1st app:The Guardian, B:Robotman,The Newsboy Legion, TNT 11,000.00
8 O:TNT & Dan the Dyna-Mite 3,500.00
9 . . . . 3,000.00
10 . . . . 3,000.00
11 . . . . 2,700.00
12 Newsboy Legion stories, Prevue of Peril!. 2,700.00
13 Kill Dat Story!. 2,700.00
14 Meanest Man on Earth 2,700.00
15 Playmates of Peril 2,700.00
16 Playboy of Suicide Slum!. . . 2,700.00
17 V:Rafferty Mob. 2,700.00
18 O:Star Spangled Kid 3,000.00
19 E:Tarantula. 2,700.00
20 B:Liberty Belle 2,700.00

Star Spangled Comics #25
© DC Comics

Star Spangled Comics #91
© DC Comics

Star Spangled War Stories #14
© DC Comics

21 . . . . 2,500.00
22 Brains for Sale 2,500.00
23 Art for Scrapper's Sake 2,500.00
24 . . . . 2,500.00
25 Victuals for Victory 2,500.00
26 Louie the Lug goes Literary. 2,500.00
27 Turn on the Heat! 2,500.00
28 Poor Man's Rich Man 2,500.00
29 Cabbages and Comics 2,500.00
30 . . . . 1,500.00
31 Questions Please! 1,500.00
32 . . . . 1,500.00
33 . . . . 1,500.00
34 From Rags to Run! 1,500.00
35 The Proud Poppas 1,500.00
36 Cowboy of Suicide Slum . . . 1,500.00
37 . . . . 1,500.00
38 . . . . 1,500.00
39 Two Guardians are a Crowd 1,500.00
40 . . . . 1,400.00
41 Back the 6th War Loan(c) . . 1,200.00
42 . . . . 1,200.00
43 American Red Cross(c) 1,200.00
44 . . . . 1,200.00
45 7th War Loan (c) 1,200.00
46 . . . . 1,200.00
47 . . . . 1,200.00
48 . . . . 1,200.00
49 . . . . 1,200.00
50 . . . . 1,200.00
51 A:Robot Robber 1,200.00
52 Rehearsal for Crime. 1,200.00
53 The Poet of Suicide Slum . . 1,200.00
54 Dead-Shot Dade's Revenge 1,200.00
55 Gabby Strikes a Gusher . . . 1,200.00
56 The Treasuer of Araby 1,200.00
57 Recruit for the Legion 1,200.00
58 Matadors of Suicide Slum . . 1,200.00
59 . . . . 1,200.00
60 . . . . 1,200.00
61 . . . . 1,200.00
62 Prevue of Tomorrow. 1,200.00
63 . . . . 1,200.00
64 Criminal Cruise 1,200.00
65 B:Robin,(c) & stories 2,700.00
66 V:No Face 1,600.00
67 The Castle of Doom. 1,500.00
68 . . . . 1,500.00
69 The Stolen Atom Bomb 2,000.00
70 V:The Clock 1,500.00
71 Perils of the Stone Age 1,500.00
72 Robin Crusoe 1,500.00
73 V:The Black Magician 1,500.00
74 V:The Clock 1,500.00
75 The State vs. Robin 1,500.00
76 V:The Fence 1,500.00
77 The Boy who Wanted Robin
for Christmas 1,500.00
78 Rajah Robin 1,500.00
79 V:The Clock,The Tick-Tock
Crimes 1,500.00
80 The Boy Disc Jockey 1,400.00
81 The Seeing-Eye Dog Crimes 1,300.00
82 The Boy who Hated Robin. . 1,200.00
83 Who is Mr. Mystery,B:Captain
Compass backup story. . . . 1,200.00
84 How can we Fight Juvenile
Delinquency? 1,400.00
85 Peril at the Pole 1,200.00
86 . . . . 1,200.00
87 V:Sinister Knight 1,500.00
88 Robin Declares War on
Batman, B:Batman app. . . . 1,400.00
89 Batman's Utility Belt? 1,400.00
90 Rancho Fear! 1,400.00
91 Cops 'n' Robbers? 1,400.00
92 Movie Hero No. 1? 1,400.00
93 . . . . 1,400.00
94 Underworld Playhouse. 1,500.00
95 The Man with the Midas Touch,
E:Robin(c),Batman story . . 1,500.00
96 B:Tomahawk(c) & stories. . . 1,000.00
97 The 4 Bold Warriors 800.00
98 . . . . 800.00
99 The Second Pocahontas 800.00
100 The Frontier Phantom 1,000.00
101 Peril on the High Seas 800.00
102 . . . . 800.00
103 Tomahawk's Death Duel! . . . 800.00
104 Race with Death! 800.00
105 The Unhappy Hunting
Grounds. 800.00
106 Traitor in the War Paint. 800.00
107 The Brave who Hunted
Tomahawk 800.00
108 'The Ghost called Moccasin
Foot!' 800.00
109 The Land Pirates of
Jolly Roger Hill! 800.00
110 Sally Raines Frontier Girl . . . 800.00
111 The Death Map of Thunder
Hill 800.00
112 . . . . 800.00
113 FF,V:The Black Cougar . . . 1,100.00
114 Return of the Black Cougar 1,100.00
115 Journey of a Thousand
Deaths 800.00
116 The Battle of Junction Fort . . 800.00
117 Siege? 800.00
118 V:Outlaw Indians 750.00
119 The Doomed Stockade? 750.00
120 Revenge of Raven Heart! . . . 800.00
121 Adventure in New York! 750.00
122 I:Ghost Breaker,(c)& stories1,000.00
123 The Dolls of Doom 700.00
124 Suicide Tower 700.00
125 The Hermit's Ghost Dog! . . . 700.00
126 The Phantom of Paris! 700.00
127 The Supernatural Alibi! 700.00
128 C:Batman,The Girl who
lived 5,000 Years! 700.00
129 The Human Orchids 750.00
130 The Haunted Town,
July, 1952 . . . . 800.00

Becomes:

STAR SPANGLED WAR STORIES

DC Comics, Aug., 1952

131 CS&StK(c),I Was A Jap
Prisoner of War 2,000.00
132 CS&StK(c),The G.I. With
The Million-Dollar Arm 1,600.00
133 CS&StK(c),Mission-San
Marino. 1,400.00
3 CS&StK(c),Hundred-Mission
Mitchell 900.00
4 CS&StK(c),The Hot Rod Tank . 900.00
5 LSt(c),Jet Pilot 900.00
6 CS(c),Operation Davy Jones. . 900.00
7 CS(c),Rookie Ranger,The 800.00
8 CS(c),I Was A
Hollywood Soldier 800.00
9 CS&StK(c),Sad Sack Squad . . 800.00
10 CS,The G.I. & The Gambler . . 800.00
11 LSt(c),The Lucky Squad 800.00
12 CS(c),The Four Horseman of
Barricade Hill 800.00
13 No Escape 800.00
14 LSt(c),Pitchfork Army 800.00
15 The Big Fish 800.00
16 The Yellow Ribbon 800.00
17 IN(c),Prize Target 800.00
18 IN(c),The Gladiator 800.00
19 IN(c),The Big Lift. 800.00
20 JGr(c),The Battle of
the Frogmen 800.00
21 JGr(c),Dead Man's Bridge . . . 600.00
22 JGr(c),Death Hurdle 600.00
23 JGr(c),The Silent Frogman . . . 600.00
24 JGr(c),Death Slide 600.00
25 JGr(c),S.S. Liferaft 600.00
26 JGr(c),Bazooka Man. 600.00
27 JGr(c),Taps for a Tail Gunner . 600.00
28 JGr(c),Tank Duel. 700.00
29 JGr(c),A Gun Called Slugger . 600.00
30 JGr(c),The Thunderbolt Tank . 600.00

St

Star Spangled War Stories #44
© DC Comics

Startling Comics #11
© Nedor Publications

Startling Terror Tales #6
© Star Publications

31 IN(c),Tank Block 400.00
32 JGr(c),Bridge to Battle 400.00
33 JGr(c),Pocket War 400.00
34 JGr(c),Fighting...Snowbirds . . 400.00
35 JGr(c),Zero Hour. 400.00
36 JGr(c),A G.I. Passed Here . . . 400.00
37 JGr(c),A Handful of T.N.T.. . . . 400.00
38 RH(c),One-Man Army 400.00
39 JGr(c),Flying Cowboy 400.00
40 JGr(c),Desert Duel 400.00
41 IN(c),A Gunner's Hands 350.00
42 JGr(c),Sniper Alley 350.00
43 JGr(c),Top Kick Brother 350.00
44 JGr(c),Tank 711
Doesn't Answer 350.00
45 JGr(c),Flying Heels. 350.00
46 JGr(c),Gunner's Seat 350.00
47 JGr(c),Sidekick 350.00
48 JGr(c),Battle Hills 350.00
49 JGr(c),Payload 350.00
50 JGr(c),Combat Dust 350.00
51 JGr(c),Battle Pigeon 250.00
52 JGr(c),Cannon-Man 250.00
53 JGr(c),Combat Close-Ups . . . 250.00
54 JGr(c),Flying Exit 250.00
55 JKu(c),The Burning Desert . . . 250.00
56 JKu(c),The Walking Sub 250.00
57 JGr(c),Call For a Frogman . . . 250.00
58 JGr(c),MD,Waist Punch 250.00
59 JGr(c),Kick In The Door 250.00
60 JGr(c),Hotbox 250.00
61 JGr(c),MD,Tow Pilot 250.00
62 JGr(c),The Three GIs 250.00
63 JGr(c),Flying Range Rider . . . 250.00
64 JGr(c),MD,Frogman Ambush . 250.00
65 JGr(c),JSe,Frogman Block . . . 250.00
66 JGr(c),Flattop Pigeon 250.00
67 RH(c),MD,Ashcan Alley 250.00
68 JGr(c),The Long Step 250.00
69 JKu(c),Floating Tank, The. . . . 250.00
70 JKu(c),No Medal For
Frogman 250.00
71 JKu(c),Shooting Star. 250.00
72 JGr(c),Silent Fish 250.00
73 JGr(c),MD,The Mouse &
the Tiger 250.00
74 JGr(c),MD,Frogman Bait. 250.00
75 JGr(c),MD,Paratroop
Mousketeers 250.00
76 MD,JKu(c),Odd Man. 250.00
77 MD,JKu(c),Room to Fight 250.00
78 MD,JGr(c),Fighting Wingman . 250.00
79 MD,JKu(c),Zero Box 250.00
80 MD,JGr(c),Top Gunner 250.00
81 MD,RH(c),Khaki Mosquito . . . 250.00
82 MD,JKu(c),Ground Flier 250.00
83 MD,JGr(c),Jet On
My Shoulder 250.00
84 MD,IN(c),O:Mademoiselle
Marie 500.00
85 IN(c),A Medal For Marie 300.00
86 JGr(c),A Medal For Marie 300.00
87 JGr(c),T.N.T. Spotlight. 300.00
88 JGr(c),The Steel Trap 300.00
89 IN(c),Trail of the Terror 300.00
90 RA(c),Island of
Armored Giants 1,000.00
91 JGr(c),The Train of Terror. . . . 250.00
92 Last Battle of the
Dinosaur Age. 400.00
93 Goliath of the Western Front . 250.00
94 JKu(c),The Frogman and
the Dinosaur 550.00
95 Guinea Pig Patrol,Dinosaurs . 400.00
96 Mission X,Dinosaur. 400.00
97 The Sub-Crusher, Dinosaur . . 400.00
98 Island of Thunder, Dinosaur . . 400.00
99 The Circus of Monsters,
Dinosaur 400.00
100 The Volcano of Monsters,
Dinosaur 450.00

STAR STUDDED

Cambridge House, 1945

N# 25 cents (c) price;128 pgs.;
32 F:stories 400.00
N# The Cadet,Hoot Gibson,
Blue Beetle 350.00

STARTLING COMICS

Better Publ./Nedor Publ., June, 1940

1 WE,LF,B&O:Captain Future,
Mystico, Wonder Man;
B:Masked Rider 7,000.00
2 Captain Future(c) 2,500.00
3 same. 2,100.00
4 same. 1,900.00
5 same. 1,800.00
6 same. 1,800.00
7 same. 1,800.00
8 ASh(c),Captain Future 1,800.00
9 Bondage(c) 1,800.00
10 O:Fighting Yank 7,000.00
11 Fighting Yank(c) 2,500.00
12 Hitler,Mussolini,Tojo (c) 2,200.00
13 JBi 1,900.00
14 JBi 1,900.00
15 Fighting Yank (c) 1,900.00
16 Bondage(c),O:Four
Comrades. 1,900.00
17 Fighting Yank (c),
E:Masked Rider 1,700.00
18 JBi,B&O:Pyroman 2,500.00
19 Pyroman(c) 1,500.00
20 Pyroman(c),B:Oracle 1,500.00
21 HcK,ASh(c)Bondage(c)
O:Ape 1,800.00
22 HcK,ASh(c),Fighting Yank(c) 1,500.00
23 HcK,BEv,ASh(c),Pyroman(c) 1,500.00
24 HcK,BEv,ASh(c),Fighting
Yank(c) 1,500.00
25 HcK,BEv,ASh(c),Pyroman(c) 1,500.00
26 BEv,ASh(c),Fighting Yank(c) 1,500.00
27 BEv,ASh(c),Pyroman(c). . . . 1,500.00
28 BEv,ASh(c),Fighting Yank(c) 1,500.00
29 BEv,ASh(c),Pyroman(c). . . . 1,500.00
30 ASh(c),Fighting Yank(c) 1,500.00
31 ASh(c),Pyroman(c). 1,500.00
32 ASh(c),Fighting Yank(c) 1,500.00
33 ASh(c),Pyroman(c). 1,500.00
34 ASh(c),Fighting Yank(c),
O:Scarab 1,800.00
35 ASh(c),Pyroman(c). 1,500.00
36 ASh(c),Fighting Yank(c) 1,200.00
37 ASh(c),Bondage (c) 1,200.00
38 ASh(c),Bondage(c). 1,500.00
39 ASh(c),Pyroman(c). 1,500.00
40 ASh(c),E:Captain Future . . . 1,500.00
41 ASh(c),Pyroman(c). 1,500.00
42 ASh(c),Fighting Yank(c) 1,500.00
43 ASh(c),Pyroman(c),
E:Pyroman 1,500.00
44 GrI(c),Lance Lewis(c) 1,700.00
45 GrI(c),I:Tygra 1,700.00
46 GrI,GrI(c),Bondage(c) 1,700.00
47 ASh(c),Bondage(c). 3,000.00
48 ASh(c),Lance Lewis(c). 1,500.00
49 ASh(c),Bondage(c),
E:Fighting Yank 7,500.00
50 ASh(c),Lance Lewis(c),
Sea Eagle. 1,100.00
51 ASh(c),Sea Eagle 1,100.00
52 ASh(c) 1,100.00
53 ASh(c),Sept., 1948. . . . . 1,100.00

STARTLING TERROR TALES

Star Publications, May, 1952

10 WW,LbC(c),The Story Starts 1,000.00
11 LbC(c),The Ghost Spider
of Death 1,700.00

Steve Roper #4
© Famous Funnies

Straight Arrow #15
© Magazine Enterprises

Strange Adventures #14
© DC Comics

12 LbC(c),White Hand Horror . . . 350.00
13 JyD,LbC(c),Love From
a Gorgor 375.00
14 LbC(c),Trapped by the
Color of Blood 350.00
4 LbC(c),Crime at the Carnival . 300.00
5 LbC(c),The Gruesome
Demon of Terror 300.00
6 LbC(c),Footprints of Death . . . 300.00
7 LbC(c),The Case of the
Strange Murder 300.00
8 RP,LbC(c),Phantom Brigade . . 300.00
9 LbC(c),The Forbidden Tomb . . 275.00
10 LbC(c),The Horrible Entity . . . 325.00
11 RP,LbC(c),The Law Will
Win, July, 1954 . . . . 300.00

STEVE CANYON COMICS

Harvey Publications, Feb., 1948–Dec., 1948

1 MC,BP,O:Steve Canyon. 275.00
2 MC,BP 175.00
3 MC,BP,Canyon's Crew 150.00
4 MC,BP,Chase of Death 150.00
5 MC,BP,A:Happy Easter 150.00
6 MC,BP,A:Madame Lynx. 165.00

STEVE ROPER

Famous Funnies, April, 1948

1 Reprints newspaper strips . . . 150.00
2 . . . . 75.00
3 . . . . 60.00
4 . . . . 60.00
5 Dec., 1948 . . . . 60.00

STEVIE

Magazine Publications (Mazie), 1952

1 teenage 80.00
2 . . . . 50.00

STONY CRAIG

Pentagon Publishing, 1945

N# 75.00

STORIES BY FAMOUS AUTHORS ILLUSTRATED

See: FAST FICTION

STORIES OF ROMANCE

Marvel Atlas, 1956

5 MB,ViC(c) 150.00
6 . . . . 100.00
7 . . . . 100.00
8 . . . . 100.00
9 ViC 125.00
10 . . . . 100.00
11 MB,ViC,JR. 150.00
12 . . . . 120.00
13 ABr 150.00

STORY OF HARRY S. TRUMAN, THE

Democratic National Committee, 1948

N# Giveaway-The Life of Our
33rd President 200.00

THE STORY OF MARTHA WAYNE

Argo Publications, 1956

1 . . . . 100.00

STRAIGHT ARROW

Magazine Enterprises, Feb.–March, 1950

1 OW,B:Straight Arrow & his
Horse Fury 1,200.00
2 BP,B&O:Red Hawk 550.00
3 BP,FF(c) 700.00
4 BP,Cave(c). 500.00
5 BP,StraightArrow'sGreatLeap . 500.00
6 BP 450.00
7 BP,The Railroad Invades
Comanche Country 450.00
8 BP 450.00
9 BP 450.00
10 BP. 450.00
11 BP,The Valley of Time. 500.00
12 thru 19 BP. . . . . @500.00
20 BP,Straight Arrow's
Great War Shield. 450.00
21 BP,O:Fury 500.00
22 BP,FF(c) 550.00
23 BP. 300.00
24 BP,The Dragons of Doom. . . . 400.00
25 BP, Secret Cave 300.00
26 BP,Red Hawk vs. Vikings 300.00
27 BP. 250.00
28 BP,Red Hawk 250.00
29 thru 35 BP. . . . . @250.00
36 BP Red Hawk, Drug 225.00
37 BP. 225.00
38 BP. 225.00
39 BP,The Canyon Beasts. 250.00
40 BP,Secret of the
Spanish Specters. 250.00
41 BP. 200.00
42 BP. 200.00
43 BP,I:Blaze 250.00
44 BP. 200.00
45 thru 53 BP . . . . @200.00
54 BP,March, 1956 . . . . 200.00

STRANGE ADVENTURES

DC Comics, 1950–74

1 The Menace of the Green
Nebula 6,000.00
2 S&K,JM(c),Doom From
Planet X 3,000.00
3 The Metal World 1,800.00
4 BP,The Invaders From the
Nth Dimension 1,800.00
5 The World Inside the Atom . . 1,800.00
6 Confessions of a Martian . . . 1,800.00
7 The World of Giant Ants 1,800.00
8 MA,ATh,Evolution Plus 1,800.00
9 MA,B:Captain Comet,The
Origin of Captain Comet. . . 3,500.00
10 MA,CI,The Air Bandits
From Space 1,800.00
11 MA,CI,Day the Past
Came Back. 1,000.00
12 MA,CI,GK(c),The Girl From
the Diamond Planet 1,000.00
13 MA,CI,GK(c),When the Earth
was Kidnapped. 1,000.00
14 MA,CI,GK(c),Destination
Doom 1,000.00
15 MA,CI,GK(c),Captain Comet-
Enemy of Earth. 1,000.00
16 MA,CI,GK(c),The Ghost of
Captain Comet 1,000.00
17 MA,CI,GK(c),Beware the
Synthetic Men. 1,000.00
18 CI,MA(c),World of Flying
Men. 1,000.00
19 CI,MA(c),Secret of the
Twelve Eternals 1,500.00
20 CI,Slaves of the Sea Master 1,500.00
21 CI,MA(c),Eyes of the
Other Worlds 800.00
22 CI,The Guardians of the
Clockwork Universe. 800.00
23 CI,MA(c),The Brain Pirates
of Planet X. 800.00

Strange Adventures #51
© DC Comics

Strange Adventures #75
© DC Comics

Strange Adventures #123
© DC Comics

24 CI,MA(c),Doomsday on Earth. 800.00
25 CI,GK(c),The Day That Vanished 800.00
26 CI,Captain Vs. Miss Universe. 800.00
27 CI,MA(c),The Counterfeit Captain Comet 800.00
28 CI,Devil's Island in Space 800.00
29 CI,The Time Capsule From 1,000,000 B.C. 800.00
30 CI,MA(c),Menace From the World of Make-Believe 750.00
31 CI,Lights Camera Action 750.00
32 CI,MA(c),The Challenge of Man-Ape the Mighty 750.00
33 CI,MA(c),The Human Beehive 750.00
34 CI,MA(c) 750.00
35 CI,MA(c),Cosmic Chessboard 750.00
36 CI,MA(c),The Grab-Bag Planet 750.00
37 CI,MA(c),The Invaders From the Golden Atom 750.00
38 CI,MA(c),Seeing-Eye Humans 750.00
39 CI,MA(c),The Guilty Gorilla. . . 750.00
40 CI,MA(c),The Mind Monster . . 750.00
41 CI,MA(c),The Beast From Out of Time. 750.00
42 CI,MD,MA(c),The Planet of Ancient Children 750.00
43 CI,MD,MA(c),The Phantom Prize Fighter 750.00
44 CI,MA(c),The Planet That Plotted Murder. 750.00
45 CI,MD,MA(c),Gorilla World . . . 750.00
46 CI,MA(c),E:Captain Comet Interplanetary War Base 750.00
47 CI,MA(c),The Man Who Sold the Earth 750.00
48 CI,MA(c),Human Phantom . . . 750.00
49 CI,MA(c),The Invasion from Indiana 750.00
50 CI,MA(c),The World Wrecker . 600.00
51 CI,MA(c),The Man Who Stole Air 600.00
52 CI,MA(c),Prisoner of the Parakeets 600.00
53 CI,MA(c),The Human Icicle. . . 600.00
54 CI,MA(c),The Electric Man . . . 500.00
55 CI,MA(c),The Gorilla Who Challanged the World,pt.I . . . 500.00
56 CI,The Jungle Emperor,pt.II . . 500.00
57 CI,The Spy from Saturn 500.00
58 CI,I Hunted the Radium Man . 500.00
59 CI,The Ark From Planet X. . . . 500.00
60 CI,Across the Ages 500.00
61 CI,The Mirages From Space. . 500.00
62 CI,The Fireproof Man 500.00
63 CI,I Was the Man in the Moon 500.00
64 CI,GK(c),Gorillas In Space . . . 500.00
65 CI,GK(c),Prisoner From Pluto. 500.00
66 CI,GK(c),The Human Battery . 500.00
67 CI,GK(c),Martian Masquerader500.00
68 CI,The Man Who Couldn't Drown 500.00
69 CI,Gorilla Conquest of Earth. . 500.00
70 CI,Triple Life of Dr. Pluto 500.00
71 CI,MSy,Zero Hour For Earth. . 400.00
72 CI,The Skyscraper That Came to Life. 400.00
73 CI,Amazing Rain of Gems . . . 400.00
74 CI,The Invisible Invader From Dimension X. 400.00
75 CI,Secret of the Man-Ape 400.00
76 CI,B:Darwin Jones,The Robot From Atlantis 400.00
77 CI,A:Darwin Jones,The World That Slipped Out of Space . . 400.00
78 CI,The Secret of the Tom Thumb Spaceman 400.00
79 CI,A:Darwin Jones,Invaders from the Ice World. 400.00
80 CI,Mind Robbers of Venus . . . 400.00
81 CI,The Secret of the Shrinking Twins 400.00
82 CI,Giants of the Cosmic Ray . 300.00
83 CI,Assignment in Eternity 300.00
84 CI,Prisoners of the Atom Universe 300.00
85 CI,The Amazing Human Race 300.00
86 CI,The Dog That Saved the Earth 300.00
87 CI,New Faces For Old 300.00
88 CI,A:Darwin Jones,The Gorilla War Against Earth 300.00
89 CI,Earth For Sale 300.00
90 CI,The Day I Became a Martian 300.00
91 CI,Midget Earthmen of Jupiter 300.00
92 CI,GK(c),The Amazing Ray of Knowledge. 300.00
93 CI,GK(c),A:Darwin Jones, Space-Rescue By Proxy 300.00
94 MA,CI,GK(c),Fisherman of Space. 300.00
95 CI,The World at my Doorstep . 300.00
96 CI,MA(c),The Menace of Saturn's Rings 300.00
97 CI,MA(c),MSy,Secret of the Space-Giant. 300.00
98 CI,GK(c),MSy,Attack on Fort Satellite 300.00
99 CI,MSy,GK(c),Big Jump Into Space. 300.00
100 CI,MSy,The Amazing Trial of John (Gorilla) Doe 400.00
101 CI,MSy,GK(c),Giant From Beyond 250.00
102 MSy,GK(c),The Three Faces of Barry Morrell 250.00
103 GK(c),The Man Who Harpooned Worlds. 250.00
104 MSy,GK(c),World of Doomed Spacemen 250.00
105 MSy,GK(c),Fisherman From the Sea 250.00
106 MSy,CI,GK(c),Genie in the Flying Saucer 250.00
107 MSy,CI,GK(c),War of the Jovian Bubble-Men 250.00
108 MSy,CI,GK(c),The Human Pet of Gorilla Land 250.00
109 MSy,CI,GK(c),The Man Who Weighed 100 Tons. 250.00
110 MSy,CI,GK(c),Hand From Beyond 250.00
111 MSy,CI,GK(c),Secret of the Last Earth-Man 250.00
112 MSy,CI,GK(c),Menace of the Size-Changing Spaceman250.00
113 MSy,CI,GK(c),Deluge From Space. 250.00
114 MSy,CI,GK(c),Secret of the Flying Buzz Saw 250.00
115 MSy,CI,GK(c),The Great Space-Tiger Hunt. 250.00
116 MSy,CI,RH,GK(c),Invasion of the Water Warriors 250.00
117 MSy,CI,GK(c),I:Atomic Knights 1,000.00
118 MSy,CI,The Turtle-Men of Space. 275.00
119 MSy,CI,MA(c),Raiders From the Giant World 250.00
120 MSy,CI,MA,Attack of the Oil Demons 500.00
121 MSy,CI,MA(c),Invasion of the Flying Reptiles. 225.00
122 MSy,CI,MA(c),David and the Space-Goliath 225.00
123 MSy,CI,MA(c),Secret of the Rocket-Destroyer. 300.00
124 MSy,CI,MA(c),The Face-Hunter From Saturn 250.00
125 MSy,CI,The Flying Gorilla Menace 225.00
126 MSy,CI,MA(c),Return of the Neanderthal Man. 400.00
127 MSy,CI,MA(c),Menace From the Earth-Globe 225.00

Strange Fantasy #6
© Farrell Publications

Strange Mysteries #19
© Superior Publications

Strange Suspense Stories #22
© Charlton Comics

128 MSy,CI,MA(c),The Man With the Electronic Brain 225.00
129 MSy,CI,MA(c),The Giant Who Stole Mountains 250.00
130 MSy,CI,MA.War With the Giant Frogs 225.00
131 MSy,CI,MA(c),Emperor of the Earth 225.00
132 MSy,CI,MA(c),The Dreams of Doom 250.00
133 MSy,CI,MA(c),The Invisible Dinosaur 225.00
134 MSy,CI,MA(c), The Aliens Who Raided New York 250.00

STRANGE CONFESSIONS

Approved Publications (Ziff-Davis), Spring, 1952

1 EK,Ph(c) 650.00
2 Ph(c) 400.00
3 EK,Ph(c),Girls Reformatory . . . 400.00
4 Ph(c),Girls Reformatory 400.00

STRANGE FANTASY

Farrell Publications/ Ajax Comics, Aug., 1952

(2)1 Jungle Princess 600.00
2 Drug & Horror 500.00
3 The Dancing Ghost 500.00
4 Demon in the Dungeon, A:Rocketman 500.00
5 Visiting Corpse 300.00
6 . . . . 300.00
7 A:Madam Satan 450.00
8 A:Black Cat 300.00
9 S&K,SD, Black Cat 400.00
10 . . . . 300.00
11 Fearful Things Can Happen in a Lonely Place 400.00
12 The Undying Fiend 300.00
13 Terror in the Attic, Bondage(c) 400.00
14 Monster in the Building, Oct.–Nov., 1954 . . . . 300.00

STRANGE JOURNEY

America's Best, 1957

1 . . . . 250.00
2 Flying Saucer 175.00
3 . . . . 150.00
4 . . . . 150.00

STRANGE MYSTERIES

Superior Publ./Dynamic Publ., 1951

1 LKa,Horror 800.00
2 . . . . 425.00
3 thru 5 . . . . @400.00
6 . . . . 350.00
7 . . . . 350.00
8 . . . . 350.00
9 Bondage,3-D type 400.00
10 . . . . 300.00
11 thru 18 . . . . @250.00
19 MB 275.00
20 reprint #1, new (c) 200.00
21 reprint 200.00

UNKNOWN WORLD

Fawcett Publications, June, 1952

1 NS(c),Ph(c),Will You Venture to Meet the Unknown 600.00

Becomes:

STRANGE STORIES FROM ANOTHER WORLD

Aug., 1952

2 NS(c),Ph(c),Will You? Dare You 750.00
3 NS(c),Ph(c),The Dark Mirror . . 500.00
4 NS(c),Ph(c),Monsters of the Mind 500.00
5 NS(c),Ph(c),Dance of the Doomed, Feb., 1953 . . . . . . 500.00

STRANGE STORIES OF SUSPENSE

See: RUGGED ACTION

STRANGE SUSPENSE STORIES

Fawcett Publications, June, 1952

1 BP,MSy,MBi 1,500.00
2 MBi,GE 1,000.00
3 MBi,GE(c) 800.00
4 BP 800.00
5 MBi(c),Voodoo(c) 800.00
6 BEv 400.00
7 BEv 400.00
8 AW 400.00
9 . . . . 400.00
10 . . . . 500.00
11 thru 13 . . . . @300.00
14 . . . . 350.00
15 AW,BEv(c) 350.00

Charlton Comics

16 . . . . 350.00
17 . . . . 300.00
18 SD,SD(c) 500.00
19 SD,SD(c) 700.00
20 SD,SD(c) 500.00
21 . . . . 250.00
22 SD(c) 450.00

Becomes:

THIS IS SUSPENSE!

Feb., 1955

23 WW 400.00
24 . . . . 150.00
25 . . . . 100.00
26 . . . . 100.00

Becomes:

STRANGE SUSPENSE STORIES

Oct., 1955

27 . . . . 200.00
28 thru 30 . . . . @150.00
31 SD(c) 300.00
32 SD 300.00
33 SD 300.00
34 SD,SD(c) 600.00
35 SD 300.00
36 SD,SD(c) 300.00
37 SD 375.00
38 . . . . 300.00
39 SD 350.00
40 SD 300.00
41 SD 300.00
42 thru 44 . . . . @125.00
45 SD 250.00
46 . . . . 125.00
47 SD 250.00
48 SD 250.00
49 . . . . 125.00
50 SD 250.00
51 SD 150.00
52 SD 150.00
53 SD 150.00
54 thru 60 . . . . @125.00
61 thru 74 . . . . @100.00
75 Capt. Atom 250.00
76 Capt. Atom 100.00
77 Capt. Atom 100.00

Strange Tales #13
© Marvel Comics Group

Strange Tales #67
© Marvel Comics Group

Strange Tales of the Unusual #8
©Marvel Comics Group

STRANGE SUSPENSE STORIES
See: LAWBREAKERS

STRANGE TALES
Marvel, June, 1951

1 The Room 4,000.00
2 Trapped In A Tomb 1,300.00
3 JMn,Man Who Never Was . . 1,000.00
4 BEv,Terror in the Morgue . . . 1,100.00
5 A Room Without A Door 1,000.00
6 RH(c),The Ugly Man 700.00
7 Who Stands Alone 700.00
8 BEv(c),Something in the Fog. . 700.00
9 Drink Deep Vampire 700.00
10 BK,Hidden Head 800.00
11 BEv(c),GC,'O'Malley's Friend . 500.00
12 Graveyard At Midnight 500.00
13 BEv(c),Death Makes A Deal . . 500.00
14 GT,Horrible Herman 500.00
15 BK,Don't Look Down. 550.00
16 Decapitation cover 500.00
17 DBr,JRo,Death Feud. 500.00
18 Witch Hunt 500.00
19 RH(c),The Rag Doll 500.00
20 RH(c),GC,SMo,Lost World . . . 500.00
21 BEv 400.00
22 BK,JF 400.00
23 Strangest Tale in the World. . . 400.00
24 The Thing in the Coffin 400.00
25 . . . . 400.00
26 . . . . 400.00
27 JF,The Garden of Death 400.00
28 Come into my Coffin. 400.00
29 Witch-Craft 400.00
30 The Thing in the Box 400.00
31 Man Who Played with Blocks . 400.00
32 . . . . 400.00
33 JMn(c),Step Lively Please . . . 400.00
34 Flesh and Blood 375.00
35 The Man in the Bottle 300.00
36 . . . . 300.00
37 Out of the Storm 300.00
38 . . . . 300.00
39 Karnoff's Plan 300.00
40 BEv,Man Who Caught
a Mermaid 300.00
41 BEv,Riddle of the Skull 325.00
42 DW,BEv,JMn,Faceless One . . 325.00
43 JF,The Mysterious Machine . . 300.00
44 . . . . 300.00
45 JKa,Land of Vanishing Men . . 325.00
46 thru 57 . . . . @300.00
58 AW 300.00
59 BK. 300.00
60 The Abyss. 275.00
61 BK. 300.00
62 . . . . 275.00
63 The Melting Pot. 300.00
64 AW 300.00
65 Afraid to Open the Door 275.00
66 . . . . 275.00
67 Trapped Between Two Worlds 350.00
68 Evacuate Earth 350.00
69 . . . . 350.00
70 When Wakes the Sphinx. 350.00
71 I Defied the Black Magic. 350.00
72 . . . . 350.00
73 . . . . 350.00
74 . . . . 350.00
75 I Am Taboo 350.00
76 I Am Dragoom. 350.00
77 Taboo Returns 350.00
78 A Martian Prowls Among Us . . 350.00
79 SD,JK,Dr.Strange Prototype . . 350.00
80 thru 83 SD,JK . . . . @250.00
84 SD,JK,Magneto Prototype . . . 250.00
85 SD,JK 250.00
86 SD,JK,I Created Mechano . . . 250.00
87 SD,JK,Return of Grogg. 250.00
88 SD,JK,Zzutak 250.00
89 SD,JK,Fin Fang Foom 700.00
90 SD,JK,Orrgo Unconquerable . 250.00
91 SD,JK,The Sacrifice 250.00
92 SD,JK,Thing That Waits 250.00
93 SD,JK,The Wax People 250.00
94 SD,JK,Pildorr the Plunderer . . 250.00
95 SD,JK,Two-Headed Thing . . . 250.00
96 SD,JK,I Dream of Doom. 250.00
97 SD,JK,When A Planet Dies. . . 600.00
98 SD,JK,No Human Can
Beat Me. 250.00
99 SD,JK,Mister Morgan's
Monster 250.00
100 SD,JK,I Was Trapped
in the Crazy Maze 250.00
101 B:StL(s),SD,JK,
B:Human Torch. 1,600.00
102 SD,JK,I:Wizard 500.00
103 SD,JK,I:Zemu 450.00
104 SD,JK,I:The Trapster 450.00
105 SD,JK,V:Wizard 450.00
106 SD,A:Fantastic Four 300.00
107 SD,V:Sub-Mariner. 375.00
108 SD,JK,A:FF,I:The Painter . . . 300.00
109 SD,JK,I:Sorcerer. 300.00
110 SD,I&B:Dr.Strange,
Nightmare. 2,000.00

STRANGE TALES OF THE UNUSUAL
Marvel, Dec., 1955—Aug., 1957

1 JMn(c),BP,DH,JR,Man Lost. . . 600.00
2 BEv,Man Afraid 300.00
3 AW,The Invaders 325.00
4 The Long Wait 225.00
5 RC,SD,The Threat. 275.00
6 BEv 225.00
7 JK,JO 225.00
8 . . . . 225.00
9 BEv(c),BK 250.00
10 GM,AT. 225.00
11 BEv(c),Aug., 1957. . . . . 225.00

STRANGE TERRORS
St. John Publishing Co., June, 1952

1 The Ghost of Castle
Karloff, Bondage(c) 900.00
2 UnshackledFlight intoNowhere 700.00
3 JKu,Ph(c),The Ghost Who
Ruled Crazy Heights 750.00
4 JKu,Ph(c),Terror from
the Tombs 900.00
5 JKu,Ph(c),No Escaping
the Pool of Death 750.00
6 LC,PMo,Bondage(c),Giant. . . . 900.00
7 JKu,JKu(c),Cat's Death,Giant 1,000.00

STRANGE WORLD OF YOUR DREAMS
Prize Group, Aug., 1952

1 S&K(c),What Do They Mean–
Messages Rec'd in Sleep . 1,200.00
2 MMe,S&K(c),Why did I Dream
That I Was Being Married
to a Man without a Face? . . . 700.00
3 S&K(c) 500.00
4 MMe,S&K(c),The Story of
a Man Who Dreamed a Murder
that Happened 450.00

STRANGE WORLDS
Avon Periodicals, Nov., 1950

1 JKu,Spider God of Akka . . . 2,200.00
2 WW,Dara of the Vikings . . . 2,000.00
3 AW&FF,EK(c),WW,JO. 3,200.00
4 JO,WW,WW(c),The
Enchanted Dagger 2,300.00

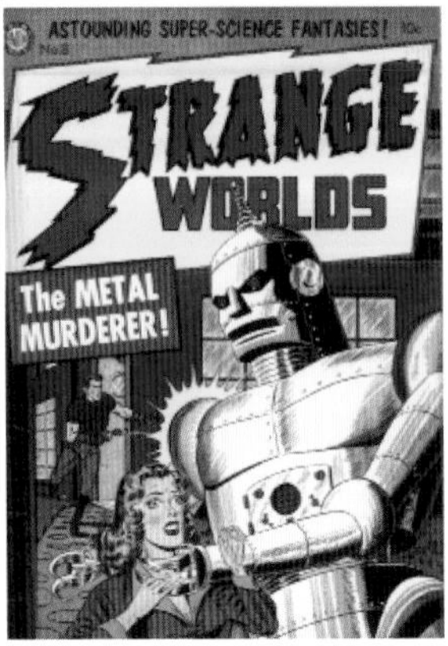

Strange Worlds #8
© Avon Periodicals

Sub-Mariner Comics #39
© Marvel Comics Group

Sun Girl #1
© Marvel Comics Group

5 WW,WW(c),JO,Bondage(c); Sirens of Space 2,400.00
6 EK,WW(c),JO,SC, Maid o/t Mist 1,000.00
7 EK, Sabotage on Space Station 1 . . . . 900.00
8 JKu,EK,The Metal Murderer . . 900.00
9 The Radium Monsters 900.00
18 JKu 800.00
19 Astounding Super Science Fantasies 800.00
20 WW(c),Fighting War Stories . . 250.00
21 EK(c) 200.00
22 EK(c),Sept.–Oct., 1955 . . . . . . 200.00

STRANGE WORLDS

Marvel, Dec., 1958

1 JK,SD,Flying Saucer 1,200.00
2 SD 650.00
3 JK 500.00
4 AW 450.00
5 SD 400.00

STRICTLY PRIVATE

Eastern Color Printing, July, 1942

1 You're in theArmyNow-Humor . 275.00
2 F:Peter Plink, 1942 . . . . 250.00

STUNTMAN COMICS

Harvey Publications, April–May, 1946

1 S&K,O:Stuntman 2,000.00
2 S&K,New Champ of Split-Second Action 1,200.00
3 S&K,Digest sized,Mail Order Only, B&W interior, Oct.–Nov., 1946 . . . . 1,500.00

SUB-MARINER COMICS

Marvel Timely, Spring, 1941

1 ASh(c),BEv,PGv,B:Sub-Mariner, The Angel 65,000.00
2 ASh(c),BEv,Nazi Submarine (c) 10,000.00
3 ASh(c),BEv,Churchill 9,500.00
4 ASh(c),BEv,BW 6,000.00
5 V:Axis Powers 5,000.00
6 ASh(c),Panama Canal 4,500.00
7 ASm&FrG(c) 4,500.00
8 ASh(c),PGv 4,500.00
9 ASh(c),BW,Flag(c) 4,500.00
10 ASh(c),GS 4,500.00
11 ASh(c),Dragon(c) 4,500.00
12 ASh(c) 3,500.00
13 ASh(c),Bondage(c) 3,500.00
14 ASh(c) 3,500.00
15 ASh(c),V:Japs 3,500.00
16 ASh(c),Cl,ASm,GS 2,500.00
17 ASh(c),V:Japs 2,500.00
18 ASh(c),ASm 2,500.00
19 . . . . 2,500.00
20 ASh(c),V:Crooks 2,500.00
21 SSh(c),BEv,Last Angel 2,200.00
22 SSh(c),BEv,A:Young Allies . . 2,200.00
23 SSh(c),BEv,Human Torch . . 2,200.00
24 MSy(c),BEv,A:Namora, bondage cover 2,200.00
25 MSy(c),HK,B:The Blonde Phantom, A:Namora, bondage(c) 2,400.00
26 BEv,SSh,A:Namora 2,000.00
27 DRi(c),BEv,A:Namora 2,000.00
28 DRi(c),BEv,A:Namora 2,000.00
29 BEv,SSh,A:Namora,Human Torch 2,000.00
30 DRi(c),BEv,Slaves Under the Sea 2,000.00
31 BEv,The Man Who Grew, A:Capt. America,E:Blonde Phantom 2,000.00
32 BEv,O:Sub-Mariner 2,500.00
33 BEv,O:Sub-Mariner,A:Human Torch,B:Namora 2,200.00
34 BEv,A:Human Torch,bondage cover 2,000.00
35 BEv,A:Human Torch 2,000.00
36 BEv,Hidden World 2,000.00
37 JMn(c),BEv 2,000.00
38 SSh(c),BEv,JMn, O:Sub-Mariner 2,300.00
39 JMn(c),BEv,Commie Frogman 2,000.00
40 JMn(c),BEv,Secret Tunnel . . 2,000.00
41 JMn(c),BEv,A:Namora 2,000.00
42 BEv,Oct., 1955 . . . . 2,400.00

SUGAR AND SPIKE

DC Comics, April-May, 1956

1 SM 3,000.00
2 SM 1,000.00
3 SM 750.00
4 SM 750.00
5 SM 750.00
6 thru 10 SM . . . . @450.00
11 thru 20 SM . . . . @350.00
21 thru 29 SM . . . . @250.00
30 SM,A:Scribbly 250.00

SUGAR BOWL COMICS

Famous Funnies, May, 1948

1 ATh,ATh(c),The Newest in Teen Age! 175.00
2 . . . . 100.00
3 ATh 125.00
4 . . . . 75.00
5 Jan., 1949 . . . . 75.00

SUN FUN KOMIKS

Sun Publications, 1939

1 F:Spineless Sam the Sweetheart 600.00

SUN GIRL

Marvel Comics, 1948

1 Miss America 2,100.00
2 Blonde Phantom 1,450.00
3 . . . . 1,450.00

SUNNY, AMERICA'S SWEETHEART

Fox Features Syndicate, Dec., 1947

11 AF,AF(c) 2,000.00
12 AF,AF(c) 1,500.00
13 AF,AF(c) 1,500.00
14 AF,AF(c) 1,500.00

SUNSET CARSON

Charlton Comics, Feb., 1951–Aug., 1951

1 Painted, Ph(c);Wyoming Mail 1,200.00
2 Kit Carson-Pioneer 800.00
3 . . . . 700.00
4 Panhandle Trouble 700.00

SUPER BOOK OF COMICS

Western Publishing Co., 1943

N# Dick Tracy 700.00
1 Dick Tracy, Smuggling 700.00
1a Smilin' Jack 400.00
2 Smitty,Magic Morro 400.00
3 Capt. Midnight 700.00
3a Moon Mullins 300.00
4 Red Ryder,Magic Morro 400.00
4a Smitty 300.00

Super-Book of Comics 2nd Series #13
© Western Publishing

Superboy #20
© DC Comics

Superboy #42
© DC Comics

5 Don Winslow,Magic Morro. . . . 400.00
5a DonWinslow,StratosphereJim 400.00
5a Terry & the Pirates. 500.00
6 Don Winslow 500.00
6a King of the Royal Mounties . . 500.00
7 Little Orphan Annie 300.00
7a Dick Tracy 600.00
8 Dick Tracy 500.00
8a Dan Dunn. 300.00
9 Terry & the Pirates. 500.00
10 Red Ryder, Magic Morro. 300.00

SUPER-BOOK OF COMICS

Western Publishing Co., 1944

1 Dick Tracy (Omar). 350.00
1 Dick Tracy (Hancock) 250.00
2 Bugs Bunny (Omar). 250.00
2 Bugs Bunny (Hancock) 250.00
3 Terry & the Pirates (Omar) . . . 300.00
3 Terry & the Pirates (Hancock) . 300.00
4 Andy Panda (Omar). 200.00
4 Andy Panda (Hancock) 200.00
5 Smokey Stover (Omar) 200.00
5 Smokey Stover (Hancock) . . . 200.00
6 Porky Pig (Omar). 250.00
6 Porky Pig (Hancock) 225.00
7 Smilin' Jack (Omar) 200.00
7 Smilin' Jack (Hancock) 200.00
8 Oswald the Rabbit (Omar). . . . 200.00
8 Oswald the Rabbit (Hancock) . 175.00
9 Alley Oop (Omar). 300.00
9 Alley Oop (Hancock) 275.00
10 Elmer Fudd (Omar). 200.00
10 Elmer Fudd (Hancock) 175.00
11 Little Orphan Annie (Omar). . . 200.00
11 Little Orphan Amnie (Hancock)200.00
12 Woody Woodpecker (Omar) . . 225.00
12 WoodyWoodpecker(Hancock) 200.00
13 Dick Tracy (Omar). 300.00
13 Dick Tracy (Hancock) 275.00
14 Bugs Bunny (Omar) 300.00
14 Bugs Bunny (Hanock). 250.00
15 Andy Panda (Omar) 200.00
15 Andy Panda (Hancock). 175.00
16 Terry & the Pirates (Omar) . . . 300.00
16 Terry & the Pirates (Hancock). 275.00
17 Smokey Stover (Omar) 200.00
17 Smokey Stover (Hancock) . . . 175.00
18 Porky Pig (Omar) 250.00
18 Smokey Stover (Hancock) . . . 175.00
19 Smilin' Jack (Omar) 175.00
N# Smilin' Jack (Hancock). 150.00
20 Oswald the Rabbit (Omar) . . . 150.00
N# Oswald the Rabbit (Hancock) 125.00
21 Gasoline Alley (Omar). 150.00
N# Gasoline Alley (Hancock). . . . 125.00
22 Elmer Fudd (Omar). 150.00
N# Elmer Fudd (Hancock) 135.00
23 Little Orphan Annie (Omar). . . 150.00
N# Little Orphan Annie (Hancock) 135.00
24 Woody Woodpecker (Omar) . . 125.00
N# WoodyWoodpecker(Hancock) 100.00
25 Dick Tracy (Omar). 175.00
N# Dick Tracy (Hancock). 150.00
26 Bugs Bunny (Omar) 150.00
N# Bugs Bunny (Hancock) 125.00
27 Andy Panda (Omar) 125.00
27 Andy Panda (Hancock). 100.00
28 Terry & the Pirates (Omar) . . . 250.00
28 Terry & the Pirates (Hancock). 225.00
29 Smokey Stover (Omar). 100.00
29 Smokey Stover (Hancock) . . . 100.00
30 Porky Pig (Omar) 150.00
30 Porky Pig (Hancock). 125.00
N# Bugs Bunny (Hancock) 125.00

SUPERBOY

DC Comics, 1949

1 Superman (c) 20,000.00
2 Superboy Day. 5,000.00
3 . . . . 3,700.00
4 The Oracle of Smallville 3,200.00
5 Superboy meets Supergirl, Pre-Adventure #252 . . . . . . 3,200.00
6 I:Humpty Dumpty,the Hobby Robber 2,700.00
7 WB,V:Humpty Dumpty 2,700.00
8 CS,I:Superbaby,V:Humpty Dumpty 2,500.00
9 V:Humpty Dumpty. 2,500.00
10 CS,I:Lana Lang 2,500.00
11 CS,2nd Lang,V:Humpty Dumpty 2,200.00
12 CS,The Heroes Club 2,000.00
13 CS,Scout of Smallville 2,000.00
14 CS,I:Marsboy. 2,000.00
15 CS,A:Superman. 2,200.00
16 CS,A:Marsboy 2,000.00
17 CS,Superboy's Double 2,000.00
18 CS,Lana Lang-Hollywood Star 2,000.00
19 CS,The Death of Young Clark Kent. 2,000.00
20 CS,The Ghost that Haunted Smallville 2,000.00
21 CS,Lana Lang-Magician . . . 1,000.00
22 CS,The New Clark Kent . . . 1,000.00
23 CS,The Super Superboy . . . 1,000.00
24 CS,The Super Fat Boy of Steel 1,000.00
25 CS,Cinderella of Smallville . 1,000.00
26 CS,A:Superbaby 1,000.00
27 CS,Clark Kent-Runaway. . . . 1,000.00
28 CS,The Man Who Defeated Superboy 1,000.00
29 CS,The Puppet Superboy . . 1,000.00
30 CS,I:Tommy Tuttle 800.00
31 CS,The Amazing Elephant Boy From Smallville. 800.00
32 CS,His Majesty King Superboy 800.00
33 CS,The Crazy Costumes of the Boy of Steel. 800.00
34 CS,Hep Cats o/Smallville 800.00
35 CS,The Five Superboys 800.00
36 . . . . 800.00
37 CS,I:Thaddeus Lang. 800.00
38 CS,Public Chimp #1 . . . . 800.00
39 CS,Boy w/Superboy Powers. . 800.00
40 CS,The Magic Necklace 700.00
41 CS,Superboy Meets Superbrave 700.00
42 CS,Gaucho of Smallville. 700.00
43 CS,Super-Farmer of Smallville 700.00
44 The Amazing Adventure of Superboy's Costume 700.00
45 A Trap For Superboy. 700.00
46 The Battle of Fort Smallville . . 700.00
47 CS,A:Superman 700.00
48 CS,Boy Without Super-Suit . . 700.00
49 I:Metallo (Jor-El's Robot) 700.00
50 The Super-Giant of Smallville 700.00
51 I:Krypto 500.00
52 CS,The Powerboy from Earth 500.00
53 CS,A:Superman 500.00
54 CS,The Silent Superboy 500.00
55 CS,A:Jimmy Olson 500.00
56 CS,A:Krypto 500.00
57 CS,One-Man Baseball Team . 500.00
58 CS,The Great Kryptonite Mystery 500.00
59 CS,A:Superbaby. 500.00
60 The 100,000 Cowboy 500.00
61 The School For Superboys. . . 400.00
62 I:Gloria Kent 400.00
63 CS,The Two Boys of Steel . . . 400.00
64 CS,A:Krypto 400.00
65 Superboy's Moonlight Spell . . 400.00
66 The Family with X-Ray Eyes . 400.00
67 I:Klax-Ar 400.00
68 O&I:Bizarro 1,400.00

Superboy #77
© DC Comics

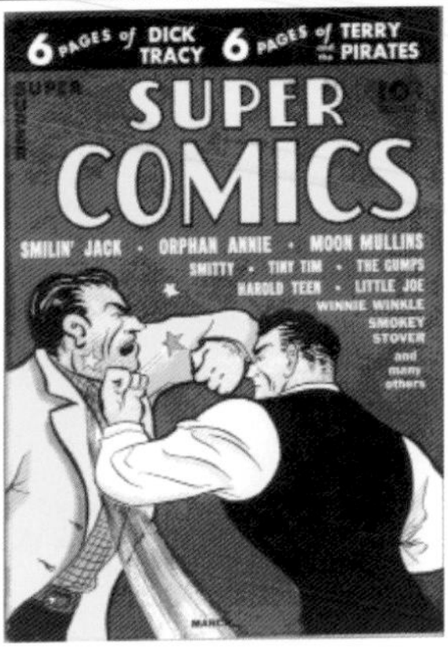

Super Comics #10
© Dell Publishing Co.

Super Comics #54
© Dell Publishing Co.

69 How Superboy Learned
To Fly 300.00
70 O:Superboy's Glasses 300.00
71 A:Superbaby 300.00
72 The Flying Girl of Smallville . . 300.00
73 CS,A:Superbaby 300.00
74 A:Jor-El & Lara 300.00
75 A:Superbaby 300.00
76 I:Super Monkey 300.00
77 Superboy's Best Friend 300.00
78 O:Mr.Mzyzptik 500.00
79 A:Jar-El & Lara 300.00
80 Superboy meets Supergirl . . . 400.00
81 The Weakling From Earth 275.00
82 A:Bizarro Krypto 275.00
83 I:Kryptonite Kid 275.00
84 A:William Tell 275.00
85 Secret of Mighty Boy 275.00
86 I:PeteRoss,A:Legion 500.00
87 I:Scarlet Jungle of Krypton . . . 275.00
88 The Invader from Earth 275.00
89 I:Mon-El 275.00
90 A:Pete Ross 150.00
91 CS,Superboy in Civil War 150.00
92 CS,I:Destructo,A:Lex Luthor . . 150.00
93 A:Legion 150.00
94 I:Superboy Revenge Squad,
A:Pete Ross 150.00
95 Imaginary Story,The Super
Family From Krypton 150.00
96 A:Pete Ross,Lex Luther 150.00
97 Krypto Story 150.00
98 Legion,I&O:Ultraboy 150.00
99 O: The Kryptonite Kid 100.00
100 I:Phantom Zone 275.00
101 The Handsome Hound
of Steel 125.00
102 O:Scarlet Jungle of Krypton . 125.00
103 CS,A:King Arthur,Jesse James
Red Kryptonite 125.00
104 O:Phantom Zone 125.00
105 CS,The Simpleton of Steel . . 125.00
106 CS,A:Brainiac 125.00
107 CS,I:Superboy Club of
Smallville 150.00
108 The Kent's First Super Son . 125.00
109 The Super Youth of Bronze . 125.00
110 A:Jor-El 125.00

SUPER BRAT

Toby Press, 1954

1 . . . . 125.00
2 . . . . 100.00
3 . . . . 100.00
4 Li'l Teevy 100.00

SUPER CAT

**Four Star Comic Corp.
(Ajax Comics/Farrell
Publ.), 1957**

1 . . . . 125.00
2 thru 4 . . . . @100.00

SUPER CIRCUS

**Cross Publishing Co.,
Jan., 1951**

1 Partial Ph(c) 150.00
2 . . . . 125.00
3 . . . . 100.00
4 . . . . 100.00
5 1951 . . . . 100.00

SUPER COMICS

**Dell Publishing Co.,
May, 1938**

1 Dick Tracy,Terry and the
Pirates,Smilin'Jack,Smokey
Stover,Orphan Annie,etc. . . 3,200.00
2 . . . . 1,400.00
3 . . . . 1,200.00
4 . . . . 1,100.00
5 Gumps(c) 1,000.00
6 . . . . 750.00
7 Smokey Stover(c) 750.00
8 Dick Tracy(c) 750.00
9 . . . . 750.00
10 Dick Tracy(c) 750.00
11 . . . . 550.00
12 . . . . 550.00
13 . . . . 550.00
14 . . . . 550.00
15 . . . . 550.00
16 Terry & the Pirates 500.00
17 Dick Tracy(c) 500.00
18 . . . . 500.00
19 . . . . 500.00
20 Smilin'Jack(c) 525.00
21 B:Magic Morro 400.00
22 Magic Morro(c) 450.00
23 all star(c) 400.00
24 Dick Tracy(c) 450.00
25 Magic Morro(c) 400.00
26 . . . . 400.00
27 Magic Morro(c) 400.00
28 Jim Ellis(c) 450.00
29 Smilin'Jack(c) 400.00
30 inc.The Sea Hawk 450.00
31 Dick Tracy(c) 350.00
32 Smilin' Jack(c) 365.00
33 Jim Ellis(c) 350.00
34 Magic Morro(c) 350.00
35 thru 40 Dick Tracy(c) . . . . @350.00
41 B:Lightning Jim 300.00
42 thru 50 Dick Tracy(c) . . . . @300.00
51 thru 54 Dick Tracy(c) . . . . @250.00
55 . . . . 250.00
56 . . . . 250.00
57 Dick Tracy(c) 250.00
58 Smitty(c) 250.00
59 . . . . 250.00
60 Dick Tracy(c) 275.00
61 . . . . 235.00
62 Flag(c) 235.00
63 Dick Tracy(c) 235.00
64 Smitty(c) 225.00
65 Dick Tracy(c) 235.00
66 Dick Tracy(c) 235.00
67 Christmas(c) 235.00
68 Dick Tracy(c) 235.00
69 Dick Tracy(c) 235.00
70 Dick Tracy(c) 235.00
71 Dick Tracy(c) 200.00
72 Dick Tracy(c) 200.00
73 Smitty(c) 200.00
74 War Bond(c) 200.00
75 Dick Tracy(c) 200.00
76 Dick Tracy(c) 200.00
77 Dick Tracy(c) 200.00
78 Smitty(c) 150.00
79 Dick Tracy(c) 150.00
80 Smitty(c) 150.00
81 Dick Tracy(c) 150.00
82 Dick Tracy(c) 150.00
83 Smitty(c) 135.00
84 Dick Tracy(c) 150.00
85 Smitty(c) 135.00
86 All on cover 150.00
87 All on cover 150.00
88 Dick Tracy(c) 150.00
89 Smitty(c) 135.00
90 Dick Tracy(c) 150.00
91 Smitty(c) 135.00
92 Dick Tracy(c) 150.00
93 Dick Tracy(c) 150.00
94 Dick Tracy(c) 150.00
95 thru 99 . . . . @135.00
100 . . . . 150.00
101 thru 115 . . . . @150.00
116 Smokey Stover(c) 100.00
117 Gasoline Alley(c) 100.00
118 Smokey Stover(c) 100.00
119 Terry and the Pirates(c) 110.00
120 . . . . 100.00
121 . . . . 100.00

Super Duck Comics #22
© Archie Publications

Super Magician Comics Vol. 3 #12
© Street & Smith Publications

Superman #14
© DC Comics

SUPER-DOOPER COMICS

Able Manufacturing Co., 1946

1 A:Gangbuster 250.00
2 . . . . 200.00
3 & 4 . . . . @150.00
5 A:Captain Freedom,Shock Gibson 150.00
6 & 7 same . . . . @150.00
8 A:Shock Gibson, 1946 . . . . . . 150.00

SUPER DUCK COMICS

MLJ Magazines/Close-Up (Archie Publ.), Autumn, 1944

1 O:Super Duck, Hitler 750.00
2 . . . . 300.00
3 I:Mr. Monster 250.00
4 & 5 . . . . @225.00
6 thru 10 . . . . @200.00
11 thru 20 . . . . @150.00
21 thru 40 . . . . @125.00
41 thru 60 . . . . @100.00
61 thru 94 . . . . @100.00

SUPER DUPER COMICS

F.E. Howard Publications, 1947

3 Mr Monster 1st. 175.00

SUPER FUN

Gilmor Magazines, 1956

1 Puzzles & comics 100.00

SUPER FUNNIES

Superior Comics Publishers, March, 1954

1 Dopey Duck 500.00
2 Out of the Booby-Hatch 200.00

Becomes:

SUPER WESTERN FUNNIES

1954

3 F:Phantom Ranger 100.00
4 F:Phantom Ranger,Sept., 1954 100.00

SUPERIOR STORIES

Nesbit Publishing Co., 1955

1 Wells-The Invisible Man 275.00
2 Ingrahams-Pirate of the Gulf . . 125.00
3 Clark-Wreck of Grosvenor 125.00
4 O'Henry-Texas Rangers 125.00

SUPER MAGICIAN COMICS

Street & Smith Publ., May, 1941

1 B:The Mysterious Blackstone . 800.00
2 V:Wild Tribes of Africa 500.00
3 V:Oriental Wizard 500.00
4 V:Quetzal Wizard,O:Transo . . . 475.00
5 A:The Moylan Sisters 475.00
6 JaB,JaB(c),The Eddie Cantor story 475.00
7 In the House of Skulls 500.00
8 A:Abbott & Costello 500.00
9 V:Duneen the Man-Ape 500.00
10 V:Pirates o/t Sargasso Sea. . . 500.00
11 JaB(c),V:Fire Wizards 500.00
12 V:Baal 500.00
2-1 A:The Shadow 500.00
2-2 Temple of the 10,000 Idols . . 250.00
2-3 Optical Illusion on (c)-turn Jap into Monkey 250.00
2-4 V:Cannibal Killers 250.00
2-5 V:The Pygmies of Lemuriai . 250.00
2-6 V;Pirates & Indians 250.00
2-7 Can Blackstone Catch the Cannonball? 250.00
2-8 V:Marabout,B:Red Dragon . . 250.00
2-9 . . . . 250.00
2-10 Pearl Dives Swallowed By Sea Demons 250.00
2-11 Blackstone Invades Pelican Islands 250.00
2-12 V:Bubbles of Death 250.00
3-1 . . . . 275.00
3-2 Bondage(c),Midsummers Eve 250.00
3-3 The Enchanted Garden 250.00
3-4 Fabulous Aztec Treasure . . . 250.00
3-5 A:Buffalo Bill 250.00
3-6 Magic Tricks to Mystify 250.00
3-7 V:Guy Fawkes 250.00
3-8 V:Hindu Spook Maker 250.00
3-9 . . . . 250.00
3-10 V:The Water Wizards 250.00
3-11 V:The Green Goliath 250.00
3-12 Lady in White. 250.00
4-1 Cannibal of Crime 225.00
4-2 The Devil's Castle 225.00
4-3 V:Demons of Golden River . . 225.00
4-4 V:Dr. Zero 225.00
4-5 Bondage(c) 225.00
4-6 V:A Terror Gang 225.00
4-7 . . . . 225.00
4-8 Mystery of the Disappearing Horse 225.00
4-9 A Floating Light? 225.00
4-10 Levitation 225.00
4-11 Lost, Strange Land of Shangri 225.00
4-12 I:Nigel Elliman 225.00
5-1 V:Voodoo Wizards of the Everglades,Bondage (c) 225.00
5-2 Treasure of the Florida Keys; Bondage (c) 225.00
5-3 Elliman Battles Triple Crime . 225.00
5-4 Can A Human Being Really Become Invisible 225.00
5-5 Mystery of the Twin Pools . . 225.00
5-6 A:Houdini 225.00
5-7 F:Red Dragon 500.00
5-8 F:Red Dragon, Feb.–March, 1947 . . . . 500.00

SUPERMAN

DC Comics, 1939

1 JoS,O:Superman,reprints Action Comics #1-#4 . . . . 280,000.00
2 JoS,I:George Taylor 18,000.00
3 JoS,V:Superintendent Lyman 11,000.00
4 JoS,V:Lex Luthor. 11,000.00
5 JoS,V:Lex Luthor 8,000.00
6 JoS,V:Brute' Bashby 4,500.00
7 JoS,I:Perry White 3,800.00
8 JoS,V:Jackal 3,600.00
9 JoS,V:Joe Gatson 3,600.00
10 JoS,V:Lex Luthor 3,500.00
11 JoS,V:Rolf Zimba 2,800.00
12 JoS,V:Lex Luthor 2,800.00
13 JoS,I:Jimmy Olsen,V:Lex Luthor,The Archer. 2,800.00
14 JoS,I:Lightning Master 4,500.00
15 JoS,V:The Evolution King . . 2,800.00
16 JoS,V:Mr. Sinus 2,300.00
17 JoS,V:Lex Luthor,Lois Lane first suspects Clark is Superman 2,300.00
18 JoS,V:Lex Luthor 2,200.00
19 JoS,V:Funnyface, 1st Imaginary story. 2,200.00
20 JoS,V:Puzzler,Leopard 2,200.00
21 JoS,V:Sir Gauntlet 1,800.00
22 JoS,V:Prankster 1,800.00
23 JoS,Propaganda story 1,800.00
24 V:Cobra King 2,500.00
25 Propaganda story 1,700.00
26 I:J.Wilbur Wolfingham, A:Mercury 1,700.00
27 V:Toyman 1,700.00
28 V:J.Wilbur Wolfingham, A:Hercules 1,700.00

Su

Superman #36
© DC Comics

Superman #95
© DC Comics

Superman #130
© DC Comics

29 V:Prankster 1,700.00
30 I&O:Mr. Mxyztplk 3,000.00
31 V:Lex Luthor. 1,400.00
32 V:Toyman 1,400.00
33 V:Mr. Mxyztptlk. 1,400.00
34 V:Lex Luthor. 1,400.00
35 V:J.Wilbur Wolfingham. 1,400.00
36 V:Mr. Mxyztptlk. 1,400.00
37 V:Prankster,A:Sinbad. 1,400.00
38 V:Lex Luthor. 1,400.00
39 V:J.Wilbur Wolfingham. 1,400.00
40 V:Mr. Mxyztplk,A:Susie Thompkins 1,400.00
41 V:Prankster 1,100.00
42 V:J.Wilbur Wolfingham. 1,100.00
43 V:Lex Luthor. 1,100.00
44 V:Toyman,A:Shakespeare . . 1,100.00
45 A:Hocus & Pocus,Lois Lane as Superwoman 1,100.00
46 V:Mr. Mxyzptlk,Lex Luthor, Superboy flashback 1,100.00
47 V:Toyman 1,100.00
48 V:Lex Luthor. 1,100.00
49 V:Toyman 1,100.00
50 V:Prankster 1,100.00
51 V:Mr. Mxyzptlk. 900.00
52 V:Prankster 900.00
53 WB,O:Superman 3,800.00
54 V:Wrecker 900.00
55 V:Prankster 900.00
56 V:Prankster 900.00
57 V:Lex Luthor 900.00
58 V:Tiny Trix 900.00
59 V:Mr.Mxyzptlk 900.00
60 V:Toyman 900.00
61 I:Kryptonite,V:Prankster 1,800.00
62 V:Mr.Mxyzptlk,A:Orson Welles 900.00
63 V:Toyman 900.00
64 V:Prankster 900.00
65 V:Mala,Kizo and U-Ban 900.00
66 V:Prankster 900.00
67 A:Perry Como,I:Brane Taylor 900.00
68 V:Lex Luthor 900.00
69 V:Prankster,A:Inspector Erskine Hawkins 900.00
70 V:Prankster 900.00
71 V:Lex Luthor 800.00
72 V:Prankster 800.00
72a giveaway 1,000.00
73 Flashback story. 800.00
74 V:Lex Luthor 800.00
75 V:Prankster 800.00
76 A:Batman, Superman & Batman reveal each other's identities 2,200.00
77 A:Pocahontas 750.00
78 V:Kryptonian snagriff, A:Lana Lang 750.00
79 V:Lex Luthor,A:Inspector Erskine Hawkins 750.00
80 A:Halk Kar. 750.00
81 V:Lex Luthor 750.00
82 V:Mr. Mxyzptlk. 650.00
83 V:The Brain. 650.00
84 Time-travel story 650.00
85 V:Lex Luthor 650.00
86 V:Mr.Mxyzptlk 650.00
87 WB,V:The Thing from 40,000 AD 650.00
88 WB,V:Lex Luthor,Toyman, Prankster team 750.00
89 V:Lex Luthor 650.00
90 V:Lex Luthor 700.00
91 The Superman Stamp. 650.00
92 Goes back to 12th Century England 650.00
93 V:The Thinker 650.00
94 Clark Kent's Hillbilly Bride. . . . 650.00
95 A:Susie Thompkins 650.00
96 V:Mr. Mxyzptlk. 475.00
97 Superboy's Last Day In Smallville 475.00
98 Clark Kent, Outlaw!. 475.00
99 V:Midnite gang 475.00
100 F:Superman-Substitute Schoolteacher. 2,800.00
101 A:Lex Luthor 475.00
102 I:Superman Stock Company 475.00
103 A:Mr.Mxyzptlk 475.00
104 F:Clark Kent,Jailbird 475.00
105 A:Mr.Mxyzptlk 475.00
106 A:Lex Luthor 500.00
107 F:Superman In 30th century (pre-Legion). 475.00
108 I:Perry White Jr. 475.00
109 I:Abner Hokum 475.00
110 A:Lex Luthor 475.00
111 Becomes Mysto the Great. . . 400.00
112 A:Lex Luthor 400.00
113 A:Jor-El 400.00
114 V:The Great Mento 400.00
115 V:The Organizer 400.00
116 Return to Smallville. 400.00
117 A:Lex Luthor 400.00
118 F:Jimmy Olsen 400.00
119 A:Zoll Orr. 400.00
120 V:Gadget Grim 400.00
121 I:XL-49 (Futureman) 350.00
122 In the White House. 350.00
123 CS,pre-Supergirl tryout A:Jor-El & Lara 375.00
124 F:Lois Lane. 350.00
125 F:Superman College Story . . 350.00
126 F:Lois Lane. 350.00
127 WB,I&O:Titano 375.00
128 V:Vard & Boka. 350.00
129 WB,I&O:Lori Lemaris 375.00
130 A:Krypto,the Superdog 350.00
131 A:Mr. Mxyzptlk. 275.00
132 A:Batman & Robin 275.00
133 F:Superman Joins Army 275.00
134 A:Supergirl & Krypto 275.00
135 A:Lori Lemaris,Mr.Mxyzptlk. . 275.00
136 O:Discovery Kryptonite 275.00
137 CS,I:Super-Menace 275.00
138 A:Titano,Lori Lemaris 275.00
139 CS,O:Red Kryptonite 275.00
140 WB,I:Bizarro Jr,Bizarro Supergirl,Blue Kryptonite. . . . 275.00
141 I:Lyla Lerrol,A:Jor-EL & Lara 225.00
142 WB,CS,A:Al Capone. 225.00
143 WB,F:Bizarro meets Frankenstein 225.00
144 O:Superboy's 1st Public Appearance 225.00
145 F:April Fool's Issue 225.00
146 F:Superman's life story 275.00
147 CS,I:Adult Legion 275.00
148 CS,V:Mxyzptlk. 225.00
149 CS:A:Luthor,C:JLA 225.00
150 CS,KS,V:Mxyzptlk. 150.00
Ann.#1 I:Supergirl Rep 1,700.00
Ann.#2 I&O:Titano 650.00
Ann.#3 I:Legion 450.00
Ann.#4 O:Legion 350.00
Ann.#5 A:Krypton. 275.00
Ann.#6 A:Legion. 275.00
Ann.#7 O:Superman,Silver Anniv. 200.00
Ann.#8 F:Secret origins 175.00

SUPERMAN'S BUDDY

DC Comics, 1954

1 w/costume, giveaway 1,800.00
1 w/out costume, giveaway 800.00

SUPERMAN'S CHRISTMAS ADVENTURE

DC Comics, 1940–44

1 (1940) giveaway 6,000.00
2 (1944) giveaway 1,500.00

Su

Superman-Tim Store Stamp Album 9-48
© DC Comics

Superman's Girl Friend, Lois Lane #37
© DC Comics

Superman's Pal Jimmy Olsen #39
© DC Comics

SUPERMAN AND THE GREAT CLEVELAND FIRE

DC Comics, 1948

1 for Hospital Fund, giveaway . . 800.00

SUPERMAN (miniature)

DC Comics, 1942

1 Py-Co-Pay Tooth Powder Give- Away 900.00
2 CS,Superman Time Capsule . . 500.00
3 CS,Duel in Space 450.00
4 CS,Super Show in Metropolis . 450.00

SUPERMAN-TIM STORE PAMPHLETS

DC Comics, 1942

Superman-Tim store Monthly Membership Pamphlets, stories, games
(1942), each 1,500.00
(1943), each 500.00
(1944), each 475.00
(1945), each 450.00
(1946), color(c) each 550.00
(1947), color(c) each 350.00
(1948), color(c) each 300.00
(1949), color(c) each 300.00
(1950), color(c) each 350.00
Superman-Tim stamp albums,
(1946) 400.00
(1947) Superman story 500.00
(1948) 400.00

SUPERMAN WORKBOOK

DC Comics, 1945

1 rep. Superman #14. . . . . 1,300.00

SUPERMAN'S GIRL FRIEND, LOIS LANE

DC Comics, 1958

1 CS,KS 6,000.00
2 CS,KS 1,500.00
3 CS,KS,spanking panel 1,000.00
4 CS,KS 750.00
5 CS,KS 750.00
6 CS,KS 550.00
7 CS,KS 550.00
8 CS,KS 450.00
9 CS,KS, A:Pat Boone 450.00
10 CS,KS 450.00
11 CS,KS 300.00
12 CS,KS 300.00
13 CS,KS 300.00
14 KS,Three Nights in the Fortress of Solitude 300.00
15 KS,I:Van-Zee. 300.00
16 KS, Lois' Signal-Watch 300.00
17 KS,CS,A:Brainiac 300.00
18 KS,A:Astounding Man. 300.00
19 KS,Superman of the Past. . . . 300.00
20 KS,A:Superman 325.00
21 KS,A:Van-Zee 225.00
22 KS,A:Robin Hood 225.00
23 KS,A:Elastic Lass, Supergirl . . 225.00
24 KS,A:Van-Zee, Bizarro 225.00
25 KS,Lois' Darkest Secret 225.00
26 KS,A:Jor-El 225.00
27 KS,CS,A:Bizarro 225.00
28 KS,A:Luthor. 225.00
29 CS,A:Aquaman,Batman,Green Arrow 225.00
30 KS,A:Krypto,Aquaman 150.00
31 KS,A:Lori Lemaris. 150.00
32 KS,CS,A:Bizarro 150.00
33 KS,CS,A:Phantom Zone,Lori Lemaris, Mon-El 150.00
34 KS,A:Luthor,Supergirl 150.00
35 KS,CS,A:Supergirl 150.00
36 KS,CS,Red Kryptonite Story . . 150.00
37 KS,CS,The Forbidden Box . . . 150.00
38 KS,CS,A:Prof.Potter, Supergirl 150.00
39 KS,CS,A:Supergirl,Jor-El, Krypto, Lori Lemaris 150.00
40 KS,Lois Lane, Hag!. 150.00
41 KS,CS,The Devil and Lois Lane. 150.00
42 KS,A:Lori Lemaris. 150.00
43 KS,A:Luthor. 150.00
44 KS,A:Lori Lemaris,Braniac, Prof. Potter 150.00
45 KS,CS,The Superman-Lois Hit Record 150.00
46 KS,A:Luthor. 150.00
47 KS,The Incredible Delusion . . 150.00
48 KS,A:Mr. Mxyzptlk. 150.00
49 KS,The Unknown Superman . 150.00
50 KS,A:Legion 160.00

SUPERMAN'S PAL, JIMMY OLSEN

DC Comics, 1954

1 CS,The Boy of 100 Faces! . . 8,500.00
2 CS,The Flying Jimmy Olsen. 2,500.00
3 CS,The Man Who Collected Excitement 1,300.00
4 CS,King For A Day! 900.00
5 CS,The Story of Superman's Souvenirs. 900.00
6 CS,Kryptonite story 650.00
7 CS,The King of Marbles 650.00
8 CS,Jimmy Olsen, Crooner. . . . 600.00
9 CS,The Missile of Steel 600.00
10 CS,Jungle Jimmy Olsen 600.00
11 CS,TNT.Olsen,The Champ . . . 400.00
12 CS,Invisible Jimmy Olsen. . . . 400.00
13 CS,Jimmy Olsen's Super Issue 400.00
14 CS,The Boy Superman. 400.00
15 CS,Jimmy Olsen,Speed Demon. 400.00
16 CS,The Boy Superman. 400.00
17 CS,J.Olsen as cartoonist 400.00
18 CS,A:Superboy 400.00
19 CS,Supermam's Kid Brother. . 400.00
20 CS,Merman of Metropolis. . . . 400.00
21 CS,The Wedding of Jimmy Olsen 250.00
22 CS,The Super Brain of Jimmy Olsen 250.00
23 CS,The Adventure of Private Olsen. 250.00
24 CS,The Gorilla Reporter 250.00
25 CS,The Day There Was No Jimmy Olsen 250.00
26 CS,Bird Boy of Metropolis . . . 250.00
27 CS,The Outlaw Jimmy Olsen . 250.00
28 CS,The Boy Who Killed Superman 250.00
29 CS,A:Krypto 250.00
30 CS,The Son of Superman . . . 250.00
31 CS,I:Elastic Lad 225.00
32 CS,A:Prof.Potter 200.00
33 CS,Human Flame Thrower. . . 200.00
34 CS,Superman's Pal of Steel . . 200.00
35 CS,Superman's Enemy 200.00
36 CS,I:Lois Lane,O:Jimmy Olsen as Superman's Pal 200.00
37 CS,O:Jimmy Olsen's SignalWatch, A:Elastic Lad(Jimmy Olsen) . 200.00
38 CS,Olsen's Super-Supper . . . 200.00
39 CS,The Super-Lad of Space. . 200.00
40 CS,A:Supergirl,Hank White (Perry White's son) 200.00
41 CS,The Human Octopus. 150.00
42 CS,Jimmy The Genie 150.00
43 WB,CS,Jimmy Olsen's Private Monster 150.00
44 CS,Miss Jimmy Olsen. 150.00
45 CS,A:Kandor. 150.00
46 CS,A:Supergirl,Elastic Lad . . . 150.00
47 CS,Monsters From Earth!. . . . 150.00

Su

Supermouse #1
© Standard Comics

Super-Mystery Comics #13 (Vol. 3 #1)
© Ace Magazines

Supersnipe Comics Vol. 2 #1
© Street & Smith Publications

48 CS,I:Superman Emergency Squad 150.00
49 CS,A:Congorilla & Congo Bill . 150.00
50 CS,A:Supergirl,Krypto,Bizarro 150.00
51 CS,A:Supergirl 125.00
52 CS,A:Mr. Mxyzptlk, Miss Gzptlsnz 125.00
53 CS,A:Kandor,Lori Lemaris, Mr.Mxyztlk 125.00
54 CS,A:Elastic Lad 125.00
55 CS,A:Aquaman,Thor 125.00
56 KS,Imaginary story 125.00

SUPERMOUSE

Standard Comics/Pines, Dec., 1948

1 FF,(fa) 350.00
2 FF,(fa) 150.00
3 FF,(fa) 135.00
4 FF,(fa) 135.00
5 FF,(fa) 135.00
6 FF,(fa) 135.00
7 thru 10 (fa) . . . . . . @125.00
11 thru 20 (fa) . . . . . . @125.00
21 thru 44 (fa) . . . . . . @100.00
45 (fa),Autumn, 1958 . . . . . . 100.00

SUPER-MYSTERY COMICS

Periodical House (Ace Magazines), July, 1940

1 B:Magno,Vulcan,Q-13,Flint of the Mountes 4,000.00
2 Bondage (c) 1,300.00
3 JaB,B:Black Spider 1,000.00
4 O:Davy;A:Captain Gallant . . . 750.00
5 JaB,JM(c),I&B:The Clown . . . 750.00
6 JM,JM(c),V:The Clown 650.00
2-1 JM,JM(c),O:Buckskin, Bondage(c) 650.00
2-2 JM,JM(c),V:The Clown 600.00
2-3 JM,JM(c),V:The Clown 600.00
2-4 JM,JM(c),V:The Nazis 600.00
2-5 JM,JM(c),Bondage(c) 600.00
2-6 JM,JM(c),Bondage(c), 'Foreign Correspondent' 600.00
3-1 B:Black Ace 600.00
3-2 A:Mr, Risk, Bondage(c) 600.00
3-3 HK,HK(c),I:Lancer;B:Dr. Nemesis, The Sword 650.00
3-4 HK 600.00
3-5 HK,LbC,A:Mr. Risk 600.00
3-6 HK,LbC,A:Paul Revere Jr. . . 600.00
4-1 HK,LbC,A:Twin Must Die . . . 550.00
4-2 A:Mr. Risk 375.00
4-3 Mango out to Kill Davey! . . . 375.00
4-4 Danger Laughs at Mr. Risk . . 375.00
4-5 A:Mr. Risk 375.00
4-6 RP,A:Mr. Risk 375.00
5-1 RP 375.00
5-2 RP,RP(c),The Riddle of the Swamp-Land Spirit 375.00
5-3 RP,RP(c),The Case of the Whispering Death 375.00
5-4 RP,RP(c) 375.00
5-5 RP,Harry the Hack 375.00
5-6 . . . . . . 375.00
6-1 . . . . . . 300.00
6-2 RP,A:Mr. Risk 300.00
6-3 Bondage (c) 300.00
6-4 E:Mango;A:Mr. Risk 300.00
6-5 Bondage(c) 300.00
6-6 A:Mr. Risk 300.00
7-1 . . . . . . 300.00
7-2 KBa(c) 300.00
7-3 Bondage(c) 300.00
7-4 . . . . . . 300.00
7-5 . . . . . . 300.00
7-6 . . . . . . 300.00
8-1 The Riddle of the Rowboat . . 275.00
8-2 Death Meets a Train 275.00
8-3 The Man Who Couldn't Die . 275.00
8-4 RP(c) 275.00
8-5 GT,MMe,Staged for Murder . 275.00
8-6 Unlucky Seven,July, 1949 . . 275.00

SUPER PUP

Avon Periodicals, 1954

4 . . . . . . 125.00
5 Robot(c) 150.00

SUPER RABBIT

Marvel Timely, 1943

1 Hitler 1,200.00
2 . . . . . . 500.00
3 . . . . . . 350.00
4 . . . . . . 350.00
5 . . . . . . 350.00
6 Origin of Super Rabbit 325.00
7 . . . . . . 225.00
8 . . . . . . 225.00
9 . . . . . . 225.00
10 . . . . . . 225.00
11 HK,Hey Look 250.00
12 . . . . . . 250.00
13 . . . . . . 250.00
14 . . . . . . 250.00

ARMY AND NAVY COMICS

Street & Smith Publ., May, 1941

1 Hawaii is Calling You,Capt. Fury,Nick Carter 750.00
2 Private Rock V;Hitler 600.00
3 The Fighting Fourth 600.00
4 The Fighting Irish 600.00
5 I:Super Snipe 700.00

Becomes:

SUPERSNIPE COMICS

Oct., 1942

6 A "Comic" With A Sense of Humor 1,300.00
7 A:Wacky, Rex King 700.00
8 Axis Powers & Satan(c), Hitler(c) 1,000.00
9 Hitler Voodoo Doll (c) 1,100.00
10 Lighting (c) 700.00
11 A:Little Nemo 700.00
12 Football(c) 700.00
2-1 B:Huck Finn 1,000.00
2-2 Battles Shark 550.00
2-3 Battles Dinosaur 500.00
2-4 Baseball(c) 500.00
2-5 Battles Dinosaur 500.00
2-6 A:Pochontas 500.00
2-7 A:Wing Woo Woo 500.00
2-8 A:Huck Finn 500.00
2-9 Dotty Loves Trouble 500.00
2-10 Assists Farm Labor Shortage 500.00
2-11 Dotty & the Jelly Beans 500.00
2-12 Statue of Liberty 500.00
3-1 Ice Skating(c) 400.00
3-2 V:Pirates(c) 400.00
3-3 Baseball(c) 400.00
3-4 Jungle(c) 400.00
3-5 Learn Piglatin 400.00
3-6 Football Hero 400.00
3-7 Saves Girl From Grisley 400.00
3-8 Rides a Wild Horse 400.00
3-9 Powers Santa's Sleigh 400.00
3-10 Plays Basketball 400.00
3-11 Is A Baseball Pitcher 400.00
3-12 Flies with the Birds 400.00
4-1 Catches A Whale 300.00
4-2 Track & Field Athlete 300.00
4-3 Think Machine(c) 300.00
4-4 Alpine Skiier 300.00
4-5 Becomes a Boxer 300.00
4-6 Race Car Driver 300.00
4-7 Bomber(c) 300.00
4-8 Baseball Star 300.00

Su

Superworld Comics #3
© Hugo Gernsback

Suspense Comics #3
© Continental Magazines

Suspense Detective #5
© Fawcett Publications

4-9 Football Hero 300.00
4-10 Christmas(c) 300.00
4-11 Artic Adventure. 300.00
4-12 The Ghost Remover 300.00
5-1 Aug.–Sept., 1949 . . . . 300.00

SUPER SPY

Centaur Publications, Oct.–Nov., 1940

1 O:Sparkler 1,500.00
2 A:Night Hawk, Drew Ghost, Tim Blain, S.S. Swanson the Inner Circle, Duke Collins, Gentlemen of Misfortune 900.00

SUPER WESTERN COMICS

Youthful Magazines, Aug., 1950

1 BP,BP,(c),B;Buffalo Bill,Wyatt Earp,CalamityJane,SamSlade150.00
2 . . . . 100.00
3 . . . . 100.00
4 March, 1951 . . . . 100.00

SUPER WESTERN FUNNIES

See: SUPER FUNNIES

SUPERWORLD COMICS

Komos Publications (Hugo Gernsback), April, 1940

1 FP,FP(c),B:MilitaryPowers,BuzzAllen Smarty Artie, Alibi Alige . . 10,000.00
2 FP,FP(c),A:Mario 6,000.00
3 FP,FP(c),V:Vest Wearing Giant Grasshoppers 4,000.00

SURE-FIRE COMICS

See: LIGHTNING COMICS

SURPRISE ADVENTURES

See: TORMENTED

SUSPENSE

Marvel Atlas, Dec., 1949

1 BP,Ph(c),Sidney Greenstreet/ Peter Lorne (Maltese Falcon) 800.00
2 Ph(c),Dennis O'Keefe/Gale Storm (Abandoned) 400.00
3 B:Horror stories,The Black Pit 450.00
4 Thing In Black 325.00
5 BEv,GT,RH,BK,DBr, Hangman's House. 350.00
6 BEv,GT,PMo,RH,Madness of Scott Mannion 350.00
7 DBr,GT,DR,Murder. 325.00
8 GC,DRi,RH,Don't Open the Door. 325.00
9 GC,DRi,Back From The Dead . 325.00
10 JMn(c),WIP,RH,Trapped In Time. 325.00
11 MSy,The Suitcase 275.00
12 GT,Dark Road. 275.00
13 JMn(c),Strange Man, bondage cover. 275.00
14 RH,Death And Doctor Parker . 400.00
15 JMn(c),OW,The Machine 275.00
16 OW,Horror Backstage. 275.00
17 Night Of Terror 275.00
18 BK,The Cozy Coffin 300.00
19 BEv,RH 275.00
20 . . . . 275.00
21 BEv(c). 275.00
22 BEv(c),BK,OW 275.00
23 BEv 275.00
24 RH,GT. 300.00
25 I Died At Midnight 350.00
26 BEv(c). 225.00
27 DBr 250.00
28 BEv 250.00
29 JMn,BF,JRo,April, 1953 . . . . . 250.00

SUSPENSE COMICS

Et Es Go Mag. Inc. (Continental Magazines), Dec., 1945

1 LbC, Bondage(c),B:Grey Mask. 6,500.00
2 DRi,I:The Mask. 4,000.00
3 LbC,ASh(c),Bondage(c) . . . 20,000.00
4 LbC,LbC(c),Bondage(c) 3,000.00
5 LbC,LbC(c) 3,000.00
6 LbC,LbC(c),The End of the Road 3,000.00
7 LbC,LbC(c) 2,700.00
8 LbC,LbC(c) 6,500.00
9 LbC,LbC(c) 2,700.00
10 RP,LbC,LbC(c). 2,700.00
11 RP,LbC,EL,LbC(c),Satan(c) . 5,000.00
12 LbC,LbC(c),Dec., 1946 . . . . 2,500.00

SUSPENSE DETECTIVE

Fawcett Publications, June, 1952

1 GE,MBi,MBi(c),Death Poised to Strike 650.00
2 GE,MSy 400.00
3 A Furtive Footstep 350.00
4 MBi,MSy,Bondage(c),A Blood Chilling Scream 350.00
5 MSy,MSy(c),MBi,A Hair-Trigger from Death, March, 1953 . . . 350.00

SUZIE COMICS

See: TOP-NOTCH COMICS

SWAT MALONE

Swat Malone Enterpriess, 1955

1 . . . . 125.00

SWEENEY

Standard Comics, June, 1949

4 Buzz Sawyer's Pal 150.00
5 Sept., 1949 . . . . 125.00

SWEETHEART DIARY

Fawcett, Winter, 1949

1 . . . . 200.00
2 . . . . 125.00
3 WW 250.00
4 WW 250.00
5 thru 10 . . . . @150.00
11 thru 14 . . . . @100.00

SWEETHEART DIARY

Charlton Comics, Jan., 1953

32 . . . . 125.00
33 thru 40. . . . . @100.00
41 thru 65. . . . . @100.00

SWEET HEART

See: CAPTAIN MIDNIGHT

SWEETHEARTS

Charlton Comics, 1954

68 . . . . 200.00
69 . . . . 150.00

Sw

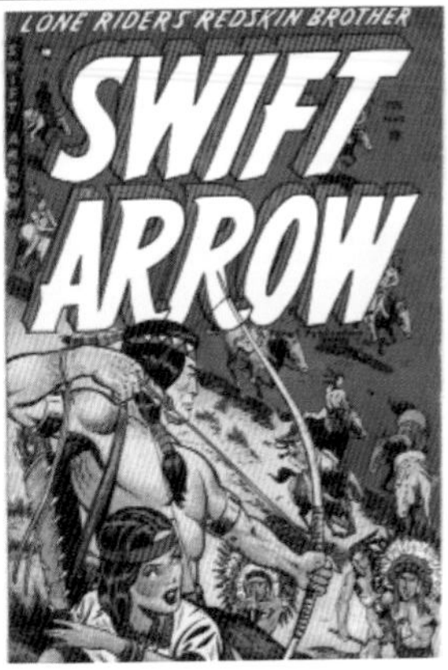

Swift Arrow #1
© Farrell Publications

Taffy #1
© Rural Home

Tales of Horror #12
© Tob Press

70 thru 80 . . . . @125.00
81 thru 99 . . . . @125.00
100 . . . . 110.00
101 thru 106 . . . . @110.00
107 BP 110.00
108 thru 110 . . . . @100.00
111 Ronald Reagan 150.00
112 thru 116 . . . . @100.00
117 GE 125.00
118 . . . . 100.00
119 Marilyn Monroe 600.00
120 A-Bomb 150.00
121 Liz Taylor 200.00
122 Marijuana 300.00

SWEETIE PIE

Farrell Publications/Pines, 1955

1 . . . . 150.00
2 . . . . 100.00
3 thru 10 . . . . @100.00
11 thru 15 . . . . @100.00

SWEET LOVE

Harvey Publications (Home Comics), Sept., 1949

1 Ph(c) 150.00
2 Ph(c) 125.00
3 BP 125.00
4 Ph(c) 100.00
5 BP,JKa,Ph(c) 100.00

Sw

SWEET SIXTEEN

Parents' Magazine Group, Aug.–Sept., 1946

1 Van Johnson story 250.00
2 Alan Ladd story 200.00
3 Rip Taylor 150.00
4 Elizabeth Taylor ph(c) 250.00
5 Gregory Peck story (c) 150.00
6 Dick Haymes(c) 150.00
7 Ronald Reagan(c) & story 300.00
8 Shirley Jones(c) 125.00
9 William Holden(c) 125.00
10 James Stewart(c) 150.00
11 . . . . 125.00
12 Bob Cummings(c) 125.00
13 Robert Mitchum(c) 150.00

SWIFT ARROW

Farrell Publications (Ajax), Feb.–March, 1954

1 Lone Rider's Redskin Brother 200.00
2 . . . . 125.00
3 . . . . 100.00
4 . . . . 100.00
5 Oct.–Nov., 1954 . . . . 100.00

(2nd Series) April, 1957

1 . . . . 100.00
2 B:Lone Rider 100.00
3 Sept., 1957 . . . . 100.00

TAFFY

Orbit Publications/Rural Home/ Taffy Publications, March–April, 1945

1 LbC(c),(fa),Bondage(c) 800.00
2 LbC(c),(fa) 350.00
3 (fa) 150.00
4 (fa) 150.00
5 LbC(c),A:Van Johnson 250.00
6 A:Perry Como 150.00
7 A:Dave Clark 150.00
8 A:Glen Ford 150.00
9 A:Lon McCallister 150.00
10 A:John Hodiak 150.00
11 A:Mickey Rooney 165.00
12 Feb., 1948 . . . . 150.00

TAILSPIN

Spotlight Publications, Nov., 1944

N# LbC(c),A:Firebird 350.00

TALE OF THE MARINES
See: DEVIL-DOG DUGAN

TALES FROM THE CRYPT
See: CRIME PATROL

TALES FROM THE GREAT BOOK

Famous Funnies, 1955

1 Samson 125.00
2 Joshua 100.00
3 Joash the Boy King 100.00
4 David 100.00

TALES OF HORROR

Toby Press/Minoan Publ. Corp, June, 1952–Oct., 1954

1 Demons of the Underworld . . . 500.00
2 What was the Thing in the Pool?,Torture 400.00
3 The Big Snake 300.00
4 The Curse of King Kala! 300.00
5 Hand of Fate 300.00
6 The Fiend of Flame 300.00
7 Beast From The Deep 300.00
8 The Snake that Held A City Captive 300.00
9 It Came From the Bottom of the World 350.00
10 The Serpent Strikes 300.00
11 Death Flower? 350.00
12 Guaranteed to Make Your Hair Stand on End,Torture . . . 350.00
13 Ghost with a Torch 350.00

TALES OF JACE PEARSON
See: JACE PEARSON

TALES OF JUSTICE
See: JUSTICE COMICS

TALES OF SUSPENSE

Marvel Atlas, 1959

1 AW,DH,JB,SD,JK 2,600.00
2 SD,JK,RH,Robot 900.00
3 SD,JK,JB(c),Flying Saucer . . . 900.00
4 AW,JK,BEv,SD 750.00
5 JK,SD,JF 600.00
6 SD,JK 600.00
7 SD,JK, ... 625.00
8 SD,BEv,JK,Lava Man 550.00
9 SD,JK,TF,Iron man type 600.00
10 SD,RH,JK 550.00
11 SD,JK 450.00
12 RC,SD,JK 450.00
13 SK,JK,Elektro 425.00
14 SD,JK,Colossus (1) 550.00
15 SD,JK 425.00
16 JK,Metallo (1) 550.00
17 JK 425 00
18 JK 425.00
19 JK 425.00
20 JK,Colossus (2) 450.00

TALES OF TERROR

Toby Press, 1952

1 Just A Bunch of Hokey Hogwash 300.00

All comics prices listed are for *Near Mint* condition.

Tales of the Mysterious Traveler #8
© Charlton Comics

Tales of the Unexpected #35
© DC Comics

Tales to Astonish #20
© Marvel Comics Group

TALES OF TERROR ANNUAL

E.C. Comics, 1951

N# AF 6,000.00
2 AF 3,000.00
3 . . . . 2,700.00

TALES OF THE MYSTERIOUS TRAVELER

Charlton Comics, 1956

1 DG 600.00
2 SD 500.00
3 SD,SD(c) 425.00
4 SD,SD(c) 500.00
5 SD,SD(c) 500.00
6 SD,SD(c) 500.00
7 thru 9 SD . . . . @450.00
10 SD,SD(c) 475.00
11 SD,SD(c) 475.00
12 . . . . 200.00
13 . . . . 225.00

TALES OF THE UNEXPECTED

DC Comics, 1956

1 The Out-Of-The-World Club . 1,700.00
2 . . . . 750.00
3 . . . . 500.00
4 Seven Steps to the Unknown . 500.00
5 . . . . 500.00
6 The Girl in the Bottle 400.00
7 NC(c),Pen That Never Lied . . . 400.00
8 . . . . 400.00
9 LSt(c),The Amazing Cube 400.00
10 MMe(c),The Strangest Show On Earth 400.00
11 LSt(c),Who Am I? 250.00
12 JK,Four Threads of Doom . . . 350.00
13 JK(c),Weapons of Destiny . . . 350.00
14 SMo(c),The Forbidden Game . 250.00
15 JK,MMe,Three Wishes to Doom 350.00
16 JK,The Magic Hammer 350.00
17 JK,Who Is Mr. Ashtar? 350.00
18 JK(c),MMe,A Man Without A World 350.00
19 NC,Man From Two Worlds . . . 325.00
20 NC(c),The Earth Gladiator . . . 325.00
21 JK,The Living Phantoms 325.00
22 JK(c),The Man From Robot Island 325.00
23 JK,The Invitation From Mars! . 325.00
24 LC,The Secret Of Planetoid Zero! 325.00
25 The Sorcerer's Asteroid! 225.00
26 MMe,The Frozem City 225.00
27 MMe,The Prison In Space . . . 225.00
28 The Melting Planet 225.00
29 The Phantom Raider 225.00
30 The Jinxed Planet 225.00
31 RH,Keep Off Our Planet 200.00
32 Great Space Cruise Mystery . . 200.00
33 The Man Of 1,000 Planets . . . 200.00
34 Ambush In Outer Space 200.00
35 MMe,I was a Space Refugee . 200.00
36 The Curse Of The Galactic Goodess 200.00
37 The Secret Prisoners Of Planet 13 . . . . 200.00
38 The Stunt Man Of Space 200.00
39 The Creatures From The Space Globe 200.00
40 B:Space Ranger,The Last Days Of Planet Mars! 1,600.00
41 SMo(c),The Destroyers From The Stars! 550.00
42 The Secret Of The Martian Helmet 550.00
43 The Riddle Of The Burning Treasures,I:Space Ranger . 1,200.00
44 DD&SMo(c),The Menace Of The Indian Aliens 375.00
45 DD&SMo(c),The Sheriff From Jupiter 375.00
46 DD&SMo(c),The Duplicate Doom! 375.00
47 DD(c),The Man Who Stole The Solar System 275.00
48 Bring 'Em Back Alive-From Space 275.00
49 RH,The Fantastic Lunar-Land 275.00
50 MA,King Barney The Ape 275.00
51 Planet Earth For Sale 275.00
52 Prisoner On Pluto 275.00
53 InterplanetaryTroubleShooter . 275.00
54 The Ugly Sleeper Of Klanth, Dinosaur 275.00
55 The Interplanetary Creature Trainer 275.00
56 B:Spaceman At Work,Invaders From Earth 275.00
57 The Jungle Beasts Of Jupiter . 275.00
58 The Boss Of The Saturnian Legion 275.00
59 The Man Who Won A World . . 275.00
60 School For Space Sleuths . . . 275.00
61 The Mystery Of The Mythical Monsters 225.00
62 The Menace Of The Red Snow Crystals 225.00
63 Death To Planet Earth 225.00
64 Boy Usurper Of Planet Zonn . 225.00
65 The Creature That Couldn't Exist 225.00
66 MMe,Trap Of The Space Convict 225.00
67 The Giant That Devoured A Village 225.00

TALES TO ASTONISH

Marvel Atlas, Jan., 1959

1 JDa,Ninth Wonder of the World 2,500.00
2 SD,Capture A Martian 1,000.00
3 SD,JK,The Giant From Outer Space 750.00
4 SD,JK,The Day The Martians Struck 750.00
5 SD,AW,The Things on Easter Island 800.00
6 SD,JK,Invasion of the Stone Men 600.00
7 SD,JK,The Thing on Bald Mountain 600.00
8 DAy,SD,JK,Mmmex, King of the Mummies 600.00
9 DAy,JK(c),SD,Droom, the Living Lizard 600.00
10 DAy,JK,SD,Titano 600.00
11 DAy,JK,SD,Monstrom, the Dweller in the Black Swamp 400.00
12 JK/DAy(c),SD,Gorgilla 400.00
13 JK,SD,Groot, the Monster From Planet X 400.00
14 JK,SD,Krang 400.00
15 JK/DAy,The Blip 550.00
16 DAy,JK,SD,Thorr 450.00
17 JK,SD,Vandoom 400.00
18 DAy,JK,SD,Gorgilla Strikes Again 400.00
19 DAy,JK,SD,Rommbu 400.00
20 JK,SD,X, The Thing That Lived 400.00
21 JK,SD,Trull the Inhuman 400.00
22 JK,SD,The Crawling Creature 300.00
23 JK,SD,Moomba is Here! 300.00
24 JK,SD,The Abominable Snowman 300.00
25 JK,SD,The Creature From Krogarr 300.00
26 JK,SD,Four-Armed Things . . . 300.00
27 StL(s),SD,JK,I:Ant-Man 7,000.00

Tally-Ho Comics #N
© Baily Publishing Co.

Target Vol. 2 #11
© Novelty Publications

Target Vol. 9 #1
© Novelty Publications

28 JK,SD,I Am the Gorilla Man . . 300.00
29 JK,SD,When the Space Beasts Attack. 300.00
30 JK,SD,Thing From the Hidden Swamp 300.00
31 JK,SD,The Mummy's Secret. . 300.00
32 JK,SD,Quicksand 300.00
33 JK,SD,Dead Storage. 300.00
34 JK,SD,Monster at Window . . . 300.00
35 StL(s),JK,SD, B:Ant-Man (2nd App.). 3,000.00
36 JK,SD,V:Comrade X 1,000.00
37 JK,SD,V:The Protector 700.00
38 JK,SD,Betrayed By the Ants. . 700.00
39 JK,DH,V:Scarlet Beetle. 700.00
40 JK,SD,DH,The Day Ant-Man Failed. 700.00

TALLY-HO COMICS

Baily Publishing Co., 1944

N# FF,A:Snowman 550.00

TASTEE-FREEZ COMICS

Harvey Comics, 1957

1 Little Dot. 60.00
2 Rags Rabbit. 30.00
3 Casper 40.00
4 Sad Sack 30.00
5 Mazie 30.00
6 Dick Tracy 50.00

TARGET COMICS

Funnnies Inc./Novelty Publ./ Premium Group/Curtis Circulation Co./Star Publications, Feb., 1940

1 BEv,JCo,CBu,JSm;B,O&I:Manowar, White Streak,Bull's-Eye;B:City Editor,High Grass Twins,T-Men, Rip Rory,Fantastic Feature Films, Calling 2-R 10,000.00
2 BEv,JSm,JCo,CBu,White Streak(c) 6,000.00
3 BEv,JSm,JCo,CBu 3,200.00
4 JSm,JCo 3,200.00
5 CBu,BW,O:White Streak . . . 9,000.00
6 CBu,BW,White Streak(c) . . . 3,500.00
7 CBu,BW,BW(c),V:Planetoid Stories,Space Hawk(c) . . . 10,000.00
8 CBu,BW,White Shark(c) 3,000.00
9 CBu,BW,White Shark(c) 3,000.00
10 CBu,BW,JK(c),The Target(c) 4,000.00
11 BW,The Target(c) 3,500.00
12 BW,same 3,200.00
2-1 BW,CBu 3,000.00
2-2 BW,BoW(c) 2,700.00
2-3 BW,BoW(c),The Target(c). . 2,500.00
2-4 BW,B:Cadet 2,500.00
2-5 BW,BoW(c),The Target(c). . 2,500.00
2-6 BW,The Target(c) 2,000.00
2-7 BW,The Cadet(c) 2,000.00
2-8 BW,same 2,000.00
2-9 BW,The Target(c) 2,000.00
2-10 BW,same 2,500.00
2-11 BW,The Cadet(c) 2,000.00
2-12 BW,same 2,000.00
3-1 BW,same 2,000.00
3-2 BW 2,000.00
3-3 BW,The Target(c) 2,000.00
3-4 BW,The Cadet(c) 2,000.00
3-5 BW 2,000.00
3-6 BW,War Bonds(c). 2,500.00
3-7 BW 2,000.00
3-8 BW,War Bonds(c). 2,500.00
3-9 BW 2,000.00
3-10 BW 2,000.00
3-11 . . . . 500.00
3-12 . . . . 500.00
4-1 JJo(c) 275.00
4-2 ERy(c) 275.00
4-3 AVi 275.00
4-4 . . . . 275.00
4-5 APl(c),Statue of Liberty(c) . . . 275.00
4-6 BW. 275.00
4-7 AVi 275.00
4-8,Christmas(c) 275.00
4-9 . . . . 275.00
4-10 . . . . 275.00
4-11 . . . . 275.00
4-12 . . . . 275.00
5-1 . . . . 250.00
5-2 The Target 125.00
5-3 Savings Checkers(c) 125.00
5-4 War Bonds Ph(c). 125.00
5-5 thru 5-12 . . . . @125.00
6-1 The Target(c) 125.00
6-2 . . . . 125.00
6-3 Red Cross(c) 125.00
6-4 . . . . 125.00
6-5 Savings Bonds(c) 150.00
6-6 The Target(c) 250.00
6-7 The Cadet(c) 250.00
6-8 AFa 250.00
6-9 The Target(c) 250.00
6-10 . . . . 250.00
6-11 . . . . 250.00
6-12 . . . . 250.00
7-1 . . . . 250.00
7-2 Bondage(c) 250.00
7-3 The Target(c) 250.00
7-4 DRi,The Cadet(c). 250.00
7-5 . . . . 250.00
7-6 DRi(c). 250.00
7-7 The Cadet(c) 250.00
7-8 DRi(c). 250.00
7-9 The Cadet(c) 250.00
7-10 DRi,DRi(c) 250.00
7-11 . . . . 250.00
7-12 JH(c) 250.00
8-1 . . . . 200.00
8-2 DRi,DRi(c),BK 200.00
8-3 DRi,The Cadet(c). 200.00
8-4 DRi,DRi(c) 200.00
8-5 DRi,The Cadet(c). 200.00
8-6 DRi,DRi(c) 200.00
8-7 BK,DRi,DRi(c) 200.00
8-8 DRi,The Cadet(c). 200.00
8-9 DRi,The Cadet(c). 200.00
8-10 DRi,KBa,LbC(c). 750.00
8-11 DRi,The Cadet. 200.00
8-12 DRi,The Cadet. 200.00
9-1 DRi,LbC(c). 750.00
9-2 DRi. 200.00
9-3 DRi,Bondage(c),The Cadet(c) 275.00
9-4 DRi,LbC(c). 750.00
9-5 DRi,Baseball(c) 250.00
9-6 DRi,LbC(c). 750.00
9-7 DRi. 250.00
9-8 DRi,LbC(c). 750.00
9-9 DRi,Football(c). 250.00
9-10 DRi,LbC(c). 750.00
9-11,The Cadet 250.00
9-12 LbC(c),Gems(c). 750.00
10-1,The Cadet 250.00
10-2 LbC(c) 750.00
10-3 LbC(c) 750.00
Becomes:

TARGET WESTERN ROMANCES

Star Publications, Oct.–Nov., 1949

106 LbC(c),The Beauty Scar. . . . 500.00
107 LbC(c),The Brand Upon His Heart 450.00

TARZAN

Dell Publishing Co., Jan.–Feb., 1948

1 V:White Savages of Vari. . . . 2,500.00
2 Captives of Thunder Valley. . 1,000.00
3 Dwarfs of Didona. 700.00
4 The Lone Hunter 700.00

Tarzan #14
© Edgar Rice Burroughs, Inc.

Teen-Age Romances #7
© St. John Publishing Co.

Teen-Age Temptations #9
© St. John Publishing Co.

5 The Men of Greed	700.00
6 Outlaws of Pal-ul-Don	600.00
7 Valley of the Monsters	600.00
8 The White Pygmies	600.00
9 The Men of A-Lur	600.00
10 Treasure of the Bolgani	600.00
11 The Sable Lion	500.00
12 The Price of Peace	500.00
13 B:Lex Barker photo(c)	450.00
14 Lex Barker ph(c)	450.00
15 Lex Barker ph(c)	450.00
16 Lex Barker ph(c)	400.00
17 Lex Barker ph(c)	400.00
18 Lex Barker ph(c)	400.00
19 Lex Barker ph(c)	400.00
20 Lex Barker ph(c)	400.00
21 thru 24 Lex Barker ph(c)	@350.00
25 Brothers of the Spear	375.00
26 thru 54 E:L.Barker ph(c)	@300.00
55 thru 70	@250.00
71 thru 79	@200.00
80 thru 90 B:ScottGordonPh(c)	@150.00
91 thru 99	@125.00
100	150.00
101 thru 110 E:S.GordonPh(c)	@150.00
111 thru 120	@125.00
121 thru 131	@100.00

TEENA

Standard Comics, 1949

20	100.00
21	100.00
22	100.00

TEEN-AGE BRIDES

Home Comics/ Harvey Publications, 1953

1 BP	150.00
2 BP	125.00
3 BP	125.00
4	100.00
5	100.00
6 BP	150.00
7	100.00

Becomes:

TRUE BRIDES' EXPERIENCES

Harvey Publications, 1954–56

8	125.00
9	100.00
10	100.00
11 thru 16	@ 100.00

Becomes:

TRUE BRIDE-TO-BE ROMANCES

Harvey Publications, 1956–58

17 S&K(c)	150.00
18 thru 30	100.00

TEEN-AGE DIARY SECRETS

St. John Publishing Co., Oct., 1949

6 MB,PH(c)	350.00
7 MB,PH(c)	300.00
8 MB,PH(c)	250.00
9 MB,PH(c)	300.00

Becomes:

DIARY SECRETS

Feb., 1952

10 MB	250.00
11 MB	200.00
12 thru 19 MB	@150.00
20 MB,JKu	200.00
21 thru 28 MB	@100.00
29 MB,Comics Code	100.00
30 MB	100.00

TEEN-AGE LOVE
See: INTIMATE

TEENAGE ROMANCE
See: MY ROMANCE

TEEN-AGE ROMANCES

St. John Publishing Co., Jan., 1949

1 MB(c),MB	500.00
2 MB(c),MB	300.00
3 MB(c),MB	350.00
4 Ph(c)	300.00
5 MB,Ph(c)	300.00
6 MB,Ph(c)	300.00
7 MB,Ph(c)	300.00
8 MB,Ph(c)	300.00
9 MB,MB(c),JKu	325.00
10 thru 27 MB,MB(c),JKu	@250.00
28 thru 30	@100.00
31 thru 34 MB(c)	@125.00
35 thru 42 MB(c),MB	@125.00
43 MB(c),MB,Comics Code	150.00
44 MB(c),MB	150.00
45 MB(c),MB	150.00

TEEN-AGE TEMPTATIONS

St. John Publishing Co., Oct., 1952

1 MB(c),MB	600.00
2 MB(c),MB	200.00
3 MB(c),MB	275.00
4 MB(c),MB	275.00
5 MB(c),MB	275.00
6 MB(c),MB	275.00
7 MB(c),MB	275.00
8 MB(c),MB,Drug	300.00
9 MB(c),MB	275.00

Becomes:

GOING STEADY

Dec., 1954

10 MB(c),MB	225.00
11 MB(c),MB	125.00
12 MB(c),MB	125.00
13 MB(c),MB	175.00
14 MB(c),MB	200.00

TEEN COMICS
See: ALL WINNERS COMICS

TEEN CONFESSIONS

Charlton Comics, 1959

1	150.00
2	125.00
3 thru 10	@100.00
11 thru 30	@100.00

TEENIE WEENIES, THE

Ziff-Davis Publishing Co., 1951

10	250.00
11	250.00

TEEN LIFE
See: YOUNG LIFE

TEEN SECRET DIARY

Charlton Comics, 1959–61

1	125.00
2	100.00
3	100.00
4	100.00
5	100.00
6 thru 11	@100.00

Television Comics #5
© Standard Comics

Tense Suspense #2
© Fago Publications

Terrors of the Jungle #21
© Star Publications

TEGRA, JUNGLE EMPRESS
See: ZEGRA, JUNGLE EMPRESS

TELEVISION COMICS
Animated Cartoons (Standard Comics), Feb., 1950

5 Humorous Format,I:Willie Nilly 300.00
6 . . . . 150.00
7 . . . . 150.00
8 May, 1950 . . . . 150.00

TELEVISION PUPPET SHOW
Avon Periodicals, 1950

1 F:Sparky Smith,Spotty, Cheeta, Speedy 250.00
2 Nov., 1950 . . . . 150.00

TELL IT TO THE MARINES
Toby Press, March, 1952

1 I:Spike & Pat 250.00
2 A:Madame Cobra 150.00
3 Spike & Bat on a Commando Raid! 125.00
4 Veil Dancing(c) 125.00
5 . . . . 125.00
6 To Paris 100.00
7 Ph(c),The Chinese Bugle 100.00
8 Ph(c),V:Communists in South Korea 100.00
9 Ph(c) 100.00
10 . . . . 100.00
11 . . . . 100.00
12 . . . . 100.00
13 John Wayne Ph(c) 150.00
14 Ph(c) 100.00
15 Ph(c),July, 1955 . . . . 100.00

TENDER ROMANCE
Key Publications, Dec., 1953

1 . . . . 200.00
2 . . . . 125.00
Becomes:

IDEAL ROMANCE
April, 1954

3 . . . . 125.00
4 thru 8 . . . . @100.00
Becomes:

DIARY CONFESSIONS
May, 1955

9 . . . . 125.00
10 . . . . 100.00

TENSE SUSPENSE
Fago Publications, 1958–59

1 . . . . 125.00
2 . . . . 100.00

TERRIFIC COMICS
See: HORRIFIC

TERRIFIC COMICS
Et Es Go Mag. Inc./ Continental Magazines, Jan., 1944

1 LbC,DRi(c),F:Kid Terrific Drug 5,000.00
2 LcC,ASh(c),B:Boomerang, 'Comics' McCormic 3,500.00
3 LbC,LbC(c) 3,500.00
4 LbC,RP(c) 6,000.00
5 LbC,BF,ASh(c),Bondage(c) . 8,000.00
6 LbC,LbC(c),BF,Nov.,1944 . . 3,200.00

TERRIFYING TALES
Star Publications, Jan., 1953

11 LbC,LbC(c),'TyrantsofTerror' . . 700.00
12 LbC,LbC(c),'Bondage(c), 'Jungle Mystery' 600.00
13 LbC(c),Bondage(c),'The Death-Fire,Devil Head(c). . . . 750.00
14 LbC(c),Bondage(c),'The Weird Idol' 550.00
15 LbC(c),'The Grim Secret', April, 1954 . . . . 550.00
Becomes:

JUNGLE THRILLS
Star Publications, Feb., 1952

16 LbC(c),'Kingdom of Unseen Terror' 700.00
Becomes:

TERRORS OF THE JUNGLE
Star Publications, May, 1952

17 LbC(c),Bondage(c) 700.00
18 LbC(c),Strange Monsters 450.00
19 JyD,LbC(c),Bondage(c),The Golden Ghost Gorilla. 400.00
20 JyD,LbC(c),The Creeping Scourge 400.00
21 LbC(c),Evil Eyes of Death! . . . 450.00
4 JyD,LbC(c),Morass of Death . 400.00
5 JyD,LbC(c),Bondage(c), Savage Train 425.00
6 JyD,LbC(c),Revolt of the Jungle Monsters 425.00
7 JyD,LbC(c) 450.00
8 JyD,LbC(c),Death's Grim Reflection 450.00
9 JyD,LbC(c),Doom to Evil-Doers 450.00
10 JyD,LbC(c),Black Magic, Sept., 1954 . . . . 450.00

TERROR ILLUSTRATED
E.C. Comics, Nov.–Dec., 1955

1 JCr,GE,GrI,JO,RC(c) 250.00
2 Spring, 1956 . . . . 150.00

BOY EXPLORERS
Harvey Comics, 1946

1 S&K(c),S&K,The Cadet 1,500.00
2 S&K(c),S&K 2,000.00
Becomes:

TERRY AND THE PIRATES
Harvey Comics, April, 1947

3 S&K,MC(c),MC,Terry and Dragon Lady 500.00
4 S&K,MC(c),MC 300.00
5 S&K,MC(c),MC,BP, Chop-Chop(c) 175.00
6 S&K,.MC(c),MC 175.00
7 S&K,MC(c),MC,BP 175.00
8 S&K,MC(c),MC,BP 175.00
9 S&K,MC(c),MC,BP 175.00
10 S&K,MC(c),MC,BP 175.00
11 S&K,MC(c),MC,BP, A:Man in Black 150.00
12 S&K,MC(c),MC,BP 150.00
13 S&K,MC(c),MC,Belly Dancers 150.00
14 thru 20 S&K,MC(c),MC . . . . @125.00
21 thru 26 S&K,MC(c),MC . . . . @110.00

Te

Terry and the Pirates #9
© Harvey Publications

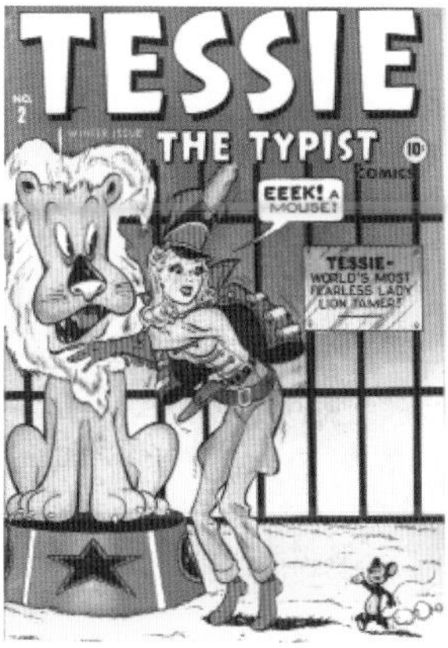

Tessie the Typist #2
© Marvel Comics Group

Tex Farrell #1
© D.S. Publishing Co.

27 Charlton Comics . . . 100.00
28 . . . 100.00
Becomes:

LONG JOHN SILVER AND THE PIRATES

Charlton Comics, 1956–57

30 . . . 125.00
31 . . . 125.00
32 . . . 125.00

TERRY-BEARS COMICS

St. John Publishing Co., June, 1952

1 . . . 125.00
2 & 3 . . . @100.00

TERRY-TOONS COMICS

Select, Timely, Marvel, St. Johns, 1942

1 Paul Terry (fa) . . . 2,500.00
2 . . . 800.00
3 thru 6 . . . @500.00
7 Hitler,Hirohito,Mussolini(c) . . . 700.00
8 thru 20 . . . @400.00
21 thru 37 . . . @300.00
38 I&(c):Mighty Mouse . . . 1,600.00
39 Mighty Mouse . . . 500.00
40 thru 49 All Mighty Mouse . . @250.00
50 I:Heckle & Jeckle . . . 600.00
51 thru 60 . . . @150.00
61 thru 70 . . . @125.00
71 thru 86 . . . @125.00
Becomes:

PAUL TERRY'S COMICS

St. John Publishing Co.

85a Mighty Mouse, etc. . . . 150.00
86a . . . 100.00
87 thru 100 . . . @100.00
101 thru 125 . . . @100.00
Becomes:

ADVENTURES OF MIGHTY MOUSE

St. John Publ. Co., 1955

126 thru 128 . . . @150.00

Pines, 1956

129 thru 143 . . . @150.00

Dell Publ. Co., 1959

144 thru 155 . . . @125.00

TESSIE THE TYPIST

Marvel Timely, Summer, 1944

1 BW,Doc Rockblock . . . 750.00
2 BW,Powerhouse Pepper . . . 400.00
3 Football cover . . . 150.00
4 BW . . . 300.00
5 BW . . . 300.00
6 BW,HK,Hey Look . . . 300.00
7 BW . . . 300.00
8 BW . . . 300.00
9 BW,HK,Powerhouse Pepper . . 325.00
10 BW,A:Rusty . . . 325.00
11 BW,A:Rusty . . . 325.00
12 BW,HK . . . 325.00
13 BW,A:Millie The Model,Rusty . 275.00
14 BW . . . 275.00
15 HK,A:Millie,Rusty . . . 275.00
16 HK . . . 150.00
17 HK,A:Millie, Rusty . . . 150.00
18 HK . . . 150.00
19 Annie Oakley story . . . 100.00
20 . . . 100.00
21 A:Lana, Millie . . . 100.00
22 . . . 100.00
23 . . . 100.00
Becomes:

TINY TESSIE

24 . . . 100.00
Becomes:

REAL EXPERIENCES

25 Ph(c),Jan., 1950 . . . 100.00

TEXAN, THE

St. John Publishing Co., Aug., 1948

1 GT,F:Buckskin Belle,The Gay Buckaroo,Mustang Jack . . . 200.00
2 GT . . . 125.00
3 BLb(c) . . . 100.00
4 MB,MB(c) . . . 200.00
5 MB,MB(c),Mystery Rustlers of the Rio Grande . . . 200.00
6 MB(c),Death Valley Double-Cross . . . 125.00
7 MB,MB(c),Comanche Justice Strikes at Midnight . . . 200.00
8 MB,MB(c),Scalp Hunters Hide their Tracks . . . 200.00
9 MB(c),Ghost Terror of the Blackfeet . . . 200.00
10 MB,MB(c),Treason Rides the Warpath . . . 125.00
11 MB,MB(c),Hawk Knife . . . 200.00
12 MB . . . 250.00
13 MB,Doublecross at Devil'sDen 200.00
14 MB,Ambush at Buffalo Trail . . 200.00
15 MB,Twirling Blades Tame Treachery . . . 200.00
Becomes:

FIGHTIN' TEXAN

Sept., 1952

16 GT,Wanted Dead or Alive . . . 125.00
17 LC,LC(c);Killers Trail, Dec., 1952 . . . 100.00

TEXAS KID

Marvel Atlas, Jan., 1951

1 GT,JMn,O:Texas Kid . . . 300.00
2 JMn . . . 200.00
3 JMn,Man Who Didn't Exist . . . 150.00
4 thru 9 JMn . . . @150.00
10 JMn,July, 1952 . . . 150.00

TEXAS RANGERS IN ACTION

Charlton Comics, 1956

5 . . . 150.00
6 and 7 . . . @100.00
8 SD . . . 100.00
9 and 10 . . . @100.00
11 AW . . . 100.00
12 . . . 100.00
13 AW . . . 150.00
14 thru 20 . . . @100.00

TEX FARRELL

D.S. Publishing Co., March–April, 1948

1 Pride of the Wild West . . . 175.00

TEX GRANGER

See: CALLING ALL BOYS

TEX MORGAN

Marvel, Aug., 1948

1 Tex Morgan & Lobo . . . 350.00
2 Boot Hill Welcome For A Bad Man . . . 225.00
3 A:Arizona Annie . . . 150.00
4 SSh,Trapped in the Outlaw's Den, A:Arizona Annie . . . 125.00
5 Valley of Missing Cowboys . . . 125.00
6 Never Say Murder, A:Tex Taylor . . . 150.00

Tex Ritter Western #13
© Fawcett Publications

The Thing #10
© Charlton Comics

This Magazine Is Haunted #8
© Fawcett Publications

7 CCB,Ph(c),Captain Tootsie, A:Tex Taylor . . . 200.00
8 Ph(c),Terror Of Rimrock Valley, A:Diablo . . . 200.00
9 Ph(c),Death to Tex Taylor, Feb., 1950 . . . 200.00

TEX RITTER WESTERN

Fawcett Publications/ Charlton Comics, Oct., 1950–May, 1959

1 Ph(c),B:Tex Ritter, his Horse White Flash, his dog Fury, and his mom Nancy . . . 900.00
2 Ph(c),Vanishing Varmints . . . 400.00
3 Ph(c),Blazing Six-Guns . . . 325.00
4 Ph(c),The Jaws of Terror . . . 275.00
5 Ph(c),Bullet Trail . . . 275.00
6 Ph(c),Killer Bait . . . 250.00
7 Ph(c),Gunsmoke Revenge . . . 225.00
8 Ph(c),Lawless Furnace Valley 225.00
9 Ph(c),The Spider's Web . . . 225.00
10 Ph(c),The Ghost Town . . . 225.00
11 Ph(c),Saddle Conquest . . . 225.00
12 Ph(c),Prairie Inferno . . . 175.00
13 Ph(c) . . . 175.00
14 Ph(c) . . . 175.00
15 Ph(c) . . . 175.00
16 thru 19 Ph(c) . . . @175.00
20 Ph(c),Stagecoach To Danger . 175.00
21 Ph(c), . . . 200.00
22 Panic at Diamond B . . . 150.00
23 A:Young Falcon . . . 125.00
24 A:Young Falcon . . . 125.00
25 A:Young Falcon . . . 125.00
26 thru 38 . . . @100.00
39 AW,AW(c) . . . 100.00
40 thru 46 . . . @100.00

TEX TAYLOR

Marvel, Sept., 1948

1 SSh,Boot Hill Showdown . . . 325.00
2 When Two-Gun Terror Rides the Range . . . 175.00
3 SSh,Thundering Hooves and Blazing Guns . . . 150.00
4 Ph(c),Draw or Die Cowpoke . . 200.00
5 Ph(c),The Juggler of Yellow Valley,A:Blaze Carson . . . 200.00
6 Ph(c),Mystery of Howling Gap. 200.00
7 Ph(c),Trapped in Time's Lost Land,A:Diablo . . . 225.00
8 Ph(c),The Mystery of Devil-Tree Plateau,A:Diablo . . . 225.00

9 Ph(c),Guns Along the Border, A:Nimo,March, 1950 . . . 225.00

THING!, THE

Song Hits/Capitol Stories/ Charlton Comics, Feb., 1952

1 Horror . . . 2,500.00
2 Crazy King(c) . . . 2,000.00
3 Green skinned creature . . . 2,000.00
4 AFa(c),I Was A Zombie . . . 1,500.00
5 LM(c),Severed Head(c) . . . 1,500.00
6 . . . 1,500.00
7 Fingernail to Eye(c) . . . 1,600.00
8 . . . 1,500.00
9 Severe cruelty . . . 2,000.00
10 Devil(c) . . . 1,250.00
11 SC,Cleaver, eye injury . . . 1,500.00
12 SD,SD(c),Neck Blood Sucking . . . 1,500.00
13 SD,SD(c) . . . 1,500.00
14 SD,SD(c) torture . . . 1,500.00
15 SD,SD(c) . . . 1,500.00
16 Eye Torture . . . 750.00
17 BP,SD(c) . . . 1,500.00

Becomes:

BLUE BEETLE

Feb., 1955

18 America's Fastest Moving Crusader Against Crime . . . 250.00
19 JKa,Lightning Fast . . . 275.00
20 JKa . . . 275.00
21 The Invincible . . . 200.00

Becomes:

MR. MUSCLES

March, 1956

22 World's Most Perfect Man. . . . 150.00
23 Aug., 1956. . . . 100.00

THIS IS SUSPENSE See: LAWBREAKERS

THIS IS SUSPENSE! See: STRANGE SUSPENSE STORIES

THIS IS WAR

Standard Comics, July, 1952

5 ATh,Show Them How To Die . 150.00
6 ATh,Make Him A Soldier . . . 125.00

7 One Man For Himself . . . 100.00
8 Miracle on Massacre Hill . . . 100.00
9 ATh,May, 1953 . . . 125.00

THIS MAGAZINE IS HAUNTED

Fawcett Publications Oct., 1951

1 MBi,F:Doctor Death . . . 850.00
2 GE . . . 650.00
3 MBi,Quest of the Vampire . . . 400.00
4 BP,The Blind, The Doomed and the Dead . . . 400.00
5 BP,GE,The Slithering Horror of Skontong Swamp! . . . 650.00
6 Secret of the Walking Dead. . . 300.00
7 The Man Who Saw Too Much . 300.00
8 The House in the Web. . . . 300.00
9 The Witch of Tarlo . . . 300.00
10 I Am Dr Death, Severed Head(c) . . . 500.00
11 BP,Touch of Death . . . 300.00
12 BP . . . 300.00
13 BP,Severed Head(c) . . . 500.00
14 BP,Horrors of the Damned . . . 300.00

Charlton Comics, 1954

15 DG(c) . . . 250.00
16 SD(c) . . . 500.00
17 SD,SD(c) . . . 600.00
18 SD,SD(c) . . . 500.00
19 SD(c) . . . 450.00
20 SMz(c) . . . 265.00
21 SD(c) . . . 400.00

Becomes:

DANGER AND ADVENTURE

Feb., 1955

22 The Viking King,F:Ibis the Invincible . . . 150.00
23 F:Nyoka the Jungle Girl Comics Code . . . 125.00
24 DG&AA(c) . . . 100.00
25 thru 27 . . . @100.00

Becomes:

ROBIN HOOD AND HIS MERRY MEN

April, 1956

28 . . . 150.00
29 thru 37 . . . @100.00
38 SD,Aug., 1958 . . . 150.00

Te

3-D Adventures of Superman
© DC Comics

3-D EC Classics #2
© E.C. Comics

3-D Sheena Jungle Queen #1
© Fiction House

THIS MAGAZINE IS HAUNTED
See: CHARLIE CHAN

3-D ACTION
Marvel Atlas 1954

1 Battle Brady. 450.00

3-D ADVENTURES OF SUPERMAN
DC Comics, 1953

N# O:Superman 1,500.00

3-D ANIMAL FUN
Premier Magazines, 1953

1 Ziggy Pig, Silly Seal,etc. 400.00

3-D BATMAN ADVENTURES
DC Comics 1953

1 with Bat-glasses 1,500.00

CAPTAIN 3-D
Harvey Publ, 1953

1 . . . . 125.00

CHERRIOS 3D CLASSICS
Walt Disney Productions, 1954

1 . . . . 150.00

3-D CIRCUS
Fiction House, 1953

1 . . . . 500.00

3-D DARING ADVENTURES
St. John Publ, 1953

1 . . . . 400.00

3-D-ELL
Dell Publishing Co., 1953

1 Rootie Kazootie 500.00
3 Flunkey Louise. 450.00

3-D DOLLY
Harvey Publ, 1953

1 Richie Rich. 850.00

3-D EC CLASSICS
E.C. Comics 1954

1 . . . . 1,200.00
2 Tales from the Crypt of Terror 1,200.00

3-D FELIX THE CAT
Toby Press, 1953

N# 350.00

3-D FIRST CHRISTMAS
Fiction House, 1953

1 . . . . 250.00

3-D FUNNY MOVIES
Comic Media, 1953

1 Bugsey Bear 425.00

FUNNY 3-D
Harvey Publ., 1953

1 . . . . 350.00

3-D HAWK, THE
St. John Publ, 1953

1 Western 350.00

3-D HOUSE OF TERROR
St. John Publ., 1953

1 . . . . 500.00

3-D I LOVE LUCY
1 Lucy, Desi, Ricky Jr. Ph(c). . . . 500.00

3-D INDIAN WARRIORS
Star Publications, 1953

1 . . . . 250.00

(3-D Features Presents) JET PUP
Dimensions Publ., 1953

1 . . . . 500.00

3-D JUNGLE THRILLS
Star Publications, 1953

1 . . . . 350.00

3-D KATY KEENE
Archie Publications, 1953

1 . . . . 500.00

3-D LITTLE EVA
St. John Publ, 1953

1 . . . . 350.00
2 . . . . 350.00

3-D LOVE
Steriographic Publ., 1953

1 . . . . 425.00

(Three Dimension Comics) MIGHTY MOUSE
St. John Publ, 1953

1 . . . . 350.00
2 . . . . 350.00
3 . . . . 350.00

3-D NOODNICK
Comic Media, 1953

1 . . . . 350.00

3-D ROMANCE
Steriographic Publ., 1954

1 . . . . 425.00

(Harvey 3-D Hits) SAD SACK
Harvey Publications, 1954

1 . . . . 350.00

3-D SHEENA, JUNGLE QUEEN
Fiction House, 1953

1 . . . . 1,000.00

3-D SPACE KAT-ETS
Power Publishing, 1953

1 . . . . 350.00

True 3-D #1
© Harvey Publications

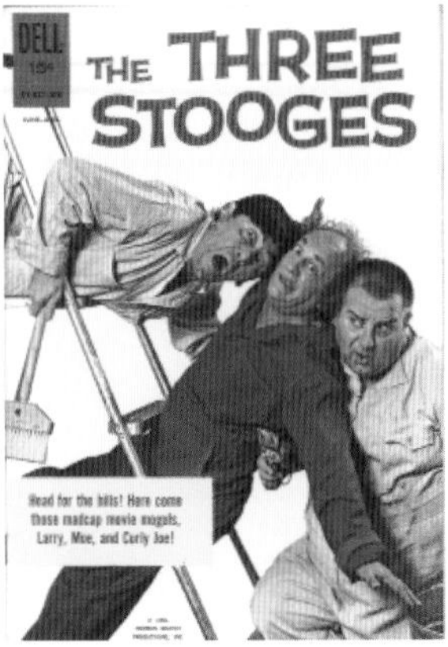

Three Stooges #9
© Dell Publishing Co.

Thrilling Comics #59
© Standard Comics

3-D SUPER ANIMALS
Star Publications, 1953

1 Pidgy and the Magic Glasses . 350.00

3-D SUPER FUNNIES
Superior Comics Publ., 1953

1 Dopey Duck 350.00

3-D TALES OF THE WEST
Marvel Atlas, 1954

1 . . . . 500.00

3-D THREE STOOGES
St. John Publ., 1953

1 . . . . 600.00
2 . . . . 600.00

3-D TRUE 3D
Harvey Publ., 1953

1 . . . . 400.00
2 . . . . 350.00

3-D WESTERN FIGHTERS
Star Publications, 1953

1 . . . . 350.00

THE THREE MOUSEKETEERS
DC Comics, 1956–60

1 . . . . 275.00
2 . . . . 150.00
3 . . . . 125.00
4 . . . . 125.00
5 . . . . 125.00
6 thru 10 . . . . @125.00
11 thru 20 . . . . @100.00
21 thru 26 . . . . @100.00

THREE RING COMICS
Spotlight Publishers, March, 1945

1 Funny Animal 200.00

THREE STOOGES
Jubilee Publ., Feb., 1949

1 JKu,Infinity(c) 1,500.00
2 JKu,On the Set of the 'The Gorilla Girl' 1,200.00

St. John Publishing Co.

1:JKu,'Hell Bent for Treasure,' Sept., 1953 . . . . 1,200.00
2 JKu. 900.00
3 JKu,3D. 900.00
4 JKu,Medical Mayhem 800.00
5 JKu,Shempador-Matador Supreme 800.00
6 JKu, ... 800.00
7 JKu,Ocotber, 1954. . . . . 800.00

THREE STOOGES
Dell Publishing Co., 1959

6 Ph(c),B:Prof. Putter 300.00
7 Ph(c) 300.00
8 Ph(c) 300.00
9 Ph(c) 300.00

THRILLING ADVENTURES IN STAMPS
See: STAMPS COMICS

THRILLING COMICS
Better Publ./Nedor/ Standard Comics, Feb., 1940

1 B&O:Doc Strange,B:Nickie Norton 5,000.00
2 B:Rio Kid,Woman in Red Pinocchio 2,500.00
3 B:Lone Eagle,The Ghost . . . 2,000.00
4 Dr Strange(c) 1,400.00
5 Bondage(c) 1,600.00
6 Dr Strange(c) 1,400.00
7 Dr Strange(c) 1,500.00
8 V:Pirates 1,500.00
9 ASh,Bondage(c) 1,500.00
10 V:Nazis. 1,700.00
11 ASh(c),V:Nazis 1,400.00
12 ASh(c) 1,400.00
13 ASh(c),Bondage(c). 1,600.00
14 ASh(c) 1,200.00
15 ASh(c),V:Nazis. 1,200.00
16 Bondage(c) 1,600.00
17 Dr Strange(c) 1,200.00
18 Dr Strange(c) 1,600.00
19 I&O:American Crusader. . . . 1,500.00
20 Bondage(c) 1,600.00
21 American Crusader(c) 1,200.00
22 Bondage(c) 1,400.00
23 American Crusader 1,200.00
24 I:Mike in Doc Strange 1,200.00
25 DR Strange(c) 1,200.00
26 Dr Strange(c) 1,200.00
27 Bondage(c) 1,400.00
28 Bondage(c) 1,400.00
29 E:Rio Kid;Bondage(c) 1,400.00
30 Bondage(c) 1,400.00
31 Dr Strange(c) 1,100.00
32 Dr Strange(c) 1,100.00
33 Dr Strange(c) 1,100.00
34 Dr Strange(c) 1,100.00
35 Dr Strange 1,100.00
36 ASh(c),B:Commando 1,200.00
37 BO,ASh(c) 1,100.00
38 ASh(c) 1,100.00
39 ASh(c),E:American Crusader1,100.00
40 ASh(c) 1,100.00
41 ASh(c),F:American Crusader, Hitler 2,000.00
42 ASh(c). 900.00
43 ASh(c). 900.00
44 ASh(c),Hitler(c). 1,400.00
45 EK,ASh(c). 800.00
46 ASh(c). 800.00
47 ASh(c). 800.00
48 EK,ASh(c). 800.00
49 ASh(c). 800.00
50 ASh(c). 800.00
51 ASh(c). 800.00
52 ASh(c),E:Th Ghost; Peto-Bondage(c) 900.00
53 ASh(c),B:Phantom Detective . 700.00
54 ASh(c),Bondage(c) 900.00
55 ASh(c),E:Lone Eagle 700.00
56 ASh(c),B:Princess Pantha . . . 900.00
57 ASh(c). 800.00
58 ASh(c). 800.00
59 ASh(c). 800.00
60 ASh(c). 800.00
61 ASh(c),Grl,A:Lone Eagle 800.00
62 ASh(c). 800.00
63 ASh(c),GT 800.00
64 ASh(c). 800.00
65 ASh(c),E:Commando Cubs, Phantom Detective 800.00
66 ASh(c). 800.00
67 FF,ASh(c) 900.00
68 FF,ASh(c) 900.00
69 FF,ASh(c) 900.00
70 FF,ASh(c) 900.00
71 FF,ASh(c) 900.00
72 FF,ASh(c),Sea Eagle 900.00
73 FF,ASh(c) 900.00
74 ASh(c),E:Princess Pantha; B:Buck Ranger 500.00
75 B:Western Front 350.00
76 Western. 350.00
77 ASh(c). 350.00

 All comics prices listed are for *Near Mint* condition.

Shocking Mystery Cases #54
© Star Publications

Thrilling True Story of the Baseball Giants N# © Fawcett Publications

Tim Holt #38
© Magazine Enterprises

78 Bondage(c) 400.00
79 BK 350.00
80 JSe,BE,April, 1951 . . . . 350.00

THRILLING CRIME CASES

Star Publications, June–July, 1950

41 LbC(c),The Unknowns 350.00
42 LbC(c),The Gunmaster. 325.00
43 LbC,LbC(c),The Chameleon. . 350.00
44 LbC(c),Sugar Bowl Murder . . . 350.00
45 LbC(c),Maze of Murder. 350.00
46 LbC,LbC(c),Modern Communications 300.00
47 LbC(c),The Careless Killer . . . 300.00
48 LbC(c),Road Black 300.00
49 LbC(c),The Poisoner. 550.00

Becomes:

SHOCKING MYSTERY CASES

Sept., 1952–Oct., 1954

50 JyD,LbC(c),Dead Man's Revenge 550.00
51 JyD,LbC(c),A Murderer's Reward 350.00
52 LbC(c),The Carnival Killer. . . . 350.00
53 LbC(c),The Long Shot of Evil . 350.00
54 LbC(c),Double-Cross of Death 350.00
55 LbC(c),Return from Death . . . 350.00
56 LbC(c),The Chase 375.00
57 LbC(c),Thrilling Cases 350.00
58 LbC(c),Killer at Large 350.00
59 LbC(c),Relentess Huntdown . . 350.00
60 LbC(c),Lesson of the Law. . . . 350.00

THRILLING ROMANCES

Standard Comics, Dec., 1949

5 Ph(c) 150.00
6 Ph(c) 100.00
7 Ph(c),JSe,BE 125.00
8 Ph(c) 100.00
9 Ph(c),GT 125.00
10 Ph(c),JSe,BE 125.00
11 Ph(c),JSe,BE. 125.00
12 Ph(c),WW 150.00
13 Ph(c),JSe 100.00
14 Ph(c),Danny Kaye. 125.00
15 Ph(c),Tony Martin,Ph(c) 100.00
16 Ph(c) 100.00
17 Ph(c) 100.00
18 thru 21 Ph(c) . . . . @100.00
22 Ph(c),ATn 125.00
23 Ph(c),ATn 125.00
24 Ph(c),ATn3 . . . . 125.00
25 Ph(c),ATn 125.00

THRILLING TRUE STORY OF THE BASEBALL GIANTS

Fawcett Publications, 1952

N# Partial Ph(c),Famous Giants of the Past, Willie Mays . . . 1,200.00
2 Yankees Ph(c),Joe DiMaggio, Yogi Berra,Mickey Mantle, Casey Stengel 900.00

THRILLS OF TOMORROW
See: TOMB OF TERROR

THUNDA
See: A-1 COMICS

TICK TOCK TALES

Magazine Enterprises, Jan., 1946

1 (fa) Koko & Kola 250.00
2 (fa) Calender 200.00
3 thru 10 (fa) . . . . @150.00
11 thru 18 (fa) . . . . @125.00
19 (fa),Flag(c) 125.00
20 thru 22 (fa) . . . . @125.00
23 (fa),Mugsy Mouse 125.00
24 thru 33 (fa) . . . . @125.00
34 (fa), 1951 . . . . 125.00

TILLY AND TED TINKERTOTLAND

W.T. Grant Co., 1945

N# Christmas 100.00

TIM HOLT

Magazine Enterprises, Jan.–Feb., 1949

1 thru 3 see: *A-1 Comics* #14, #17, #19
4 FBe,Ph(c) 1,200.00
5 FBe,Ph(c). 700.00
6 FBe,Ph(c),I:Calico Kid 600.00
7 FBe,Ph(c),Man-Killer Mustang 500.00
8 FBe,Ph(c) 500.00
9 FBe,DAy(c),TerribleTenderfoot 500.00
10 FBe,DAy(c),The Devil Horse . 500.00
11 FBe,DAy(c),O&I:Ghost Rider . 750.00
12 FBe,DAy(c),Battle at Bullock Gap. 250.00
13 FBe,DAy(c),Ph(c) 250.00
14 FBe,DAy(c),Ph(c),The Honest Bandits 250.00
15 FBe,DAy,Ph(c) 250.00
16 FBe,DAy,Ph(c) 250.00
17 FBe,DAy,Ph(c) 750.00
18 FBe,DAy,Ph(c) 300.00
19 FBe,DAy,They Dig By Night . . 175.00
20 FBe,DAy,O:Red Mask. 300.00
21 FBe,DAy,FF(c) 600.00
22 FBe,DAy 175.00
23 FF,FBe,DAy. 500.00
24 FBe,DAy,FBe(c) 175.00
25 FBe,DAy,FBe(c) 350.00
26 FBe,DAy,FBe(c) 175.00
27 FBe,DAy,FBe(c),V:Straw Man. 175.00
28 FBe,DAy,FBe(c),Ph(c) 175.00
29 FBe,DAy,FBe,Ph(c), ... 175.00
30 FBe,DAy,FBe(c),Lady Doom & The Death Wheel. 200.00
31 FBe,DAy,FBe(c) 200.00
32 FBe,DAy,FBe(c) 200.00
33 FBe,DAy,FBe(c) 200.00
34 FBe,DAy,FBe(c) 250.00
35 FBe,DAy,FBe(c) 250.00
36 FBe,DAy,FBe(c),Drugs 350.00
37 FBe,DAy,FBe(c) 250.00
38 FBe,DAy,FBe(c) 250.00
39 FBe,DAy,FBe(c),3D Effect . . . 200.00
40 FBe,DAy,FBe(c) 200.00
41 FBe,DAy,FBe(c) 200.00

Becomes:

RED MASK

June–July, 1954

42 FBe,DAy,FBe(c),3D 250.00
43 FBe,DAy,FBe(c),3D 225.00
44 FBe,DAy,FBe(c),Death at Split Mesa,3D 225.00
45 FBe,DAy,FBe(c),V:False Red Mask 225.00
46 FBe,DAy,FBe(c) 225.00
47 FBe,DAy,FBe(c) 225.00
48 FBe,DAy,FBe(c),Comics Code 200.00
49 FBe,DAy,FBe(c) 200.00
50 FBe,DAy 200.00
51 FBe,DAy,The Magic of 'The Presto Kid' 200.00
52 FBe,DAy,O:Presto Kid 225.00
53 FBe,DAy 150.00
54 FBe,DAy,Sept., 1957 . . . . 225.00

Tim Tyler Cowboy #11
© Standard Comics

Tip Top Comics #34
© St. John Publishing Co.

T-Man #3
© Quality Comics Group

TIM McCOY
See: ZOO FUNNIES

TIMMY THE TIMID GHOST
See: WIN A PRIZE COMICS

TIM TYLER COWBOY
Standard Comics, Nov., 1948

11 . . . 150.00
12 . . . 100.00
13 The Doll Told the Secret . . . 100.00
14 Danger at Devil's Acres . . . 100.00
15 Secret Treasure . . . 100.00
16 . . . 100.00
17 . . . 100.00
18 1950 . . . 100.00

TINY TESSIE
See: TESSIE THE TYPIST

TINY TOT FUNNIES
See: FAMILY FUNNIES

TINY TOTS COMICS
Dell Publishing Co., 1943

1 WK,fairy tales . . . 500.00

TINY TOTS COMICS
E.C. Comics, March, 1946

N# Your First Comic Book
B:Burton Geller(c) and art . . . 500.00
2 . . . 275.00
3 Celebrate the 4th . . . 225.00
4 Go Back to School . . . 250.00
5 Celebrate the Winter . . . 225.00
6 Do Their Spring Gardening . . . 225.00
7 On a Thrilling Ride . . . 225.00
8 On a Summer Vacation . . . 225.00
9 On a Plane Ride . . . 225.00
10 Merry X-Mas Tiny Tots
E:Burton Geller(c)and art . . . 225.00

TIP TOP COMICS
United Features, St. John, Dell, 1936

1 HF,Li'l Abner . . . 10,000.00
2 HF . . . 2,600.00
3 HF,Tarzan(c) . . . 2,400.00
4 HF,Li'l Abner(c) . . . 1,500.00
5 HF,Capt&Kids(c) . . . 1,000.00
6 HF . . . 900.00
7 HF . . . 900.00
8 HF,Li'l Abner(c) . . . 900.00
9 HF,Tarzan(c) . . . 1,200.00
10 HF,Li'L Abner(c) . . . 900.00
11 HF,Tarzan(c) . . . 850.00
12 HF,Li'l Abner . . . 800.00
13 HF,Tarzan(c) . . . 850.00
14 HF,Li'L Abner(c) . . . 800.00
15 HF,Capt&kids(c) . . . 800.00
16 HF,Tarzan(c) . . . 850.00
17 HF,Li'L Abner(c) . . . 800.00
18 HF,Tarzan(c) . . . 850.00
19 HF,Football(c) . . . 750.00
20 HF,Capt&Kids(c) . . . 750.00
21 HF,Tarzan(c) . . . 750.00
22 HF,Li'l Abner(c) . . . 500.00
23 HF,Capt&Kids(c) . . . 500.00
24 HF,Tarzan(c) . . . 750.00
25 HF,Capt&Kids(c) . . . 500.00
26 HF,Li'L Abner(c) . . . 500.00
27 HF,Tarzan(c) . . . 750.00
28 HF,Li'l Abner(c) . . . 500.00
29 HF,Capt&Kids(c) . . . 500.00
30 HF,Tarzan(c) . . . 750.00
31 HF,Capt&Kids(c) . . . 500.00
32 HF,Tarzan(c) . . . 700.00
33 HF,Tarzan(c) . . . 750.00
34 HF,Capt&Kids(c) . . . 750.00
35 HF . . . 450.00
36 HF,HK,Tarzan(c) . . . 750.00
37 HF,Tarzan . . . 750.00
38 HF . . . 450.00
39 HF,Tarzan . . . 700.00
40 HF . . . 450.00
41 Tarzan(c) . . . 750.00
42 . . . 450.00
43 Tarzan(c) . . . 400.00
44 HF . . . 450.00
45 HF,Tarzan(c) . . . 400.00
46 HF . . . 450.00
47 HF,Tarzan(c) . . . 400.00
48 HF . . . 450.00
49 HF . . . 450.00
50 HF,Tarzan(c) . . . 400.00
51 . . . 375.00
52 Tarzan(c) . . . 450.00
53 . . . 375.00
54 . . . 475.00
55 . . . 350.00
56 . . . 350.00
57 BHg . . . 400.00
58 . . . 300.00
59 BHg . . . 400.00
60 . . . 300.00
61 and 62 BHg . . . @400.00
63 thru 90 . . . @200.00
91 thru 99 . . . @150.00
100 . . . 175.00
101 thru 150 . . . @125.00
151 thru 188 . . . @100.00
189 thru 225 . . . @75.00

TIP TOPPER COMICS
United Features Syndicate, 1949

1 Abbie & Slats, Li'l Abner, etc. . . 200.00
2 . . . 150.00
3 . . . 125.00
4 . . . 125.00
5 Fearless Fosdick . . . 125.00
6 Fearless Fosdick . . . 125.00
7 . . . 100.00
8 . . . 100.00
9 . . . 100.00
10 . . . 100.00
11 thru 16 . . . @100.00
17 Peanuts (c) . . . 150.00
18 thru 24 . . . @100.00
25 Peanuts . . . 110.00
26 Peanuts . . . 110.00

T-MAN
Comics Magazines (Quality Comics Group), Sept., 1951

1 JCo,Pete Trask-the
Treasury Man . . . 500.00
2 RC(c),The Girl with Death
in Her Hands . . . 250.00
3 RC(a&c),Death Trap in Iran . . 250.00
4 RC(a&c),Panama Peril . . . 250.00
5 RC(a&c),Violence in Venice . . 250.00
6 RC(c),The Man Who
Could Be Hitler . . . 225.00
7 RC(c),Mr. Murder & The
Black Hand . . . 225.00
8 RC(c),Red Ticket to Hell . . . 225.00
9 RC(c),Trial By Terror . . . 200.00
10 . . . 200.00
11 The Voice of Russia . . . 175.00
12 Terror in Tokyo . . . 175.00
13 Mind Assassins . . . 175.00
14 Trouble in Bavaria, Hitler . . . 200.00
15 The Traitor,Bondage(c) . . . 175.00
16 Hunt For a Hatchetman . . . 175.00
17 Red Triggerman . . . 175.00
18 Death Rides the Rails . . . 175.00

Ti

 All comics prices listed are for *Near Mint* condition.

Tomahawk #5
© DC Comics

Tomahawk #31
© DC Comics

Tom and Jerry Summer Fun #1
© Dell Publishing Co.

19 Death Ambush 175.00
20 The Fantastic H-Bomb Plot. . . 200.00
21 The Return of Mussolini 150.00
22 Propaganda for Doom 165.00
23 Red Intrigue in Parid,H-Bomb. 150.00
24 Red Sabotage. 150.00
25 RC,The Ingenious Red Trap. . 150.00
26 . . . . 125.00
27 . . . . 125.00
28 . . . . 125.00
29 . . . . 125.00
30 thru 37. . . . . @125.00
38 Dec., 1956 . . . . 125.00

TNT COMICS

Charles Publishing Co., Feb., 1946

1 FBI story,YellowJacket. 400.00

TODAY'S BRIDES

Ajax/Farrell Publishing Co., Nov., 1955

1 . . . . 125.00
2 thru 4 Nov., 1956 . . . . @100.00

TODAY'S ROMANCE

Standard Comics, March, 1952

5 Ph(c) 100.00
6 ATh, Ph(c) 125.00
7 and 8 Ph(c) . . . . @100.00

TOMAHAWK

DC Comics, 1950

1 Prisoner Called Tomahawk. . 2,500.00
2 FF(4pgs),Four Boys
Against the Frontier 1,000.00
3 Warpath 800.00
4 Tomahawk Wanted: Dead
or Alive. 800.00
5 The Girl Who Was Chief 800.00
6 Tomahawk-King of the Aztecs . 700.00
7 Punishment of Tomahawk 700.00
8 The King's Messenger. 700.00
9 The Five Doomed Men 700.00
10 Frontied Sabotage 700.00
11 Girl Who Hated Tomahawk . . . 500.00
12 Man From Magic Mountain. . . 500.00
13 Dan Hunter's Rival 500.00
14 The Frontier Tinker 500.00
15 The Wild Men of
Wigwam Mountain. 500.00
16 Treasure of the Angelique. . . . 500.00
17 Short-Cut to Danger 500.00
18 Bring In M'Sieur Pierre 500.00
19 The Lafayette Volunteers 500.00
20 NC(c),The Retreat of
Tomahawk 500.00
21 NC(c),The Terror of the
Wrathful Spirit 350.00
22 CS(c),Admiral Tomahawk 350.00
23 CS(c),The Indian Chief
from Oxford 350.00
24 NC(c),Adventure In the
Everglades. 350.00
25 NC(c),The Star-Gazer of
Freemont 350.00
26 NC(c),Ten Wagons For
Tomahawk 350.00
27 NC(c),Frontier Outcast 350.00
28 I:Lord Shilling 375.00
29 Conspiracy of Wounded Bear. 400.00
30 The King of the Thieves 350.00
31 NC(c),The Buffalo Brave
From Misty Mountain. 350.00
32 NC(c),The Clocks That
Went to War. 350.00
33 The Paleface Tribe 350.00
34 The Capture of General
Washington 350.00
35 Frontier Feud 350.00
36 NC(c),A Cannon for Fort
Reckless 350.00
37 NC(c),Feathered Warriors. . . . 350.00
38 The Frontier Zoo. 350.00
39 The Redcoat Trickster. 350.00
40 Fearless Fettle-Daredevil 350.00
41 The Captured Chieftain. 350.00
42 The Prisoner Tribe 350.00
43 Tomahawk's Little Brother. . . . 350.00
44 The Brave Named Tomahawk 350.00
45 The Last Days of Chief Tory . . 350.00
46 The Chief With 1,000 Faces. . 200.00
47 The Frontier Rain-Maker. 200.00
48 Indian Twin Trouble. 200.00
49 The Unknown Warrior. 200.00
50 The Brave Who Was Jinxed . . 200.00
51 General Tomahawk. 200.00
52 Tom Thumb of the Frontier . . . 200.00
53 The Four-Footed Renegade . . 200.00
54 Mystery of the 13th Arrows. . . 200.00
55 Prisoners of the Choctaw 200.00
56 The Riddle of the
Five Little Indians 200.00
57 The Strange Fight
at Fort Bravo 250.00
58 Track of the Mask. 150.00
59 The Mystery Prisoner of
Lost Island. 150.00
60 The Amazing Walking Fort . . . 150.00
61 Tomahawk's Secret Weapons. 100.00
62 Strongest Man in the World . . 100.00
63 The Frontier Super Men 100.00
64 The Outcast Brave 100.00
65 Boy Who Wouldn't Be Chief. . 100.00
66 DD&SMo(c),A Trap For
Tomahawk 100.00
67 DD&SMo(c),Frontier Sorcerer 100.00
68 DD&SMo(c),Tomahawk's
Strange Ally 100.00
69 DD&SMo(c),Tracker-King
of the Wolves. 100.00
70 DD&SMo(c),Three Tasks
for Tomahawk 100.00
71 DD&SMo(c),The Boy Who
Betrayed His Country 100.00
72 DD&SMo(c),The Frontier Pupil 100.00
73 DD&SMo(c),The Secret of
the Indian Sorceress 100.00
74 DD&SMo(c),The Great
Paleface Masquerade 100.00
75 DD&SMo(c),The Ghost of
Lord Shilling. 100.00
76 DD&SMo(c),The Totem-Pole
Trail 100.00
77 DD&SMo(c),The Raids of
the One-Man Tribe 100.00

TOM AND JERRY

DELL GIANT EDITIONS
Dell Publishing Co., 1952–58

Back to School. 300.00
Picnic Time. 250.00
Summer Fun 1. . . . . 350.00
Summer Fun 2. . . . . 200.00
Winter Carnival 1 . . . . 500.00
Winter Carnival 2. . . . . 350.00
Winter Fun 3 . . . . 200.00
Winter Fun 4 . . . . 175.00
Winter Fun 5 . . . . 150.00
Winter Fun 6 . . . . 150.00
Winter Fun 7 . . . . 150.00

TOM AND JERRY

See: OUR GANG COMICS

TOMB OF TERROR

Harvey Publications, June, 1952

1 BP,The Thing From the
Center of the Earth 750.00

Tom Corbett Space Cadet #4
© Dell Publishing Co.

Tom Mix Comics #8
© Ralston-Purina Co.

Tom Mix Western #56
© Fawcett Publications

2 RP,The Quagmire Beast 600.00
3 BP,RP,Caravan of the Doomed, Bondage(c) 600.00
4 RP,I'm Going to Kill You, Torture 500.00
5 RP 500.00
6 RP,Return From the Grave . . . 500.00
7 RP,Shadow of Death 500.00
8 HN,The Hive 500.00
9 BP,HN,The Tunnel 500.00
10 BP,HN,The Trial 500.00
11 BP,HN,The Closet 500.00
12 BP,HN,Tale of Cain 550.00
13 BP,What Was Out There 600.00
14 BP,SC,End Result 600.00
15 BP,HN,Break-up, Exploding Head 1,000.00
16 BP,Going,Going,Gone 600.00

Becomes:

THRILLS OF TOMORROW

Oct., 1954

17 RP,BP,The World of Mr. Chatt. 300.00
18 RP,BP,The Dead Awaken 200.00
19 S&K,S&K(c),A:Stuntman 600.00
20 S&K,S&K(c),A:Stuntman 500.00

TOM CAT

See: BO

TOM CORBETT SPACE CADET

Dell Publishing Co., Jan., 1952

See also Dell Four Color
4 based on TV show 200.00
5 . . . . 150.00
6 . . . . 100.00
7 . . . . 100.00
8 . . . . 100.00
9 . . . . 100.00
10 and 11 . . . . @100.00

TOM CORBETT SPACE CADET

Prize Publications, May–June, 1955

1 Robot(c) 400.00
2 . . . . 300.00
3 Sept.–Oct., 1955 . . . . 300.00

TOM MIX COMICS

Ralston-Purina Co., Sept., 1940

1 O:Tom Mix 4,500.00
2 . . . . 1,500.00
3 . . . . 800.00
4 thru 9 . . . . @750.00

Becomes:

TOM MIX COMMANDOS COMICS

Nov., 1942

10 . . . . 700.00
11 Invisible Invaders 700.00
12 Terrible Talons Of Tokyo 700.00

TOM MIX WESTERN

Fawcett Publications, Jan., 1948

1 Ph(c),Two-Fisted Adventures 1,500.00
2 Ph(c),Hair-Triggered Action . . 600.00
3 Ph(c),Double Barreled Action . 500.00
4 Ph(c),Cowpunching 500.00
5 Ph(c),Two Gun Action 500.00
6 CCB,Most Famous Cowboy . . 350.00
7 CCB,A Tattoo of Thrills 250.00
8 EK,Ph(c),Gallant Guns 325.00
9 CCB,Song o/t Deadly Spurs . . 325.00
10 CCB,Crack Shot Western 325.00
11 CCB,EK(C),Triple Revenge . . 325.00
12 King of the Cowboys 250.00
13 Ph(c),Leather Burns 250.00
14 Ph(c),Brand of Death 250.00
15 Ph(c),Masked Treachery 250.00
16 Ph(c),Death Spurting Guns . . . 250.00
17 Ph(c),Trail of Doom 250.00
18 Ph(c),Reign of Terror 225.00
19 Hand Colored Ph(c) 250.00
20 Ph(c),CCB,F:Capt Tootsie 225.00
21 Ph(c) 225.00
22 Ph(c),The Human Beast 225.00
23 Ph(c),Return of the Past 225.00
24 Hand Colored Ph(c), The Lawless City 225.00
25 Hand Colored Ph(c), The Signed Death Warrant . . 225.00
26 Hand Colored Ph(c), Dangerous Escape 225.00
27 Hand Colored Ph(c), Hero Without Glory 225.00
28 Ph(c),The Storm Kings 225.00
29 Hand Colored Ph(c),The Case of the Rustling Rose . . 225.00
30 Ph(c),Disappearance in the Hills 225.00
31 Ph(c) 175.00
32 Hand Colored Ph(c), Mystery of Tremble Mountain 175.00
33 . . . . 175.00
34 . . . . 175.00
35 Partial Ph(c),The Hanging at Hollow Creek 175.00
36 Ph(c) 175.00
37 Ph(c) 175.00
38 Ph(c),36 pages 150.00
39 Ph(c) 175.00
40 Ph(c) 175.00
41 Ph(c) 175.00
42 Ph(c) 175.00
43 Ph(c) 150.00
44 Ph(c) 150.00
45 Partial Ph(c),The Secret Letter 150.00
46 Ph(c) 150.00
47 Ph(c) 150.00
48 Ph(c) 150.00
49 Partial Ph(c),Blind Date With Death 150.00
50 Ph(c) 150.00
51 Ph(c) 150.00
52 Ph(c) 150.00
53 Ph(c) 150.00
54 Ph(c) 150.00
55 Ph(c) 150.00
56 Partial Ph(c),Deadly Spurs . . . 150.00
57 Ph(c)5 . . . . 150.00
58 Ph(c) 150.00
59 Ph(c) 150.00
60 Ph(c) 150.00
61 Partial Ph(c),Lost in the Night,May, 1953 . . . . 175.00

TOMMY OF THE BIG TOP

King Features/ Standard Comics, 1948

10 Thrilling Circus Adventures . . . 150.00
11 . . . . 100.00
12 March, 1949 . . . . 100.00

TOM TERRIFIC!

Pines Comics

Summer, 1957

1 . . . . 250.00
2 thru 5 . . . . @175.00
6 Fall, 1958 . . . . 175.00

All comics prices listed are for *Near Mint* condition.

Topix Comics Vol. 8 #19
© Topix/Catechetical Guild

Top-Notch Comics #10
© MLJ Magazines

Suzie Comics #64
© MLJ Magazines

TOM-TOM THE JUNGLE BOY

Magazine Enterprises, 1946

1 (fa) 200.00
2 (fa) 150.00
3 Winter 1947,(fa),X-mas issue . 125.00
1 . . . . 100.00

TONTO
See: LONE RANGER'S COMPANION TONTO

TONY TRENT
See: FACE, THE

TOODLES

Approved Comics (Ziff-Davis Publ.), 1951

10 . . . . 125.00

THE TOODLES TWINS

Argo Publ., 1956

1 . . . . 100.00

TOP FLIGHT COMICS

Four Star/St. John Publ. Co., July, 1949

1 . . . . 125.00
1 Hector the Inspector 100.00

TOPIX COMICS

Topix/Catechetical Guild, 1942

1 Catholic 350.00
2 . . . . 250.00
3 . . . . 250.00
4 . . . . 200.00
5 . . . . 200.00
6 . . . . 200.00
7 . . . . 200.00
8 . . . . 200.00
Volume 2, any, except #5 . . . . . . 200.00
5 Pope Pius XII. 250.00
Volume 3, any 200.00
Volume 4, any 175.00
Volume 5, any, except #12 . . . . . 150.00
12 Life of Christ 175.00
Volume 6, any 125.00
Volume 7, any 100.00
Volume 8, any #4. . . . . 150.00
4 Dagwood Splits Atom. 150.00
Volume 9, any, except #12 . . . . . 100.00
12 Christmas issue 100.00
Volume 10, any 100.00

TOP LOVE STORIES

Star Publications, May, 1951

3 LbC(c) 300.00
4 LbC(c) 200.00
5 LbC(c) 200.00
6 LbC(c),WW 300.00
7 LbC(c) 250.00
8 LbC(c), WW Story 275.00
9 LbC(c) 250.00
10 thru 16 LbC(c) . . . . @250.00
17 LbC(c),WW 275.00
18 LbC(c). 250.00
19 LbC(c),JyD 250.00

TOP-NOTCH COMICS

MLJ Magazines, Dec., 1939

1 JaB,JCo,B&O:The Wizard, B:Kandak,Swift of the Secret Service,The Westpointer, Mystic, Air Patrol,Scott Rand, Manhunter 12,000.00
2 JaB,JCo,B:Dick Storm, E:Mystic, B:Stacy Knight . . 7,600.00
3 JaB,JCo,EA(c),E:Swift of the Secret Service,Scott Rand 4,000.00
4 JCo,EA(c),MMe,O&I:Streak, Chandler 3,500.00
5 Ea(c),MMe,O&I:Galahad, B:Shanghai Sheridan 3,500.00
6 Ea(c),MMe,A:The Shield . . . 3,000.00
7 Ea(c),MMe,N:The Wizard . . 3,800.00
8 E:Dick Sorm,B&O:Roy The1 Super Boy,The Firefly 3,500.00
9 O&I:Black Hood, B:Fran Frazier 10,000.00
10 A:Black Hood 3,500.00
11 . . . . 2,800.00
12 . . . . 2,800.00
13 . . . . 2,800.00
14 Bondage(c) 2,800.00
15 MMe. 2,800.00
16 . . . . 2,500.00
17 Bondage(c) 2,800.00
18 . . . . 2,500.00
19 Bondage(c) 2,800.00
20 . . . . 2,500.00
21 . . . . 2,000.00
22 . . . . 2,000.00
23 Bondage(c) 2,200.00
24 Black Hood Smashes Murder Ring 2,000.00
25 E:Bob Phantom 2,000.00
26 . . . . 2,000.00
27 E:The Firefly 2,000.00
28 B:Suzie,Pokey Okay, Gag Oriented 2,000.00
29 E:Kandak. 2,000.00
30 . . . . 2,000.00
31 . . . . 900.00
32 . . . . 900.00
33 BWo,B:Dotty&Ditto 900.00
34 BWo 900.00
35 BWo 900.00
36 BWo 900.00
37 thru 40 BWo . . . . @900.00
41 . . . . 900.00
42 BWo 900.00
43 . . . . 900.00
44 EW:Black Hood,I:Suzie. 900.00
45 Suzie(c) 1,000.00
Becomes:

LAUGH COMIX

Summer, 1944

46 Suzie & Wilbur 500.00
47 Suzie & Wilbur 400.00
48 Suzie & Wilbur 400.00
Becomes:

SUZIE COMICS

Spring, 1945

49 B:Ginger 600.00
50 AFy(c) 400.00
51 AFy(c) 400.00
52 AFy(c) 400.00
53 AFy(c) 400.00
54 AFy(c) 500.00
55 AFy(c) 500.00
56 BWo,B;Katie Keene 300.00
57 thru 70 BWo . . . . @300.00
71 thru 79 BWo . . . . @200.00
80 thru 99 BWo . . . . @200.00
100 Aug., 1954, BWo. 200.00

TOPS

Tops Mag. Inc. (Lev Gleason), July, 1949

1 RC&BLb,GT,DBa,CBi(c),I'll Buy That Girl,Our Explosive Children 1,500.00
2 FGu,BF,CBi(c),RC&BLb 1,400.00

Top Secrets #8
© Street & Smith Publications

Torchy #3
© Quality Comics Group

Trapped N#
© Harvey Publications

TOPS COMICS

Consolidated Book Publishers, 1944

2000 Don on the Farm. 400.00
2001 The Jack of Spades
V:The Hawkman 300.00
2002 Rip Raiders 250.00
2003 Red Birch 200.00

TOP SECRET

Hillman Publications, Jan., 1952

1 The Tricks of the Secret
Agent Revealed 250.00

TOP SECRETS

Street & Smith Publ., Nov., 1947

1 BP,BP(c),Of the Men Who
Guard the U.S. Mail 400.00
2 BP,BP(c),True Story of Jim
the Penman 350.00
3 BP,BP(c),Crime Solved by
Mental Telepathy 300.00
4 Highway Pirates. 300.00
5 BP,BP(c),Can Music Kill 300.00
6 BP,BP(c),The Clue of the
Forgotten Film 300.00
7 BP,BP(c),Train For Sale. 375.00
8 BP,BP(c) 300.00
9 BP,BP(c) 300.00
10 BP,BP(c),July–Aug., 1949. . . . 375.00

TOPS IN ADVENTURE

Approved Comics (Ziff-Davis), Autumn, 1952

1 BP,Crusaders From Mars 600.00

TOP SPOT COMICS

Top Spot Publishing Co., 1945

1 The Duke Of Darkness 450.00

TOPSY-TURVY

R.B. Leffingwell Publ., April, 1945

1 I:Cookie 200.00

TOR

St. John Publishing Co., Sept., 1953

1 JKu,JKu(c),O;Tor,One Million
Years Ago 150.00
2 JKu,JKu(c),3-D Issue 100.00
3 JKu,JKu(c),ATh,historic Life . . 125.00
4 JKu,JKu(c),ATh 125.00
5 JKu,JKu(c),ATh,Oct., 1954 . . . 125.00

TORCHY

Quality Comics Group, Nov., 1949

1 GFx,BWa(c),The Blonde
Bombshell 2,200.00
2 GFx(a&c),Beauty at Its Best. 1,100.00
3 GFx,GFx(c),You Can't
Beat Nature 1,100.00
4 GFx,GFx(c),The Girl to
Keep Your Eye On 1,400.00
5 BWa,GFx,BWa(c),At the
Masquerade Party 1,800.00
6 Sept., 1950,BWa,GFx,
BWa(c),The Libido Driven
Boy Scout. 1,800.00

TORMENTED, THE

Sterling Comics, July, 1954

1 Buried Alive 400.00
2 Sept., 1954,The Devils Circus 250.00
Becomes:

SURPRISE ADVENTURES

Sterling Comics, 1955

3 MSy 250.00
4 . . . . 150.00
5 MSy 200.00

TOUGH KID SQUAD COMICS

Marvel Timely, March, 1942

1 AAv,SSh,O:The Human Top,
Tough Kid Squad,A:The Flying
Flame, V:Doctor Klutch . . 15,000.00

TOYLAND COMICS

Fiction House Magazines, Jan., 1947

1 Wizard of the Moon 400.00
2 Buddy Bruin & Stu Rabbit 200.00
3 GT,The Candy Maker 250.00
4 July, 1947 . . . . 200.00

TOY TOWN COMICS

Toytown Publ./Orbit Publ., Feb., 1945

1 LbC,LbC(c)(fa) 500.00
2 LbC,(fa) 300.00
3 LbC,LbC(c),(fa) 250.00
4 thru 7 LbC,(fa) May, 1947 . . @250.00

TRAIL BLAZERS See: RED DRAGON COMICS

TRAPPED

Harvey Publications, 1951

N# 150.00

TRAPPED!

Periodical Magazines (Ace Magazines), 1954

1 . . . . 125.00
2 and 3 . . . . @60.00

TREASURE CHEST

George A Pflaum Publ., Inc., 1946

1 . . . . 300.00
2 thru 4 . . . . @150.00
5 Dr Styx. 160.00
6 . . . . 150.00
Vol 2, 1 thru 20 . . . . @150.00
Vol 3, 1 thru 5 (1947–48). . . . . @150.00
Vol 3, #6 Verne,Voyage to Moon, 135.00
Vol 3, 7 thru 20 . . . . @110.00
Vol 4, 1 thru 20 (1948–49). . . . @135.00
Vol 5, 1 thru 20 (1949–50). . . . @125.00
Vol 6, 1 thru 20 (1950–51). . . . @125.00
Vol 7, 1 thru 20 (1951–52). . . . @125.00
Vol 8, 1 thru 20 (1952–53). . . . @125.00
Vol 9, 1 thru 20 (1953–54). . . . @100.00
Vol 10, 1 thru 10 (1954–55). . . @100.00
Vol 10, #11 BP. 100.00
Vol 10, 12 thru 20 . . . . @100.00
Vol 11, 1 thru 20 (1955–56). . . @100.00
Vol 12, 1 thru 20 (1956–57). . . @100.00
Vol 13, 1 thru 20 (1957–58). . . . @75.00
Vol 14, 1 thru 20 (1958–59). . . . @75.00
Vol 15, 1 thru 20 (1959–60). . . . @75.00
Vol 16, 1 thru 20 (1960–61). . . . @75.00
Vol 17, 1 thru 20 (1962–63)
odd #s . . . . @75.00
even #s "Godless Communism"

Treasure Comics #4
© Prize Publications

True Aviation Picture Stories #1
© Parent's Institute

True Comics #14
© Parents' Magazine Press

2 RC 275.00
4 and 6 . . . . @275.00
8 thru 14 Stalin, WWII . . . . @275.00
14 thru 20 Kruschev . . . . . @225.00

TREASURE COMICS
Prize Comics Group, 1943

1 S&K,Reprints of Prize Comics #7 through #11 . . . . 3,000.00

TREASURE COMICS
American Boys Comics (Prize Publications), June–July, 1945

1 HcK,B:PaulBunyan,MarcoPolo 500.00
2 HcK(a&c),B:Arabian Knight, Gorilla King,Dr.Styx 300.00
3 HcK 250.00
4 HcK 250.00
5 HcK,JK, Marco Polo 300.00
6 BK,HcK(a&c) 250.00
7 FF,HcK(a&c),Capt.Kidd, Jr. . . . 500.00
8 HcK,FF 500.00
9 HcK,DBa 250.00
10 JK,DBa,JK(c) 400.00
11 BK,HcK,DBa,The Weird Adventures of Mr. Bottle 300.00
12 DBa,DBa(c),Autumn, 1947 . . . 250.00

TREASURY OF COMICS
St. John Publishing Co., 1947

1 RvB,RvB(c),Abbie an' Slats . . 150.00
2 Jim Hardy 125.00
3 Bill Bimlin 125.00
4 RvB,RvB(c),Abbie an' Slats . . 125.00
5 Jim Hardy,Jan., 1948 . . . . 100.00

TREASURY OF COMICS
St. John Publishing Co., 1948

1 Abbott & Costello, Little Audrey. 250.00
2 . . . . 125.00
3 thru 5 . . . . @110.00

TRIPLE THREAT
Gerona Publications, Winter, 1945

1 F:King O'Leary,The Duke of Darkness,Beau Brummell . . . 350.00

TRUE ADVENTURES
See: TRUE WESTERN

TRUE ANIMAL PICTURE STORIES
True Comics Press, 1947

1 . . . . 125.00
2 . . . . 125.00

TRUE AVIATION PICTURE STORIES
Parents' Institute/P.M.I., Aug., 1942

1 How Jimmy Doolittle Bombed Tokyo 300.00
2 Knight of the Air Mail 250.00
3 The Amazing One-Man Air Force 200.00
4 Joe Foss America's No. 1 Air Force 200.00
5 Bombs over Germany 200.00
6 Flight Lt. Richard Hillary R.A.F. 200.00
7 "Fatty" Chow China's Sky Champ 200.00
8 Blitz over Burma 200.00
9 Off the Beam 200.00
10 "Pappy" Boyington 200.00
11 Ph(c) 200.00
12 . . . . 200.00
13 Ph(c),Flying Facts. 200.00
14 . . . . 200.00
15 True Aviation Adventures 200.00
Becomes:

AVIATION AND MODEL BUILDING
Dec., 1946

16 . . . . 125.00
17 Feb., 1947. . . . . 150.00

TRUE BRIDES' EXPERIENCES
See: TEEN-AGE BRIDES

TRUE BRIDE-TO-BE ROMANCES
See: TEEN-AGE BRIDES

TRUE COMICS
True Comics/ Parents' Magazine Press, April, 1941–Aug., 1950

1 My Greatest Adventure-by Lowell Thomas, Churchill . . . 450.00
2 BEv,The Story of the Red Cross 200.00
3 Baseball Hall of Fame 225.00
4 Danger in the Artic 150.00
5 Father Duffy-the Fighting Chaplain, Joe Louis. 165.00
6 The Capture of Aquinaldo 175.00
7 JKa,Wilderness Adventures of George Washington 165.00
8 U.S. Army Wings 125.00
9 A Pig that Made History 125.00
10 Adrift on an Ice Pan 125.00
11 Gen. Douglas MacArthur. 110.00
12 Mackenzie-King of Cananda . . 110.00
13 The Real Robinson Crusoe. . . 110.00
14 Australia war base of the South Pacific 110.00
15 The Story of West Point 125.00
16 How Jimmy Doolittle Bombed Tokyo. 120.00
17 The Ghost of Captain Blig, B.Feller 125.00
18 Battling Bill of the Merchant Marine 135.00
19 Secret Message Codes. 110.00
20 The Story of India 100.00
21 Timoshenko the Blitz Buster . . 110.00
22 Gen, Bernard L. Montgomery . 100.00
23 The Story of Steel 100.00
24 Gen. Henri Giraud-Master of Escape 100.00
25 Medicine's Miracle Men 100.00
26 Hero of the Bismarck Sea. . . . 100.00
27 Leathernecks have Landed. . . 110.00
28 The Story of Radar 100.00
29 The Fighting Seabees. 100.00
30 Dr. Norman Bethune-Blood Bank Founder 100.00
31 Our Good Neighbor Bolivia, Red Grange 110.00
32 Men against the Desert 125.00
33 Gen.Clark and his Fighting 5th 150.00
34 Angel of the Battlefield 125.00
35 Carlson's Marine Raiders 125.00
36 Canada's Sub-Busters 125.00
37 Commander of the Crocodile Fleet. 125.00
38 Oregon Trailblazer 125.00
39 Saved by Sub, FBI 125.00

True Comics #84
© Parents Magazine Press

True Crime Comics #3
© Magazine Village, Inc.

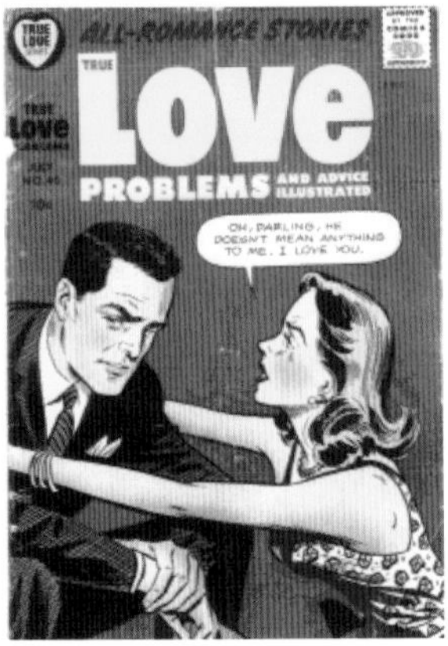

True Love Problems and Advice Illustrated #40 © Harvey Publications

40 Sea Furies 125.00
41 Cavalcade of England. 100.00
42 Gen. Jaques Le Clerc-Hero of Paris 100.00
43 Unsinkable Ship 100.00
44 El Senor Goofy, Truman 100.00
45 Tokyo Express 100.00
46 The Magnificent Runt 100.00
47 Atoms Unleashed, Atomic Bomb 175.00
48 Pirate Patriot 100.00
49 Smoking Fists 100.00
50 Lumber Pirates 100.00
51 Exercise Musk-Ox. 100.00
52 King of the Buckaneers 100.00
53 Baseline Booby. 100.00
54 Santa Fe Sailor. 100.00
55 Sea Going Santa 100.00
56 End of a Terror 100.00
57 Newfangled Machines 100.00
58 Leonardo da Vinci-500 years too Soon, Houdini 100.00
59 Pursuit Pirates, Bob Hope . . . 100.00
60 Emmett Kelly-The World's Funniest Clown 100.00
61 Peter Le Grand-Bold Buckaneer. 100.00
62 Sutter's Gold. 100.00
63 Outboard Outcome 100.00
64 Man-Eater at Large. 100.00
65 The Story of Scotland Yard. . . 100.00
66 Easy Guide to Football Formations, Will Rogers 100.00
67 The Changing Zebra. 100.00
68 Admiral Byrd 100.00
69 FBI Special Agent Steve Saunders, Jack Benny 100.00
70 The Case of the Seven Hunted Men. 100.00
71 Story of Joe DiMaggio 150.00
72 FBI,Jackie Robinson. 100.00
73 The 26 Mile Dash-Story of the Marathon, Walt Disney . . 100.00
74 A Famous Coach's Special Football Tips, Amos & Andy . 100.00
75 King of Reporters 100.00
76 Story of a Buried Treasure . . . 100.00
77 France's Greatest Detective . . 100.00
78 Cagliostro-Master Rogue 100.00
79 Ralph Bunche-Hero of Peace. 100.00
80 Rocket Trip to the Moon 200.00
81 Red Grange 200.00
82 Marie Celeste Ship of Mystery 175.00
83 Bullfighter from Brooklyn. 175.00
84 King of the Buckaneers 175.00

Tr

TRUE COMPLETE MYSTERY
See: COMPLETE MYSTERY

TRUE CONFIDENCES
Fawcett Publications, Autumn, 1949

1 . . . . 200.00
2 and 3 . . . . @125.00
4 DP 125.00

TRUE CRIME COMICS
Magazine Village, Inc., May, 1947

2 JCo(c),James Kent-Crook, Murderer,Escaped Convict; Drug 2,000.00
3 JCo(a&c),Benny Dickson-Killer;Drug. 1,500.00
4 JCo(a&c),Little Jake-Big Shot 1,400.00
5 JCo(c),The Rat & the Blond Gun Moll;Drug 1,000.00
6 Joseph Metley-Swindler, Jailbird, Killer 800.00
2-1(7) ATh,WW,Ph(c),Phil Coppolla,Sept., 1949 . . . . . 1,200.00

TRUE LIFE ROMANCES
Ajax/Farrell Publications, Dec., 1955

1 . . . . 125.00
2 and 3 . . . . @75.00

TRUE LIFE SECRETS
Romantic Love Stories/ Charlton Comics, March–April, 1951

1 Ph(c) 150.00
2 . . . . 75.00
3 thru 11 . . . . @60.00
12 Escort Girl. 65.00
13 thru 20. . . . . @60.00
21 thru 25 . . . . @50.00
26 thru 29 . . . . @40.00

TRUE LIFE TALES
Marvel Comics, 1949

1 (8) Ph(c). 125.00
2 Ph(c) 125.00

TRUE LOVE CONFESSIONS
Premier Magazines, 1954

1 Marijuana. 135.00
2 . . . . 65.00
3 thru 11 . . . . @50.00

TRUE LOVE PICTORIAL
St. John Publishing Co., 1952

1 Ph(c) 350.00
2 MB 450.00
3 MB(c),MB,JKu 750.00
4 MB(c),MB,JKu 750.00
5 MB(c),MB,JKu 750.00
6 MB(c) 350.00
7 MB(c) 350.00
8 MB(c) 300.00
9 MB(c) 300.00
10 MB(c),MB 300.00
11 MB(c),MB 300.00

TRUE LOVE PROBLEMS AND ADVICE ILLUSTRATED
Harvey Publications, 1949–57

1 . . . . 150.00
2 . . . . 125.00
3 thru 10 . . . . @100.00
11 thru 20 . . . . @100.00
21 thru 37 . . . . @100.00
38 S&K(c). 125.00
39 thru 44. . . . . @100.00

Becomes:

ROMANCE STORIES OF TRUE LOVE
Harvey Publications, 1957–58

45 thru 51 . . . . 100.00
52 . . . . 125.00

TRUE MOVIE AND TELEVISION
Toby Press, Aug., 1950

1 Liz Taylor, Ph(c) 650.00
2 FF,Ph(c),John Wayne, L.Taylor 500.00
3 June Allyson,Ph(c) 350.00
4 Jane Powell,Ph(c),Jan.,1951. . 200.00

All comics prices listed are for *Near Mint* condition.

True Sport Picture Stories #10
© Street & Smith Publications

True Sport Picture Stories
Volume 3, #11 © Street & Smith Publ.

True-To-Life Romances #22
© Star Publications

TRUE SECRETS

Marvel Atlas, 1950–56

Previously LOVE DIARY or OUR LOVE, depending on who you believe.

3 ... 150.00
4 ... 125.00
5 ... 125.00
6 BEv ... 135.00
7 ... 125.00
8 ... 125.00
9 ... 125.00
10 ... 125.00
11 thru 21 ... @110.00
22 BEv ... 125.00
23 ... 110.00
24 ViC ... 125.00
25 thru 28 ... @110.00
29 thru 39 ... @100.00
40 Sept., 1956 ... 100.00

SPORT COMICS

Street & Smith Publ., Oct., 1940

1 F:Lou Gehrig ... 700.00
2 F:Gene Tunney ... 400.00
3 F:Phil Rizzuto ... 450.00
4 F:Frank Leahy ... 300.00

Becomes:

TRUE SPORT PICTURE STORIES

Street & Smith Publ., Feb., 1942–July-Aug., 1949

5 Joe DiMaggio ... 400.00
6 Billy Confidence ... 250.00
7 Mel Ott ... 275.00
8 Lou Ambers ... 250.00
9 Pete Reiser ... 250.00
10 Frankie Sinkwich ... 250.00
11 Marty Serfo ... 250.00
12 JaB(c),Jack Dempsey ... 265.00
2-1 JaB(c),Willie Pep ... 250.00
2-2 JaB(c) ... 250.00
2-3 JaB(c),Carl Hubbell ... 265.00
2-4 Advs. in Football & Battle ... 275.00
2-5 Don Hutson ... 250.00
2-6 Dixie Walker ... 275.00
2-7 Stan Musial ... 300.00
2-8 Famous Ring Champions of All Time ... 275.00
2-9 List of War Year Rookies ... 300.00
2-10 Connie Mack ... 275.00
2-11 Winning Basketball Plays ... 250.00
2-12 Eddie Gottlieb ... 250.00
3-1 Bill Conn ... 250.00
3-2 Philadelphia Athletics ... 200.00
3-3 Leo Durocher ... 250.00
3-4 Rudy Dusek ... 200.00
3-5 Ernie Pyle ... 200.00
3-6 Bowling with Ned Day ... 200.00
3-7 Return of the Mighty (Home from War);Joe DiMaggio(c) ... 400.00
3-8 Conn V:Louis ... 300.00
3-9 Reuben Shark ... 200.00
3-10 BP,BP(c),Don "Dopey" Dillock ... 200.00
3-11 BP,BP(c),Death Scores a Touchdown ... 200.00
3-12 Red Sox V:Senators ... 200.00
4-1 Spring Training in Full Spring ... 200.00
4-2 BP,BP(c),How to Pitch 'Em Where They Can't Hit 'Em ... 200.00
4-3 BP,BP(c),1947 Super Stars ... 235.00
4-4 BP,BP(c),Get Ready for the Olympics ... 235.00
4-5 BP,BP,(c),Hugh Casey ... 200.00
4-6 BP,BP(c),Phantom Phil Hergesheimer ... 200.00
4-7 BP,BP(c),How to Bowl Better 200.00
4-8 Tips on the Big Fight ... 235.00
4-9 BP,BP(c),Bill McCahan ... 200.00
4-10 BP,BP(c),Great Football Plays ... 200.00
4-11 BP,BP(c),Football ... 200.00
4-12 BP,BP(c),Basketball ... 200.00
5-1 Satchel Paige ... 250.00
5-2 History of Boxing ... 200.00

TRUE STORIES OF ROMANCE

Fawcett Publications, 1950

1 Ph(c) ... 150.00
2 Ph(c) ... 100.00
3 Ph(c) ... 100.00

TRUE SWEETHEART SECRETS

Fawcett Publications, May, 1950

1 Debbie Reynolds,Ph(c) ... 150.00
2 WW ... 250.00
3 BD ... 125.00
4 BD ... 125.00
5 BD ... 125.00
6 thru 11 ... @125.00

TRUE TALES OF ROMANCE

Fawcett Publications

4 Ph(c) ... 100.00

TRUE-TO-LIFE ROMANCES

Star Publications, Nov.–Dec., 1949

3 LbC(c),GlennFord/JanetLeigh . 300.00
4 LbC(c) ... 200.00
5 LbC(c) ... 200.00
6 LbC(c) ... 200.00
7 LbC(c) ... 200.00
8 LbC(c) ... 200.00
9 LbC(c) ... 200.00
10 LbC(c) ... 200.00
11 LbC(c) ... 200.00
12 LbC(c) ... 200.00
13 LbC(c),JyD ... 200.00
14 LbC(c),JyD ... 200.00
15 LbC(c),WW,JyD ... 250.00
16 LbC(c),WW,JyD ... 250.00
17 LbC(c),JyD ... 175.00
18 LbC(c),JyD ... 175.00
19 LbC(c),JyD ... 175.00
20 LbC(c),JyD ... 175.00
21 LbC(c),JyD ... 175.00
22 LbC(c) ... 175.00
23 LbC(c) ... 175.00

TRUE WAR EXPERIENCES

Harvey Publications, 1952

1 ... 150.00
2 thru 4 ... @100.00

TRUE WAR ROMANCES

Comic Magazines, Inc. (Quality Comics), Sept., 1952

1 Ph(c) ... 150.00
2 ... 125.00
3 thru 10 ... @100.00
11 thru 20 ... @100.00
21 Comics Code ... 100.00

Becomes:

EXOTIC ROMANCES

Oct., 1955

22 ... 125.00
23 thru 26 ... @100.00
27 MB ... 150.00

True Western #1
© Marvel Comics Group

Turok, Son of Stone #15
© Dell Publishing Co.

Two-Fisted Tales #18
© E.C. Comics

28 MB. 125.00
29 . . . . 100.00
30 MB. 125.00
31 MB. 150.00

TRUE WESTERN

Marvel, Dec., 1949

1 Ph(c),Billy the Kid 200.00
2 Ph(c),Alan Ladd,Badmen vs. Lawmen 250.00

Becomes:

TRUE ADVENTURES

3 BP,MSy,Boss of Black Devil . . 200.00

Becomes:

MEN'S ADVENTURES

4 AvB,He Called me a Coward . 400.00
5 AvB,Brother Act 225.00
6 AvB,Heat of Battle 200.00
7 AvB,The Walking Death 200.00
8 AvB,RH,Journey Into Death . . 200.00
9 AvB,Bullets,Blades and Death 125.00
10 BEv,The Education of Thomas Dillon 125.00
11 Death of A Soldier 125.00
12 Firing Squad 125.00
13 RH(c),The Three Stripes. 125.00
14 GC,BEv,Steel Coffin 125.00
15 JMn(c). 125.00
16 . . . . 125.00
17 . . . . 125.00
18 . . . . 125.00
19 JRo 125.00
20 GC,RH(c) 125.00
21 BEv(c),JSt,The Eye of Man . . 225.00
22 BEv,JR,Mark of the Witch. . . . 225.00
23 BEv(c),RC,The Wrong Body. . 225.00
24 RH,JMn,GT,Torture Master. . . 225.00
25 SSh(c),Who Shrinks My Head 400.00
26 Midnight in the Morgue 225.00
27 BP,CBu(c),A:Capt.America, Human Torch,Sub-Mariner . 1,400.00
28 BEv,A:Capt.America,Human Torch, Sub-Mariner,July, 1954. . . . 1,300.00

TUBBY
See: MARGE'S TUBBY

TUFFY

Best Books, Inc.
(Standard Comics) 1949

5 . . . . 125.00
6 true 9 . . . . @100.00

TUROK, SON OF STONE

Dell Publishing Co., Dec., 1954

(1) *see Dell Four Color #596*
(2) *see Dell Four Color #656*
3 Cavemen 350.00
4 & 5 . . . . @300.00
6 & 7 . . . . @250.00
8 Dinosaur, Lost Valley 275.00
9 thru 16 . . . . @150.00
17 Prehistoric Pigmies 175.00
18 thru 29. . . . . @125.00

TV SCREEN CARTOONS
(see REAL SCREEN COMICS)

TV TEENS

Charlton Comics, 1954

1 Ozzie & Babs. 125.00
2 . . . . 100.00
3 . . . . 100.00
4 . . . . 100.00
5 . . . . 100.00
6 Don Winslow 100.00
7 B:Mopsy. 100.00
8 . . . . 100.00
9 . . . . 100.00
10 . . . . 100.00
11 thru 13 . . . . @100.00

TWEETY AND SYLVESTER

Dell Publishing Co., June, 1952

(1) *see Dell Four Color #406*
(2) *see Dell Four Color #489*
(3) *see Dell Four Color #524*
4 thru 20 . . . . @125.00
21 thru 37. . . . . @100.00

TWINKLE COMICS

Spotlight Publications, May, 1945

1 Humor Format 300.00

TWO-BIT WACKY WOODPECKER

Toby Press, 1952

1 . . . . 150.00
2 . . . . 120.00
3 . . . . 120.00

TWO-FISTED TALES

Fables Publications (E.C. Comics), Nov.–Dec., 1950–March, 1955

18 JCr,WW,JSe,HK(a&c) 2,000.00
19 JCr,WW,JSe,HK(a&c) 1,500.00
20 JDa,WW,JSe,HK(a&c) 900.00
21 JDa,WW,JSe,HK(a&c) 800.00
22 JDa,WW,JSe,HK(a&c) 800.00
23 JDa,WW,JSe,HK(a&c) 600.00
24 JDa,WW,JSe,HK(a&c) 500.00
25 JDa,WW,JSe,HK(a&c) 500.00
26 JDa,JSe,HK(c),Action at the Changing Reservoir. 400.00
27 JDa,JSe,HK(c) 400.00
28 JDa,JSe,HK(c) 400.00
29 JDa,JSe,HK(c) 450.00
30 JSe,JDa(a&c) 450.00
31 JDa,JSe,HK(c),Civil War Story. 400.00
32 JDa,JKu,WW(c) 400.00
33 JDa,JKu,WW(c),A-Bomb 500.00
34 JSe,JDa(a&c) 400.00
35 JSe,JDa(a&c),Civil War Story. 400.00
36 JDa,JSe(a&c),A Difference of Opinion. 500.00
37 JSe(a&c),Bugles & Battle Cries 500.00
38 JSe(a&c). 500.00
39 JSe(a&c). 500.00
40 JDa,JSe,GE(a&c) 550.00
41 JSe,GE,JDa(c) 500.00
Ann. 1952 (#1) 1,750.00
Ann. 1953 (#2) JDa(c) 1,400.00

2-GUN KID
See: BILLY BUCKSKIN

TWO-GUN KID

Marvel Atlas, March, 1948

1 SSh,B:Two-Gun Kid,The Sheriff 1,400.00
2 Killers of Outlaw City 600.00
3 RH,SSh,A:Annie Oakley 400.00
4 RH,A:Black Rider 400.00
5 RH 500.00
6 . . . . 400.00
7 RH,Brand of a Killer 400.00
8 Secret of the Castle of Slaves 400.00
9 JSe,SSh,Trapped in Hidden Valley, A:Black Rider 400.00

 All comics prices listed are for *Near Mint* condition.

Two-Gun Kid #52
© Marvel Comics Group

Uncanny Tales #48
© Marvel Comics Group

Uncle Scrooge #4
© Walt Disney

10 JK(c),The Horrible Hermit of Hidden Mesa 400.00
11 JMn(c),GT,A:Black Rider. 250.00
12 JMn(c),GT,A:Black Rider 250.00
13 . . . . 225.00
14 . . . . 225.00
15 thru 24. . . . . @225.00
25 AW,JMn. 225.00
26 DAy,JMn 150.00
27 DAy,JMn 150.00
28 JMn. 150.00
29 . . . . 150.00
30 AW 150.00
31 thru 44. . . . . @125.00
45 JDa 100.00
46 JDa 100.00
47 JDa 100.00
48 . . . . 100.00
49 JMn. 100.00
50 . . . . 100.00
51 AW 100.00
52 thru 59. . . . . @100.00
60 DAy,New O:Two-Gun Kid . . . 125.00

TWO GUN WESTERN
See: CASEY–CRIME PHOTOGRAPHER

TWO-GUN WESTERN
See: BILLY BUCKSKIN

UNCANNY TALES
Marvel Atlas, June, 1952

1 RH,While the City Sleeps . . 1,200.00
2 JMn,BEv 600.00
3 Escape to What 500.00
4 JMn,Nobody's Fool 500.00
5 Fear 500.00
6 He Lurks in the Shadows 550.00
7 BEv,Kill,Clown,Kill 550.00
8 JMn,Bring Back My Face. 450.00
9 BEv,RC,The Executioner. 450.00
10 JMn,RH(c),JR,The Man Who Came Back To Life 450.00
11 GC,The Man Who Changed . . 350.00
12 BP,BEv,Bertha Gets Buried . . 350.00
13 RH,Scared Out of His Skin. . . 350.00
14 RH,TLw,Victims of Vonntor. . . 350.00
15 RA,JSt,The Man Who Saw Death. 350.00
16 JMn,GC,Zombie at Large 350.00
17 GC,TLw,I Live With Corpses . 350.00
18 JF,BP,Clock Face(c) 350.00
19 DBr,RKr,TLw,The Man Who Died Again. 350.00
20 DBr,Ted's Head 350.00
21 . . . . 300.00
22 DAy. 300.00
23 TLw. 300.00
24 . . . . 300.00
25 MSy. 300.00
26 Spider-Man prototype story . . 400.00
27 RA,TLw. 275.00
28 TLw. 275.00
29 JMn. 200.00
30 . . . . 200.00
31 . . . . 200.00
32 BEv. 200.00
33 . . . . 200.00
34 BP. 200.00
35 TLw,JMn. 200.00
36 BP,BEv. 200.00
37 MD 200.00
38 BP. 200.00
39 BEv. 200.00
40 . . . . 200.00
41 . . . . 200.00
42 MD 225.00
43 . . . . 200.00
44 . . . . 200.00
45 MD 200.00
46 GM 200.00
47 TSe 200.00
48 BEv. 200.00
49 JO 200.00
50 JO 200.00
51 GM 225.00
52 GC. 200.00
53 JO,AT 200.00
54 . . . . 220.00
55 . . . . 200.00
56 Sept., 1957. . . . . 225.00

UNCLE CHARLIE'S FABLES
Lev Gleason Publications, Jan., 1952

1 CBi(c),Ph(c) 200.00
2 BF,CBi(c),Ph(c) 125.00
3 CBi(c),Ph(c) 135.00
4 CBi(c),Ph(c) 135.00
5 CBi,Ph(c),Sept., 1952 . . . . 135.00

UNCLE JOE'S FUNNIES
Centaur Publications, 1938

1 BEv,Puzzles & Comics 650.00

UNCLE MILTY
Victoria Publications (True Cross Comic), 1950

1 Milton Berle 600.00
2 . . . . 400.00
3 . . . . 350.00
4 . . . . 325.00

UNCLE SAM
See: BLACKHAWK

UNCLE SCROOGE
Dell Publishing Co., March, 1952

(1) *see Dell Four Color #386*
(2) *see Dell Four Color #456*
(3) *see Dell Four Color #495*
4 Gladstone Album #11 . . . . 600.00
5 Gladstone Special 450.00
6 . . . . 350.00
7 CB, Seven Cities of Cibola . . . 325.00
8 thru 10 . . . . @300.00
11 thru 23. . . . . @275.00
24 Christmas issue 275.00
25 thru 30. . . . . @250.00
31 thru 39. . . . . @200.00

UNDERWORLD
D.S. Publishing Co., Feb.–March, 1948

1 SMo(c),Violence 600.00
2 SMo(c),Electrocution 600.00
3 AMc,AMc(c),The Ancient Club 500.00
4 GrI,The Beer Baron Murder . . 450.00
5 GrI,The Postal Clue. 300.00
6 The Polka Dot Gang 250.00
7 Mono-The Master 250.00
8 The Double Tenth 250.00
9 Thrilling Stories of the Fight against Crime,June, 1953 . . 250.00

UNDERWORLD CRIME
Fawcett Publications, June, 1952

1 The Crime Army 500.00
2 Jailbreak 350.00
3 Microscope Murder 300.00
4 Death on the Docks 300.00
5 River of Blood 300.00
6 The Sky Pirates 300.00
7 Bondage & Torture(c) 500.00
8 and 9 June, 1953. . . . . @300.00

Un

United States Marines #3
© Magazine Enterprises

Unusual Tales #1
© Charlton Comics

U. S. A. Comics #4
© Marvel Comics Group

UNITED COMICS
See: FRITZI RITZ

UNITED STATES FIGHTING AIR FORCE
Superior Comics, Ltd., Sept., 1952

1 Coward's Courage 150.00
2 Clouds that Killed 125.00
3 Operation Decoy 100.00
4 thru 28 . . . . @100.00
29 Oct., 1959 . . . . 100.00

UNITED STATES MARINES
Wm. H. Wise/Magazine Ent/ Toby Press, 1943–52

N# MBi,MBi(c),Hellcat out of Heaven 200.00
2 MBi,Drama of Wake Island, Tojo 450.00
3 A Leatherneck Flame Thrower, Tojo. 350.00
4 MBi 125.00
5 BP 100.00
6 BP 100.00
7 BP 100.00
8 thru 11 . . . . @100.00

UNKEPT PROMISE
Legion of Truth, 1949

1 Anti:Alcoholic Drinking 100.00

UNKNOWN WORLDS
See: STRANGE STORIES FROM ANOTHER WORLD

UNSANE
See: HOLIDAY COMICS

UNSEEN, THE
Visual Editions (Standard Comics), 1952

5 ATh,The Hungry Lodger 500.00
6 JKa,MSy,Bayou Vengeance . . 350.00
7 JKz,MSy,Time is the Killer . . . 350.00
8 JKz,MSy,The Vengeance Vat . 300.00
9 JKz,MSy,Your Grave is Ready 350.00
10 JKz,MSy 350.00
11 JKz,MSy 300.00
12 ATh,GT,Till Death Do Us Part . 350.00
13 . . . . 250.00
14 . . . . 250.00
15 ATh,The Curse of the Undead!, July, 1954. . . . . 350.00

UNTAMED LOVE
Comic Magazines (Quality Comics Group), Jan., 1950

1 BWa(c),PGv. 300.00
2 Ph(c) 175.00
3 PGv, Ph(c) 200.00
4 Ph(c) 175.00
5 PGv, Ph(c) 200.00

UNUSUAL TALES
Charlton Comics, 1955–65

1 . . . . 300.00
2 . . . . 150.00
3 thru 5 . . . . @100.00
6 SD,SD(c) 225.00
7 SD,SD(c) 275.00
8 SD,SD(c) 275.00
9 SD,SD(c) 300.00
10 SD,SD(c). 325.00
11 SD 300.00
12 SD. 200.00
13 . . . . 125.00
14 SD. 200.00
15 SD,SD(c). 225.00
16 thru 20. . . . . @125.00
21 . . . . 100.00
22 SD. 150.00
23 . . . . 100.00
24 . . . . 100.00
25 thru 27 SD. . . . . @135.00
28 . . . . 100.00
29 SD. 125.00
30 thru 49. . . . . @100.00

U.S.A. COMICS
Marvel Timely, Aug., 1941

1 S&K(c),BW,AAv,SSh,Bondage(c), The Defender(c) 20,000.00
2 S&K(c),BW,SSh, Capt. Terror(c) 6,000.00
3 S&K(c),SSh,Capt.Terror(c) . . 4,000.00
4 SSh,Major Liberty 3,500.00
5 Hitler(c),O:AmericanAvenger 3,800.00
6 ASh(c),Capt.America(c) 4,000.00
7 BW,O:Marvel Boy 3,800.00
8 ASh(c),Capt.America (c). . . . 3,500.00
9 ASh(c),Bondage(c), Captain America 3,500.00
10 ASh(c),Bondage(c), Captain America 3,500.00
11 SSh(c),Bondage(c), Captain America 2,000.00
12 ASh(c),Capt.America 2,000.00
13 ASh(c),Capt.America 2,000.00
14 AyB(c),Capt.America 1,500.00
15 Capt.America 1,500.00
16 ASh(c),Bondage(c), Capt.America 1,500.00
17 Bondage(c),Capt.America . . 1,500.00

USA IS READY
Dell Publishing Co., 1941

1 Propaganda WWII 500.00

U.S. JONES
Fox Features Syndicate, Nov., 1941

1 Death Over the Airways 1,900.00
2 Nazi (c),Jan., 1942 . . . . 1,400.00

U.S. MARINES
See: A-1 COMICS

U.S. MARINES IN ACTION!
Avon Periodicals, Aug.–Dec., 1952

1 On Land,Sea & in the Air 125.00
2 The Killer Patrol 100.00
3 EK(c),Death Ridge. 100.00

U.S. PARATROOPS
Avon Periodicals, 1951

1 WW 200.00
2 EK 125.00
3 . . . . 100.00
4 thru 6 EK . . . . @125.00

U.S. TANK COMMANDOS
Avon Periodicals, June, 1952

1 EK(c),Fighting Daredevils of the USA 150.00

V... Comics #2
© Fox Features Syndicate

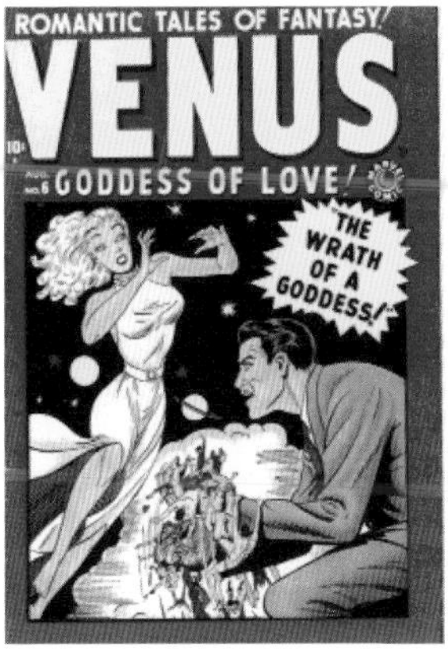

Venus #6
© Marvel Comics Group

Victory Comics #2
© Hillman Periodicals

2 EK(c) 100.00
3 EK,EK(c),Robot Armanda 100.00
4 EK,EK(c),March, 1953 . . . . . . 100.00

VALOR

E.C. Comics, March, 1955

1 AW,AT,WW,WW(c),Grl,BK 800.00
2 AW(c),AW,WWGrl,BK 700.00
3 AW,RC,BK,JOc(c) 500.00
4 WW(c),RC,Grl,BK,JO 500.00
5 WW(c),WW,AW,GE,Grl,BK . . . 450.00

VARIETY COMICS

Rural Home Publ./ Croyden Publ. Co., 1944

1 MvS,MvS(c),O:Capt, Valiant . . 300.00
2 MvS,MvS(c) 250.00
3 MvS,MvS(c) 200.00
4 . . . . 150.00
5 1946 . . . . 150.00

VAULT OF HORROR See: WAR AGAINST CRIME

V...COMICS

Fox Features Syndicate, Jan., 1942

1 V:V-Man, Nazi(c) 1,800.00
2 The Horror of the Dungeons, March, 1942 . . 1,400.00

VENUS

Marvel Atlas, Aug., 1948

1 B:Venus,Hedy Devine,HK,Hey Look 2,000.00
2 Venus(c) 1,300.00
3 Carnival(c) 1,400.00
4 Cupid(c).HK,Hey Look 1,400.00
5 Serenade(c) 1,400.00
6 SSh(c),Wrath of a Goddess, A:Loki 1,000.00
7 Romance that Could Not Be. 1,000.00
8 The Love Trap 1,000.00
9 Whom the Gods Destroy . . . 1,000.00
10 JMn,B:Science Fiction/Horror, Trapped On the Moon 1,300.00
11 RH,The End of the World. . . 1,500.00
12 GC,The Lost World 1,300.00
13 BEv,King o/t Living Dead . . . 1,300.00
14 BEv,The Fountain of Death . 1,300.00
15 BEv,The Empty Grave 1,300.00
16 BEv,Where Gargoyles Dwell 1,500.00
17 BEv,Tower of Death, Bondage(c). 1,300.00
18 BEv,Terror in the Tunnel . . . 1,300.00
19 BEv,PMo, Kiss Of Death . . . 1,300.00

VERI BEST SURE FIRE COMICS

Holyoke Publishing Co., 1945

1 . . . . 250.00

VERI BEST SURE SHOT COMICS

Holyoke Publishing Co., 1945

1 reprint Holyoke One-Shots . . . 500.00

VIC FLINT

St. John Publishing Co., Aug., 1948

1 ...Crime Buster 200.00
2 . . . . 175.00
3 . . . . 150.00
4 . . . . 150.00
5 April, 1949 . . . . 150.00

VIC FLINT

Argo Publ., 1956

1 . . . . 125.00
2 . . . . 100.00

VIC JORDAN

Civil Service Publications, April, 1945

1 Escape From a Nazi Prison . . 150.00

VICKY

Ace Magazines, 1948

N# Teenage 150.00
2 . . . . 125.00
3 . . . . 125.00
4 . . . . 125.00
5 A:Dotty 125.00

VIC TORRY AND HIS FLYING SAUCER

Fawcett Publications, 1950

1 Ph(c),Revealed at Last. 1,000.00

VICTORY COMICS

Hillman Periodicals, Aug., 1941

1 BEv,BEv(c),F:TheConqueror 4,200.00
2 BEv,BEv(c) 1,900.00
3 The Conqueror(c) 1,200.00
4 Dec., 1941 . . . . 1,100.00

VIC VERITY MAGAZINE

Vic Verity Publications, 1945

1 CCB,CCB(c),B:Vic Verity,Hot-Shot Galvan, Tom Travis . . . 250.00
2 CCB,CCB(c),Annual Classic Dance Recital 150.00
3 CCB 125.00
4 CCB,I:Boomer Young;The Bee-U-TiFul Weekend 125.00
5 CCB,Championship Baseball Game 125.00
6 CCB,High School Hero 125.00
7 CCB,CCB(c),F:Rocket Rex . . 125.00

VOODOO

Four Star Publ./Farrell/ Ajax Comics, May, 1952

1 MB,South Sea Girl. 800.00
2 MB 600.00
3 Face Stabbing 500.00
4 MB,Rendezvous 500.00
5 Ghoul For A Day,Nazi 350.00
6 The Weird Dead, Severed Head 400.00
7 Goodbye World 350.00
8 MB, Revenge 450.00
9 Will this thing Never Stew? . . . 350.00
10 Land of Shadows & Screams . 350.00
11 Human Harvest. 300.00
12 The Wazen Taper 300.00
13 Bondage(c),Caskets to Fit Everybody 325.00
14 Death Judges the Beauty Contest, Zombies . . . 300.00
15 Loose their Heads, Opium . . . 325.00
16 Fog Was Her Shroud 300.00
17 Apes Laughter,Electric Chair . 325.00
18 Astounding Fantasy 300.00
19 MB,Bondage(c); Destination Congo. 450.00
Ann.#1 100-pg. 1,250.00
Becomes:

Voodoo #12
© Ferrell Publications

Walt Disney's Comics and Stories #38
© Walt Disney

Walt Disney's Comics and Stories #100
© Walt Disney

VOODA
April, 1955

20 MB,MB(c),Echoes of an A-Bomb . . . 500.00
21 MB,MB(c),Trek of Danger . . . 400.00
22 MB,MB(c),The Sun Blew Away, Aug., 1955 . . . 400.00

WACKY DUCK
See: DOPEY DUCK

WALT DISNEY'S COMICS & STORIES
Dell Publishing Co.

N# 1943 dpt.store giveway . . . 750.00
N# 1945 X-mas giveaway . . . 350.00

WALT DISNEY'S COMICS & STORIES
Dell Publishing Co., Oct., 1940

1 (1940)FGu,Donald Duck & Mickey Mouse . . . 25,000.00
2 . . . 9,000.00
3 . . . 3,000.00
4 1st Huey, Dewey & Louie Christmas(c) . . . 2,500.00
4a Promo issue . . . 3,500.00
5 Goofy(c) . . . 1,700.00
6 . . . 1,500.00
7 . . . 1,500.00
8 Clarabelle Cow(c) . . . 1,500.00
9 . . . 1,500.00
10 . . . 1,500.00
11 2nd Huey,Louie,Dewey(c) . . 1,500.00
12 . . . 1,200.00
13 . . . 1,100.00
14 . . . 1,100.00
15 3 Little Kittens . . . 1,000.00
16 3 Little Pigs . . . 1,000.00
17 The Ugly Ducklings . . . 1,000.00
18 . . . 850.00
19 . . . 800.00
20 . . . 800.00
21 . . . 850.00
22 . . . 750.00
23 . . . 750.00
24 Flying Gauchito . . . 700.00
25 . . . 700.00
26 . . . 700.00
27 Jose Carioca . . . 700.00
28 . . . 750.00
29 . . . 700.00
30 . . . 700.00
31 CB; Donald Duck . . . 6,000.00
32 CB . . . 2,500.00
33 CB . . . 1,700.00
34 CB;WK; Gremlins . . . 1,500.00
35 CB;WK; Gremlins . . . 1,500.00
36 CB;WK; Gremlins . . . 1,500.00
37 CB;WK; Gremlins . . . 800.00
38 CB;WK; Gremlins . . . 1,000.00
39 CB;WK; Gremlins, X-mas . . 1,000.00
40 CB;WK; Gremlins . . . 1,000.00
41 CB;WK; Gremlins . . . 900.00
42 CB . . . 800.00
43 CB,Seven Dwarfs . . . 800.00
44 CB . . . 800.00
45 CB,Nazis in stories . . . 800.00
46 CB,Nazis in stories . . . 800.00
47 CB,Nazis in stories . . . 800.00
48 CB,Nazis in stories . . . 800.00
49 CB,Nazis in stories . . . 800.00
50 CB,Nazis in stories . . . 800.00
51 CB,Christmas . . . 700.00
52 CB; Li'l Bad Wolf begins . . . 700.00
53 CB . . . 700.00
54 CB . . . 700.00
55 CB . . . 700.00
56 CB . . . 700.00
57 CB . . . 700.00
58 CB . . . 700.00
59 CB . . . 700.00
60 CB . . . 700.00
61 CB; Dumbo . . . 600.00
62 CB . . . 600.00
63 CB; Pinocchio . . . 600.00
64 CB; Pinocchio, X-mas . . . 600.00
65 CB; Pluto . . . 600.00
66 CB . . . 600.00
67 CB . . . 600.00
68 CB, Mickey Mouse . . . 600.00
69 CB . . . 600.00
70 CB . . . 600.00
71 CB . . . 500.00
72 CB . . . 500.00
73 CB . . . 500.00
74 CB . . . 500.00
75 CB; Brer Rabbit . . . 500.00
76 CB; Brer Rabbit, X-mas . . . 500.00
77 CB; Brer Rabbit . . . 500.00
78 CB . . . 500.00
79 CB . . . 500.00
80 CB . . . 500.00
81 CB . . . 500.00
82 CB;Bongo,Googy . . . 500.00
83 CB;Bongo . . . 500.00
84 CB;Bongo . . . 500.00
85 CB . . . 500.00
86 CB;Goofy & Agnes . . . 500.00
87 CB;Goofy & Agnes . . . 375.00
88 CB;Goofy & Agnes, I:Gladstone Gander . . . 500.00
89 CB;Goofy&Agnes,Chip'n'Dale 375.00
90 CB;Goofy & Agnes . . . 375.00
91 CB . . . 300.00
92 CB . . . 300.00
93 CB . . . 300.00
94 CB . . . 300.00
95 CB(c) . . . 300.00
96 Little Toot . . . 300.00
97 CB; Little Toot . . . 300.00
98 CB; Uncle Scrooge . . . 600.00
99 CB . . . 300.00
100 CB . . . 400.00
101 CB . . . 300.00
102 CB . . . 300.00
103 CB . . . 275.00
104 . . . 275.00
105 CB . . . 300.00
106 CB . . . 300.00
107 CB, Donald super-powers . . 500.00
108 . . . 275.00
109 . . . 275.00
110 CB . . . 300.00
111 CB . . . 300.00
112 CB; drugs . . . 400.00
113 CB . . . 300.00
114 CB . . . 300.00
115 WK(c) . . . 300.00
116 Dumbo . . . 150.00
117 . . . 150.00
118 . . . 150.00
119 . . . 150.00
120 . . . 150.00
121 Grandma Duck begins . . . 150.00
122 . . . 150.00
123 . . . 300.00
124 CB,Christmas . . . 250.00
125 CB;I:Junior Woodchucks . . . 400.00
126 CB . . . 450.00
127 CB . . . 250.00
128 CB . . . 250.00
129 CB . . . 250.00
130 CB . . . 250.00
131 CB . . . 250.00
132 CB A:Grandma Duck . . . 250.00
133 CB . . . 250.00
134 I:The Beagle Boys . . . 500.00
135 CB . . . 250.00
136 CB . . . 250.00
137 CB . . . 250.00
138 CB,Scrooge & Money . . . 350.00
139 CB . . . 250.00

Walt Disney's Comics and Stories #146
© Walt Disney

Walt Disney's Dell Giant Silly Symphonies #1 © Walt Disney

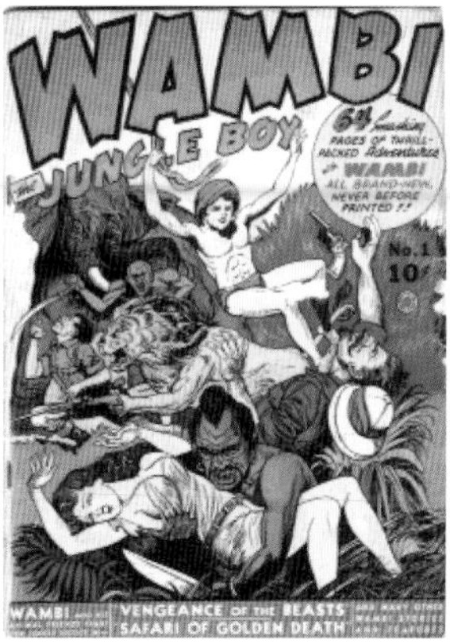

Wambi Jungle Boy #1
© Fiction House

140 CB; I:Gyro Gearloose 500.00
141 CB. 200.00
142 CB. 200.00
143 CB; Little Hiawatha 200.00
144 CB; Little Hiawatha 200.00
145 CB; Little Hiawatha 200.00
146 CB; Little Hiawatha 200.00
147 CB; Little Hiawatha 200.00
148 CB; Little Hiawatha 200.00
149 CB; Little Hiawatha 200.00
150 CB; Little Hiawatha 200.00
151 CB; Little Hiawatha 200.00
152 thru 200 CB. . . . . @150.00
201 thru 203 CB. . . . . @125.00
204 CB, Chip 'n' Dale & Scamp. . 125.00
205 thru 240 CB. . . . . @125.00
241 CB; Dumbo x-over 125.00
242 CB. 125.00
243 CB. 125.00
244 CB. 125.00
245 CB. 125.00
246 CB. 125.00
247 thru 255 CB;GyroGearloose . . . . . . @125.00
256 thru 263 CB;Ludwig Von Drake & Gearloose . . . . . . @125.00

WALT DISNEY'S DELL GIANT EDITIONS

Dell Publishing Co.

1 CB,W.Disney'sXmas Parade('49) 1,200.00
2 CB,W.Disney'sXmas Parade('50). 1,000.00
3 W.Disney'sXmas Parade('51) . 300.00
4 W.Disney'sXmas Parade('52) . 250.00
5 W.Disney'sXmas Parade('53) . 250.00
6 W.Disney'sXmas Parade('54) . 250.00
7 W.Disney'sXmas Parade('55) . 250.00
8 CB,W.Disney'sXmas Parade('56) 500.00
9 CB,W.Disney'sXmas Parade('57) 500.00
1 CB,W.Disney's Christmas in Disneyland (1957). 600.00
1 CB,W.Disney's Disneyland Birthday Party (1958) 600.00
1 W.Disney's Donald and Mickey in Disneyland (1958) 250.00
1 W.Disney's Donald Duck Beach Party (1954) 300.00
2 W.Disney's Donald Duck Beach Party (1955) 250.00
3 W.Disney's Donald Duck Beach Party (1956) 250.00
4 W.Disney's Donald Duck Beach Party (1957) 250.00
5 W.Disney's Donald Duck Beach Party (1958) 250.00
6 W.Disney's Donald Duck Beach Party (1959) 250.00
1 W.Disney's Donald Duck Fun Book (1954). 1,200.00
2 W.Disney's Donald Duck Fun Book (1954). 1,100.00
1 W.Disney's Donald Duck in Disneyland (1955) 275.00
1 W.Disney's Huey, Dewey and Louie (1958). 175.00
1 W.Disney's DavyCrockett('55) . 350.00
1 W.Disney's Lady and the Tramp (1955). 400.00
1 CB,W.Disney's Mickey Mouse Almanac (1957). 600.00
1 W.Disney's Mickey Mouse Birthday Party (1953) 700.00
1 W.Disney's Mickey Mouse Club Parade (1955). 600.00
1 W.Disney's Mickey Mouse in Fantasyland (1957) 275.00
1 W.Disney's Mickey Mouse in Frontierland (1956) 275.00
1 W.Disney's Summer Fun('58) . 275.00
2 CB,W.Disney'sSummer Fun('59). 275.00
1 W.Disney's Peter Pan Treasure Chest (1953) 2,200.00
1 Disney Silly Symphonies('52) . 600.00
2 Disney Silly Symphonies('53) . 500.00
3 Disney Silly Symphonies('54) . 450.00
4 Disney Silly Symphonies('54) . 450.00
5 Disney Silly Symphonies('55) . 400.00
6 Disney Silly Symphonies('56) . 400.00
7 Disney Silly Symphonies('57) . 400.00
8 Disney Silly Symphonies('58) . 400.00
9 Disney Silly Symphonies('59) . 400.00
1 Disney SleepingBeauty('59) . . 600.00
1 CB,W.Disney's Uncle Scrooge Goes to Disneyland (1957) . . 550.00
1 W.Disney's Vacation in Disneyland (1958). 250.00
1 CB,Disney's Vacation Parade('50). 1,700.00
2 Disney'sVacation Parade('51) . 600.00
3 Disney'sVacation Parade('52) . 300.00
4 Disney'sVacation Parade('53) . 300.00
5 Disney'sVacation Parade('54) . 300.00
6 Disney's Picnic Party (1955) . . 250.00
7 Disney's Picnic Party (1956) . . 250.00
8 CB,Disney's Picnic Party (1957). 500.00

WALT DISNEY'S DELL JUNIOR TREASURY

1 W.Disney's Alice in Wonderland (1955) 250.00

WALT DISNEY PRESENTS

Dell Publishing Co., June–Aug., 1952

1 Ph(c), Four Color. 200.00
2 Ph(c) 150.00
3 Ph(c) 150.00
4 Ph(c) 150.00
5 and 6 Ph(c) . . . . @150.00

WAMBI JUNGLE BOY

Fiction House Magazines, Spring, 1942–Winter, 1952

1 HcK,HcK(c),Vengence of the Beasts 1,200.00
2 HcK,HcK(c),Lair of the Killer Rajah 650.00
3 HcK,HcK(c) 500.00
4 HcK,HcK(c),The Valley of the Whispering Drums 250.00
5 HcK,HcK(c),SwamplandSafari. 250.00
6 Taming of the Tigress 225.00
7 Duel of the Congo Kings 225.00
8 AB(c),Friend of the Animals . . 225.00
9 Quest of the Devils Juju 225.00
10 Friend of the Animals 200.00
11 . . . . 200.00
12 Curse of the Jungle Jewels . . 200.00
13 New Adventures of Wambi . . . 175.00
14 . . . . 175.00
15 The Leopard Legions 175.00
16 . . . . 175.00
17 Beware Bwana!. 175.00
18 Ogg the Great Bull Ape. 175.00

WANTED COMICS

Toytown Comics/ Orbit Publications, Sept.–Oct., 1947

9 Victor Everhart. 250.00
10 Carlo Banone 150.00
11 Dwight Band 150.00
12 Ralph Roe. 165.00

Wanted Comics #16
© Toytown Comics

War Against Crime #9
© E. C. Comics

The Vault of Horror #35
© E. C. Comics

13 James Spencer;Drug 175.00
14 John "Jiggs" Sullivan;Drug . . . 175.00
15 Harry Dunlap;Drug 125.00
16 Jack Parisi;Drug 135.00
17 Herber Ayers;Drug 135.00
18 Satan's Cigarettes;Drug 250.00
19 Jackson Stringer 125.00
20 George Morgan 125.00
21 BK,Paul Wilson 135.00
22 Strong violence 135.00
23 George Elmo Wells 125.00
24 BK,Bruce Cornett;Drug 135.00
25 Henry Anger 125.00
26 John Wormly 125.00
27 Death Always Knocks Twice . . 125.00
28 Paul H. Payton 125.00
29 Hangmans Holiday 125.00
30 George Lee 125.00
31 M Consolo 125.00
32 William Davis 125.00
33 The Web of Davis 125.00
34 Dead End 125.00
35 Glen Roy Wright 125.00
36 SSh,SSh(c),Bernard Lee
Thomas 100.00
37 SSh,SSh(c),Joseph M. Moore 100.00
38 SSh,SSh(c) 100.00
39 The Horror Weed;Drug 175.00
40 . . . . 100.00
41 . . . . 100.00
42 . . . . 100.00
43 . . . . 100.00
44 . . . . 100.00
45 Killers on the Loose;Drug 125.00
46 Charles Edward Crews 100.00
47 . . . . 100.00
48 SSh,SSh(c) 100.00
49 . . . . 100.00
50 JB(c),Make Way for Murder . . 150.00
51 JB(c),Dope Addict on a
Holiday of Murder;Drug 135.00
52 The Cult of Killers;
Classic Drug 135.00
53 April, 1953 . . . . 100.00

WAR ACTION

Marvel Atlas, April, 1952

1 JMn,RH,War Stories, Six Dead
Men 250.00
2 GT 125.00
3 Invasion in Korea 100.00
4 thru 10 . . . . @100.00
11 and 12 . . . . @125.00
13 BK 125.00
14 Rangers Strike,June, 1953 . . . 100.00

WAR ADVENTURES

Marvel Atlas, Jan., 1952

1 GT,Battle Fatigue 200.00
2 The Story of a Slaughter 125.00
3 JRo 100.00
4 RH(c) 100.00
5 RH,Violent(c) 100.00
6 Stand or Die 100.00
7 JMn(c) 100.00
8 BK 125.00
9 RH(c) 100.00
10 JRo(c),Attack at Dawn 100.00
11 Red Trap 100.00
12 . . . . 100.00
13 RH(c),The Commies Strike
Feb., 1953 . . . . 100.00

WAR AGAINST CRIME

L.L. Publishing Co. (E.C. Comics), Spring, 1948

1 Grl, Stories from Police 1,000.00
2 Grl,Guilty of Murder 700.00
3 JCr(c) 700.00
4 AF,JCr(c) 600.00
5 JCr(c) 600.00
6 AF,JCr(c) 600.00
7 AF,JCr(c) 600.00
8 AF,JCr(c) 600.00
9 AF,JCr(c),The Kid 600.00
10 JCr(c),I:Vault Keeper 2,800.00
11 JCr(c) 1,600.00
Becomes:

VAULT OF HORROR, THE

April–May, 1950–Jan., 1955

12 AF,JCr(a&c),Wax Museum . . 6,700.00
13 AF,WW,JCr(c),Grl,Drug 2,500.00
14 AF,WW,JCr(c),Grl 2,500.00
15 AF,JCr(a&c),Grl,JKa 2,500.00
16 Grl,JKa,JCr(a&c) 1,800.00
17 JDa,Grl,JKa,JCr(a&c) 1,800.00
18 JDa,Grl,JKa,JCr(a&c) 1,500.00
19 JDa,Grl,JKa,JCr(a&c) 1,500.00
20 JDa,Grl,JKa,JCr(a&c) 1,600.00
21 JDa,Grl,JKa,JCr(a&c) 1,600.00
22 JDa,JKa,JCr(a&c) 1,600.00
23 JDa,Grl,JCr(a&c) 1,600.00
24 JDa,Grl,JO,JCr(a&c) 1,600.00
25 JDa,Grl,JKa,JCr(a&c) 1,600.00
26 JDa,Grl,JCr(a&c) 1,200.00
27 JDa,Grl,GE,JCr(a&c) 1,500.00
28 JDa,Grl,JCr(a&c) 1,500.00
29 JDa,Grl,JKa,JCr(a&c),
Bradbury Adapt. 1,500.00
30 JDa,Grl,JCr(a&c) 1,500.00
31 JDa,Grl,JCr(a&c),
Bradbury Adapt. 1,200.00
32 JDa,Grl,JCr(a&c) 1,200.00
33 JDa,Grl,RC,JCr(c) 1,200.00
34 JDa,Grl,RC,JCr(a&c) 1,200.00
35 JDa,Grl,JCr(a&c),X-mas . . . 1,200.00
36 JDa,Grl,BK,JCr(a&c),Drug . . 1,200.00
37 JDa,Grl,AW,JCr(a&c)
Hanging 1,200.00
38 JDa,Grl,BK,JCr(a&c) 1,200.00
39 Grl,BK,RC,JCr(a&c)
Bondage(c) 1,200.00
40 Grl,BK,JO,JCr(a&c) 1,400.00

WAR BATTLES

Harvey Publications, Feb., 1952

1 BP,Devils of the Deep 175.00
2 BP,A Present From Benny . . . 125.00
3 BP 100.00
4 . . . . 100.00
5 . . . . 100.00
6 HN 100.00
7 BP 125.00
8 . . . . 100.00
9 Dec., 1953 . . . . 100.00

WAR BIRDS

Fiction House Magazines, 1952

1 Willie the Washout 175.00
2 Mystery MIGs of Kwanjamu . . 110.00
3 thru 6 . . . . @100.00
7 Winter, 1953,Across the
Wild Yalu 100.00

WAR COMBAT

Marvel Atlas, March, 1952

1 JMn,Death of Platoon Leader . 175.00
2 . . . . 125.00
3 JMn(c) 100.00
4 JMn(c) 100.00
5 The Red Hordes 100.00
Becomes:

COMBAT CASEY

6 BEv,Combat Casey cont 175.00
7 . . . . 125.00
8 JMn(c) 100.00
9 . . . . 100.00
10 RH(c) 125.00
11 . . . . 100.00
12 . . . . 100.00
13 thru 19 . . . . @125.00
20 . . . . 100.00

War Comics #2
© Marvel Comics Group

War Heroes #5
© Ace Magazines

Wartime Romances #16
© St. John Publishing Co.

21 thru 33 . . . . @100.00
34 July, 1957 . . . . 100.00

WAR COMICS

Dell Publishing Co., May, 1940

1 AMc,Sky Hawk 800.00
2 O:Greg Gildam 450.00
3 . . . . 350.00
4 O:Night Devils 400.00

WAR COMICS

Marvel Atlas, Dec., 1950

1 You Only Die Twice 300.00
2 Infantry's War 150.00
3 . . . . 125.00
4 GC,The General Said Nuts . . 125.00
5 . . . . 125.00
6 The Deadly Decision of General Kwang 125.00
7 RH,JMn 125.00
8 RH,No Survivors 125.00
9 RH,JMn 125.00
10 . . . . 125.00
11 Flame thrower 135.00
12 thru 21 . . . . @100.00
22 . . . . 100.00
23 thru 37 . . . . @100.00
38 JKu 125.00
39 . . . . 100.00
40 . . . . 100.00
41 . . . . 100.00
42 JO 100.00
43 AT,MD 125.00
44 . . . . 100.00
45 . . . . 100.00
46 RC 125.00
47 . . . . 100.00
48 MD,JO 100.00
49 Sept., 1957 . . . . 125.00

WARFRONT

Fighting Forces Publ./ Harvey Publications

1 Korean War 200.00
2 . . . . 150.00
3 . . . . 125.00
4 . . . . 125.00
5 . . . . 125.00
6 thru 10 . . . . @125.00
11 thru 21 . . . . @100.00
22 HN 125.00
23 thru 33 . . . . @100.00

34 JK 100.00
35 . . . . 100.00

WAR FURY

Comic Media/Harwell, 1952

1 DH,RP,hole in head 300.00
2 Violent 150.00
3 Violent 150.00
4 PMo,Violent 150.00

WAR HEROES

Dell Publishing Co., July–Sept., 1942

1 Gen. Douglas MacArthur (c) . . 400.00
2 . . . . 300.00
3 Pro-Soviet 250.00
4 A:Gremlins 350.00
5 . . . . 250.00
6 . . . . 200.00
7 . . . . 200.00
8 thru 11 . . . . @200.00

WAR HEROES

Ace Magazines, May, 1952

1 Always Comin' 150.00
2 LC,The Last Red Tank 125.00
3 You Got it 100.00
4 A Red Patrol 100.00
5 Hustle it Up 100.00
6 LC,Hang on Pal 125.00
7 LC 125.00
8 LC, April, 1953 . . . . 125.00

WARPATH

Key Publications/ Stanmore, Nov., 1954

1 Red Men Raid 125.00
2 AH(c),Braves Battle 100.00
3 April, 1955 . . . . 100.00

WARRIOR COMICS

H.C. Blackerby, 1944

1 Ironman wing Brady 400.00

WAR REPORT

Excellent Publ. (Ajax/Farrell Publ.), 1952

1 . . . . 150.00
2 Burning bodies 250.00

3 . . . . 125.00
4 . . . . 125.00
5 . . . . 125.00

WAR SHIPS

Dell Publishing Co., 1942

1 AMc 200.00

WAR STORIES

Dell Publishing Co., 1942

5 O:The Whistler 300.00
6 A:Night Devils 250.00
7 A:Night Devils 250.00
8 A:Night Devils 250.00

WARTIME ROMANCES

St. John Publishing Co., July, 1951

1 MB(c),MB 400.00
2 MB(c),MB 300.00
3 MB(c),MB 250.00
4 MB(c),MB 250.00
5 MB(c),MB 225.00
6 MB(c),MB 250.00
7 MB(c),MB 225.00
8 MB(c),MB 225.00
9 MB(c),MB 200.00
10 MB(c),MB 200.00
11 MB(c),MB 200.00
12 MB(c),MB 200.00
13 MB(c) 100.00
14 MB(c) 100.00
15 MB(c) 100.00
16 MB(c),MB 175.00
17 MB(c) 100.00
18 MB(c),MB 175.00

WAR VICTORY COMICS

U.S. Treasury/War Victory/ Harvey Publ., Summer, 1942

1 Savings Bond Promo with Top Syndicated Cartoonists, benefit USO 500.00

Becomes:

WAR VICTORY ADVENTURES

Summer, 1942

2 BP,2nd Front Comics 300.00
3 BP,F:Capt Cross of the Red Cross 250.00

Web of Mystery #7
© Ace Magazines

The Weekender, Vol. 2 #1
© Rucker Publishing Co.

Weird Comics #20
© Fox Features Syndicate

WASHABLE JONES AND THE SHMOO

Toby Press Publ., 1953

1 Super Shmoo . . . 225.00

WEB OF EVIL

Comic Magazines, Inc. (Quality Comics Group), Nov., 1952

1 Custodian of the Dead . . . 750.00
2 JCo,Hangmans Horror . . . 500.00
3 JCo . . . 500.00
4 JCo(a&c),Monsters of the Mist . . . 500.00
5 JCo(a&c),The Man who Died Twice,Electric Chair(c) . . . 600.00
6 JCo(a&c),Orgy of Death . . . 500.00
7 JCo(a&c),The Strangling Hands . . . 500.00
8 JCo,Flaming Vengeance . . . 450.00
9 JCo,The Monster in Flesh . . . 450.00
10 JCo,Brain that Wouldn't Die . . 450.00
11 JCo,Buried Alive . . . 450.00
12 Phantom Killer . . . 300.00
13 Demon Inferno . . . 300.00
14 RC(c),The Monster Genie . . . 300.00
15 Crypts of Horror . . . 300.00
16 Hamlet of Horror . . . 300.00
17 Terror in Chinatown, Drug . . . 325.00
18 Scared to Death,Acid Face . . . 300.00
19 Demon of the Pit . . . 275.00
20 Man Made Terror . . . 275.00
21 Dec., 1954, Death's Ambush . 275.00

WEB OF MYSTERY

A.A. Wyn Publ. (Ace Magazines), Feb., 1951

1 MSy,Venom of the Vampires . 700.00
2 MSy,Legacy of the Accursed . 350.00
3 MSy,The Violin Curse . . . 300.00
4 GC . . . 300.00
5 . . . 300.00
6 LC . . . 300.00
7 MSy . . . 300.00
8 LC,LC(c),MSy,The Haunt of Death Lake . . . 300.00
9 LC,LC(c) . . . 300.00
10 . . . 300.00
11 MSy . . . 300.00
12 LC . . . 275.00
13 LC,LC(c)Surrealist . . . 275.00
14 MSy . . . 275.00
15 . . . 275.00
16 . . . 275.00
17 LC,LC(c) . . . 275.00
18 LC . . . 275.00
19 LC . . . 275.00
20 LC, Beyond . . . 275.00
21 MSy . . . 275.00
22 . . . 275.00
23 . . . 275.00
24 LC . . . 275.00
25 LC . . . 275.00
26 . . . 275.00
27 LC, Beyond . . . 275.00
28 RP,1st Comics Code issue . . . 200.00
29 MSy,Sept., 1955 . . . 200.00

WEDDING BELLS

Quality Comics Group, Feb., 1954

1 OW . . . 175.00
2 . . . 125.00
3 . . . 125.00
4 . . . 125.00
5 . . . 125.00
6 . . . 125.00
7 . . . 125.00
8 . . . 125.00
9 Comics Code . . . 125.00
10 BWa . . . 200.00
11 . . . 100.00
12 . . . 100.00
13 . . . 100.00
14 . . . 100.00
15 MB(c) . . . 100.00
16 MB(c),MB . . . 150.00
17 . . . 100.00
18 MB . . . 125.00
19 MB . . . 125.00

WEEKENDER, THE

Rucker Publishing Co., Sept., 1945

1-1 rep.(c), As Zip . . . 175.00
1-2 thru 1-4 . . . @175.00
2-1 rep.(c), As Dynamic . . . 200.00
2-2 Jco,rep.(c), As Dynamic . . . 175.00
2-3 WMc,Jan., 1946 . . . 175.00

WEIRD ADVENTURES

P.L. Publishing, May, 1951–Oct., 1951

1 MB,Missing Diamonds . . . 700.00
2 Puppet Peril . . . 600.00
3 Blood Vengeance . . . 500.00

WEIRD ADVENTURES

Approved Comics (Ziff-Davis), July–Aug., 1951

10 P(c),Seeker from Beyond . . . 500.00

WEIRD CHILLS

Key Publications, July, 1954

1 MBi(c),BW . . . 1,100.00
2 Eye Torture(c) . . . 1,000.00
3 Bondage(c),Nov., 1954 . . . 600.00

WEIRD COMICS

Fox Features Syndicate, April, 1940

1 LF(c),Bondage(c),B:Birdman, Thor,Sorceress of Doom, BlastBennett,Typhon,Voodoo Man, Dr.Mortal . . . 7,000.00
2 LF(c),Mummy(c) . . . 3,000.00
3 JSm(c) . . . 1,500.00
4 JSm(c) . . . 1,500.00
5 Bondage(c),I:Dart,Ace; E:Thor . . . 1,700.00
6 Dart & Ace(c) . . . 1,400.00
7 Battle of Kooba . . . 1,400.00
8 B:Panther Woman,Dynamo, The Eagle . . . 1,400.00
9 V:Pirates . . . 1,000.00
10 A:Navy Jones . . . 1,000.00
11 Dart & Ace(c) . . . 800.00
12 Dart & Ace(c) . . . 800.00
13 Dart & Ace(c) . . . 800.00
14 The Rage(c) . . . 800.00
15 Dart & Ace (c) . . . 800.00
16 Flag,The Encore(c) . . . 800.00
17 O:Black Rider . . . 775.00
18 . . . 750.00
19 . . . 750.00
20 Jan., 1941,I'm The Master of Life and Death . . . 950.00

WEIRD FANTASY

I.C. Publishing Co. (E.C. Comics), May–June, 1950

13(1)AF,HK,JKa,WW,AF(c), Roger Harvey's Brain . . . 3,500.00
14(2)AF,HK,JKa,WW,AF(c),Cosmic Ray Brain Explosion . . . 2,500.00
15(3)AF,HK,JKa,WW,AF(c),Your Destination is the Moon . . . 1,800.00

All comics prices listed are for *Near Mint* condition.

Weird Fantasy #17
© E. C. Comics

Weird Science #19
© E. C. Comics

Weird Science-Fantasy #23
© E. C. Comics

16(4)AF,HK,JKa,WW,AF(c) . . . 1,800.00
17(5)AF,HK,JKa,WW,AF(c),Not Made by Human Hands . . . 1,600.00
6 AF,HK,JKa,WW,AF(c),Robot. 1,500.00
7 AF,JKa,WW,AF(c) 1,500.00
8 AF,JKa,WW,AF(c) 1,500.00
9 AF,Jka,WW,JO,AF(c) 1,500.00
10 AF,Jka,WW,JO,AF(c) 900.00
11 AF,Jka,WW,JO,AF(c) 1,500.00
12 AF,Jka,WW,JO,AF(c) 1,500.00
13 AF,Jka,WW,JO,AF(c) 1,500.00
14 AF,JKa,WW,JO,AW&FF, AF(c). 1,200.00
15 AF,JKa,JO,AW&RKr,AF(c), Bondage(c). 1,500.00
16 AF,JKa,JO,AW&RKr,AF(c) . . 2,000.00
17 AF,JOP,JKa,AF(c),Bradbury 1,500.00
18 AF,JO,JKa,AF(c),Bradbury. . 1,500.00
19 JO,JKa,JO(c),Bradbury 1,500.00
20 JO,JKa,FF,AF(c) 1,500.00
21 JO,JKa,AW&FF(c) 1,800.00
22 JO,JKa,JO(c),Nov.,1953 . . . 1,100.00
With Weird Science, Becomes:

WEIRD SCIENCE FANTASY

WEIRD HORRORS

St. John Publishing Co., June, 1952

1 GT,Dungeon of the Doomed . . 750.00
2 Strangest Music Ever 400.00
3 PMo,Strange Fakir From the Orient, Drug 400.00
4 Murderers Knoll 350.00
5 Phantom Bowman 350.00
6 Monsters from Outer Space . . 600.00
7 LC,Deadly Double 700.00
8 JKu,JKu(c),Bloody Yesterday . 500.00
9 JKu,JKu(c),Map Of Doom 500.00
Becomes:

NIGHTMARE

Dec., 1953

10 JKu(c),The Murderer's Mask . 800.00
11 BK,Ph(c),Fangs of Death 600.00
12 JKu(c),The Forgotten Mask . . 500.00
13 BP,Princess of the Sea 350.00
Becomes:

AMAZING GHOST STORIES

Oct., 1954

14 EK,MB(c),Pit & Pendulum. . . . 400.00
15 BP,Weird Thrillers 300.00
16 Feb., 1955, EK,JKu. 350.00

WEIRD JUNGLE TALES

Star Publications, 1953

202 . . . . 150.00

WEIRD MYSTERIES

Gilmore Publications, Oct., 1952

1 BW(c) 1,100.00
2 BWi, Robot Woman 1,500.00
3 Severed Heads(c) 750.00
4 BW,Human headed ants(c) . 1,300.00
5 BW,Brains From Head(c) . . . 1,500.00
6 Severed Head(c) 750.00
7 Used in "Seduction" 1,100.00
8 The One That Got Away 800.00
9 Epitaph,Cyclops, Violence 750.00
10 The Ruby 600.00
11 Voodoo Dolls. 550.00
12 Sept., 1954 . . . . 550.00

WEIRD SCIENCE

E.C. Comics, 1950

1 AF(a&c),JKu,HK,WW 6,000.00
2 AF(a&c),JKu,HK,WW,Flying Saucers(c) 3,000.00
3 AF(a&c),JKu,HK 2,000.00
4 AF(a&c),JKu,HK 2,000.00
5 AF(a&c),JKu,HK,WW, Atomic Bomb(c) 2,000.00
6 AF(a&c),JKu,HK 2,000.00
7 AF(a&c),JKu,HK,Classic(c). . 2,000.00
8 AF(a&c),JKu 2,000.00
9 WW(c),JKu,Classic(c). 2,200.00
10 WW(c),JKu,JO,Classic(c) . . 2,000.00
11 AF,JKu,Space war 1,200.00
12 WW(c),JKu,JO,Classic(c) . . 1,200.00
13 WW(c),JKu,JO, ... 1,200.00
14 WW(a&c),JO 1,500.00
15 WW(a&c),JO,Grl,AW, RKr,JKa 1,500.00
16 WW(a&c),JO,AW,RKr,JKa . . 1,400.00
17 WW(a&c),JO,AW,RKr,JKa . . 1,400.00
18 WW(a&c),JO,AW,RKr, JKa,Atomic Bomb. 1,400.00
19 WW(a&c),JO,AW, FF,Horror(c) 1,500.00
20 WW(a&c),JO,AW,FF,JKa . . . 1,500.00
21 WW(a&c),JO,AW,FF,JKa . . . 1,500.00
22 WW(a&c),JO,AW,FF 1,500.00
Becomes:

WEIRD SCIENCE FANTASY

March, 1954

23 WW(a&c),AW,BK 1,300.00
24 WW,AW,BK,Classic(c) 1,300.00
25 WW,AW,BK,Classic(c) 1,400.00
26 AF(c),WW,RC, Flying Saucer(c) 1,200.00
27 WW(a&c),RC 1,200.00
28 AF(c),WW 1,400.00
29 AF(c),WW,Classic(c) 3,500.00
Becomes:

INCREDIBLE SCIENCE FANTASY

July–Aug., 1955

30 WW,JDa(c),BK,AW,RKr,JO . . 600.00
31 WW,JDa(c),BK,AW,RKr 750.00
32 JDa(c),BK,WW,JO 750.00
33 WW(c),BK,WW,JO 750.00

WEIRD TALES OF THE FUTURE

S.P.M. Publ./ Aragon Publications, March, 1952

1 RA 2,000.00
2 BW,BW(c), Jumpin Jupiter . . 3,000.00
3 BW,BW(c) 3,000.00
4 BW,BW(c) 2,000.00
5 BW,BW(c),Jumpin' Jupiter Lingerie(c) 3,000.00
6 Bondage(c) 1,500.00
7 BW,Devil(c). 2,000.00
8 July–Aug., 1953 . . . . 2,500.00

WEIRD TERROR

Allen Hardy Associates (Comic Media), Sept., 1952

1 RP,DH,DH(c),Dungeon of the Doomed;Hitler 750.00
2 HcK(c),PMo, Torture 600.00
3 PMo,DH,DH(c),Strong Violence. 600.00
4 PMo,DH,DH(c),Severed Head. 600.00
5 PMo,DH,RP,DH(c),Hanging(c). 550.00
6 DH,RP,DH(c),Step into My Parlour, Severed Head . . 550.00
7 DH,PMo,DH(c),Blood o/t Bats . 500.00
8 DH,RP,DH(c),Step into My Parlour, Severed Head . . 550.00
9 DH,PMo,DH(c),The Fleabite . . 450.00

Weird Thrillers #1
© Ziff-Davis Publications

Western Comics #23
© DC Comics

Western Crime Busters #9
© Trojan Magazines

10 DH,BP,RP,DH(c) 450.00
11 DH,DH(c),Satan's Love Call . . 500.00
12 DH,DH(c),King Whitey 450.00
13 DH,DH(c),Wings of Death,
Severed Head, Sept. 1954 . . 450.00

WEIRD THRILLERS
Approved Comics (Ziff-Davis), Sept.–Oct., 1951

1 Ph(c),Monsters & The Model 1,200.00
2 AW,P(c),The Last Man 850.00
3 AW,P(c),Princess o/t Sea . . 1,100.00
4 AW,P(c),The Widows Lover . . . 800.00
5 BP,Oct., 1952,AW,P(c),
Wings of Death 800.00

WENDY PARKER COMICS
Marvel Atlas, 1953

1 . . . . 150.00
2 . . . . 100.00
3 . . . . 125.00
4 . . . . 125.00
5 . . . . 125.00
6 . . . . 125.00
7 . . . . 125.00
8 . . . . 125.00

WESTERN ACTION THRILLERS
Dell Publishing Co., April, 1937

1 Buffalo Bill, Texas Kid 1,200.00

WESTERN ADVENTURES COMICS
A.A. Wyn, Inc. (Ace Magazines), Oct., 1948

N#(1)Injun Gun Bait 275.00
N#(2)Cross-Draw Kid 150.00
N#(3)Outlaw Mesa 150.00
4 Sheriff, Sal 125.00
5 . . . . 125.00
6 Rip Roaring Adventure 125.00
Becomes:

WESTERN LOVE TRAILS
Nov., 1949

7 . . . . 150.00
8 Maverick Love 125.00
9 March, 1950 . . . . 100.00

WESTERN BANDIT TRAILS
St. John Publishing Co., Jan., 1949

1 GT,MB(c), Blue Monk 300.00
2 GT,MB(c) 250.00
3 GT,MB,MB(c),Gingham Fury . 275.00

WESTERN COMICS
DC Comics, Jan.–Feb., 1948

1 MMe,B:Vigilante,Rodeo Rick,
Wyoming Kid, Cowboy
Marshal. 1,500.00
2 MMe,Vigilante vs. Dirk Bigger . 600.00
3 MMe,Vigilante vs. Pecos Kid . . 700.00
4 MMe,Vigilante as Pecos Kid . . 700.00
5 I:Nighthawk 500.00
6 Wyoming Kid vs. The
Murder Mustang 300.00
7 Wyoming Kid in The Town
That Was Never Robbed. . . . 300.00
8 O:Wyoming Kid 500.00
9 Wyoming Kid vs. Jack
Slaughter 300.00
10 Nighthawk in Tunnel ofTerror . 300.00
11 Wyoming Kid vs. Mayor Brock 275.00
12 Wyoming Kid vs. Baldy Ryan . 275.00
13 I:Running Eagle 275.00
14 Wyoming Kid in The Siege
of Prairie City. 275.00
15 Nighthawk in Silver, Salt
and Pepper 275.00
16 Wyoming Kid vs. Smilin' Jim. . 275.00
17 BP,Wyoming Kid vs. Prof.
Penny 275.00
18 LSt on Nighthawk,Wyoming Kid
in Challenge of the Chiefs. . . 275.00
19 LSt,Nighthawk in The
Invisible Rustlers 275.00
20 LSt,Nighthawk in The Mystery
Mail From Defender Dip 250.00
21 LSt,Nighthawk in Rattlesnake
Hollow 250.00
22 LSt,I:Jim Pegton 250.00
23 LSt,Nighthawk reveals
ID to Jim 250.00
24 The $100,000 Impersonation . 250.00
25 V:Souix Invaders. 250.00
26 The Storming of the Sante
Fe Trail 250.00
27 The Looters of Lost Valley . . . 250.00
28 The Thunder Creek Rebellion. 250.00
29 Six Guns of the Wyoming Kid. 250.00
30 V:Green Haired Killer 250.00
31 The Sky Riding Lawman. 250.00
32 Death Rides the Stage Coach 250.00
33 . . . . 250.00
34 Prescription For Killers 250.00
35 The River of Rogues. 250.00
36 Nighthawk(c),Duel in the Dark 200.00
37 The Death Dancer 200.00
38 Warpath in the Sky 200.00
39 Death to Fort Danger 200.00
40 Blind Man's Bluff 200.00
41 thru 60. . . . . @175.00
61 thru 85. . . . . @150.00

WESTERN CRIME BUSTERS
Trojan Magazines, Sept., 1950–April, 1952

1 Gunslingin' Galoots 400.00
2 K-Bar Kate 250.00
3 Wilma West 250.00
4 Bob Dale 250.00
5 Six-Gun Smith 250.00
6 WW 400.00
7 WW,Wells Fargo Robbery . . . 400.00
8 . . . . 250.00
9 WW,Lariat Lucy 400.00
10 WW,Tex Gordon 400.00

WESTERN CRIME CASES
See: OUTLAWS, THE

WESTERNER, THE
Wanted Comics Group/ Toytown Publ., June, 1948

14 F:Jack McCall 250.00
15 F:Bill Jamett 200.00
16 F:Tom McLowery 200.00
17 F:Black Bill Desmond 200.00
18 BK,F:Silver Dollar Dalton 250.00
19 MMe,F:Jess Meeton 150.00
20 . . . . 150.00
21 BK,MMe 200.00
22 BK,MMe 200.00
23 BK,MMe 200.00
24 BK,MMe 200.00
25 O,I,B:Calamity Jane 200.00
26 BK,F:The Widowmaker. 250.00
27 BK. 250.00
28 thru 31. . . . . @125.00
32 E:Calamity Jane 125.00
33 A:Quest. 125.00
34 . . . . 125.00

Western Fighters #1
© Hillman Periodicals

Western Killers N#
© Fox Features Syndicate

Western Outlaws #19
© Marvel Comics Group

35 SSh(c) 125.00
36 . . . . 125.00
37 Lobo-Wolf Boy 125.00
38 . . . . 125.00
39 . . . . 125.00
40 SSh(c) 125.00
41 Dec., 1951 . . . . 125.00

WESTERN FIGHTERS

Hillman Periodicals, April–May, 1948

1 S&K(c) 450.00
2 BF(c) 200.00
3 BF(c) 150.00
4 BK,BF 175.00
5 . . . . 125.00
6 . . . . 125.00
7 BK 150.00
8 . . . . 125.00
9 . . . . 125.00
10 BK 150.00
11 AMC&FF 400.00
2-1 BK 150.00
2-2 BP 125.00
2-3 thru 2-12 . . . . @100.00
3-1 thru 3-11 . . . . @100.00
3-12 BK 125.00
4-1 . . . . 100.00
4-2 BK 150.00
4-3 BK 150.00
4-4 BK 150.00
4-5 BK 150.00
4-6 BK 150.00
4-7 March–April, 1953 . . . . 100.00

WESTERN FRONTIER

P.L. Publishers (Approved Comics), May, 1951

1 Flaming Vengeance 150.00
2 . . . . 125.00
3 Death Rides the Iron Horse . . 100.00
4 thru 6 . . . . @100.00
7 1952 . . . . 100.00

WESTERN GUNFIGHTERS

See: APACHE KID

WESTERN HEARTS

Standard Magazine, Inc., Dec., 1949

1 JSe, Whip Wilson, Ph(c) 275.00
2 AW,FF, Palomino, Ph(c) 275.00
3 Rex Allen, Ph(c) 150.00
4 JSe,BE, Ph(c) 150.00
5 JSe,BE,Ray Milland, Ph(c) . . . 150.00
6 JSe,BE,Irene Dunn, Ph(c) 150.00
7 JSe,BE,Jock Mahoney Ph(c) . . 150.00
8 Randolph Scott, Ph(c) 150.00
9 JSe,BE, Whip Wilson, Ph(c) . . 150.00
10 JSe,BE, Bill Williams,Ph(c) . . . 150.00

WESTERN HERO

See: WOW COMICS

WESTERN KID

Marvel, [1st Series] Dec., 1954

1 JR,B:Western Kid,O:Western Kid (Tex Dawson) 250.00
2 JMn,JR,Western Adventure . . . 125.00
3 JMn(c),JR,Gunfight(c) 100.00
4 JMn(c),JR,The Badlands 100.00
5 JR 100.00
6 JR 100.00
7 JR 100.00
8 JR 100.00
9 JR,AW 125.00
10 JR,AW,Man in the Middle 125.00
11 thru 16 . . . . @100.00
17 Aug., 1957 . . . . 100.00

WESTERN KILLERS

Fox Features Syndicate, 1948

N# Lingerie 280.00
60 Violence 300.00
61 JCo,LSe 250.00
62 . . . . 225.00
63 . . . . 225.00
64 . . . . 225.00

WESTERN LIFE ROMANCES

See: MY FRIEND IRMA

WESTERN LOVE

Feature Publications (Prize Comics Group), July–Aug., 1949

1 S&K, Randolph Scott 350.00
2 S&K, Whip Wilson 250.00
3 JSe,BE, Reno Brown 200.00
4 JSe,BE 200.00
5 JSe,BE, Dale Robertson 250.00

WESTERN LOVE TRAILS

See: WESTERN ADVENTURE COMICS

WESTERN OUTLAWS

Marvel Atlas, Feb., 1954—Aug., 1957

1 JMn(c),RH,BP,The Greenville Gallows,Hanging(c) 250.00
2 . . . . 125.00
3 thru 10 . . . . @100.00
11 AW,MD 125.00
12 JMn 100.00
13 MB,JMn 125.00
14 AW 125.00
15 AT,GT 100.00
16 BP,JMn,JSe,AW 100.00
17 JMn,AW 100.00
18 JSe 100.00
19 JMn,JSe,RC 100.00
20 and 21 JSe . . . . @100.00

WESTERN OUTLAWS & SHERIFFS

See: BEST WESTERN

WESTERN PICTURE STORIES

Comics Magazine Co., Feb., 1937–June, 1937

1 WE,Treachery Trail, 1st Western 2,500.00
2 WE,Weapons of the West . . 1,500.00
3 WE,Dragon Pass 1,200.00
4 CavemanCowboy 1,200.00

WESTERN ROUGH RIDERS

Stanmor Publ. (Gilmore Magazines), 1954

1 . . . . 125.00
2 . . . . 125.00
3 . . . . 125.00
4 . . . . 125.00

WESTERN TALES

See: WITCHCRAFT

Western Thrillers #5
© Fox Features Syndicate

WESTERN TALES OF BLACK RIDER See: ALL WINNERS COMICS

WESTERN THRILLERS

Fox Features Syndicate, Aug., 1948

1 Velvet Rose 600.00
2 . . . . 250.00
3 GT,RH(c) 225.00
4 . . . . 250.00
5 Butch Cassidy 250.00
6 June, 1949 . . . . 225.00

Becomes:

MY PAST CONFESSIONS

Aug., 1949

7 . . . . 225.00
8 . . . . 150.00
9 . . . . 150.00
10 . . . . 150.00
11 WW 300.00
12 Crimes Inc. 125.00

WESTERN THRILLERS

Marvel, Nov., 1954

1 JMn,Western tales 175.00
2 . . . . 100.00
3 . . . . 100.00
4 . . . . 100.00

Becomes:

COWBOY ACTION

Marvel, March, 1955–March, 1956

5 JMn(c),The Prairie Kid. 150.00
6 . . . . 100.00
7 . . . . 100.00
9 . . . . 100.00
10 . . . . 100.00
11 MN,AW,The Manhunter, ... 125.00

Becomes:

QUICK-TRIGGER WESTERN

Marvel, May, 1956–Sept., 1957

12 Bill Larson Strikes. 175.00
13 AW,The Man From Cheyenne 175.00
14 BEv,RH(c) 175.00
15 AT,RC 150.00
16 JK,JD 125.00

Western True Crime #2 (#16)
© Fox Features Syndicate

17 GT. 125.00
18 GM 125.00
19 JSe 100.00

WESTERN TRAILS

Marvel Atlas, 1957

1 MMe,FBe,JSe(c),Ringo Kid . . . 165.00
2 MMe,FBe,JSe(c) 100.00

WESTERN TRUE CRIME

Fox Features Syndicate, Aug., 1948

1 (#15) JKa, Zoot 14. . . . . 450.00
2 (#16) JKa, Violence 300.00
3 JKa. 250.00
4 JCr. 300.00
5 . . . . 200.00
6 . . . . 200.00

Becomes:

MY CONFESSION

Aug., 1949–Feb., 1950

7 WW 400.00
8 WW,My Tarnished Reputation 350.00
9 I:Tormented Men 150.00
10 I Am Damaged Goods 150.00

WESTERN WINNERS See: ALL WINNERS COMICS

WHACK

St. John Publishing Co., Dec., 1953

1 3-D 400.00
2 Steve Crevice,Flush Jordan V:Bing (Crosby)The Merciful 300.00
3 F:Little Awful Fannie 200.00

WHAM COMICS

Centaur Publications, Nov., 1940

1 PG,The Sparkler & His Disappearing Suit. 2,400.00
2 Dec., 1940,PG,PG(C), Men Turn into Icicles 1,500.00

WHIP WILSON See: BLAZE CARSON

White Princess of the Jungle #3
© Avon Periodicals

WHIRLWIND COMICS

Nita Publications, June, 1940

1 F:The Cyclone 2,500.00
2 A:Scoops Hanlon,Cyclone(c) 1,500.00
3 Sept., 1940,A:Magic Mandarin,Cyclone(c) 1,400.00

WHITE INDIAN See: A-1 COMICS

WHITE PRINCESS OF THE JUNGLE

Avon Periodicals, July, 1951

1 EK(c),Terror Fangs 750.00
2 EK,EK(c),Jungle Vengeance . 500.00
3 EK,EK(c),The Blue Gorilla . . . 450.00
4 Fangs of the Swamp Beast . . 400.00
5 EK,Coils of the Tree Snake Nov., 1952 . . . . 400.00

WHITE RIDER AND SUPER HORSE See: OUTLAWS, THE

WHIZ COMICS

Fawcett Publications, Feb., 1940

1 O:Captain Marvel,B:Spy Smasher, Golden Arrow,Dan Dare, Scoop Smith, Ibis the Invincible, Sivana 125,000.00
2 . . . . 15,000.00
3 Make way for Captain Marvel 10,000.00
4 Captain Marvel Crashes Through 7,500.00
5 Captain Marvel Scores Again! 7,000.00
6 Circus of Death 4,800.00
7 B:Dr Voodoo,Squadron of Death 4,800.00
8 Saved by Captain Marvel! . . 4,800.00
9 MRa,Captain Marvel on the Job. 4,800.00
10 Battles the Winged Death . . 4,800.00
11 Hurray for Captain Marvel . . 3,000.00
12 Captain Marvel rides the Engine of Doom 3,000.00
13 Worlds Most Powerful Man!. 3,000.00
14 Boomerangs the Torpedo . . 3,000.00

We

Whiz Comics #19
© Fawcett Publications

Whiz Comics #88
© Fawcett Publications

Wilbur Comics #7
© Archie Publications

15 O:Sivana	2,500.00
16 Dr. Voodoo	2,500.00
17 Knocks out a Tank	2,500.00
18 V:Spy Smasher	2,500.00
19 Crushes the Tiger Shark	2,200.00
20 V:Sivana	2,200.00
21 O:Lt. Marvels	2,300.00
22 Mayan Temple	1,500.00
23 GT,A:Dr. Voodoo	1,500.00
24	1,500.00
25 O&I:Captain Marvel Jr., Stops the Turbine of Death	12,000.00
26	1,400.00
27 V:Death God of the Katonkas	1,500.00
28 V:Mad Dervish of Ank-Har	1,500.00
29 Three Lt. Marvels (c), Pan American Olympics	1,500.00
30 CCB(c)	1,400.00
31 Douglass MacArthur & Spy Smasher(c)	1,300.00
32 Spy Smasher(c)	1,300.00
33 Spy Smasher(c)	1,600.00
34 Three Lt. Marvels (c)	1,000.00
35 Capt. Marvel and the Three Fates	1,200.00
36 Haunted Hallowe'en Hotel	1,000.00
37 Return of the Trolls	1,000.00
38 Grand Steeplechase	1,000.00
39 A Nazi Utopia	1,000.00
40 A:Three Lt. Marvels, The Earth's 4 Corners	1,000.00
41 Captain Marvel 1,000 years from Now	800.00
42 Returns in Time Chair	800.00
43 V:Sinister Spies, Spy Smasher(c)	800.00
44 Life Story of Captain Marvel	900.00
45 Cures His Critics	800.00
46	800.00
47 Captain Marvel needs a Birthday	800.00
48	800.00
49 Writes a Victory song	800.00
50 Captain Marvel's most embarrassing moment	800.00
51 Judges the Ugly-Beauty Contest	700.00
52 V:Sivana, Chooses His Birthday	700.00
53 Captain Marvel fights Billy Batson	700.00
54 Jack of all Trades	700.00
55 Family Tree	700.00
56 Tells what the Future Will Be	700.00
57 A:Spy Smasher,Golden Arrow, Ibis	700.00
58	700.00
59 V:Sivana's Twin	700.00
60 Missing Person's Machine	700.00
61 Gets a first name	650.00
62 Plays in a Band	650.00
63 Great Indian Rope Trick	650.00
64 Suspected of Murder	650.00
65 Lamp of Diogenes	650.00
66 The Trial of Mr. Morris!	650.00
67	650.00
68 Laugh Lotion, V:Sivana	650.00
69 Mission to Mercury	1,000.00
70 Climbs the World's Mightiest Mountain	650.00
71 Strange Magician	600.00
72 V:The Man of the Future	600.00
73 In Ogre Land	600.00
74 Old Man River	600.00
75 The City Olympics	600.00
76 Spy Smasher become Crime Smasher	600.00
77	600.00
78 Golden Arrow	600.00
79	600.00
80	600.00
81	600.00
82 The Atomic Ship	600.00
83 Magic Locket	600.00
84	600.00
85 The Clock of San Lojardo	600.00
86 V:Sinister Sivanas	600.00
87 The War on Olympia	600.00
88 The Wonderful Magic Carpet	600.00
89 Webs of Crime	600.00
90	600.00
91 Infinity (c)	600.00
92	600.00
93 Captain America become a Hobo?	600.00
94 V:Sivana	600.00
95 Captain Marvel is grounded	600.00
96 The Battle Between Buildings	600.00
97 Visits Mirage City	600.00
98	600.00
99 V:Menace in the Mountains	600.00
100 Anniversary Issue	700.00
101	600.00
102 A:Commando Yank	600.00
103	600.00
104 Flag(c)	600.00
105	600.00
106 A:Bulletman	600.00
107 The Great Experiment	700.00
108 thru 114	@500.00
115 The Marine Invasion	500.00
116	500.00
117 V:Sivana	500.00
118 thru 121	@500.00
122 V:Sivana	500.00
123	500.00
124	500.00
125 Olympic Games of the Gods	500.00
126	500.00
127	500.00
128	500.00
129	400.00
130	400.00
131 The Television Trap	400.00
132 thru 142	@400.00
143 Mystery of the Flying Studio	400.00
144 V:The Disaster Master	400.00
145	400.00
146	400.00
147	400.00
148	400.00
149	400.00
150 V:Bug Bombs	450.00
151	450.00
152	450.00
153 V:The Death Horror	700.00
154 Horror Tale, I:Dr.Death	700.00
155 V:Legend Horror,Dr.Death	750.00

WHODUNIT?

D.S. Publishing Co.,
Aug.–Sept., 1948

1 MB,Weeping Widow	300.00
2 Diploma For Death	150.00
3 Dec.–Jan., 1949	150.00

WHO IS NEXT?

Standard Comics,
Jan., 1953

5 ATh,RA,Don't Let Me Kill	250.00

WILBUR COMICS

MLJ Magazines
(Archie Publications),
Summer, 1944

1 F:Wilbur Wilkin-America's Song of Fun	700.00
2	350.00
3	250.00
4	200.00
5 I:Katy Keene	1,200.00
6 F:Katy Keene	350.00

Wild Bill Elliot #9
© Dell Publishing Co.

7 F:Katy Keene 350.00
8 F:Katy Keene 350.00
9 F:Katy Keene 350.00
10 F:Katy Keene 350.00
11 thru 20 F:Katy Keene @300.00
21 thru 30 F:Katy Keene @250.00
31 thru 40 F:Katy Keene @150.00
41 thru 56 F:Katy Keene @125.00
57 thru 89 @100.00
90 Oct., 1965 100.00

WILD

Marvel Atlas, Feb., 1954

1 BEv,JMn,Charlie Chan Parody 300.00
2 BEv,RH,JMn,Witches(c) 175.00
3 CBu(c),BEv,RH,JMn, 150.00
4 GC,Didja Ever See a Cannon Brawl 150.00
5 RH,JMn,Aug., 1954 150.00

WILD BILL ELLIOT

Dell Publishing Co., May, 1950

(1) *see Dell Four Color #278*
2 125.00
3 thru 5 @100.00
6 thru 10 @100.00
(11-12) *see Four Color #472, 520*
13 thru 17 @100.00

WILD BILL HICKOK AND JINGLES
See: YELLOWJACKET COMICS

WILD BILL HICKOK

Avon Periodicals, Sept.–Oct., 1949

1 Grl(c),Frontier Fighter 275.00
2 Ph(c),Gambler's Guns 150.00
3 Ph(c),Great Stage Robbery 100.00
4 Ph(c),Guerilla Gunmen 100.00
5 Ph(c),Return of the Renegade 100.00
6 EK,EK(c),Along the Apache Trail 100.00
7 EK,EK(c)Outlaws of Hell's Bend 100.00
8 Ph(c),The Border Outlaws 100.00
9 PH(c),Killers From Texas 100.00
10 Ph(c) 100.00

Wild Boy of the Congo #11
© Ziff-Davis Publications

11 EK,EK(c),The Hell Riders 100.00
12 EK,EK(c),The Lost Gold Mine 100.00
13 EK,EK(c),Bloody Canyon Massacre 125.00
14 125.00
15 100.00
16 JKa,Bad Men of Deadwood 100.00
17 JKa 100.00
18 JKa,Kit West 100.00
19 thru 23 @100.00
24 EK,EK(c) 100.00
25 EK,EK(c) 100.00
26 EK,EK(c) 100.00
27 EK,EK(c) 100.00
28 EK,EK(c),May–June, 1956 100.00

WILD BOY OF THE CONGO

Approved(Ziff-Davis)/ St. John Publ. Co., Feb.–March, 1951

10(1)NS,PH(c),Bondage(c),The Gorilla God 500.00
11(2)NS,Ph(c),Star of the Jungle 250.00
12(3)NS,Ph(c),Ice-Age Men 250.00
4 NS.Ph(c),Tyrant of the Jungle 350.00
5 NS,Ph(c),The White Robe of Courage 200.00
6 NS,Ph(c) 200.00
7 MB,EK.Ph(c) 250.00
8 Ph(c),Man-Eater 200.00
9 Ph(c),Killer Leopard 200.00
10 200.00
11 MB(c) 250.00
12 MB(c) 250.00
13 MB(c) 250.00
14 MB(c) 250.00
15 June, 1955 200.00

WILD FRONTIER

Charlton Comics, 1955

1 Davy Crockett 125.00
2 same 100.00
3 same 100.00
4 same 100.00
5 same 100.00
6 same 100.00
7 O:Cheyenne Kid 100.00

Becomes:

CHEYENNE KID

8 125.00
9 100.00
10 AW,AT,SD(c) 125.00

Wild Western #3
© Marvel Comics Group

11 Giant,Geronimo 125.00
12 AW,AT 125.00
13 AW,AT 125.00
14 AW 125.00
15 125.00
16 100.00
17 100.00
18 100.00
19 100.00
20 JSe 100.00
21 JSe 125.00
22 JSe 125.00
23 75.00
24 JSe 100.00
25 JSe 100.00
26 JSe 100.00
27 75.00
28 75.00
29 75.00
30 JSe 100.00

WILD WEST

Marvel, Spring, 1948

1 SSh(c),B:Two Gun Kids,Tex Taylor,Arizona Annie 400.00
2 SSh(c),CCb, Captain Tootsie 250.00

Becomes:

WILD WESTERN

Marvel, 1948

3 SSh(c),B:Tex Morgan,Two Gun Kid,Tex Taylor,Arizona Annie 350.00
4 Rh,SSh,CCB,Capt. Tootsie. A:Kid Colt,E:Arizona Annie 250.00
5 RH,CCB,SSh,Captain Tootsie A;Black Rider,Blaze Carson 250.00
6 A:Blaze Carson,Kid Colt 200.00
7 Two-Gun Kid 200.00
8 RH 200.00
9 Ph(c),B:Black Rider, Tex Morgan 225.00
10 Ph(c), Black Rider 250.00
11 Black Rider 200.00
12 Black Rider 200.00
13 Black Rider 200.00
14 Prairie Kid,Black Rider 175.00
15 Black Rider 175.00
16 thru 18 Black Rider @175.00
19 Black Rider 185.00
20 thru 29 Kid Colt @150.00
30 JKa, Kid Colt 150.00
31 thru 40 @100.00
41 thru 47 @100.00
48 AW 125.00
49 thru 53 @100.00

Wi

 All comics prices listed are for *Near Mint* condition.

Will Rogers Western #2
© Fox Features Syndicate

Wings Comics #6
© Fiction House Magazines

Wings Comics #80
© Fiction House Magazines

54 AW . . . 125.00
55 AW . . . 125.00
56 and 57 Sept., 1957 . . . @100.00

WILLIE COMICS
See: IDEAL COMICS

WILLIE THE PENGUIN
Animated Cartoons (Standard Comics), 1951

1 Funny animal . . . 125.00
2 . . . 100.00
3 . . . 100.00
4 . . . 100.00
5 . . . 100.00
6 . . . 100.00

WILLIE THE WISE-GUY
Marvel Atlas, 1957

1 MMe . . . 125.00

WILL ROGERS WESTERN
Fox Features Syndicate, 1950

1 (5) . . . 400.00
2 Ph(c) . . . 350.00

WIN A PRIZE COMICS
Charlton Comics, 1955

1 S&K,Edgar Allen Poe adapt. . . 900.00
2 S&K . . . 600.00

Becomes:

TIMMY THE TIMID GHOST
Charlton Comics, 1957

3 . . . 150.00
4 . . . 125.00
5 . . . 125.00
6 . . . 100.00
7 . . . 100.00
8 . . . 100.00
9 . . . 100.00
10 . . . 100.00
11 giant . . . 125.00
12 giant . . . 125.00
13 . . . 100.00
14 . . . 100.00
15 . . . 100.00
16 . . . 100.00
17 . . . 100.00
18 . . . 100.00
19 . . . 100.00
20 thru 25 . . . @100.00

WINGS COMICS
Wings Publ. (Fiction House Magazines), Sept., 1940

1 HcK,AB,GT,Ph(c),B:Skull Squad, Clipper Kirk,Suicide Smith, War Nurse,Phantom Falcons, GreasemonkeyGriffin,Parachute Patrol,Powder Burns . . . 6,000.00
2 HcK,AB,GT,Bomber Patrol . . 3,000.00
3 HcK,AB,GT . . . 1,700.00
4 HcK,AB,GT,B:Spitfire Ace . . . 1,700.00
5 HcK,AB,GT,Torpedo Patrol . 1,700.00
6 HcK,AB,GT,Bombs for Berlin 1,500.00
7 HcK,AB . . . 1,500.00
8 HcK,AB,The Wings of Doom 1,500.00
9 Sky-Wolf . . . 1,400.00
10 The Upside Down . . . 1,400.00
11 . . . 1,300.00
12 Fury of the fire Boards . . . 1,300.00
13 Coffin Slugs For The Luftwaffe . . . 1,300.00
14 Stuka Buster . . . 1,300.00
15 Boomerang Blitz . . . 1,300.00
16 O:Capt.Wings . . . 1,500.00
17 Skyway to Death . . . 1,200.00
18 Horsemen of the Sky . . . 1,200.00
19 Nazi Spy Trap . . . 1,200.00
20 The One Eyed Devil . . . 1,200.00
21 Chute Troop Tornado . . . 1,000.00
22 TNT for Tokyo . . . 1,000.00
23 RP,Battling Eagles of Bataan 1,000.00
24 RP,The Death of a Hero . . . 1,000.00
25 RP,Suicide Squeeze . . . 1,000.00
26 Tojo's Eagle Trap . . . 1,000.00
27 BLb,Mile High Gauntlet . . . 1,000.00
28 BLb,Tail Gun Tornado . . . 1,000.00
29 BLb,Buzzards from Berlin . . 1,000.00
30 BLb,Monsters of the Stratosphere . . . 950.00
31 BLb,Sea Hawks away . . . 950.00
32 BLb,Sky Mammoth . . . 950.00
33 BLb,Roll Call of the Yankee Eagles . . . 950.00
34 BLb,So Sorry,Mr Tojo . . . 950.00
35 BLb,RWb,Hell's Lightning . . . 950.00
36 RWb,The Crash-Master . . . 950.00
37 RWb,Sneak Blitz . . . 950.00
38 RWb,Rescue Raid of the Yank Eagle . . . 950.00
39 RWb,Sky Hell/Pigboat Patrol . 950.00
40 RWb,Luftwaffe Gamble . . . 950.00
41 RWb,.50 Caliber Justice . . . 900.00
42 RWb,PanzerMeat forMosquito 900.00
43 RWb,Suicide Sentinels . . . 900.00
44 RWb,Berlin Bombs Away . . . 900.00
45 RWb,Hells Cargo . . . 900.00
46 RWb,Sea-Hawk Patrol . . . 900.00
47 RWb,Tojo's Tin Gibraltar . . . 900.00
48 RWb . . . 900.00
49 RWb,Rockets Away . . . 900.00
50 RWb,Mission For a Madman . 900.00
51 RWb,Toll for a Typhoon . . . 800.00
52 MB,Madam Marauder . . . 800.00
53 MB,Robot Death Over Manhattan . . . 800.00
54 MB,Juggernauts of Death . . . 800.00
55 MB . . . 800.00
56 MB,Sea Raiders Grave . . . 800.00
57 MB,Yankee Warbirds over Tokyo . . . 800.00
58 MB . . . 800.00
59 MB,Prey of the Night Hawks . . 800.00
60 MB,E:Skull Squad, Hell's Eyes . . . 800.00
61 MB,Raiders o/t Purple Dawn . 750.00
62 Twilight of the Gods . . . 750.00
63 Hara Kiri Rides the Skyways . 750.00
64 Taps For Tokyo . . . 750.00
65 AB,Warhawk for the Kill . . . 750.00
66 AB,B:Ghost Patrol . . . 750.00
67 AB . . . 750.00
68 AB,ClipperKirkBecomesPhantom Falcon;O:Phantom Falcon . . . 750.00
69 AB,O:cont,Phantom Falcon . . 750.00
70 AB,N:Phantom Falcon; O:Final Phantom Falcon . . . 750.00
71 Ghost Patrol becomes Ghost Squadron . . . 750.00
72 V:Capt. Kamikaze . . . 750.00
73 Hell & Stormoviks . . . 750.00
74 BLb(c),Loot is What She Lived For . . . 750.00
75 BLb(c),The Sky Hag . . . 750.00
76 BLb(c),Temple of the Dead . . . 750.00
77 BLb(c),Sky Express to Hell . . . 750.00
78 BLb(c),Loot Queen of Satan's Skyway . . . 750.00
79 BLb(c),Buzzards of Plunder Sky . . . 750.00
80 BLb(c),Port of Missing Pilots . 750.00
81 BLb(c),Sky Trail of the Terror Tong . . . 750.00
82 BLb(c),Bondage(c),Spider & The Fly Guy . . . 800.00
83 BLb(c),GE,Deep Six For Capt. Wings . . . 750.00
84 BLb(c),GE,Sky Sharks to the Kill . . . 750.00
85 BLb(c),GE . . . 750.00
86 BLb(c),GE,Moon Raiders . . . 750.00

Winnie Winkle #1
© Dell Publishing Co.

Witchcraft #2
© Avon Periodicals

Witty Comics #1
© Irwin H. Rubin

87 BLb(c),GE 750.00
88 BLb(c),GE,Madmans Mission . 750.00
89 BLb(c),GE,Bondage(c), Rockets Away 900.00
90 BLb(c),GE,Bondage(c),The Radar Rocketeers 900.00
91 BLb(c),GT,Bondage(c),V-9 for Vengeance. 900.00
92 BLb(c),GE,Death's red Rocket 750.00
93 BLb(c),GE,Kidnap Cargo . . . 1,100.00
94 BLb(c),GE,Bondage(c),Ace of the A-Bomb Patrol 1,200.00
95 BLb(c),GE,The Ace of the Assassins 750.00
96 BLb(c),GE 750.00
97 BLb(c),GE,The Sky Octopus . 750.00
98 BLb(c),GE,The Witch Queen of Satan's Skyways 750.00
99 BLb(c),GE,The Spy Circus . . . 750.00
100 BLb(c),GE,King o/t Congo . . 800.00
101 BLb(c),GE,Trator of the Cockpit 700.00
102 BLb(c),GE,Doves of Doom . . 700.00
103 BLb(c),GE 700.00
104 BLb(c),GE,Fireflies of Fury . . 700.00
105 BLb(c),GE 700.00
106 BLb(c),GE,Six Aces & A Firing Squad 700.00
107 BLb(c),GE,Operation Satan . 700.00
108 BLb(c),GE,The Phantom of Berlin 700.00
109 GE,Vultures of Vengeance Sky 700.00
110 GE,The Red Ray Vortex 700.00
111 GE,E:Jane Martin 500.00
112 The Flight of the Silver Saucers 500.00
113 Suicide Skyways 500.00
114 D-Day for Death Rays. 500.00
115 Ace of Space 500.00
116 Jet Aces of Korea 500.00
117 Reap the Red Wind 500.00
118 Vengeance Flies Blind 500.00
119 The Whistling Death 500.00
120 Doomsday Mission 500.00
121 Ace of the Spyways 500.00
122 Last Kill Korea 500.00
123 The Cat & the Canaries 500.00
124 Summer, 1954, Death Below Zero 500.00

WINNIE WINKLE
Dell Publishing Co., 1941

1 . . . . 250.00
2 . . . . 200.00
3 thru 7 . . . . @200.00

WITCHCRAFT
Avon Periodicals, March–April, 1952

1 SC,JKu,Heritage of Horror . . . 900.00
2 SC,JKu,The Death Tattoo 700.00
3 EK,Better off Dead 500.00
4 Claws of the Cat, Boiling Humans 525.00
5 Ph(c),Where Zombies Walk . . 550.00
6 March, 1953 Mysteries of the Moaning Statue 500.00

WITCHES TALES
Harvey Publications, Jan., 1951

1 RP,Bondage(c),Weird Yarns of Unseen Terror 900.00
2 RP,AAv,We Dare You 600.00
3 RP,Bondage(c)Forest of Skeletons. 400.00
4 BP 400.00
5 BP,Bondage(c),Share My Coffin 450.00
6 BP,Bondage(c),Servants of the Tomb 400.00
7 BP,Screaming City. 400.00
8 Bondage(c) 450.00
9 Fatal Steps. 400.00
10 BP,....,IT! 400.00
11 BP,Monster Maker. 350.00
12 Bondage(c);The Web of the Spider 350.00
13 The Torture Jar 350.00
14 AAv,Transformation. 350.00
15 Drooling Zombie 350.00
16 Revenge of a Witch 350.00
17 Dimension IV 350.00
18 HN,Bird of Prey. 400.00
19 HN,The Pact 400.00
20 HN,Kiss & Tell. 400.00
21 HN,The Invasion. 400.00
22 HN,A Day of Panic 400.00
23 HN,The Wig Maker. 400.00
24 HN,The Undertaker. 425.00
25 What Happens at 8:30 PM? Severed Heads(c) 500.00
26 Up There. 350.00
27 The Thing That Grew 350.00
28 AAv,Demon Flies. 350.00
Becomes:

WITCHES WESTERN TALES
Feb., 1955

29 S&K(a&c),F:Davy Crockett . . . 450.00
30 S&K(a&c) 400.00
Becomes:

WESTERN TALES
Oct., 1955

31 S&K(a&c),F:Davy Crockett . . . 250.00
32 S&K(a&c),F:Davy Crockett . . . 250.00
33 S&K(a&c),July–Sept.,1956 . . . 250.00

WITH THE MARINES ON THE BATTLEFRONTS OF THE WORLD
Toby Press, June, 1953

1 Flaming Soul, John Wayne, Ph(c) 325.00
2 Mar., 1954, Monty Hall, Ph(c) . 100.00

WITNESS, THE
Marvel, Sept., 1948

1 . . . . 2,200.00

WITTY COMICS
Irwin H. Rubin/Chicago Nite Life News, 1945

1 Pioneer, Jr. Patrol 325.00
2 1945. . . . . 150.00
3 thru 7 . . . . @125.00

WOMEN IN LOVE
Fox Features Synd./ Hero Books/ Ziff-Davis, Aug., 1949

1 . . . . 700.00
2 . . . . 400.00
3 . . . . 250.00
4 WW 300.00

WOMEN OUTLAWS
Fox Features Syndicate, July, 1948

1 . . . . 1,000.00
2 . . . . 800.00
3 . . . . 800.00
4 . . . . 700.00
5 thru 8 . . . . @550.00
N# Cody of the Pony Express . . . 400.00

Wonder Comics #10
© Better Publications

Wonderworld #32
© Fox Features Syndicate

Wonder Woman #17
© DC Comics

Becomes:

MY LOVE MEMORIES

Fox Features Syndicate, Nov., 1949

9 . . . . 250.00
10 . . . . 150.00
11 . . . . 175.00
12 WW. 200.00

WONDERBOY
See: HORRIFIC

WONDER COMICS

Great Publ./Nedor/ Better Publications, May, 1944

1 SSh(c),B:Grim Reaper, Spectro Hitler(c) 2,500.00
2 ASh(c),O:Grim Reaper,B:Super Sleuths,Grim Reaper(c) . . . 1,800.00
3 ASh(c),Grim Reaper(c) 1,500.00
4 ASh(c),Grim Reaper(c) 1,000.00
5 ASh(c),Grim Reaper(c) 1,000.00
6 ASh(c),Grim Reaper(c) 900.00
7 ASh(c),Grim Reaper(c) 900.00
8 ASh(c),E:Super Sleuths, Spectro 900.00
9 ASh(c),B:Wonderman 900.00
10 ASh(c),Wonderman(c) 950.00
11 Grl(c),B:Dick Devins 1,000.00
12 Grl(c),Bondage(c) 1,000.00
13 ASh(c),Bondage(c). 1,000.00
14 ASh(c),Bondage(c) E:Dick Devins 1,000.00
15 ASh(c),Bondage(c),B:Tara . . 1,700.00
16 ASh(c),A:Spectro, E:Grim Reaper 1,000.00
17 FF,ASh(c),A:Super Sleuth . . 1,600.00
18 ASh(c),B:Silver Knight 1,500.00
19 ASh(c),FF. 1,500.00
20 FF,ASh(c),Oct., 1948 . . . . . . 1,700.00

WONDER COMICS

Fox Features Syndicate, May, 1939

1 BKa,WE,WE(c),B:Wonderman, DR.Kung,K-51 . . . . 28,000.00
2 WE,BKa,LF(c),B:Yarko the Great,A:Spark Stevens. . . . 9,000.00

Becomes:

WONDERWORLD COMICS

Fox Features Syndicate, July, 1939–Jan., 1942

3 WE,LF,BP,LF&WE,I:Flame . 14,000.00
4 WE,LF,BP,LF(c) 7,000.00
5 WE,LF,BP,GT,LF(c),Flame . . 4,000.00
6 WE,LF,BP,GT,LF(c),Flame . . 4,000.00
7 WE,LF,BP,GT,LF(c),Flame . . 5,000.00
8 WE,LF,BP,GT,LF(c),Flame . . 5,000.00
9 WE,LF,BP,GT,LF(c),Flame . . 3,800.00
10 WE,LF,BP,LF(c),Flame. 3,800.00
11 WE,LF,BP,LF(c),O:Flame . . . 3,800.00
12 BP,LF(c),Bondage(c),Flame. 3,500.00
13 LF(c),E:Dr Fung,Flame 3,500.00
14 JoS,Bondage(c),Flame 3,000.00
15 JoS&LF(c),Flame. 2,200.00
16 Flame(c). 1,600.00
17 Flame(c). 1,600.00
18 Flame(c). 1,600.00
19 Male Bondage(c),Flame . . . 1,800.00
20 Flame(c). 1,500.00
21 O:Black Club &Lion,Flame. . 1,400.00
22 Flame(c). 1,200.00
23 Flame(c). 1,000.00
24 Flame(c). 1,000.00
25 A:Dr Fung,Flame 1,000.00
26 Flame(c). 1,000.00
27 Flame(c). 1,000.00
28 Bondage(c)I&O:US Jones, B:Lu-nar,Flame. 1,600.00
29 Bondage(c),Flame 1,000.00
30 O:Flame(c),Flame 1,700.00
31 Bondage(c),Flame 1,000.00
32 Hitler(c),Flame 1,100.00
33 Male Bondage(c) 1,000.00

WONDER DUCK

Marvel, Sept., 1949

1 Whale(c) 175.00
2 . . . . 125.00
3 March, 1950 . . . . 125.00

WONDERLAND COMICS

Feature Publications (Prize Comics Group), Summer, 1945

1 (fa),B:Alex in Wonderland 250.00
2 . . . . 150.00
3 thru 8 . . . . @125.00
9 1947. 125.00

WONDER WOMAN

DC Comics, 1942

1 O:Wonder Woman,A:Paula Von Gunther 40,000.00
2 I:Earl of Greed,Duke of Deception and Lord Conquest. 7,500.00
3 Paula Von Gunther reforms . 3,500.00
4 A:Paula Von Gunther 2,600.00
5 I:Dr. Psycho,A:Mars 2,600.00
6 I:Cheetah 2,000.00
7 . . . . 2,000.00
8 I:Queen Clea. 2,000.00
9 I:Giganto 2,000.00
10 I:Duke Mephisto Saturno . . . 2,400.00
11 I:Hypnoto 1,700.00
12 I:Queen Desira. 1,700.00
13 V:King Rigor & the Seal Men 1,700.00
14 I:Gentleman Killer 1,700.00
15 I:Solo 1,700.00
16 I:King Pluto 1,700.00
17 Wonder Woman goes to Ancient Rome. 1,700.00
18 V:Dr. Psycho 1,700.00
19 V:Blitz. 1,700.00
20 V:Nifty and the Air Pirates . . 1,700.00
21 I:Queen Atomia 1,500.00
22 V:Saturno. 1,500.00
23 V:Odin and the Valkyries . . . 1,500.00
24 I:Mask 1,500.00
25 V:Purple Priestess 1,500.00
26 I:Queen Celerita. 1,500.00
27 V:Pik Socket. 1,500.00
28 V:Cheetah,Clea,Dr. Poison, Giganta,Hypnata,Snowman, Zara (Villainy,Inc.). 2,000.00
29 V:Paddy Gypso 2,000.00
30 The Secret of the Limestone Caves 2,000.00
31 V:Solo 1,000.00
32 V:Uvo 1,000.00
33 V:Inventa 1,000.00
34 V:Duke of Deception 1,000.00
35 Jaxo,Master of Thoughts . . . 1,000.00
36 V:Lord Cruello 1,000.00
37 A:Circe 1,000.00
38 V:Brutex 1,000.00
39 The Unmasking of Wonder Woman 1,000.00
40 Hollywood Goes To Paradise Island 1,000.00
41 Wonder Woman,Romance Editor. 900.00
42 V:General Vertigo 900.00
43 The Amazing Spy Ring Mystery 900.00

Wonder Woman #49
© DC Comics

Wonder Woman #98
© DC Comics

The World Around Us #15
© Gilberton Publications

44 V:Master Destroyer 900.00
45 The Amazon and the Leprachaun 1,500.00
46 V:Prof. Turgo 800.00
47 V:Duke of Deception 800.00
48 V:Robot Woman 800.00
49 V:Boss 800.00
50 V:Gen. Voro 800.00
51 V:Garo 600.00
52 V:Stroggo 600.00
53 V:Crime Master of Time 600.00
54 A:Merlin 600.00
55 The Chessmen of Doom 600.00
56 V:Plotter Gang 600.00
57 V:Mole Men 600.00
58 V:Brain 600.00
59 V:Duke Dozan 600.00
60 A:Paula Von Gunther 600.00
61 Earth's Last Hour 500.00
62 V:Angles Andrews 500.00
63 V:Duke of Deception 500.00
64 V:Thought Master 500.00
65 V:Duke of Deception 500.00
66 V:Duke of Deception 500.00
67 Confessions of a Spy 500.00
68 Landing of the Flying Saucers 500.00
69 A:Johann Gutenberg,Chris. Columbus, Paul Revere and the Wright Brothers 500.00
70 I:Angle Man 500.00
71 One-Woman Circus 500.00
72 V:Mole Goldings 500.00
73 V:Prairie Pirates 500.00
74 The Carnival of Peril 450.00
75 V:Angler 450.00
76 . . . . 450.00
77 V:Smokescreen gang 450.00
78 V:Angle Man 450.00
79 V:Spider 450.00
80 V:Machino 450.00
81 V:Duke of Deception, Angle Man 450.00
82 A:Robin Hood 450.00
83 The Boy From Nowhere 450.00
84 V:Duke of Deception, Angle Man 450.00
85 V:Capt. Virago 450.00
86 V:Snatcher 450.00
87 The Day the Clocks Stopped . 450.00
88 V:Duke of Deception 450.00
89 The Triple Heroine 450.00
90 Wonder Woman on Jupiter . . . 450.00
91 The Interplanetary Olympics . . 400.00
92 V:Angle Man 400.00
93 V:Duke of Deception 400.00
94 V:Duke of Deception, A:Robin Hood 400.00
95 O:Wonder Woman's Tiara 400.00
96 V:Angle Man 400.00
97 The Runaway Time Express . . 400.00
98 . . . . 400.00
99 V:Silicons 400.00
100 Anniversary Issue 450.00
101 V:Time Master 350.00
102 F:Steve Trevor 350.00
103 V:Gadget-Maker 350.00
104 A:Duke of Deception 350.00
105 O,I:Wonder Woman 1,500.00
106 W.Woman space adventure . 350.00
107 Battles space cowboys 350.00
108 Honored by U.S. Post Off. . . 350.00
109 V:Slicker 350.00
110 I:Princess 1003 . . . . 350.00
111 I:Prof. Menace 350.00
112 V:Chest of Monsters 300.00
113 A:Queen Mikra 300.00
114 V:Flying Saucers 300.00
115 A:Angle Man 300.00
116 A:Professor Andro 300.00
117 A:Etta Candy 300.00
118 A:Merman 300.00
119 A:Mer Boy 300.00
120 A:Hot & Cold Alien 300.00
121 A:Wonder Woman Family . . . 250.00
122 I:Wonder Tot 250.00
123 A:Wonder Girl,Wonder Tot . . 250.00
124 A:Wonder Girl,Wonder Tot . . 250.00
125 WW-Battle Prize 250.00
126 I:Mr.Genie 250.00

WONDERWORLD
See: WONDER COMICS

WOOLWORTH'S CHRISTMAS STORY BOOK
Western Printing Co., 1954

N# 100.00

THE WORLD AROUND US
Gilberton Publications, 1958

1 GE,Dogs 125.00
2 SC,Indians 125.00
3 LbC,Horses 125.00
4 LbC,Railroads 100.00
5 GrI,Space 125.00
6 GE,The FBI 125.00
7 GrI,Pirates 100.00
8 GE,GrI,Flight 100.00
9 GrI,EK,Army 100.00
10 EK,Navy 100.00
11 Marines 100.00
12 GrI,Coast Guard 100.00
13 JCo,Air Force 100.00
14 GE,EK,The French Revolution 125.00
15 AW,GM,EK,Prehistoric Animals 135.00
16 EK,The Crusades 100.00
17 GE,RC,Festivals 100.00
18 GE,RC,Great Scientists 100.00
19 AW,GM,The Jungle 125.00
20 RC,GE,AT,Communications . . 125.00
21 RC,GE,GM,American Presidents 125.00
22 GE,Boating 100.00
23 RC,GE,Great Explorers 100.00
24 GM,GE,Ghosts 125.00
25 GM,GE,Magic 125.00
26 The Civil War 150.00
27 RC,GE,CM,AT,High Adventure 100.00
28 RC,GE,GM,AT,LbC(c),Whaling 110.00
29 RC,GE,AT,GM,Vikings 125.00
30 RC,GE,JK,AT,Undersea Adventures 125.00
31 RC,GE,GrI,EK,JK,Hunting . . . 100.00
32 GM,JK,RC,GE,For Gold and Glory 100.00
33 AT,GE,RC,Famous Teens 110.00
34 RC,GE,Fishing 100.00
35 LcM,JK,GM,GE,Spies 110.00
36 JK,Fight For Life 100.00

WORLD FAMOUS HEROES MAGAZINE
Comic Corp. of America (Centaur) Oct., 1941

1 BLb,Paul Revere 1,600.00
2 BLb,Andrew Jackson,V: Dickinson, Lou Gehrig 750.00
3 BLb,Juarez-Mexican patriot . . 600.00
4 BLb,Canadian Mounties 600.00

WORLD FAMOUS STORIES
Croyden Publ., 1945

1 Rip Van Winkle,Ali Baba 150.00

THE WORLD IS HIS PARISH
George A. Pflaum, 1953

N# Pope Pius XII 75.00

World of Fantasy #11
© Marvel Comics Group

World's Best Comics #1
© DC Comics

World's Finest Comics #35
© DC Comics

WORLD OF FANTASY

Marvel Atlas, May, 1956

1 The Secret of the Mountain . . . 600.00
2 JMn,AW,Inside the Tunnel 400.00
3 DAy,SC, The Man in the Cave. 350.00
4 BEv(c),BP,JF,Back to the Lost City 250.00
5 BEv(c),BP,In the Swamp 250.00
6 BEv(c),BP,The Strange Wife of Henry Johnson 250.00
7 BEv(c),GM,Man in Grey 250.00
8 GM,JO,MF,The Secret of the Black Cloud 275.00
9 BEv,BK. 250.00
10 . . . . 200.00
11 AT 200.00
12 BEv(c) 200.00
13 BEv,JO 200.00
14 JMn(c),GM,JO,CI,JM 200.00
15 JK(c) 200.00
16 AW,SD,JK 275.00
17 JK(c),SD 275.00
18 JK(c) 275.00
19 JK(c),SD,Aug., 1959 . . . . 275.00

WORLD OF MYSTERY

Marvel Atlas, 1956–57

1 BEv(c),AT,JO,The Long Wait . 600.00
2 BEv(c),The Man From Nowhere 225.00
3 SD,AT,JDa, The Bugs 300.00
4 SD(c),BP,What Happened in the Basement 300.00
5 JO,She Stands in Shadows . . 225.00
6 AW,SD,GC,Sinking Man 300.00
7 GC,JSe,Pick A Door 225.00

WORLD OF SUSPENSE

Marvel Atlas, April, 1956

1 JO,BEv,JMn,A Stranger Among Us 500.00
2 SD,LC,JMN(c),When Walks the Scarecrow 300.00
3 AW,JMN(c),The Man Who Couldn't Be Touched 300.00
4 Something is in This House . . 225.00
5 BEv,DH,JO. 225.00
6 BEv(c),BP 225.00
7 AW,The Face 300.00
8 Prisoner of the Ghost Ship . . . 225.00

WORLD'S BEST COMICS

DC Comics, Spring, 1941

1 Superman vs. the Rainmaker, Batman vs. Wright 27,000.00

Becomes:

WORLD'S FINEST COMICS

DC Comics, 1941

2 Superman V:The Unknown X, Batman V:Ambrose Taylor 12,000.00
3 I&O:Scarecrow 9,000.00
4 Superman V:Dan Brandon, Batman V:Ghost Gang 7,000.00
5 Superman V:Lemuel P.Potts, Batman V:Brains Kelly 6,500.00
6 Superman V:Metalo,Batman meets Scoop Scanlon 5,200.00
7 Superman V:Jenkins,Batman V:Snow Man Bandits 5,200.00
8 Superman:Talent Unlimited Batman V:Little Nap Boyd, B:Boy Commandos 5,000.00
9 Superman:One Second to Live,Batman V:Bramwell B. Bramwell. 5,200.00
10 Superman V:The Insect Master, Batman reforms OliverHunt 5,000.00
11 Superman V:Charlie Frost, Batman V:Rob Calendar . . 4,200.00
12 Superman V:Lynx,Batman: Alfred Gets His Man 4,200.00
13 Superman V:Dice Dimant, Batman,V:Swami Pravhoz . 4,200.00
14 Superman V:Al Bandar,Batman V:Jib Buckler. 4,200.00
15 Superman V:Derby Bowser, Batman V:Mennekin 4,200.00
16 Superman:Music for the Masses, Batman V:Nocky Johnson . 4,200.00
17 Superman:The Great Godini, Batman V:Dr.Dreemo 4,200.00
18 Superman:The Junior Reporters, Batman V:Prof.Brane 4,000.00
19 A:The Joker 4,000.00
20 A:Toyman 4,000.00
21 Superman:Swindle in Sweethearts!. 3,000.00
22 Batman V:Nails Finney 3,000.00
23 Superman:The Colossus of Metropolis. 3,000.00
24 . . . . 3,000.00
25 Superman V:Ed Rook,Batman: The Famous First Crimes. . 3,000.00
26 Confessions of Superman . . 3,000.00
27 The Man Who Out-Supered Superman. 3,000.00
28 A:Lex Luther,Batman V:Glass Man. 3,000.00
29 Superman:The Books that Couldn't Be Bound 3,000.00
30 Superman:Sheriff Clark Kent, Batman V:Joe Coyne 3,000.00
31 Superman's Super-Rival,Batman: Man with the X-Ray Eyes. . 2,700.00
32 Superman Visits Ancient Egypt 2,700.00
33 Superman Press, Inc., Batman V:James Harmon . 2,700.00
34 The Un-Super Superman. . . 2,700.00
35 Daddy Superman,A:Penguin 2,700.00
36 Lois Lane,Sleeping Beauty . 2,700.00
37 The Superman Story,Batman V:T-Gun Jones 2,700.00
38 If There were No Superman 2,700.00
39 Superman V:Big Jim Martin, Batman V:J.J.Jason 2,700.00
40 Superman V:Check,Batman:4 Killers Against Fate! 2,700.00
41 I:Supermanium, E:Boy Commandos 2,000.00
42 Superman goes to Uranus, A:Marco Polo & Kubla Khan2,000.00
43 A:J.Wilbur Wolfingham. 2,000.00
44 Superman:The Revolt of the Thought Machine 2,000.00
45 Superman:Lois Lane and Clark Kent,Private Detectives . . . 2,000.00
46 Superman V:Mr. 7 . . . . 2,000.00
47 Superman:The Girl Who Hated Reporters 2,000.00
48 A:Joker. 2,000.00
49 Superman Meets the Metropolis Shutterbug Society, A:Penguin 2,000.00
50 Superman Super Wrecker . . 2,000.00
51 Superman:The Amazing Talents of Lois Lane 2,000.00
52 A:J.Wilbur Wolfingham. 2,000.00
53 Superman V:Elias Toomey. . 2,000.00
54 The Superman Who Avoided Danger!. 2,000.00
55 A:Penguin. 2,000.00
56 Superman V:Dr.Vallin,Batman V:Big Dan Hooker. 2,000.00
57 The Artificial Superman 2,000.00
58 Superman V:Mr.Fenton 2,000.00
59 A:Lex Luthor,Joker. 2,000.00
60 A:J.Wilbur Wolfingham. 2,000.00
61 A:Joker,Superman's Blackout 1,500.00

World's Finest Comics #88
© DC Comics

Worlds of Fear #5
© Fawcett Publications

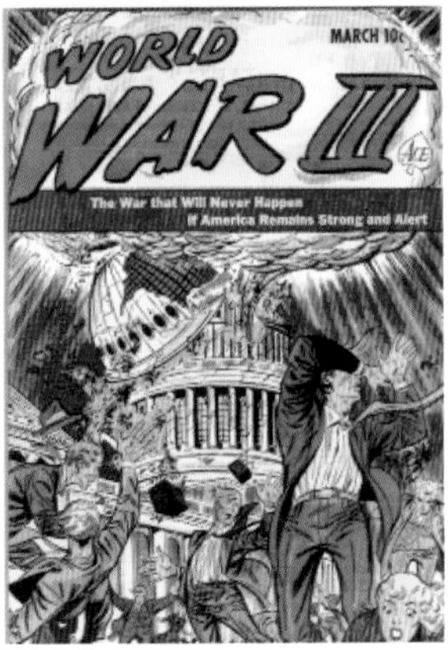

World War III #1
© Ace Periodicals

62 A:Lex Luthor. 1,500.00
63 Superman:Clark Kent, Gangster. 1,500.00
64 Superman:The Death of Lois Lane,Batman:Bruce Wayne... Amateur Detective 1,500.00
65 The Confessions of Superman, Batman V:The Blaster 2,500.00
66 Superman,Ex-Crimebuster; Batman V:Brass Haley 1,500.00
67 Superman:Metropolis-Crime Center! 1,500.00
68 Batman V:The Crimesmith. . 1,500.00
69 A:Jor-El,Batman V:Tom Becket 1,500.00
70 The Two Faces of Superman, Batman:Crime Consultant . 1,500.00
71 B:Superman/Batman team-ups. 3,000.00
72 V:Heavy Weapon gang 2,000.00
73 V:Fang 2,000.00
74 The Contest of Heroes 1,600.00
75 V:The Purple Mask Mob . . . 1,500.00
76 When Gotham City Challenged Metropolis 1,200.00
77 V:Prof.Pender 1,200.00
78 V:Varrel mob 1,200.00
79 A:Aladdin 1,200.00
80 V:Mole 1,200.00
81 Meet Ka Thar from future 900.00
82 A:Three Musketeers 900.00
83 The Case of the Mother Goose Mystery 900.00
84 V:Thad Linnis Gang 900.00
85 Meet Princess Varina 900.00
86 V:Henry Bartle. 900.00
87 V:Elton Craig. 900.00
88 1st team-up Luthor & Joker . . 950.00
89 I:Club of Heroes 900.00
90 A:Batwoman 900.00
91 V:Rohtul,Descendent of Lex Luthor 700.00
92 Ist & only A:Skyboy. 700.00
93 V:Victor Danning 700.00
94 O:Superman/Batman team, A:Lex Luthor. 1,200.00
95 Battle o/t Super Heroes 700.00
96 Super-Foes from Planet X . . . 700.00
97 V:Condor Gang. 700.00
98 I:Moonman 700.00
99 JK,V:Carl Verril 700.00
100 A:Kandor, Lex Luthor. 1,200.00
101 A:Atom Master 450.00
102 V:Jo-Jo Groff gang, B:Tommy Tomorrow. 450.00
103 The Secrets of the Sorcerer's Treasure. 450.00
104 A:Lex Luthor 450.00
105 V:Khalex 450.00
106 V:Duplicate Man 450.00
107 The Secret of the Time Creature. 450.00
108 The Star Creatures 450.00
109 V:Fangan 450.00
110 The Alien Who Doomed Robin! 450.00
111 V:Floyd Frisby 450.00
112 . . . . 450.00
113 1st Bat-Mite/Mr.Mxyzptlk team-up 450.00
114 Captives o/t Space Globes . . 450.00
115 The Curse That Doomed Superman 350.00
116 V:Vance Collins 350.00
117 A:Batwoman,Lex Luthor 350.00
118 V:Vath-Gar. 350.00
119 V:General Grambly 350.00
120 V:Faceless Creature 350.00
121 I:Miss Arrowette 350.00

WORLD'S GREATEST SONGS
Marvel Atlas, 1954

1 Eddie Fisher, Frank Sinatra. . . 500.00

WORLD'S GREATEST STORIES
Jubilee Publications Jan., 1949

1 F:Alice in Wonderland 450.00
2 F:Pinocchio 400.00

WORLDS BEYOND
Fawcett Publications, 1951

1 BP,BBa. 500.00

Becomes:

WORLDS OF FEAR
Fawcett Publications, 1952

2 BP. 1,200.00
3 GE 900.00
4 BP,MSy 750.00
5 BP,MSy 750.00
6 . . . . 750.00
7 . . . . 750.00
8 . . . . 750.00
9 . . . . 750.00
10 no-eyed man, eyeballs(c) . . 2,200.00

WORLD WAR III
Ace Periodicals, March–May, 1953

1 Atomic Bomb (c). 1,000.00
2 The War That Will Never Happen 750.00

WOTALIFE COMICS
See: PHANTOM LADY

WOW COMICS
David McKay/Henle Publ., July, 1936–Nov., 1936

1 WE,DBr(c),Fu Manchu, Buck Jones. 3,800.00
2 WE,Little King 2,800.00
3 WE,WE(c), Popeye. 2,500.00
4 WE,BKa,AR,DBr(c),Popeye, Flash Gordon 3,000.00

WOW COMICS
Fawcett Publications, Winter, 1940

N#(1)S&K,CCB(c),B&O:Mr Scarlett; B:Atom Blake,Jim Dolan,Rick O'Shay,Bondage(c) 27,000.00
2 B:Hunchback 4,500.00
3 V:Mummy Ray Gun 3,000.00
4 O:Pinky 3,200.00
5 F:Pinky the Whiz Kid 2,000.00
6 O:Phantom Eagle; B:Commando Yank 2,000.00
7 Spearhead of Invasion 1,500.00
8 All Three Heroes. 1,500.00
9 A:Capt Marvel,Capt MarvelJr. Shazam,B:Mary Marvel . . . 3,200.00
10 The Sinister Secret of Hotel Hideaway 1,500.00
11 . . . . 1,400.00
12 Rocketing adventures 1,400.00
13 Thrill Show 1,400.00
14 V:Mr Night 1,400.00
15 Shazam Girl of America . . . 1,200.00
16 Ride to the Moon 1,200.00
17 V:Mary Batson,Alter Ego Goes Berserk 1,200.00
18 I:Uncle Marvel,Infinity(c) V is For Victory. 1,200.00
19 A Whirlwind Fantasy 1,200.00
20 Mary Marvel's Magic Carpet 1,200.00
21 Word That Shook the World . . 500.00

Wow Comics #38
© Fawcett Publications

Real Western Hero #75
© Fawcett Publications

Wyatt Earp #10
© Dell Publishing Co.

22 Come on Boys-
Everybody Sing 500.00
23 Trapped by the Terror of
the Future 500.00
24 Mary Marvel 500.00
25 Mary Marvel Crushes Crime. . 500.00
26 Smashing Star-
Studded Stories 400.00
27 War Stamp Plea(c) 400.00
28 Pinky 400.00
29 . . . . 400.00
30 In Mirror Land 400.00
31 Stars of Action. 350.00
32 The Millinery Marauders 350.00
33 Mary Marvel(c) 350.00
34 A:Uncle Marvel 350.00
35 I:Freckles Marvel 500.00
36 Secret of the Buried City. 350.00
37 7th War loan plea 350.00
38 Pictures That Came to Life . . . 350.00
39 The Perilous Packages. 350.00
40 The Quarrel of the Gnomes . . 350.00
41 Hazardous Adventures 300.00
42 . . . . 300.00
43 Curtain Time 300.00
44 Volcanic Adventure 300.00
45 . . . . 300.00
46 . . . . 300.00
47 . . . . 300.00
48 . . . . 300.00
49 . . . . 300.00
50 Mary Marvel/Commando Yank 300.00
51 Command Yank 250.00
52 . . . . 250.00
53 Murder in the Tall Timbers . . . 250.00
54 Flaming Adventure 250.00
55 Earthquake!. 250.00
56 Sacred Pearls of Comatesh . . 250.00
57 . . . . 250.00
58 E:Mary Marvel;The Curse
of the Keys 250.00
59 B:Ozzie the Hilarious
Teenager 250.00
60 thru 64. . . . . @250.00
65 A:Tom Mix 250.00
66 A:Tom Mix 250.00
67 A:Tom Mix 250.00
68 A:Tom Mix 250.00
69 A:Tom Mix,Baseball 250.00
Becomes:

REAL WESTERN HERO

Sept., 1948

70 It's Round-up Time 500.00
71 CCB,P(c),A Rip
Roaring Rodeo 325.00
72 w/Gabby Hayes 325.00
73 thru 75. . . . . @325.00
Becomes:

WESTERN HERO

March, 1949

76 Partial Ph(c)&P(c). 350.00
77 Partial Ph(c)&P(c). 200.00
78 Partial Ph(c)&P(c). 200.00
79 Partial Ph(c)&P(c),
Shadow of Death. 175.00
80 Partial Ph(c)&P(c). 200.00
81 CCB,Partial Ph(c)&P(c),
F:Tootsie 200.00
82 Partial Ph(c)&P(c),
A:Hopalong Cassidy 200.00
83 Partial Ph(c)&P(c). 200.00
84 Ph(c) 175.00
85 Ph(c) 175.00
86 Ph(c),The Case of the
Extra Buddy, giant 175.00
87 Ph(c),The Strange Lands 175.00
88 Ph(c),A:Senor Diablo 175.00
89 Ph(c),The Hypnotist 175.00
90 Ph(c),The Menace of
the Cougar, giant. 150.00
91 Ph(c),Song of Death. 150.00
92 Ph(c),The Fatal Hide-out,
giant. 150.00
93 Ph(c),Treachery at
Triple T, giant. 150.00
94 Ph(c),Bank Busters,giant 150.00
95 Ph(c),Rampaging River 150.00
96 Ph(c),Range Robbers,giant . . 150.00
97 Ph(c),Death on the
Hook,giant 150.00
98 Ph(c),Web of Death,giant 150.00
99 Ph(c),The Hidden Evidence . . 150.00
100 Ph(c),A:Red Eagle,Giant . . . 150.00
101 Red Eagle, Ph(c) 150.00
102 thru 111 Ph(c) . . . . @150.00
112 Ph(c),March, 1952 . . . . 175.00

WYATT EARP

Marvel Atlas, Nov., 1955

1 JMn,F:Wyatt Earp 250.00
2 AW,Saloon(c). 150.00
3 JMn(c),The Showdown,
A:Black Bart 125.00
4 Ph(c),Hugh O'Brian,JSe,
India Sundown 125.00
5 Ph(c),Hugh O'Brian,DW,
Gun Wild Fever 125.00
6 BEv(c) 125.00
7 AW 125.00
8 JMn,Wild Bill Hickok 125.00
9 and 10 . . . . @125.00
11 . . . . 125.00
12 AW,JMn. 125.00
13 . . . . 100.00
14 . . . . 100.00
15 thru 20. . . . . @100.00
21 JDa(c). 100.00
22 thru 29. . . . . @100.00

WYATT EARP

Dell Publishing Co., 1957

1 RsM 175.00
2 RsM 125.00
3 RsM 110.00
4 . . . . 100.00
5 Ph(c) 100.00
6 . . . . 100.00
7 . . . . 100.00
8 . . . . 100.00
9 . . . . 100.00
10 . . . . 100.00
11 . . . . 100.00
12 RsM. 100.00
13 AT 100.00

XMAS COMICS

Fawcett Publications, 1941

1 Whiz #21. . . . . 5,500.00
2 Capt. Marvel 2,200.00
7 Hoppy, Funny Animal. 900.00
Second Series, 1949–52
4 Whiz, Capt. Marvel, Nyoka . . . 900.00
5 . . . . 700.00
6 . . . . 700.00
7 Bill Boyd. 700.00

X-VENTURE

Victory Magazines, 1947

1 Mystery Shadow, Atom
Wizard 1,500.00
2 same 750.00

YANKEE COMICS

Chesler Publications (Harry A. Chesler), Sept., 1941–March, 1942

1 F:Yankee Doodle Jones . . . 2,400.00
2 The Spirit of '41 . . . . 1,100.00
3 Yankee Doodle Jones 800.00
4 JCo,Yankee Doodle Jones . . . 800.00

Cowboy Western Comics #27
© Charlton Comics

Space Western Comics #43
© Charlton Comics

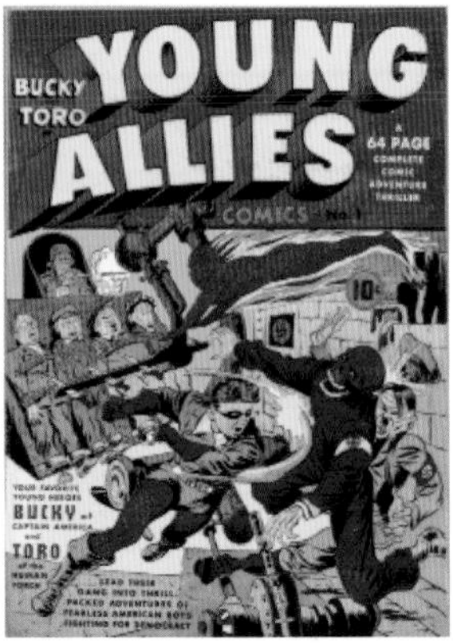

Young Allies #1
© Marvel Comics Group

YANKS IN BATTLE
Comic Magazine, Inc. (Quality Comics Group), 1956

1 CCv 125.00
2 CCv 100.00
3 CCv 100.00
4 CCv 100.00

THE YARDBIRDS
Ziff-Davis Publishing Co., 1952

1 . . . . 125.00

YELLOW CLAW
Marvel Atlas, 1956

1 MMe 1,300.00
2 JK,JSe 1,000.00
3 BEv 975.00
4 JK,JSe 975.00

YELLOWJACKET COMICS
Levy Publ./Frank Comunale/ Charlton, Sept., 1944

1 O&B:Yellowjackets,B:Diana the Huntress 1,500.00
2 Rosita &The Filipino Kid 750.00
3 . . . . 700.00
4 Fall of the House of Usher. . . . 750.00
5 King of Beasts 750.00
6 . . . . 800.00
7 I:Diane Carter;The Lonely Guy 2,000.00
8 The Buzzing Bee Code 800.00
9 . . . . 750.00
10 Capt Grim V:The Salvage Pirates 800.00
Becomes:

JACK IN THE BOX
Charlton, Feb., 1946

11 Funny Animal,Yellow Jacket . . 300.00
12 Funny Animal 200.00
13 BW,Funny Animal 300.00
14 thru 16 Funny Animal . . . . . @200.00
Becomes:

COWBOY WESTERN COMICS
Charlton, July, 1948

17 Annie Oakley,Jesse James. . . 250.00
18 JO,JO(c) 200.00
19 JO,JO(c),Legends of Paul Bunyan 200.00
20 JO(c),Jesse James. 125.00
21 Annie Oakley VisitsDryGulch . 125.00
22 Story of the Texas Rangers . . 125.00
23 . . . . 125.00
24 Ph(c),F:James Craig. 125.00
25 Ph(c),F:Sunset Carson 125.00
26 Ph(c) 150.00
27 Ph(c),Sunset Carson movie . . 750.00
28 Ph(c),Sunset Carson movie . . 400.00
29 Ph(c),Sunset Carson movie . . 400.00
30 Ph(c),Sunset Carson movie . . 400.00
31 Ph(c) 100.00
32 thru 34 Ph(c) . . . . @100.00
35 thru 37 Sunset Carson . . . . @350.00
38 and 39 . . . . @100.00
Becomes:

SPACE WESTERN COMICS
Charlton Comics, Oct., 1952

40 Spurs Jackson,V:The Saucer Men 1,100.00
41 StC(c),Space Vigilantes 750.00
42 StC(c),Atomic Bomb 900.00
43 StC(c),Battle of Spacemans Gulch 800.00
44 StC(c),The Madman of Mars . 750.00
45 StC(c),The Moon Bat,Hitler. . . 775.00
Becomes:

COWBOY WESTERN COMICS
Oct., 1953

46 . . . . 250.00
Becomes:

COWBOY WESTERN HEROES
Dec., 1953

47 . . . . 150.00
48 . . . . 150.00
Becomes:

COWBOY WESTERN
May–June, 1954

49 . . . . 125.00
50 F:Jesse James 125.00
51 thru 57. . . . . @100.00
58, Wild Bill Hickok, giant 125.00
59 thru 66. . . . . @100.00
67 AW&AT 150.00
Becomes:

WILD BILL HICKOK AND JINGLES
Aug., 1958

68 AW 125.00
69 AW 100.00
70 AW 100.00
71 thru 73. . . . . @100.00
74 1960 . . . . 100.00

YOGI BERRA
Fawcett, 1957

1 Ph(c). 1,000.00

YOUNG ALLIES COMICS
Marvel Timely, Summer, 1941—Oct., 1946

1 S&K,SSh,Hitler(c),I&O:Young Allies 1st meeting Capt. America & Human Torch,A:Red Skull 45,000.00
2 S&K,A;Capt.America,Human Torch. 9,000.00
3 Remember Pearl Harbor(c) . 8,000.00
4 A;Capt. America,Torch,Red Skull ASh(c),Horror In Hollywood A:Capt.America,Torch. 9,000.00
5 ASh(c),AAv,Capt.America . . . 3,500.00
6 ASh(c) 2,800.00
7 ASh(c),SSh 2,800.00
8 ASh(c),WW2,Bondage 2,800.00
9 ASh(c),Axis leaders(c), B:Tommy Type,Hitler 3,000.00
10 ASh(c),O:Tommy Type. 2,800.00
11 ASh(c) 2,000.00
12 ASh(c),Decapitation 2,000.00
13 ASh(c) 2,000.00
14 ASh(c) 2,000.00
15 ASh(c),AAv. 2,000.00
16 ASh(c) 2,000.00
17 ASh(c),SSh 2,000.00
18 ASh(c) 1,800.00
19 ASh(c),E:Tommy Type 1,800.00
20 SSh 1,800.00

YOUNG BRIDES
Feature Publications (Prize Comics), Sept.–Oct., 1952

1 S&K,Ph(c) 400.00
2 S&K,Ph(c) 225.00
3 S&K,Ph(c) 200.00
4 S&K 200.00
5 S&K 200.00
6 S&K 200.00

Young Eagle #1
© Fawcett Publications

Young King Cole Vol 2 #5
© Novelty Press

Young Love #2
© Prize Publications

2-1 S&K 175.00
2-2 S&K 100.00
2-3 S&K 175.00
2-4 S&K 175.00
2-5 S&K 175.00
2-6 S&K 175.00
2-7 S&K 175.00
2-8 S&K 100.00
2-9 S&K 100.00
2-10 S&K 175.00
2-11 S&K 175.00
2-12 S&K 175.00
3-1 thru 4-1 . . . . @100.00
4-2 S&K 150.00
4-3 . . . . 100.00
4-4 S&K 150.00
4-5 . . . . 100.00

YOUNG EAGLE

Fawcett Publications/ Charlton Comics, Dec., 1950

1 Ph(c) 200.00
2 Ph(c),Mystery of Thunder Canyon 125.00
3 Ph(c),Death at Dawn 100.00
4 Ph(c) 100.00
5 Ph(c),The Golden Flood 100.00
6 Ph(c),The Nightmare Empire . . 100.00
7 Ph(c),Vigilante Vengeance . . . 100.00
8 Ph(c),The Rogues Rodeo 100.00
9 Ph(c),The Great Railroad Swindle 100.00
10 June, 1952, Ph(c),Thunder Rides the Trail,O:Thunder 100.00

YOUNG HEARTS

Marvel, Nov., 1949—Feb., 1950

1 . . . . 150.00
2 Feb., 1950 . . . . 100.00

YOUNG HEROES

Titan Publ. (American Comics Group), 1955

35 Frontier Scout 125.00
36 . . . . 125.00
37 . . . . 125.00

YOUNG KING COLE

Novelty Press/Premium Svcs. Co., Autumn, 1945

1-1 Detective Toni Gayle 400.00
1-2 . . . . 250.00
1-3 . . . . 200.00
1-4 . . . . 200.00
2-1 . . . . 150.00
2-2 . . . . 150.00
2-3 . . . . 150.00
2-4 . . . . 150.00
2-5 . . . . 150.00
2-6 . . . . 150.00
2-7 . . . . 150.00
3-1 . . . . 175.00
3-2 LbC 250.00
3-3 The Killer With The Hat 150.00
3-4 The Fierce Tiger 150.00
3-5 AMc 150.00
3-6 . . . . 175.00
3-7 LbC(c),Case of the Devil's Twin 250.00
3-8 . . . . 150.00
3-9 The Crime Fighting King 150.00
3-10 LbC(c) 250.00
3-11 LbC(c) 250.00
3-12 July, 1948,AMc(c) 150.00

YOUNG LIFE

New Age Publications, Summer, 1945

1 Partial Ph(c),Louis Prima 175.00
2 Partial Ph(c),Frank Sinatra . . . 200.00

Becomes:

TEEN LIFE

Winter, 1945

3 Partial Ph(c),Croon without Tricks,June Allyson(c) 150.00
4 Partial Ph(c),Atom Smasher Blueprints,Duke Ellington(c) . 125.00
5 Partial Ph(c), Build Your Own Pocket Radio, Jackie Robinson(c) 150.00

YOUNG LOVE

Feature Publ. (Prize Comics Group), Feb.–March, 1949

1 S&K,S&K(c) 600.00
2 S&K,Ph(c) 300.00
3 S&K,JSe,BE,Ph(c) 250.00
4 S&K,Ph(c) 150.00
5 S&K,Ph(c) 150.00
2-1 S&K,Ph(c) 250.00
2-2 Ph(c) 135.00
2-3 Ph(c) 135.00
2-4 Ph(c) 135.00
2-5 Ph(c) 135.00
2-6 S&K(c) 200.00
2-7 S&K(c),S&K 200.00
2-8 S&K 200.00
2-9 S&K(c),S&K 200.00
2-10 S&K(c),S&K 200.00
2-11 S&K(c),S&K 200.00
2-12 S&K(c),S&K 200.00
3-1 S&K(c),S&K 200.00
3-2 S&K(c),S&K 200.00
3-3 S&K(c),S&K 200.00
3-4 S&K(c),S&K 200.00
3-5 Ph(c) 175.00
3-6 BP,Ph(c) 175.00
3-7 Ph(c) 175.00
3-8 Ph(c) 175.00
3-9 MMe,Ph(c) 175.00
3-10 Ph(c) 175.00
3-11 Ph(c) 175.00
3-12 Ph(c) 175.00
4-1 S&K 175.00
4-2 Ph(c) 150.00
4-3 Ph(c) 150.00
4-4 Ph(c) 150.00
4-5 Ph(c) 150.00
4-5 Ph(c) 150.00
4-6 S&K,Ph(c) 150.00
4-7 thru 4-12 Ph(c) . . . . @125.00
5-1 thru 5-12 Ph(c) . . . . @125.00
6-1 thru 6-9 . . . . @100.00
6-10 thru 6-12 . . . . @100.00
7-1 thru 7-7 . . . . @100.00
7-8 thru 7-11 . . . . @100.00
7-12 thru 8-5 . . . . @100.00
8-6 thru 8-12 . . . . @100.00

YOUNG MARRIAGE

Fawcett Publications, 1950

1 BP,Romance,Ph(c) 150.00

YOUNG MEN
See: COWBOY ROMANCES

YOUNG ROMANCE COMICS

Feature Publ./Headline/ Prize Publ., Sept.–Oct., 1947

1 S&K(c),S&K 650.00
2 S&K(c),S&K 350.00
3 S&K(c),S&K 300.00
4 S&K(c),S&K 300.00
5 S&K(c),S&K 300.00
6 S&K(c),S&K 300.00

Young Romance Comics #11
© Prize Publications

Zago, Jungle Prince #2
© Fox Features Syndicate

Zegra, Jungle Empress #2
© Fox Features Syndicate

2-1 S&K(c),S&K 275.00
2-2 S&K(c),S&K 275.00
2-3 S&K(c),S&K 275.00
2-4 S&K(c),S&K 275.00
2-5 S&K(c),S&K 275.00
2-6 S&K(c),S&K 250.00
3-1 thru 3-12 S&K(c),S&K . . . . @250.00
4-1 thru 4-12 S&K . . . . @250.00
5-1 ATh,S&K 250.00
5-2 . . . . 250.00
5-3 . . . . 225.00
5-4 thru 5-12 S&K . . . . @225.00
6-1 . . . . 100.00
6-2 . . . . 100.00
6-3 . . . . 100.00

YOUR UNITED STATES

Lloyd Jacquet Studios, 1946

1N# Teeming Nation of Nations . 300.00

YOUTHFUL HEARTS

Youthful Magazines, May, 1952

1 Frankie Lane(c) 350.00
2 Vic Damone 250.00
3 Johnnie Ray 250.00

Becomes:

DARING CONFESSIONS

Nov., 1952

4 DW,Tony Curtis 175.00
5 Ray Anthony 125.00
6 DW 135.00
7 . . . . 125.00
8 DW 125.00

YOUTHFUL ROMANCES

Pix Parade/Ribage/ Trojan, Aug.–Sept., 1949

1 . . . . 300.00
2 Walter Johnson 200.00
3 Tex Beneke 150.00
4 . . . . 150.00
5 . . . . 150.00
6 . . . . 125.00
7 Tony Martin(c) 150.00
8 WW(c), Frank Sinatra 250.00
9 . . . . 125.00
10 Mel Torme 135.00
11 . . . . 125.00
12 Tony Benett 135.00
13 Richard Hays 125.00
14 . . . . 125.00

Becomes:

DARLING LOVE

Oct.–Nov., 1949

15 WD,Spike Jones, Ph(c). 125.00
16 Tony Bavaar, Ph(c) 125.00
17 DW,Ph(c). 125.00

also continues as

YOUTHFUL ROMANCES

Ribage/Trojan 1953

15 (1) Ph(c),Spike Jones 125.00
16 (2) Ph(c) 125.00
17 (3) Ph(c) 125.00
18 (4) 125.00
5 Les Paul & Mary Ford 110.00
6 Debbie Reynolds 100.00
7 Tony Martin 100.00
8 Aydrey Hepburn 100.00

ZAGO, JUNGLE PRINCE

Fox Features Syndicate, Sept., 1948

1 A:Blue Beetle 900.00
2 JKa. 750.00
3 JKa. 600.00
4 MB(c) 600.00

Becomes:

MY STORY

May, 1949

5 JKa,Too Young To Fall in Love 250.00
6 I Was A She-Wolf 125.00
7 I Lost My Reputation 125.00
8 My Words Condemned Me . . . 125.00
9 WW,Wayward Bride 250.00
10 WW,March, 1950,Second Rate Girl 250.00
11 . . . . 125.00
12 Ph(c) 125.00

ZAZA THE MYSTIC

See: CHARLIE CHAN

TEGRA, JUNGLE EMPRESS

Fox Features Syndicate Aug., 1948

1 Blue Bettle,Rocket Kelly 750.00

Becomes:

ZEGRA, JUNGLE EMPRESS

Oct., 1948

2 JKa 750.00
3 . . . . 600.00
4 . . . . 600.00
5 . . . . 600.00

Becomes:

MY LOVE LIFE

June, 1949–Aug., 1950

6 I Put A Price Tag On Love . . . 175.00
7 An Old Man's Fancy 125.00
8 My Forbidden Affair 125.00
9 I Loved too Often 125.00
10 My Secret Torture 125.00
11 I Broke My Own Heart 125.00
12 I Was An Untamed Filly 125.00
13 I Can Never Marry You 100.00

ZIGGY PIG, SILLY SEAL

Marvel Timely, 1944

1 Funny Animals vs. Japs. 300.00
2 . . . . 150.00
3 . . . . 125.00
4 . . . . 125.00
5 . . . . 125.00
6 . . . . 150.00

ZIP COMICS

MLJ Magazines, Feb., 1940–Summer, 1944

1 MMe,O&B:Kalathar,The Scarlet Avenger,Steel Sterling,B:Mr Satan,Nevada Jones,War Eagle Captain Valor 7,500.00
2 MMe,CBi(c)B:Steel Sterling(c) 3,000.00
3 MMe,CBi(a&c) 2,500.00
4 MMe,CBi(a&c) 2,000.00
5 MMe,CBi(a&c) 2,000.00
6 MMe,CBi(a&c) 1,700.00
7 MMe,CBi(a&c) 1,700.00
8 MMe,CBi(a&c),Bondage(c) . 1,700.00
9 CMMe,CBi(a&c),E:Kalathar, Mr Satan;Bondage(c) 2,000.00
10 MMe,CBi(a&c),B:Inferno . . . 1,800.00
11 MMe,CBi(a&c) 1,500.00
12 MMe,CBi(a&c),Bondage(c) . 1,500.00
13 MMe,CBi(a&c),E:Inferno, Bondage(c),Woman in Electric Chair 1,600.00
14 MMe,CBi(a&c),Bondage(c) . 1,500.00

Zip-Jet 1
© St. John Publishing Co.

Zoo Funnies 1st Series #2
© Charlton Comics

Rulah, Jungle Goddess #17
© Fox Features Syndicate

15 MMe,CBi(a&c),Bondage(c) . 1,600.00
16 MMe,CBi(a&c),Bondage(c) . 1,500.00
17 CBI(a&c),E:Scarlet
Avenger Bondage(c) 1,500.00
18 IN(c),B:Wilbur 1,500.00
19 IN(c),Steel Sterling(c) 1,500.00
20 IN(c),O&I:Black Jack
Hitler(c) 2,400.00
21 IN(c),V:Nazis 1,200.00
22 IN(c) 1,200.00
23 IN(c),Flying Fortress 1,200.00
24 IN(c),China Town Exploit . . . 1,200.00
25 IN(c),E:Nevada Jones 1,200.00
26 IN(c),B:Black Witch,
E:Capt Valor 1,200.00
27 IN(c),I:Web,V:Japanese 2,000.00
28 IN(C),O:Web,Bondage(c) . . . 1,600.00
29 Steel Sterling & Web 750.00
30 V:Nazis 750.00
31 IN(c) 650.00
32 Nazi Skeleton, WWII 800.00
33 Bondage(c) 700.00
34 I:Applejack;Bondage(c) 700.00
35 E:Zambini 650.00
36 I:Senor Banana 650.00
37 . . . . 650.00
38 E:Web 650.00
39 O&B:Red Rube 650.00
40 . . . . 550.00
41 . . . . 550.00
42 . . . . 550.00
43 . . . . 550.00
44 Red Rube 550.00
45 E:Wilbur 550.00
46 Red Rube 550.00
47 Crooks Can't Win 550.00

ZIP-JET

St. John Publishing Co., Feb., 1953

1 Rocketman 1,000.00
2 April–May, 1953, Assassin
of the Airlanes 650.00

ZIPPY THE CHIMP

Pines Comics, 1957

50 . . . . 70.00
51 . . . . 70.00

ZOO FUNNIES

Charlton Magazines, 1945

1 Funny Animals (1st Charlton) . 250.00
2 . . . . 125.00
3 . . . . 125.00
4 . . . . 125.00
5 . . . . 125.00
6 . . . . 100.00
7 . . . . 100.00
8 Diana the Huntress 100.00
9 . . . . 100.00
10 . . . . 100.00
11 thru 15 . . . . @100.00

Becomes:

TIM MCCOY

Charlton Comics, 1948

16 Western Movie Stories,
John Wayne 600.00
17 Rocky Lane 500.00
18 Rod Cameron 500.00
19 Jessie James 500.00
20 Jimmy Wakley 500.00
21 Johnny Mack Brown 500.00

Becomes:

PICTORIAL LOVE STORIES

Charlton Comics, 1949

22 B:Me-Dan Cupid 225.00
23 . . . . 225.00
24 Fred Astaire 250.00
25 . . . . 225.00
26 . . . . 225.00

ZOO FUNNIES

Charlton Comics, 1953–55

1 Timothy the Ghost 150.00
2 Leo the Lyin' Lion 100.00
3 thru 7 . . . . @125.00
8 Nyoka 150.00
9 Nyoka 150.00
10 Nyoka 150.00
11 Nyoka 150.00
12 Nyoka 150.00
13 Nyoka 150.00

ZOOM COMICS

Carlton Publishing Co., Dec., 1945

N# O:Captain Milksop 600.00

ZOOT COMICS

Fox Features Syndicate, Spring, 1946

N#(1)(fa) 250.00
2 A:Jaguar(fa) 250.00
3 (fa) 150.00
4 (fa) 150.00
5 (fa) 125.00
6 (fa) 125.00
7 B:Rulah 1,300.00
8 JKa(c),Fangs of Stone 850.00
9 JKa(c),Fangs of Black Fury . . 850.00
10 JKa(c),Inferno Land 850.00
11 JKa,The Purple Plague,
Bondage(c) 900.00
12 JKa(c),The Thirsty Stone,
Bondage(c) 800.00
13 Bloody Moon 650.00
14 Pearls of Pathos,Woman
Carried off by Bird 850.00
15 Death Dancers 650.00
16 . . . . 650.00

Becomes:

RULAH, JUNGLE GODDESS

Aug., 1948

17 JKa(c),Wolf Doctor 1,300.00
18 JKa(c),Vampire Garden 900.00
19 JKa(c) 850.00
20 . . . . 850.00
21 JKa(c) 850.00
22 JKa(c) 850.00
23 . . . . 750.00
24 . . . . 650.00
25 . . . . 650.00
26 . . . . 650.00
27 . . . . 700.00

Becomes:

I LOVED

July, 1949–March, 1950

28 . . . . 150.00
29 thru 31 . . . . @100.00
32 My Poison Love 100.00

ZORRO

Dell Publ. Co., 1959–61

1 thru 8, see Dell 4-Color
8 . . . . 125.00
9 . . . . 150.00
10 . . . . 110.00
11 . . . . 110.00
12 ATh 150.00
13 . . . . 100.00
14 . . . . 100.00
15 . . . . 100.00

GRADING/PRICE GUIDE

Grading comics is an objective art. This grading guide outlines the many conditions you should look for when purchasing comics, from the highest grade and top condition to the lowest collectible grade and condition. Your own comics will fall into one of these categories. A more complete description and our comments on comics grades can be found inside. We would like to point out, however, that no reader or advertiser is required to follow this or any other standard. All prices in this guide are for comics in Near Mint condition. Happy collecting!

Mint: Perfect, pristine, devoid of any trace of wear or printing or handling flaws. Covers must be fully lustrous with sharply pointed corners. No color fading. Must be well centered. Many "rack" comics are not "Mint" even when new.

Near Mint: Almost perfect with virtually no wear. No significant printing flaws. Covers must be essentially lustrous with sharp corners. Spine is as tight as new. In older comics, minimal color fading is acceptable, as is slight aging of the paper. Most price guides, including this one, quote prices in this grade.

Very Fine: Well preserved, still pleasing in appearance. Small signs of wear, most particularly around the staples. Most luster is readily visible. Corners may no longer be sharp, but are not rounded. Typical of a comic read only a few times and then properly stored.

Fine: Clean, presentable, with noticeable signs of wear. Some white may show through enamel around staples, and moderate rounding of corners. No tape or writing damage. Book still lies flat.

Very Good: A well worn reading copy with some minor damage such as creasing, small tears or cover flaking. Some discoloration may be evident, with obvious wear around the staples. Little luster remains, and some rolling of the spine may be seen when comic is laid flat on the table.

Good: A fully intact comic with very heavy wear. Tears, cover creases and flaking, and rolled spine will all be evident. No tape repairs present. Only very scarce or valuable issues are collected in this state.

The adjoining price table shows the prices for the other collectible grades which correspond to any "near mint" price given in this book.

Mint	Near Mint	Very Fine	Fine	Very Good
$60,000	**$50,000**	$35,000	$20,000	$10,000
48,000	**40,000**	28,000	16,000	8,000
36,000	**30,000**	21,000	12,000	6,000
24,000	**20,000**	14,000	8,000	4,000
18,000	**15,000**	10,500	6,000	3,000
12,000	**10,000**	7,000	4,000	2,000
10,800	**9,000**	6,300	3,600	1,800
9,600	**8,000**	5,600	3,200	1,600
9,000	**7,500**	5,250	3,000	1,500
8,400	**7,000**	4,900	2,800	1,400
7,800	**6,500**	4,550	2,600	1,300
7,200	**6,000**	4,200	2,400	1,200
6,600	**5,500**	3,850	2,200	1,100
6,000	**5,000**	3,500	2,000	1,000
4,800	**4,000**	2,800	1,600	800
3,600	**3,000**	2,100	1,200	600
2,400	**2,000**	1,400	800	400
1,800	**1,500**	1,050	600	300
1,200	**1,000**	700	400	200
1,080	**900**	630	360	180
960	**800**	560	320	160
900	**750**	525	300	150
840	**700**	490	280	140
780	**650**	455	260	130
720	**600**	420	240	120
660	**550**	385	220	110
600	**500**	350	200	100
570	**475**	332	190	95
540	**450**	315	180	90
510	**425**	297	170	85
480	**400**	280	160	80
450	**375**	262	150	75
420	**350**	245	140	70
390	**325**	227	130	65
360	**300**	210	120	60
330	**275**	192	110	55
300	**250**	175	100	50
270	**225**	157	90	45
240	**200**	140	80	40
210	**175**	122	70	35
180	**150**	105	60	30
150	**125**	87	50	25
120	**100**	70	40	20
114	**95**	66	38	19
108	**90**	63	36	18
102	**85**	59	32	17
96	**80**	56	32	16
90	**75**	52	30	15
84	**70**	49	28	14
78	**65**	45	26	13
72	**60**	42	24	12
66	**55**	38	22	11
60	**50**	35	20	10